# Lecture Notes in Computer Science     8696

Commenced Publication in 1973
Founding and Former Series Editors:
Gerhard Goos, Juris Hartmanis, and Jan van Leeuwen

T0236170

Andrea Bondavalli   Andrea Ceccarelli
Frank Ortmeier (Eds.)

# Computer Safety, Reliability, and Security

SAFECOMP 2014 Workshops:
ASCoMS, DECSoS, DEVVARTS, ISSE, ReSA4CI, SASSUR
Florence, Italy, September 8-9, 2014
Proceedings

Springer

Volume Editors

Andrea Bondavalli
University of Florence
Department of Mathematics and Informatics
Florence, Italy
E-mail: bondavalli@unifi.it

Andrea Ceccarelli
University of Florence
Department of Mathematics and Informatics
Florence, Italy
E-mail: andrea.ceccarelli@unifi.it

Frank Ortmeier
Otto-von-Guericke-University Magdeburg
Computer Systems in Engineering
Magdeburg, Germany
E-mail: frank.ortmeier@ovgu.de

ISSN 0302-9743　　　　　　　　　　e-ISSN 1611-3349
ISBN 978-3-319-10556-7　　　　　　e-ISBN 978-3-319-10557-4
DOI 10.1007/978-3-319-10557-4
Springer Cham Heidelberg New York Dordrecht London

Library of Congress Control Number: Applied for

LNCS Sublibrary: SL 2 – Programming and Software Engineering

*Typesetting:* Camera-ready by author, data conversion by Scientific Publishing Services, Chennai, India

Printed on acid-free paper

Springer is part of Springer Science+Business Media (www.springer.com)

# Preface

To accompany the 33rd edition of SAFECOMP, and the overarching FLO-
RENCE 2014, the one-week scientific event on the development of safe, secure,
dependable, and performing systems, we selected workshops covering different
partially overlapping application areas and different phases of the lifecyle of such
safety-critical systems. We decided to give various domain experts a common
meeting place at SAFECOMP in the format of domain-specific workshops. The
joining aspects are always safety and security. Bringing these experts together
at one place and collecting their articles in one volume fosters collaboration and
exchange of ideas.

For SAFECOMP 2014, we accepted 6 domain-specific, high-quality workshops, each with well-known chairs and an International Program Committee:

- 3rd Workshop on Architecting Safety in Collaborative Mobile Systems (AS-
  CoMS 2014) (Chairs Renato Librino and Martin Törngren)
- ERCIM/EWICS/ARTEMIS Workshop on Dependable Embedded and Cy-
  berphysical Systems and Systems-of-Systems (DECSoS 2014) (Chairs Erwin
  Schoitsch and Amund Skavhaug)
- Workshop on DEvelopment, VeriFIcation and VAlidation of cRiTical Sys-
  tems (DEVVARTS 2014) (Chairs Francesco Brancati, Nuno Laranjeiro, and
  Ábel Hegedüs)
- 1st International Workshop on the Integration of Safety and Security Engi-
  neering (ISSE 2014) (Chairs Laurent Rioux and John Favaro)
- Workshop on Reliability and Security Aspects for Critical Infrastructure
  Protection (ReSA4CI 2014) (Chairs: Silvia Bonomi and Ilaria Matteucci)
- Workshop on Next Generation of System Assurance Approaches for Safety-
  Critical Systems (SASSUR 2014) (Chairs: Alejandra Ruiz, Tim Kelly, and
  Jose Luis de la Vara)

Altogether 92 researchers from 21 countries reviewed the following 42 articles.
Summarizing, we have to say that the correspondence and organization of these 6
workshops for SAFECOMP took a lot of time. But when looking at the program
now, we are very proud of it and wish to thank all workshop chairs, their Program
Committee members and all the people involved in the organization. You did a
fantastic job.

We hope readers and attendees share our opinion that this will be a great
extension to SAFECOMP 2014.

July 2014

Andrea Bondavalli
Andrea Ceccarelli
Frank Ortmeier

# Organization

## EWICS TC7 Chair

Francesca Saglietti      University of Erlangen-Nuremberg, Germany

## General Chair

Andrea Bondavalli      University of Florence, Italy

## Program Co-chairs

Andrea Bondavalli      University of Florence, Italy
Felicita Di Giandomenico      ISTI-CNR, Italy

## Workshop and Tutorial Chair

Frank Ortmeier      Otto -v.-Guericke-University, Germany

## Industry-liaison Chair

Michael Paulitsch      AIRBUS Group, Germany

## Finance Chair

Ettore Ricciardi      ISTI-CNR, Italy

## Publication Chair

Andrea Ceccarelli      University of Florence, Italy

## Publicity Chair

Francesco Flammini      Ansaldo STS, Italy

## Local Organizing Chair

Paolo Lollini                    University of Florence, Italy

## ASCoMS Program Committee

Luis Almeida                    FEUP, Portugal
Abele Andreas                   Bosch, Germany
Fredrik Asplund                 KTH, Sweden
António Casimiro                FCUL, Portugal
Karl Goeschka                   TUWIEN, Austria
Teruo Higashino                 Osaka University, Japan
Per Johannessen                 Volvo AB, Sweden
Rolf Johansson                  SP, Sweden
Jörg Kaiser                     OVGU, Germany
Vana Kalogeraki                 Athens University of Economics and Business,
                                    Greece
Marc-Olivier Killijian          Laas, France
Renato Librino                  4S s.r.l, Italy
Henrik Lönn                     Volvo AB, Sweden
Mattias Nyberg                  Scania and KTH, Sweden
Elad Michael Schiller           Chalmers University of Technology, Sweden
Erwin Schoitsch                 AIT, Austria
Martin Törngren                 KTH, Sweden

## DECSoS Program Committee

Bettina Buth                    HAW Hamburg, Germany
Francesco Flammini              Ansaldo STS Italy, University "Federico II"
                                    of Naples, Italy
Denis Hatebur                   Universität Duisburg-Essen, Germany
Floor Koornneef                 TU Delft, The Netherlands
Michael Lipaczweski             Otto-von-Guericke-Universitaet, Germany
Dejan Nickovic                  AIT Austrian Institute of Technology, Austria
Frank Ortmeier                  Otto-von-Guericke-Universitaet, Germany
Thomas Pfeiffenberger           Salzburg Research Forschungsgesellschaft
                                    m.b.H, Austria
Francesca Saglietti             University of Erlangen-Nuremberg, Germany
Christoph Schmitz               Zühlke Engineering AG, Switzerland
Erwin Schoitsch                 AIT Austrian Institute of Technology, Austria
Rolf Schumacher                 Ingenievr-Büro, Germany
Amund Skavhaug                  NTNU, Norway
Mark-Alexander Sujan            University of Warwick, UK
Meine van der Meulen            DNV, Norway

# DEVVARTS Program Committee

| | |
|---|---|
| Andrea Ceccarelli | Università di Firenze, Italy |
| Alessandro Cimatti | Bruno Kessler Foundation, Italy |
| Barbara Gallina | Mälardalen University, Sweden |
| Michaela Huhn | Technische Universität Clausthal, Germany |
| Hardi Hungar | German Aerospace Center - Braunschweig, Germany |
| Melinda Kocsis-Magyar | PROLAN zrt, Hungary |
| Rui Lopes | Airbus Defence and Space, UK |
| Henrique Madeira | University of Coimbra, Portugal |
| Istvan Majzik | Budapest University of Technology and Economics, Hungary |
| Roberto Natella | University of Naples Federico II, Italy |
| Francesco Rossi | ResilTech s.r.l., Italy |
| Stefano Russo | University of Naples Federico II, Italy |
| Marco Vieira | University of Coimbra, Portugal |

# ISSE Program Committee

| | |
|---|---|
| Pasi Ahonen | VTT, Finland |
| Julien Brunel | Onera, France |
| Adele-Louise Carter | KITEWAY, UK |
| Barbara Czerny | Chrysler Group LLC, USA |
| Gjalt de Jong | Melexis, Belgium |
| Rami Debouk | General Motors, USA |
| Huascar Espinoza | Tecnalia, Spain |
| Anthony Faucogney | ALL4TEC, France |
| Donald Firesmith | SEI, USA |
| Jarkko Holappa | NIXU, Finland |
| Flemming Nielson | DTU, Denmark |
| Stephane Paul | Thales, France |
| Michael Paulitsch | Airbus Group, Germany |
| Giovanni Sartori | Yogitech, Italy |
| Erwin Schoitsch | AIT, Austria |
| Michal Sojka | Czech Technical University, Czech Republic |
| Lorenzo Strigini | City University, UK |
| Robert Stroud | Adelard, UK |
| Timo Wiander | Stuk, Finland |

# ReSA4CI Program Committee

| | |
|---|---|
| Valentina Bonfiglio | University of Florence, Italy |
| Silvia Bonomi | University of Rome La Sapienza, Italy |

| Felicita Di Giandomenico | ISTI-CNR, Italy |
| Maria Gradinariu | |
| Potop-Butucaru | UPMC Paris 6, France |
| Karama Kanoun | LAAS, France |
| Ilaria Matteucci | IIT-CNR, Italy |
| Alessia Milani | University of Bordeaux, France |
| Simin Nadjm-Tehrani | Linkoeping University, Sweden |
| Federica Paci | University of Trento, Italy |
| Marta Patino Martinez | Technical University of Madrid, Spain |
| Marinella Petrocchi | IIT-CNR, Italy |
| Sara Tucci Piergiovanni | CEA, France |

## SASSUR Program Committee

| Michael Armbruster | Siemens, Germany |
| Ronald Blanrue | EADS/Eurocopter, France |
| Markus Borg | Lund University, Sweden |
| Marc Born | ikv++, Germany |
| Daniela Cancila | CEA, France |
| Ibrahim Habli | University of York, UK |
| Tudor Ionescu | TTTech, Austria |
| Sunil Nair | Simula Research Laboratory, Norway |
| Paolo Panaroni | Intecs, Italy |
| Ansgar Radermacher | CEA, France |
| Laurent Rioux | Thales Research and Technology, France |
| Mehrdad Sabetzadeh | University of Luxemburg, Luxemburg |
| Kenji Taguchi | AIST, Japan |
| Martin Wassmuth | EADS, Germany |
| Gereon Weiß | Fraunhofer, Germany |
| Ji Wu | Beihang University, China |

# Sponsors

## Scientific Sponsors

EWICS TC7

Università degli Studi di
Firenze

Consiglio Nazionale delle Ricerche
(CNR) - Istituto di Scienza e Tecnologie
dell'Informazione (ISTI) "A. Faedo"

## Industrial Sponsors

# Technical Co-sponsors

Associazione Italiana Esperti in
Infrastrutture Critiche (AIIC)

Austrian Institute of Technology

European Network of Clubs for
Reliability and Safety of Software

European Research Consortium for Informatics and Mathematics (ERCIM)

Gesellschaft für Informatik e. V

International Federation for Information
Processing

Oesterreichische Computer Gesellschaft-
Austrian Computer Society

# Table of Contents

## Architecting Safety in Collaborative Mobile Systems (ASCoMS'14)

# ERCIM/EWICS/ARTEMIS Workshop on Dependable Embedded and Cyberphysical Systems and Systems-of-Systems (DECSoS'14)

## DEvelopment, Verification and VAlidation of cRiTical Systems (DEVVARTS'14)

## Integration of Safety and Security Engineering (ISSE'14)

## Reliability and Security Aspects for Critical Infrastructure Protection (ReSA4CI'14)

## Next Generation of System Assurance Approaches for Safety-Critical Systems (SASSUR'14)

# 3rd Workshop on Architecting Safety in Collaborative Mobile Systems (ASCoMS)

Renato Librino[1] and Martin Törngren[2]

[1] 4S s.r.l, Italy
[2] Kungliga Tekniska Hoegskolan, Sweden

This volume contains the papers presented at ASCoMS 2014: the 3rd Workshop on Architecting Safety in Collaborative Mobile Systems held on September 8, 2014 in Firenze as part of SAFECOMP Conference 2014. As for the two previous years the workshop was held at SAFECOMP.

ASCoMS 2014 focuses on fundamental challenges in ensuring that safety requirements are satisfied despite the increased system complexity and the uncertainties introduced by operation in open and not well defined environments, motivated by new systems of systems that will be established in the era of Cyber-Physical Systems.

New and improved sensor and communication technologies create opportunities for designing embedded and mobile systems that are able to interact with their environment, and exhibit "smart" and autonomous behavior. Furthermore, collaboration between mobile entities can also be envisaged for improving their functionality as well as performance. Example applications include unmanned aerial vehicles (UAVs) and smart cars, where for instance, UAVs can be used for environmental surveillance and control, and smart vehicles coordinating their behaviors can be used to increase traffic throughput and improve mobility without the need of using more space for the respective traffic infrastructures.

A fundamental challenge is then to ensure that safety requirements are satisfied despite the increased system complexity and the uncertainties introduced by the operation in open and not well defined environments. In general, the problem might be equated in terms of achieving system safety for potentially mass consumer products. From an application perspective, the workshop focuses on distributed and cooperative safety-critical systems. So far, the existing solutions are still insufficient or inadequate and therefore these systems are not allowed to operate in the public air space or on public roads because the risk of causing severe damage or even threaten human lives cannot be excluded with sufficient certainty. This justifies the importance of research in this area, and explains the interest on the subject by the academia and the industry.

The papers for ASCoMS 2014 consider different aspects of future mobile systems and their safety concerns, including communication and performance adaptation aspects, safety constraints and verification, to collaborative development and ITS design perspectives.

A. Bondavalli et al. (Eds.): SAFECOMP 2014 Workshops, LNCS 8696, pp. 1–2, 2014.

Two papers consider the challenge of adapting the system to different performance levels as needed to ensure safety according to the existing operational conditions, e.g., system and environment state.

Related to this, another paper treats safety rules for run-time monitoring based on safety rules. Two further papers treat safety aspects in relation to design time verification through formal methods and testing, respectively. A paper on information modeling for holistic safety management unifies the design- and run-time perspectives by treating what information is required for design, verification and run-time decision making. Communication protocols and aspects of relevance for collaborative systems are investigated in two papers. Finally, one paper is devoted to support for collaborative development with specific consideration of the development of safety critical automotive systems.

The workshop program comprises four regular papers and five invited papers, providing a basis for comprehensive discussions at ASCoMS 2014. We believe the workshop program provides a good basis for future research initiatives. The organization of this workshop was partially supported by the EC, through project FP7-STREP-288195, KARYON (Kernel-based ARchitecture for safetY-critical cONtrol) and the FUSE project (Functional Safety and Evolvable architectures for autonomy, a Swedish national project support by Vinnova).

# Intelligent Transport Systems - The Role of a Safety Loop for Holistic Safety Management

Kenneth Östberg[1], Martin Törngren[2], Fredrik Asplund[2], and Magnus Bengtsson[3]

[1] Electronics / Software, SP Technical Research Institute of Sweden, Borås, Sweden
kenneth.ostberg@sp.se
[2] KTH, Stockholm, Sweden
{martint,fasplund}@kth.se
[3] Chalmers University of Technology, SE-41296, Göteborg, Sweden
magnus.bengtsson@chalmers.se

**Abstract.** An ITS represents a Cyber-Physical System (CPS), which will involve information exchange at operational level as well as potential explicit collaboration between separate entities (systems of systems). Specific emphasis is required to manage the complexity and safety of such future CPS. In this paper we focus on model-based approaches for these purposes for analyzing and managing safety throughout the lifecycle of ITS. We argue that: (1) run-time risk assessment will be necessary for efficient ITS; (2) an information centric approach will be instrumental for future ITS to support all aspects of safety management – a "safety loop"; (3) a formal basis is required to deal with the large amounts of information present in an ITS. We elaborate these arguments and discuss what is required to support their realization.

**Keywords:** ITS, traffic management, safety management, information model, ontology.

## 1 Introduction

The promises and anticipation of the positive effects of the Intelligent Transport System (ITS) are huge. The hope is that ITS will help road users utilize the infrastructure in a more efficient way, thereby enabling better comfort, efficiency and safety. Secondary effects also promise to be significant, e.g. if ITS succeeds with increasing road safety the reduced number of severely injured or killed persons in traffic could decrease rehabilitation and hospital cost enormously (see e.g. [15, 16, 17]).

However, with the upcoming capabilities of autonomous driving, ITS will probably become among the most complex cyber-physical system human has ever invented. It will involve many entities, have control loops at different levels with properties like self-organization and self-adaptation, and include huge amounts of information, providing a number of implications for the way that systems are engineered. Specific emphasis will be required to manage the complexity and safety correctly.

A. Bondavalli et al. (Eds.): SAFECOMP 2014 Workshops, LNCS 8696, pp. 3–10, 2014.

In this paper we focus on model-based approaches for these purposes based on the following prerequisites:

- Run-time risk assessment will be necessary for efficient ITS, where both local and global information will provide the basis for run-time decision making.
- An information centric approach will be instrumental for future ITS to support all aspects of safety management, from design, over run-time risk assessment and diagnostics, through to system improvements.
- A formal basis is required to deal with the large amounts of information present in an ITS.

In particular we propose the use of an information model for ITS to support both the system design process and the safety process.

In the remainder of Section 1, we provide perspectives to areas related to ITS efforts. Section 2 presents fundamental concepts for, and characteristics of ITS. Section 3 concludes the paper and provides ideas for future work.

## 1.1     Related Work for ITS

The development of ITS has seen significant effort since the 1990s, [1, 2], [5]. Enabling technologies that provide sensing, location, communication and processing in real-time have made it possible to develop new schemes for information sharing and collaboration and slowly transformed both infrastructure and vehicles. Technical aspects in addressing ITS thus include data gathering and analysis at transportation system level (see e.g. the Mobile Millennium project [19]), control for individual and collaborating vehicles (see e.g. the Sartre project [20]) and research addressing safety and architectures for autonomous automotive systems (see e.g. [21, 22]). ITS represents a truly multidisciplinary field that spans multiple abstractions and domains, from entire regions and cities down to smart devices, and encompasses e.g. road and communication infrastructure and vehicle development. ITS will be made up of Cyber-Physical Systems (CPS), which will form socio-technical systems where a number of technological, economical and societal aspects will be of key importance for successful deployment [18].

Apart from the technical aspects, ITS will benefit from multiple perspectives that have proven to be important when developing similar systems. These include different views on traffic management systems, legislation and standards. In the following we provide some snapshots on these perspectives, highlighting a few aspects of state of the art.

In Europe an ITS standardization initiative has already begun by European Telecommunications Standardizations Institute (ETSI), [3, 4, 5]. Furthermore, projects that focus on actually ensuring particular benefits of ITS, such as intersection safety [6] and certification of autonomous cars [7], has already been a reality for quite some time.

Safety standardization has not yet been proven with regards to highly automated ITS, but new safety standards of importance to CPS development in the transportation sector are currently being released at a fast pace [8, 9, 10].

Air Traffic Management encompasses the multiple concerns required for safe coordination of air traffic, taking into account the multitude of stakeholders involved and the system life-cycle process. Increasing air traffic loads have been driving renewed efforts in Air Traffic Management, in particular to ensure safety [11, 12]. These efforts include the creation of the SESAR joint undertaking. The high-level goals of SESAR include a 40% reduction in accident risk per flight hour [13]. One should note that a Safety management system is now required by International Civil Aviation Organization (ICAO) and FAA international safety standards [12].

# 2    ITS Characteristics and Fundamental Concepts

In the following we discuss these topics:

- Life cycle perspective and safety aspects of ITS
- ITS station
- Traffic simulation and the safety loop

## 2.1    Lifecycle Perspective and Safety Aspects

If a larger CPS system is designed using traditional methods, the development process can help establish clear boundaries for system development activities and system properties. For instance ISO 26262, the functional safety standard for road vehicles, points at two primary possibilities for addressing safety. Firstly, redundancy can be introduced in the design phase. Secondly, in the verification phase more rigorous verification techniques can be used. Through these two means a vehicle can be released with no **unacceptable** risks left in the vehicle's electrical and/or electronic (E/E) system. The idea behind ISO26262 is thus to establish that safety is sufficiently ensured at a particular point in time (considering all efforts done prior to this time and all efforts planned after it), i.e. the vehicle release time. One may also note that there is also an entity that takes responsibility for ensuring this safety, i.e. the automotive manufacturer.

An important property of ITS is that its development process will have no well-defined start or points of update. Instead ITS will be a slowly emerging system that will be expanded, updated and adjusted continuously. The ITS safety process, indeed the safety process of every CPS deployed into ITS, will therefore benefit from being a continuous life-cycle process and not a onetime design activity during development. For automotive manufacturers to do otherwise would imply a conservative approach, since they can then only trust the information available at design time. At most such information could rely on ITS information with a very small scope and associated contracts between legal entities, such as requests for all vehicles in a particular area to stop that all automotive manufacturers respect. Fine-grained analyses will have to rely either on vehicle-specific, or at most fleet-specific, information, since the design choices and legal obligations by other CPS developers might change. The resulting conservative approach will most probably preclude many of the benefits that motivates the launch of ITS to begin with. Alternatively automotive manufacturers will have to sign far-reaching legal agreements with other automotive manufacturers to ensure the correctness of certain information at all times, with subsequent legal battles when this fails.

The implications of this is therefore that part of the systems safety properties needs to be designed to be monitored and handled during run time. If (when) accidents occur they can then be analyzed, off-line, so that the events that led to the accidents can be understood and similar scenarios prevented in the future. This continuous process of interplay between design-time safety assessments, run-time safety assessments and off-line post analysis is what we term a **safety loop**.

## 2.2   ITS Station

Entities participating in ITS and sharing information will have to comply with a number of standards concerning communication interfaces and how to interact. In Europe ETSI has defined a reference architecture for an ITS-Station [3]. One of the purposes with this standard is to define a common data model of information that can be shared among the ITS-Stations. All stations have local sensors that collect information about their vicinity which gives them a local perspective. This information is then shared among the participants to achieve global awareness.

In current standards there are two fundamental message types, Cooperative Awareness Messages (CAM) and Decentralized environmental Notification Messages (DNM). Specifically, there are dedicated messages from these two types to support a "Driving Assistance" application named "Road Hazard Warning". Current standards are thus an initial effort to address safety, but the shared information holds a greater potential in achieving safety. The information in the system taken together, not only dedicated hazard messages, can be used to identify hazards, perform risk assessment and risk management.

ITS exists today in form of Advanced Traffic Management Systems. These are centralized system and mainly monitoring and controlling traffic at **macroscopic** and **mesoscopic** views, e.g. whole cities or large city blocks, at traffic operations centers (TOCs). These systems operate more at a **strategic** and **tactic** level than an **operational** level. Operational level and **microscopic** view is defined as where traffic can be monitored and controlled at vehicle level. With the introduction of ITS-stations and their in-station sensors which acquire detailed-level of operational data, it will become possible to decentralize traffic management and perform traffic management at microscopic view.

Level-of-service is a traffic management term that is used to describe different properties of a traffic system, e.g. traffic flow and traffic density. Increasing traffic density and traffic flow means that vehicles have lesser spacing between them and travel at higher speed. This traffic behavior has potential for severe accidents. To match these efficiency properties there needs to be a way to identify hazards and have risk management strategies at operational level. This is where the previously discussed, shared information can make a difference. Detailed, consistent, trusted information about the capabilities of the involved systems can enable risk management in different operational situations.

One way to achieve the required trust and management can be to extend the ITS reference architecture with a safety manager responsible for run time safety handling to work in cooperation with the traffic management system.

## 2.3    Traffic Simulation and the Safety Loop

Traffic simulators are important tools in traffic system planning and developing traffic control strategies. The simulators range from macroscopic to microscopic views. Microscopic view and operational situations demands a detailed representation of the system and the situation in order reflect real scenarios and being valuable for analysis. This detailed representation will include detailed models of the road network, the road surface, dynamic models of the entities, wheatear models and models of communication networks. All these information sources are necessary to have at an approximated level to calculate risks.

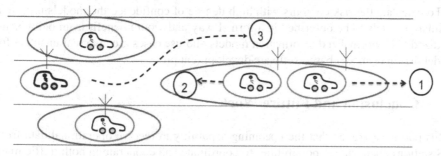

**Fig. 1.** Safety zone and risk contours

With all this detailed information an important aspect is that it must be possible to tune the system parameters in a structured way to find conditions where the risks are at acceptable levels while achieving high efficiency.

One way to handle this is to apply virtual risk contours around potential sources of harm (see Fig. 1). In other words, to apply a virtual dynamic zone around objects within an operational situation which are likely to be part of a scenario resulting in an accident. All the entities will then have a corresponding virtual comfort zone, or a safety shield, protecting its neighborhood. No other entities or their risk contour at certain level are allowed within this area. From the ego perspective, using information from own sensors together with shared information, local hazards are identified. The risk classification can be handled by having a virtual risk potential field around the hazards and the risk contours showing curves with equal risks. The velocity, or relative velocity, of other objects will certainly affect their perceived risk. Risk contours can thus give an indication of how dense traffic can be packed while still maintaining safety.

For safety management the risk contours describe the available time and space to perform collision mitigation strategies. In [23, 24] such strategies are discussed and two parameters are defined as quantifiers for collision risk; braking threat number (BTN) and steering threat number (STN). These parameters are dependent on physical capabilities such as tire-to-road friction but also distance between the safety zone and a risk contour.

Risk contours may also be a useful concept for planning safe trajectories for fully autonomous vehicles and not just collision mitigation strategies. In future where there will be different levels of automation, risk contours may be one way to assert that the transitioning process from self-driving mode to automated model is safe because it has a notion of safe distance in form of timing.

Risk contours may therefore be a unifying concept to give meaningful metrics to safety and a possibility to connect different level-of-service parameters to each other in order to tune system parameters in a structured way to find a good balance in the system.

Risk contours can be designed to be monitored and handled during run time, but still analyzed, off-line using traffic simulators with input from actual diagnostic feedback information from real life situations. They therefore also agree with the previously mentioned safety loop concept.

To calculate the risk contours with high degree of confidence the models used in a simulation needs to be described in a formal way and would benefit from being standardized [14]. Formalized information models and use cases are also real enablers for model driven or model based software development processes.

## 3    Conclusion and Future Work

In his paper we argued that the upcoming capability to receive operational data from ITS stations opens up for possibilities to coordinate and cooperate in both traffic management and safety management at a microscopic decentralized level in real time. To support such initiatives there needs to be a formalized description of shared concepts, an ontology and a formal information model, to support all aspects of safety management, from simulation and design, over run-time risk assessment and diagnostics, through to system improvements. The safety process will be a continuous iterative process between these phases, what we term a safety loop.

Future research work is to realize an ontology, and a formal information model, for traffic management and safety management within ITS. In order to understand parts needed to support our safety loop the ontology has to be investigated in the light of a simulation environment, model driven software development and tested at run time in an ITS station. To close the loop, diagnostic information collected at run time should be feed back into the simulation environment.

**Acknowledgement.** This work has been supported by the EU under the FP7-ICT programme, through project 288195 "Kernel-based ARchitecture for safetY-critical cONtrol" (KARYON).

# References

1. Sussman, J.M.: Perspectives on Intelligent Transportation Systems. Springer, New York (2005)
2. Vision for ITS. Proc. of the National Workshop on Intelligent Vehicle/Highway systems sponsored by Mobility 2000, Dallas, TX (1990),
   http://ntl.bts.gov/lib/jpodocs/repts_te/9063.pdf
   (accessed June 2014)
3. ETSI, EN. 302 665 (V1. 1.1), Intelligent Transport Systems (ITS) (2010).
4. ETSI TR 102 863 Intelligent Transport Systems (ITS); Local Dynamic Map (LDM)
5. ETSI on Intelligent Transport Systems, http://www.etsi.org/technologies-clusters/technologies/intelligent-transport (accessed June 2014)
6. Fuerstenberg, K.C.: A New European Approach for Intersection Safety – The EC-Project INTERSAFE. In: Proceedings of the 8th International, IEEE Conference on Intelligent Transportation Systems, Vienna, Austria, September 13-16 (2005)
7. van Dijke, J., van Schijndel, M., Nashashibi, F., de la Fortelle, A.: Certification of Automated Transport Systems. Procedia - Social and Behavioral Sciences 48, 3461–3470 (2012), http://dx.doi.org/10.1016/j.sbspro.2012.06.1310, ISSN 1877-0428
8. ISO 26262:2011, road vehicles - functional safety (2011)
9. DO-178C, software considerations in airborne systems and equipment certification (2011)
10. BS/EN 50128:2011, railway applications - communications, signalling and processing systems - software for railway control and protection systems (2011)
11. Kirwan, B., Perrin, E.: Imagining Safety in European Air Traffic Management. Short paper prepared for 3rd Int. Conf. on Occupational Risk Prevention (ORP 2004), Santiago, Spain, June 2-4 (2004)
12. FAA presentation on Safety Management System for Air Traffic Control Safety by Joseph Teixeira at NSF, https://www.faa.gov/about/office_org/headquarters_offices/ato/service_units/safety/media/NSF-Presentation-final-for-web.pdf (accessed June 2014)
13. SESAR joint undertaking,
    http://www.sesarju.eu/discover-sesar/objectives
    (accessed June 2014)
14. Dupuis, M., Strobl, M., Grezlikowski, H.: OpenDRIVE 2010 and Beyond–Status and Future of the de facto Standard for the Description of Road Networks. In: Proceedings of the Driving Simulation Conference DSC Europe 2010 (2010)
15. U.S. Department of Transportation. Policy on Automated Vehicle Development, http://www.nhtsa.gov/staticfiles/rulemaking/pdf/Automated_Vehicles_Policy.pdf (accessed June 2014)
16. ETSI – Intelligent Cooperative Transportation Systems,
    http://www.etsi.org/technologies-clusters/technologies/intelligent-transport/cooperative-its (accessed June 2014)
17. Human error accounts for 90% of road accidents, FleetAlert, International News (April 2011), http://www.alertdriving.com/home/fleet-alert-magazine/international/human-error-accounts-90-road-accidents (accessed June 2014)
18. CyPherS – Deliverable D2.2,
    http://www.cyphers.eu/sites/default/files/D2.2.pdf
    (accessed June 2014)
19. Mobile Millenium Project, http://traffic.berkeley.edu/ (accessed June 2014)

20. SARTRE - Safe Road Trains for the Environment,
    http://www.sartre-project.eu/en/Sidor/default.aspx
    (accessed June 2014)
21. Karyon - Kernel-Based ARchitecture for safetY-critical Control,
    http://www.karyon-project.eu/ (accessed June 2014)
22. FUSE – Functional safety and evolving architectures for Autonomy,
    http://www.fuse-project.se/ (accessed June 2014)
23. Ali, M., Gelso, E.R., Sjoberg, J.: Automotive Threat Assessment Design for Combined
    Braking and Steering Maneuvers. IEEE Transactions on Vehicular Technology 62(4),
    1519–1526 (2013)
24. Sjöberg, J., et al.: Driver Models To Increase The Potential Of Automotive Active Safety
    Functions. In: Proceedings of 18th European Signal Processing Conference 2010, Aalborg,
    Denmark, August 23-27 (2010)

# Safety Verification of Multiple Autonomous Systems by Formal Approach

Kozo Okano[1] and Toshifusa Sekizawa[2]

[1] Osaka University, Japan
okano@ist.osaka-u.ac.jp
[2] Nihon University, Japan
sekizawa@cs.ce.nihon-u.ac.jp

**Abstract.** We have studied verification of a line tracing robot using model checking. In this paper, we extend the model to multiple autonomous systems, and describe the advantages of applying model checking and difficulties. The targeted line tracing robot usually has only one or two sensors to detect a line painted on white background, and it traces the line according to the read value of the sensors. It is easy to trace if the line is simple straight line. However, lines sometimes become complicated by existence of random sequential corners. Those robots are often used in robot competitions for university students in Japan. Driving time, accuracy and robustness are evaluated in such competitions. The robot is usually designed as a stand-alone. Here, we extend such line tracing robots to multiple autonomous robots by adding communication functions and proximity sensors. We consider multiple lines to be crossed where robots might hit each other. Although the introduced model is simple, it has enough power to provide a structure where we can discuss safety and robustness using model checking. Our proposed method can also treat time constraints of robot controls.

## 1 Introduction

Recently, embedded systems have become important in our society. Embedded systems exist everywhere in our daily life including public facilities. Therefore, to ensure safety properties of the embedded systems becomes much important. We have studied verification of a line tracing robot using model checking.

In order to model such systems (real-time systems), several models have been proposed. Timed automaton is proposed by Alur and Dill[1]. The most interesting point of timed automaton is that it uses clock variables where the range of a clock variable is real numbers. Locations and transitions of timed automaton have constraints on clocks in limited syntax forms. Timed automaton, therefore, can naturally represent behavior of real-time systems. The famous verifier for timed automaton is UPPAAL[2]. The timed automaton used in UPPAAL is a strong extension of the original timed automaton. It can deal with bounded integer variables and guard expressions on its transitions can express constraints on such variables. Several success applications of verification have reported, including verification of audio-video protocols[3], a gear controller[4], timeliness properties of multimedia systems [5], and so on.

A. Bondavalli et al. (Eds.): SAFECOMP 2014 Workshops, LNCS 8696, pp. 11–18, 2014.

The line tracing robot usually has only one or two sensors to detect a line painted on white background, and it traces the line according to the read value of the sensors. It is easy to trace if the line is simple straight line. The line sometimes becomes complicated by existence of random sequential corners. However, the line is topologically the same as a simple straight line. The robots are often used in robot competitions in Japan. Driving time, accuracy and robustness are usually evaluated in such competitions. The robot is usually designed as a stand-alone. Thus it does not communicate with each other. Also it does not have sensors to detect others. Only one robot runs in the same time, thus functions for communication are not needed in competitions.

There is room to extend the line tracing robot to multiple autonomous systems. We can do it by adding a simple communication function and a proximity sensor to each of robots. With these robots, we can extend the lines to be crossed. Such extensions provide a moderate abstract model for real autonomous automobile systems. It is very simple if we compare it to the real world, but it has enough power to provide a structure where we can discuss safety and robustness from the view point of formal techniques, such as model checking. We describe applicability of model checking based on our past experience[8] on model checking for a stand-alone robot using UPPAAL, a model checker for network of timed automata.

In this paper, we extend the stand-alone model to multiple autonomous systems, and describe advantages of applying model checking. Difficulties of such approach are also described.

The rest of the paper is organized as follows. Sec. 2 provides preliminaries. Sec. 3 will describe both of the stand-alone and multiple models. Sec. 4 discusses model checking possibilities. Finally, Sec. 5 concludes the paper.

## 2   Preliminaries

We provide several definitions and notions used in this paper.

### 2.1   Line Tracing Robot

A line tracing robot is a vehicle robot tracing a course. The course is assumed to be painted in black color on white background with the same width. Figure 1 shows a typical line tracing robot and a course layout for the robots.

**Fig. 1.** A Line Tracing Robot and an Oval Course

LEGO® Mindstorms NXT is a kit for assembling robots with various actuators and sensors. The actuators include stepping motors which users can accurately control rotation angles. The sensors include color sensors, touch sensors, ultrasonic sensors and so on. Various programming languages are provided for control of the NXT kit, including NXC (Not eXactly C) and LeJOS[7]. LeJOS is a development environment for Java. NXC and LeJOS have classes for the above-mentioned sensors and actuators. Users can program its behavior. This research uses LeJOS for developing the line tracing robot.

### 2.2 Model Checking

In general, the behavior of a line tracing robot can be modeled in a state machine, where signals from sensors and commands to actuators are abstracted into actions of the state machine.

For a given state machine $M$ and a temporal logic expression $e$, we can perform model checking. A model checker searches all possibilities of behaviors produced by $M$ and checks whether the behaviors satisfy the expression $e$. If the behaviors satisfy $e$ then the model checker outputs "yes" otherwise "no." For the latter case, it also produces a counter-example which is a concrete trace that violates $e$.

For real-time systems, it is desired to support time properties in a state machine. A timed automaton is an extension of the conventional automaton with clock variables and constraints for expressing real-time dynamics. They are widely used in the modeling and analyses of real-time systems.

UPPAAL[2] is a famous model checker for extended timed automata by Wang-Yi et al. It also supports model checking for the conventional timed automata. In addition, it supports local and global integers and primitive operations on integers, such as addition, subtract and multiplication with constants. The model of the system can be created from multiple timed automata which are synchronized together via CCS-like synchronization mechanisms.

## 3   Multiple Autonomous Systems Model

We give our model of multiple autonomous systems. First, we describe a model for a stand-alone tracing robot. Next, we extend the model to multiple autonomous systems.

### 3.1   Stand-Alone Tracing Robot

A model for a line tracing robot consists of the following three sub-models:

- Controller Behavior Model (CM),
- State Transition of Environment Model (EM), and
- Disturbance Model (DM).

CM can be modeled in a network of timed automata to represent behavior of robot's controller program. A controller program usually changes values of some of state variables based on values of some state variables. For example, the state variables of a line tracing robot will be the location of the robot, the locations of the right and left sensors, the output values of the right and left sensors, direction of the robot, the rotation speed of left and right wheels, and so on. The output values of the right and left sensors are used as inputs of the controller. The rotation speed of left and right wheels are used as outputs of the controller.

EM can be normally represented in differential equations on state variables. In a hybrid system, such equations are used, while in a finite state model, differential-difference equations are used as approximation.

DM can be modeled as uncertain error for each of observation variables.

For a line tracing robot, the principle state variables are summarized in Table 1.

**Table 1.** State Variables of a Line Tracing Robot

| variable | description |
|----------|-------------|
| $x$: | x-coordinate of the center of a line tracing robot |
| $y$: | y-coordinate of the center of a line tracing robot |
| $\theta$: | direction of a line tracing robot |
| $slx$: | x-coordinate of the left sensor of a line tracing robot |
| $sly$: | y-coordinate of the left sensor of a line tracing robot |
| $srx$: | x-coordinate of the right sensor of a line tracing robot |
| $sry$: | y-coordinate of the right sensor of a line tracing robot |
| $wl$: | revolution speed of the left wheel of a line tracing robot |
| $wr$: | revolution speed of the right wheel of a line tracing robot |
| $sl$: | the sensed value of the left color sensor |
| $sr$: | the sensed value of the right color sensor |

We need some other constants to model, especially constants on the size of the line tracing robot.

Assume that a line tracing robot turns with the speed of left and right wheels at $h_s$ and $l_s$. Then equations of motion can be given as follows.

$$\frac{d\theta}{dt} = \frac{h_s - l_s}{w} \qquad (1) \qquad\qquad \frac{dy}{dt} = r_c \cdot \cos\theta \cdot \frac{d\theta}{dt} \qquad (3)$$

$$\frac{dx}{dt} = -r_c \cdot \sin\theta \cdot \frac{d\theta}{dt} \qquad (2) \qquad\qquad r_c = \frac{w}{2} \cdot \frac{h_s + l_s}{h_s - l_s}, \qquad (4)$$

where $w$ is the width of the robot.

## 3.2  Multiple Tracing Robots

The model for multiple tracing robots divides each robot's CM into two levels of controllers, namely upper controller model (UCM) and lower controller model (LCM). The upper controller model deals with proximity sensors and wireless communication devices, while the lower controller model deals with color sensors and motors. Figure 2 shows the overview of the whole model. In Figure 2, Communication Medium Model is also used, which supports modeling for communication among proximity sensors and wireless communication devices.

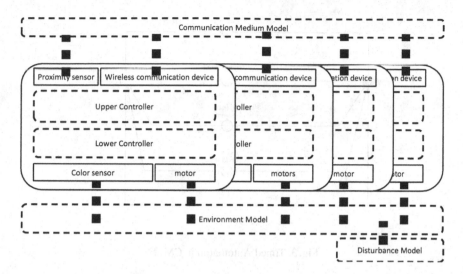

**Fig. 2.** Model Overview of Multiple Tracing Robots

We can easily implement a proximity sensor for the robot with a combination of ultrasonic sensors and touch sensors provided by the latest LEGO Mindstorms. A communication device for the robot can be also implemented with a bluetooth device built in the main block of LEGO Mindstorms.

## 4   Formal Verification

We describe two results of model checking on our models. The first is the stand-alone system model and the other is the multiple autonomous systems model.

### 4.1   Stand-Alone Tracing Robot

In this experiment, we use a simple controller program, where the rotation speed of wheels has only two values, $h_s$ and $l_s$. Moreover we assume that sensors only tell white and black colors on the track. In other words, the values of $sl$ and $sr$ are determined by only the position of the line tracing robot. On the other hand, we model the delay of sensors and actuators. Concretely, we have parameters $d_s$, $d_a$, and $d_t$ for delay between the time when program senses color and the time when the sensors obtain the values of colors, delay between the time when program issues a command and the time when the motor reacts, and sleeping time for next sense-act loop, respectively. This modeling represents real behaviors of a line tracing robot.

Figure 3 shows the control behavior model of the program.

As EM, we use sampling abstraction, which updates the values of environment state variables at fixed intervals[8].

We verified the following queries on an ideal model consisting of CM and EM (without DM):

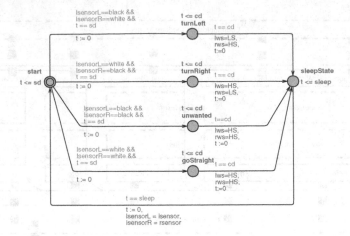

**Fig. 3.** Timed Automaton in CM

1. $\mathbb{E}\Diamond(900 < x)$.
2. $\mathbb{E}\Diamond(\text{C.turnRight})$.
3. $\mathbb{E}\Diamond(\text{C.turnLeft})$.
4. $\mathbb{E}\Diamond(\text{C.unwanted})$.
5. $\mathbb{A}\Box\neg(\text{C.unwanted})$.
6. $\mathbb{E}\Diamond(\text{C.goStraight})$.
7. $\mathbb{A}\Box((x > 280) \Rightarrow (-100 < y < 100))$.
8. $\mathbb{A}\Box((x > 280) \Rightarrow (\theta < 10 \lor 350 < \theta))$.
9. $\mathbb{E}\Diamond((x > 280) \Rightarrow \text{C.turnRight})$.
10. $\mathbb{E}\Diamond((x > 280) \Rightarrow \text{C.turnLeft})$.

The first query (1) means that the line tracing robot will reach the area $x > 900$. Queries (2) and (3) mean that the controller eventually reaches state C.turnRight and C.turnLeft. Queries (4) and (5) mean that the controller eventually reaches state C.unwanted and that the controller never reaches state C.unwanted, respectively, where both of sensors detect black color. Please note that query (4) and (5) contradict each other, i.e., query (5) is negation of query (4). Query (6) means that the controller eventually reaches state C.goStraight. Queries (7) and (8) mean that the line tracing roughly keeps the track and appropriate direction, respectively, after 280 unit length point. The last two queries mean that the line tracer eventually turns left or right even if the tracer is in stable state.

Every of the verifications (except the query (4)) has succeeded[8].

### 4.2   Multiple Tracing Robots

In order to communicate between the upper level control and the lower level control, we introduce a state variable *command*. If the value of *command* is stop then LCM sets the values of speed of motors to 0. The revised version of LCM is shown in the left of Figure 4.

UCM has to control the value of *command* according to the values of proximity sensors. In order to select one robot to enter an intersection among robots at the intersection, robots have to negotiate the selection with them when each of them senses its neighbors by its proximity sensors. We can choose an algorithm for such a problem from many distributed algorithm. If we assume that every intersection has its associated

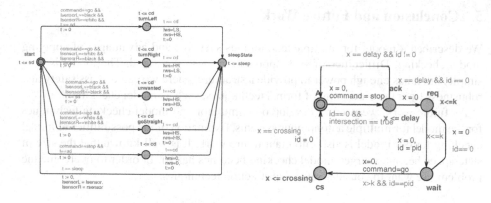

**Fig. 4.** Timed Automata for LCM and UCM

whiteboard and any robot at the intersection can access the whiteboard, then we can use Fischer's protocol. It is well-known that Fischer's protocol can be model checked in UPPAAL. We modify the model served as a demo example in UPPAAL distribution by adding some transitions with extra actions and guards.

The right of Figure 4 shows the modified Fischer's protocol model with wireless communication delay and intersection crossing time, as UCM. The variable *id* shows the whiteboard. If the value of *id* is 0, it means that no robots is in the intersection. A robot which wants to enter the intersection overwrites the value of *id* to its own id. After some units of time, if the value is the same as its own id, the robot enter the intersection. The modified version has two more locations than the original model Fischer's model. However, we think that the modified model is still too abstract. If we want more detailed behaviors, we need more clocks, transitions, events, and other automata.

We can successfully perform model checking that at most one robot exists in the intersection with the model in Figure 4. In general, if the size of models becomes larger, the model checking costs (CPU time) become larger.

At first we wrongly modeled UCM as an automaton without a transition from location ack to A. Also the guard of the transition from ack to req is not "x== delay && id ==0," but "x==delay." Such a small defect leads the result of model checking to fail. Therefore, model checking on a high-level specification is very useful to avoid unwanted design.

To model check some important properties based on our model is one of future work. If we cannot assume that every intersection has its whiteboard, then making mutual agreements among the robots become harder. Some algorithms for it might be hard to be modeled.

Once we have modeled all of sub-models in timed automata, we can simulate several concrete behaviors using simulator function in UPPAAL. However its visualization is based on message sequence charts. For our model, it is desired to visualize more concrete views such as location and moving speed of every robot in a 2D map. LTSA tool[9] has such a function. In LTSA tool, users can configure animation objects and their behaviors for abstract specification of concurrent systems by editing configure files in XML format. We want to extend the simulation viewer of UPPAAL with a similar as LTSA tool.

## 5   Conclusion and Future Work

We described a model for multiple autonomous systems, and advantages of applying model checking. Difficulties of such approach are also described. The model is very simple, but it has enough power to provide a structure where we can discuss safety and robustness from the view point of formal techniques, such as model checking.

As future work, we want to develop our simulator and model checking techniques for the model for multiple autonomous systems. Evaluation of the possibilities of model checking for our model is also important future work. It is well-known that the size of state space becomes larger, model checking becomes harder. In order to overcome the problem, we want to consider several abstraction techniques.

## References

1. Alur, R., Dill, D.L.: A theory of timed automata. Journal of Theoretical Computer Science 126(2), 183–235 (1994)
2. Bengtsson, J., Yi, W.: Timed Automata: Semantics, Algorithms and Tools. In: Desel, J., Reisig, W., Rozenberg, G. (eds.) ACPN 2003. LNCS, vol. 3098, pp. 87–124. Springer, Heidelberg (2004)
3. Bengtsson, J., Griffioen, W.O.D., Kristoffersen, K.J., Larsen, K.G., Larsson, F., Pettersson, P., Yi, W.: Verification of an Audio Protocol with bus collision using UPPAAL. In: Alur, R., Henzinger, T.A. (eds.) CAV 1996. LNCS, vol. 1102, pp. 244–256. Springer, Heidelberg (1996)
4. Lindahl, M., Pettersson, P., Yi, W.: Formal Design and Analysis of a Gear Controller. In: Steffen, B. (ed.) TACAS 1998. LNCS, vol. 1384, pp. 281–297. Springer, Heidelberg (1998)
5. Bordbar, B., Okano, K.: Verification of Timeliness QoS Properties in Multimedia Systems. In: Dong, J.S., Woodcock, J. (eds.) ICFEM 2003. LNCS, vol. 2885, pp. 523–540. Springer, Heidelberg (2003)
6. Fitzgerald, J., Larsen, P.G., Pierce, K., Verhoef, M., Wolff, S.: Collaborative Modelling and Co-simulation in the Development of Dependable Embedded Systems. In: Méry, D., Merz, S. (eds.) IFM 2010. LNCS, vol. 6396, pp. 12–26. Springer, Heidelberg (2010)
7. LeJOS, Java for LEGO Mindstorms, http://lejos.sourceforge.net
8. Okano, K., Sekizawa, T., Shimba, H., Kawai, H., Hanada, K., Sasaki, Y., Kusumoto, S.: Verification of Safety Properties of a Program for Line Tracing Robot using a Timed Automaton Model. International Journal of Informatics Society 5(3), 147–155 (2013)
9. Magee, J., Kramer, J.: Concurrency: State Models and Java Programs, 2nd edn. John Wiley and Sons (April 2006)

# Checking Verification Compliance of Technical Safety Requirements on the AUTOSAR Platform Using Annotated Semi-formal Executable Models

Martin Skoglund[1], Hans Svensson[2], Henrik Eriksson[1], Thomas Arts[2], Rolf Johansson[1], and Alex Gerdes[2]

[1] SP - Technical Research Institute of Sweden, Dep. of Electronics, SE-501 15 Borås, Sweden
{martin.skoglund,henrik.eriksson,rolf.johansson}@sp.se
[2] Quviq AB, SE-412 88 Gothenburg, Sweden
{hans.svensson,thomas.arts,alex.gerdes}@quviq.com

**Abstract.** Implementing AUTOSAR-based embedded systems that adhere to ISO 26262 is not trivial. High-level safety goals have to be refined to functional safety requirements and technical HW and SW safety requirements. SW safety requirements allocated to the application as well as the underlying AUTOSAR platform. Finding relevant safety requirements on the AUTOSAR basic software are a challenge. AUTOSAR specifications provide incomplete lists of requirements which might be relevant. In this paper we address this challenge by providing tool support to automatically extract relevant functional requirements for given safety scenarios. A conservative estimation gives that the safety-relevant part of the overall requirements can be as small as 30%, which reduce the necessary rigid testing effort. An electronic parking brake example is presented as a demonstration of concept.

**Keywords:** Technical Safety Concept, Technical Safety Requirements, Safety Verification, Safety arguing, Automotive, ISO 26262, AUTOSAR.

## 1 Introduction – The Automotive Safety Problem

The ISO 26262 standard has been developed to address the exponential growth in complexity of the software integrated into automotive systems, and the inherent potential for catastrophic failure. The standard aims to address these failures, by defining a safety lifecycle-process to ensure that safety is taken into account in the design of electronic systems in automotive applications.

The functional safety requirements are refined to technical safety requirements and HW and SW safety requirements respectively, on the application level, as well as on all underlying software levels, e.g., the AUTOSAR basic software platform. To verify the top-level safety requirements, safety goals, we therefore need to verify that the AUTOSAR platform implementation in its context can meet the strict requirements of ISO 26262. This is in practice a challenge. There is evidence that production ready

A. Bondavalli et al. (Eds.): SAFECOMP 2014 Workshops, LNCS 8696, pp. 19–26, 2014.
© Springer International Publishing Switzerland 2014

AUTOSAR software may still contain deviations against the standard [6]. Thus, a safety argument based upon the argument that the basic software has been QA tested is in practice insufficient. The least we would like to know is that all requirements important for safety analysis are tested well enough for the claimed safety integrity level. Requirements that are not important for the safety argument can then be ignored. This in accordance with the ISO 26262 reference life cycle, that assumes that it is possible to identify where the safety requirements are allocated. However, this is in general only considered feasible for application software, for platform software it is usual to consider all functional requirements as safety related. Such a strategy might be very costly, and therefore it would be beneficial to reduce the scope for safety argumentation to only the requirements that are safety relevant in the actual context.

In this paper, we address the challenge to identify safety-relevant requirements in the AUTOSAR basic software. As an example, we gather all technical requirements from a set of functional safety requirements that demand that a car CAN network is accessible (i.e. wake up from sleep mode).

## 2     Background

The overall objective of the AUTOSAR standard [4] is to define a platform upon which future vehicle applications will be developed. In this paper focus is placed on the safety critical software features of AUTOSAR Basic Software (BSW) that is closely linked to the functional safety standard ISO 26262.

Safety requirements allocated on the BSW have propagated down from the application software it serves in an assumed context. Typically, one can only assume the level of intended integrity for the BSW module because it is developed before and separate from an application. This kind of development is covered by the guideline for Safety Element out of Context (SEooC) in the ISO 26262 [2]. The SEooC can typically be an AUTOSAR BSW module. The process directs the developer to make assumptions on the scope of the SEooC, which entails listing circumstances of use, that can be foreseen e.g. the software will be integrated in a specific layered architecture or that the module should detect errors or to delegate the error detection. The next step is to make assumptions on the safety requirements of the SEooC. When all assumptions on the SEooC have been documented, the development of the software SEooC can be started according to the requirements of ISO 26262-6 [1] for the selected ASIL level. During the integration of the SEooC in a new particular context, the validity of all assumptions is checked and if the not all assumptions are valid, an impact analysis should be carried out. This may lead to a redesign of the SEooC software or adjustments to its environment.

In order, for concepts like SEooC to be applicable and practical it is required that the AUTOSAR platform can meet the rigorous verification requirements of ISO 26262 with confidence. The ambition is to build that confidence and to identify a method to aid the confirmation of compliance with the stringent requirements on the verification of safety requirements stated in Table 2 *Methods for the verification of safety requirements* in clause 6.4.3.3 of ISO 26262-8 [2].

The big advantage is to be able to point directly to a common ground like the AUTOSAR standard requirements on a module when allocating and verifying safety integrity. The proposed method in this paper aims to bridging the gap between application and platform seen in Figure 1.

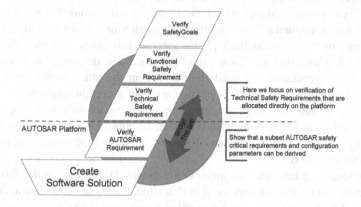

**Fig. 1.** Right side of the V-model development process focused on safety

# 3    Our Approach

## 3.1    Identify Safety Critical Features Allocated to Platform

In general, it is hard to know which functional requirements are important for the fulfilment of a safety requirement. The basic assumption is that all functional requirements are correctly implemented and that this is verified in some way. The safety analysis should not need to repeat this work, but just assuming correct implementation of all-important requirements seems precarious.

The minimum we want to establish is what requirements we should have well tested. To attain a relevant set of safety requirements we will go through the safety lifecycle process described in ISO 26262. First, identify the *item* and its top-level system functionality then make a comprehensive set of *hazardous events* identified for the item and assign an ASIL to each event. Each *hazardous event* is assigned a *safety goal*, with the purpose of reducing of the risk to an acceptable level, inheriting the ASIL of the hazardous event. *Safety goals* are refined into lower-level *functional safety requirements* that have been assigned to system architectural elements. *Functional safety requirements* can be refined or decomposed further to *technical safety requirements* allocated to hardware and software components, here of special interest is the *technical safety requirements* allocated direct on the software platform. This process is also applicable for a SEooC but then all the entities that govern safety are assumed. If we have *technical safety requirements* allocated on the platform they generally state that some platform mechanism has to behave a certain way with ASIL integrity. Even if the mechanism falls under one of the predefined *technical safety concepts* of AUTOSAR [4], the problem of tracing what functional requirements are relevant for this particular mechanism still remain, but we now know what mechanism and behavior that is safety related.

## 3.2    Identify Relevant Test Scenarios

We use the scenarios to identify relevant requirements. Basically, for each performed API call, one should know what requirements apply to that call. This is problematic, since the requirements depend not only on the API call, but also on the present system state. Therefore, we use a model implementing the specifications that we use for testing AUTOSAR components. These models are written in the programming language Erlang [9] and used by QuickCheck [7] to generate test cases. The models are templates for the implementations. Each model has a state to determine which consecutive calls can be generated and what their effect on the state should be. The state contains all information needed to determine whether a certain requirement is applicable to a specific call. We therefore can annotate the model with those requirements that are relevant at a certain moment of time. The requirements are manually added to the model by carefully reading the specification. We assume that this annotation has carefully been validated.

When generating a test case, we traverse the model. Depending on the function arguments and the state the software is in at that time, the model code is traversed differently. On the code path, we have annotated requirements and as soon as we pass one of these, that is recorded. The model can also replay generated test cases; we use that to run the actual test case against the software. We can during this replay also save the requirements encountered during that test run. Thus, a test case always corresponds to a set of requirements that we encountered in the code when running that test case. A scenario is just a large test case and by executing the scenario, we automatically derive all requirements that we encountered during the run of this scenario. Note that we do not need any code for executing a scenario in the model, since we have the possibility with these models to not execute, but just simulate a test run.

## 4    Application of the Method on Parking Brake

To demonstrate the method we will use a small part of a larger safety life cycle work done on an electronic parking brake (EPB) item [10]. No assertion to comprehensiveness is being made on the item presented here. We have conducted the process prescribed in ISO 26262 with a minimal but illustrative example. The goal is to have a set of technical safety requirements allocated to the platform that states that some platform mechanism has to behave in a certain way, with ASIL integrity. Then use a call trace in the requirement annotated executable model of the relevant modules to yield a complete list of the affected AUTOSAR requirements for the technical safety requirement of interest.

### 4.1    Identify Safety Critical Features Allocated on Platform

Electronic parking brakes are used on passenger vehicles to hold the vehicle stationary on grades and flat roads. This was traditionally accomplished using a manual parking brake. With an EPB, the driver engages the holding mechanism with a button and the brake pads are then electrically applied onto the rear brake discs. Releasing the brakes are done the similar way. However if considering the situation when the vehicle is parked on a railway crossing with EPB engaged, the EBP needs to know that there is a driver present, to not risk violating the safety goal for "Parked slope, driver not present" (unintended release). This is implemented by pressing the gas pedal in order to discern that release is valid. The <gas pedal pressed> sensor is allocated to a different node and the signal is sent via a CAN bus to the EPB.

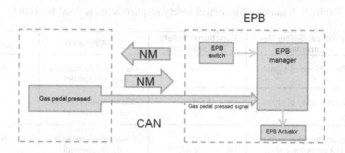

**Fig. 2.** EPB System view with network management (NM) included

If the EPB under some circumstance is unaware that the <gas pedal pressed> signal is being sent and therefore unable to mitigate with a safe state, we have an "Intended release omission". This is unlikely to happen but have severe consequences, see Table 1. This safety goal will be considered for the rest of the paper.

**Table 1.** Hazard analysis for parked on train track

| Hazard id | Failure mode | Situation | Hazard | E | S | C | ASIL | Safety goal id | Safety goal |
|---|---|---|---|---|---|---|---|---|---|
| Haz1 | Release Omission | Parked railway crossing Driver pressing the gas pedal | Intended release omission | E0 Incredible rare | S3 Life-threatening or fatal injuries | C3 Difficult to control or uncontrollable | A | SG1 | Shall release on train track |

Proposed functional safety requirements on EPB item are listed in Table 2, which meet the level of detail required by the example, but they will not reflect the complete set of functional safety requirements. It adheres to the principle that at least one functional safety requirement shall be specified for each safety goal. In a complete set, consideration has to be taken to operating modes, fault tolerant time interval, safe states, emergency operation interval, and functional redundancies (e.g. fault tolerance). A warning and degradation concept should also be specified.

**Table 2.** Functional safety requirement

| Tag | Functional Safety Requirement | Safety Goal | Allocated | ASIL |
|---|---|---|---|---|
| FSR1 | \<Gas pedal pressed\> signal max age 1 second +-200ms | SG1 | \<Gas pedal pressed\> signal channel | ASIL A |

**Table 3.** A sample of technical safety requirements refined for FSR1

| Tag | Technical Safety Requirement | Functional Safety Requirement | Allocated | ASIL |
|---|---|---|---|---|
| TSR2 | Detect loss of signal | FSR1 | \<Gas pedal pressed\> signal channel | ASIL A |
| TSR3 | Detect delay of signal | FSR1 | \<Gas pedal pressed\> signal channel | ASIL A |
| TSR6 | Detect blocking access to a communication | FSR1 | \<Gas pedal pressed\> signal channel | ASIL A |

The EPB item has full AUTOSAR network management implemented. The CanNm module has the following states; here we focus on the external states (observable): `Network Mode`, `Prepare Bus-Sleep Mode`, and `Bus-Sleep Mode`.

If the receiving node (EPB) is in Bus-Sleep Mode it has no possibility to fulfill the technical safety requirements placed on *Detect loss of signal*, *Detect delay of signal*, and *Detect blocking access to a communication channel*. Protective features placed on these are put out of play when in Bus-Sleep Mode because it has no possibility to detect the absence of a signal on a sleeping net. The transition from `Bus-Sleep Mode` to `Network Mode` is safety related since the node has to have the ability to leave sleep mode, and the transition from `Prepare Bus-Sleep Mode` to `Bus-Sleep Mode` is important because the node should not go to sleep without just cause. The initialization is obviously also important; the node should not get stuck in the startup phase. Tracing these transitions in the AUTOSAR specification is quite simple, but deriving the related functional requirements that support these features is more challenging.

### 4.2    Identify Relevant Test Scenario of Network Management

The first step in our approach is to reduce the safety goals to scenarios that need to work in order to fulfil the safety requirements. For instance, in our parking brake example, we want to be able to get the network to full communication, bring it to sleep, and get it to full communication again as explained in Section 4.1. Such a scenario is not the same as a test case, in order to make a test case, one need to call a number of API functions in BSW modules CanNm, CanIf, and CanSM. At the moment we manually create this test case from such scenario. For the above example, this test case consists of 546 calls to 10 different API functions. From these API functions, 4 functions are specified in CanNm, 2 are specified in CanIf and 3 are specified in CanSM. Thus even such a simple scenario points to three different specifications and a large number of functions that should be correctly implemented.

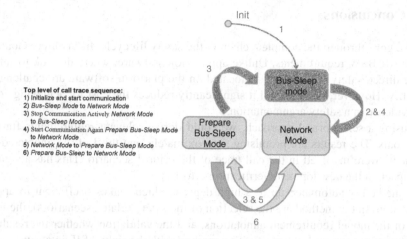

**Top level of call trace sequence:**
1) Initialize and start communication
2) *Bus-Sleep Mode to Network Mode*
3) Stop Communication Actively *Network Mode*
   to *Bus-Sleep Mode*
4) Start Communication Again *Prepare Bus-Sleep Mode*
   to *Network Mode*
5) *Network Mode to Prepare Bus-Sleep Mode*
6) *Prepare Bus-Sleep to Network Mode*

**Fig. 3.** Schematic test scenario description

## 4.3    Result of Call Trace

For each transition made in Figure 3, the relevant AUTOSAR requirements can be listed. Here we are only interested in transitions 1, 2, 3 and 4. The relevant requirements are grouped by module and presented in Figure 4.

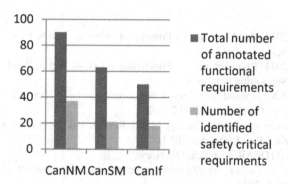

**Fig. 4.** Result summary of call trace for requirements

The total number of 203 requirements was annotated in the three modules and out of those 76 was involved in the call trace. Approximately one third of the annotated requirements on module level where in some way involved in the call trace, and thus are safety related. This is a promising technique to fulfil item 1c in clause 6.4.3.3 of ISO 26262-8 [2].

## 5     Conclusions

We have gone through the complete chain in the safety lifecycle, from Safety Goals to AUTOSAR BSW requirements. Unlike application software, where the link to safety is more direct, safety requirements allocated on the platform software are challenging to identify. However, if successful it significantly reduces the cost for achieving complete evidence in a safety argumentation.

By using a semi-formal approach, we could derive relevant requirements for our safety goals. The results are promising, approximately one third of the annotated requirements were involved in the call trace of the critical scenario. This has a significant impact on the development/verification effort.

The method is automated up to a high degree, which makes it efficient to apply. Manual steps in the method are the selection of the safety related scenario(s), the validation of the model requirement annotations, and the validation whether the resulting requirements are covered in a verification method with the right ASIL integrity.

Altogether, the presented method was shown to be a viable way to derive a limited amount of safety requirements on platform components.

**Acknowledgements.** We acknowledge the Swedish research foundation Vinnova for its support of the AcSäPt project (ref. 2012-00943) and the European Commission for its support of the nSafeCer project, ARTEMIS (ref. 295373).

## References

1. ISO, 26262-6:2011, Road vehicles — Functional safety — Part 6, Product development at the software level
2. ISO, 26262-8:2011, Road vehicles — Functional safety — Part 8, Road vehicles — Functional safety - Supporting processes
3. ISO, 26262-10:2011, Road vehicles — Functional safety — Part 10, Road vehicles — Functional safety - Guideline on ISO 26262
4. AUTOSAR, Technical Safety Concept Status Report, vol. Document Version 1.2.0, no. Part of Release 4.1 Rev 1 (October 2013)
5. AUTOSAR, AUTOSAR Technical Overview, http://www.autosar.org/index.php?p=1&up=2&uup=0 (retrieved March 5, 2014)
6. Arts, T., Johansson, R., Svensson, D., Kallerdahl, A.: Model Based Testing of AUTOSAR components. In: Proceedings of the 3rd AUTOSAR Open Conference, Frankfurt, Germany, May 11 (2011)
7. Arts, T., Hughes, J., Johansson, J., Wiger, U.: Testing telecoms software with Quviq QuickCheck. In: ACM SIGPLAN Workshop on Erlang (2006)
8. Svenningsson, R., Johansson, R., Arts, T., Norell, U.: Formal Methods Based Acceptance Testing for AUTOSAR Exchangeability. SAE Int. J. Passeng. Cars - Electron. Electr. Syst. 5(1), 209–213 (2012)
9. Armstrong, J.L., Williams, M., Virding, R., Wilkström, C.: ERLANG for Concurrent Programming. Prentice-Hall, Inc. (1993)
10. Skoglund, M.: AP1, Quality criteria for supporting the ISO 26262, AcSäPt project (ref. 2012-00943)

# Evaluation of Safety Rules in a Safety Kernel-Based Architecture

Eric Vial and António Casimiro

Universidade de Lisboa, Faculdade de Ciências, Portugal
evial@lasige.di.fc.ul.pt, casim@di.fc.ul.pt

**Abstract.** Kernel-based architectures have been proposed as a possible solution to build safe cooperative systems with improved performance. These systems adjust their operation mode at run-time, depending on the actual quality of sensor data used in control loops and on the execution timeliness of relevant control functions. Sets of safety rules, defined at design-time, express the conditions concerning data quality and timeliness that need to be satisfied for the system to operate safely in each operation mode.

In this paper we propose a solution for practically expressing these safety rules at design-time, and for evaluating them at run-time. This evaluation is done using periodically collected information about safety-related variables. For expressing the rules we adopt the XML language. The run-time solution is based on a safety rules evaluation engine, which was designed for efficiency and scalability. We describe the architecture of the engine, the solution for structuring data in memory and the rule evaluation algorithm. A simple sensor-based control system is considered to exemplify how the safety rules are expressed.

## 1 Introduction

Safety is typically a fundamental concern when designing and developing vehicular autonomous systems like autonomous cars, airplanes or boats. System safety is usually proved at design-time, for which assumptions on system properties have to be made (e.g., fault and timeliness assumptions). These assumptions are required to hold with very high probability when developing safety-critical systems. A difficult problem when moving towards more complex systems performing more complex functions is that failure modes also become more complex and the system behavior tends to be less predictable. This is amplified when considering cooperative systems, which need to interact over wireless communication networks. In such systems, making assumptions on bounded message delays becomes a hard exercise: either these assumptions are pessimistic, leading to inefficient solutions, or additional resources must be used to improve the characteristics of communication subsystem, increasing the cost of the solution.

To address this problem, the solutions proposed in literature typically suggest to separate the system in different parts. The properties assumed for each part will be different, resulting in systems with a hybrid architecture. Notable examples include the Simplex model [4] and the Timely Computing Base model [5].

A. Bondavalli et al. (Eds.): SAFECOMP 2014 Workshops, LNCS 8696, pp. 27–35, 2014.
© Springer International Publishing Switzerland 2014

In both cases, part of the functions will be executed in a more predictable way (under a stronger failure or timeliness model), while other functions, the complex ones, will execute in a less predictable part of the system. The system separation in two parts makes it easier to enforce the properties assumed for the "better" part, while safety is ensured by making the system adjustable at run-time: the complex functions will only be used for control when a certain set of assumptions is satisfied. For that, the system must encompass a safety manager that observes relevant variables, verifies if predefined safety rules (assumptions) are met, and adjusts the system configuration and operation whenever necessary.

This idea was explored in the KARYON project, which defined a generic architectural pattern for the development of sensor-based autonomous and co-operative systems [2]. The KARYON architecture is based on a safety kernel that performs the mentioned observation of safety-related variables and determines the adequate operation mode. The safety kernel is also responsible to drive the necessary adjustments or reconfiguration actions, according to the operation mode that was determined as the safe one. There is a set of safety rules that has been defined at design-time for each mode of operation to perform the desired functions safely. They are used at run-time by the safety kernel, which periodically evaluates if they are being satisfied, given the collected safety information. KARYON also proposes solutions to abstract specific sensor faults, defining an abstract sensor model that allows sensor data to be characterized by a *validity* attribute [1]. Therefore, safety rules are expressed in terms of *validity requirements*, as well as in terms of *timeliness requirements*. We note that safety rules, once defined in design-time, and once being considered for safety analysis, will not change in run-time.

This paper focusses on the design and the implementation of an engine that performs the run-time verification of safety requirements expressed in safety rules. This engine is one of the main components the safety kernel and hence has to perform the verification efficiently. In addition, we also devised a solution that deals with scalability issues and may thus be useful for more realistic applications, involving a large number of safety rules. The paper explain how the safety rules can be expressed using the XML notation, how they are parsed and stored in memory and what is the algorithm performed by the safety manager engine to evaluate safety based on collected safety information.

The paper is structured as follows. In Section 2 we provide a brief overview of the safety kernel components. The design and the implementation of the relevant components for evaluating safety at run-time are presented in Section 3. An example case is considered in section4, to illustrate how safety rules are defined. Finally, Section 5 concludes the paper.

## 2 Definitions and Concepts

We consider a system in which several (possibly cooperative) functions can be executed. Nominal system components required for the execution of these functions include: *sensors, actuators, computation* and *communication* components. Each of these components can be used to support multiple functions. Each function can be provided with several *levels of service* (LoS), depending on the components that are being used and/or the *performance level* of each component. Some components can exhibit uncertain timeliness, but some of them (used to execute the functions with a minimum guaranteed LoS) must always be timely.

Besides the nominal system components, the system includes a safety kernel that is responsible for adjusting the performance level of specific components or reconfiguring the system, such that each function will be executed with a desired level of service (LoS). The safety kernel is necessarily in the predictable part of the system. For its operation, the safety kernel collects timeliness and sensor data validity information. It then uses this information to verify if safety rules are satisfied, determining the adequate LoS for each function. Depending on the combination of LoS for the different functions, a specific system configuration and/or component performance level is enforced.

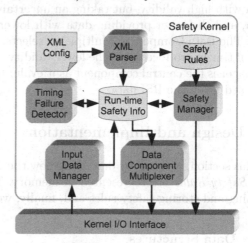

**Fig. 1.** Safety kernel components

Figure 1 gives an overview of the safety kernel components. At startup the *XML Parser* reads the local configuration, builds a *Safety Rules* repository and initializes *Run-time Safety Information* (RSI) structures. Therefore, the configuration file includes both safety rules and *unit* definitions. A unit corresponds to a safety kernel input (collected data), output (adjustment data – typically a component performance level) or locally calculated values (for instance, the acceptable LoS for some function). A safety rule is a boolean expression involving combinations of static values (bounds) and unit identifiers. A safety rule is meaningful for a specific LoS of some function. For instance, function $F_2$ can only be safely executed in LoS 1 when data validity $V_0$ is greater than 50 and $V_1$ greater than 70. This is expressed as:

$$F_2(LoS1) \rightarrow V_0 > 50 \wedge V_1 > 70$$

The *Input Data Manager* receives data inputs from the external (nominal system) components and updates the RSI. The *Timing Failure Detector* (TFD) is responsible for checking if certain data inputs have been received from external components within predefined temporal bounds. This TFD executes periodically, during each execution round of the safety kernel. When the TFD detects a timing failure (some data, which might be just an heartbeat, has not been timely produced at the safety kernel interface), it stores this information in the RSI unit corresponding to the untimely data. The *Data Component Multiplexer* selects, from two or more data inputs (collected from nominal components), one that is forwarded to its output. This is useful, for instance, when the nominal has two components providing the same data (e.g., a front distance value), one providing data with high validity, but taking an uncertain amount of time to produce this data, and the other providing data with lower validity, but always in a timely way. The Data Component Multiplexer selects, among the two values, the better one, if timely produced, and the lower validity one, otherwise. Finally, the Safety Manager is the central component as it evaluates at run-time if *Safety Rules* are satisfied given the RSI data.

## 3   Design and Implementation

In this section, we start by describing how the *Run-time Safety Information* and the *Safety Rules* are represented in memory. Then we explain the solution for parsing and storing safety rules and, finally, we address the safety manager.

### 3.1   Data Structures

Data structures must be simple to provide code robustness, but they are designed as well with the aim of reducing the computation time during the rule evaluation phase. The Run-time Safety Information (RSI) repository is initialized during system bootstrap and is updated at run-time with collected safety-related information. The RSI size depends on the number of units (inputs, outputs and internal variables) declared in the configuration file. As this size is not changed at run-time, we use a single dimension array to store the units. Each unit structure contains several fields, including a pointer to related safety rules, which set requirements on this unit, a timeliness status, which may be relevant for units with timeliness constraints, a data validity value, a level value that may be used to store performance levels or levels of service (this is clarified ahead in the text), and some other attributes.

The safety rules are also built at bootstrap from the configuration file. We note that one possible design approach would be to simply hard code the safety rules within the safety kernel, thus avoiding the need for specifying them in a configuration file, and consequently processing them at bootstrap. However, we decided to follow an approach that provides some additional flexibility and leads to a generic safety kernel implementation. Safety rules can be updated without the need for recompiling the code and loading it on the board, which is particularly advantageous during the development process. And the safety kernel core is totally independent of the specific application, which can facilitate verification and validation activities.

Given that safety rules need to be checked in every execution cycle, within a limited amount of time, a fundamental requirement is to devise a solution for storing them in memory, such that safety management is efficient and scalable.

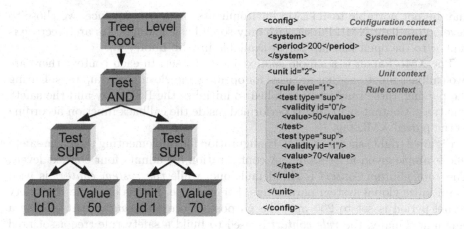

**Fig. 2.** Basic safety rule definition

This is particularly necessary if considering that in real systems the number of safety rules will tend to be very high. The concrete number will depend on the amount of functionalities that may be performed by an autonomous vehicle, on the number of system variables that may have to be checked in run-time, and on the number of levels of service considered for each functionality. We addressed this requirement by adopting a tree-based data organization, where the root node for each safety rule contains the associated level of service (LoS) and a pointer to the top child node of the tree. This tree is created during the XML Parsing. This kind of structure allows for efficient rule parsing at run-time, using the algorithm described in Section 3.3.

The tree corresponding to the basic rule example from Section 2 is shown in Figure 2 (left). Three different types of nodes can be used in the tree: test nodes, unit id nodes and value nodes. Test nodes store boolean operations, like *AND*, *OR*, *EQUAL*, *DIFF* or *SUP*, among others. Each unit id node contains the index of a unit in the RSI array. According to the way a unit id is defined in the configuration, it contains either a data validity value or a level of service/performance level value. In the example, the two units (ids 0 and 1) will contain data validity values. Different rule trees can refer to a single unit when there are multiple constrains (safety rules) related to a certain safety-related variable. When this happens, the several rule trees are level-sorted (from the higher to the lower level, as defined in the root node) in a linked list to which the unit will point. Finally, value nodes contain constants (bounds) against which the unit values will be checked.

## 3.2   XML Parsing

A lot of *XML Parsers* are described in the literature and many of them are available for free. These parsers usually offer a large range of functionalities and may be not portable to RTEMS environments. As a consequence, we chose to develop our light XML Parser with only some basic features. Its architecture is similar to the open markup parser available in Glib library [3].

The XML Parser is a simple context-based parser. In each context there are two callback functions that are used for opening and closing markup tags. During the parsing, these functions are called to initialize the RSI array and the safety rule trees. Context switching is performed inside the callback function according to the parsed XML tag.

Figure 2 (right) shows an XML configuration file implementing the basic safety rule example given in Section 2. A configuration file admits four context levels. The *configuration context* is the default one, while the *system context* is used to initialize global system parameters. For instance, in this example the safety kernel period is set to 200 ms. The purpose of the *unit context* is to define a new unit. Finally, the *rule context* is used to build a safety rule tree associated to a given unit. Note that besides the output unit with id 2 (which allows to set the performance level of some application component), two additional units are created (ids 0 and 1) to store data validity values. The output unit will hold the value 1 when the (only) rule evaluates to true, and 0 otherwise. A node stack allows to internally store the nodes and assemble the tree.

## 3.3 Safety Rules Evaluation

At run-time the Safety Manager will periodically scan the RSI array. For each unit with at least one defined rule (some units, like units 0 and 1 from the example, do not have any associated rule), the Safety Manager evaluates them starting with the rule with the highest level. The rationale is to first evaluate if the conditions to perform some function at the highest level of service are satisfied. When they are not, then other safety rules will be checked. Therefore, the evaluation stops when a rule is satisfied or when the end of the rule list is reached. In the latter case, this means that the function has to be executed at the lowest LoS (level 0). At the end of the process, the Safety Manager updates the level field of internal units (those holding the acceptable LoS for some function) and of output units (holding the performance level level of specific components). The rule evaluation functions are the following:

```
 1: function LEVEL(rule_list)
 2:    for all rule ∈ rule_list do
 3:        node_list ← rule.root
 4:        if AND(node_list) then
 5:            return rule.level
 6:        end if
 7:    end for
 8:    return 0
 9: end function
10:
11: function AND(node_list)
12:    for all node ∈ node_list do
```

```
13:        if ¬EVAL(node) then
14:            return false
15:        end if
16:    end for
17:    return true
18: end function
19:
20: function EVAL(node)
21:    switch node.type do
22:        case test
23:            return TEST(node)
24:        end case
```

```
25:        case unit                          39:              return false
26:            return UNIT(node)              40:          end if
27:        end case                           41:          return COMPARE(node) > 0
28:        case value                         42:      end case
29:            return true                    43:      ...
30:        end case                           44:  end switch
31:    end switch                             45: end function
32: end function                              46:
33:                                           47: function UNIT(node)
34: function TEST(node)                       48:    id ← node.unit.id
35:    node_list ← node.test.childs           49:    unit ← unit_array[id]
36:    switch node.test.type do               50:    return unit.status
37:        case sup                           51: end function
38:            if ¬AND(node_list) then
```

The *level* function (line 1) evaluates the unit rule list. The *and* function is first called, as the top-level node is always an *AND* in any rule tree. This first node gathers all conditions required for the rule to be satisfied. The *eval* function (line 20) evaluates a node according to its type. In the *test* function (line 34) we only show the SUP operator (line 37). First we check the timeliness status of both operands by recursively calling the *and* function. If the evaluation returns true, we compare the values of both operands (line 41). The *unit* function (line 47) is called to evaluate a unit and returns its timeliness status.

# 4   Example Application

We consider an example application in which two cooperative functions, $CF_A$ and $CF_B$, are implemented. These functions use two sensors, *S1* and *S2*, and five functional components, from *C1* to *C5*. Both sensors provide a data validity value associated to the sensor data they produce, which is sent to the safety kernel (*V1* and *V2*). *C4* is a multi-component with two implementations, *C4'* and *C4"*, corresponding, respectively, to performance levels *PL1* and *PL0*. According to the execution timeliness of *C4'*, called $ET_{C4-PL1}$, the *Data Component Multiplexer* will forward the selected value from *C4* to *C5*. Finally, *C1* is a component below the hybridization line able to execute with three different performance levels (from PL2 to PL0). We also consider that the safety rules for both functions are the following (the bounds have to be defined at design-time, and it must be proven that the functions will be safely performed in each LoS when the safety rules are met):

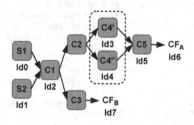

**Fig. 3.** Example functions

$CF_A\_LoS(LoS3) \rightarrow V1 > 80 \wedge ET_{C4-PL1} < D_{C4}$     $CF_B\_LoS(LoS3) \rightarrow V1 > 80 \wedge V2 > 70$

$CF_A\_LoS(LoS2) \rightarrow V1 > 60 \wedge ET_{C4-PL1} < D_{C4}$     $CF_B\_LoS(LoS2) \rightarrow V1 > 80$

$CF_A\_LoS(LoS1) \rightarrow V1 > 60$     $CF_B\_LoS(LoS1) \rightarrow V1 > 60$

$CF_A\_LoS(LoS0), otherwise$     $CF_B\_LoS(LoS0), otherwise$

The next table shows the performance levels of *C1* and *C4* in dependence of the *LoS* of both functions. All invalid combinations have been removed. On the right side of the table, we provide a possible set of expressions that can be used to calculate these performance levels.

| $CF_A$ | $CF_B$ | C1 | C4 |
|--------|--------|-----|-----|
| LoS3 | LoS3 | PL2 | PL1 |
| LoS1 | LoS3 | PL2 | PL0 |
| LoS3 | LoS2 | PL1 | PL1 |
| LoS2 | LoS1 | PL1 | PL1 |
| LoS1 | LoS1 | PL1 | PL0 |
| LoS0 | LoS0 | PL0 | PL0 |

$C1\_PL(PL2) \rightarrow CF_B\_LoS = 3$

$C1\_PL(PL1) \rightarrow CF_B\_LoS > 0$

$C1\_PL(PL0), otherwise$

Given all the above expressions, required to determine the feasible LoS for each function and the corresponding component performance levels, it is possible to create an XML configuration file. An identifier must be first assigned to each unit (e.g., ID0 for *S1*, ID1 for *S2*, ...), and this allows the proper references to be made in the configuration file. Note that there are no IDs for *C2* ad *C3* as they are not involved in any expressions. A subset of the resulting configuration file is presented below.

```
1  <?xml version="1.0"?>
2  <config>
3      <!-- C1 component -->
4      <unit id="2">
5          <mode>update</mode>
6          <rule level="2">
7              <test type="equal">
8                  <level id="7"/>
9                  <value>3</value>
10             </test>
11         </rule>
12         <rule level="1">
13             <test type="sup">
14                 <level id="7"/>
15                 <value>0</value>
16             </test>
17         </rule>
18     </unit>
19     ...
20     <!-- Function A -->
21     <unit id="6">
22         <rule level="3">
23             <test type="sup">
24                 <validity id="0"/>
25                 <value>80</value>
26             </test>
27             <test type="equal">
28                 <level id="5"/>
29                 <value>1</value>
30             </test>
31         </rule>
32         <rule level="2">
33             <test type="sup">
34                 <validity id="0"/>
35                 <value>60</value>
36             </test>
37             <test type="equal">
38                 <level id="5"/>
39                 <value>1</value>
40             </test>
41         </rule>
42         <rule level="1">
43             <test type="sup">
44                 <validity id="0"/>
45                 <value>60</value>
46             </test>
47         </rule>
48     </unit>
49     <!-- Function B -->
50     <unit id="7">
51         ...
52     </unit>
53  </config>
```

# 5   Conclusion

This paper describes the solutions developed in the KARYON project for specifying safety rules in configuration files, for storing safety rules and safety data in memory, and for evaluating safety at run-time. They were designed with the objective of being simple but effective, addressing performance and scalability requirements. This simplicity facilitates the calculation of upper bounds for safety rule evaluation time. These solutions have been implemented and are being used in the KARYON vehicular demonstration prototypes.

**Acknowledgements.** This work was partially supported by the EU's FP7 through project KARYON, under grant agreement No. 288195, and by the FCT, through the Multiannual program.

# References

1. Brade, T., Zug, S., Kaiser, J.: Validity-based failure algebra for distributed sensor systems. In: SRDS, pp. 143–152 (2013)
2. Casimiro, A., Kaiser, J., Schiller, E.M., Costa, P., Parizi, J., Johansson, R., Librino, R.: The karyon project: Predictable and safe coordination in cooperative vehicular systems. In: 2013 43rd Annual IEEE/IFIP Conference on Dependable Systems and Networks Workshop (DSN-W), pp. 1–12. IEEE (2013)
3. GLib Project: Rsimple xml subset parser, version 2.37 (2014)
4. Sha, L.: Using simplicity to control complexity. IEEE Software 18(4), 20–28 (2001)
5. Verissimo, P., Casimiro, A.: The timely computing base model and architecture. IEEE Transactions on Computers 51(8), 916–930 (2002)

# Driving with Confidence: Local Dynamic Maps That Provide LoS for the Gulliver Test-Bed*

Christian Berger, Oscar Morales, Thomas Petig, and Elad Michael Schiller

Computer Science and Engineering,
Chalmers University of Technology, Sweden
{christian.berger,mooscar,petig,elad}@chalmers.se

**Abstract.** The design of automated driving systems aims at reducing the human error and increasing the fuel efficiency by letting the vehicles map their surroundings and drive autonomously. One of the system challenges on the road is that at any time the environment can stop meeting the system's operational conditions (and then resume meeting the requirements at some later point in time). Thus, as vehicles map their surroundings, they should also provide information that can help the vehicles to know whether the operational conditions are met with respect to the confidence that they have about the mapped information.

We design and implement key services of *Local Dynamic Maps* (LDMs) that are based on on-board and remote sensory information. The LDM provides the position of all nearby noticeable objects along with the LDM's confidence about these positions. The design also includes an extension that allows the vehicular system to agree on the lowest common ability to meet the operational conditions.

We evaluate the performance of a key component in our pilot implementation together with a set of test cases that validate the proposed design. Our current findings show that the presented ideas can accelerate the deployment of automated driving systems.

## 1 Introduction

Self-driving cars will be the next big step in vehicular technology as several important automotive original equipment manufacturers (OEMs) have recently announced [9]. However, their specific challenge besides deploying a robust and reliable technology throughout a vehicle's lifetime [5] is to bring down the technology's costs. Therefore, expensive sensors that perceive a vehicle's surroundings need to be substituted by cheaper counterparts. Cheap sensors normally have a reduced accuracy. This is addressed by sensor fusion with information provided by other vehicles and the infrastructure.

---

* The work of this author was partially supported by the EC, through project FP7-STREP-288195, KARYON (Kernel-based ARchitecture for safetY-critical cONtrol).

A. Bondavalli et al. (Eds.): SAFECOMP 2014 Workshops, LNCS 8696, pp. 36–45, 2014.

Research in this area however is time-consuming, error-prone, expensive, and tedious, when several cars need to be coordinated within a real-scale experiment on a real proving ground. As an intermediate for instance, preliminary experiments can be planned and conducted with miniaturized counterparts. We maintain such a fleet of scaled autonomous and cooperative vehicles using the Gulliver Testbed [15]. Different use cases with our test-bed have successfully shown [2, 3] that it is possible to bridge between purely virtual experiments as carried out in simulations and physical experiments on real-scale proving grounds [4].

Our system design has two distinct parts that each has different timing properties, following the architectural hybridization concept [8]. Given the uncertainties affecting the system operation and the confidence in the data used in control processes, we use the architectural concept of safety kernel. This concept is responsible for managing the task, in a way, that ultimately ensures the required safety goals. The vehicle limited ability to communicate prevents centralized solutions and open the door to cooperative ones. We consider sensory data that has validity attributes attached that defines that accuracy and conference in the data. The (decartelized) safety kernel uses these attributes to decide on a system service level that in turn will set the system performance level after cooperatively evaluating the service level. This version of the paper refers to the work that was done in KARYON with respect to local dynamic maps. We note that cooperation to construction of localization maps was earlier discussed in other projects, such as Hidenets.[1]

We have designed and implemented the Gulliver testbed [4, 15] with an emphasis on demonstrating safety aspects of cooperative systems, and system architecture to the concrete implementation of fundamental components. The software architecture within each vehicle follows the proposed architectural pattern and, in particular, uses a safety kernel for safety management. For that, the hardware and software so-

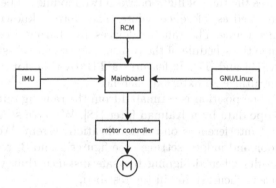

**Fig. 1.** Gulliver vehicle (hardware) architecture

lution presented in this paper are based on an earlier design in which we have implemented and integrated the safety kernel in Gulliver vehicles [8]. Thus, the test-bed is adequate to demonstrate the architectural concept, and to show that it is possible to manage the performance level depending on the operational conditions while ensuring that the functions always perform safely.

---

[1] www.hidenets.aau.dk

## 2  System Overview

We present the key implementation issues of the Gulliver test-bed, which we have further developed based on an earlier design [4, 15].

**Hardware Architecture.** The hardware architecture is sketched in Figure 1. The central component is the mainboard. Further components are the inertial measurement unit (IMU), the ranging device (RCM), a GNU/Linux system and the motor controller.

The IMU provides heading information that is derived from a gyroscope. The RCM provides position information and allows communication between the mainboards of different vehicles. The GNU/Linux system supervises the operation of the vehicle and provides a platform for cooperative algorithms. The vehicles can communicate with each other and the test-bed control client via Wifi links. The motor and the steering servos are controlled by the motor controller. Additionally, it provides odometry information.

Further vehicles from the Gulliver Testbed [2, 3] comprise components that also enable experiments for self-driving vehicular technology. These vehicles participate in the annual international competition CaroloCup[2] for miniature self-driving cars.

**Localization.**  The localization system is based on two different sensors, a ranging device and an inertial measurement unit. The ranging device is P410 RCM produced by timedomain. It uses an ultra-wide band transceiver and measures the time of flight between two modules. Therefore, three stationary anchors are used as reference points. They have a known position and define the reference frame. The ranging devices are sharing a common wireless and, hence, we have the schedule of the transmissions. Our self-stabilizing approach is presented in [16] and [17]. It features a TDMA timeslot assignment algorithm that does not utilize an external reference.

The position is estimated from the ranging outcome, the odometry, and gyroscope data by a Kalman filter [18]. We have studied the influence of reflections and interferences on our localization system. We have experimented both outdoor and indoor settings, see figures 2 and 3, respectively. We have used these results when designing the safe distance that vehicles should keep from each other when driving in the test-bed.

**Path Planning and Following.**  The Gulliver demonstrator uses a set of predefined paths during a demonstration. The paths are defined by the operator especially for the application that is to be demonstrated.

A waypoint is defined as $(x, y, v)$, where $x, y \in \mathbb{Z}$ is the position of the waypoint on the plane and $v \in \mathbb{Z}$ is the proposed maximum speed used to reach this waypoint. The vehicles follow predefined paths; each is a finite ordered sequence of waypoints, where the last waypoint follows the first.

For some test cases, e.g., it is useful to define multiple waypoints. Thus, we support several paths and we allow the vehicle to switch between them.

---

[2] www.carolocup.de

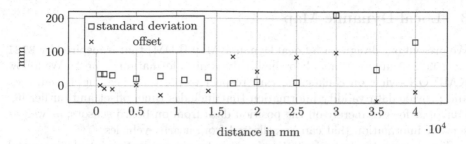

**Fig. 2.** Outdoor accuracy of the RCM. The offset (difference of measured mean and actual distance) and the standard deviation of 10k measurements each.

**External Vision Based Localization.** An external localization system can help to supervise the operation of the demonstrator. A vision based system can give, after calibration, absolute coordinates of the vehicles with respect to a given reference frame. Our system uses inexpensive standard USB cameras as external references. Each vehicle is equipped with a unique tag that can be recognized by image processing software.

We are using OpenCV, a software toolkit that was originally introduced in [7] as CVLib. It provides a programming interface for acquiring frames from the camera, as well as composable algorithms for image processing. The vehicles are equipped with unique AprilTags [14]. These tags allow the vision-based localization system to compute the vehicle id, position and orientation. The computation is done for every frame separately. The position of the camera is automatically determined by a group of four reference tags on the floor with known positions. These can be used to compute a perspective transformation matrix $P$. Using this matrix, a vehicle's position can be computed directly from the coordinates in the captured frame. The resulting vehicle positions are sent in User Datagram Protocol (UDP) to the test-bed control client and integrated with LDM, as well as with the Gulliver software.

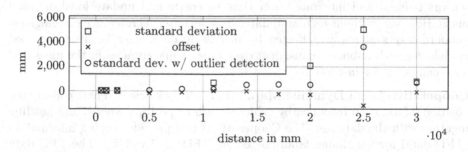

**Fig. 3.** Indoor accuracy of the RCM. The offset (difference of measured mean and actual distance) and the standard deviation of 10k measurements each. The standard deviation increases due to reflections.

## 3   Local Dynamic Map

We present our design for a Local Dynamic Map (LDM) that is inspired by ETSI TR 102 863 and focus mainly on highly dynamic information (type 4). We follow KARYON's view on confidence, with respect to position, heading, speed, etc., and provide data validity information that includes time, offset and outlier [6]. Our pilot focuses merely on the position data from on-board sensors, as well as sensory information that can be collected from nearby vehicles.

Since remote sensory information is prone to communication interferences and delays, we use a hybrid architecture, in which the architecture is divided into one real-time part and another in which complex computations are allowed, such as vehicle-to-vehicle communication. Thus, the system can always rely on a baseline service that is provided by on-board sensors. When the opportunity occurs and the operational conditions improve, the system upgrades its performance by using remote sensory information for gaining more confidence. Note that one of the key advantages of this hybrid approach is that the system design does not require the access to communication systems that never fail (or with very high probability). In case that those communication failures bring the confidence level below the operational requirements, the system can always rely on the baseline service until better confidence is gained and the system can upgrade its service. Our design assumes the existence of a safety kernel that sets the system performance level according to the recent events [8].

**On-board Local Dynamic Map.**   The on-board part uses merely on-board sensors that can be implemented in a real-time manner. On-board maps, for instance, are built and updated while the vehicle is driving through an unknown or previously mapped environment to realize a self-localization and mapping algorithm. Sensors that can be used for this purpose include: rotary encoders like wheel encoders, incremental encoders, hall-effect sensors, mice-based odometers; distance sensors like ultra-sonic sensors, infrared sensors, or depth sensors like laser or radar sensors; even vision sensors can be used to analyze the optical flow for instance. In combination with an IMU device, the input data from such sensors is fused and integrated over time to create and update local onboard maps. However, without regular updates from an external reference system, such onboard-only systems are affected by increasing data error because the used models, for such onboard maps, drift over time as inaccuracies in the measured data can occur for instance.

**Cooperative Local Dynamic Map.**   This network-oriented part collects the position information from nearby vehicles, such as position, speed, and heading together with the data age. The Cooperative LDM provides timing information (TFD data) for the timing failure detector (TFD) and validity. The TFD data allows the TFD to detect the liveliness of the Cooperative LDM. Note that this does not contain information about the data age that is collected from other vehicles. The validity contains information on how certain the Cooperative LDM is about the position information stored, whereas certainty is meant over the coordinates and time.

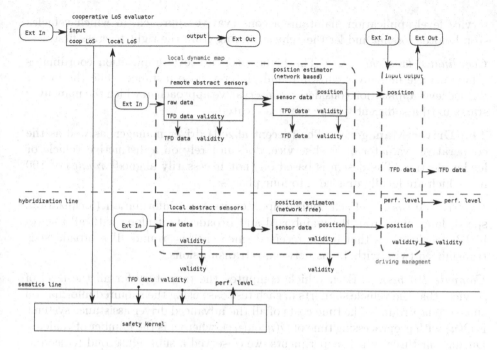

**Fig. 4.** Gulliver software architecture of a single vehicle

# 4 Cooperative Vehicular Algorithms

We selected test cases for which we can define two applications; a fully cooperative one that we associate with the highest service level, and autonomous one that we associate with the lowest service level. We explain how the vehicles' driver manager can act upon the operation service level, which the Cooperative Service Level Evaluator can provide. We present a pilot implementation for this feasibility study.

**Test Cases.**   We considered three test-cases for performing the experiments.[3] For the completeness sake, this paper includes a brief description of these test cases. More details can be found in [1].

*Adaptive cruise control and vehicular platooning.*   Vehicles maintain a safety distance from the vehicle ahead. We set to 3 sec the headway for the Vehicular Adaptive Cruise Control (lowest service level) and 1 second for platooning (Highest service level).

*Intersection crossing.*   The highest service level application coordinates the intersection crossing so that the waiting time is minimized while the lowest

---

[3] See demonstration videos at www.chalmers.se/hosted/gulliver-en/documents

service level application maintains a conservative approach, in which vehicles stop before crossing and let the vehicle coming from the right to cross first.

*Coordinated lane change.*     The highest service level application coordinates a lane change maneuver with minimum inter-vehicle distance while the lowest service level application considers a conservative approach in which the maneuver starts until a sufficiently large space is created.

**The Driver Manager.**     The (decentralized) driver manager, as well as the cooperative evaluator of level service, does not rely on a distinctive vehicle or leader election. The design is based on (not necessarily aligned) *rounds* of 190 ms, which are locally divided into four phases:

*Observe (80 ms).*     Each vehicle updates its local information (localization, speed, lane, etc.) from the mainboard and broadcasts it along with all the vehicle's localizations that it has received since the last round. The broadcast is transmitted twice with 40 ms between retransmissions.

*Compute (10 ms).*     Each vehicle computes the trajectory for all the level of services that the vehicle supports in each test case using the acquired information since the last round. The time costs of all the advanced driver assistance systems is $O(n)$ with preprocessing time of $O(n\log(n))$, where $n$ is the number of vehicles. During our three vehicle experiments, we observed a sub-millisecond trajectory computation cost but for redundancy reasons we assume 10 ms.

*Agreement (80 ms).*     Each vehicle executes the cooperative service level evaluator to agree on the cooperative service level that all the vehicles will run in the next round. Essentially, each vehicle broadcasts its maximum local level of service as well as the maximum level of service from the vehicle that it has received since the last round. The broadcast is transmitted twice with 40 ms between retransmissions. Thus, the phase can be completed within 80 ms. Note that the vehicles operate in distinct level of service for no longer than two consecutive rounds.

*Move (20 ms).*     Each vehicle determines the trajectory to operate according to the cooperative service level obtained for the current round. The trajectory is then sent to the mainboard. It takes around 10 ms to send the trajectory through the serial port to the mainboard and receive the acknowledge, but for redundancy reasons we assume 20 ms.

**Cooperative Service Level Evaluator.**     This fault-tolerant distributed vehicular system must ensure its safe operation. Each vehicle implements a *cooperative service level evaluator* that on every round decides what would be the lowest common ability to meet the operational conditions for the next round. Therefore, the decision and its dissemination must be done in bounded time. Due to communication failures, the cooperative service level evaluator must be able to cope with participants or communication failures.

We consider $n$ vehicles; each has a unique id. The vehicles create an ad-hoc network, i.e., no access points or base stations [10–13]. For the communication protocol, we consider UDP in order to avoid the retransmission overheads, and thus messages can be lost due to noise or interference.

The cooperative service level evaluator aims at allowing the vehicles to operate at the highest service level. It can do so when allow vehicles can support the highest service level, and the communication network delivers messages in a timely manner. Since wireless communications can experience periods of arbitrary packet drops, the cooperative service level evaluator has to lower the service level when the vehicles fail to exchange their service level reports in a timely manner. Our feasibility tests focused on the scalability of this component in ns3 and aimed at validating its behavior with respect to scenarios that involve several vehicles. For the simulation, we consider a wireless ad-hoc network with a standard channel IEEE 802.11b. We used the log distance propagation loss model with exponent 3 and reference loss of 60.0. We assume that the vehicles are deployed uniformly at random in a rectangle with dimension $30 \times 150$ meters. Vehicles move at a constant speed chosen randomly and uniformly between 0 and $20\frac{m}{s}$. We perform experiments with a variant number of vehicles between 2 and 30, and the number of transmissions between 2 and 4. We run each experiment for $1,200$ sec.

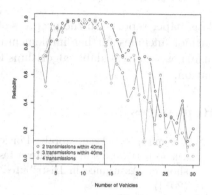

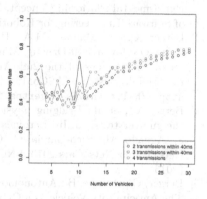

**Fig. 5.** Reliability of the consensus algorithm (Proportion of rounds in high service level) and packet drop rate

We estimate the reliability aspects of our implementation by considering the time that the system operates on the highest service level. We compare that time and the packet drop rate. The plot on the left of Figure 5 shows that, as the number of vehicles increases, the time that the system operates on the highest service level decreases. This is due to the increment on the packet drop rate since the medium is shared with more vehicles, as depicted on the right of Figure 5. We also validated our results via experiments that used (physical) scaled-vehicles in which the number of vehicles was between two and five. We observed that 90% of the time that the system operated on the highest service level when the number of vehicles was between two and four. This validates our computer simulations. However, there was a drop to 60% when we tested five vehicles. We believe that the reason is due to the use of network adapters from different vendors during the experiments. Further tests are needed for this case.

## 5  Conclusions

This paper reports on the progress of the development work. The development outlook includes further implementation of the different data validity mechanisms as well as scalable algorithms for achieving cooperative service level evaluation.

## References

[1] Casimiro, A., Oscar Morales-Ponce, T.P., Schiller, E.M.: Vehicular coordination via a safety kernel in the gulliver test-bed. In: The Thirteenth International Workshop on Assurance in Distributed Systems and Networks (ADSN 2014). IEEE (2014)

[2] Berger, C.: From a Competition for Self-Driving Miniature Cars to a Standardized Experimental Platform: Concept, Models, Architecture, and Evaluation. Journal of Software Engineering for Robotics 5(1), 63–79 (2014)

[3] Berger, C., Al Mamun, M.A., Hansson, J.: COTS-Architecture with a Real-Time OS for a Self-Driving Miniature Vehicle. In: Schiller, E.M., Lönn, H. (eds.) Proceedings of the 2nd Workshop on Architecting Safety in Collaborative Mobile Systems (ASCoMS), Toulouse, France, pp. 1–12 (September 2013), http://hal.archives-ouvertes.fr/docs/00/84/81/01/PDF/00010133.pdf

[4] Berger, C., et al.: Bridging physical and digital traffic system simulations with the gulliver test-bed. In: Berbineau, M., Jonsson, M., Bonnin, J.-M., Cherkaoui, S., Aguado, M., Rico-Garcia, C., Ghannoum, H., Mehmood, R., Vinel, A. (eds.) Nets4Trains/Nets4Cars 2013. LNCS, vol. 7865, pp. 169–184. Springer, Heidelberg (2013)

[5] Berger, C., Rumpe, B.: Autonomous Driving - 5 Years after the Urban Challenge: The Anticipatory Vehicle as a Cyber-Physical System. In: Goltz, U., Magnor, M., Appelrath, H.J., Matthies, H.K., Balke, W.T., Wolf, L. (eds.) Proceedings of the INFORMATIK 2012, pp. 789–798. Braunschweig, Germany (2012)

[6] Brade, T., Zug, S., Kaiser, J.: Validity-based failure algebra for distributed sensor systems. In: SRDS, pp. 143–152. IEEE (2013)

[7] Bradski, G.R., Pisarevsky, V.: Intel's computer vision library: Applications in calibration, stereo, segmentation, tracking, gesture, face and object recognition. In: 2013 IEEE Conference on Computer Vision and Pattern Recognition, vol. 2, p. 2796 (2000)

[8] Casimiro, A., Rufino, J., Pinto, R.C., Vial, E., Schiller, E.M., Morales-Ponce, O., Petig, T.: A kernel-based architecture for safe cooperative vehicular functions. In: 9th IEEE International Symposium on Industrial Embedded Systems, SIES 2014 (2014)

[9] Hirsch, J.: Self-driving cars inch closer to mainstream availability (October 2013), http://www.latimes.com/business/autos/la-fi-adv-hy-self-driving-cars-20131013,0,5094627.story

[10] Leone, P., Papatriantafilou, M., Schiller, E.M.: Relocation analysis of stabilizing MAC algorithms for large-scale mobile ad hoc networks. In: Dolev, S. (ed.) ALGOSENSORS 2009. LNCS, vol. 5804, pp. 203–217. Springer, Heidelberg (2009)

[11] Leone, P., Papatriantafilou, M., Schiller, E.M., Zhu, G.: Chameleon-MAC: Adaptive and self-★ algorithms for media access control in mobile ad hoc networks. In: Dolev, S., Cobb, J., Fischer, M., Yung, M. (eds.) SSS 2010. LNCS, vol. 6366, pp. 468–488. Springer, Heidelberg (2010)

[12] Leone, P., Schiller, E.M.: Self-stabilizing TDMA algorithms for dynamic wireless ad-hoc networks. Int. J. Distributed Sensor Networks, 639761 (2013)

[13] Mustafa, M., Papatriantafilou, M., Schiller, E.M., Tohidi, A., Tsigas, P.: Autonomous TDMA alignment for VANETs. In: 76th IEEE Vehicular Technology Conf. (VTC-Fall 2012), pp. 1–5. IEEE (2012)

[14] Olson, E.: AprilTag: A robust and flexible visual fiducial system. In: Proceedings of the IEEE International Conference on Robotics and Automation (ICRA), pp. 3400–3407. IEEE (May 2011)

[15] Pahlavan, M., Papatriantafilou, M., Schiller, E.M.: Gulliver: a test-bed for developing, demonstrating and prototyping vehicular systems. In: Proceedings of the 9th ACM International Symposium on Mobility Management and Wireless Access, pp. 1–8. ACM (2011)

[16] Petig, T., Schiller, E.M., Tsigas, P.: Self-stabilizing tdma algorithms for wireless ad-hoc networks without external reference. CoRR abs/1308.6475 (2013)

[17] Petig, T., Schiller, E.M., Tsigas, P.: Self-stabilizing TDMA algorithms for wireless ad-hoc networks without external reference. In: Higashino, T., Katayama, Y., Masuzawa, T., Potop-Butucaru, M., Yamashita, M. (eds.) SSS 2013. LNCS, vol. 8255, pp. 354–356. Springer, Heidelberg (2013)

[18] Thrun, S., Burgard, W., Fox, D.: Probabilistic Robotics (Intelligent Robotics and Autonomous Agents). The MIT Press (2005)

# Sensor- and Environment Dependent Performance Adaptation for Maintaining Safety Requirements

Tino Brade, Georg Jäger, Sebastian Zug, and Jörg Kaiser

Otto-von-Guericke-University of Magdeburg,
Institute for Distributed Systems (IVS), Germany
{brade,jaeger,zug,kaiser}@ivs.cs.uni-magdeburg.de

**Abstract.** Driving assistance or automated driving depends to a large extent on the correct perception of the environment. Because automated driving functions have to be proven safe under all operational conditions, worst-case assumptions concerning the sensors and also the environment have to be assumed. In this paper, we propose a scheme that allows taking weaker assumptions. This is based on a continuous assessment of the quality of sensor data, a model of the interaction between the control process and the environment and the possibility to adapt the performance. We present an example of a car autonomously driving a simple course and adapting its speed according to the environment and the confidence in the perceived sensor data. We derive a set of simple safety rules used to adjust performance that, in the case given in the example affects the cruising speed.

## 1 Introduction

Functional safety is a non-debatable property for automotive systems. The requirements and procedures for functional safety are fixed in a respective standard [1]. At the same time, it is one of the most challenging tasks ensuring functional safety for sophisticated driver assistance systems or complex automatic driving functions. One of the reasons is that assurance means that a function has to be proven safe before it can be put into operation in a car. Consequently, it has to be proven safe at design time for all driving situations and failures that may occur during operation. This results in worst-case assumptions about the environment, the perception system and the control application. Particularly, the control application makes implicit assumptions about the quality of sensor input by tolerating acceptable error margins due to a robust design of the control algorithm. The correct functionality is usually carefully checked during the testing phase. Statically assuming worst-case conditions at design time has some undesirable consequences. Firstly, it leads to high costs of the sensors because lower cost sensors, although in most cases will comply with the requirements, cannot ensure this at any time during a mission. Secondly, because perception and control are tightly intertwined, the test only provides a validation for a

A. Bondavalli et al. (Eds.): SAFECOMP 2014 Workshops, LNCS 8696, pp. 46–54, 2014.
© Springer International Publishing Switzerland 2014

specific set of sensors. If sensors have to be replaced, only the same or very similar sensors can be used. Finally, because a system has to show that safety is guaranteed under all conditions, the requirements will be overly strict.

In this paper we will present a scheme for adapting performance according to environmental conditions and erroneous sensor information without sacrificing safety. This scheme is based on a number of system functions that have been elaborated during the KARYON project [2].

1. The KARYON architecture defines a safety kernel that allows to put the system in different levels-of-performance according to a set of safety rules. The safety rules specify the conditions in terms of system health state and the quality of sensor data.
2. Separating the design of the perception system from the design of the control application. The main advance over other systems is that on the control application side, we present a way, how the control application can specify the quality of sensor data explicitly. On the sensor side, we provide a concept, how to quantify the confidence in sensor data. Instead of having to validate a single sensor-control block, we can validate these blocks separately. This allows dealing with a changing set of sensors easily. Additionally, it is a prerequisite when assuming remote sensors that are not known at design time. A more detailed discussion about this point can be found in [3].
3. The scheme to quantify the confidence in sensor data called "validity" allows the dynamic assessment of sensor data during run-time. Because the KAYON safety kernel allows to react if the validity is too low, we are able to handle this situation dynamically. The example below explains this in more detail.
4. Knowledge about the road is exploited to define the tolerable error margins in which safety can be ensured. In our example, we simulate a simple course and build a model of the process that relates speed, validity of sensor data and the position of the car to define safe conditions for controlling the car

The contribution of this paper is firstly showing how the notion of validity can be used to express error margins and secondly how the knowledge about the course of a road, the speed of a car, its position and orientation can be described by a mathematical model allowing to determine the adequate level of performance for a given safety level.

The paper is organized as follows: In the next section we briefly introduce the notion of validity and its relation to a failure model. This is needed to understand how error margins are expressed by a validity. Chapter 3 provides introduction and evaluation of the simulation example. Chapter 4 discusses the results and related work and the summary in chapter 5 concludes the paper.

## 2   Assessing the Quality of Sensor Data

Sensors deliver a continuous range of values and often exhibit a subtle behaviour in case of external or internal disturbances. In our work, we use a data centric approach [4] to identify sensor failures, i.e. we try to infer faulty sensor data from

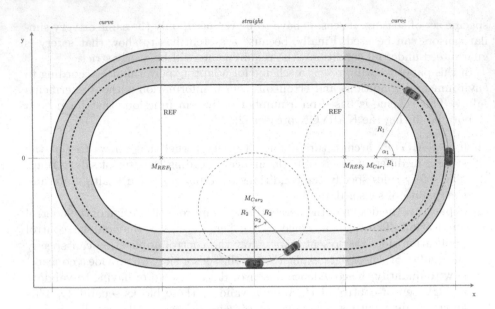

**Fig. 1.** Illustration of the environment

certain failure characteristics rather than applying space or time redundancy mechanisms. These parameters are derived empirically from testing a sensor exhaustively under many typical operational conditions and internal and external disturbances (e.g. voltage drops, electromagnetic glitches, intensive light for IR sensors and laser sensors etc.). A discussion of the resulting failure model can be found in [5]. Basically, we characterize a failure according to its amplitude and its occurrence probability. From these parameters, we calculate the anticipated validity of sensor data at design-time. A system performs at its best when no failures occur. With occurring sensor failures, additional robustness is required which has implications on the performance. The KARYON system allows to trade fading functionality against the level of system performance. The more failures will occur, the lower the performance that can be achieved safely by the system. For choosing an adequate performance level without violating safety, actual sensor data needs to be assessed at run-time. The key for achieving this is a consistent representation of the validity at design-time and at run-time. This allows proving the system to be safe for a given set of failures. By using the run-time validity, the system is switched to a performance level that is proven to cope with the occurred failures.

## 3   An Automated Driving Scenario

This section considers a lane tracing application, which is a common task when building an autonomous car. Fig. 1 illustrates an example course for the automated car. In order to prove the system to be safe, we have to model the environment, specify system parameters and we make assumption regarding the operational context. This allows us to statically prove the compliance of our setup with requirements. Based on this prove, we identify conditions under which the car follows the line although sensor failures are present. Such conditions are expressed in terms of safety rules, which are used at run-time to choose the highest possible performance setting (LoS) of the application without risking safety. By analysing validity ranges at design-time we can derive safety rules, which are checked at run-time by the safety kernel. This is the basis to trigger switching the level of service (LoS).

The following example will explain how to derive these safety rules. For sake of clarity, we consider a simple course with straight and curved lanes. The course is modelled by the straight-line equation $REF = |y|$ and the circle equation $REF = \sqrt{(x-a)^2 + (y-b^2)}$. Clearly, such an environment model leads to an over-determined set of equations. For deriving safety rules, we have to assign system variables to define the basic kinematics of the car, to map the requirements and to make assumptions on which the system will be proven to be safe.

First, we assign system variables as follows: the steering angle $(\alpha)$ in a range of $-45°$ and $45°$, the highest maximum velocity of the car $(v \leq 15\frac{m}{s})$, the wheelbase of the car is set to $3m$ and the distance to the rear axle $(a_2)$ assigned as $1.5m$. Theses system variables describe the kinematics of the car so that the anticipated position of the car can be calculated. Additionally, we have to define the sample time $(t = 0.5s)$, which is the update rate of the observation and of the calculation of the steering command. This means that the perception-action loop of the car is periodically executed every 0,5 seconds.

Second, the kinematics of the car is required to calculate the impact of a certain steering angel on its position and orientation in the environment. For resolving this relation, we make use of the Ackerman condition: $R = \sqrt{a_2^2 + l^2 \cdot \cot^2(\alpha)}$. This condition allows us to calculate the deviation of the car from its ideal track assuming the current position and orientation of the car.

Third, in order to decide whether the deviation of the car from the ideal track is in line with requirements, we have to specify what is tolerable. In our scenario, we define a deviation of plus/minus one meter $(th_{err} \leq \pm1m)$ as acceptable.

Finally, we have to make assumptions in terms of the position and the orientation of the car with respect to the validity. In cases where the position sensor data has a high validity, the PID controller will keep the car very close to the ideal track. When sensor failures occur and the observed position is not accurate, the validity in sensor data drops and, as a result, the car deviates considerably in terms of position and orientation from the ideal track. The key for making such an analysis is the concept of design-time validity that specifies failure cases. This allows proving the system being safe under a set of assumptions. Without such assumptions, these check whether the system acts safe, could not be made at design time. This is because the equations representing the environment stays over-determined without assumptions regarding the quality of sensor inputs. Consequently, the combination of system variables, sensor inputs, and the controller output together with the environment model would be checked at

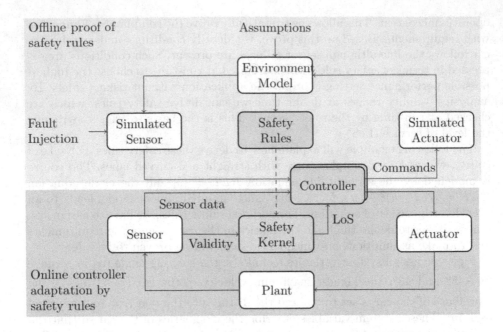

**Fig. 2.** Schematic overview of the concept

run-time. Obviously, run-time checking does not provide guarantees and so the response of the system is unknown when sensor failures occur.

### 3.1   Deriving Safety Rules at Design-Time

The objective of safety rules is to calculate the performance that can be reached without violating requirements. Fig. 3 depicts the problem of adjusting the steering angle based on an erroneous observation. $C_1$ shows the observed position of the car based on which a steering command is computed. By applying the steering command, the car drives to $C_2$. In case of sensor failures, the computed steering angle violates the requirement. The actual position now would be $C_3$ and the car moves to $C_4$ then. This shows the effect of erroneous observations. To maintain a safe behaviour we use the notion of sensor data validity to adapt the performance, which in this simple example means to adjust the velocity.

Safety rules define conditions under which the system operates safe. In our case, we observe the position of the car and compute a respective steering command in order to keep the car on track. As illustrated in Fig. 2, we derive safety rules by simulating the perception-action loop under a simple environment model. This setup allows us to check the compliance of the controller with requirements. It requires knowing the environment model, defining the system parameters and considering sensor failures that need to be handled at run-time. As shown in Fig. 2, the controller receives observations of a (simulated) sensor, which allows us to record the reaction of the controller on sensor failures that

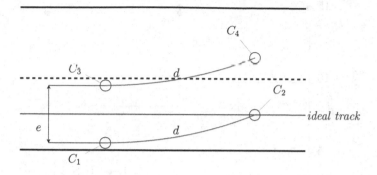

**Fig. 3.** The effect of sensor failures ($e$) without adapting the velocity ($d$)

have been injected. Consequently, we can check the controller response for every anticipated failure case. Based on this analysis we can define safety rules. Safety rules relate the validity of perception data to the level of service for the controller, which specifies system parameters, in our case the velocity of the car. The LoS may be translated to specific configurations or even different versions of the controller.

The following safety rules respect the validity of sensor data to calculate the highest velocity without violating requirements. Therefore, we compute the intersection point $I(x_i, y_i)$ between the requirement and the erroneous position, which is in fact unknown but estimated by the validity $C(x_c, y_c)$. By exploiting the time-space-relation $v = \dfrac{s}{t}$, we determine the distance of the actual position of the car to the intersection point $I$ and so we receive the velocity for adapting the performance.

*Safety rule for driving on the straight track.* In cases where the steering angle is zero ($\alpha = 0°$), the highest maximal velocity is then given by $v = \dfrac{|\overrightarrow{CI}|}{t}$. Otherwise, the car drives a circular path that is given by the Ackermann-condition ($R = \sqrt{a_2^2 + l^2 \cdot \cot^2(\alpha)}$) and correlates to the second safety rule.

*Safety rule for driving on the curved track.* When driving a curve, we calculate the angle ($\gamma$) between the actual position of the car and the intersection point with the requirement: $\cos(\gamma) = \dfrac{\overrightarrow{MI} \times \overrightarrow{MC}}{|\overrightarrow{MI}| \cdot |\overrightarrow{MC}|}$ where M is the center of the steering cycle as shown in Fig. 1. The velocity that should not be exceeded, is therefore given by: $v = \dfrac{\pi \cdot R \cdot \dfrac{\gamma}{180°}}{t}$.

### 3.2   Checking Safety Rules at Run-Time

At run-time, detection mechanisms are used to assess the sensor data of the positioning sensor. The better an observation, the higher the validity of sensor

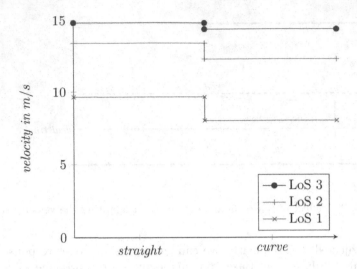

**Fig. 4.** Proven velocities of different performance levels to cope with positioning failures

data. As shown in Fig. 2, the safety kernel switches the controller into a level of service (LoS) dependent on the validity of actual sensor data. The safety rules thus specify the required validity for performing a certain level of service and serve as a decision basis to switch configurations of the controller. Whether the system operates safe by using this LoS setup was proven at design-time while deriving the safety-rules. This results in an approach that reduces the LoS in order to operate safe in case of sensor failures. Otherwise, the safety kernel switches to a higher LoS without jeopardizing safety.

## 4   Discussion

The proposed scheme is implemented in Simulink where V-Rep is used as for simulating the environment. We obtain reproducible results and are able to analyse the effect of observation failures on the performance of the system. By using a fault injection framework, we compare test cases with and without failures. In accordance to the injected failure amplitude, the car degraded its performance in order to comply with requirements. It should be noted that the system stops if the car is not able to keep within the lane due to injected failures or limitations of the steering angle.

In Fig 4, we plotted the resulting velocity of different LoS as a result of the derived safety rules. The blue curve (LoS 3) shows the highest performance level that can be reached when no failure occurs. Therefore, the velocities of the blue curve corresponds to the performance of an ideal system. The red curve labeled LoS 2 gives the velocity that can be set in cases where the positioning sensor suffers from noise. The violet curve (LoS 1) states the system performance when outliers and noise failures are considered. When making only worst case assumptions, the system performance would be statically set to the violet curve (LoS 1). In contrast our approach degrades the performance level only if necessary.

Comparing our approach to related work, we found approaches either dealing with sensor failures at design-time or at run-time only. Uncertainty margins [6] describe the characteristics of a sensor but they fail to distinguish failure types. The separation of failure types is provided by FMEA [7] that is limited to design-time analysis. On the other hand, confidence intervals [8], confidence classes [9] and also validates [10] provide a run-time representation but do no support design-time analysis. None of them can be used both at design-time as well as at run-time. Without such a consistent representation, the service levels of a system cannot statically proven safe at design-time and switched at run-time. On the side of an application, we found approaches [11], [12] for adapting the configuration in accordance to failures but such approaches ignore the operational context and the consideration of the environment. Nevertheless, those aspects are essential when proving the system to be safe.

## 5 Conclusion

The KARYON project developed an architectural pattern, which allows to react on a degraded functionality by switching to different levels of service, i.e. to differnt control schemes. The decision is based on the assessment of system health in a broad sense. In this paper, we focussed on failures of the sensor system. For a simple example we showed how the notion of validity can be used for design time analysis and also in run-time assessment of sensor data. A reliable safety kernel monitors the validity and takes actions if validity drops below a predefined bound. The bounds on validity and the necessary knowledge for the controller can be statically analysed at design time and transformed into safety rules to be executed at run-time for configuring controller functions.

**Acknowledgment.** This work has been supported by the EU under the FP7-ICT programme, through project 288195 Kernel-based ARchitecture for safetY-critical cONtrol (KARYON).

## References

1. (ISO), ISO 26262-1 to ISO 26262-9, 1st edn. (2011)
2. Casimiro, A., Kaiser, J., Schiller, E.M., Costa, P., Parizi, J., Johansson, R., Librino, R.: The karyon project: Predictable and safe coordination in cooperative vehicular systems. In: 2013 43rd Annual IEEE/IFIP Conference on Dependable Systems and Networks Workshop (DSN-W), pp. 1–12. IEEE (2013)
3. Brade, T., Zug, S., Kaiser, J.: Validity-based failure algebra for distributed sensor systems. In: 2013 IEEE 32nd International Symposium on Reliable Distributed Systems (SRDS), pp. 143–152. IEEE (2013)

4. Ni, K., Ramanathan, N., Chehade, M.N.H., Balzano, L., Nair, S., Zahedi, S., Kohler, E., Pottie, G., Hansen, M., Srivastava, M.: Sensor network data fault types. ACM Transactions on Sensor Networks (TOSN) 5(3), 25 (2009)
5. Zug, S., Dietrich, A., Kaiser, J.: Fault-handling in networked sensor systems. In: Fault Diagnosis in Robotic and Industrial Systems (2012)
6. Moffat, R.J.: Describing the uncertainties in experimental results. Experimental Thermal and Fluid Science 1(1), 3–17 (1988)
7. Stamatis, D.H.: Failure Mode and Effect Analysis: Fmea from Theory to Execution. ASQ Quality Press, Milwaukee (2003)
8. Elmenreich, W.: Fusion of continuous-valued sensor measurements using confidence-weighted averaging. Journal of Vibration and Control 13(9-10), 1303–1312 (2007)
9. Piontek, H.-M.: Self-description mechanisms for embedded components in cooperative systems. Der Andere Verlag (2007)
10. Duta, M., Henry, M.: The fusion of redundant seva measurements. IEEE Transactions on Control Systems Technology 13(2), 173–184 (2005)
11. Blanke, M., Schröder, J.: Diagnosis and fault-tolerant control, vol. 115. Springer (2003)
12. Frank, P.M.: Fault diagnosis in dynamic systems using analytical and knowledge-based redundancy: A survey and some new results. Automatica 26(3), 459–474 (1990)

# Collaborative Development of Safety-Critical Automotive Systems: Exchange, Views and Metrics[*]

Johan Ekberg[1], Urban Ingelsson[2], Henrik Lönn[3], Magnus Skoog[4], and Jan Söderberg[5]

[1] Arccore AB, Gothenburg, Sweden
[2] Semcon Sweden AB, Linköping, Sweden
[3] Volvo Group, Advanced Technology and Research,
Gothenburg, Sweden
[4] Autoliv Electronics, Linköping, Sweden
[5] Systemite AB, Gothenburg, Sweden

**Abstract.** Automotive system development involves a large set of organizations and disciplines. In particular, vehicle manufacturers rely on a large set of suppliers to provide components and systems. To successfully develop and integrate these components, stakeholders exchange requirement specifications that define in detail the component properties. Because of the complexity of a typical automotive system, requirement specifications are error prone and time consuming to negotiate with a correct result. In addition, most systems have safety implications and require rigorous means to achieve and argue safety. Recent autonomous and semi-autonomous systems are particularly complex and critical.

The Synligare project addresses these challenges by providing model-based technologies to assist collaborative development of safety critical systems. The project is working along three lines as explained below.

**Model Exchange:** Being able to exchange models rather than documents to convey engineering information improves efficiency and precision in collaboration between stakeholders. Version and variant information is an important aspect to secure validity of information.

**Views:** Understanding system solutions and analysis results is difficult as more and more aspects need to be considered. Appropriate views, based on formalized system representations, makes engineering information more accessible.

**Metrics:** Development status and system properties can sometimes be represented and tracked by means of metrics. Such automatically and continuously provided measures, makes development effort more predictable and indirectly ensure safety.

This paper will describe aspects on exchange, views and metrics identified in the Synligare project, and illustrate with examples how it can be applied in practical system development.

---

[*] This work was supported by VINNOVA under the FFI Programme.

A. Bondavalli et al. (Eds.): SAFECOMP 2014 Workshops, LNCS 8696, pp. 55–62, 2014.

# 1    Background

Automotive system development involves a large set of organizations and disciplines. In particular, vehicle manufacturers rely on a large set of suppliers to provide components and systems. To successfully develop and integrate these components, stakeholders exchange requirement specifications that define in detail the component properties. Because of the complexity of a typical automotive system, requirement specifications are error prone and time consuming to negotiate with a correct result. In addition, most systems have safety implications and require rigorous means to achieve and argue safety. Recent systems for autonomous and semi-autonomous driving are particularly complex and critical.

The Synligare project addresses these challenges by providing model-based technologies to assist collaborative development of safety critical systems.

This paper will describe preliminary results from the project and starts with a description of the modelling and tooling infrastructure used. It then goes on to discuss technology for exchange, views and metrics. The paper concludes with a summary.

# 2    Infrastructure

The modelling approach from AUTOSAR [1] and the EAST-ADL [3] architecture description language is used as basis for the views and metrics identified, detailed and prototyped in Synligare. Tooling is developed based on the SystemWeaver enterprise modelling platform from Systemite AB, Enterprise Architect from Sparx Inc. and the Eclipse tool platforms EATOP [4] and Artop [2] for EAST-ADL and AUTOSAR, respectively.

# 3    Collaboration

Collaboration between stakeholders occurs in various engineering phases and regarding phase-specific kinds of engineering artefacts. In this paper we will focus on collaboration between manufacturers of automotive products and suppliers of automotive components. The relation can be considered recursively, i.e. Tier-1 suppliers rely on Tier-2 suppliers for their deliveries, etc.

One style of collaboration, with low level of interaction is illustrated in Fig. 1. The vehicle manufacturer provides high level requirements together with a limited but detailed interface specification in the early engineering phase. In the early phase, modified models are exchanged as a handshake, but not until the end of development, the supplier comes back with a component implementation.

In a more cohesive development scenario, the vehicle manufacturer and it suppliers exchange engineering artifacts continuously, Fig. 2. The collaboration starts as before with a description of high level requirements and intentions from the vehicle manufacturer, which the supplier inspects, corrects and returns. But in this scenario, the supplier soon returns an abstract solution, which the vehicle manufacturer can analyse and integrate with existing functionality. After corrections and suggestions, the supplier gets an updated version of the solution and continues to add details, gradually fulfilling more of the requirements.

We will use the reference model in Fig. 3 as a basis for characterizing engineering artefacts. The reference model uses abstractions from Vehicle Level capturing vehicle needs and requirements without solution information, down to Implementation Level with complete specifications. Operational Level corresponds to the final product. The right side of each "V" is concerned with verification and validation of detailed up to overall aspects (altitude). V&V may concern different degrees of integration from individual functions up to complete vehicle (thickness of V).

With this reference model in mind, the kind of information exchanged in the early phase would be requirements, use cases and vehicle features from vehicle level, to characterize the high level requirements. In the same phase, some of the detailed interfacing requirements would be known which can be captured by AUTOSAR elements on the Implementation level and complemented with textual requirements.

In the low interaction scenario, the next delivery from the supplier would be AUTOSAR models and corresponding code.

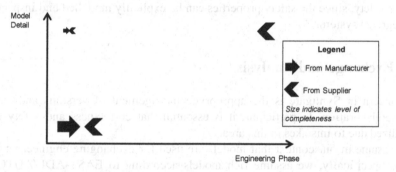

**Fig. 1.** Illustration of collaboration style with little exchange

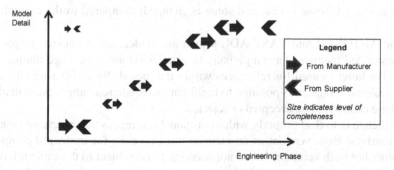

**Fig. 2.** Illustration of collaboration style with frequent exchange

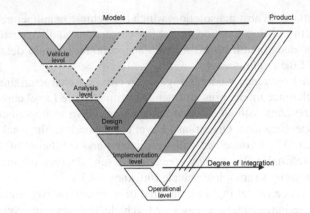

**Fig. 3.** Reference model for the engineering life cycle and engineering artifacts

In the more coupled scenario, the supplier would deliver models representing solutions of the agreed features, with more details as development progresses. The vehicle manufacturer would integrate and verify, and thus be able to detect mistakes in the manufacturer's specifications or in the supplier's solutions. It is also an opportunity to improve safety, since the safety properties can be explicitly modelled and inspected in the integrated system.

## 4    Exchange and Analysis

One concern in Synligare is the appropriate management of versions and variants during collaboration. In particular, it is essential that correctness and safety is not jeopardized due to mistakes in this area.

We assume in our context that models are used for exchanging engineering information. Specifically, we assume rich models according to EAST-ADL/AUTOSAR with content of various categories such as requirements, software components, timing annotations and variability.

When a stakeholder receives a model from another stakeholder, some of the content is unchanged, some is new and some is changed, compared to the current, local version.

In the AUTOSAR and EAST-ADL standards, models are organized in packages where contained elements have a globally unique UUID and a package-unique "short name". The latter is used for references within the model. By comparing an existing and an acquired model, it is possible to highlight areas where changes were made and allow these changes to be accepted or rejected.

A challenge is to deal properly with intra-model references when new version of an element arrives. Both versions of an element must co-exist for backward compatibility reasons, but both versions should not necessarily be subject to the same references. The project is investigating concepts and views to assist the engineering effort in this area.

# 5    Views

Views represent the system under development from a certain perspective or viewpoint [1]. By collecting relevant elements in a view, adequate information for a certain role in a certain method or process phase can be presented. Fig. 4 shows examples of criteria for viewpoints onto a system model, which would result in several useful views.

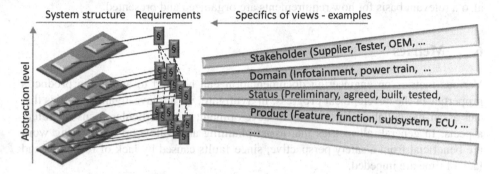

**Fig. 4.** Example of viewpoints on a multi-aspect system model

## 5.1    Structural Viewpoints

The model structure is a fundamental basis for defining effective viewpoints that helps understanding product models.

Based on the SystemModel element, model artifacts on a specific abstraction level can be viewed. By combining with a VehicleFeature, only parts relevant for that VehicleFeature would be exposed.

Another useful view is the set of functions that are allocated to a specific ECU, or the set of signals that communicate over a certain bus. The latter can be established by investigating the functions allocated to ECUs that are linked with the chosen bus, and/or where allocation constraints tie function connectors to such bus.

## 5.2    Safety Viewpoints

Viewpoints useful for working with functional safety include in particular those that show safety artifacts. Showing all safety goals for a certain item provides overview of the top level safety concerns. Showing in a specific architecture all components that are realizing the features contained in an Item, provides understanding for the system solutions to be secured. Showing requirements and elements that make up the functional or technical safety concept assists working with the safety mechanisms.

## 5.3    Requirements-Related Viewpoints

Views that expose requirements in an effective way are particularly important when multiple stakeholders collaborate. Showing requirements clustered on features, functions, components, or other designated architectural elements, make a large set of requirements more tangible. Showing requirements together with relevant attributes gives an overview of the status, responsibilities or other markings of the requirements. Requirements may have different kinds and may concern different aspects, which is also a relevant basis for how requirements are organized and presented.

# 6    Metrics

Various metrics on engineering documentation can be used to assess the product's properties or the development progress. In Synligare, we are investigating metrics that can assist the collaborative aspects of development, with particular focus on safety aspects. In general, all metrics that assist planning and follow-up engineering work are beneficial from a safety perspective, since faults caused by lack of resources and lack of time are impeded.

A metric is calculated on the basis of an entire system specification or parts thereof. Examples of delimitations include

- Architecture part - The metric concerns a particular architecture or parts thereof
- Requirement set - The metric concerns a particular requirement set
- Project - the metric concerns a particular project

A hierarchy of metrics based e.g. on the structural hierarchy of the system (system, subsystem, etc.) is conceivable. Depending on character, metrics can in a tool or in a report be visually represented as lists, flags and colors in addition to plain numbers.

### 6.1    Progress Metrics

Development progress can be assessed based on the status of the model or based on assessments of actual status that is reflected in the model.

**Requirement Progress**

Assuming that requirements are used to specify what the product shall do, they can also be the basis for assessing progress. Progress of requirement allocation is measured as the fraction of requirements allocated to architectural elements. Because requirements may be derived to more specific requirements, a requirement with one or more derived requirements is also considered as allocated. Progress of requirement implementation is measured as the fraction of requirements that are implemented in the product. This criterion is not well-defined, as it may concern requirements with a final design, final software specification, final code, compiled code, etc. On computing this metric, the model can be inspected for one of the criteria mentioned, or a specific flag that is manually set by the engineer is used as a basis.

**Verification Progress**

In EAST-ADL, verification is linked to requirements. For each requirement one or several verification cases can be defined, each of which may pass or fail.

Verification progress may thus concern the fraction of requirements that are verified or where a verification method is defined. If multiple verification cases are defined per requirement, the fraction may be based on verification cases instead. In case verification is done, a useful metric is the fraction of passed vs. failed requirements.

**Realization Progress**

The EAST-ADL model provides means to relate model elements to its abstract counterpart. For example, a function or ECU is linked to the Vehicle Feature it is realizing. In the end all Vehicle Features should be realized down to the Software or hardware Component level. On computing realization progress, one must decide which criterion to use, for example realization in software, function or hardware architecture. One must also be aware that it is not possible to know how many concrete elements are required for realizing an abstract element. For this reason, an alternative approach is to use a specific flag which is manually set when a feature is deemed to be realized.

**Safety-related Progress Metrics**

The ISO26262 functional safety standard defines a number of engineering artifacts that shall be defined in the context of its Item. One of these artifacts is the safety goal, which is the starting point for organizing safety requirements. Examples of metrics include the fraction of Items with safety goals defined or the fraction of safety goals with functional safety requirements. Because it is system specific, it is not possible to know how many safety goals or safety requirements are needed. It is still a useful metric, since the amount must be non-zero.

Another safety-related metric is the fraction of functional safety concepts that are matched by a technical safety concept. This can be computed based on derivation relations between functional and technical safety requirements combined with realization relations between analysis functions and design functions making up the architectural aspects of the functional and technical safety concepts, respectively.

## 6.2    Product Metrics

As opposed to progress metrics, product related metrics are typically absolute. One metric that is relevant for strategic decisions regarding development rigor or priority, is the number of manufactured vehicles that are impacted by a certain engineering artifact. This can be computed based on the take rate annotations of vehicle features realized by the engineering artifact considered. Similarly, total revenue or cost can be computed by combining take rate information with financial annotations.

Various dependability metrics are of course safety relevant too. These include failure rate and other hardware architecture metrics.

### 6.3    Identifying Context

In general, it is necessary to be aware of context when computing metrics based on fractions. The AUTOSAR/EAST-ADL notion of package is one possible context. Another is to consider a certain feature, function, hardware component and compute a fraction among the related elements.

## 7    Summary

Model based software and systems engineering represents state-of-the-art technology and is a key enabler for better products and development methodology in the automotive industry. By taking advantage of the fact that engineering information is more precise and organized systematically compared to document-based practice, collaboration between stakeholders, most notably vehicle manufacturers and its suppliers can be enhanced.

This paper has described preliminary results and directions from the Synligare project. As a means to work efficiently with model-based exchange of engineering information, the project is identifying views and metrics that allow exchanged information to be investigated and assessed conveniently. Tool prototypes based on EAST-ADL and AUTOSAR are built on the SystemWeaver, EATOP and Artop platforms.

## References

1. AUTOSAR Development Partnership: AUTOSAR web site,
   http://www.autosar.org/
2. AUTOSAR Tool Platform User Group: AUTOSAR Tool platform,
   http://www.artop.org/
3. EAST-ADL Association: EAST-ADL web site, http://www.east-adl.info/
4. EATOP Eclipse Open Source Project: EAST-ADL Tool platform,
   http://www.eclipse.org/eatop
5. International Organization for Standardization: Systems and software engineering — Architecture description. International Standard ISO/IEC/IEEE 42010:2011 (2011)
6. International Organization for Standardization: Road Vehicles – Functional Safety – Part 1 to 9. International Standard ISO/FDIS 26262 (November 2011)
7. Synligare Consortium: Synligare Project website, http://www.synligare.eu/

# Towards Energy Efficient, High-Speed Communication in WSNs

Attila Nagy and Olaf Landsiedel

[1] Gothenburg University, Sweden
[2] Chalmers University of Technology, Sweden
nagat@student.chalmers.se, olafl@chalmers.se

**Abstract.** Traditionally, protocols in wireless sensor networks focus on low-power operation with low data-rates. In addition, a small set of protocols provides high throughput communication. With sensor networks developing into general propose networks, we argue that protocols need to provide both: low data-rates at high energy-efficiency and, additionally, a high throughput mode. This is essential, for example, to quickly collect large amounts of raw-data from a sensor.

This paper presents a set of practical extensions to the low-power, low-delay routing protocol ORW. We introduce the capability to handle multiple, concurrent bulk-transfers in dynamic application scenarios. Overall, our extensions allow ORW to reach an almost 500% increase in the throughput with less than a 25% increase of the power consumption during a bulk transfer. Thus, we show that instead of developing a new protocol from scratch, we can carefully enhance an existing, energy-efficient protocol with high-throughput extensions. Both the energy-efficient low data-rate mode and the high throughput extensions transparently co-exist inside a single protocol.

**Keywords:** high-throughput, opportunistic routing, Wireless Sensor Network.

## 1 Introduction

In *wireless sensor networks (WSNs)*, most protocol stacks are designed for low data-rates. This is a widespread application scenario in WSNs and matches the limited resources of sensor nodes in terms of bandwidth and energy. However, there is a set of situations, in which we demand for high-speed bulk-transfers: the energy efficient transport of large amounts of data through the resource constrained WSNs. Such scenarios, for example, include the distribution of OS updates and configurations, or the collection of raw measurement traces and logs from individual nodes.

In this paper we argue that instead of developing a new protocol, it is sufficient to extend an existing energy-efficient, low data-rate protocol with a set of carefully designed high-throughput extensions. For this, we base our design on the existing energy-efficient, opportunistic routing protocol, ORW [6]. Our extensions cover a wide range of scenarios including intra-path interference, inter-path interference and concurrent bulk transfers. We provide three key mechanisms:

A. Bondavalli et al. (Eds.): SAFECOMP 2014 Workshops, LNCS 8696, pp. 63–70, 2014.

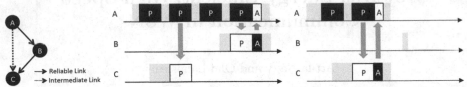

(a) Sample topology: Node $A$ reaches $C$ via $B$ on reliable links or directly on an unreliable link.

(b) Traditional unicast routing in WSNs: Although $C$ might overhear some transmission from $A$, packets are addressed to $B$ to ensure stable routing.

(c) Opportunistic Routing in ORW: The first node that wakes up, receives a packet, and provides sufficient routing progress acknowledges and forwards it.

**Fig. 1.** Basic idea of ORW: Utilizing the first woken neighbor as forwarder, ORW reduces energy consumption and delay. This exploiting of spatial and temporal link diversity also increase resilience to link dynamics.

1. Our first extension to the ORW protocol initiates a novel collision avoidance method for high-throughput scenarios. It is applied beside the already existing, well functioning collision detection technique for low data-rate settings.
2. The second extension's purpose is to stabilize the EDC routing metric used by the ORW protocol to estimate the latency, i.e., duty-cycled wake-ups, required for a packet to reach the sink from a given node.
3. The third extension disables duty-cycling during a bulk transfer for the nodes that are participating in an ongoing bulk transfer.

The remainder of this paper continues by briefly discussing the ORW protocol to provide the required background in Section 2. We describe related work in Section 3, and show the design of our high-throughput extensions to the ORW protocol in Section 4. Section 5 evaluates these extensions and we conclude in Section 6.

## 2   Background

ORW targets duty-cycled protocol stacks. For simplicity we here illustrate the basic concept of ORW utilizing an asynchronous low-power-listening MAC, such as in X-MAC [1]. In low-power-listening a sender transmits a stream of packets until the intended receiver wakes up and acknowledges it (see Fig. 1b). To integrate opportunistic routing into duty cycled environments, we depart from this traditional unicast forwarding scheme in one key aspect: The first node that (a) wakes up, (b) receives the packet, and (c) provides routing progress, acknowledges and forwards the packet, see Fig. 1c. For example, in Figure 1a node $A$ can reach node $C$ either directly via an unreliable link or via $B$. Commonly, traditional routing ignores the unreliable link $A \to C$ and relies on $A \to B \to C$ for forwarding. ORW extends this, by also including $A \to C$ into the routing process: If $A \to C$ is temporary available and $C$ wakes up before $B$, ORW will utilize it for forwarding. This reduces the energy consumption and delay (see Fig. 1c). To select forwarders, ORW introduces EDC (Expected Duty Cycled wakeups) as routing metric. EDC is an adaptation of ETX [2] to energy-efficient, anycast routing in duty-cycled WSNs.

Our design enables an efficient adaptation of opportunistic routing to the specific demands of wireless sensor networks: (1) In contrast to opportunistic routing in mesh networks, forwarder selection in ORW focuses on energy efficiency and delay instead of network throughput: It minimizes the number of probes until a packet is received by a potential forwarder. (2) It integrates well into duty-cycled environments and ensures that many potential forwarders can overhear a packet in a single wake-up period. Thereby, ORW exploits spatial and temporal link-diversity to improve resilience to wireless link dynamics. (3) The fact that only a small number of nodes receive a probe at a specific point in time simplifies the design of a coordination scheme to select a single forwarder. This limits overhead of control traffic.

However, in the design of ORW we focused on low data-rate traffic, as this is the most common scenario in WSNs. In this paper, we now take the next step and widen our application scenarios: We extend ORW to high-throughput settings, i.e., to support bulk transfers.

## 3 Related Work

There exist several approaches to high-throughput communication in WSNs. For instance, *Packet in Pipe* [7] (PIP) is a connection-oriented, multi-hop, multi-channel, TDMA-based solution. Another approach is *Flush* [5], a CSMA-based protocol applying a rate-control algorithm along with end-to-end acknowledgments. Both of these protocols are not designed to handle multiple concurrent bulk transfers. Moreover, they do not integrate well with other routing protocols. Their design is tailored to being the only routing protocol in place at a specific point in time. We argue that this assumption is not practical as low data-rate applications are the common application scenario in WSN. Thus, we believe any high-throughput protocol must co-exist efficiently with low-data rate protocols.

On the other hand, the *Lossy Link, Low Power, High Throughput* [4] protocol (LLH) allows for several concurrent bulk transfers crossing each others paths. This protocol uses duty-cycling with low-power listening, has a high resistance against both intra-path and inter-path interference, and applies a CSMA based MAC protocol. From these three high-throughput solutions the LLH resembles the most to the extended ORW protocol due to its low-power property and the capability to handle concurrent bulk transfers. However, in contrast to our work, LLH assembles a new protocol to be deployed alongside with existing low-power, low-rate protocols. This leads to an increased code base and potentially additional energy consumption, as two protocols need to be operated in parallel. As a result, the may both have own state and each map apply own network maintenance such neighbor discovery or wireless link estimation.

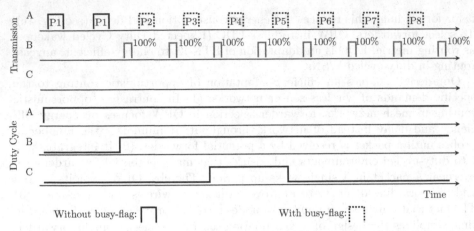

**Fig. 2. Collision avoidance by the extensions:** Node $B$ forwards all the packets from node $A$. When node $C$ starts its duty cycle, it receives the packets with busy-flag, and therefore does not acknowledge them.

## 4  Design

In this section, we identify the limitations of ORW in high-throughput scenarios and next introduce three extensions to enable high-throughput communication in ORW.

### 4.1  Limitations of ORW in High-Throughput Scenarios

We begin with a discussion of the limitations of ORW in presence of high data-rates. The base ORW protocol performs poorly in the bulk transfer scenario due to the following key problems: (1) contention and packet collisions, (2) unstable routing metrics, and (3) early termination of duty cycles.

1. **Problem: High Contention and Packet Collisions.** Bulk transfers are streams of packets leading to many, concurrent transmissions in the network. This inherently increases contention and as a result the possibility of collisions, especially when there are multiple possible paths for a packet between the source node and the sink node.

2. **Problem: Unstable EDC Routing Metric.** EDC as routing metric in ORW estimates the expected duty cycles that are required for a packet to traverse the topology from a node to the sink. Our analysis indicates that this metrics tends to fluctuate rapidly in case of high contention. This is especially the case in topologies where the path of a bulk packet has a high number of hops but just a few possible paths exist for the packet. The result of this fluctuation are loops in the packet's path and, via these loops, packet loss.

3. **Problem: Nodes do not stay awake until burst is completed.** Duty-cycling during a bulk transfer can lead to situations where nodes that are

heavily used turn off their radio receiver, as their duty cycles have expired. This forces ORW to find a new, alternative forwarder or to wait for that particular forwarder to wake-up again. As a result, it increases the transmission time of packets and the power consumption of the whole network.

## 4.2  Extending ORW to High-Throughput Scenarios

In the following, we present our extensions to ORW to mitigate the challenges discussed above and to enable energy-efficient and reliable high-throughput communication.

**Collision Avoidance:** Our collision avoidance extension is divided into two parts: a sender and a receiver part. In the sender part, the design contains a special flag, the *busy-flag*. A sender sets it to indicate that it has locked onto a specific forwarder to transfer a bulk of packets. A forwarder shall only forward packets from senders that have locked onto it. Other potential forwarders shall, upon receiving packets with the the flag set, not forward it and quickly go back to sleep to safe energy. As a result, this extensions limits contentions between nodes to be elected as forwarder. Figure 2 illustrates how this collision avoidance extension works with one sender node $A$ and two receiver nodes $B$ and $C$.

**Stabilizing the EDC Routing Metric:** ORW, by default, updates its routing estimates after each transmission. Thus, based on its success or failure the quality estimation of the wireless link to the neighboring nodes is updated. In high-throughput scenarios, with many current transmissions this leads to erroneous estimates. Our solution is to simply prohibit the EDC update of a node if it is involved in a bulk transfer. Thus, we update the routing metric at the end of each bulk transfer, i.e., after 10 to 20 packets, and not during it.

**Keeping Nodes Awake:** Finally, we prohibit nodes that are involved in a bulk transfer from going back to sleep before the bulk transfer has completed.

## 5  Evaluation

Our evaluation presents two types of benchmarks: (1) micro-benchmarks and (2) macro-benchmarks. For the micro-benchmarks we use a WSN simulation environment, Cooja, and for the macro-benchmark we utilize Indriya [3], a three-dimensional wireless sensor network deployed across three floors of the National University of Singapore.

The micro-benchmarks use two types of metrics: (1) reliability, (2) power consumption of the whole bulk transfer. We evaluate each of our three extensions separately and we show their combination:

1. ORWE-BF: busy-flag extension to avoid contention and collisions.
2. ORWE-EDC: stabilization of the EDC routing metric.
3. ORWE-DC: stabilization of the duty-cycle.
4. ORWE: the combination of all three extensions.

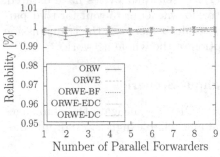

(a) **Reliability:** Our extensions have the same level of reliability as the base ORW design.

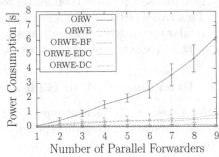

(b) **Power consumption:** Drastic increase in the ORW design when the topology increases. In contrast, our extensions show only a minimal increase.

**Fig. 3.** Parallel forwarder nodes

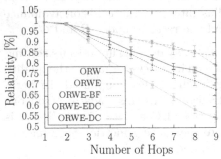

(a) **Reliability:** ORWE has a higher reliability than the base ORW protocol.

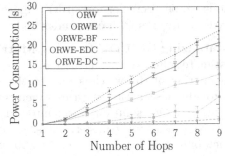

(b) **Power consumption:** ORWE has the lowest power consumption.

**Fig. 4.** Intra-path interference

Our micro-benchmarks evaluate three types of scenarios in a controlled environment. The first scenario, inter-path interference, shows the best performance improvement. The topology we use for this type contains a set of parallel forwarder nodes between the source and sink nodes. The more potential forwarders we deploy, the higher the chance for collisions of acknowledgments is. While the base ORW protocol resolves collisions per packet, our extensions allow to lower this intensity to one collision per bulk transfer. Figure 3 shows the reliability and power consumption of this scenario: The power consumption stays on a low level without any performance degradation in the reliability.

The second type of scenario, intra-path interference, aims to show the performance of our extensions in a topology where there is only one path between the source and the sink, but that path contains a high number of hops. In this scenario, the extensions perform significantly better than the base protocol in all

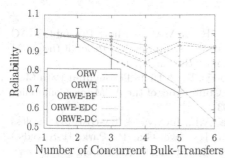
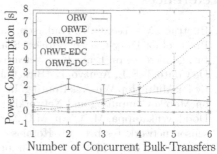

(a) **Reliability:** The bottleneck scenario highlights the limitations of all design: the contention leads to packet losses in all designs. Nonetheless, ORWE improves over default ORW.

(b) **Power consumption:** ORWE has the lowest power consumption.

**Fig. 5.** Bottleneck scenario: Multiple sources with 4 potential forwarders

the metrics. For instance, ORWE uses the 10% of the power that is used by the base ORW protocol for the same bulk transfer. Moreover, we increase the reliability in the meantime. Figure 4 shows the reliability and power consumption for this scenario. The third type of scenario shows that our extensions are capable of handling multiple concurrent bulk transfers with only a minor performance degradation.

The third type of topology evaluates a case when a number of source nodes concurrently sending bulk packets exceeds the number of forwarders, see Figure 5. This topology formulates a bottleneck scenario in the sense that the number of forwarder nodes are not able to serve the performance demand generated by the source nodes creating a special collision critical situation.

The macro-benchmark serves as a platform for the evaluation on a larger scale. Overall, our results show that our extensions use 25% of the power that are used by the base ORW protocol with a slightly higher reliability.

# 6 Conclusion

In this paper we show, that by adding three carefully designed extensions to the ORW protocols, we can extend it from a low data-rate protocol to also support high-throughput scenarios at high energy-efficiency. Our future work includes a detailed testbed evaluation and an experimental comparison to the state of the art.

Conversely, by applying our extensions we obtain a significant performance improvement in all the metrics that we presented in this paper. Lastly, these extensions have no effect on the non-bulk packet transfer, since they are only activated when the transmission rate exceeds a certain level. Thus, these extensions transparently integrate into ORW and are backwards compatible with the base protocol.

# References

1. Buettner, M., Yee, G.V., Anderson, E., Han, R.: X-MAC: a Short Preamble MAC Protocol for Duty-Cycled Wireless Sensor Networks. In: SenSys: Proc. of the ACM Int. Conference on Embedded Networked Sensor Systems (2006)
2. De Couto, D.S.J., Aguayo, D., Bicket, J., Morris, R.: A High-Throughput Path Metric for Multi-Hop Wireless Routing. In: MobiCom: Proc. of the ACM Int. Conference on Mobile Computing and Networking (2003)
3. Doddavenkatappa, M., Chan, M.C., Ananda, A.L.: Indriya: A low-cost, 3D wireless sensor network testbed. In: Korakis, T., Li, H., Tran-Gia, P., Park, H.-S. (eds.) TridentCom 2011. LNICST, vol. 90, pp. 302–316. Springer, Heidelberg (2012)
4. Duquennoy, S., Österlind, F., Dunkels, A.: Lossy links, low power, high throughput. In: Proceedings of the 9th ACM Conference on Embedded Networked Sensor Systems, SenSys 2011 (2011)
5. Kim, S., Fonseca, R., Dutta, P., Tavakoli, A., Culler, D., Levis, P., Shenker, S., Stoica, I.: Flush: A reliable bulk transport protocol for multihop wireless networks. In: Proceedings of the 5th International Conference on Embedded Networked Sensor Systems, SenSys 2007 (2007)
6. Landsiedel, O., Ghadimi, E., Duquennoy, S., Johansson, M.: Low power, low delay: Opportunistic routing meets duty cycling. In: IPSN 2012: Proceedings of the 11th ACM/IEEE International Conference on Information Processing in Sensor Networks (April 2012)
7. Raman, B., Chebrolu, K., Bijwe, S., Gabale, V.: Pip: A connection-oriented, multi-hop, multi-channel tdma-based mac for high throughput bulk transfer. In: Proceedings of the 8th ACM Conference on Embedded Networked Sensor Systems, SenSys 2010 (2010)

# Comparing Adaptive TDMA against a Clock Synchronization Approach

Luis Almeida[1], Frederico Santos[2], and Luis Oliveira[1]

[1] IT/FEUP, University of Porto, Portugal
{lda,dee10023}@fe.up.pt
[2] DEE-ISEC, Polytechnic Institute of Coimbra, Portugal
fred@isec.pt

**Abstract.** Teams of cooperating robots are getting more popular fostered by hardware platforms as well as technologies and techniques for coordination that are becoming widely available. The wireless communication is one such technology that impacts directly on the quality provided by the cooperative applications running atop. In cases where the team robots transmit periodically, it has been shown that synchronizing their transmissions so that they occur out of phase is beneficial, e.g. in a TDMA manner. However, persisting periodic interfering traffic may increase collisions with the team traffic and thus downgrade the channel quality. The Adaptive TDMA self-synchronized protocol was then proposed to improve the resilience to this type of interference. In this paper we assess the effectiveness of Adaptive TDMA in comparison with a traditional TDMA implementation based on clock synchronization. The results of practical experiments show a reduction in packet losses when the interfering traffic is short, typically single packet.[1]

**Keywords:** TDMA, synchronization, adaptation, cooperation, information exchange.

## 1 Introduction

Cooperative robotics has been motivating substantial research work since several years [1,2,3]. It is a useful approach to many practical robotic applications for both military and civil purposes, from search and rescue in catastrophic situations, to demining or maneuvers in contaminated areas.

Recently, the availability of hardware platforms as well as technologies and techniques needed for coordination of autonomous agents is fostering the use of teams of cooperating robots. One such technology is wireless communication but its use still raises several challenges. In fact, the wireless medium is open, prone to errors, and fast fading, thus leading to limited communication range and problems such as hidden

---

[1] This work was partially supported by the Portuguese Government through FCT grant CodeStream PTDC/EEI-TEL/3006/2012.

A. Bondavalli et al. (Eds.): SAFECOMP 2014 Workshops, LNCS 8696, pp. 71–79, 2014.

and exposed nodes. Moreover, being an inherently shared medium, some kind of access control is required.

The option for an existing wireless communication standard, such as the IEEE 802.11, solves those problems up to a certain extent, particularly using the infra-structured mode. In fact, this mode implies that all the communications pass through an Access Point (AP), which enforces team membership consistency, i.e., an agent is considered as part of the team whenever it has an active link with the AP [4]. Nevertheless, despite the existence of a fairly complex distributed arbitration mechanism in IEEE 802.11, access collisions can still occur and their probability raises significantly with the network load as well as with certain transmission patterns, e.g., periodic transmissions with coherent periods[2] [5,6].

In this work we address the problem of packet losses due to medium access collisions in IEEE 802.11 infra-structured networks using the common Distributed Coordination Function (DCF) access control method. This is likely the most common communications technology used today in teams of cooperating robots. We follow a previous line of work that proposed synchronizing the team transmissions in a round in a Time-Division Multiple Access (TDMA) manner [4]. We then propose an improvement to the adaptation mechanism proposed therein that is more robust to timing interferences caused by the AP itself. Moreover, we present a comparison with a traditional TDMA implementation based on clock synchronization in the presence of coherent periodic interfering traffic. This comparison was still lacking in the referred framework. We will see that the adaptive version achieves lower packet losses when the interfering traffic is short, typically a single packet per transaction.

The paper is organized as follows. Section 2 presents a brief survey of related work, Section 3 discusses the implementation of TDMA over IEEE 802.11 networks, Section 4 compares a clock-synchronized with the adaptive implementations of TDMA while Section 5 concludes the paper.

## 2    Related Work

The work on slotted approaches in wireless communications, both for data and voice, is rather vast and old. For example, in [9,10,11] the authors propose using dynamic TDMA frameworks where slots in a static round structure are assigned dynamically to nodes. However, these approaches are normally centralized in which a master receives slot requests and assigns slots to nodes dynamically. The original Point Coordination Function (PCF), as well as the more recent Controlled Channel Access (HCCA) of the Hybrid Coordination Function (HCF), of IEEE 802.11 also work in a similar manner with the AP scheduling the nodes traffic in a centralized collision-free way. Conversely to these approaches, we seek a fully distributed access coordination scheme, which is a typical property of TDMA protocols.

---

[2] We use the expression "coherent periods" to refer to periods in which one is equal or an integer multiple of the other one.

Following an approach similar to [4] the authors of RI-EDF [8] synchronize slots based on the reception time instants of the transmission of other nodes in a distributed fashion. However, the protocol was not developed to cope with uncontrolled non-complying traffic in the channel.

A well-known and widely used distributed access control technique is Carrier Sense Multiple Access with Collision Avoidance (CSMA-CA), which is the basic mechanism of IEEE 802.11 DCF. However, this technique may behave poorly in the presence of interfering periodic flows [4,6] and this is why we are pursuing the use of TDMA techniques. Finally, TDMA techniques are typically developed atop clock synchronization mechanisms that provide a consistent global clock [7]. In this case, the slots structure in the round is fixed during all system operation. In our work we will use an open software package named Chrony [12] to achieve such global clock and drive the clock-synchronized version of TDMA that will be used for comparison.

## 3    TDMA Communication Framework

TDMA is a common temporal multiplexing scheme for periodic communications that provides each node with an exclusive fixed duration transmission window (or slot). These slots are organized in a round that repeats continuously. For cooperating robots in a team that frequently share their state in a periodic fashion, TDMA is rather convenient. In this case, assigning a slot to each robot[3], its transmissions will be separated in time from those of the other nodes (they occur in different slots) and thus the occurrence of in-team medium access collisions is precluded.

However, if uncontrolled interfering traffic cannot be avoided, herein called *external traffic*, which is the general case we are considering, then two issues must be addressed. On one hand, there must be a collision resolution mechanism since access collisions are now possible. This is granted by the underlying IEEE 802.11 protocol (DCF). On the other hand, the nodes in the team must use windows that are sufficiently large ($T_{xwin}$) to accommodate both their own transmissions ($M_{k,i}$) and the expected external traffic (Fig. 1). Note that under heavy external traffic load, it is still possible that the transmissions of a node in the team are significantly delayed and fall inside the following window, creating interference within the team.

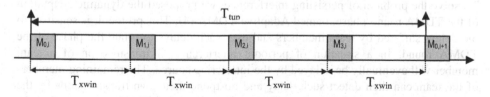

**Fig. 1.** TDMA transmission control of wireless communications within a team of 4 nodes considering equal slots (i.e., all robots have similar communication requirements)

---

[3] In the scope of this work we will use *robot*, *agent* and *node* interchangeably.

The implementation using clock-synchronization is straight forward once the global clock $G(t)$ is in place. Node $k$ is allowed to transmit whenever:

$$G(t) \bmod T_{tup} = k * T_{xwin}, \quad k = 0 \ldots n - 1 \quad (n \text{ nodes})$$

In practice this is achieved with timers that trigger the respective transmissions. However, this approach may perform poorly, with high significant packet losses during certain periods of time, herein called *critical periods*, independently of the network load. This is the case in the presence of interfering external periodic traffic with approximately coherent periods. In this case, given the fixed TDMA round structure, the protocol will continue triggering transmissions at the same time as the interference source, until the clock drifts eventually set those instants apart (Fig. 2).

Consequently, a periodic interference with a coherent period will cause persistent interference, independently of the load, increasing the probability of collisions and consequent packet losses. In fact, this pernicious phenomenon also happens when the robots in the team transmit periodically, with similar periods, but unsynchronized. In this case, each one will be a coherent periodic interference for the others, which is the motivation to use a TDMA approach in the team.

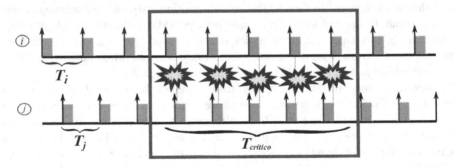

**Fig. 2.** Critical interference period arising from approximately coherent periodic transmissions

### 3.1    Adaptive TDMA

To solve the problem of persisting interference, we proposed the dynamic adaptation of the TDMA round phase, named Adaptive TDMA [4]. This protocol, is sensitive to the delays suffered by team members and uses such delays to rotate the phase of the TDMA round. In a situation of periodic interference, a transmission of a team member will eventually be delayed by the interfering source. The remaining members of the team can then detect such delay and postpone their own transmissions by the same amount of time, effectively shifting the phase of the TDMA round so that the following transmissions would not collide with the interfering source again.

Moreover, this technique also carries along a further benefit since each node now synchronizes with the others in the team by measuring the reception instants of the respective packets and thus clock synchronization is no longer needed.

The work in [4] includes both the adaptation mechanism as well as a dynamic reconfiguration of the round structure, according to robots that dynamically join and leave the team. This is orthogonal to the current work and thus it will not be considered here. The focus will thus be on the adaptive TDMA mechanism, only.

Moreover, we use an improved version of the adaptive mechanism proposed in [4] in which just an automatically elected reference node, namely the one with the lowest ID among the active ones, senses the delays in the team transmissions and adjusts the round phase. All other nodes transmit after receiving from the reference node in each round and with an offset equal to that of the respective slot (Fig. 3). The reference node is automatically reassigned in case the current one leaves the team.

The reference node (node 0) determines its transmission instant in the following round ($i+1$) as follows, considering the previously computed transmission instant for the current round ($i$) and the delays $\delta_k$ suffered by nodes 1 to $k$ in this round (if lower than the maximum allowed $\Delta$ adjustment):

$$T_{0,i+1} = T_{0,i} + T_{tup} + \max_{k=1..n-1, \delta_k < \Delta} \delta_k$$

The transmission instants for the remaining nodes are defined as follows, where $\hat{T}_{0,i}$ is an estimation of $T_{0,i}$ considering the wireless transmission latency:

$$T_{k,i} = \hat{T}_{0,i} + k * T_{xwin}, \qquad k = 1..n-1$$

If the reference node does not receive from any of the other nodes during one round (or receives with a delay larger than $\Delta$) then it transmits $T_{tup}$ later. Similarly, if the other nodes do not receive from the reference node in one round, they transmit $T_{tup}$ after their previous transmission.

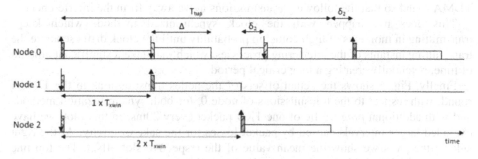

**Fig. 3.** The improved Adaptive TDMA protocol with a single adapting reference node

This mechanism is particularly better than the originally proposed one when in the presence of an AP with the power management feature active and a fairly long DTIM period. In such case the transmissions instants in the former approach would be altered and the team would not synchronize. With the new mechanism, the reference node transmission instants may still be altered (implying a potential large error in $\hat{T}_{0,i}$) but this will impact the start of the round, only. The remaining transmissions in the team are still separated in time according to the respective slots in the round.

## 4     Comparing Clock-Synchronized and Adaptive TDMA

When comparing Adaptive TDMA with clock synchronized TDMA there is one immediate difference. The former merges synchronization and data transmission while the latter needs a clock synchronization service and then implements data transmission alone. Moreover, the clock synchronization service requires transmissions of its own that must be accommodated by the data protocol. For these reasons we believe that Adaptive TDMA is simpler to deploy and use.

Moreover, clock synchronization algorithms are typically master-slave such as Chrony [12], frequently without master redundancy, which makes them sensitive to single point failures. Conversely, Adaptive TDMA is fully distributed and thus resilient by nature to the failure of any of its nodes.

Finally, to compare both approaches quantitatively with respect to packet losses in the presence of near coherent periodic interference we carry out several experiments using the *ping* command issued from an external computer. The results were extracted from a sequence of logs of a team with four nodes, during 5min of operation, using a round of 99.5ms. The reason for such period is to make it slightly different from that of the ping traffic, which was set to sub-multiples of 100ms with 1kB packets. With this difference in periods, we expect a high contention interval between both types of traffic to occur recurrently approximately every 20s, resulting from the difference of the frequencies of the interfering periodic processes.

The clock synchronized TDMA results are shown as *chrony*. Those concerning Adaptive TDMA appear as Rec Adap TDMA (since the actual protocol includes the reconfigurable part). Note that there is still a certain residual level of external traffic that was circulating in the medium at the time the experiments were carried out.

The results shown in Fig. 4 reveal an advantage of Adaptive TDMA that is expected. If the team transmissions collide at a given moment with the interfering ping packets, eventually a team transmission will be delayed shifting the whole TDMA round so that the following transmissions move away from the interference.

This does not happen with the clock synchronized method, which keeps transmitting in moments of high collision probability until the clock drifts separate the transmitting instants of the interfering processes, which may take a significant amount of time, potentially creating a long critical period.

Finally, Fig. 5 shows the actual offsets of the nodes transmissions in the TDMA round, with respect to the transmissions of node 0, for both synchronization methods and with additional *ping* traffic of one 1KB packet every 20ms. In this plot, we have excluded larger intervals caused by packet losses for the sake of clarity. At the right side of the plots we show the mean value of the respective slot offset. The top line represents the interval between consecutive transmissions of node 0, thus showing the effective round period.

In general, the clock synchronized approach exhibits more symmetrical variations in the slot intervals, which is expected given the fixed regular average slot offsets. The adaptive approach shows essentially positive variations, only, due to the sliding phase mechanism that absorbs delays into the round period. This can be seen in the larger average period than the programmed value of 9.5ms, as opposed to the clock synchronized case that maintains an average round period very close to the programmed one.

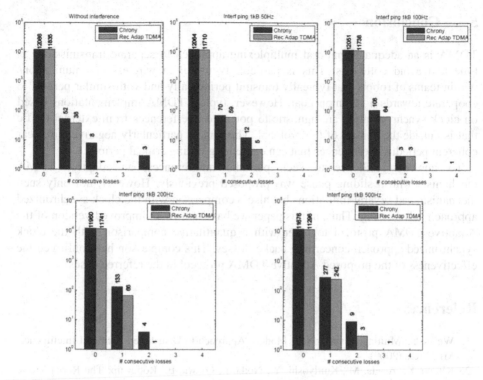

**Fig. 4.** Histograms of consecutive lost packets with *no ping*, or *1KB single packet ping* traffic with variable frequency

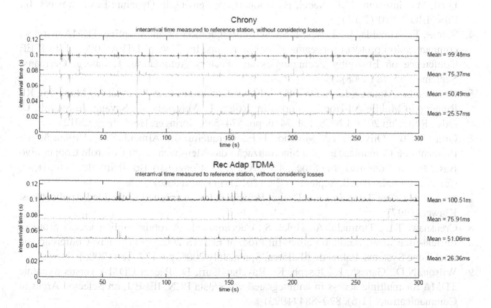

**Fig. 5.** Transmission offsets in the round with respect to the reference node in both clock synchronized and Adaptive TDMA with 1KB ping every 20ms of external traffic

## 5    Conclusion

TDMA is an adequate temporal multiplexing approach to separate transmissions in time and avoid collisions. This is particularly useful in wireless communications within teams of robots that typically transmit periodically and with similar periods to cooperate towards a common goal. However, typical TDMA implementations based on clock synchronization are agnostic to potential interferences from external traffic that is outside the control of the protocol. This can be particularly negative with near coherent periodic interferences that can cause long lasting critical periods.

To improve resilience to such periodic interferences, an adaptive TDMA mechanism with a sliding phase was proposed previously. However, not only such mechanism had several limitations but also a comparison with the clock synchronized approach was missing. Thus, in this paper we have shown an improved version of the Adaptive TDMA protocol together with a quantitative comparison with the clock synchronized approach concerning packet losses. This comparison has confirmed the effectiveness of the proposed Adaptive TDMA protocol in the referred cases.

## References

1. Weiss, G.: Multiagent systems. A Modern Approach to Distributed Artificial Intelligence. MIT Press (2000)
2. Kitano, K., Asada, M., Kuniyoshi, Y., Noda, I., Osawa, E.: RoboCup: The Robot World Cup Initiative. In: Proc. of IJCAI 1995 Workshop on Entertainment and AI/Alife, Montreal (1995)
3. Dietl, M., Gutmann, J.-S., Nebel, B.: Cooperative Sensing in Dynamic Environments. In: Proc. IROS 2001 (2001)
4. Santos, F., Almeida, L., Lopes, L.S.: Self-configuration of an Adaptive TDMA wireless communication protocol for teams of mobile robots. In: Proc. of ETFA 2008 - 13th IEEE Conference on Emerging Technologies and Factory Automation, Hamburg, Germany, September 15-18 (2008)
5. Oliveira, L., Almeida, L., Santos, F.: A Loose Synchronisation Protocol for Managing RF Ranging in Mobile Ad-Hoc Networks. In: Röfer, T., Mayer, N.M., Savage, J., Saranlı, U. (eds.) RoboCup 2011. LNCS, vol. 7416, pp. 574–585. Springer, Heidelberg (2012)
6. Ordoñez, B., Oliveira, L., Moreno, U.F., Cerqueira, J., Almeida, L.: Utilização de Protocolo de Comunicação para Sincronização das Mensagens para Controle Cooperativo Baseado em Consenso. In: Proc. of CBA 2012 - Congresso Brasileiro de Automação, Campina Grande, Brasil, September 2-6 (2012) (in Portuguese)
7. Kopetz, H.: Real-Time Systems Design Principles for Distributed Embedded Applications. Kluwer (1997)
8. Crenshaw, T.L., Tirumala, A., Hoke, S., Caccamo, M.: A robust inplicit access protocol for real-time wireless collaboration. In: Proc. of ECRTS 2005 – Euromicro Conference on Real-Time Systems, Palma de Mallorca, Spain, July 2005, pp. 177–186 (2005)
9. Wilson, N.D., Ganesh, R., Joseph, K., Raychaudhuri, D.: Packet CDMA versus dynamic TDMA for multiple access in an integrated voice/data PCN. IEEE J. on Selected Areas in Communications 11(6), 870–884 (1993)

10. Young, C.D.: Usap: A unifying dynamic distributed multichannel TDMA slot assignment protocol. In: Proc. of MILCOM 1996 - Military Communications Conference, vol. 1, pp. 235–239 (October 1996)
11. Kanzaki, A., Uemukai, T., Hara, T., Nishio, S.: Dynamic TDMA slot assignment in ad hoc networks. In: Proc. of AIDA 1996 - Advanced Information and Networking Applications, pp. 330–335 (March 1996)
12. Mora, F.: Bring an Atomic Clock to Your Home with Chrony. Linux Journal 2002(101) (September 2002), http://chrony.tuxfamily.org

# Introduction:
# ERCIM/EWICS/ARTEMIS Workshop on Dependable Embedded and Cyberphysical Systems and Systems-of-Systems (DECSoS'14) at SAFECOMP 2014

## A European Approach to Critical Systems Engineering

Erwin Schoitsch[1] and Amund Skavhaug[2]

[1] AIT Austrian Institute of Technology GmbH, Vienna, Austria
erwin.schoitsch@ait.ac.at
[2] NTNU, Trondheim, Norway
Amund.Skavhaug@ntnu.no

## 1 Introduction

This workshop at SAFECOMP follows already its own tradition since 2006. In the past, it focussed on the conventional type of "embedded systems", covering all dependability aspects (in the meaning of IFIP WG 10.4, defined by Avizienis, Lapries, Kopetz, Voges and others). To emphasize more the relationship to physics, mechatronics and the notion of interaction with an unpredictable environment, the terminology changed to "cyber-physical systems" (CPS). Collaboration and co-operation of these systems with each other and humans, and the interplay of safety and security are leading to new challenges in verification, validation and certification/qualification.

In a highly interconnected world, a finite number of independently operable and manageable systems are networked together for a period of time to achieve a certain higher goal as constituent systems of a so-called "system-of-systems". Examples are the smart power grid with power plants and power distribution and control, smart transport systems (rail, traffic management with V2V and V2I facilities, air traffic control systems), advanced manufacturing systems, mobile co-operating autonomous robotic systems, smart buildings up to smart cities and the like.

The impact on society as a whole is considerable - thus dependability (safety, reliability, availability, security, maintainability, etc.) evaluated in a holistic manner becomes an important issue, including resilience, robustness, and sustainability. CPSs are a targeted research area in Horizon 2020 and public-private partnerships such as ECSEL (Electronic Components and Systems for European Leadership), which integrates the former ARTEMIS, ENIAC and EPoSS efforts, where industry and research ("private") are represented by the industrial associations ARTEMIS-IA (for ARTEMIS, embedded intelligence and systems), AENEAS (for ENIAC, semiconductor industry) and EPoSS (for "Smart Systems Integration"), and the public part is represented by the EC and the national public authorities of the member states which take part in the ECSEL Joint Undertaking. Funding comes from the EC and the national public authorities ("tri-partite funding": EC, member states, project partners).

A. Bondavalli et al. (Eds.): SAFECOMP 2014 Workshops, LNCS 8696, pp. 80–83, 2014.

# 2    ARTEMIS/ECSEL: The European Cyber-Physical Systems Initiative

This year the workshop is co-hosted by the ARTEMIS projects

- MBAT[1] ("Combined Model-based Analysis and Testing of Embedded Systems", http://www.mbat-artemis.eu) and
- nSafeCer[1] ("Safety Certification of Software-intensive Systems with Reusable Components", http://www.safecer.eu),
- CRYSTAL[1] ("Critical Systems Engineering Factories", http://www.crystal-artemis.eu),
- ARROWHEAD[1] ("Ahead of the Future", http://www.arrowhead.eu/) and
- EMC² (Embedded multi-core systems for mixed criticality applications in dynamic and changeable real-time environments, http://www.emc2-project.eu)[1].

ARTEMIS (Advanced Research and Technology for Embedded Intelligence and Systems) was one of the European, industry-driven research initiatives. The economic impact in terms of jobs and growth is expected to exceed € 100 billion over ten years.

As a Joint Undertaking it is funding mainly a set of rather big projects, following the ARTEMIS Strategic Research Agenda in its work program and conducting each year a separate call for proposals based on its work program. From Mid 2014 onwards ARTEMIS has become part of the ECSEL PPP, but the current ARTEMIS projects will be continued according to the ARTEMIS rules, but managed by the ECSEL JU. The five co-hosting ARTEMIS projects will be described briefly:

MBAT will achieve better results by combining test and analysis methods. A new leading-edge Reference Technology Platform (RTP) for effective and cost-reducing validation and verification of Embedded Systems will be developed. MBAT project will strongly foster the development of high-quality embedded systems in the transportation sector at reduced costs (in short: higher quality embedded systems at lower price). Higher quality embedded systems will in turn increase the overall quality and market value of the transportation products. This will be of high value for the European industry and future projects, and contribute to the overarching ARTEMIS Goal of a Common Technology Reference Platform. Therefore close co-operation with related projects is envisaged, especially with those of the ARTEMIS Safety & High-reliability Cluster (e.g. CESAR, MBAT, SafeCer, iFEST, R3-COP).

nSafeCer aims at increased efficiency and reduced time-to-market together with increased quality and reduced risk through composable certification of safety-relevant embedded systems in the industrial domains of automotive and construction equipment, avionics, and rail. nSafeCer will also develop certification guidelines for other domains, including cross-domain qualification and the application of the nSafeCer Certification framework in new domains. nSafeCer will provide support for efficient reuse of safety certification arguments and prequalified components within and across

[1] The projects MBAT (grant agreement n° 269335), nSafeCer (grant agreement n° 295373), CRYSTAL (grant agreement n° 332830), ARROWHEAD (grant agreement n° 332987) and EMC² (grant agreement n° 621429) received funding from the EU ARTEMIS Joint Undertaking and the partners' national programmes/funding authorities.

industrial domains. This addresses the overarching goal of the ARTEMIS JU strategy to overcome fragmentation in the embedded systems markets.

CRYSTAL, a large ARTEMIS Innovation Pilot Project (AIPP), aims at fostering Europe's leading edge position in embedded systems engineering by facilitating high quality and cost effectiveness of safety-critical embedded systems and architecture platforms. Its overall goal is to enable sustainable paths to speed up the maturation, integration, and cross-sector reusability of technological and methodological bricks in the areas of transportation (aerospace, automotive, and rail) and healthcare providing a critical mass of European technology providers. CRYSTAL will integrate the contributions of previous ARTEMIS projects (CESAR, MBAT, iFEST, SafeCer etc.) and further develop the ARTEMIS RTP (Reference Technology Platform) and Interoperability Specification and create a sustainable innovative eco-system in the area of critical embedded systems engineering.

ARROWHEAD, a large AIPP addressing the areas production and energy system automation, intelligent-built environment and urban infrastructure, is aiming at enabling collaborative automation by networked embedded devices (from enterprise/worldwide level in the cloud down to device level at the machine in the plant) and achieving efficiency and flexibility on a global scale for five application verticals: production (manufacturing, process, energy), smart buildings and infrastructures, electro-mobility and virtual market of energy.

EMC² is up to now the largest ARTEMIS AIPP with EMC2 bundling the power for innovation of 97 partners from embedded industry and research from 19 European countries and Israel with an effort of about 800 person years and a total budget of about 100 million Euro. It started April 2014. The objective of the EMC² project is to develop an innovative and sustainable service-oriented architecture approach for mixed criticality applications in dynamic and changeable real-time environments.

It provides the paradigm shift to a new and sustainable system architecture which is suitable to handle open dynamic systems:

- Dynamic Adaptability in Open Systems, scalability and utmost flexibility,
- Utilization of expensive system features only as Service-on-Demand in order to reduce the overall system cost,
- Handling of mixed criticality applications under real-time conditions,
- Full scale deployment and management of integrated tool chains, through the entire lifecycle.

The AIPPs ARROWHEAD and EMC² are addressing "Systems-of-Systems" aspects in context of critical systems, whereas SafeCer, MBAT and CRYSTAL are devoting their major efforts towards creating a sustainable eco-system of a CRTP (Collaborative Reference Technology Platform) based on an ARTEMIS common IOS (Interoperability Specification).

## 3    This Year's Workshop

The workshop DECSoS'14 comprises the following sessions (in brackets: Acronym of the related ARTEMIS project if it is basis of the work reported):

### Introduction
- Erwin Schoitsch, Amund Skavhaug. *ERCIM, EWICS, ARTEMIS: An (European) introduction to different aspects of critical systems engineering.*

**Formal Analysis and Verification**

- S. Salvi, D. Kästner, T. Bienmüller and Ch. Ferdinand: *True Error or False Alarm? Refining Astree's Abstract Interpretation Results by EmbeddedTester's Automatic Model-based Testing*     [MBAT]
- M. Oertel, O. Kacimi and E. Boede: *Formal Verification of Implementation Models against Safety Specifications*     [MBAT]
- Ch. Ellen, M. Böschen and T. Peikenkamp: *MTBF Inconsistency Analysis on Inferred Product Breakdown Structures*     [CRYSTAL]
- F. Moscato, R. Aversa and B. Di Martino: *Critical Systems Verification in MetaMORP(h)OSY*     [CRYSTAL]

**Railway Applications: Safety Analysis and Verification**

- V. Frédérique, A. Ginisty, E. Soubiran and V.- D. Tchapet-Nya: *Report on the Railway Use case of the Crystal project: Objectives and Progress* [CRYSTAL]
- M. Carloni, O. Ferrante, A. Ferrari, G. Massaroli, A. Orazzo, L. Velardi and Ida Petrone: *Contract-based Analysis for verification of Communication-Based Train Control (CBTC) system.*     [MBAT]
- G. Barberio, B. Di Martino, N. Mazzocca, L. Velardi, A. Amato, R. De Guglielmo, U. Gentile, S. Marrone, R. Nardone, A. Peron and V. Vittorini: *An Interoperable Testing Environment for ERTMS/ETCS control systems.* [CRYSTAL]

**Resilience and Trust: Dynamic Issues**

- L. Laibinis, I. Pereverzeva and E. Troubitsyna: *Modelling Resilient Systems-of-Systems in Event-B.*
- N. Kajtazovic, Ch. Preschern, A. Höller and Ch. Kreiner: *Towards Assured Dynamic Configuration of Safety-critical Embedded Systems.*
- D. Schneider, E. Armengaud and E. Schoitsch: *Towards Trust Assurance and Certification in Cyber-Physical Systems.*     [EMC²]

The workshop will hopefully provide some insight into the topics, and enable fruitful discussions during the meeting and afterwards. As chairpersons of the workshop we want to thank all authors and contributors who submitted their work, and want to express our thanks to the SAFECOMP organizers who provided us the opportunity to organize the workshop at SAFECOMP 2014 in Florence. Particularly we want to thank the EC and national public authorities who made the research work possible. We want not to forget the continued support of our companies and organizations, of ERCIM (European Research Consortium for Informatics and Mathematics, with its Working Group on Dependable Embedded Software-intensive Systems) and EWICS, the creator and main sponsor of SAFECOMP, with its working groups, who always helped us to learn from their networks.

We hope that all participants will benefit from the workshop, enjoy the conference and will join us again in the future!

Erwin Schoitsch                                             Amund Skavhaug
AIT Austrian Institute of Technology GmbH          NTNU, Trondheim, Norway

# True Error or False Alarm?
# Refining Astrée's Abstract Interpretation Results by Embedded Tester's Automatic Model-Based Testing

Sayali Salvi[1], Daniel Kästner[1], Tom Bienmüller[2], and Christian Ferdinand[1]

[1] AbsInt GmbH, Science Park 1, 66123 Saarbrücken, Germany
[2] BTC Embedded Systems AG, Gerhard-Stalling-Str. 19, D-26135 Oldenburg, Germany

**Abstract.** A failure of safety-critical software may cause high costs or even endanger human beings. Contemporary safety standards require to identify potential functional and non-functional hazards and to demonstrate that the software does not violate the relevant safety goals. Typically for ensuring functional program properties model-based testing is used while non-functional properties like occurrence of runtime errors are addressed by abstract interpretation-based static analysis. Hence the verification process is split into two distinct parts – currently without any synergy between them being exploited. In this article we present an approach to couple model-based testing with static analysis based on a tool coupling between Astrée and BTC Embedded*Tester*®. Astrée reports all potential runtime errors in C programs. This makes it possible to prove the absence of runtime errors, but typically users have to deal with false alarms, i.e. spurious notifications about potential runtime errors. Investigating alarms to find out whether they are true errors which have to be fixed, or whether they are false alarms can cause significant effort. The key idea of this work is to apply model-based testing to automatically find test cases for alarms reported by the static analyzer. When a test case reproducing the error has been found, it has been proven that it is a true error; when no error has been found with full test coverage, it has been proven to be a false alarm. This can significantly reduce the alarm analysis effort and reduces the level of expertise needed to perform the code-level software verification. We describe the underlying concept and report on experimental results and future work.

## 1 Introduction

Safety-related software has to satisfy stringent quality requirements. The complexity of software-implemented functionality grows at a fast pace. Development teams have to meet tight budget constraints and face increasing pressure to reduce time-to-market. To meet these conflicting goals the development process has to be sound and efficient.

A leap in development efficiency can be reached by a holistic model-centric approach to software development, testing and verification. In model-based development the software is graphically developed at a high abstraction level, typically by hierarchical finite state machines and data flow diagrams which represent specification and model at the same time. From this high-level model the implementation is automatically generated by configurable code generators, often in the form of C code. Model-based testing aims

A. Bondavalli et al. (Eds.): SAFECOMP 2014 Workshops, LNCS 8696, pp. 84–96, 2014.

at automating testing activities and integrating the development of both design artifacts and test artifacts in a unified framework. This makes it possible to automatically create test architectures, and generate and execute the test cases.

All contemporary safety standards require to identify functional and non-functional hazards and to demonstrate that the software does not violate the relevant safety goals. Depending on the criticality level of the software the absence of safety hazards has to be demonstrated by formal methods or testing with sufficient coverage. This holds not only for DO-178B/DO-178C, but also for related norms like ISO 26262, and IEC-61508. Functional properties can be efficiently addressed by automatic model-based testing. The critical non-functional safety-relevant software characteristics are essentially implementation-level properties, e.g., whether real-time requirements can be met, whether stack overflows can occur, and whether there can be runtime errors like invalid pointer accesses, or divisions by zero. Because of the high abstraction level of model-based development these properties are largely hidden from the developers. Moreover they are very hard to check experimentally, i.e., by testing and measurements. Identifying safe end-of-test criteria for program properties like timing, stack size, and runtime errors is an unsolved problem. In consequence the required test effort is high, the tests require access to the physical hardware and the results are not complete.

Formal verification methods provide an alternative, in particular for safety-critical applications. One such method is abstract interpretation, which allows properties to be proven for all program runs with all inputs [8]. Nowadays, abstract interpretation-based static analyzers that can detect stack overflows [14] and violations of timing constraints [16], and that can prove the absence of runtime errors, are widely used in industry [15] (cf. Sec. 2). The advantage of abstract interpretation is that it enables full control and data coverage, but can be easily automatized and can reduce the testing effort.

In consequence, from a workflow perspective the verification process is split into two parts: model-based testing is used for showing functional program properties, and static analysis to prove the absence of non-functional program errors. In the course of the MBAT project[1] a concept for integrating model-based testing and static analysis has been developed which enables both aspects to be addressed seamlessly [13]. This concept has been realized by a tool coupling between BTC Embedded*Tester®* [7], and the static analysis tools aiT WCET Analyzer [1], StackAnalyzer [2], and Astrée [3] from AbsInt. Model-level information like execution model or environment specifications are automatically taken into account, reducing setup for test and analysis efforts and improving analysis precision. Tests and analyses can be launched seamlessly and produce unified result reports. While significantly improving the efficiency of the V&V process the tool coupling as described in [13] is mostly limited to workflow aspects and does not yet exploit the full potential of a combination of the two verification technologies, static analysis and model-based testing.

In this article we describe a deep technical integration between static runtime error analysis and model-based testing, implemented as a tool coupling between Astrée and BTC Embedded*Tester®*. Astrée is a sound static analyzer which can find all potential runtime errors in C programs. It works with an abstract semantics of the program which makes it possible to compute results even for big applications – the largest

---

[1] http://www.mbat-artemis.eu/

application investigated so far contains more than two million LOC. The downside of the abstraction mechanism is that there can be false alarms, i.e. spurious notifications about potential runtime errors, which are not actual bugs. Therefore, all alarms have to be investigated by the developers to determine whether they correspond to true errors which have to be fixed, or whether they are false alarms. This can cause significant effort. The key idea of this work is to apply model-based testing to automatically find test cases for alarms reported by Astrée. When BTC Embedded Tester® finds a test case reproducing the error, it has not only been proven that it is a true error, but users can directly investigate the situation in a debugger. When no test case reproducing the error could be found, the interpretation depends on the test model generation: when full test coverage can be achieved, the absence of the error has been proven. Situations where no full test coverage was possible, or where the error could not be reproduced in the given amount of time, have to be manually investigated – but even here the test coverage obtained is a valuable feedback for the user. With this coupling the effort for alarm analysis can be significantly reduced. Preliminary experimental results demonstrate the viability of our approach.

The article is structured as follows: we introduce the key concepts of static runtime error analysis in Sec. 2. Sec. 3 gives an overview of model-based testing with a focus on the concept of C observers which provide the basis for our methodological integration. The concept to automatically generate test cases for Astrée alarms is explained in Sec. 4. Experimental results are presented in Sec. 5 and Sec. 6 concludes.

## 2    Static Runtime Error Analysis

Over the last few years static analyzers based on abstract interpretation have evolved to be the state of the art for verifying non-functional software properties. A static analyzer is a software tool which computes information about the software under analysis without executing it. Abstract interpretation is a semantics-based method for program analysis which belongs to the formal verification methods. Its results are sound, i.e., they are valid for all program runs with all inputs and achieve full data and control coverage. The soundness of the analysis can be formally proven. Examples of abstract interpretation based static analyzers are tools to compute safe upper bounds on the worst-case execution time and the maximal stack usage of tasks [11] and to prove the absence of runtime errors [15]. Runtime errors like arithmetic overflows, array bound violations, divisions by zero, and invalid pointer accesses are critical programming errors. They can destroy the data integrity of a program, causing the program to behave erroneously, or to crash altogether. A well-known example for the possible effects of runtime errors is the explosion of the Ariane 5 rocket in 1996. The analyzer Astrée [3] is an abstract interpretation based static runtime error analyzer which finds all potential runtime errors in C programs, thereby enabling users to prove the absence of runtime errors [6]. Astrée analyzes structured C programs with the sole restrictions that no dynamic memory allocation and no recursion should be used, which is typically the case for safety-critical applications. The class of errors reported includes out-of-bound array accesses, erroneous pointer manipulations and dereferencing, integer and floating-point division by zero, integer and floating point overflows and invalid operations. Astrée also detects read accesses to uninitialized variables, detects shared variables accessed by asynchronous threads and performs a sound value analysis for them, and enables users to prove user-defined static assertions. The static assertions can be applied to arbitrary C expressions so that functional program properties can be addressed. When Astrée does not report an assertion failure alarm, the correctness of the asserted expression has been formally proven. The core of Astrée is a sophisticated analysis engine which allows to fine-tune the analysis precision to the software under analysis. This makes very low false alarm rates possible: safety-critical avionics software of several 100,000 lines of C code could be analyzed successfully with Astrée without any false alarm [4,15].

Since Astrée is based on an abstract semantics of the program there can be false alarms, i.e. spurious notifications about potential runtime errors which are caused by the overapproximation inherent to the analysis. False alarms can also be caused by preconditions that have not been made known to Astrée. Therefore, all alarms have to be investigated by the developers to determine whether they correspond to true errors which have to be fixed, or whether they are false alarms. This can cause significant effort.

## 2.1 Runtime Errors and Alarms

Runtime errors can occur in situations where the behavior of the C program is undefined, or unspecified according to the C semantics [12]. A notification about a potential runtime error is termed as *Alarm*. Astrée distinguishes two main types of alarms:

**Type A:** alarm about a runtime error which has unpredictable results. The analyzer reports the alarm and continues the analysis for scenarios where the error does not occur. For contexts where the error definitely occurs, the analyzer reports a definite runtime error and stops the analysis as there is no feasible continuation. Examples are out-of-bound array accesses, or write accesses via dangling pointers.

**Type C:** alarm about a runtime error which has a predictable outcome. The analyzer continues the analysis by overapproximating all possible results, including the effect of the error. Examples are integer overflows, invalid shifts, invalid cast operations.

The alarm messages displayed in the Astrée GUI possess a well-defined format. It provides details such as execution context of the alarm scenario, alarm location, type of alarm and the actual alarm text message. In addition to this, users can also request for program invariants, i.e., access the value ranges of variables the analyzer has computed for each specific context. The alarm messages have the following syntax:

(*context* at *filename*:*line1*.*column1*–*line2*.*column2*)$^+$ ALARM(*class*) : *alarm message*

The *context* information provides a forward sequence of unfinished function calls to reach the alarm location, loops encountered in these functions before reaching the alarm location and disambiguated conditional statements encountered before reaching the alarm location. The syntax is the following:

call#*f*@*line*
    function *f* is called at line *line*.

loop@*line*=*n*/*m* or loop@*line*>=*m+1*
    *n* is the rank of loop iteration and *m* is the unroll level. The first *n* iterations of the
    loop at line *line* are unrolled by the analyzer.
if@*line*=true or if@*line*=false
    if condition at line *line* is evaluated to true or false resp.

The location information provides start coordinates *line1*.*column1* and end coordinates *line2*.*column2* of the code fragment in the file *filename* for which the *alarm message* is issued. The *class* is one of the alarm types, i.e., A or C. An example of an alarm message is shown here:

```
[ call#analysis_wrapper@4 at astree.cfg:4.5-21
  loop@17=1/3 at astree.cfg:17.2-25.3
  call#fuelratecontroller@23 at astree.cfg:23.4-22
  call#IntakeAirflowEstimation@9921 at frc.c:9921.3-26
  call#Tab2DS17I2T4169_a@10221 at frc.c:10221.4-21
  loop@9554>=2 at frc.c:9554.3-9558.24
  ALARM (C): implicit signed int->unsigned char conversion range
  [-1, 254] not included in [0, 255] at frc.c:9555.6-16 ]
```

The alarm is reported for a potential overflow which occurs in the second or later iteration of the loop from line 9554 to line 9558 in file frc.c. The lines above describe the precise call stack traversed to reach the loop in the potential error scenario.

Astrée uses various abstract domains to compute program invariants providing detailed information about the values of variables and the relations between them in every possible execution context [6]. All computed invariants can be inspected by the users; depending on the option setting they can be observed either at each statement or in the beginning of each function, and they can be context-insensitive or context-sensitive. In the latter case the computed abstract values are shown separately for each execution context.

Note that Astrée computes an abstract semantics and provides local abstract invariants attached to program points. Thus, in case of a potential runtime error users can access the alarm message along with its context and the invariants. But it does not provide a concrete execution trace for the alarm, since each abstract trace represents a set of concrete execution traces.

## 3 Model-Based Testing

In this section we give an overview of model-based testing with the example of BTC Embedded *Tester*® (ET). ET provides an automated test and verification environment for Simulink/TargetLink and also for handwritten C code. It is capable of performing various tasks such as automatic test case generation and execution, back-to-back testing, automatic test analysis, automatic test and coverage reporting, debugging, and import/export of test cases.

### 3.1 Test Case Generation

ET can generate input stimuli vectors and test vectors. Input stimuli vectors represent a set of input values per execution step for a number of execution steps. They can be either imported or generated using vector generation engines. ET uses two engines: the Automatic Test vector Generation engine (ATG) and the Code Verification analysis engine (CV). ATG is a random engine based on well-tuned heuristics which is fast, but not complete. If a test goal cannot be reached, it is unclear whether the goal is unreachable or the engine just could not reach it. In contrast, the CV engine is complete. It tries to generate vectors by claiming that a certain test goal is unreachable [5]. A counterexample, if there is one, is provided as a vector, otherwise the goal is proven unreachable because it uses an exhaustive technique based on symbolic model checking that checks the full search space. The input stimuli vectors can then be used to generate test vectors. Test vectors represent a set of input and output values per step. The output values in a test vector are the expected values. So, when test vectors are generated using simulation with input stimuli vectors, the output values in them need to be reviewed. ET also supports back-to-back testing in which case the output values are not required to be reviewed. Test vectors with expected values can also be imported in ET. ET supports various kinds of simulations like MIL (model-in-the-loop), SIL (software-in-the-loop) and PIL (processor-in-the-loop).

## 3.2 Observer

ET provides the possibility to define evaluation functions (C code) which can be used to decide if the behaviour of the system under test is correct or invalid. These evaluation functions are called *observers*. Observers are integrated automatically into the test execution/simulation environment of a system under test by ET. ET generates tests that cover observers and performs automatic test execution of the system under test in co-execution/simulation with observers. Observers are used in ET, e.g., for requirement verification, standard analysis, or additional test (e.g., equivalence class test cases) generation.

A C-observer (more precisely a *commitment observer*) is a small C function that evaluates some property of the system under test. It returns a boolean value indicating whether the observed property is valid or invalid. C-observer code can check conditions on interface objects of the system under test, i.e., inputs, outputs, calibration variables and display variables. An example of an observer is shown here:

```
/* Observer Evaluation Function */
unsigned char eval_OBS_2_RV_fuel_rate() {
  unsigned char evalResult = 1;
  if (!(fuel_rate >= 0 && fuel_rate <= 32358))
    evalResult = 0;
  return evalResult;
}
```

## 3.3 Property Location Language – PLL

ET uses the Property Location Language (PLL) for uniquely identifying code properties (i.e., test cases). For example, to generate input stimuli vectors for a code property the corresponding PLL expression of the code property has to be provided.

In general, a PLL expression has three parts, identifying code properties relevant for testing: 1) one or several property classes like Statement (STM), Relation Operator (RO), Decision (D), Division by 0 (DZ) etc. ; 2) a unique ID of a specific entity of this property class in the code; 3) a specific property value of this entity. One example is **D:3:1**, where "D" denotes the decisions in the code, "3" is the unique ID of a decision in the code (IDs are automatically generated by ET) and "1" represents the case that the decision evaluates to true. In case of observers, the PLL expression has two additional parts in the beginning i.e., in total five parts: it starts with "O:[OBSID]:...", where [OBSID] is a unique identifier of an observer. e.g., **O:OBS_1:D:3:1**.

### 3.4   Integration of C-Observer in ET

**Step1.** An observer is defined by a user or it is generated automatically from some source, e.g., requirement specification.

**Step2.** Stimuli vectors are generated for the observer. Using the right PLL formulation to indicate the desired observer test properties is important.

**Step3.** The generated stimuli vectors are used to generate the corresponding test vectors.

**Step4.** The ET debugging feature can be used to perform step-by-step debugging and analysis of the behaviour of the generated vector. Alternatively, in some use cases like requirement verification, the test vectors are automatically executed. During test execution, the observer is run in parallel with the system under test and the return value of the observer is used to check whether the system execution is valid. The execution is valid when the return value is 1 and invalid when it is 0.

## 4   Combining the Two Worlds

Our goal is to combine the static analyzer Astrée with BTC Embedded*Tester*® in order to validate whether an alarm is a true error or a false alarm. The key idea is to automatically transform an alarm reported by Astrée (described in Sec. 2.1) into a C-observer that can be integrated in ET (described in Sec. 3.2). This transformation includes inserting some code fragments into the source code under test and generating the observer code that exploits the information provided by the inserted code. The code modifications are free of side effects and do not interfere with normal program execution. The integration includes creating an ET profile for the modified version of system under test and importing the observer into the profile. ET supports generating test vectors from the observers. This approach can be applied to any category of errors detected by Astrée. In the following we demonstrate our approach with four exemplary alarm categories.

As already stated in Sec. 2.1, alarm messages contain the precise location of the code fragment that is responsible for the alarm. The code insertion phase uses the alarm message and its location information to store the error condition into variables at the appropriate location. These variables include one flag variable which indicates if the alarm condition is reachable. Note that the flag variable needs to be global so that it becomes a part of an interface of the system under test: only then it becomes observable by ET. The code insertion is explained in detail for each of the four selected alarm categories in the following subsections. The observer code just consists of checking the flag value. If the flag value is true, an error condition has been reached. The observers are designed to return 0 when the flag value is true. Our generic observer code is shown in Fig.1.

```
unsigned char eval_OBS_1() {
  unsigned char evalResult = 1;
  if (__ET_flag_1 != 0)
    evalResult = 0;
  return evalResult;
}
```

**Fig. 1.** Generic Observer Code

## 4.1 Division by Zero

The alarm message for divisions by zero is `<type> division by zero [interval]`, where "type" can be either integer or float. A simple example of an integer division by zero alarm is shown below.

```
[ call#analysis_wrapper@3 at astree.cfg:3.5-21
  loop@16=1/3 at astree.cfg:16.2-24.3
  call#fuelratecontroller@22 at astree.cfg:22.4-22
  call#IntakeAirflowEstimation@9931 at fuelratecontroller.c:9931.3-26
  call#Tab2DS1712T4169_a@10231 at fuelratecontroller.c:10231.4-21
  ALARM (A): integer division by zero [0, 65535] at fuelratecontroller.c:9596.27-9597.66 ]
```

The location details `fuelratecontroller.c:9596.27-9597.66` in the alarm message provide the code fragment for which the alarm is issued: it extends from column 27 in line 9596 to column 66 in line 9597. The corresponding code fragment, a division expression, is highlighted after clicking on the alarm message in the GUI:

```
9594        /* 1. Y-Interpolation. */
9595        __ET_flag_1 = (Aux_U16_b == 0);
9596        Aux_U16_c = (UInt16) ((((UInt32) (((UInt32) Aux_U16_a) * ((UInt32) z_table[0]))) + ((UInt32)
9597          (((UInt32) Aux_U16) * ((UInt32) z_table[1])))) / Aux_U16_b);
9598        z_table += Aux_U8;
```

We parse the division expression to retrieve its denominator and then generate code which stores the condition under which the denominator becomes zero into a flag variable. We assume that execution of the denominator expression has no side effects. The generated assignment is put at the program point just before the division expression (cf. line 9595 in the above image). The flag variable `__ET_flag_1` is then used in an observer as shown in Fig.1.

## 4.2 Overflow in Arithmetic

The alarm message for arithmetic overflows of numerical types reads `<type> arithmetic range [interval] not included in [interval]`.

The two intervals in the message show the actual value range computed for the expression and the acceptable value range, respectively. Here is an example of an alarm message on an overflow of an `unsigned int`.

```
[ call#analysis_wrapper@3 at astree.cfg:3.5-21
  loop@5~1/3 at astree.cfg:5.2-13.3
  call#fuelratecontroller@11 at astree.cfg:11.4-22
  call#IntakeAirflowEstimation@1888 at fuelratecontroller.c:1888.3-26
  call#Tab2DS1712T4169_a@2165 at fuelratecontroller.c:2165.4-21
  ALARM (C): unsigned long arithmetic range [0, 6516407190] not included in [0, 4294967295] at fuelratecontroller.c1600.28-1601.53 ]
```

The message gives the location `fuelratecontroller.c:1600.28-1601.53` of the code fragment i.e., the arithmetic expression for which the alarm is issued. The fragment is highlighted at lines 1600 and 1601 in the image below.

```
1595    __ET_var_1 = ((UInt32) (((UInt32) Aux_U16_a) * ((UInt32) z_table[0])));
1596    __ET_var_2 = ((UInt32) (((UInt32) Aux_U16) * ((UInt32) z_table[1])));
1597
1598    __ET_flag_1 = (4294967295 - __ET_var_2 < __ET_var_1);
1599
1600    Aux_U16_c = (UInt16) (((((UInt32) (((UInt32) Aux_U16_a) * ((UInt32) z_table[0]))) + ((UInt32)
1601    (((UInt32) Aux_U16) * ((UInt32) z_table[1])))) / Aux_U16_b);
```

The arithmetic expression is parsed in order to retrieve its operator and the corresponding operands. In this example, it is '+' operator. Now we have to check if the operands can evaluate to such values that when are added to each other they cause an overflow. The corresponding code is shown in lines 1595-1598 in the above image. Note that the operands, which may be complex expressions, are stored into variables of type "type" and it is ensured that the inserted code does not raise the overflow alarm itself. The code generated for this category of alarm can vary based on the arithmetic operator (i.e., whether it is + or - etc. ), whether it is signed or unsigned arithmetic and whether the overflow is w.r.t. minimum and/or maximum bound.

### 4.3  Overflow in Conversion

The third category of alarms is associated with overflows in conversions, i.e., type casts. The alarm message reads `<type1>-><type2>` conversion range `[interval]` not included in `[interval]`. An expression responsible for this alarm evaluates to a value of type "type1". An overflow may occur when a type of an expression value is converted implicitly or explicitly to type "type2". This alarm message shows the range of potential values of the expression before and after conversion in the first and second interval, respectively. We determine the region of the first interval that does not overlap with the second interval. The required instrumentation then consists of storing the expression value into a variable of type "type1" and checking whether a value of this variable is in the non-overlapping region of the first interval. The check is put at a location just before the expression that is responsible for an alarm.

### 4.4  Invalid Dereference

The fourth category of alarms considered is associated with invalid pointer dereferences: `Invalid dereference: dereferencing <value> byte(s)` at offset(s) <value> may overflow the variable <name> of byte-size <value>. This alarm is raised when dereferencing a pointer expression that points to an invalid location, e.g., because it has not been properly initialized. The message indicates the offset, expressed in bytes, and the byte size of the dereferenced variable "name". An example of alarm message is shown below:

```
[ call#analysis_wrapper@4 at astree.cfg:4.5-21
loop@17=2/3 at astree.cfg:17.2-27.3
call#f0@24 at astree.cfg:24.4-6
call#f1@1884 at controller.c:1884.3-5
call#f2@2187 at controller.c:2187.16-18
ALARM (A): invalid dereference: dereferencing 2 byte(s) at offset(s) 34+2*[0;305] may overflow the variable global_array of byte-size 612 at controller.c:1480.13-21 ]
```

and the corresponding code fragment array[n] is highlighted at line 1480 in the image below:

```
1471    int __ET_var_1 = 0;
1472    if (array == (const UInt16 *)global_array)
1473        __ET_var_1 = 1;
1474
1475    array += ((UInt16) (((UInt16) (((UInt16) v1) * ((UInt16) n))) + ((UInt16) v2)));
1476    val1 = array[0];
1477    if (v3 == 0) {
1478        if (__ET_var_1 == 1)
1479            __ET_flag_1 = (((array + n) - (const UInt16 *)global_array) >= 306);
1480        val2 = array[n];
1481    }
```

In the specific case of the pointer dereference in the example message above, array+n accesses offsets from 34 to 34 + 610 bytes, which exceeds the valid offset range of [0, 612 − 2] bytes. To capture the error condition here we have to check whether dereferencing array+n would leave the feasible range as shown at lines 1471-1473 and 1478-1479 in the image above. The comparison (array == (const UInt16*) global_array) is used to identify the correct alarm context. In general the function f2 containing the code with the alarm is invoked from different call sites with different parameters. The specific alarm under analysis is for one specific context where f2 is called with global_array as a parameter. Generating the instrumentation code for pointer dereferences currently is ongoing work. We plan to use program slicing to explicitly construct the possibly invalid pointer value and check it for feasibility. Astrée already provides a program slicer which can be reused for this purpose.

## 5   Experiments and Practical Experience

We performed experiments to investigate the applicability of our approach with a couple of control applications: namely, a fuel rate controller from the automotive domain and a simple flight control system from the avionics domain. The fuel rate controller is a fixed-point implementation generated by dSPACE TargetLink [9] from a MATLAB/Simulink model and consists of 2837 lines of code. Also the avionics example is a model-based design; here Esterel SCADE [10] has been used as a code generator. The implementation consists of 2205 lines of floating-point C code.

Executing an Astrée analysis on each of the two applications provides us with a list of alarms. The obtained alarms did not include division by zero alarms. Thus, for our purpose we modified the fuel rate controller code to induce an integer division by zero alarm and the flight controller code to induce a float division by zero alarm.

In our implementation we have extended Astrée to automatically generate observers and insert the associated instrumentation code snippets into the source code for each alarm selected by the user. The implementation is ongoing work: so far we have successfully accomplished the automatic handling of division by zero alarms; the support of overflow alarms currently is restricted to a limited set of C-operators. For the examples where the implementation is not available yet, we have manually written the observers and the instrumentation code snippets in the same form as the implementation shall provide.

The generated observers have been verified with ET. This includes generating the ET profiles from the instrumented source code, importing the observers into those profiles, and generating the stimuli vectors that cover the observer properties. As explained in Sec. 3.3, a PLL string is used to represent the observer property. In our case, we are interested in generating a stimuli vector for the trace that demonstrates the actual alarm condition. This is the case when the flag variable is true, i.e., when the corresponding observer returns 0. So, the PLL string that is used during verification is "O:[OBSID]:V:0", where "V:0" stands for the return value zero. It is possible that no vector is generated during stimuli vector generation. This indicates that the specified code properties are not reachable during any execution. In our case, it means that the alarm under investigation is a false alarm. Table 1 shows the result of stimuli vector generation for our observers performed at the highest level of the subsystem hierarchy of the software under analysis.

In order to ascertain the correctness of the obtained results, we debug the generated stimuli vectors when the status is *covered*, whereas we do a manual inspection of the code when the status is *unreachable*. ET provides a feature to produce a debugging

**Table 1.** Stimuli Vector Generation Results: *covered* - stimuli vector is generated (true error); *unreachable(inf)* - stimuli vector is not generated (false alarm)

| Alarm Category | Controller | Alarm Message | Status |
|---|---|---|---|
| Integer division by zero | fuel rate | ALARM (A): integer division by zero [0, 65535] at fuelratecontroller.c:9596.27-9597.66 | unreachable(inf) |
| Float division by zero | flight | ALARM (A): float division by zero [0., 10000.] at ComputePitchRoll_FlightControl.c:512.28-54 | covered |
| Arithmetic overflow | fuel rate | ALARM (C): unsigned long arithmetic range [0, 6516407190] not included in [0, 4294967295] at fuelratecontroller.c:1600.28-1601.53 | unreachable(inf) |
| Conversion overflow | fuel rate | ALARM (C): implicit signed int->unsigned char conversion range [-1, 254] not included in [0, 255] at fuelratecontroller.c:9568.6-16 | unreachable(inf) |
| Invalid dereference | fuel rate | ALARM (A): invalid dereference: dereferencing 2 byte(s) at offset(s) 34+2*[0;305] may overflow the variable PressEst_z_table of byte-size 612 at fuelratecontroller.c:9449.18-28 | covered |

environment directly from the vector. Through debugging it is possible to analyze the execution trace covered by the vector. In our case, we check if the trace reaches the alarm condition.

The results show that all alarm categories investigated can be successfully handled for both input applications.

## 6 Future Work and Conclusion

In this article, we have presented an approach to automatically classify the alarms produced by a static analyzer as true errors or false alarms by applying model-based testing techniques to stimulate appropriate error conditions. We have described the principles of this interaction between static analysis and model-based testing and have developed an implementation based on a tool coupling between the static runtime error analyzer Astrée and the model-based testing tool BTC Embedded *Tester*®. Our approach significantly reduces the effort for alarm analysis, i.e., investigating alarms to find out whether they are true errors which have to be fixed, or whether they are false alarms. As the tool coupling can run fully automatically it also opens the alarm investigation process to users with less experience than manual investigation requires. Preliminary experiments demonstrate the viability of our approach with fixed-point and floating-point applications from the automotive and aerospace domains. To the best of our knowledge this is the first successful combination of static analysis and model-based testing to exploit synergies between these techniques in the V&V process of safety-critical software.

Our future work, in a first step, aims at completing the implementation to handle all four exemplary alarm categories automatically. In a further step, the mechanism has to be extended to cover the full set of Astrée alarms. Also further experiments on industry-relevant applications will be conducted to check how the proposed method scales with large-scale software projects.

**Acknowledgement.** The work presented in this paper has been supported by the ITEA2 project TIMMO-2-USE and the EU ARTEMIS Joint Undertaking under grant agreement no. 269335 with the German BMBF (MBAT project).

## References

1. AbsInt GmbH. aiT Worst-Case Execution Time Analyzer Website, http://www.AbsInt.com/ait
2. AbsInt GmbH. StackAnalyzer Website, http://www.AbsInt.com/sa.
3. AbsInt GmbH. Astrée Website, http://www.AbsInt.com/astree.
4. Bertrane, J., Cousot, P., Cousot, R., Feret, J., Mauborgne, L., Miné, A., Rival, X.: Static analysis and verification of aerospace software by abstract interpretation. In: AIAA Infotech@Aerospace 2010, number AIAA-2010-3385, pp. 1–38. American Institue of Aeronautics and Astronautics (April 2010)
5. Biere, A., Cimatti, A., Clarke, E., Zhu, Y.: Symbolic model checking without BDDs. In: Cleaveland, W.R. (ed.) TACAS 1999. LNCS, vol. 1579, pp. 193–207. Springer, Heidelberg (1999)

6. Blanchet, B., Cousot, P., Cousot, R., Feret, J., Mauborgne, L., Miné, A., Monniaux, D., Rival, X.: A Static Analyzer for Large Safety-Critical Software. In: Proceedings of the ACM SIGPLAN 2003 Conference on Programming Language Design and Implementation (PLDI 2003), San Diego, California, USA, June 7-14, pp. 196–207. ACM Press (2003)
7. BTC Embedded Systems AG. BTC BTC Embedded*Tester*® Website, http://www.btc-es.de/index.php?idcatside=2.
8. Cousot, P., Cousot, R.: Abstract interpretation: a unified lattice model for static analysis of programs by construction or approximation of fixpoints. In: POPL 1977: Proceedings of the 4th ACM SIGACT-SIGPLAN Symposium on Principles of Programming Languages, pp. 238–252. ACM Press, New York (1977)
9. dSPACE GmbH. TargetLink Website, http://www.dSPACE.com/go/TargetLink
10. Esterel Technologies. SCADE Suite, http://www.esterel-technologies.com/products/scade-suite
11. Ferdinand, C., Heckmann, R.: Static Memory and Execution Time Analysis of Embedded Code. SAE 2006 Transactions Journal of Passenger Cars - Electronic and Electrical Systems 9 (2007)
12. ISO/IEC 9899:1999 (E). Programming languages – C (1999)
13. Kästner, D., Brockmeyer, U., Pister, M., Nenova, S., Bienmüller, T., Dereani, A., Ferdinand, C.: Combining Model-based Analysis and Testing. In: Embedded Real Time Software and Systems Congress ERTS$^2$ (2014)
14. Kästner, D., Ferdinand, C.: Proving the Absence of Stack Overflows. In: SAFECOMP 2014: Proceedings of the 33th International Conference on Computer Safety, Reliability and Security (to appear, 2014)
15. Kästner, D., Wilhelm, S., Nenova, S., Cousot, P., Cousot, R., Feret, J., Mauborgne, L., Miné, A., Rival, X.: Astrée: Proving the Absence of Runtime Errors. In: Embedded Real Time Software and Systems Congress ERTS$^2$ (2010)
16. Souyris, J., Pavec, E.L., Himbert, G., Jégu, V., Borios, G., Heckmann, R.: Computing the Worst Case Execution Time of an Avionics Program by Abstract Interpretation. In: Proceedings of the 5th International Workshop on Worst-case Execution Time (WCET 2005), Mallorca, Spain, pp. 21–24 (2005)

# Proving Compliance of Implementation Models to Safety Specifications*

Markus Oertel, Omar Kacimi, and Eckard Böde

OFFIS e.V., Eschwerweg 1, 26121 Oldenburg, Germany
{oertel,kacimi,boede}@offis.de

**Abstract.** Current safety standards like the ISO 26262 require a continuous safety argumentation starting from the initial hazard and risk assessment, down to the implementation of hardware and software. To enable re-use of components and ease handling of changes in the system, modular safety cases are addressed by many research projects. Current approaches are focusing on hierarchical safety specifications describing the relevant fault propagation behavior. Nevertheless, it needs to be ensured that the final implementation meets the safety specification. Currently, this is at most a manual and error prone process of matching fault trees or test results to the specification. In this paper, we present an automated approach based on fault-injection and model checking for proving the compliance of an implementation to a safety specification. In our multi-aspect analysis, (safety and functional aspect) we rely on the popular specification mechanism of safety contracts and implementations modeled in Matlab/Stateflow.

**Keywords:** Verification and Validation, Safety Critical Systems, Model-based Design, Fault-Injection, Fault Modeling, Model Checking, Formal Methods.

## 1  Introduction and Related Work

Safety standards like the ISO 26262[8] or the DO178c[17] require a safety case to argue the absence of unreasonable risk for humans caused by the item to be developed. The safety concepts that describe the architectural decisions regarding the detection and the mitigation of faults are important elements of the safety case. Starting from a functional safety concept at very early stages of the system development, this fault propagation specification is further refined at lower abstraction levels, e.g. the hardware and software implementation level. If this safety specification and the functional requirements are refined to an acceptable level, the specification can be implemented in terms of hardware and

---

* The research leading to these results has received funding from the ARTEMIS Joint Undertaking under grant agreement n°269335 (MBAT), and the German Federal Ministry of Education and Research (BMBF) under the funding ID 01IS11019 (SAFE, an ITEA2 Project) and ID 01IS12005M (SPES_XT Project).

A. Bondavalli et al. (Eds.): SAFECOMP 2014 Workshops, LNCS 8696, pp. 97–107, 2014.

software. Nevertheless, to complete the safety case, an argumentation about the compliance of the implementation to the requirements needs to be provided.

This is typically done by reviews or testing[6]. Although advances have been made in the field of automatic testcase generation, testing techniques suffer from their incompleteness, since only a selection of all possible test-vectors are applied to the system. To test safety properties, fault injection[20] can be used. Another possibility consists on comparing existing Fault tree analyzes(FTA) or Failure modes and effects analyzes (FMEA) with the safety specification. Again, this is a manual error prone process.

In this paper we present a formal approach allowing to automate the process of analyzing the compliance of the fault detection and mitigation capabilities of an implementation with the safety specification. To achieve this, the safety requirements need to be stated in a formal way. There are multiple formalization approaches for safety concepts, starting from the very theoretical "function-structure-models" [5] or the notion of processes and channels [12], which are both not suitable for production use, since they require a special structural model. The HipHops approach [15,14] can be applied to development models like Simulink, but lacks some important features such as timing support. In this paper we are focusing on the concept of safety contracts [13].

Contracts separate a requirement into *assumptions* and a *promise* [2]. The assumptions specify the required behavior of the environment, while the promise states the expected functionality provided by the component. This separation allows to reason about the correct decomposition of requirements [4,7], which is essential for a modular safety case. The assertions themselves are described in a formal, pattern-based language, which can be translated to many target languages such as LTL or timed-automata [1] in order to enable automated verification .

In addition to a formal specification, we need a technique to analyze the fault tolerance behavior of a component in a formal way. Approaches such as [19] verify formalized fault trees against formal implementation models. Furthemore, several fault injection analyzes that rely on model checking like [3] and [9] have been presented. In this paper we focus on a fault injection based-technique [16], [10] that is called model-based safety analysis *MBSA*. The *MBSA* processes functional requirements and provides complete results as cut-sets and allows to define custom faulty behavior in the implementation model, which is specified using Matlab/Stateflow. Cut-sets are unique combinations of malfunctions occurrences that can cause a system failure. A cut-set is said to be minimal if no event can be removed from the set and the combination of malfunctions still leads to a failure[11].

We introduce safety contracts and the MBSA in section 2. In section 3, we explain how the MBSA is used to prove the correct implementation of a safety contract. We apply this procedure to an example in section 4 and finally conclude the work in section 5 with an outlook on improvements and future research directions.

## 2    Background

We briefly introduce the pattern language for safety together with the predefined contract templates as well as the model-based safety analysis.

### 2.1    Safety Contracts

Safety contracts[13] are a technique for specifying fault propagation. The *assumption* and the *promise* of a contract are expressed using safety pattern which are textual building bricks, with user filled attributes. The most commonly used pattern describes, that a combination of faults and failures does not occur in a run of the system. These expression sets may contain one or more faults and failures.

**none of** {expr-set1, expr-set2,...} **occurs**

the LTL semantics of this pattern are defined as:

$$(\mathbf{G}!e_1 \vee \mathbf{G}!e_2) \wedge (\mathbf{G}!e_3 \vee \mathbf{G}!e_4),$$

with $expr\_set1 = \{e_1, e_2\}$ and $expr\_set2 = \{e_3, e_4\}$. I.e., that in every expr-set one fault occurs at most. The fault are generally assumed to be independent, but dependence between them can be separately specified. There exists a abbreviated pattern which just considers a single expression-set, with identical semantics as described above:

{expr-set} **does not occur**

In a top-down approach the faults are typically expected defects in functions selected by experts. If they are refined to a particular level it needs to be shown that the selected hardware and software component match the expectations. In a bottom-up approach, the potential malfunctions of a component can be found in the safety manual or identified by techniques like FMEA.

Patterns are formally defined on traces, i.e. system runs with an evolution over its variables [7]. Hence, a requirement pattern restricts the possible runs of a system. Pattern 1 and its derived Pattern 2 state that only system runs in which the combination of malfunctions (stated in the expression sets) is absent are accepted.

Oertel et.al [13] presented several contract templates that can be used to describe typical safety concepts. In this work we focus on the most commonly used templates that we want to connect to implementation models. The basic template is depicted in contract $C_1$ that describes the propagation of input and internal faults ($mf$ in the assumption) to a failure at the level of one of the component's outputs.

$C_1$ 
A: none of {{mf_$1_1$ ...,mf_$1_n$}, ..., {mf_$n_1$ ...,mf_$n_m$}} occurs.
P: {output_mf} does not occur.

Safety contracts are able to express the degradation of a system as required by the ISO 26262, i.e. switching to a safe-state. This safe-state is expressed in functional terms (e.g. functional variables need to be in a defined range), and is therefore just considered as an identifier in safety contracts. Contract template $C_2$ is using this mechanisms to state, that a system is either operating normally or that it is in a safe-state, if the combination of malfunctions in the assumption is not present.

$C_2$
A: none of $\{\{\text{mf\_l}_1 \ldots, \text{mf\_l}_n\}, \ldots, \{\text{mf\_}n_1 \ldots, \text{mf\_}n_m\}\}$ occurs.
P: {output_fail and !safestate} does not occur.

This contract implies that there is never a situation in which a wrong output is present in the absence of the safe-state. This timing behaviour might be correct for safety concepts using multi-channel architectures and voting, but it is not correct in case malfunctions are detected by periodic tests. Therefore the **perm** operator has been introduced, leading to an additional contract template $C_3$

$C_3$
A: none of $\{\{\text{mf\_l}_1 \ldots, \text{mf\_l}_n\}, \ldots, \{\text{mf\_}n_1 \ldots, \text{mf\_}n_m\}\}$ occurs.
P: {perm(output_fail and !safestate)} does not occur.

In terms of LTL, **perm** is just a "globally" operator. This contract template guarantees, that the system is not permanently failing, without eventually switching to a safe-state. i.e., finally the safe-state will be established.

## 2.2  The Model-Based Safety Analysis

The MBSA [16] performs fault injection in a model of the system's nominal behavior. The correctness of this model can be checked with typical model checking techniques against the functional requirements. The MBSA can be used to automatically assess which combinations of malfunctions lead to the violation of a selected functional requirement. The resulting cut-sets (of malfunctions) can be represented as a fault-tree. The analysis currently supports nominal behavioral models formalized in Matlab/Stateflow[1] while requirements are provided in a formal language called RSL [1] to enable automatic processing.

The faults to be injected can have different types specified in a library. This library defines the deviation of a variable in the implementation model from its intended value. Commonly used deviations are:

**Stuck-at:** this pattern describes the case an internal variable of the system model is stuck at an erroneous value.
**Random:** this pattern is used to describe cases in which random changes to the value of an internal variable occur.
**User defined:** This pattern is used in case the desired fault behavior can't be modeled using the fault library. The pattern allows then the custom modeling of this fault behavior in the same language of the implementation model. Accordingly, the fault is not injected later in the process in the nominal model but it

---

[1] http://www.mathworks.de/products/simulink/

is rather embedded in the nominal model. Additional input variables are then added to the model to control the activation of the injected fault.

The current implementation supports two analysis engines as a backend. The first one is based on the VIS model checker [2]. The VIS based backend guarantees complete results since the full state space is checked. The monte-carlo simulation based engine can be used to cope with models that are more challenging in terms of the state space size. In this case however, the completeness is not guaranteed anymore. In the present work, we use the VIS based engine.

At runtime, the nominal model is injected with the faults. Additionally, an observer automaton for the analyzed requirement is generated and injected in the model. The resulting overall model is finally translated to the VIS format and passed to the model checker. The analysis identifies all state sequences leading from the set of initial system states over the activation of faults to the observation of the violation of the functional requirement. These paths are the basis for computing the set of minimal cut-sets leading to the failure.

For convenience, we will refer from now on to the MBSA as a function with three arguments: an Implementation $I$ and a set of faults $F$ and the functional requirement $r$ that the system shall implement. Each fault $f \in F$ is a tuple $(id, fm)$ consisting of a name of the fault $(id)$ and a formal description of the deviation the fault causes. The result is a set $C$ of fault combinations leading to the violation of $r$.

$$\text{MBSA}(r, I, F) = C \subseteq \mathcal{P}(F),$$

with $\mathcal{P}$ denoting the powerset.

## 3    Verifying Safety Contracts Using the MBSA

The safety contracts specify the propagation of faults in the system, addressing the correctness of a signal. In contrast, functional specifications are concerned about the occurrence and order of signals. While the incorrectness of an output signal with respect to internal faults of a component can be expressed in functional terms (e.g. that a calculation does not deliver the expected result) the combination of input faults and internal faults cannot be put in the functional context of a component, since the propagating correctness refers to signals and calculations outside of the scope of a single component.

Nevertheless, the safety mechanisms themselves are described in a functional way. E.g., "a watchdog is periodically sending a signal to a component. After a timeout a default value is used to override the components output". Still, this description is not talking about malfunctions in any way.

The MBSA is a multi-aspect analysis, since it analyzes a functional implementation model and injects faults, described in the safety aspect. Figure 1 describes the principal relation between a safety contract, the malfunctions of a system and the result of the MBSA on the example of a simple fault propagation contract $C_1$.

---

[2] http://vlsi.colorado.edu/~vis/

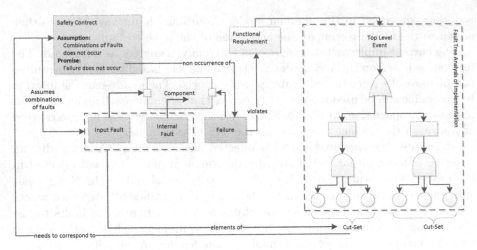

**Fig. 1.** Relation of a Safety Contract to an FTA results

$$C_1 \quad \begin{aligned} &\text{A: } \left| \texttt{none of } \{\{\texttt{mf\_}1_1 \ldots, \texttt{mf\_}1_n\}, \ldots, \{\texttt{mf\_}n_1 \ldots, \texttt{mf\_}n_m\}\} \right. \\ &\phantom{\text{A: }}\left| \texttt{occurs.} \right. \\ &\text{P: } \left| \{\texttt{output\_mf}\} \texttt{ does not occur.} \right. \end{aligned}$$

The assumption of a safety contract specifies the combination of malfunctions that potentially leads to a wrong output which is described in the promise. If the output of a component $C$ is wrong, this means that the requirement $r$ describing the expected value is violated. $r$ is passed to the MBSA, together with all malfunctions $f \in F$ that might occur in a component. The resulting cut-sets of the MBSA need to comply with the assumptions of the safety contract $C_{ass}$:

$$MBSA(r, I, F) \subseteq C_{ass}$$

The MBSA is not capable of injecting input faults, i.e. a wrong signal that is propagating to this component. Restricting the input variables would potentially only reduce the cut-sets, not enlarge them. I.e., the model checker evaluates less paths in the state-space of the system. In order to provide a possibility to identify an input signal as faulty, the intended value must be known. Therefore, we extend the model with an additional component that simulates the input malfunction by an internal malfunction.

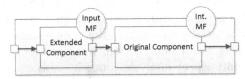

**Fig. 2.** Extending the system model to represent input malfunctions

Safety contracts describing safety mechanisms (see Contract $C_2$) can include a reference to the *safe-state* of the system.

$$C_2 \quad \begin{array}{l} \text{A:} \\ \\ \text{P:} \end{array} \begin{array}{|l} \texttt{none of } \{\{\texttt{mf\_l}_1 \ldots, \texttt{ mf\_l}_n\}, \ldots, \{\texttt{mf\_n}_1 \ldots, \texttt{mf\_n}_m\}\} \\ \texttt{occurs.} \\ \{\texttt{output\_fail and !safestate}\} \texttt{ does not occur.} \end{array}$$

The `safestate` is a placeholder in the safety specification, since the safe-state *is* a functional state of the system. E.g. the safe-state for an engine cooling system is the maximum fan speed to avoid that the engine overheats. To be able to check the safety contract with the MBSA, we need to provide a functional requirement, that uses this functional representation of the safe-state (safestate_fun). For contract $C_2$ the requirement $r$ that is passed to the MBSA is:

$$r = G(fr(output\_fail) \vee safestate\_fun),$$

where $fr(output\_fail)$ is the functional requirement that the failure is violating. The cut-sets returned by the MBSA for the specified requirement specify cases in which neither the correct value is calculated, nor the safe-state is set.

An additional feature of safety contracts is the possibility to represent time in the safety concept. Contract $C_3$ uses the `perm` operator to indicate that *finally* the wrong output will be detected and a safe-state will be established.

$$C_3 \quad \begin{array}{l} \text{A:} \\ \\ \text{P:} \end{array} \begin{array}{|l} \texttt{none of } \{\{\texttt{mf\_l}_1 \ldots, \texttt{ mf\_l}_n\}, \ldots, \{\texttt{mf\_n}_1 \ldots, \texttt{mf\_n}_m\}\} \\ \texttt{occurs.} \\ \{\texttt{perm(output\_fail and !safestate)}\} \texttt{ does not occur.} \end{array}$$

It may be sufficient for an abstract safety concept to specify that the wrong result is not permanently in the system, however, for a concrete implementation it is necessary to specify a time bound. This time bound, the *Fault Tolerant Time Interval* specifies the maximum time between the occurrence of the fault and the attainability of the safe-state. Hence, the requirement statement to be checked by the MBSA is, informally:

**whenever failure occurs then (safestate or !failure) occurs within the FTTI**

The semantics of this requirement are depicted in the observer automaton in figure 3.

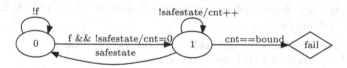

**Fig. 3.** Automaton for Perm with a given Bound

## 4   Example

We demonstrate the check of safety contracts using the MBSA on a highly simplified light manager system of a road vehicle. The purpose of this system is to decide on an analog environment light signal (`aLightIn1`) if the front light of the vehicle shall be switched on. The system has one potential hazard: switching

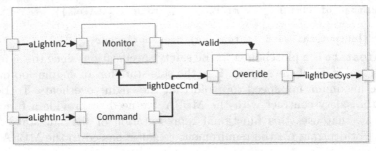

**Fig. 4.** Architecture of the Light Manager System

off the lights while driving in the dark. This hazard has been discovered and classified by the regular *Hazard and Risk Analysis* (HARA) of the ISO 26262. To prevent the hazard a redundant architecture is used (see Figure 4). The command component computes the switching decision (lightDecCmd) and communicates it to a Monitor and a Override component. The Monitor independently computes a switching decision based on a redundant analog environment light signal. If the computed value deviates from the one coming from the Command unit, the valid signal is set to false. In this case, either one component is dysfunctional or one of the input signals is not correct. Accordingly, The Override establishes the safe-state. The safe-state for this system is lightDecSys==1 i.e. that it is recommended to turn on the light.

The safety contract for the complete system (see $C_4$) guarantee that the system will create a correct output or is in the safe-state, if there is only one malfunction in the system.

$C_4$ A: |{more_than_1_malfunction} does not occur.
P: |{lightDecSys_fail and !SafeState} does not occur.

more_than_1_malfunction is a textual macro that can be used to avoid typing all double cut-sets of the identified faults of the system (which are depicted in table 1.

This top level requirement is split up into three contracts belonging to the sub-components of the system. The Command component delivers a correct output if the input is correct and the command itself does not fail. This behaviour is represented by Contract $C_5$.

$C_5$ A: |none of {{aLightIn1_fail},{command_fail}} occurs.
P: |{lightDecCmd_fail} does not occur.

The valid signal of the Monitor is correct if the input is correct and the monitor itself does not fail (see contract $C_6$

$C_6$ A: |none of {{aLightIn2_fail},{monitor_fail}} occurs.
P: |{valid_fail} does not occur.

The Override component fails only in establishing the safe-state or delivering a correct output if both, the valid signal and the output of the Command are wrong.

$C_7$ A: |none of {{valid_fail, lightDecCmd_fail}} occurs.
P: |{lightDecSys_fail AND !SafeState} does not occur.

**Table 1.** Malfunctions and Functional Requirements of the Automatic Light Manager

| Malfunction | Violated Functional Requirement / Unintended Behaviour |
|---|---|
| aLightIn1_fault | in1 stuck at 0 |
| aLightIn2_fault | in 2 stuck at 0 |
| command_fault | cmd out random |
| lightDecCmd_fail | command shall determine if the light should be switched on according to the sensed environment light |
| monitor_fault | valid random |
| valid_fail | monitor shall calculate if the light shall be switched on and compare the results with the value calculated by the command unit. If they differ, set valid to false |
| lightDecSys_fail (override view) | if valid is true, pass through lightDecCmd_out, otherwise return 1 as light-DecSys. |
| lightDecSys_fail (top level view) | The component shall calculate if the front lights need to be switched on, according to the environment light situation. |

Table 1 lists all malfunctions in the system. For internal or input malfunctions the corresponding faulty behaviour is represented in a monospaced font.

We can now check e.g. the safety contract $C_5$ against the implementation of the Command component. The Stateflow model is depicted in figure 5. It consists out of two states and calculates the light recommendation based on the analog input value. If the input is greater than two the output will be set to true, otherwise to false. This easy one-step calculation as been chosen to keep the example simple, more complicated and timed executions are not restricted by the approach.

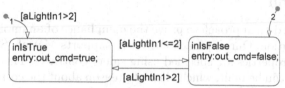

**Fig. 5.** Stateflow model of the command

Now, the requirement for the MBSA needs to be generated. The Command component has the formalized requirement $r_{cmd}$.

$$r_{cmd} = G(((\text{aLightIn1} > 2) \rightarrow (\text{lightDecCmd} == 1))$$
$$\&\&((\text{aLightIn1} \leq 2) \rightarrow (\text{lightDecCmd} == 0)))$$

Running the MBSA, we obtain the following results:

$$\text{MBSA}(r_{cmd}, I_{cmd}, \{(\text{aLightIn1\_fault}, \text{stuck-at}), (\text{command\_fault}, \text{random})\})$$
$$= \{\{\text{aLightIn1\_fault}\}, \{\text{command\_fault}\}\}$$

The resulting cut-sets are identical to the assumption of contract $C_5$, the implementation is compliant to the contract.

This component did not include any safety mechanisms. As an example for a more complex system, we perform the same steps again on contract $C_4$ for the complete light manager. The requirement $r_{top}$ of the top level component is nearly identical to the one of the command, in addition the safe-state (lightDec-Sys==1) is a valid output.

$$r_{top} = ((\texttt{aLightIn1} > 2) \rightarrow (\texttt{lightDecSys} == 1))$$
$$\&\&((\texttt{aLightIn1} <= 2) \rightarrow (\texttt{lightDecSys} == 0))$$
$$\|(\texttt{lightDecSys} == 1)$$

It is not surprising that the requirement is very similar, since the functionality of the command is the base functionality of the whole system, the additional components (monitor and override) have been only added to gain a certain level of fault tolerance. Therefore we do not need to consider in_2 in the description of the functionality, since its only purpose is redundancy. Running the MBSA, we get the following results:

$$MBSA(r_{top}, I_{System}, \{//\text{all faults from table } 1//\}) =$$
$$\{\{\texttt{aLightIn1\_fault}, \texttt{aLightIn2\_fault}\}, \{\texttt{aLightIn2\_fault}, \texttt{monitor\_fault}\},$$
$$\{\texttt{aLightIn1\_fault}, \texttt{command\_fault}\}, \{\texttt{aLightIn1\_fault}, \texttt{monitor\_fault}\},$$
$$\{\texttt{aLightIn2\_fault}, \texttt{command\_fault}\}\{\texttt{monitor\_fault}, \texttt{command\_fault}\}\}$$

Since no single cut-set has been identified, the top level contract has been respected.

## 5    Conclusion

We have presented an approach to prove the compliance of an implementation to a safety specification. Our approach currently supports Matlab/Stateflow models. The safety properties are specified using safety contracts. Therefore, a safety view of a system can be built, which allows to reason about the correct refinement of safety requirements (by using virtual integration techniques for contracts) and an correct fulfillment of these requirements by an implementation. This reduces verification effort, since integration tests can be replaced to a certain extent.

The use of model checking makes the approach prone to the state-space explosion problem. Nevertheless, we are able to check realistic functional safety concepts (braking system example from the ARP 4761 [18]) within minutes. A more detailed benchmarking still needs to be performed. Furthermore we are restricted to discrete time, which is a limitation introduced by the stateflow semantics and the LTL-based backend.

Although the majority of safety concept is can already be analyzed with our approach, we plan to cover the remaining language constructs in the pattern language of the safety contracts. On a larger time scale we plan to integrate also stochastical safety specifications in the approach, verifying if the implementation behaves es expected w.r.t quantified faults.

## References

1. Baumgart, A., Böde, E., Büker, M., Damm, W., Ehmen, G., Gezgin, T., Henkler, S., Hungar, H., Josko, B., Oertel, M., Peikenkamp, T., Reinkemeier, P., Stierand, I., Weber, R.: Architecture modeling. Tech. rep., OFFIS (March 2011)

2. Benveniste, A., Caillaud, B., Nickovic, D., Passerone, R., baptiste Raclet, J., Reinkemeier, P., Sangiovanni-vincentelli, A., Damm, W., Henzinger, T., Larsen, K.: Contracts for systems design. Tech. rep., Research Centre Rennes – Bretagne Atlantique (2012)
3. Bozzano, M., Villafiorita, A.: Improving system reliability via model checking: The FSAP/NuSMV-SA safety analysis platform. In: Anderson, S., Felici, M., Littlewood, B. (eds.) SAFECOMP 2003. LNCS, vol. 2788, pp. 49–62. Springer, Heidelberg (2003)
4. Damm, W., Hungar, H., Josko, B., Peikenkamp, T., Stierand, I.: Using contract-based component specifications for virtual integration testing and architecture design. In: Design, Automation Test in Europe Conference Exhibition (2011)
5. Echtle, K.: Fehlertoleranzverfahren. Springer (1990)
6. Ellims, M., Bridges, J., Ince, D.: The economics of unit testing. Empirical Software Engineering 11(1), 5–31 (2006)
7. Hungar, H.: Compositionality with strong assumptions. In: Nordic Workshop on Programming Theory (November 2011)
8. ISO: Road Vehicles - Functional Safety. International Standard Organization, iSO 26262 (November 2011)
9. Joshi, A., Heimdahl, M.P.E.: Model-based safety analysis of simulink models using SCADE design verifier. In: Winther, R., Gran, B.A., Dahll, G. (eds.) SAFECOMP 2005. LNCS, vol. 3688, pp. 122–135. Springer, Heidelberg (2005)
10. Kacimi, O., Ellen, C., Oertel, M., Sojka, D.: Creating a reference technology platform: Performing model-based safety analysis in an heterogeneous development environment. In: Proceedings of the MODELSWARD Conference (2014)
11. Kececioglu, D.: Reliability engineering handbook, vol. i. PTR Prentice Hall, Englewood Cliffs (1991)
12. Lamport, L., Merz, S.: Specifying and verifying fault-tolerant systems. In: Langmaack, H., de Roever, W.-P., Vytopil, J. (eds.) FTRTFT 1994 and ProCoS 1994. LNCS, vol. 863, pp. 41–76. Springer, Heidelberg (1994)
13. Oertel, M., Mahdi, A., Böde, E., Rettberg, A.: Contract-based safety: Specification and application guidelines. In: Proceedings of the 1st International Workshop on Emerging Ideas and Trends in Engineering of Cyber-Physical Systems (2014)
14. Papadopoulos, Y., Maruhn, M.: Model-based synthesis of fault trees from matlab-simulink models. In: International Conference on Dependable Systems and Networks, DSN 2001, pp. 77–82 (2001)
15. Papadopoulos, Y., McDermid, J.A.: Hierarchically performed hazard origin and propagation studies. In: Felici, M., Kanoun, K., Pasquini, A. (eds.) SAFECOMP 1999. LNCS, vol. 1698, pp. 139–152. Springer, Heidelberg (1999)
16. Peikenkamp, T., Cavallo, A., Valacca, L., Böde, E., Pretzer, M., Hahn, E.M.: Towards a unified model-based safety assessment. In: Górski, J. (ed.) SAFECOMP 2006. LNCS, vol. 4166, pp. 275–288. Springer, Heidelberg (2006)
17. RTCA: DO-178C: Software Considerations in Airborne Systems and Equipment Certification. Radio Technical Commission for Aeronautics (RTCA) (2011)
18. SAE: ARP4761: Guidelines and Methods for Conducting the Safety Assessment Process on Civil Airborne Systems and Equipment (1996)
19. Schäfer, A.: Combining real-time model-checking and fault tree analysis. In: Araki, K., Gnesi, S., Mandrioli, D. (eds.) FME 2003. LNCS, vol. 2805, Springer, Heidelberg (2003)
20. Svenningsson, R., Vinter, J., Eriksson, H., Törngren, M.: MODIFI: A MODel-Implemented Fault Injection Tool. In: Schoitsch, E. (ed.) SAFECOMP 2010. LNCS, vol. 6351, pp. 210–222. Springer, Heidelberg (2010)

# MTBF Inconsistency Analysis on Inferred Product Breakdown Structures

Christian Ellen, Martin Böschen, and Thomas Peikenkamp

OFFIS - Institute for Information Technology
Escherweg 2,26121 Oldenburg, Germany
{ellen,boeschen,peikenkamp}@offis.de

**Abstract.** This article describes our current work on the combination of an ontology-based knowledge representation and formal analysis procedures. We use formalized system engineering knowledge and partial architectural information (induced by a set of requirements) to formalize natural language requirements and to identify inconsistencies based on this formalization. Our analysis combines requirements specified by patterns and an ontology-based product breakdown structure. As an example, we identify inconsistencies between Mean Time Between Failure (MTBF) specifications of systems and their subsystems.

**Keywords:** MTBF Analysis, Ontology, Requirements Engineering, Verification.

## 1 Introduction

In system design, using natural language requirements is the most common way for people to express their needs and there are good reasons for that: Compared with the modeling formalisms used in industry today, natural language is more expressive, thus allowing an efficient and comprehensive capturing of the problem. An additional benefit is that requirement engineers do not have to learn a new specification mechanism or — even worse — have to learn several of them including their usually non-trivial relationships. The major drawback of natural language requirements is their ambiguity which has two important negative consequences: First, the risk of misinterpretation of the needs of the users expressed by these requirements. This risk increases when the requirements are refined and may lead to expensive design iterations. Second, the inconsistencies in (the original or refined) requirements are difficult to detect not only because of the aforementioned ambiguity, but also because even trivial inconsistencies can only be detected by humans.

In this article we present current work done in the CRYSTAL Project[1] where we use information from three sources to disambiguate and analyze requirements:

1. Information defined by physical laws and/or agreed rules to determine typical system parameters (like the MTBF)

---

[1] http://www.crystal-artemis.eu/

A. Bondavalli et al. (Eds.): SAFECOMP 2014 Workshops, LNCS 8696, pp. 108–118, 2014.
© Springer International Publishing Switzerland 2014

2. Ontological knowledge about the domain or the system under construction
3. Information extracted from the requirement text itself.

We present a simple example in this article in which information is provided as follows: For (1) we use the classical equation to determine a system MTBF out of the component MTBFs. More precisely, we analyze if the required *Mean Time Between Failures* (MTBF) and *Mean time to Repair* (MTTR) values of parent systems and their subsystems are consistent. For (2), the example shows how to extract information about the system structure and how to organize it in an ontology-like structure called *Product Breakdown Structure* (PBS). Such information is typically present in structural models available in many industrial contexts. In our example we show moreover, how this information can also be extracted from the requirement text itself. For (3) we show how to use a set of boilerplates or patterns[4], which force a certain structure on requirements, resembling the structure of the natural language text. This similarity can be used to perform on-the-fly analysis of natural language requirements. In the CRYS-TAL project, the *Requirements Authoring Tool* from the Reuse Company[12] is used for this step. While entering a new requirement, it guides the requirement engineer to the best boilerplate by making suggestions. The boilerplates used in the example are equipped with a formal, trace-based semantical model, which allows formal analysis methods to be applied. This approach has been investigated for example within the CESAR project [11] and is starting to get tool support [3] as well as some industrial acceptance.

Although we are using an existing technical infrastructure, the overall approach is independent to any tool or format and can be tailored to different ontology formats, like OWL[5] or RSHP[8].

The rest of the article is structured as follows: Section 2 introduces the PBS as our main ontology structure and Section 3 outlines the specification of MTBF requirements as well as methods to identify inconsistencies. The article concludes with Section 4.

## 2 Product Breakdown Structure

In the early requirements elicitation phase, a detailed component model of the system with interfaces and interconnection may not be available. But for the initial specification of MTBF a very abstract view of the system and of its subsystems is already enough. This abstract representation of the system is called the product breakdown structure (PBS). In the following, we use a very simple ontology, defined along the lines of [1].

### 2.1 Definitions

A formal definition of the ontology structure used in a PBS is provided by Definition 1. It defines the elements of a PBS by using standard ontology terms like concepts and relations[5].

**Definition 1.** *PBS A PBS is an ontology* $\mathcal{S} = \{\mathcal{C}, \mathcal{C}_{type}, \overset{part}{\longrightarrow}, \overset{is\_a}{\longrightarrow}, \overset{con}{\longleftrightarrow}\}$ , *s.t.:*

- $c_1, c_2 \in \mathcal{C}$ *are concepts denoting system and subsystem elements,*
- $t_1, t_2 \in \mathcal{C}_{type}$ *are concepts denoting types of system elements,*
- $\overset{part}{\longrightarrow}$: *defines pairwise relationships* $c_1 \overset{part}{\longrightarrow} c_2$ *between two system elements denoting their direct hierarchical relationship,*
- $\overset{is\_a}{\longrightarrow}$: *defines pairwise relationships* $c_1 \overset{is\_a}{\longrightarrow} t_1$ *between a system element and a type,*
- $\overset{con}{\longleftrightarrow}$: *defines pairwise relationships* $c_1 \overset{con}{\longleftrightarrow} c_2$ *denoting the existence of a connection between* $c_1$ *and* $c_2$

In the following, we use the short form $\mathcal{C}_{type}(c)$ to represent the set of all $t \in \mathcal{C}_{type}$ for which $c \overset{is\_a}{\longrightarrow} t$ is defined within the PBS ontology.

A PBS is a reduced component model which defines some of the system elements and parts of their decomposition hierarchy into subsystems. Such a simple view is available even in early stages of the development process and can be refined during further development. For example in early stages of the design of a car breaking system, the fact that it will at least consists of different actuators, a breaking pedal and a computational ABS unit can be used as a first PBS. This PBS can be refined if more detailed information of the system becomes available, like the different types of actuators used.

Therefore, the PBS also includes a *weak* typing of systems and subsystems by allowing, but not requiring, the definition of an is_a relationship between a system and a type. By using this concept it is for example possible to express that a refined *disc brake* system is an *actuator* of the braking system. A PBS may also include information about the connection between systems. In fact, it is not limited to the concepts and relations of Def. 1. The PBS ontology can be extended with any additional knowledge of the system.

To avoid inconsistent structures, e.g. in the hierarchy of the elements, some additional constraints have to be met:

**Definition 2.** *PBS Consistency A PBS $\mathcal{S}$ is consistent, iff for all $c_1, c_2 \in \mathcal{C}$:*

- $\mathcal{C} \cap \mathcal{C}_{type} = \emptyset$
- $\overset{part}{\longrightarrow}$ *induces a forest of directed tree*
- $\overset{is\_a}{\longrightarrow}$ *induces a directed acyclic graph*
- $\overset{con}{\longleftrightarrow}$ *is symmetric*

These simple constraints can be checked by an ontology reasoner (e.g. HermiT[2]).

An example of a PBS is shown in Figure 1. It shows a braking system, which consists of a pedal, an ABS-Controller and a brake actuator. The ABS-Controller can be further divided into two ABS-Systems, which are redundant for safety reasons, and a voter, which compares their output values.

---

[2] http://hermit-reasoner.com/

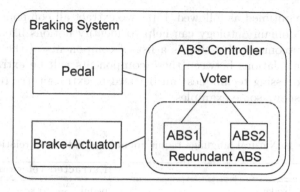

**Fig. 1.** Example PBS of a car braking system and the decomposition of its ABS-Controller

Using the concepts of Definition 1, the set of components for the braking system is: $\mathcal{C} = \{$ Braking System, Pedal, ABS-Controller, Brake-Actuator$\}$. Furthermore, we have the following relations:

$$\text{Pedal} \xrightarrow{part} \text{Braking System}$$

$$\text{Brake-Actuator} \xrightarrow{part} \text{Braking System}$$

$$\text{ABS-Controller} \xleftrightarrow{con} \text{Pedal}$$

$$\text{ABS-Controller} \xleftrightarrow{con} \text{Brake-Actuator}$$

## 2.2 Creation of the PBS

The PBS can be created by using different means, like a component modeling tool (e.g. Papyrus for EAST-ADL[3]). The downside of this approach is that the usage of a dedicated modeling tool may introduce additional constraints or the need to specify not yet available information. This requires design decisions which reduce the freedom for design space exploration in later stages of the development process.

As we defined the PBS as an ontology, a more natural option is to use an ontology-editor like Protégé. It is a very generic tool that doesn't force a specific methodology. Missing information is assumed to be not modeled yet, it is not interpreted as not existent.

Finally, another option is to derive the PBS knowledge directly from the current set of already defined requirements. The inferred information may not be as accurate and complete as an explicit model, but can be sufficient for early analysis activities in cases where no explicit model is available.

In this article, we present the third approach, which uses only the information in the requirements to create the PBS. A PBS can be generated in several

---

[3] http://www.papyrusuml.org

steps, which are outlined as followed. First we extract all components from the requirement. A domain ontology can help to identify notions like system components. The outcome of this step is a list of components of the system. In a second step, the relations between these components will be extracted. Natural language processing techniques can be used to extract these relations. The following table shows some examples:

Table 1. Natural language requirements and extracted relations

| Requirement | Extracted relation |
|---|---|
| The pedal of the brake .... | pedal $\xrightarrow{part}$ brake |
| If the Braking System controller outputs .. | controller $\xrightarrow{part}$ Braking system |
| The pedal sends its signal to the controller | controller $\xleftrightarrow{con}$ pedal |
| The signals of the control unit will be processed in the voter | control unit $\xleftrightarrow{con}$ voter |

### 2.3 Incompleteness

With the definitions we have so far, it is already possible to perform a first analysis. One example is to check the requirements for completeness. We won't go into a philosophical discussion what completeness means, but rather take a practical approach and search for indications of incompleteness. This is a common approach for analyzing requirements for completeness [11]. The motivation is, that it is hard to define completeness in an ontology which only captures parts of a system architecture. Therefore, we only try to identify incomplete structures. For example, a connection between two components $c_1 \xleftrightarrow{con} c_2$ (i.e. $c_1 \xleftrightarrow{con} c_2$) induces the fact that they are part of a higher level component. If such a system is not specified, this is an indication of incompleteness within the specification. This motivates our next definition:

**Definition 3.** *PBS Incompleteness (Ancestor) A PBS is ancestor-incomplete if there exists $c_1, c_2 \in C$ s.t. $c_1 \xleftrightarrow{con} c_2$ and $c_1$ and $c_2$ have no common $\xrightarrow{part}$-ancestor.*

## 3   Analysis

The mean time between failures (MTBF) is an important concept in the development of safety critical systems [2]. It describes the mean time between the beginning of the up-time of a system to the beginning of the next unplanned downtime due to a failure. In this section we will discuss, how MTBF requirements can be specified using simple patterns and how an early consistency analysis may be applied to this requirements by using the partial architectural information provided by the PBS.

Some standards like the ISO26262 [6] use the concept of failures in time (FIT) rather than MTBF and there are other important safety measures, e.g. mean time to failure (MTTF). In this article, we use the MTBF calculations as an example. In addition, there are many valid means to estimate the MTBF and compute the composition of systems in the literature (e.g. [2]) or more practical by engineers (e.g. [7]). Here, we use one rather simple way and provide the necessary assumptions. Formally the MTBF can be defined as:

$$MTBF = \int_0^\infty tf(t)dt$$

Here, $f(t)$ denotes the failure probability density function which describes the probability of an component-failure at time $t$.

For a simplified computation of the MTBF compositions, we apply some assumptions. The first assumption is that for the consistency analysis all occurrences of failures are independent. This assumption is motivated by the fact that the consistency of the MTBF specification is evaluated purely on the PBS structure and that no information on failure dependencies is available. The computations can be adapted if such information is available. The second assumption is that $f(t)$ is instantiated by an exponential distribution, i.e. $f(t) = \lambda e^{-\lambda t}$, with a constant failure rate $\lambda$. This assumption is typical, if only the "useful life period" of a component according to the so called "bathtube"[2] distribution is relevant. By using this assumption the MTBF is given by $\frac{1}{\lambda}$.

## 3.1   MTBF Pattern

Similar to a boilerplate, a pattern defines a textual structure of a requirement to support the requirements engineer to write unified requirements. A pattern is more restrictive than a boilerplate because it not only defines a textual base structure with open parameters, but restricts the instantiation of the parameters to specific syntax [4,9]. This allows a strict formal interpretation of a pattern. In this case the pattern to define a requirement on the MTBF of components expects two parameters: $\mathcal{C}' \subseteq \mathcal{C}$ a subset of components for which the MTBF shall be defined and $\Theta \in \mathcal{T}$ a time value from the current time domain. This pattern is defined in Table 2.

The formal semantics of the pattern defines the minimum MTBF values for any component $c \in \mathcal{C}'$ as entry in the partial function $MTBF_p : \mathcal{C} \cup \mathcal{C}_{type} \rightsquigarrow \mathcal{T}$. The function is only partially defined, because not all elements of the PBS may have a MTBF definition. It defines for a subset of PBS concepts $Def(MTBF_p) \subseteq \mathcal{C} \cup \mathcal{C}_{type}$ a MTBF value from the time domain which is lower bounded by the $\Theta$ value of a requirement.

The pattern No. 1 can be used to specify the minimal MTBF for a single component as well as for a group of components, which shall have the same MTBF. The second pattern (Table 3) defines the MTBF for a specific type of component. Its semantics are that every instance $c \in \mathcal{C}$ within the PBS which is of one of the types $t \in \mathcal{C}'_{type} \subseteq \mathcal{C}_{type}$ has to have at least an MTBF of $\Theta$. Both patterns are explicitly naming components or types. Therefore, they can be linked to existing components or types in the PBS or can be used to infer new elements of the ontology.

**Table 2.** MTBF Pattern No. 1

| Structure | The MTBF of $C'$ shall be at least $\Theta$ |
|---|---|
| Meaning | The pattern specifies a lower bound $\Theta$ on the MTBF of the components listed in the set $C'$. |
| Intuition | With this pattern a requirement engineer can directly specify the target MTBF for a single component of the PBS, as well as, for a set of components which shall have the same target MTBF. |
| Example | The MTBF of {BrakingSystem} shall be at least 16.605$h$<br>The MTBF of {ABS1, ABS2} shall be at least 20.000$h$ |
| Formal semantic | $\forall c \in C' : MTBF_p(c) \geq \Theta$ |

**Table 3.** MTBF Pattern No. 2

| Structure | The MTBF of each $C'_{type}$ shall be at least $\Theta$ |
|---|---|
| Meaning | The pattern specifies a lower bound $\Theta$ on the MTBF of all instances within the PBS of the component types listed in the set $\mathcal{C}_{type}$. |
| Intuition | With this pattern, a requirement engineer can directly specify the target MTBF of a component type. The requirement is applied to each instance defined by $\xrightarrow{is\text{-}a}$ within the PBS. |
| Example | The MTBF of each {brake-actuator} shall be at least 16.000$h$ |
| Formal semantic | $\forall t \in C'_{type}, \forall c \in \mathcal{C}, \mathcal{C}_{type}(c) = t : MTBF_p(c) \geq \Theta$ |

An MTBF specification is considered inconsistent with the typing of a PBS, if there is an entry defined in the partial function $MTBF_p$ s.t. the type requires a higher MTBF value than an instance of the type:

**Definition 4.** *MTBF Inconsistency (typing) A partial function $MTBF_p$ is inconsistent for a consistent PBS $\mathcal{S}$, iff there exists a $c \in \mathcal{C}$, with $c \in Def(MTBF_p)$ $\wedge \mathcal{C}_{type}(c) \neq \emptyset$, s.t:*

$$MTBF_p(c) < \max_{t \in \mathcal{C}_{type}(c)} (MTBF_p(t))$$

Such inconsistencies may arise during the requirement elicitation phase and can be identified using the (implicit) PBS structure.

The MTBF information specified using both patterns can be combined to a single function $MTBF : \mathcal{C} \rightarrow \mathcal{T}$. The function uses $\bot$ as a special symbol denoting that no MTBF specification is provided for a PBS component:

$$MTBF(c) = \begin{cases} MTBF_p(c) & \text{if } c \in Def(MTBF_p) \\ \max_{t \in C_{type}(c)}(MTBF_p(t)) & \text{if } c \notin Def(MTBF_p) \\ & \text{and } C_{type}(c) \neq \emptyset \\ \bot & \text{else} \end{cases} \quad (1)$$

This function assigns an MTBF value to every PBS component instance and resolves the $MTBF_p$ specifications of the type by giving precedence to directly specified MTBF values over values derived from the types of a component. If $MTBF_p$ is consistent, $MTBF$ will return the value of the hardest (highest) applying MTBF requirement or $\bot$. The function can be used to analyze further sources of inconsistencies between the specification and the PBS structure. The most interesting one is the correct relation of the MTBF values defined on a parent component to the specification of its sub-components. The combination of the MTBF values of the sub-components must at least match the required MTBF of the parent component.

## 3.2   Compositional MTBF

For the computation of the combined MTBF of several sub-components, the pure knowledge of the individual MTBF of the components is not sufficient, also the mean time to repair (MTTR) needs to be specified. This can be done by using a specific MTTR pattern as defined in Table 4.

**Table 4.** MTTR Pattern

| Structure | The MTTR of $C'$ shall be at most $\Theta$ |
|---|---|
| Meaning | The pattern specifies an upper bound $\Theta$ on the MTTR of the components listed in the set $C'$. |
| Intuition | With this pattern a requirement engineer can directly specify an individual MTTR for a single component of the PBS, as well as, for a set of components. |
| Example | The MTTR of {BrakingSystem} shall be at most 2000$h$<br>The MTTR of {ABS,Brake} shall be at most 1500$h$ |
| Formal semantic | $\forall c \in C' : MTTR_p(c) \leq \Theta$ |

Analogue to the MTBF functions, the semantic of the MTTR defines entries of a partial function $MTTR_p : C \rightsquigarrow \mathcal{T}$. The pattern allows the definition of individual MTTR values for each component.

In a typical application many other aspects will be captured by requirements, e.g. safety contracts [10] can be used to define the dependencies or independence between failures. This knowledge has to be taken into account for the analysis of inconsistencies.

The combination of different MTBF values is based on the type of composition of the sub-components and can either be serial or parallel. So far the PBS definition 1 only defines the part relation and does not define the type of decomposition. Our assumption is that if not otherwise stated, a component has a serial decomposition. This means that any failure of a sub-component results in an failure of the parent component. For example, the Braking System of Figure 1 is assumed to be serial decomposed into the *Pedal* component, the *ABS-Controller*, and the *Brake-Actuator* system.

Under the stated assumptions, the combined value $MTBF_{serial}$ for a serial composed component can be computed by adding the individual failure rates of the sub-components $\lambda_{serial} = \sum \lambda$ and using the assumption $MTBF = \frac{1}{\lambda}$:

$$MTBF_{serial}(\mathcal{C}') = \frac{\prod_{c \in \mathcal{C}'} MTBF(c)}{\sum_{c \in \mathcal{C}'} MTBF(c)} \quad (2)$$

Here, $\mathcal{C}'$ is a set of sub-components which have an MTBF specification (i.e. $MTBF(c) \neq \bot$). Sub-components without an MTBF specification are explicitly ignored in the formula. The function $MTBF_{serial}$ defines an upper bound on the combined MTBF, since adding an MTBF specification to one of the sub-components only decreases the value of the function. Therefore, an analysis which checks the consistency of the $MTBF_{serial}$ with the parent $MTBF$ value may only be used to identify inconsistencies in the specification:

**Definition 5.** *MTBF Inconsistency (serial composition) Let S be a consistent PBS, $c \in \mathcal{C}$ be a serial composed component, $\mathcal{C}' \subset \mathcal{C}$ the set of sub-components of c, with $\forall s \in \mathcal{C}' : s \xrightarrow{part} c \in S$ and $MTBF(c) \neq \emptyset$. The MTBF specification of $\mathcal{C}'$ is inconsistent to the MTBF of c, iff*

$$MTBF_{serial}(\mathcal{C}') < MTBF(c)$$

This definition can be used to identify inconsistencies in early phases of the design. In case an MTBF specification is inconsistent, an engineer may decide to plan for a redundant implementation of a component to increase its overall MTBF value. This can be specified in the PBS by the pattern defined in Table 5. The pattern only provides a very simple mean to express some safety concept and is only suitable for the early stages of the design. Refinements of such specifications may be done by using more elaborated concepts like safety patterns [10].

The combined MTBF of parallel sub-components can be computed by multiplying their failure rates $\lambda$ which are scaled down by the MTTR of the sub-components: $\lambda_{par} = \prod \lambda \cdot \sum MTTR$

The scaling with MTTR is motivated by the fact, that if a failure of a component occurs, another sub-component may already be in its failure state[4] and

---

[4] The full derivation can be found in [7].

**Table 5.** Redundancy Pattern

| Structure | $C'$ shall be implemented redundant |
|-----------|--------------------------------------|
| Meaning   | The pattern specifies that each of the components in $C'$ shall be composed of redundant sub-components. |
| Intuition | A requirement engineer may use this pattern to specify that a component is part of a safety concept in which it consists of a several redundant components which are composed in parallel. |
| Example   | $\{ABS_{par}\}$ shall be implemented redundant |

therefore the associated MTTR has to be accounted for. Using $MTBF = \frac{1}{\lambda}$ results in:

$$MTBF_{par}(C') = \frac{\prod_{c \in C'} MTBF(c)}{\sum_{c \in C'} MTTR(c)} \qquad (3)$$

If the MTTR information is not available for every component, a global common MTTR value can be assumed.

**Definition 6.** *MTBF Inconsistency (parallel composition) Let $S$ be a consistent PBS, $c \in C$ be a parallel composed component, $C' \subset C$ the set of sub-components of $c$, with $\forall s \in C' : s \xrightarrow{part} c \in S$ and $MTBF(c) \neq \emptyset$. The MTBF specification of $C'$ is inconsistent to the MTBF of $c$, iff*

$$MTBF_{par}(C') < MTBF(c)$$

The combinations of the different inconsistency statements from Def. 4,5, and 6 may be applied to different layers within the PBS structure to find inconsistencies within the MTBF specifications. For example, the main *ABS-Controller* of Figure 1 is a serial composition of a *Voter* and a subsystem consisting of two redundant *ABS-Controllers*. In general, the analysis has to check the tree structures induced by the $\xrightarrow{part}$-Relation starting from the leafs to check the MTBF consistency for each sub-component and the complete system.

## 4    Conclusion

In this article we have briefly discussed the idea to infer implied structures of a potential system model in the early stages of the development process and how to manage this knowledge using a PBS. Furthermore, we introduced a set of patterns which allows a requirement engineer to specify MTBF and MTTR values on elements of this PBS and defined formally statements to identify inconsistencies between the different MTBF specification. The presented approach shows the benefits of the combination of ontology knowledge and consistency analysis tasks.

In future work, we will evaluate this approach in case studies and thereby extend the means to extract PBS knowledge. An integration into the Requirements Quality Toolchain [12] and an application of more complex analysis tasks is planned.

**Acknowledgments.** The research leading to these results has received funding from the ARTEMIS Joint Undertaking under Grant Agreement N°332830 (CRYSTAL) and German national funding from BMBF N°01$IS$13001$A$.

# References

1. Baader, F., Horrocks, I., Sattler, U.: Description logics. In: Staab, S., Studer, R. (eds.) Handbook on Ontologies. International Handbooks on Information Systems, pp. 3–28. Springer (2004)
2. Bozzano, M., Villafiorita, A.: Design and Safety Assesment of Critical Systems. Auerbach Publications (2011)
3. BTC Embedded Systems: BTC Embedded Specifier, http://www.btc-es.de/index.php?idcatside=52 (last visited May 27, 2014)
4. Damm, W., Hungar, H., Henkler, S., Stierand, I., Josko, B., Oertel, M., Reinkemeier, P., Baumgart, A., Büker, M., Gezgin, T., Ehmen, G., Weber, R.: SPES2020 Architecture Modeling. Tech. rep., OFFIS e.V. (2011)
5. Hitzler, P., Krötzsch, M., Parsia, B., Patel-Schneider, P.F., Rudolph, S.: Owl 2 web ontology language primer. W3C Recommendation 27(1), 123 (2009)
6. International Standard Organization: Road Vehicles - Functional Safety (November 2011)
7. Lin, D.L.: Reliability characteristics for two subsystems in series or parallel or n subsystems in m_out_of_n arrangement. Tech. rep., Aurora Consulting Engineering LLC (2006), http://auroraconsultingengineering.com/doc_files/ Reliability_series_parallel.doc
8. Llorens, J., Morato, J., Genova, G.: RSHP: an information representation model based on relationships. In: Damiani, E., Madravio, M., Jain, L. (eds.) Soft Computing in Software Engineering. STUDFUZZ, vol. 159, pp. 221–253. Springer, Heidelberg (2004)
9. Mitschke, A., Loughran, N., Josko, B., Oertel, M., Rehkop, P., Häusler, S., Benveniste, A.: RE Language Definitions to formalize multi-criteria requirements V2. Tech. rep., The CESAR Consortium (2010), http://cesarproject.eu/fileadmin/user_upload/ CESAR_D_SP2_R2.2_M2_v1.000.pdf
10. Oertel, M., Mahdi, A., Böde, E., Rettberg, A.: Contract-based safety: Specification and application guidelines. In: Proceedings of the 1st International Workshop on Emerging Ideas and Trends in Engineering of Cyber-Physical Systems, EITEC 2014 (2014)
11. Rajan, A., Wahl, T. (eds.): CESAR - Cost-efficient Methods and Processes for Safety-relevant Embedded Systems, No. 978-3709113868. Springer (2013)
12. The Reuse Company: Requirements Quality Suite, http://www.reusecompany.com/requirements-quality-suite (last visited May 27, 2014)

# Critical Systems Verification in MetaMORP(h)OSY

Rocco Aversa, Beniamino Di Martino, and Francesco Moscato*

DIII, Second University of Naples
DiSciPol, Second University of Naples, Italy
{rocco.aversa,beniamino.dimartino,francesco.moscato}@unina2.it

**Abstract.** Multi Agent Systems (MAS) methodologies are emerging as a new approach for modeling and developing complex distributed systems. When complex constraints have to be verified on critical systems Model Driven Engineering (MDE) methodologies allow for the design and implementation of systems *correct by construction*. Usually verification is enforced by formal analysis. This paper presents MetaMORP(h)OSY (Meta-modeling of Mas Object-based with Real-time specification in Project Of complex SYstems) methodology and framework. They provide a mean for building MAS models used to verify properties (and requirements) of Critical Systems following a MDE approach. In particular, this work describes model transformation algorithms used in Meta-MORP(h)OSY to verify real-time and timed reachability requirements.

**Keywords:** Formal Models, Reliability, Model Driven Engineering.

## 1   Introduction

Complexity of Software and Hardware systems is growing more and more day by day. Errors in any phase of the life cycle of these systems may lead to significant consequences ([1, 2]).

The growing of complexity is coupled with the raising difficulties in distinguishing hardware from software components in critical systems. Embedded systems in automotive and aerospace industries are made up of billion of line of source code that are also used for describing behaviors of reconfigurable hardware components [3]. Due to this complexity, it has been predicted that "the current development process is reaching the limit of affordability of building safe..." critical systems [4]. Novel technologies are going to be used in critical environments in order to improve safety and security, but the introduction on new components in a complex system makes it more complex and design and implementation require proper methodologies in order to validate requirements.

Model-Driven Engineering (MDE) methods and techniques try to solve this problem by facilitating definition, composition, implementation and verification

---

* Corresponding author.

A. Bondavalli et al. (Eds.): SAFECOMP 2014 Workshops, LNCS 8696, pp. 119–129, 2014.
© Springer International Publishing Switzerland 2014

of complex systems. Nowadays very few enterprises use MDE in their development cycles and they usually performs verification by using other techniques (testing above all). This problem is discussed in [5] that reports a study of MDE practices in industries. In brief, the survey describes how very few enterprises (especially in the field of critical systems development) use Model-Based techniques in order to verify requirements and how many of these enterprises have interests in introducing MDE techniques in their development processes in order to improve it. In addition, the survey shows that UML is the preferred modeling language that enterprises would use in their MDE frameworks.

CRYSTAL[1] project aims at fostering Europes leading edge position in embedded systems engineering in particular regarding quality and cost effectiveness of safety-critical embedded systems and architecture platforms. Its overall goal is to enable sustainable paths to speed up the maturation, integration, and cross-sectoral reusability of technological and methodological bricks of the factories for safety-critical embedded systems engineering in the areas of transportation (aerospace, automotive, and rail) and healthcare providing a critical mass of European technology providers. In particular, one of the goal of the project is the definition of proper tool chain and methodologies based on formal models for verification and test definition process. Traceability of the model, both on system requirements and on generated tests, may support users in the analysis of the impact of modification in system requirements during the whole life cycle of the system, reducing time needed to modify test cases after changes in requirements. The graphic approach is a good method in order to understand the test and to manage test suite (revisions, recycled tests..). While the object-oriented meta-language allows to adopt features such as data abstraction, encapsulation, messaging, modularity, polymorphism, and inheritance.

This work describes some of the results obtained during the investigation of research activities performed by The Second University of Naples in CRYSTAL project. In particular, we will describe the MetaMORP(h)OSY Model Driven Engineering Framework that copes with several goals of CRYSTAL project.

This paper describes the model transformations techniques used in MetaMORP(h)OSY, (Meta-modeling of Mas Object-based with Real-time specification in Project Of complex SYstems) in order to verify requirements at design time, and to build testbeds at run-time for verification of same properties. Formal modeling and analysis of Multi-Agent Systems (MAS) form the basis for the application for aforementioned techniques. MAS represent a model for designing and developing complex systems[6] coping with their increasing complexity.

Several methodologies have been proposed for MAS design and development [7, 8]. However software engineering has not provided yet any approach to model and verify dependability during all the life cycle.

*MetaMORP(h)OSY*([9]) framework is based on Papyrus [10] and it defines modeling profiles (or meta-models) for the definition of real-time MAS models. Verification at every life-cycle step is performed by implementing translation

---

[1] http://http://www.crystal-artemis.eu/

algorithms which translate design, simulation and run-time description into formal models [11–13].

## 2 State of The Art

The use of MDE techniques in modeling and verification of complex and critical systems is growing more and more, especially in industrial domain.

Usually UML could be considered as the standard modeling language to use, but it is not the best tool for modeling agent based systems[14]. The problem in standard UML-based languages for multi-agent systems, is that agents pro-activity is hard to describe. This is why several languages for Agent Based models have been developed like Agent-UML [15], Agent Modeling Language (AML)[16] (a semi-formal visual modeling language based on the UML 2.0 superstructure) or the one defined for the Prometheus methodology [17]. The Prometheus methodology has been coped with INGENIAS[18]: it consists of a meta-model describing MAS from different perspectives like environment, goals and tasks, specifying the behavior of each agent. Anyway INGENIAS focuses only on the generation of executable software and no verification issues are addressed especially for critical systems.

A tool that uses an approach similar to MetaMORP(h)OSY is SCADE[19]. It enacts model checking to verify properties at design time and implements them onto embedded systems. It is nowadays at a mature implementation stage, but unlike MetaMORP(h)OSY, it implements only verification of state reachability properties (by mean of Model Checking) and it focuses on embedded and control system. Model transformation focused on a single domain is common for MDE tools and methodologies. For example, another framework which focuses on the generation of executable embedded code in TOPCASED [20].

The MetaMORP(h)OSY modeling methodology is oriented towards requirements verification. Differently from other proposed approaches, it uses both vertical and horizontal transformation in order to follow requirement verification during all life cycle of the system. The design model (DSML) is based on UML and it is an extension of AML with time support. It also allows to specify properties to evaluate by means of definition of proper Observers. Model Transformation algorithms can be coped with different Observers by including proper plugins in the framework. Model transformations are used both for the analyses of design models, and for the implementation of run-time components. Hence MetaMORP(h)OSY is a more versatile framework and at the state of the art it has been used both for verification of properties and generation of running embedded systems (like in this work), and also to provide support for design and provisions of cloud services[13, 21]. It also supports different verification techniques (and new ones can be plugged in) including multi-formalisms and multi-solution approaches [12].

The use of Formal models in ERTMS verification is not a new approach: in [22], authors translates ERTMS subsystems into a State-based transition system, which is analyzed by using model checking techniques, but no MDE methodology is defined in their work; in [23] (and [24]) an MDE methodology is described for the verification of a Movement Authority (MA): it uses an UML-based (CSP Process Algebra - based) modeling language, but only structural and functional properties of the system are considered.

# 3    MetaMORP(h)OSY

MetaMORP(h)OSY framework (see [25, 9, 13] for further descriptions) allows for definition of design models by using a proper META-Model (or modeling profile) which is based on UML diagrams. The MetaMORP(h)OSY methodology uses MAS abstraction at design stage. MAS definition follows the Beliefs, Desires, Intentions (BDI[26]) paradigm. Formal rules for MAS design are defined in a Unified Modeling Language (UML) profile called RT-AML (Real Time - Agent Modelling Language). In MetaMORP(h)OSY, the definition of properties is also assured by the definition of a common ontology which describes formally cloud components and services and a taxonomy of properties which is possible to analyze on different MAS models components[9, 27]. Proper annotation techniques and models (like the one discussed in [28, 29]) should be coped with agents definition to specify requirements.

The MDE methodology in MetaMORP(h)OSY is enacted by means of two main components: *Observer* and *Translators Observers* are used in order to evaluate properties both on (abstract) models and (real) running systems. *Translators* implement both vertical and horizontal transformation [30]. Horizontal transformations translate models into other (formal) ones at the same level of abstraction: they are used in order to create analyzable models from descriptive ones (for example: real time properties are verified on design models translating UML models into timed automata). Vertical transformation are usually used in MetaMORP(h)OSY in order to translate *abstract* models into *finer grained* models. This kind of transformation usually usually is not fully automated. Requirements tracing in vertical transformations requires the creation of proper *Observers* able to verify abstract requirements on finer grained models.

Requirements in MetaMORP(h)OSY are tracked during all system life cycle: this involves the definition of proper MDE techniques and transformation able to define properties to verify on system components at design, simulation and run-time stages.

The modeling profile in MetaMORP(h)OSY is named RT-AML (Real Time - Agent Modeling Language). In RT-AML, agents behavior is defined by using BDI logic in terms of *beliefs* of an agent, *goals* they want to achieve and the *plans* available to reach the goals. RT-AML is compliant with MARTE profiles [9] for modeling of real-time properties in UML profiles. They main components of an Agent Diagram are: **AgentRT**, **PlanRT**, **DgoalRT** and **BeliefRT**. They are defined as UML stereotypes which contains all properties needed to describe Agent structures and behaviors (like temporal properties: arrival time, execution time, deadlines; availability etc.) AgentRTs define agents structures with their attributes; PlanRTs defines agents Intentions while reaching a goal state; DgoalRTs declare decidable goals for AgentRTs (i.e. goals whose reachability can be determined under real-time constraints). Descriptions of RT-AML Activity and Sequence Diagrams are omitted for the lack of space. Anyway, they are similar to UML Activity and Sequence. In order to define properties that can be evaluated on models by proper Observers an *Observer Diagram* must be defined. It must contain the specification of requirements to verify, the elements on which requirements are defined, the life cycle phase when analysis has to be performed and the kind of analysis to perform. Supported requirements are defined in another profile. It mainly consists in a taxonomy of dependability properties and it was introduced in [21].

# 4   Case Study

As proof of concept we show the use of MetaMORP(h)OSY in the design prototyping and monitoring of Movement Authority (MA) in an ERTMS (European Rail Traffic Management System) level 2 system [31]. The model we propose analyzes a specification consisting in the verification of a real-time property. We consider the case when an authorization to move must be sent. Because of the lack of space, we do not model here the variables considered to decide for an authorization or not (i.e. distances, dynamics, timestamps, vitality checks etc.). In this example, we take in account only the events (and not their contents, assuming that the decision if for movement) exchanged during the protocol, time elapsed to take decisions and deadlines to respect in each action. A MA is an authorization to move for a train (EuroCab). The Authorization is grant by the Radio Block Center (RBC) that analyzes EuroCab position (transmitted by the EuroCab itself) and other environment information and decides for movement authorization or not. MetaMORP(H)OSY modeling of this system requires the definition of an RT-AML model. Fig.1 reports the structure of the two AgetRTs

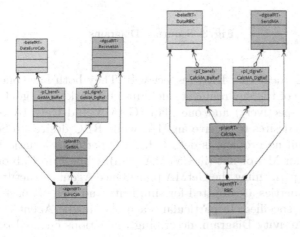

**Fig. 1.** Agent Diagram

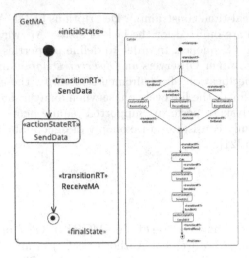

**Fig. 2.** Activity Diagram

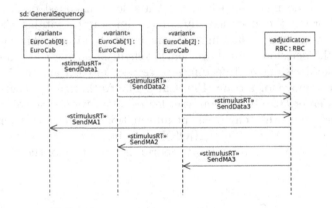

**Fig. 3.** Sequence Diagrams

used to model Eurocab and RBC respectively. They both have one belief (containing the state of the environment, including network), one goal (ReceiveMA and SendMA respectively) and one plan (GetMA and CalcMA respectively). Hence, EuroCab desires to receive an MA, while RBC desires to Send the MA to the EuroCab if no problem is detected. RBC performs a majority voting in order to decide for MA or not (in CalcMA plan), while EuroCab only wants to acquire its MA (performing the GetMA plan).Once Agents structure are defined (stereotypes properties are omitted for simplicity and lack of space), behavioral diagrams can be specified. In particular, each plan in the Agent Diagram is associated to an Activity Diagram, describing the actions enacted to reach goals during plan execution.

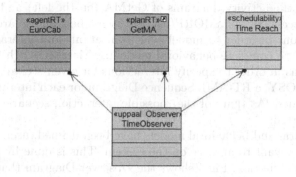

**Fig. 4.** Schedulability Observer

---

**Algorithm 1.** Timed Schedulability Translator

---

Identify all *ActionStates* and *Transitions* in Activity Diagrams of all Agents.

**for** act in ActivityDiagrams **do**

  create a new TimedAutomaton

  **for** i in *ActionStates* of act **do**

    Create a new Node in TimedAutomaton[act] with proper properties from agents model;

    Node Invariants depend on properties of Action States and AgentRT stereotypes.

  **end for**

  **for** j in *Transitions* of act **do**

    Create a new Transition in TimedAutomaton[act];

    **if** *Transition*[j] has a guard **then**

      create a channel in the Timed Automaton with the guard's name

      Define a "?" synchronization on the newly created Transition

      Create a new Transition in TimedAutomaton[act];

      Transition Guards and time resets depend on properties of Action States and AgentRT stereotypes.

    **end if**

  **end for**

  Select a Sequence Diagram

  Create a New Product Automaton

  **for** obj in Agent in Sequence Diagram **do**

    Add the Timed Automaton related to the agent to the product Automaton

  **end for**

  Add a new Timed Automaton to the Product Automaton for stimula.

  **for** stim in Stimulus of Sequence Diagram **do**

    Add a New Node in the Stimulus Timed Automaton

    Add a New Transition in the Stimulus Timed Automaton with a channel with the same name of the Stimulus

  **end for**

**end for**

Verify Property

---

Fig. 2 shows the activity diagrams of GetMA (on the left) and CalcMA (on the right). Notice that MetaMORP(h)OSY uses labels and guards on *TransitionRT* transitions in order to model synchronizations and interactions among agents. In order to complete behavioral modeling, MetaMORP(h)OSY uses Sequence Diagrams in order to specify interactions for given scenarios. Finally, in MetaMORP(h)OSY, a RT-AML Sequence Diagram for each interaction scenario has to be provided. As (part of the) possible interaction scenario the sequence in Fig.3 is reported.

Once structural and behavioral models have been defined, users must declare which properties want to analyze on the system. This is done by means of *Observer Diagram* definition. Fig.4 shows the Observer Diagram that requires the verification of *schedulability* property on GetMA plan.

In this example, the schedulability property is equivalent to a timed state reachability problem. The depicted Observer enact a model transformation by mean of a Translator, from RT-AML to Timed Automata which is analyzed by model checking. This translation algorithm works as described in Alg.1.

Fig.5 shows part of the obtained result. The model is analyzable by the UP-PAAL Model Checker.

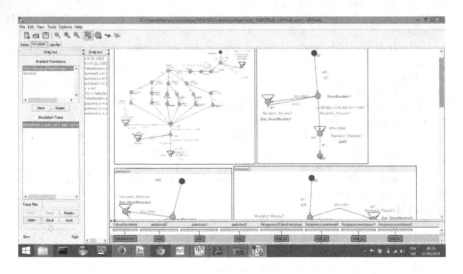

**Fig. 5.** Translated Model

## 5    Conclusions and Future Work

In this work we have described a methodology that supports the design, verification and validation of multi-agent systems, in particular, has been described the framework to support these activities, focusing on each phase. The methodology can be used in the design of MAS real-time and design models to allow to verify the requirements in a MDE scenario. This work has showed Model Driven

Engineering techniques in order to realize complex monitoring and testing environments in embedded system development. Thank to the flexibility of the framework design and implementation by using MDE techniques it is general enough for managing a wide range of systems. The framework has been developed with an high modularity to allow a rapid extension of it. To prove the actual flexibility, MetaMORP(h)OSY has been used for a test case, a 2-out-3 railway safety system, that permit to show the framework at work in all phases.

The framework covers the entire design phase of models of systems, going beyond the abstraction, next releases will cover largest and varied application contexts in which it makes sense to model the interaction between the components as a multi-agent system for example, anyone familiar with UML models may use the framework and shape it with a MAS system. As already discussed, have been provided tools to extend the framework, that in later versions, could be expanded with new formal verification methods or new properties to be checked on the system.

**Acknowledgement.** The research leading to these results has received funding from CRYSTAL: the ARTEMIS Joint Undertaking under Grant Agreement N 332830 and from specific national programs and / or funding authorities.

# References

1. Bureau, A.T.S.: Ao-2008-070: In-flight upset, 154 km west of learmonth, wa, 7 october 2008. In: Airbus A330-303. Tech. rep (October 2008)
2. Williams, M.: Toyota to recall prius hybrids over abs software. In: Computerworld (2010)
3. Charette, R.N.: This car runs on code. IEEE Spectrum 46 (2009)
4. Feiler, P.H.: Model-based validation of safety-critical embedded systems. In: 2010 IEEE Aerospace Conference, pp. 1–10. IEEE (2010)
5. Hutchinson, J., Rouncefield, M., Whittle, J.: Model-driven engineering practices in industry. In: 2011 33rd International Conference on Software Engineering (ICSE), pp. 633–642 (May 2011)
6. Guessoum, Z., Briot, J.P., Faci, N., Marin, O.: Towards reliable multi-agent systems: An adaptive replication mechanism. Multiagent Grid Syst. 6, 1–24 (2010)
7. Kavi, K.M., Aborizka, M., Kung, D., Texas, N.: A framework for designing, modeling and analyzing agent based software systems. In: Proc. of 5th International Conference on Algorithms and Architectures for Parallel Processing, pp. 23–25 (2002)
8. Da Silva, V.T., De Lucena, C.J.P.: From a conceptual framework for agents and objects to a multi-agent system modeling language. Autonomous Agents and Multi-Agent Systems 9, 145–189 (2004)
9. Moscato, F., Aversa, R., Amato, A.: Describing cloud use case in metamorp(h)osy. In: IEEE Proc. of CISIS 2012 Conference, pp. 793–798 (2012)
10. PapyrusGroup: Papyrus uml, http://www.papyrusuml.org
11. Franceschinis, G., Gribaudo, M., Iacono, M., Marrone, S., Moscato, F., Vittorini, V.: Interfaces and binding in component based development of formal models. In: IEEE Proc. of VALUETOOLS 2009 Conference, vol. 44 (2009)

12. Moscato, F., Vittorini, V., Amato, F., Mazzeo, A., Mazzocca, N.: Solution workflows for model-based analysis of complex systems. IEEE T. Automation Science and Engineering 9(1), 83–95 (2012)
13. Moscato, F., Martino, B.D., Aversa, R.: Enabling model driven engineering of cloud services by using mosaic ontology. Scalable Computing: Practice and Experience 13(1) (2012)
14. Bauer, B.: UML class diagrams revisited in the context of agent-based systems. In: Wooldridge, M.J., Weiß, G., Ciancarini, P. (eds.) AOSE 2001. LNCS, vol. 2222, pp. 101–118. Springer, Heidelberg (2002)
15. Bauer, B., Müller, J.P., Odell, J.: Agent uml: A formalism for specifying multiagent software systems. Int. Journal of Software Engineering and Knowledge Engineering 11, 91–103 (2000)
16. Trencansky, I., Cervenka, R.: Agent modeling language (aml): A comprehensive approach to modeling mas. Whitestein Series in Software Agent Technologies and Autonomic Computing 29, 391–400 (2005)
17. Gascueña, J.M., Navarro, E., Fernández-Caballero, A.: Model-driven engineering techniques for the development of multi-agent systems. Engineering Applications of Artificial Intelligence 25(1), 159–173 (2012)
18. Fernández-Caballero, A., Gascueña, J.M.: Developing multi-agent systems through integrating prometheus, INGENIAS and ICARO-T. In: Filipe, J., Fred, A., Sharp, B. (eds.) ICAART 2009. CCIS, vol. 67, pp. 219–232. Springer, Heidelberg (2010)
19. Abdulla, P.A., Deneux, J., Stålmarck, G., Ågren, H., Åkerlund, O.: Designing safe, reliable systems using scade. In: Margaria, T., Steffen, B. (eds.) ISoLA 2004. LNCS, vol. 4313, pp. 115–129. Springer, Heidelberg (2006)
20. Farines, J., De Queiroz, M., da Rocha, V., Carpes, A., Vernadat, F., Cregut, X.: A model-driven engineering approach to formal verification of plc programs. In: 2011 IEEE 16th Conference on Emerging Technologies Factory Automation (ETFA), pp. 1–8 (September 2011)
21. Moscato, F., Aversa, R., Martino, B.D., Fortis, T.F., Munteanu, V.I.: An analysis of mosaic ontology for cloud resources annotation. In: IEEE Proc. of FedCSIS 2011 Conference, pp. 973–980 (2011)
22. Ghazel, M.: Formalizing a subset of ertms/etcs specifications for verification purposes. Transportation Research Part C: Emerging Technologies 42, 60–75 (2014)
23. Ayed, R.B., Collart-Dutilleul, S., Bon, P., Idani, A., Ledru, Y.: B formal validation of ERTMS/ETCS railway operating rules. In: Ait Ameur, Y., Schewe, K.-D. (eds.) ABZ 2014. LNCS, vol. 8477, pp. 124–129. Springer, Heidelberg (2014)
24. James, P., Moller, F., Nguyen, H., Roggenbach, M., Schneider, S., Treharne, H.: Techniques for modelling and verifying railway interlockings. International Journal on Software Tools for Technology Transfer, 1–27 (2014)
25. Moscato, F., Venticinque, S., Aversa, R., Di Martino, B.: Formal modeling and verification of real-time multi-agent systems: The REMM framework. In: Badica, C., Mangioni, G., Carchiolo, V., Burdescu, D. (eds.) Intelligent Distributed Computing, Systems and Applications. SCI, vol. 162, pp. 187–196. Springer, Berlin (2008)
26. Wooldridge, M.: Agent-based software engineering. In: IEE Proceedings on Software Engineering, pp. 26–37 (1997)
27. Amato, F., Casola, V., Mazzocca, N., Romano, S.: A semantic-based document processing framework: a security perspective. In: 2011 International Conference on Complex, Intelligent and Software Intensive Systems (CISIS), pp. 197–202. IEEE (2011)

28. Amato, F., Casola, V., Mazzocca, N., Romano, S.: A semantic approach for fine-grain access control of e-health documents. Logic Journal of IGPL 21(4), 692–701 (2013)
29. Amato, F., Casola, V., Mazzeo, A., Romano, S.: A semantic based methodology to classify and protect sensitive data in medical records. In: 2010 Sixth International Conference on Information Assurance and Security (IAS), pp. 240–246. IEEE (2010)
30. Mens, T., Gorp, P.V.: A taxonomy of model transformation. Electronic Notes in Theoretical Computer Science 152, 125–142 (2006); Proceedings of the International Workshop on Graph and Model Transformation (GraMoT 2005) (2005)
31. Bloomfield, R.: Fundamentals of european rail traffic management system-ertms. IET Standards (2006)
32. Ciccozzi, F., Sjodin, M.: Enhancing the generation of correct-by-construction code from design models for complex embedded systems. In: 2012 IEEE 17th Conference on Emerging Technologies Factory Automation (ETFA), pp. 1–4 (September 2012)
33. Altera: Quartus ii,
    http://www.altera.com/products/software/quartus-ii/about/
    qts-performance-productivity.html
34. Hirel, C., Sahner, R., Zang, X., Trivedi, K.S.: Reliability and performability modeling using SHARPE 2000. In: Haverkort, B.R., Bohnenkamp, H.C., Smith, C.U. (eds.) TOOLS 2000. LNCS, vol. 1786, pp. 345–349. Springer, Heidelberg (2000)
35. Červenka, R., Trenčanský, I., Calisti, M., Greenwood, D.P.A.: AML: Agent modeling language toward industry-grade agent-based modeling. In: Odell, J.J., Giorgini, P., Müller, J.P. (eds.) AOSE 2004. LNCS, vol. 3382, pp. 31–46. Springer, Heidelberg (2005)
36. Nicol, D., Sanders, W., Trivedi, K.: Model-based evaluation: from dependability to security. IEEE Transactions on Dependable and Secure Computing 1(1), 48–65 (2004)
37. Panesar-Walawege, R.K., Sabetzadeh, M., Briand, L.: Supporting the verification of compliance to safety standards via model-driven engineering: Approach, tool-support and empirical validation. Information and Software Technology 55(5), 836–864 (2013)

# Report on the Railway Use-Case of the Crystal Project: Objectives and Progress

Alexandre Ginisty[1], Frédérique Vallée[1],
Elie Soubiran[2], and Vidal-delmas Tchapet-Nya[2]

[1] All4tec, Massy 91300 France
{frederique.vallee,alexandre.ginisty}@all4tec.net
[2] IRT SystemX Integration Center Nano-Innov
Building N3 - 8, avenue de la Vauve
91120 Palaiseau, France
{elie.soubiran,vidal-delmas.tchapet-nya-ext}@transport.alstom.com

**Abstract.** This paper aims at describing the contribution of the technological brick Safety Architect to the CRYSTAL project. The goal of the CRYSTAL project is to provide a platform of interoperability between tools supporting all the steps constituting the lifecycle of a product.

Based on a railway use-case, the goal is to provide support for realization of safety analysis with All4tec tool Safety Architect (especially automating the filling of safety documents). The first steps have consisted in the automatic generation of FMEA. The automatic management of the Hazard Log through DOORS is currently in development, and the next steps will deal with the change management facilities.

**Keywords:** MBSA, Safety Architect, FMEA, Fault Tree, Interoperability.

## 1 CRYSTAL Project: CRitical sYSTem engineering AcceLeration

The overall project goal of CRYSTAL is to foster Europe's leading edge position in the design, development, and deployment of interoperable safety-critical embedded systems in particular regarding quality, cost effectiveness, flexibility, reusability, acceleration of time to market, continuous integration of innovations, and sustainability.

CRYSTAL gathers and connects the main European players regarding embedded systems engineering in the areas of Aerospace (onboard and ground systems), Automotive (onboard systems and parts of the roadside infrastructure), Rail (onboard and interlocking systems), and Healthcare(patient and hospital staff safety, new medical procedures, medical apparatus) providing a critical mass of European technology providers to achieve both societal impact regarding future safer transport and Healthcare and technological advances in terms of cross domain platform-based reusability.

A. Bondavalli et al. (Eds.): SAFECOMP 2014 Workshops, LNCS 8696, pp. 130–136, 2014.
© Springer International Publishing Switzerland 2014

CRYSTAL wants to have a significant impact to strengthen European competitiveness, increase the efficiency of the embedded software development in the industry and allow the emergence of new markets and societal applications. The primary objective of CRYSTAL is to increase the maturity, reusability, and the ease of integration of technology bricks – which are defined as building blocks of integrated tool chains including e.g. software components, specific tools, engineering methods, interfaces, or even standards – and to demonstrate their impact through both domain and cross-domain environments.

CRYSTAL will exploit domain-specific insights into embedded system design and safety processes to investigate and establish cross-domain synergies. Consequently, currently fragmented research results will be integrated into a harmonized framework for safety-critical systems development. This will build on and extend existing domain-specific and domain-independent standards.

## 2    Case-Study: MBSE-MBSA Interaction in the Development of a Signalling System

### Description

The use-case is oriented on the development of a signalling system and more precisely on interactions that take place between safety and system design teams including transverse activities such as requirement management and traceability, and change management.

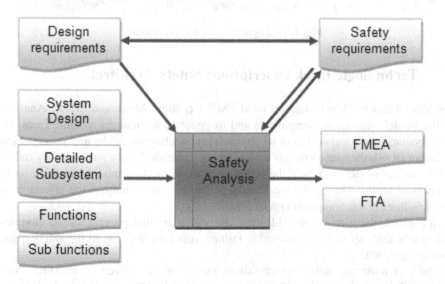

**Fig. 1.** Safety Analysis workflow

The applicative case-study that supports the evaluation of the methodology and its associated tools is a system function called "Compute traction orders". While being limited to one single system function, this case-study is representative of the system since it contains both critical and non-critical sub-functions and considers both real-time and operational constraints. The use-case will allow to structure and strengthen the development platform and framework of such systems, especially in the scope of multi-viewpoint system modelling (e.g. operational, functional, constructional, dysfunctional...). A simplified view of interoperability needs between system model, safety analysis and requirement management is represented in the following workflow:

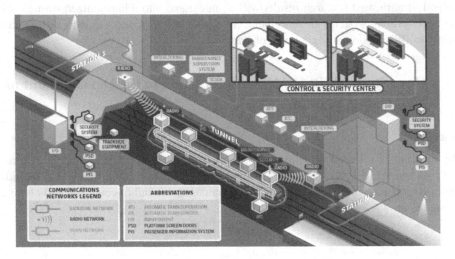

**Fig. 2.** Description of the CBTC system

## 3      Technologic Brick Description: Safety Architect

The aim of this brick is to support local FMEA (Failure Mode and Effects Analysis) on the model elementary components and to generate automatically Fault Trees. Using a system functional design or its physical architecture model by any interoperability mean (IOS), the user performs a local analysis inside Safety Architect, by linking failure modes of the outputs of the components to the failure modes identified on the component inputs. During the local analysis, the user also analyses the effects of internal failures of the component on its outputs.

In parallel, the user can also identify safety barriers that prevent the development of a single fault up to an unacceptable failure, participating thus to the safety objectives compliance.

The user must also define which failure modes are the feared events (FE). These events will be studied by the global analysis provided by the tool Safety Architect. A dysfunctional simulation of the system is then executed by propagating failures along the dataflow dependencies of components and until a feared event is reached.

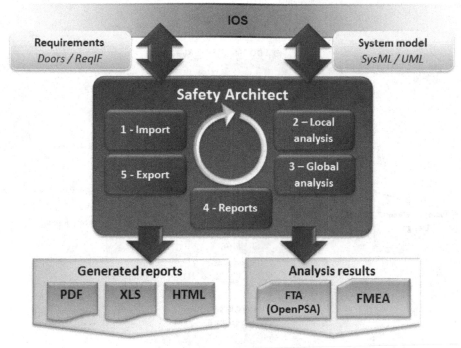

**Fig. 3.** Safety Architect Workflow

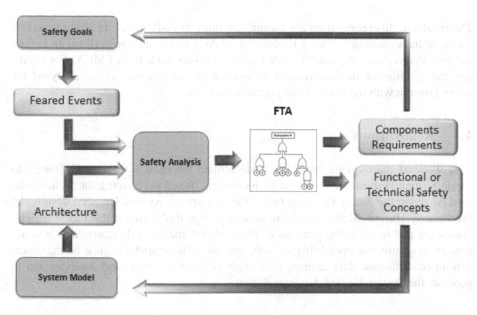

**Fig. 4.** Data model: Engineering loop

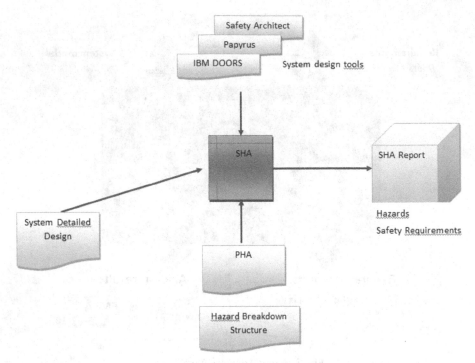

**Fig. 5.** SHA needs for interoperability

The results of this propagation are formulated through Fault Trees. In case of modification of the system or software model, Safety Architect is able to perform an impact analysis that reduces the rework costs that can be very high for a FMEA. For example, the addition or modification of a function or component can be analysed for safety concern with the reuse of the previous analysis.

## 4      Realizations

First work on the use-case has been made around the need for Safety Engineers to create System Hazard Analysis (SHA) documents. When performing the System Hazard Analysis, the Safety Engineer takes into account the System Detailed design, the Preliminary Hazard Analysis[1] and the system design tools. Given the fact that SHA makes use and traces heterogeneous elements that come from these artefacts it is necessary to ensure interoperability of tools and data. These artifacts must be interoperable in order to ease data exchange, to improve the System Hazard Analysis and to generate the System Hazard Analysis Report.

---

[1] The preliminary hazard analysis is performed by a consequence to cause analysis and describes exhaustively the accident scenario.

In term of interoperability needs, the following information is required:

- Traceability Relationships between the safety requirements and the systems
- Traceability Relationships between the system functions and theirs failure modes
- Traceability Relationships between the safety requirements and the failure modes they mitigate
- Traceability Relationships between the safety requirements and the system requirements in order to update and improve system requirements
- Traceability matrix of all failure modes to failure causes and failure effects

Starting from a functional architecture model, Safety Engineers are performing local analysis using Safety Architect, consisting in linking failure modes of inputs of a block to failure modes in outputs. Safety Engineers have also to create a feared event library (or reuse a previous one, for an analysis in the same domain for example). After putting feared events from the library to the failure modes in the model, they can export their work to generate automatically FMEA documents.

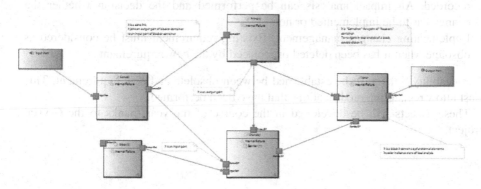

**Fig. 6.** Example of Safety Architect view

| | ID | System function | Function | Failure mode | RRF | Mode | Option | Cause | Effect | Potential accident |
|---|---|---|---|---|---|---|---|---|---|---|
| 1 | ⊟(Recovery) | Recovery | | | | | | | | |
| 2 | System Failure | | | System Failure | NONE | | | | | |
| 3 | ⊟(Recovery) | Recovery | | | | | | | | |
| 4 | ⊟(Recovery::Sensor) | | Sensor | | | | | | | |
| 5 | Internal Failure | | | Internal Failure | NONE | | | | | |
| 6 | ⊟(Recovery::Sensor) -> [SensorDF] | | | | | | | | | |
| 7 | (Recovery::Sensor)->[SensorDF](A) | | | A | NONE | | | | | |
| 8 | (Recovery::Sensor)->[SensorDF](U) | | | U | NONE | | | | | |
| 9 | (Recovery::Sensor)->[SensorDF](E) | | | E | NONE | | | | | |
| 10 | ⊟(Recovery::Sensor) -> [Input Port] | | | | | | | | | |
| 11 | (Recovery::Sensor)->[Input Port](A) | | | A | NONE | | | | | |
| 12 | (Recovery::Sensor)->[Input Port](U) | | | U | NONE | | | | | |
| 13 | (Recovery::Sensor)->[Input Port](E) | | | E | NONE | | | | | |
| 14 | ⊟(Recovery::Primary) | | Primary | | | | | | | |
| 15 | Internal Failure | | | Internal Failure | NONE | | | | | |

**Fig. 7.** Example of generated FMEA for a generic system. Includes the functions/components, the ports, the failure modes concerned, the cause, effect and potential accident of a failure mode, and some specific properties (Risk Reduction Factor, Mode, etc.)

## 5    Ongoing Work

The work achieved on the case-study has demonstrated that Safety Architect was suitable to capture a dysfunctional specification and to generate FT or FMEA. The next challenge is to integrate SA in a complex engineering environment that gathers change management tools, configuration tools, quality tools etc… Indeed, considering traceability needs, the tool that ensures safety analysis has to manage the evolution of system architecture and configuration as well as requirements evolution. We require configuration management in order to control changes throughout the system life-cycle. So we can evaluate changes before they are approved. We need to control product releases and updates, to record and report components status, to manage the process execution and its tools. Configuration management must facilitate team work. It can also manage revision of requirements through version control.

Requirements change management activities include:

- Analyzing changes management: Any change request must be documented and recorded. An impact analysis can be performed and the decision whether the change has to be implemented or not.
- Implementing changes management: Existing requirement must be considered as obsolete when it has been deleted or replaced by the new requirement.

A traceability links must be established between obsolete and new requirement. This must allow registering modifications that have been performed.

These aspects will be developed in the course of the year thanks to the Crystal project.

# Contract-Based Analysis for Verification
# of Communication-Based Train Control (CBTC) System

Marco Carloni[1], Orlando Ferrante[1], Alberto Ferrari[1],
Gianpaolo Massaroli[2], Antonio Orazzo[2], Ida Petrone[2], and Luigi Velardi[2]

[1] Advanced Laboratory on Embedded Systems, via Barberini, 50, Rome, Italy
[2] Ansaldo Signalling and Transportation Solutions, via Argine, 425, Naples, Italy
{marco.carloni,orlando.ferrante,alberto.ferrari}@ales.eu.com,
{gianpaolo.massaroli.prof644,antonio.orazzo,
ida.petrone.prof423,luigi.velardi}@ansaldo-sts.com

**Abstract.** In this paper we apply the contract theory to the analysis of the door control functionality in a metro train. The system under development is specified and modeled by rail domain experts. Contract theory is used to formalize some safety requirements that can be then automatically analyzed by our developed tool suite, Formal Specs Verifier (FSV). The produced work that derives by working with and on FSV represents a good starting point for matching the industrial needs in the field of system analysis and testing and for the definition of new analysis methods that provides indications on how to efficiently reduce the effort of making an exhaustive testing.

**Keywords:** requirement engineering, model-based design, contract theory, semi-formal verification, model checking.

## 1    Introduction

In requirements engineering the need to fix the specification of the system under design through the adoption of an unambiguous language is paramount. This goal improves both automation, i.e. the minimization of the human intervention in the development process of services and/or goods, and traceability, i.e. the connection of models, tests, and analyses with requirement definitions to help manage changes and reduce waste in the design flow.

The main contribution of this work is the application of Contract-Based Design for the analysis of a part of the on-board sub-system of the Ansaldo STS CBTC System, which commands the passengers' doors of a metro train. This analysis is performed as part of the MBAT European Project (2011-2014) that aims at exploiting synergies between formal analysis and testing for the verification and validation (V&V) of embedded systems. We use ALES tool suite Formal Specs Verifier [1] to model the requirements as contracts and to perform automatic analyses that formally verify the contracts against the model. The interesting results we get give us the right stimulus to progress this activity on the implementation of new techniques for reducing the effort of V&V of complex systems.

A. Bondavalli et al. (Eds.): SAFECOMP 2014 Workshops, LNCS 8696, pp. 137–146, 2014.

The paper is organized as follows: in section 2 the railway use case is presented. Section 3 shortly describes the developed technology conforms to the applied Contract-based Analysis principles. In section 4 the activities of requirements formalization, modelling, and analyses are illustrated. Finally, section 5 summarizes the performed activity and outlines the future steps.

## 2     The Use Case Under Investigation

As said before, the use case provided by ASTS (Ansaldo STS) derives from CBTC, an automatic innovative system for the management of railway traffic in an urban area. It is particularly used for metropolitan projects with the aim to overcome the limitations of conventional fixed-block systems optimizing the transportation levels and ensuring safety and shortest headways in the newest Rapid Transit Metro systems.

CBTC technology ensures that the trains stop at the right position at the stations, open and close the doors, leave the stations, keep the correct speed and the secure distance between them, and so on, by means of systems integrated in the trains, on the tracks, on the stations and in the control room, which have the capability to exchange real-time data in continuous way.

The correct integration of these different sub-systems and the consequent proper operation of the final system in compliance with the given requirements, involves deep and extensive activities of analysis and testing on the CBTC functions. Due to the high costs of the traditional development process, in this work we adopt the new tools and methods to reduce the effort through the combination of analysis and testing techniques developed in MBAT project and described in the next sections.

## 3     The Formal Specs Verifier (FSV) Tool-Suite

ALES laboratory has recently implemented the Formal Specs Verifier (FSV) tool-suite to support Contract-based Design (CBD) for analysis and testing. CBD methodology was proposed in [2], [3], [4] to facilitate the development of the work among different design groups. The contract definition relies on the concept of system/component interface in a component-based model. A system/component is a hierarchical entity that represents a unit of design and components are interconnected and communicate through ports carrying discrete or event values. The interface of a system/component is defined by its ports. Moreover, implementations and requirements can be attached to components. Requirements are expressed as contracts. Finally, a contract formalizes expectations between the system/component and its environment. In this context, the models are "rich" - not only profiles, types, or taxonomy of data, but also models describing the functions, performances of various kinds (time and energy), and safety[5].

FSV is presently capable of automatically processing a Matlab Simulink model file producing an internal representation for execution of formal verification and test generation. In this work we exploit two specific tools of the suite: the BCL toolbox and the Formal Verification tool.

## 3.1    FSV-BCL Toolbox

The FSV-BCL toolbox is a Simulink library implementation of the Block-based Contract Language (BCL), a ALES proprietary language for requirement formalization [6], that we developed during the evolution of this activity. This toolbox is a graphical editor built to assist the engineers in tackling the complexity of requirement formalization by providing a library of patterns to univocally define requirements.

## 3.2    FSV-Formal Verification

The analysis execution, performed by FSV-Formal Verification, allows for checking the satisfaction relation using formal verification by the implementation of the model checking technique [1]. The implementation of this technique is sketched in Figure 1. The implementation provides different method engines according to the designer needs.

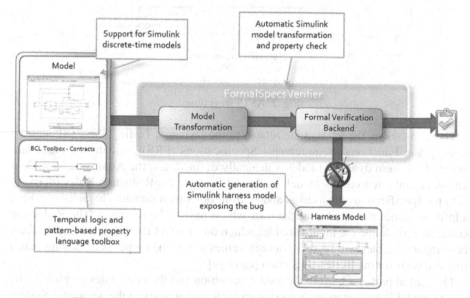

**Fig. 1.** FSV - Formal Verification, model checking implementation

Basically, FSV-Formal Verification takes as inputs a model of the system and a description of the requirement specification, i.e. the desirable behavior, provided by the FSV-BCL tool. Once the designer has selected the contract to be verified, FSV-Formal Verification automatically checks if this contract is not violated. If an error is recognized the tool provides an executable counter-example, technically named harness model, showing that the model behaves in an undesired way when stimulated by a particular input trace produced by the tool. Thus the harness model provides evidence that the model is faulty and needs to be revised. If no errors are found, the model description can be refined by taking new design decisions that make the model more concrete and the verification process can be restarted.

# 4    Modeling, Requirements Formalization, and Analysis

Figure 2 depicts the ASTS workflow for combination of Analysis & Testing (A&T) [7]. The workflow is composed of three main parts.

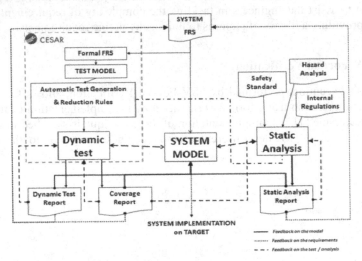

**Fig. 2.** ASTS workflow

The elements on the left part are related to the Dynamic Testing phase [8]: starting from system Functional Requirements Specifications (FRS), written in natural language, the system dynamic model is manually defined, and the Automatic Test Generation is calibrated on this model. In the ATG phase the Reduction Rules (deriving from the specifications themselves and/or from one's own domain characteristics) are helpful to reduce the number of the tests which have to be executed. The Reduction Rules, indeed, define the input variables which don't affect the output ones; therefore, these input variables will be set to default values to test the output ones, saving hence time and costs during the test execution phase [9].

The central part is related to the model definition and the system design phases: the system model is built starting from system FRS, and it leads to the automatic System Implementation on Target.

The right part concerns the Contract-based Analysis we perform in this work on the system model, aiming, through the exploitation of synergies with the dynamic testing phase (which are described hereinafter), to achieve a more efficient workflow in terms of number of discovered errors and effort spent to perform the V&V activities [10] [11].

## 4.1    System Modeling

The system function under investigation is the implementation of an on-board functionality of the ASTS CBTC system. The role of this function is to manage the set of actions related to the opening and the closing of the train doors for safe passenger transfer. This includes: 1) ensuring that the train is stopped and correctly aligned at the platform; 2) the safe immobilization of the train during the passenger exchange; 3) the safe management of the opening and the closing of the train doors and 4) the safe departure of the train when the train doors are closed and locked. Following a component-based methodology, the system behavior (architecture and functionality) is modeled using the MATLAB Simulink/Stateflow software [12].

## 4.2    Requirements Formalization

The requirements taken into account are specified in natural language and classified in 2 categories: safety (Table 1) and reachability (Table 2). For space limitations only one contract for each category is presented. In applying the contract formalization, the first step consists in finding out the signals included in each requirement; signal labels are included in brackets after the relevant text object in Table 1. The second step is to map each requirement, according to the signals, to a specific system component or to the system itself that has those signals entering to its ports. Next, from the point of view of the system/component, the assumptions on the input signals are defined and the promises on the signals are set with respect to the related requirement and by using a formal notation. Table 3 and Table 4 show the requirements translated in the contract formalization.

**Table 1.** Safety

| Req. ID | Natural Language Description |
|---|---|
| RS01 | if train's polarity (TP_train_polarity) is positive, the right platform side is not to be opened at some point while that train is at that platform (current_platform_side), and the driver has commanded the doors on the right side of the train to open (driver_door_open_rqst_right) then it never happens that the check of the manual door selection (manual_door_selection_error) won't be failed. |

**Table 2.** Reachability

| Req. ID | Natural Language Description |
|---|---|
| RR01 | During the life of the system there must exist a combination of values for the inputs signals that produces the following output combination: both the check of the manual door open right selection (manual_door_open_right_selection_error) fails and the check of the manual door open left selection (manual_door_open_left_selection_error) fails. |

**Table 3.** Safety Contract

| Contract ID | | Formal Language Description |
|---|---|---|
| CS01 | ASSS01 | TP_train_polarity in {"positive","negative","unspecified"} && current_platform_side in {"left","right","left_then_right", right_then_left","none"} |
| | PRMS01 | (TP_train_polarity = "positive") && (current_platform_side = "left") && (driver_door_open_rqst_right = TRUE) → !(!manual_door_selection_error) |

**Table 4.** Reachability Contract

| Contract ID | | Formal Language Description |
|---|---|---|
| CR01 | ASSR01 | TP_train_polarity in {"positive","negative","unspecified"} && current_platform_side in {"left","right","left_then_right", "right_then_left","none"} && platform_tp_line_direction in {"TRUE", "FALSE"} |
| | PRMR01 | F((manual_door_open_right_selection_error) && (manual_door_open_left_selection_error)) |

The formal notation is suitable for a machine going to process the contracts, as FSV-Formal Verification, but it does not result really "polite" to the engineer that has to formalize the requirements. This is the main reason to motivate the ALES engineer to implement the graphical editor of the BCL. By using the FSV-BCL toolbox, developed for the Simulink environment, the contracts are graphically modeled enriching the functional model of the system. Figure 3 shows the FSV-BCL model of the safety contract CS01: system inputs are colored in green while system outputs are colored in red. For CS01 there are 3 system inputs and 1 system output. All these signals are inputs for the contract. By exploiting the pattern blocks for the specification of the contracts, provided by the BCL toolbox, we rapidly build the logic describing the assumption and the promise of CS01. Finally, the "P" block allows us fixing the final logic value we expect to be kept during the analysis. Following the BCL guidelines, we repeat the model construction for all the contracts we are going to analyze.

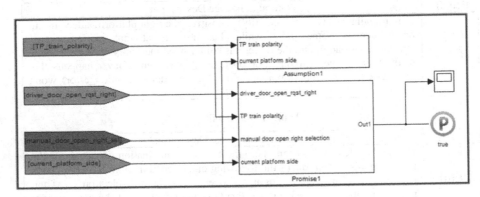

**Fig. 3.** Safety Contract (CS01)

### 4.3    Contract-Based Analysis

FSV supports a rich subset of the language constructs provided by Simulink and STATEFLOW software. Therefore, we use the FSV-Formal Verification tool to process the overall Simulink schematic (system model and contracts) and perform the following Contract-based Analyses: 1) safety analysis; 2) coverage analysis. The results of the analyses consist in a text report showing if the contract is verified or violated. The evidence of a contract violation is eventually provided by a simulation trace through the generation of an executable Simulink test harness model.

**Safety Analysis.** The safety analysis aims to ensure that the hazardous scenarios listed in Table 1 will never occur. An example of hazard identified in the ASTS system is the case of a driver which attempts to manually open the doors on the wrong side of the train: the platform is on the left of the train current direction, but the driver tries to open the right side doors. This situation can cause serious injuries to the passengers like traumas and fulguration (if the train line is electrified). To avoid these bad situations, the system has to be explored in order to detect the hazardous states/combination of hazardous conditions. If the exploration is complete on the state space, it is possible to demonstrate that the hazardous scenario is not reachable; otherwise, if the dangerous situation is reached, the analysis indicates the erroneous design of the system and/or the erroneous definition of requirements. On the contrary, when the exploration is not complete, it is possible to state that the unwanted scenario could not occur with a certain value of probability [13]. In the performed safety analysis, the contracts declare in their promises that some situation will never happen. Therefore, each contract will be never violated if the relative system states will be unreachable. The screenshot of Figure 4 shows the output of FSV that states that the promise of contract CS01 is verified (VERIF. STATUS=TRUE).

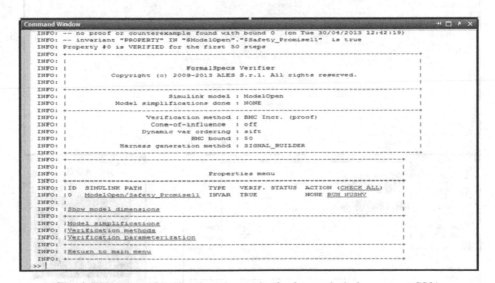

**Fig. 4.** FSV-Formal Verification: the result of safety analysis for contract CS01

**Coverage Analysis.** The coverage analysis provides a measure of the states/parts of the system not stimulated by the test set. As a consequence, the combination of this result with static analysis allows justifying the not covered branches of the model. We applied the static analysis with contracts in carrying out this operation. In particular, as shown in Figure 5, starting from the not covered branches, the FSV-Formal Verification can provide two results: 1) The state is reachable. This implies that the corresponding test case is missing. Through the counter-example provided by the analysis

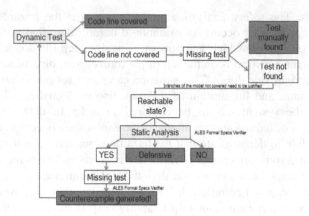

**Fig. 5.** Coverage Analysis: an A&T technique

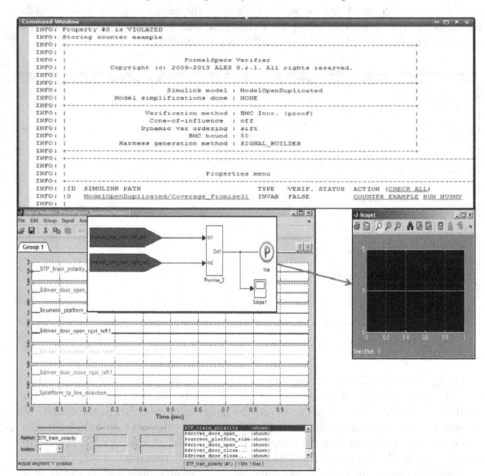

**Fig. 6.** FSV-Formal Verification: test harness generation and execution for the coverage analysis of contract CR01

tool, it's possible to achieve a feedback between analysis and testing phases, i.e. the test to include in the dynamic analysis phase itself or 2) the state is not-reachable. This last condition has to be justified by the user. The possible explanations are two. The state is effectively not-reachable (similar to "dead code"), likely due to the modifications occurred during the system development phases. This state has to be deleted or the state is a "defensive state" and it has been intentionally added in order to be not-reachable in correspondence of any input combination (mandatory for SIL4). The coverage analysis was executed for the contract in Table 4 must happen at least one time during the system lifetime. Even in this case, we can use FSV to explore that this liveness property occurs: we negate the requirement and we find that the negated property is violated. Therefore, the produced counter-example gives the sequence of input values that leads to the reachability of the required condition that thus results covered.

Figure 6 collects some images of the FSV processing for this coverage analysis: in the upper image the result of the negated contract violation is shown, on the left the model of the negated contract and the input traces for the test harness are illustrated, and, finally, on the right side the simulation output produced by the Simulink test harness is visualized in the moment when the property fails. In this case, since the contract was defined on a combinatorial part of the system, the desired result, i.e. the false condition, is obtained in the first step of the simulation.

## 5    Conclusion and Future Work

In this work, we applied the contract-based design methodology for analyzing the model of the Ansaldo STS CBTC System. The safety and coverage requirements were formalized as contracts to be processed by FSV, a tool suite we are developing for the verification of the embedded systems. FSV aided us to automatically verify the contracts against the modeled system through the satisfaction relation checking technique. In order to reduce the overall effort of complex systems design, we plan to extend our work on the following three main axes: methodology refinement, analysis testing tool suite improvement, enlargement of the set of analyses to perform through the implementation of other interesting analyses based on the definition of new categories of identified requirements.

**Acknowledgements.** The research leading to these results was partially funded by the EU ARTEMIS Joint Undertaking under grant agreement no. 269335 (project MBAT) and the Italian Ministry of Education, University and Research (MIUR).

## References

1. Ferrante, O., Benvenuti, L., Mangeruca, L., Sofronis, C., Ferrari, A.: Parallel NuSMV: A NuSMV Extension for the Verification of Complex Embedded Systems. In: Ortmeier, F., Daniel, P. (eds.) SAFECOMP 2012 Workshops. LNCS, vol. 7613, pp. 409–416. Springer, Heidelberg (2012)

2. Benveniste, A., Caillaud, B., Passerone, R.: Multi-viewpoint state machines for rich component models. In: Model-Based Design for Embedded Systems. CRC Press (November 2009)

3. Benvenuti, L., Ferrari, A., Mangeruca, L., Mazzi, E., Passerone, R., Sofronis, C.: A contract-based formalism for the specification of heterogeneous systems. In: Forum on Specification & Design Languages (FDL 2008) (September 2008)

4. Mangeruca, L., Ferrante, O., Ferrari, A.: Formalization and completeness of evolving requirements using Contracts. In: 2013 8th IEEE International Symposium on Industrial Embedded Systems, SIES (2013)

5. Benveniste, A., Caillaud, B., Nickovic, D., Passerone, R., Raclet, J.-B., Reinkemeier, P., Sangiovanni-Vincentelli, A., Damm, W., Henzinger, T., Larsen, K.: Contracts for System Design (2012)

6. Ferrante, O., Passerone, R., Ferrari, A., Mangeruca, L., Sofronis, C., D'Angelo, M.: Monitor-Based Run-Time Contract Verification of Distributed Systems. In: 9th IEEE International Symposium on Industrial Embedded Systems, SIES, Pisa (2014)

7. Marrone, S., Nardone, R., Orazzo, A., Petrone, I., Velardi, L.: Improving Verification Process in Driverless Metro Systems: The MBAT Project. In: Margaria, T., Steffen, B. (eds.) ISoLA 2012, Part II. LNCS, vol. 7610, pp. 231–245. Springer, Heidelberg (2012)

8. CESAR: CESAR Project, Cost-efficient methods and processes for safety relevant embedded systems, http://www.cesarproject.eu/ (accessed 2012)

9. Bonifacio, G., Marmo, P., Orazzo, A., Petrone, I., Velardi, L., Venticinque, A.: Improvement of Processes and Methods in Testing Activities for Safety-Critical Embedded Systems. In: Flammini, F., Bologna, S., Vittorini, V. (eds.) SAFECOMP 2011. LNCS, vol. 6894, pp. 369–382. Springer, Heidelberg (2011)

10. De Nicola, G., di Tommaso, P., Rosaria, E., Francesco, F., Pietro, M., Antonio, O.: A Grey-Box Approach to the Functional Testing of Complex Automatic Train Protection Systems. In: Dal Cin, M., Kaâniche, M., Pataricza, A. (eds.) EDCC 2005. LNCS, vol. 3463, pp. 305–317. Springer, Heidelberg (2005)

11. De Nicola, G., di Tommaso, P., Esposito, R., Flammini, F., Marmo, P., Orazzo, A.: ERTMS/ETCS: Working Principles and Validation. In: Proceedings of the International Conference on Ship Propulsion and Railway Traction Systems, SPRTS 2005, Bologna, Italy, pp. 59–68 (2005)

12. MathWorks In: Simulink - Simulation and Model-Based Design, http://www.mathworks.com/products/simulink

13. di Tommaso, P., Esposito, R., Marmo, P., Orazzo, A.: Hazard Analysis of Complex Distributed Railway Systems. In: Proc. of International Symposium on Reliable Distributed Systems, SRDS 2003, Florence, Italy, pp. 283–292 (2003)

# An Interoperable Testing Environment for ERTMS/ETCS Control Systems

Gregorio Barberio[1], Beniamino Di Martino[2], Nicola Mazzocca[3], Luigi Velardi[4],
Aniello Amato[1], Renato De Guglielmo[4], Ugo Gentile[3], Stefano Marrone[5],
Roberto Nardone[3], Adriano Peron[3], and Valeria Vittorini[3]

[1] MATE Consulting s.r.l., Salerno, Italy
{g.barberio,a.amato}@tabit.it
[2] Seconda Università di Napoli, DIII, Aversa, Italy
beniamino.dimartino@unina2.it
[3] Università di Napoli "Federico II", DIETI, Napoli, Italy
{nicola.mazzocca,ugo.gentile,roberto.nardone,
adrperon,valeria.vittorini}@unina.it
[4] AnsaldoSTS, Napoli, Italy
{Luigi.Velardi,Renato.DeGuglielmo}@ansaldo-sts.com
[5] Seconda Università di Napoli, DMF, Caserta, Italy
stefano.marrone@unina2.it

**Abstract.** Verification of functional requirements of critical control systems requires a hard testing activity regulated by international standards. As testing often forms more than fifty percent of the total development cost, to support the verification processes by automated solutions is a key factor for achieving lower effort and costs and reducing time to market. The ultimate goal of the ongoing work here described is the development of an interoperable testing environment supporting the *system level testing* of railway ERTMS/ETCS control systems. The testing environment will provide a standardized interface to enable the integration testing between sub-systems developed by different companies/suppliers. We present the first outcomes obtained within the ARTEMIS project CRYSTAL which tackles the challenge to establish and push forward an Interoperability Specification (IOS) as an open European standard for the development of safety-critical embedded systems.

**Keywords:** Functional Testing, Railway Control System, Model-Based System Testing, Model Driven Engineering, Test Case Generation.

## 1 The RBC Use Case within the Crystal Project

The ARTEMIS Joint Undertaking project CRYSTAL (CRitical sYSTem engineering AcceLeration) [2] takes up the challenge to establish and push forward an Interoperability Specification (IOS) and a Reference Technology Platform (RTP) as a European standard for safety critical systems. CRYSTAL is strongly industry-oriented and will provide ready-to-use integrated *tool chains* having a mature technology-readiness-level. To achieve technical innovations ("technology

A. Bondavalli et al. (Eds.): SAFECOMP 2014 Workshops, LNCS 8696, pp. 147–156, 2014.
© Springer International Publishing Switzerland 2014

*bricks*"), CRYSTAL adopts a user-driven approach based on applying engineering methods to industrially relevant *Use Cases* from the automotive, aerospace, rail and health-care sectors [15] and *increases the maturity of existing concepts* developed in previous European and national projects like CESAR [1], iFEST [3], MBAT [4]. The work described in this paper was born in the rail domain, and specifically from the needs expressed by Ansaldo STS (ASTS), an international transportation leader in the field of signalling and integrated transport systems for passenger traffic (Railway/Mass Transit) and freight operation. The industry needs expressed by the ASTS's *Use Case* are oriented to improve the quality and the efficiency of existing Verification & Validation (V&V) processes. In fact, testing activities are time-consuming tasks whose efficiency is a primary issue in a global competitive market and whose quality can not be decreased due to the adherence to international standards.

The ASTS's Use Case is centred on the Radio Block Centre (RBC) system, a computer-based system whose aim is to control the movements of the set of trains on a track area under its supervision, in order to guarantee a safe inter-train distance according to the ERTMS/ETCS specifications. ERTMS/ETCS (European Rail Traffic Management System/European Train Control System) [16] is a standard for the interoperability of the European railway signalling systems ensuring both technological compatibility among trans-European railway networks and integration of the new signalling system with the existing national train interlocking systems. Each ERTMS/ETCS controlled track is usually divided into several sub-tracks, each of them is supervised by a single RBC in charge of *concurrently and continuously* controlling a number of connections with trains. The main objective of the train control system is to timely transmit to each train its up-to-date Movement Authority (MA) and the related speed profile. The MA contains information about the distance the train may safely cover, depending on the status of the forward track. RBC is also in charge of managing emergency situations if the communication with one or more trains is compromised.

In this context, this paper presents an interoperable testing environment supporting the *system level testing* of railway ERTMS/ETCS control systems being developed within CRYSTAL. The paper is organized as follows: Section 2 provides a bird-eye view of the testing environment and related technological bricks involved in the ASTS *Use Case*. The subsequent Sections contain more information about the state of development of each Brick: Section 3 addresses modelling and test case generation carried out in the *Rail Model* Brick; Section 4 and Section 5 describe the architecture of the *IOP Test Writer* and *Log Analyzer* Bricks, respectively. Finally Section 6 describes how the Bricks are integrated into the CRYSTAL RTP/IOS.

## 2    An Environment for ERTMS/ETCS Interoperable Testing

The user needs expressed by ASTS within the CRYSTAL project are oriented to the automation of the system level testing activities, and to the realisation of a tool chain providing full support to interoperable testing. In this Section the complete workflow of the automated testing process is described as well as the components of the tool chain and their relationships.

The proposed workflow complies with the ASTS *Use Case* requirements and will improve the current testing process, starting from the definition of the system specification to the generation of test reports. In detail, it enables semi-automatic generation of test cases from a set of test specifications, relying on a Model-Driven methodology. The generated test cases are then automatically transformed into executable test scripts, which can be executed on the real system or on simulation environments. Test logs are then analysed and test reports are automatically generated.

In Fig. 1 (a) the complete workflow is represented by an activity diagram, the tool chain and the involved technological bricks are described in Fig. 1 (b). The same figure also reports the links between each activity of the workflow and its supporting brick.

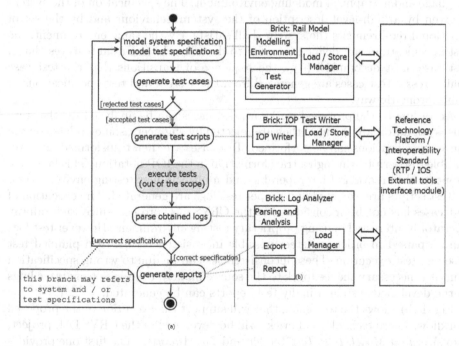

**Fig. 1.** CRYSTAL enhancements: the testing workflow (a) and the bricks implementing the tool chain (b)

With respect to the current process implemented in ASTS, this workflow introduces three main advantages:

- *automatic generation of test cases from test specification*: in the current process, adopted by ASTS, test cases are manually generated by domain experts which are able to control the high complexity of these systems. This activity is heavy and error prone, in addition the training of new testers is very expensive as they must have a great experience, that could be acquired only working on several different projects.

- *generation of test script in IOP notation*: due to the heterogeneity of simulation environments, system level testing requires an interoperable testing environment where different simulators can exchange information. The generation of test scripts in IOP notation, under development by UNISIG, allows for the execution of interoperable tests in a multi-suppliers environment.
- *tool supported analysis of test logs*: the decision about the outcomes of test cases is currently performed by inspecting big log files; the adoption of a tool which is able to parse generated logs reduces the efforts of navigating them and generating reports.

The first activity of the testing workflow is the realization of a system specification, performed manually by V&V engineers by using a proper modeling language and a graphical modeling environment. The specification of the system is given by a high-level description of the system behaviour and by the set of functional requirements the system shall satisfy. By the same environment, the test specifications are defined in order to describe the essential features that a test case must accomplish (e.g., the sequence of transitions that the test case shall stress). Test cases are generated from the system and test specifications in semi-automatic way.

According to the proposed workflow, test cases can be analyzed (at the state this is not automated) and, if they are rejected by engineers, some updates on the source specifications can be performed. Test cases are then transformed into executable test scripts, through a transformation in the IOP notation. This language supports the creation of interoperable and multi-supplier testing environments.

Test scripts are executed and proper test logs are generated. The execution of test cases has not been considered in the CRYSTAL project, since each railway operator is interested in using proprietary testing environment. However test logs can be parsed in order to detect possible inconsistencies between planned test case and test execution. These inconsistencies can be due to wrong specification (and it is necessary the feedback to the source model), otherwise they trace bugs in the developed system. Finally test reports can be generated.

Fig. 1 (b) shows the tool chain that will support the execution of the proposed workflow. Three technological bricks will be developed in the CRYSTAL project, they are: *Rail Model*, *IOP Test Writer* and *Log Analyzer*. The first one provides the modeling environment to describe the system and the test specifications, it is also able to generate test cases implementing the appropriate transformations to and from the specific model checker, as explained in the next Section. The second brick supports the generation of test scripts written in IOP Language (according to the concept of an interoperable testing environment). The last one is able to parse the test logs and to generate test reports from them. Some details about these technological bricks are given in the following Sections, as well as some technological hints.

# 3    Rail Model: Model-Based Test Sequences Generation

The inputs of the *Rail Model* brick are a formal state based specification of the system behaviour and of its requirements. From them, chains of model transformations allows to obtain Test Cases by applying model checking techniques. This approach is based on the previous experiences on extending UML with the V&V UML Profile [10,14]. The approach under development envisages a) the definition of a proper formal state-based language (DSTM4Rail) to be used for modeling the behaviour of the system under test and to formalize the requirements from which the test specifications are obtained; b) the implementation of the transformation chains in order to obtain the test cases; c) and the definition of a proper set of test specification patterns which will provide general reusable models for recurrent classes of requirements.

The CENELEC standards [6,7] explicitly recommend the usage of state-based formalisms, as the dynamic of critical control systems, based on a sequential computation, can be abstracted as a state-transition system. Despite the great number of works addressing the usage of state machine and their extensions, within CRYSTAL the railway industry expressed the need for a concise formal modeling notation, able to easily capture some characteristic features of the specific domain, to be used in model-driven test automation environments. In particular, at the state, ASTS keeps out the possibility of using several UML diagrams and prefers an ad-hoc formal language, developed from scratch, with the objective to be as simple as possible and as rich as needed for modeling the behaviour and the requirements of a railway control system for system testing purposes.

DSTM4Rail extends Hierarchical State Machines [5]. Its peculiarity mainly resides in the semantics of fork-and-join which allows dynamic (bounded) instantiation of machines (processes) and parallel execution of machines inside a box. Each state machine may be parametric over a finite set of dynamically evaluated parameters; in addition the same machine may be dynamically instantiated many times without explicitly replicating its entire structure.

DSTM4Rail also allows to model the requirements and add proper information to the behavioural models for implementing requirement traceability. ATL (Atlas Transformation Language) [13] is used to translate the DSTM4Rail model of the system to a NuSMV [8] or Promela [12] specification and the DSTM4Rail model of the requirement to verify into a CTL/LTL specification or into a Promela property (e.g., a never claim) which are added to the NuSMV or Promela model, respectively. Indeed, it is well known that test case generation may be obtained by using the ability of a model checker to construct counterexamples to violated properties: a counterexample defines the sequence of steps which are interpreted as a test case [11].

Fig. 2 shows a DSTM4Rail specification model of a particular functionality of RBC (i.e., *Management of the train movement* in the box) and its realization in the prototype modeling environment.

During the movement of the train, RBC periodically sends the Movement Authority (MA) to the train (Section 1). Concurrently, RBC has to monitor the

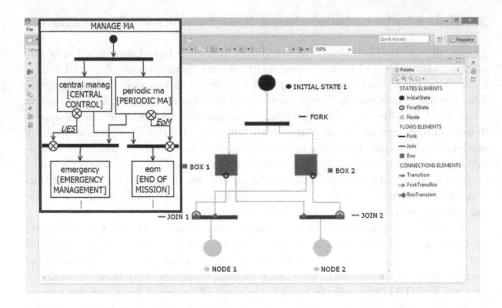

**Fig. 2.** A DSTM4Rail model and a tool screenshoot

commands that come from the Centralized Traffic Control (CTC) where a human operator may raise an alarm which requires the train to brake: in this case an Unconditional Emergency Stop (UES) message is sent to the train. On the other hand, when the train successfully ends its trip, it performs the End of Mission (EoM) procedure. This scenario needs for representing concurrently executing machines, one of whom may force the termination of the others. DSTM4Rail models this situation by a preemptive join, as shown in Fig. 2 where the processes CENTRAL CONTROL and PERIODIC MA are executed concurrently but, when the first machine reaches the UES exiting node, the join on the left forces with preemption the process PERIODIC MA to terminate. In this case the machine EMERGENCY MANAGEMENT is instantiated. On the contrary, if the process PERIODIC MA terminates in the EoM exiting node, the join on the right forces with preemption the CENTRAL CONTROL to terminate, and the END OF MISSION machine is instantiated.

*State of the development* : up to date a first and stable version of the DSTM4Rail formalism has been implemented, within the Eclipse Modelling Framework (EMF), by an Ecore metamodel. To represent DSTM4Rail in a user-friendly way, a graphical editor has been realized through functionalities provided by the Eclipse Graphical Modeling Framework (GMF). A screen shot of the graphical environment is shown in Fig. 2.

The implementation of the transformations is an ongoing activity. At the state, a set of test specification patterns has been also defined, based on the notion of Dwyers's property specification patterns [9].

## 4  IOP Test Writer

The *Rail Model* brick, described in Section 3, generates the sequence of the steps specifying the test case. These traces need to be translated into an concrete notation in order to be executed on simulated environments. Since ERTMS/ETCS based infrastructures are composed by different subsystems that can be supplied by different technology providers, the testing and simulation environments reflect this heterogeneity being a federation of different simulators developed by different teams. One of the requirements for a an interoperable testing environment is that each component must speak a common "testing" language. The IOP Notation is developed by the UNISIG (Union Industry of Signaling). Properly interpreted by vendor-specific adapters, IOP can support the creation of integrated testing environments. The aim of the IOP notation is not limited to simulated environments as it can be used to give commands and interpreting the states of real systems: the scenario depicted in the Fig. 3 exemplifies its usage in on-field testing.

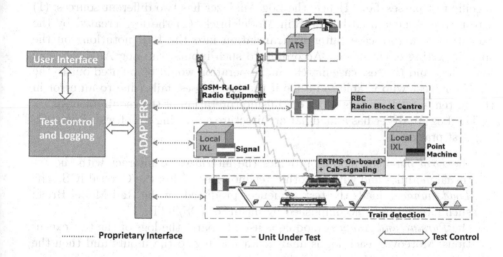

**Fig. 3.** IOP Test Writer

Since all the ERTMS technology providers are interested in increasing the level of interoperability of their products, ASTS is moving its testing tool set and environments to the IOP notation. According to this wish, the IOP Test Writer can extremely accelerate the test implementation phase by automatically generating the test scripts written in IOP language from the test cases created by Rail Model.

The IOP Test Writer tool will consists of two modules according to software engineering best practises: the *TestWriter* and the *Load/Store Manager*. Each module performs some specific tasks and shows a set of interfaces used to interact with the other module. More specifically:

- the *Load/Store manager* module provides the interfaces to interact with the external modules (for example the RailModel) and with the other technologies within the Crystal IOS. *Load/Store manager* module loads the test sequences produced by the Rail Model Brick and stores their results in the system: such interaction is accomplished by means of IOS/RTP;
- the *IOP Writer* module provides the transformation of the test cases expressed in a Ecore language to a test cases expressed in IOP notation by means of a Model-to-Text (M2T) transformation.

*State of the development:* up to date, the IOP Test Writer is in its design phase. The idea is to develop it in Java as an Eclipse plug-in to make the integration with the Rail Model brick easier.

## 5   Log Analyzer

The Log Analyzer brick aids the V&V engineer to state if the execution of a specific test passes/fails. Hence, the Log Analyzer has two different sources: (1) a test case as generated by the Rail Model brick, (2) the logs created by the execution of a test case (after its translation into the IOP notation) on the specific testing environment. According to such inputs, the Log Analyzer may find if logs and the test case match. Such operation would be pointed out to the V&V engineer who is able to decide if the test passes, fails (due to an error in the system model) or fails (due to a misinterpretation of the requirements).

The Log Analyzer has a modular architecture according to software engineering best practises:

- the *Load manager* module provides the interfaces to interact with the external modules and with the other technologies within the Crystal IOS. The *Load manager* loads the test sequences produced by the Rail Model Brick: such interaction is accomplished by means of IOS/RTP;
- the *Parsing and Analysis* module is used to parse the logs of the test executions. Moreover, each log is analyzed according to the inputs and then the fail/pass decision is taken for the single log.
- the *Report* module focuses on building up summary information about the entire testing campaign and in generating supporting tables for traceability, coverage, etc.;
- the *Export* module has the role to export the report of a testing campaign and the related execution logs. The target report will be conform to widespread document formats (e.g. pdf files or spreadsheets).

*State of the development:* up to date, the Log Analyzer is in its design phase. As it is not called automatically after the first two bricks, the design teams of this tool is evaluating the possibility to implement it as a stand-alone tool.

# 6   Integration in RTP/IOS

As shown in Figure 1, each Technology Brick interacts with an External Tool Interface module. This External Tool Interface module implements a custom solution for the integration of RailModel, IOP Test Writer and Log Analyzer or a flexible solution for a generic integration, based on the technologies available in Crystal Reference Technology Platform / Interoperability Specifications (RTP/IOS). The RTP is a generic platform for the integration of model-based tools. It is composed by a set of interoperable tools, methods and processes designed to increase the quality of development processes of safety critical embedded systems. This integration platform will host tools coming from different stakeholders (vendors, industrial & academic partners, etc.) that realise Bricks within the project. Therefore there is the need for a common non-proprietary standard to realise this interoperability functionality within the RTP.

The CRYSTAL IOS would accomplish this task by adopting the Open Services for Lifecycle Collaboration (OSLC), a framework that moves to the integration of data, workflows and processes among product lifecycles. OSLC is divided in several workgroups each of which addressing specific integration scenariosThe set of scenarios and specifications are named *OSLC Domain*. The presence of different domains introduces the necessity to manage the coherence among them. This need is satisfied by a set of standard rules and patterns, contained in the OSLC Core Specification, and all the domain groups must adopt these rules for the specifications. The union of a OSLC Core Specification and a OSLC Domain constitutes a OSLC protocol that is used in order to add interoperability to a specific tool chain, as in CRYSTAL. Some work packages in CRYSTAL are devoted to the study of existing standards and to the proposition of proper technological solutions in order to integrate the Technology Bricks with the RTP/IOS.

Here a brief description of how the tool chain presented in this paper will be integrated in the RTP/IOS is reported. According to the Fig. 1, the tool chain uses the RTP by loading/storing the artifacts generated during the process. Each brick interacts with the RTP/IOS via its Load/Store Manager. More specifically:

- Rail Model loads existing DSTM model of the system/test specification previously defined and stores DSTM models created with the Modelling Environment. The module may store test cases generated by the Test Generator module;
- IOP Test Writer loads existing test cases from the RTP/IOS. In addition it stores IOP compliant test cases generated by the IOP Writer;
- Log Analyzer loads existing test cases from the RTP/IOS. Both the logs of the test executions and the report are stored out of the RTP/IOS.

**Acknowledgments.** This paper is supported by research project CRYSTAL (Critical System Engineering Acceleration), funded from the ARTEMIS Joint Undertaking under grant agreement number 332830 and from ARTEMIS member states Austria, Belgium, Czech Republic, France, Germany, Italy, Netherlands, Spain, Sweden, United Kingdom.

# References

1. CESAR: Cost-Efficient methods and proceses for SAfety Relevant embedded systems, http://www.cesarproject.eu/
2. CRYSTAL: CRitical sYSTem engineering AcceLeration, http://www.crystal-artemis.eu/
3. iFEST: industrial Framework for Embedded Systems Tools, http://www.artemis-ifest.eu/
4. MBAT: Combined Model-based Analysis and Testing of Embedded Systems, http://www.mbat-artemis.eu/
5. Alur, R., Kannan, S., Yannakakis, M.: Communicating hierarchical state machines. In: Wiedermann, J., Van Emde Boas, P., Nielsen, M. (eds.) ICALP 1999. LNCS, vol. 1644, pp. 169–178. Springer, Heidelberg (1999)
6. CENELEC. Cenelec, en 50128: Railway applications - communication, signalling and processing systems - software for railway control and protection systems (2011)
7. CENELEC. Cenelec, en 50126: Railway applications - demonstration of reliability, availability, maintainability and safety (rams) - part 1: Generic rams process (2012)
8. Cimatti, A., Clarke, E., Giunchiglia, F., Roveri, M.: Nusmv: a new symbolic model checker. International Journal on Software Tools for Technology Transfer 2 (2000)
9. Dwyer, M.B., Avrunin, G.S., Corbett, J.C.: Patterns in property specifications for finite-state verification. In: Proceedings of the 21st International Conference on Software Engineering, ICSE 1999, pp. 411–420. ACM, New York (1999)
10. Flammini, F., Marrone, S., Mazzocca, N., Nardone, R., Vittorini, V.: Model-driven V&V processes for computer based control systems: A unifying perspective. In: Margaria, T., Steffen, B. (eds.) ISoLA 2012, Part II. LNCS, vol. 7610, pp. 190–204. Springer, Heidelberg (2012)
11. Gargantini, A., Heitmeyer, C.: Using model checking to generate tests from requirements specifications. SIGSOFT Softw. Eng. Notes 24(6), 146–162 (1999)
12. Holzmann, G.: Spin Model Checker, the: Primer and Reference Manual, 1st edn. Addison-Wesley Professional (2003)
13. Jouault, F., Kurtev, I.: Transforming models with ATL. In: Bruel, J.-M. (ed.) MoDELS 2005. LNCS, vol. 3844, pp. 128–138. Springer, Heidelberg (2006)
14. Marrone, S., Flammini, F., Mazzocca, N., Nardone, R., Vittorini, V.: Towards model-driven v&v assessment of railway control systems. International Journal on Software Tools for Technology Transfer, 1–15 (2014)
15. Pflügl, H., El-Salloum, C., Kundner, I.: CRYSTAL, CRitical sYSTem engineering AcceLeration, a Truly European Dimension. ARTEMIS Magazine 14, 12–15 (2013)
16. UIC. ERTMS/ETCS class1 system requirements specification, ref. SUBSET-026, issue 2.2.2 (2002)

# Modelling Resilient Systems-of-Systems
# in Event-B

Linas Laibinis[1], Inna Pereverzeva[1,2], and Elena Troubitsyna[1]

[1] Åbo Akademi University, Turku, Finland
[2] Turku Centre for Computer Science, Turku, Finland
{linas.laibinis,inna.pereverzeva,elena.troubitsyna}@abo.fi

**Abstract.** Ensuring resilience – the ability to remain dependable in dynamic environment – constitutes a major challenge for engineering systems-of-systems (SoS). In this paper, we take a mission-centric view on the behaviour of SoS and demonstrate how to formally reason about their dependability. We use Event-B as our modelling framework and demonstrate how to formally specify and verify generic system-wide dependability properties as well as the dynamic behaviour of SoS. The proposed approach is exemplified by a case study – a flight formation system. As a result, we argue that Event-B offers a scalable approach to formal modelling of SoS and facilitates engineering of resilient SoS.

**Keywords:** Systems-of-systems, formal modelling, Event-B, refinement.

## 1 Introduction

Systems-of-Systems (SoS) are characterised by high complexity, reconfigurability and adaptability. Usually a SoS consists of loosely coupled systems (we will further call them components) that interact with each other to achieve common goals [3]. Typically, the constituting systems autonomously decide on their actions to accomplish the desired collaborative behaviour. Since there is no centralised component that would orchestrate functioning of the constituting systems, ensuring resilience of SoS becomes especially challenging.

To address this problem, in this paper we propose a formal generic approach to modelling dependable SoS. We structure the behaviour of SoS in terms of missions – the collaborative actions of the SoS components working on achieving the required goals. In our modelling, we follow the systems approach and define the behaviour of the overall system and the relevant part of its environment within a common specification. This allows us to express and verify system-wide properties. By decomposing the obtained model of a SoS into the respective specifications of its components, we ensure that, despite their autonomy, the constituents will act in a dependability-preserving way.

We rely on the Event-B formalism and its associated Rodin platform to formally specify and verify behaviour of resilient SoS. Event-B [2] is a state-based framework that relies on abstract modelling, refinement, and theorem proving to create and verify specifications of complex systems. To create such a specification, the designers start with an abstract model that only captures the

A. Bondavalli et al. (Eds.): SAFECOMP 2014 Workshops, LNCS 8696, pp. 157–166, 2014.

most essential system behaviour and its properties. In a number of correctness-preserving steps – refinements, the abstract model is transformed into a detailed specification of the overall system. The resultant specification is further decomposed into specifications of the independent subsystems that are guaranteed to preserve the system-level properties through their interactions. The Rodin platform [9] automates the development and verification in Event-B.

In this paper, we propose a generic model of a resilient SoS and exemplify the proposed approach by its instantiation to a flight formation case study. Our generic development defines the methodology of specifying the behaviour and properties of a SoS without cluttering the reasoning with application-specific details. When applied to a particular system, the proposed generic pattern is instantiated and populated with application-specific details, as we demonstrate by the flight formation example. We believe that the formal system-level reasoning is essential for modelling resilient SoS and argue that Event-B constitutes a suitable basis for achieving this goal.

The paper is organised as follows. In Section 2 we give an overview of the Event-B formalism. In Section 3 we present our generic model of a resilient SoS derived by refinement in Event-B. In Section 4 we exemplify the proposed approach by a case study – a satellite flight formation. Finally, in Section 5 we present some concluding remarks and discuss the future work.

## 2    Modelling and Refinement in Event-B

Event-B is a state-based formal approach that promotes the correct-by-construction development paradigm and formal verification by theorem proving [2]. In Event-B, a system model is specified using the notion of an *abstract state machine*. An abstract state machine encapsulates the model state represented as a collection of variables, and defines operations on this state, i.e., it describes the *behaviour* of the modelled system. A machine usually has the accompanying component, called *context*. A context may include user-defined carrier sets, constants and their properties (model *axioms*). In Event-B, the model variables are strongly typed by the constraining predicates called *invariants*. Moreover, the invariants specify important properties that should be preserved during the system execution.

The dynamic behaviour of the system is defined by a set of atomic *events*. An event is essentially a *guarded command* that can be defined as follows:

$$\text{evt} \mathrel{\widehat{=}} \textbf{any } vl \textbf{ where } g \textbf{ then } S \textbf{ end}$$

where $vl$ is a list of new local variables, $g$ is the *guard*, and $S$ is the *action*. The guard is a state predicate that defines the conditions under which the action can be executed. In general, the action of an event is a parallel composition of deterministic or non-deterministic assignments.

Event-B employs a top-down *refinement-based* approach to system development. A development starts from an *abstract* system specification that nondeterministically models the most essential functional requirements. In a sequence of refinement steps, we gradually reduce non-determinism and introduce detailed design decisions. In particular, we can add new events, split events as well as replace abstract variables by their concrete counterparts, i.e., perform *data refinement*. When data refinement is performed, we should define so called *gluing invariant* as a part of the invariant of the refined machine. The gluing invariant defines the relationship between the abstract and concrete variables.

The Event-B refinement process allows us to gradually introduce implementation details, while preserving functional correctness. The consistency of Event-B models, e.g., invariant preservation, should be formally demonstrated by discharging the relevant proof obligations. The verification efforts, in particular, automatic generation and proving of the required proof obligations, are significantly facilitated by Event-B tool support – the Rodin platform [9].

There are several features of Event-B that make the framework an attractive option for modelling SoS. Firstly, abstraction allows us to define system-wide properties of complex systems and verify them over all execution traces. Secondly, refinement enables system modelling at different architectural layers. Furthermore, proofs in combination with refinement allow us to verify complex systems in a highly automated manner. Finally, a special form of refinement – decomposition – allows us to derive specifications of constituent systems in such a way that system-level properties would be preserved despite their autonomy. In the next section, we will demonstrate how to derive a generic specification of a SoS by refinement in Event-B.

## 3   Deriving a Generic Specification of a SoS

The aim of our development is to derive a detailed yet generic specification of resilient SoS. The resulting generic Event-B development can be applied (by formal instantiation) to a family of systems sharing similar traits. We cover a class of SoS that have the following characteristics:

- A SoS should accomplish a number of pre-defined missions;
- The current mission can be changed or restarted depending on the internal system state or changes in the system environment;
- Each mission has the associated *scenario* that contains a number of steps (phases), reaching the last of which indicates completion of the mission;
- SoS functioning can be disrupted by internal or external events (e.g., hardware or communication failures, adverse environment changes) that can put the SoS into an unsafe state. In that case, the SoS should react by switching to a degraded yet safe state (mode) of functioning;
- At different architectural levels the system behaviour is governed by the $SENSE \rightarrow PLAN \rightarrow ACT$ pattern, i.e., the system first senses the environment changes and/or its internal failures, then plans on how to react on those, and finally acts on its decisions either changing its course of actions of by continuing the current mission;
- A SoS consists of a number of constituent systems coordinating their activities to achieve the common mission. The coordination is achieved by inter-component communication to ensure that they are in the same mission and its phase, or that that they all are in the degraded state.

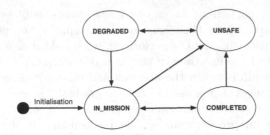

**Fig. 1.** System meta-states and their transitions

Next, we will outline our formal development of such a mission-oriented SoS in Event-B. We will start with a very abstract description of a SoS (consisting of a single event) and then unfold the system complexity by four refinement steps, gradually introducing the notions of missions and their scenarios, the system environment and communication, the cyclic behaviour pattern, and finally decomposing the SoS into its constituent systems.

**Abstract Model.** In the initial specification, we abstractly model the system state and state transitions. We partition the system state space into four groups (*meta-states*): IN_MISSION (i.e., the system is progressing towards the current mission), COMPLETED (i.e., the current mission is completed or in the last completing phase), UNSAFE (i.e., the system is disrupted by external or internal adverse events) and DEGRADED (i.e., the system is in a degraded yet safe state). The possible transitions between the meta-states are shown on Fig.1.

In the model context component, we introduce the abstract type $STATES$ and its partitioning into disjoint subsets $IN\_MISSION$, $COMPLETED$, $UNSAFE$, and $DEGRADED$. Moreover, we define the relation *Trans* modelling possible transitions between states. The allowed transitions depicted in Fig.1 are formulated as a number of axioms constraining *Trans*, as shown below:

```
axm7:  Trans ∈ STATES ↔ STATES
axm8:  ∀s·s ∈ IN_MISSION ⇒ Trans[{s}] = IN_MISSION ∪ COMPLETED ∪ UNSAFE
axm9:  ∀s·s ∈ COMPLETED ⇒ Trans[{s}] = IN_MISSION ∪ COMPLETED ∪ UNSAFE
axm10: ∀s·s ∈ UNSAFE ⇒ Trans[{s}] = UNSAFE ∪ DEGRADED
axm11: ∀s·s ∈ DEGRADED ⇒ Trans[{s}] = IN_MISSION ∪ UNSAFE ∪ DEGRADED
```

The dynamic system behaviour is represented by the single event ChangeState:

$$\text{ChangeState} \; \widehat{=} \; \textbf{begin} \; state :\in Trans[\{state\}] \; \textbf{end}$$

Here the variable $state \in STATES$ models the current system state. The event allows for nondeterministic state change, restricted only by the relation *Trans*. In our abstract specification, *Trans* imposes very loose constraints on possible state transitions. In the following refinements, we gradually unfold both SoS structure and its behaviour, constraining at the same time allowed state transitions.

**First Refinement.** In the first refinement step, we focus on the pre-defined system missions and their scenarios. In the model context, we introduce the abstract sets $MISSIONS$ and $PHASES$, as well as several abstract constants and functions interrelating system missions, scenarios, and phases.

$$
\begin{array}{l}
\text{axm6: } init\_mission \in MISSIONS \\
\text{axm7: } Scenarios \in MISSIONS \to (PHASES \leftrightarrow PHASES) \\
\text{axm9: } fnc \in MISSIONS \to (PHASES \leftrightarrow \mathbb{N}) \\
\text{axm10: } \forall m, ph1, ph2 \cdot (ph1 \mapsto ph2) \in Scenarios(m) \Rightarrow fnc(m)(ph2) < fnc(m)(ph1)
\end{array}
$$

Here the constant *init_mission* stands for the initial system mission, the function *Scenarios* formally relates each mission with some pre-defined chain of the mission phases. The function *fnc* is needed to guarantee that each such scenario is well-defined, i.e., there exists a decreasing measure (variant) for each scenario, therefore it cannot continue indefinitely and mission will be either accomplished or abandoned.

To model the dynamic behaviour of the SoS, we introduce new variables *mission*, *phase*, and *failure*, standing respectively for the current system mission, its current phase, and a detected failure. The abstract event ChangeState is now refined into a number of events specifying under what conditions the system may enter a particular meta-state or stay within it (e.g., see the events *Progressing* and *Completion* given below). Moreover, the introduced notions of SoS mission and scenario allow us to elaborate on the *IN_MISSION* meta-state as well as distinguish between the mission progressing and completing steps.

$$
\begin{array}{l}
\text{Progressing } \;\widehat{=}\; \text{refines ChangeState} \\
\quad \textbf{any } new\_ph \\
\quad \textbf{when } state \in IN\_MISSION \land failure = FALSE \land \\
\qquad (phase \mapsto new\_ph) \in Scenarios(mission) \\
\quad \textbf{then } \; state :\in IN\_MISSION \parallel phase := new\_ph \; \textbf{end} \\
\text{Completion } \;\widehat{=}\; \text{refines ChangeState} \\
\quad \textbf{when } state \in IN\_MISSION \cup COMPLETED \land failure = FALSE \land \\
\qquad \neg(\exists ph \cdot ph \in PHASES \land (phase \mapsto ph) \in Scenarios(mission)) \\
\quad \textbf{then } \; state :\in COMPLETE \; \textbf{end}
\end{array}
$$

Finally, we also add a new event ChangeMission allowing the system to non-deterministically change its current mission (if the system is not in the *UNSAFE* or *DEGRADED* states). In the later refinement steps, this event will be constrained to model a reaction on communication or a detected environment change.

**Second Refinement.** In the second refinement step, we elaborate on the system communication aspect. In particular, the current mission can be changed as a reaction to a received message. Moreover, the system may enter a degraded state as a result of incoming communication or, vice versa, the system is required to send an outgoing message if some internal error is detected, thus resulting in a degraded system state. For brevity, we omit a detailed description of this refinement step. Later, when the SoS will be decomposed into its constituent systems, we will further elaborate on the communication mechanisms to ensure dependability preserving communication.

**Third Refinement.** In the third refinement step, we introduce the behavioural pattern *SENSE* $\to$ *PLAN* $\to$ *ACT* typically governing behaviour of autonomic systems. At each cycle, the system checks (senses) the environment for possible changes (failures, arrived messages, etc.), then decides on a system reaction (e.g., moving to a degraded state, changing its current mission), and finally continues its mission execution in a possibly changed (as a result of the previous $PLAN$ step) state. If no changes are detected, only the $ACT$ step is executed.

We extend the model context by a new enumerated set, $STEPS$, consisting of the constants $SENSE$, $PLAN$, and $ACT$. A new variable, $step$, is introduced to reflect the current step of the cycle and is used (in the event guards and actions) to enforce the fixed order of execution. The existing model events are consequently partitioned into the three groups associated to the above steps.

To illustrate the performed model transformation, below we present the event ToUnsafe_LocFailure that models detection of a local failure that consequently brings the system into an unsafe state.

> ToUnsafe_LocFailure  $\widehat{=}$ refines ToUnsafe_LocFailure
>   **where** $state \in IN\_MISSION \cup COMPLETED \cup DEGRADED \ \wedge step = SENSE$
>   **then**  $state :\in UNSAFE \parallel failure := TRUE \parallel step := PLAN$ **end**

The event is a part of the $SENSE$ step. As a result, the system moves to the following step $PLAN$, where the corresponding event(s) will be triggered, trying to bring the system into a degraded system state. Moreover, in the $ACT$ step, this failure also leads to sending an outgoing message to the involved parties.

In this refinement, we are able to prove the invariant property
$$failure = TRUE \Rightarrow step = PLAN,$$
which states that we only allow the system to enter an unsafe state right after the $SENSE$ step is finished (i.e., when $step = PLAN$). It essentially means that during the $PLAN$ step the system must be able to react immediately to this situation, bringing the system into a degraded yet safe state, if necessary.

**Fourth Refinement.** In the last refinement step, we decompose the SoS into its constituents coordinating their activities in order to accomplish a common mission. For brevity, we demonstrate our approach on two constituent systems.

As a result of this refinement step, the system state, $state \in STATES$, is data refined by a combination of separate states $state1 \in STATES1$ and $state2 \in STATES2$ belonging to the separate constituting systems. The corresponding state spaces $STATES1$ and $STATES2$ are introduced in the model context. Similarly, these state spaces are partitioned into the disjoint subsets: $IN\_MISSION1$, $COMPLETED1$, $UNSAFE1$, $DEGRADED1$ for $STATES1$, and $IN\_MISSION2$, $COMPLETED2$, $UNSAFE2$, $DEGRADED2$ for $STATES2$.

The context also introduces a function $Map$ (a partial injection), mapping two new states (from the same meta-state) into the corresponding old one. This function formally defines a gluing invariant for the performed data refinement step, i.e., it establishes a correspondence between the state of the SoS and the states of its constituting systems.

> axm17: $Map \in STATES1 \times STATES2 \rightarrowtail STATE$
> axm18: $\forall st1, st2 \cdot st1 \in UNSAFE1 \wedge st2 \in UNSAFE2 \Rightarrow Map(st1 \mapsto st2) \in UNSAFE$
> axm19: $\forall st1, st2 \cdot st1 \in DEGRADED1 \wedge st2 \in DEGRADED2 \Rightarrow Map(st1 \mapsto st2) \in DEGRADED$

In the machine part, we duplicate all the model events, allocating them to the first and second systems respectively. The main difference between the duplicated events is, of course, that these events now update either $state1$ or $state2$ of the constituting systems. The gluing invariant formally expresses the relationships between these states and the abstract variable $state$ they replaced:

$$in\_sync = TRUE \Rightarrow state = Map(state1 \mapsto state2).$$

The additional condition in this invariant reflects the fact that, once the SoS is decomposed, we cannot guarantee that certain state changes that should be coordinated between the constituting systems will happen synchronised. A certain synchronisation delay caused by necessary extra communication between the systems is needed to re-establish a consistent state of the overall SoS.

The new global variable $in\_sync$ reflects whether the system is currently synchronised or not. Once any of the components gets "de-synchronised", $in\_sync$ becomes $FALSE$, blocking its nominal activities until synchronisation is confirmed by communication with the other component. The new events modelling this communication are also introduced in the model. Note that a communication failure is treated as a failure leading to an unsafe state by both systems, which forces both of them to move to a degraded state.

**Further Possible Refinements.** In the following refinements the system model can be further extended. Introducing details of communication protocols would allow us to replace (data refine) the global variable $in\_sync$ by its local counterparts $in\_sync1$ and $in\_sync2$, thus making the system decentralised and autonomous. The meta-state $DEGRADED$ can be elaborated by introducing concrete fault tolerance and recovery mechanisms. Also, separate components can be refined in different ways thus implementing different component roles.

As a result of our formal modelling, we have formally defined the relationships between the SoS mission, states of the constituting systems and faults. We have clearly defined the situations under which the system goes through unsafe states and enforced transitions that bring it to a safe state.

# 4    Case Study: Satellite Flight Formation

In this section we will briefly describe our case study – *Satellite Flight Formation* [10] – and illustrate how the proposed generic approach can be applied to model a SoS from the space domain.

**Case Study Description.** Satellite flight formation is a mission critical SoS. The main goal of the system is acquisition of valuable scientific data. The scientific instruments are distributed over two satellites flying in a formation with the relative position control. The spacecrafts operate on an elliptical orbit where the mission objectives are performed at apogee (low gravity region of the orbit). The formation is periodically broken and reacquired since it cannot be maintained at particular orbit regions (e.g., perigee). The satellites flying in a formation must act collaboratively by coordinating their activities via frequent communication.

The satellites *autonomously* manage the formation and, in most cases, take mission critical decisions with no ground supervision. The used metrology sensors allow for formation acquisition and relative position determination maintenance. Thus, even in majority of the off-nominal situations, the constituent spacecrafts are able to autonomously re-adjust and continue the mission.

The main mission of the Satellite Flight Formation system is organised into several sub-missions (also called modes), such as *Science* and *Parking*. The *Science* mode is an operational system mode during which the scientific data are obtained, while the *Parking* mode is used to perform maintenance activities when it is not possible to get scientific data. In their turn, *Science* and *Parking* consist of a number of sequential stages, called *phases*. For instance, *Science* mode consists of the preparation phase, the science phase (when scientific experiments are performed at apogee), the preparation to the drifting phase, and the free drifting phase (at perigee). In some cases, the ground control may change the current sub-mission (e.g., may order to go to *Parking* from the *Science* mode).

During the mission execution a number of off-nominal situations may occur. Some of them may lead to potential collision between the satellites. For instance, an internal failure may result in a wrong satellite attitude or communication between both satellites can be lost. In these cases, both spacecrafts should coordinate by switching to the *Manual* mode (with the pre-defined safe orbits and no other manoeuvres allowed). When the communication between satellites is lost, both satellites should go to the *Manual* mode independently. Recovery from such dangerous situations is performed under ground supervision.

**Supporting Formal Modelling of Satellite Flight Formation.** The formal development presented in Section 3 is generic, since its parameters (abstract constants defined in the context) can be instantiated in different ways, provided that their expected properties are provably shown to be true. To apply the proposed generic approach in the flight formation modelling, we can interpret the *Science* and *Parking* modes as two concrete missions of the system to be developed, i.e., the abstract set *MISSIONS* in our generic models can be instantiated with the concrete set {*Science, Parking*}. The pre-defined sequences of their phases can be formalised as concrete instances of the *Scenarios* function. The system operating in the *Manual* mode corresponds to the model states belonging to *DEGRADED*.

Each SoS component adjusts its behaviour by sensing (detecting) changes in its environment or the internal state. For the case study, they correspond to the changed orbit segment (perigee, apogee), communication from the ground control or other components, an internal failure. As a result, it can move to a different mission or its phase, or enter a degraded state. It also has an obligation to inform the other components to coordinate their activities in achieving the joint mission. These aspects of the case study fit very well with the behavioural pattern $SENSE \rightarrow PLAN \rightarrow ACT$ specified in our generic models.

In this paper, the presented generic development stops at the decomposition of the overall system into several components with identical basic functionality. In the case study, one of the satellites (called *master*) has a higher degree of control over coordination of joint activities. Moreover, different protocols are used for inter-component communication in different situations. We believe that these implementation details can be introduced in additional refinement steps of our formal development.

# 5   Conclusions and Related Work

In this paper, we presented an approach to formal modelling of SoS in Event-B. In particular, we have proposed a generic development pattern that allowed us to develop a complex SoS in a correctness-preserving way. In addition, we have briefly discussed how the proposed generic development can be instantiated to model a flight formation – a SoS consisting of two autonomous spacecrafts.

Engineering of SoS is an actively developing research area. In general, there are two main directions that are pursued – integration of the development techniques to address the variety of issues associated with engineering of SoS and extension of specific existing frameworks to achieve versatility. Among the approaches pertaining to the former, a work has been done within the COMPASS project [3] on unifying several formal frameworks. Among the latter ones, there are the works dedicated to extending formal frameworks, e.g., by integrating modelling of the continuous behaviour into a system model, see [1]. Moreover, a verification-centric approach has been put forward by Ortmeier [8], while agile development techniques have been experimented with by Gorski [4].

The approach presented in this paper is more focused and pragmatic – we have investigated how to use a mature technology of Event-B to model and verify system-wide properties of SoS and derive the conditions that the constituent systems should preserve to guarantee overall system dependability. Among obvious advantages of the proposed approach is a good scalability and the availability of industrial strength automated tool support. The generic development, proposed in the paper, essentially defines the reusable modelling patterns that can further facilitate the use of the proposed technology for SoS development.

The approach proposed in the paper continues our line of research on formal modelling of complex dependable systems from various domains. It builds on the ideas of goal-oriented modelling [7], resilient agent systems [6], fault tolerant systems [11] and layered architectures [5]. As a future work, it would be interesting to further experiment with the decomposition methods needed to derive communication protocols and dependability contracts verifiable at run-time.

# References

1. Abrial, J.-R., Su, W., Zhu, H.: Formalizing Hybrid Systems with Event-B. In: Derrick, J., Fitzgerald, J., Gnesi, S., Khurshid, S., Leuschel, M., Reeves, S., Riccobene, E. (eds.) ABZ 2012. LNCS, vol. 7316, pp. 178–193. Springer, Heidelberg (2012)
2. Abrial, J.R.: Modeling in Event-B. Cambridge University Press (2010)
3. COMPASS, EU FP7 project, http://www.compass-research.eu/
4. Górski, J., Lukasiewicz, K.: Towards Agile Development of Critical Software. In: Gorbenko, A., Romanovsky, A., Kharchenko, V. (eds.) SERENE 2013. LNCS, vol. 8166, pp. 48–55. Springer, Heidelberg (2013)
5. Iliasov, A., Troubitsyna, E., Laibinis, L., Romanovsky, A., Varpaaniemi, K., Ilic, D., Latvala, T.: Developing mode-rich satellite software by refinement in Event-B. Sci. Comput. Program. 78(7), 884–905 (2013)
6. Pereverzeva, I., Troubitsyna, E., Laibinis, L.: A refinement-based approach to developing critical multi-agent systems. IJCCBS 4(1), 69–91 (2013)

7. Pereverzeva, I., Troubitsyna, E., Laibinis, L.: Formal Goal-Oriented Development of Resilient MAS in Event-B. In: Brorsson, M., Pinho, L.M. (eds.) Ada-Europe 2012. LNCS, vol. 7308, pp. 147–161. Springer, Heidelberg (2012)
8. Ortmeier, F.: Dependability in Pervasive Computing: Challenges and Chances. JITR 5(1), 1–17 (2012)
9. Rodin: Event-B Platform, http://www.event-b.org/
10. Tarabini, L., Castellani, A., Llorente, S., Fernandez, J.M., Ruiz, M., Mestreau-Garreau, A., Cropp, A., Santovincenzo, A.: PROBA-3 MISSION. In: 5th International Conference on Spacecraft Formation Flying Missions and Technologies (2013)
11. Tarasyuk, A., Pereverzeva, I., Troubitsyna, E., Latvala, T., Nummila, L.: Formal Development and Assessment of a Reconfigurable On-board Satellite System. In: Ortmeier, F., Lipaczewski, M. (eds.) SAFECOMP 2012. LNCS, vol. 7612, pp. 210–222. Springer, Heidelberg (2012)

# Towards Assured Dynamic Configuration of Safety-Critical Embedded Systems

Nermin Kajtazovic, Christopher Preschern,
Andrea Höller, and Christian Kreiner

Institute for Technical Informatics,
Graz University of Technology,
Infeldgasse 16, Graz, Austria
{nermin.kajtazovic,christopher.preschern,
andrea.hoeller,christian.kreiner}@tugraz.at

**Abstract.** Assuring systems quality is an inherent part of developing safety-critical embedded systems. Currently, continuous increase of systems complexity, in particular that of software, makes this development challenging. In response, more and more software faults are remaining unidentified at design-time so that changes and maintenance need to be performed at an increased rate. Unfortunately, today's safety-critical systems are not designed to be upgraded or maintained in a seamless way, so that the overhead of performing changes may be considerable, especially when such changes require to re-verify and re-validate the whole system.

In this paper, we present an approach to perform software changes in the operation and maintenance phase of the systems lifecycle. Changes are performed dynamically, by replacing parts of software (i.e., software components) with their functionally equal out-of-the-box instances. In order to prevent the impact of changes on systems integrity, we provide a support to model and to analyze the system. The main outcome here is that specific kind of changes can be maintained without adding any development costs.

**Keywords:** safety-critical embedded systems, component-based systems, dynamic configuration.

## 1 Introduction

Maintaining a correct function even in presence of faults is an important characteristic of safety-critical embedded systems. In order to reduce the risk of failures, and thus to avoid the potential environmental damages or harm on humans, their hardware/software development has to be rigorous and quality assured.

Currently, rapid and continuous increase of systems complexity, in particular that of software, makes the development of these systems challenging [4] [12]. In response, more and more software faults are remaining unidentified at design-time so that changes and maintenance need to be performed at an increased rate. Concrete examples of such change and maintenance demands are quite often

A. Bondavalli et al. (Eds.): SAFECOMP 2014 Workshops, LNCS 8696, pp. 167–179, 2014.

recalls of vehicles, medical devices, and other products. Some of these recalls are related to faults located in the software functions, such as the control algorithms, libraries, flaws in modification or adaptation, and other. According to recent studies related to defect analysis in recalls, those faults are getting more frequent, as more and more functions are being implemented in software [2]. Eliminating those faults in most current safety-critical systems is quite difficult, in particular because it has to be evidenced that the changed system still maintains certain level of quality – a so called safety integrity in the notation of safety standards. To provide such an evidence, many steps in the development lifecycle have to be repeated. In addition, depending on the impact of changes and regulations of the considered safety standard, new certification might be required.

In this paper, we present an approach to perform software changes in the operation and maintenance phase of the systems lifecycle. Changes are performed dynamically, by replacing parts of software (software components [5]) with their functionally equal out-of-the-box instances. Before any change can be performed, a new system configuration is analyzed against the violation of the safety integrity. Thus, only the configurations that pass this analysis step can be installed into the system dynamically. To enable such assured dynamic configurations, we have provided the following basis in our previous work: (a) a runtime mechanism that allows to load the out-of-the-box software components into a real-time operating system dynamically – the dynamic linker [10], and (b) a design-time mechanism to ensure the consistency of new system configurations [11]. This consistency mechanism performs the analysis of a changed system based on modelled properties which describe certain system attributes, such as memory and timing budgets for example[1]. In order to determine whether changes caused by replacing software components have an impact on the safety integrity, there is a need to identify which attributes may be relevant here. For this purpose, we analyze in this paper how the change management is regulated in some safety standards, and under which conditions the replacements of components are allowed.

The main outcome here is that for specific kind of changes, in which software components can be replaced, the system does not need to be turned back into the development phase. Furthermore, if the re-certification of the system is required, the original certification data can be reused, since they are not impacted by those changes. In response, replacements of software components can be maintained without any development costs.

The remainder of this paper is organized as follows: Section 2 provides a brief overview of relevant related work. Section 3 describes how changes are handled in safety standards, and which system attributes have to be considered when analyzing changes. In Section 4 the proposed approach is described, and a short discussion is given in Section 5. Finally, concluding remarks are given in Section 6.

---

[1] We use the notation *system attributes* to identify various functional and non-functional system aspects, such as performance requirements, constraints, etc.

## 2    Related Work

Now we turn to a brief overview of related studies. We summarize here some relevant articles that handle the analysis of changes in safety-critical embedded systems.

To date, much research has been done on analyzing planned changes in software architectures for safety-critical systems [1] [15] [13] . In the work by Adler et al. [1], an adaptive architecture for safety-critical automotive systems is proposed. The main goal here is to increase the systems availability by allowing software components to implement diverse behaviours, so that in the event of failures or degradation of quality, the automotive system can continue operating by switching between correct implementations. Since different implementations of components may have different quality, the authors provide a design-time analysis to prevent mixing not allowed combinations of component implementations. For this purpose, they define a quality system, with a set of fixed quality types. A more advanced framework for dynamic adaptation of avionics systems was developed by Montano [15]. The goal is to adapt the system to new, correct configurations, in case of failures. To perform this, a common quality system defines the contracts between functions and available static resources (e.g. memory consumption, CPU utilization, etc.) and in this way it restricts the possible set of correct configurations. An important aspect of this work is that it demonstrates the CP approach to solving the composition problem. However, the quality type system only considers static resources, and does not consider contracts between functions. Ultimately, the approach is strongly focused on dynamic adaptation with human-assisted decision making. Similar reconfiguration strategy is used in [13], but the consistency of the reconfiguration here is ensured by the runtime mechanisms (partitioning).

There are also some works which focus on upgrading safety-critical systems [20] [16] [19]. One of the most notable is work done in the scope of the project PINCETTE, which has as a goal to perform live upgrades of software systems that control the safety-critical processes [20]. Although the topic is beyond the scope of available validation methods in the practice, the aim is to evaluate the feasibility of formal methods to such use cases. In contrast to our data flow-oriented analysis, the focus here is on validating the interaction between upgraded behaviours. Another work [16], done in the scope of the RECOMP project, addresses also live upgrades as one of the goals to reduce the costs for certifying systems. However, only dynamic linker has been realized here, without considering the analysis of changes. Finally, the work in [19] shows how to validate changes of upgraded safety-critical system. Here, model checker is used to verify changed behaviour.

In summary, various analysis methods have been developed to validate changes. However, none of the approaches discussed here consider regulations of standards, to identify whether changes they support are allowed and, if so, to which extent.

# 3    Addressing Changes in Engineering of Safety-Critical Embedded Systems

Identifying system requirements affected by changes is a crucial step in the change management process. To determine which requirements and which related system attributes influence the systems safety integrity, we analyze in the following how changes are regulated in safety standards. Based on this analysis, we build a list of system attributes that we further use to construct our software architecture, and to build properties for our software components.

## 3.1    Change Management in Safety Standards

In general, standards for functional safety provide the guidelines on how to align the system development with the safety lifecycle in each phase. One aspect of these guidelines are activities related to maintenance and operation phase of the systems lifecycle. Changes in the operation phase are usually handled in the context of the supporting processes defined in standards, such as the maintenance, the configuration management, and the change management [18]. In the following, we describe the change management defined in the IEC 61508, which is a generic safety standard applied in the industry. We align our approach to this standard, because many guidelines it provides can also be found in other standards applied in specific industrial sectors, since they represent derivatives of the IEC 61508 (e.g., the ISO26262 standard provides similar guidelines for maintaining changes in automotive systems).

The lifecycle of the IEC 61508 standard comprises the engineering activities for software and systems scope. Changes in the operation and maintenance phase of systems are described in parts 1, 2 and 3 of the standard, in the context of the supporting processes: maintenance, configuration management, and change management. Each of these processes has defined steps, the inputs and the work products it shall produce. To ensure the safety integrity after implementing changes, the standard prescribes requirements that have to be fulfilled and a list of possible techniques and measures to apply within these processes. The requirements are mainly related to activities that need to be performed if safety integrity is affected by changes. In Table 1, we have filtered out the most relevant requirements. Basically, if safety integrity is affected by changes the standard recommends to (i) perform the hazard and risk analysis in order to identify additional faults that might be introduced by such changes and (ii) to return to the appropriate phase in the software lifecycle to implement changes. On the system level (part IEC61508-2), it is recommended to use the same development equipment and expertise (e.g., tools, previous system configuration, project artifacts, etc.), in order to just focus on changed parts only. In addition to requirements, developers have the option to choice which techniques and measures to perform, based on the level of safety integrity they want to achieve after implementing changes (bottom part of the table). Among them, the most influential measure here from the aspect of costs is a need for the verification and validation. For the highest levels of safety integrity, the standard recommends to

**Table 1.** IEC 61508 requirements, measures and techniques related to change management (an excerpt)

| | Requirements on software change management, IEC 61508-3 |
|---|---|
| 7.8.2.3 | An analysis shall be carried out on the impact of the proposed software modification on the functional safety of the E/E/PE safety-related system: a) to determine whether or not a hazard and risk analysis is required; b) to determine which software safety lifecycle phases will need to be repeated. |
| 7.8.2.5 | All modifications which have an impact on the functional safety of the E/E/PE safety-related system shall initiate a return to an appropriate phase of the software safety lifecycle. All subsequent phases shall then be carried out in accordance with the procedures specified for the specific phases in accordance with the requirements in this standard. Safety planning (see Clause 6) shall detail all subsequent activities. |
| | Requirements on system change management, IEC 61508-2 |
| 7.8.2.3 | Modifications shall be performed with at least the same level of expertise, automated tools (see 7.4.4.2 of IEC 61508-3), and planning and management as the initial development of the E/E/PE safety-related systems. |
| 7.8.2.4 | After modification, the E/E/PE safety-related systems shall be reverified and revalidated. |
| | Recommended techniques and measures, IEC 61508-3 A.8 |
| 2 | Reverify changed software module |
| 3 | Reverify affected software modules |
| 4a/4b | Revalidate complete system or Regression validation |

perform the re-verification and re-validation of the complete system (measures 2, 3, 4a in the Table 1). Alternatively, regression validation would also suffice (measure 4b). Nevertheless, changed artifacts (from the work products of the hazard and risk analysis down to the test reports) have to be newly certified.

In summary, the change impact on safety integrity implies to update many work products throughout the systems lifecycle, to repeat particular steps of that lifecycle and to re-verify and re-validate the system. However, according to requirements 7.8.2.3 and 7.8.2.5, those activities have to be performed only if there is an impact on the functional safety (i.e., the systems safety integrity is changed). Our goal in this context is to allow changes to an extent to which they have no impact on the systems safety integrity. For this purpose, we need to evaluate the requirement 7.8.2.3-a, for every change request. If there is no need for the hazard and risk analysis, changes are allowed, otherwise not. To realize this, we first need to identify the system attributes that have an impact on systems safety integrity. Based on these attributes, we can set constraints on the architectural level (e.g., software components, layers, operating system configuration, etc.) that would allow us to evaluate the requirement 7.8.2.3-a. In the following, we introduce these attributes.

## 3.2 Impact of Changes on System Requirements

Safety standards set requirements to achieve the functional safety, while leaving the space for the developers on details on how they should implement those requirements. The same holds for the change management, i.e., the IEC 61508 does not specify which system attributes have to be considered when analysing the impact of changes. More concrete guidelines about this can be found in the avionics domain, concretely in the concept Reusable Software Component (RSC) from the Federal Aviation Administration (FAA) that was developed for the standard

DO-178B, to enable reuse of software components and their late integration into a certified safety-critical system [7]. Similar to change management, the aim is to maintain the functional safety after integrating components. Although RSC provides concrete information about reusing pre-fabricated components, no focus has been given on how to design such components for reuse – for example, how to describe the context in which components have to operate (embedded system, environment, etc.) and which system attributes contribute to that context. Similar to RSC, the concept Safety Element out of Context (SEooC) as part of the automotive standard ISO26262 defines reuse for the sub-systems, but on the abstraction level of requirements.

To our knowledge, the only available official publication that handles change management in detail and is related to safety standards are the FAA guidelines on analyzing the impact of changes in software [6] [17]. Here, a collection of the concrete system attributes that might be affected by changes is presented. This collection is made to help developers in the post-certification process of the DO-178B standard to ensure the safety integrity of the changed system by determining the impact of changes on the system, and by estimating the overhead to re-verify, re-validate and re-certify the system. Although avionics domain is addressed here, most of those attributes are common to embedded systems in general. In Table 2, we summarize the common system attributes.

**Table 2.** Considered system attributes to analyze impact of changes, according to Federal Administration Aviation (FAA) [6]

| System attribute | Description |
|---|---|
| traceability | requirements, design, tests, procedures |
| memory margin | memory allocation requirements (volatile, non-volatile memory) |
| timing margin | timing requirements (task scheduling, interface timing, ...) |
| data flow | coupling between software components (data syntax, semantics) |
| control flow | coupling between software components (events, calls, ...) |
| input/output | interfaces with the external world (bus, hardware, memory, ...) |
| development environment and process | compilers, linkers, loaders, tools |
| operational characteristics | runtime mechanisms (changes on limits, i.e. contracts, exception handling, ...) |
| partitioning | change on protective safety mechanisms |

We use some of the FAA attributes as the first class entities to maintain the consistency of the system, and to estimate the impact of changes. We discuss the selection of attributes in the following section more in detail.

## 4    Ensuring Consistency of System Configurations

In this section, we introduce our approach to ensuring the consistency of system configurations. To this end, we show how we define a system using attributes

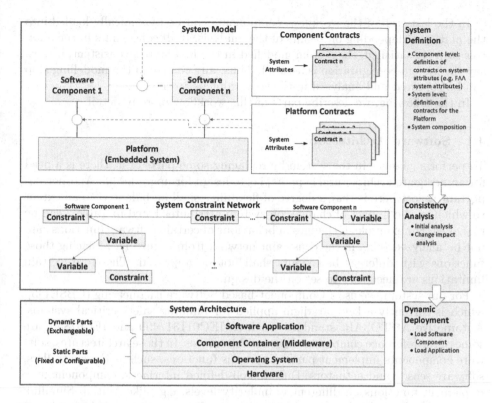

**Fig. 1.** Proposed workflow for ensuring systems consistency: system modelling using contracts to describe attributes (top), consistency analysis (middle) and dynamic deployment of software components (bottom)

described in the previous section, and how we analyze the impact of changes. All information about systems consistency is contained in those attributes.

The proposed approach in the workflow form is depicted in Figure 1. On the top, a model of the system is defined. This model consists of the two elements: software components which implement certain application-level functions, and the platform, which is a model of an embedded system. Both software components and the platform implement certain contracts, in order to express relations to other dependent components or platform. These contracts are the fundamental elements of the system model that allow us to maintain the consistency of the system. They contain the information about system attributes discussed in the previous section, and provide means to build relationships to other contracts. Based on those relationships, impact of changes in one particular contract can be tracked throughout the complete system. We introduce contracts later in Section 4.2. In the next step of the workflow, the system in terms of contracts is translated into a so called constraint network, i.e., a set of inter-connected variables and constraints. This constraint network represent contracts and their relationships in another problem domain, which allows us to automatically analyze the consistency of the system by evaluating constraints.

In the last step of the workflow, components can be dynamically loaded into the platform, depending on results of the analysis. If all constraints in the analysis step are satisfied, the system modelled in the first step is consistent, i.e., we say the system configuration is assured. Thus, any change in the modelling step can be captured and analyzed in the constraint network.

In the following, we describe parts of this workflow more in detail.

## 4.1 Software Architecture

To perform changes in the system by replacing some parts of it, there is a need for an adequate architectural support, i.e. a design for upgrades [9]. Another important aspect here is that a degree of flexibility shall be balanced to an extent to which an the impact of changes on system attributes listed in Table 2 can be managed. For example, if changes in behaviour of certain software functions cannot be analyzed (e.g., in the constraint network from Figure 1), replacing those functions with different behaviours shall not be approved. Therefore, certain limitations are necessary to set on the design.

For our system, we use a Component-based Software Engineering (CBSE) [5], which is currently a key paradigm applied for building safety-critical systems. Automotive AUTOSAR, standards such as IEC61131/499 and IEC61850, are some of the reference component-based architectures. In those architectures, software components implement parts of systems functions, such as the controllers, software sensor and actuators. Due to well-defined interfaces, component may implement functions on different granularity levels, e.g., like Matlab Simulink function blocks and sub-systems, thus allowing for compositional (hierarchical) design. Moreover, well-defined interfaces allow their reuse, customization for the use in different contexts, and so forth.

Our software architecture is depicted in Figure 1 (bottom part). Here, software components implement certain software functions composed into an application, whereas their lifecycle, their coordination and resources from the operating system are managed by the underlying middleware, i.e., a component container. Changes related to software may impact any of these layers, and therefore any of the introduced system attributes. In order to be able to analyze such an impact, we set limitation on the design so that replacements of software components are allowed only. That means, some of the system attributes are fixed at design-time so that changes have no influence on those attributes. For example, connections between software components have to be static, since they may affect the functional requirements if changed (e.g., adding/removing software components, or changing connectors may affect systems behaviour), and this can only be analyzed manually.

With our limitations, the impact of changes is related to software components and their interaction with the platform only. However, such cases are also not trivial, since changes may still have an impact on systems consistency. For example, the consistency may be compromised if the replaced software component implements interfaces with different semantics, e.g. different value intervals provided to dependent components, and new intervals were not considered during the system verification. Similarly, mixing components with different quality levels may cause the same effects, e.g. deploying components qualified for the lower level of the safety integrity than the integrity of the platform.

The main impact of changes here is on (i) resource management, in particular on task and memory management for components, and on (ii) interfaces between components and their interfaces to the platform. From the perspective of the software architecture, the configuration of tasks (i.e., number of tasks, their scheduling policy, etc.) and the organisation of memory (i.e., memory layout, size of the heap, and allocation to tasks) are static features. However, they have to be included in the analysis since exchanged components may have different demands with regard to resources (timing, memory).

Similarly, the connections and interfaces between components are static, but many details have to be considered in order to ensure that the integration or the composition is correct (i.e., the syntax and the semantics, such as units, valid intervals of certain data values, etc.). In addition, some components may implement many alternative behaviours so that different configurations of interfaces are possible. Therefore, we consider interfaces in our analysis. Finally, details with regard to the development process and the operational profile are also parts of the analysis. In Table 3, we summarize system attributes that we include in the analysis, and possible types of changes (right column). The systems consistency is therefore analysed based on these changes only. The remaining systems attributes from Table 2 are fixed at design time, and cannot be influenced, i.e., the control flow of components, their interaction semantics and behaviour are implemented as a static part of the architecture.

**Table 3.** System attributes considered in the consistency analysis, selected from FAA attribute collection [6]

| System attributes | Allowed changes |
| --- | --- |
| memory margin | components: volatile and non-volatile memory<br>platform: volatile memory (allocated to tasks), non-volatile memory |
| timing margin | components: execution time<br>platform: task execution time |
| data flow | components/platform: syntax (datatype, interface), semantics (intervals, values, specific constraints (units, standard compliance, configuration and calibration data, ...)) |
| development environment and process | components/platform: tools (compiler, linker, specific constraints (build options, ...)), version |
| execution platform | components/platform: architecture (cpu, floating point support, ...), safety integrity level |

## 4.2   System Modelling

To integrate the information about selected attributes from Table 3 into the systems structure, we use Contract-based Design paradigm (CBD) [3]. According to CBD, software components and the platform implement certain contracts, which capture part of that information (i.e., a quality stamps or properties). In addition to capturing information, contracts provide means to integrate components and platform.

Among few types of different contract available, such as state transition-based contracts like interface automata, probabilistic contracts, etc., we use a form that is based on data semantics, i.e., data flow contracts [3]. According to this type, every contract consists of data parameters, and expressions (or properties) on those data parameters in form of assumption and guarantees. The guarantees describe a valid behaviour in form of expressions, that can evaluate to true/-false, depending on the evaluation of expressions in assumptions. For specifying contracts, various formalisations can be used, for example logic languages such as propositional logic, first order logic, their extensions, and other.

In Figure 2, we show how the structure of our software components is defined to match with used contracts, and how different types of system attributes are modelled using contracts. A trivial example is shown here just to simplify the demonstration. Similar to the structure of contracts, every software component and the platform are defined as a set of data parameters, input and output data variables. In addition to this information, they contain a list of implemented contracts. Thus, data parameters in contracts relate to data parameters of their corresponding components/platform.

Another essential aspect of CBD are the relationships between contracts, which allow to verify the composition between two contracts, if their assumptions and guarantees are defined in a formal way. In our example, the contracts of components $M_{IS}$ and $M_{IIAS}$ are related with each other using a composition relation, which is valid only if these contracts are compatible and can interact. Concretely, this means the relation is valid if the contract of a component which accepts data, the $C1$ implemented by component $M_{IIAS}$, can be satisfied by

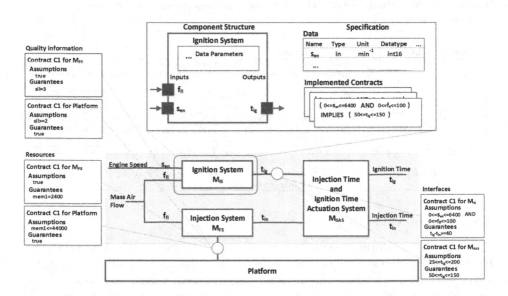

**Fig. 2.** Structure definition of software components and the platform, and supported types of contracts shown on an example of the engine controller, adopted from [8]

the guarantees of the providing component. In the example, this can evaluate to true only if the assumption $(25 \leq t_{ig} \leq 200)$ can also evaluate to true[2]. This can only be satisfied, if the guarantee of the contract $C1$ of $M_{IS}$, $(50 \leq t_{ig} \leq 150)$, matches with the assumption $(25 \leq t_{ig} \leq 200)$, which is the case in the example, since $M_{IIAS}$ can accept more values of $t_{ig}$ (for more details, please refer to [11]). Therefore, guarantees and assumptions of dependent components are interrelated by their expressions. In a similar way, we define contracts for resources and quality information, as shown in the figure.

Based on relationships between contracts, information about the system attributes on a system level is maintained. Changes in any contract (or exchanges of contracts) can be captured by evaluating assumptions/guarantees of other dependent contracts.

### 4.3   Consistency Analysis

The consistency analysis is based on verifying relations between contracts, in particular, by evaluating their assumptions and guarantees. As a background technology, we use Constraint Programming paradigm (CP) [14], which is a widely applied method to solve decision and optimization problems. The essential aspect of CP is a problem definition, which is represented as a network of variables of various types and constraints. Here, constraints represent various kinds expressions on variables (logical, arithmenic, etc.), and can be related to other constraints. Solving that problem means evaluating all constraints in the network. Thus, there is a solution if all constraints in the network are satisfied.

In our approach, we translate the system modelled in form of contracts into such a constraint network. For this purpose, we have defined a model of a contract, its variables, assumptions and guarantees, and relations between contracts as network elements, i.e., variables and constraints. The systems consistency is therefore analyzed by evaluating constraints that are derived from contracts (for more details, please refer to [11]).

## 5   Discussion

We showed in this paper that simple replacements of software components are not trivial. Many details about functional and non-functional aspects of software components have to be considered to ensure that replacements have no impact on systems integrity. One of the major challenges here is to determine how much information should be considered in the analysis, to have a confidence in its results. With the list of systems attributes we introduced in this work, some fundamental aspects are covered, but much more details might be required, depending on the specific domain. This collection of attributes can be extended according to types of contracts introduced.

---

[2] This data is related to the ignition time of an engine controller $t_{ig}$. The components modelled here implement contracts in order to satisfy the timing requirement on allowed difference between injection and ignition time, i.e. $(t_{ig} - t_{in})$.

The analysis method presented here can also be applied to some existing component-based systems, but in some cases with certain limitations. In AU-TOSAR for example, changes would be possible on a level of Runnables, which are units of the execution inside of AUTOSAR software components, and have a generalized standard behaviour (read, execute, write) [12]. In contrast, changes of complete software components could not be supported, because events for the execution of Runnables are user-defined, and other techniques are required here to analyze the interaction between those events. Generally, for synchronous data flow systems, such as IEC61131-based systems, or Matlab Simulink function blocks, it is more easily to apply the analysis, since software components used here have a standard behaviour and standard execution semantics.

## 6    Conclusion

In this paper, we presented an approach to perform changes on safety-critical embedded systems in the operation and maintenance phase. Changes are limited to replacements of software components. To prevent the impact of such type of changes on systems integrity, we have analyzed which related system attributes might be affected when replacing software components. Based on those attributes, we provided a modelling means to build a system including attributes on the level of software components and their platform (embedded system), and we provided a consistency analysis of such a modelled system. The main outcome of this work is that for replacements of software components the system does not need to be turned back into the development phase.

The collection of attributes described here provides a foundation for the future work. One of the major challenges here is to determine how much information is required to describe software components and their platform, in order to have a confidence on results of the consistency analysis. This may depend on many factors, such as used software architecture, domain-specific details, and so forth.

As part of our ongoing work, we will analyse different component-based architectures with regard to the use case of replacing software components, and derive specific system attribute out of them. The aim is to extend the proposed modelling and analysis support to system attributes, which can be commonly used in safety domains.

## References

1. Adler, R., Schaefer, I., Trapp, M., Poetzsch-Heffter, A.: Component-based modeling and verification of dynamic adaptation in safety-critical embedded systems. ACM Trans. Embed. Comput. Syst. 10(2), 20:1–20:39 (2011)
2. Alemzadeh, H., Iyer, R., Kalbarczyk, Z., Raman, J.: Analysis of safety-critical computer failures in medical devices. IEEE Security Privacy 11(4), 14–26 (2013)
3. Benveniste, A., Caillaud, B., Nickovic, D., Passerone, R., Raclet, J.B., Reinkemeier, P., Sangiovanni-Vincentelli, A., Damm, W., Henzinger, T., Larsen, K.: Contracts for Systems Design. Tech. rep., Research Report, Nr. 8147, 2012, Inria (2012)

4. Butz, H.: Open integrated modular avionic (ima): State of the art and future development road map at airbus deutschland. Department of Avionic Systems at Airbus Deutschland GmbH Kreetslag 10, D-21129 Hamburg, Germany (-)
5. Crnkovic, I.: Building Reliable Component-Based Software Systems. Artech House, Inc., Norwood (2002)
6. FAA: Guidelines for the Oversight of Software Change Impact Analyses used to Classify Software Changes as Major or Minor. Notice 8110.85, FAA (2000)
7. FAA: AC20-148 Reusable Software Components. Tr, FAA (2004)
8. Frey, P.: Case Study: Engine Control Application. Tech. rep., Ulmer Informatik-Berichte, Nr. 2010-03 (2010)
9. Gluch, D., Weinstock, C.: Workshop on the State of the Practice in Dependably Upgrading Critical Systems: April 16-17, 1997. Special report, Carnegie Mellon University, Software Engineering Institute (1997)
10. Kajtazovic, N., Preschern, C., Kreiner, C.: A component-based dynamic link support for safety-critical embedded systems. In: 20th IEEE ECBS (2013)
11. Kajtazovic, N., Preschern, A., Hoeller, C., Kreiner, C.: Constraint-based verification of compositions in safety-critical component-based systems. In: IEEE/ACIS SNPD (June 2014)
12. Kindel, O., Friedrich, M.: Softwareentwicklung mit AUTOSAR: Grundlagen, Engineering, Management in der Praxis. dpunkt Verlag, Auflage: 1 (2009)
13. Lopez-Jaquero, V., Montero, F., Navarro, E., Esparcia, A., Catal'n, J.: Supporting arinc 653-based dynamic reconfiguration. In: 2012 Joint WICSA and ECSA (2012)
14. Marriott, K., Stuckey, P.J.: Programming with Constraints: An Introduction. The MIT Press (March 1998)
15. Montano, G.: Dynamic reconfiguration of safety-critical systems: Automation and human involvement. PhD Thesis (2011)
16. Pop, P., Tsiopoulos, L., Voss, S., Slotosch, O., Ficek, C., Nyman, U., Ruiz, A.: Methods and tools for reducing certification costs of mixed-criticality applications on multi-core platforms: the recomp approach. In: WICERT (2013)
17. Rierson, L.: A systematic process for changing safety-critical software. In: Proceedings of the 19th Digital Avionics Systems Conference, DASC, vol. 1, pp. 1B1/1–1B1/7 (2000)
18. Smith, D., Simpson, K.: A Straightforward Guide to Functional Safety, IEC 61508 (2010 Edition) and Related Standards, Including Process IEC 61511 and Machinery IEC 62061 and ISO 13849. Elsevier Science (2010)
19. Soliman, D., Thramboulidis, K., Frey, G.: A methodology to upgrade legacy industrial systems to meet safety regulations. In: 2011 3rd International Workshop on Dependable Control of Discrete Systems (DCDS), pp. 141–147 (June 2011)
20. Zhang, M., Ogata, K., Futatsugi, K.: Formalization and verification of behavioral correctness of dynamic software updates. Electronic Notes in Theoretical Computer Science 294, 12–23 (2013); Proceedings of the 2013 VSSE Workshop

# Towards Trust Assurance and Certification
# in Cyber-Physical Systems

Daniel Schneider[1], Eric Armengaud[2], and Erwin Schoitsch[3]

[1] Fraunhofer IESE, Kaiserslautern, Germany
daniel.schneider@iese.fraunhofer.de
[2] AVL List GmbH, Graz, Austria
eric.armengaud@avl.com
[3] AIT Austrian Institute of Technology GmbH, Vienna, Austria
erwin.schoitsch@ait.ac.at

**Abstract.** We are currently witnessing a 3rd industrial revolution, driven by ever more interconnected distributed systems of systems, running under the umbrella term of cyber-physical systems (CPS). In the context of this paradigm, different types of computer-based systems from different application domains collaborate with each other in order to render higher level services that could not be rendered by single systems alone. However, the tremendous potential of CPS is inhibited due to significant engineering challenges with respect to the systems safety and security. Traditional methodologies are not applicable to CPS without further ado and new solutions are therefore required. In this paper, we present potential solution ideas that are currently investigated by the European EMC² research project.

**Keywords:** Cyber-physical systems, trust, safety, security, system engineering.

## 1 Introduction

The introduction of electronic control systems has revolutionized almost all technology domains (e.g., transportation, home and factory automation, energy, health and all kinds of services) by providing major cost decrease and quality increase of the existing functionalities, and even by enabling new functionalities. For example, today's cars are controlled by a computing network of up to 100 electronic control units taking over the optimal energy distribution and transfer between the different sources (hybrid vehicle) according to the chosen road and traffic situation, and today's planes are providing fly-by-wire in order to improve controllability, safety and comfort.

Moore´s law [12], stating the doubling of the computer capacity every 2 years, is still a strong enabler for this fast function increase and at the same time cost-per-function decrease. The current development trend for computing platforms has moved from increasing the frequency of single cores to increasing the parallelism (increasing the number of cores on the same die). Multi-core and many-core technologies have strong potential to further support the different technology domains, but at the same time present new challenges. From the potentials point of view they provide:

A. Bondavalli et al. (Eds.): SAFECOMP 2014 Workshops, LNCS 8696, pp. 180–191, 2014.
© Springer International Publishing Switzerland 2014

- *More computing resources*, thus enabling more complex algorithms and / or integration of different functionalities on a single platform, finally leading to cost reduction and efficiency increase for the intended application
- *Integrated mechanisms and new CPU architectures,* e.g. built-in memory protection mechanisms, trusted Networks on Chip (NoC), as developed in the ARTEMIS project ACROSS [28], thus enabling the development of new safety / security concepts and reducing the SW related efforts for providing trust and dependability of the application

At the same time, new challenges arise due to the existing integration needs and the computing platform enabling this high degree of integration. From the dependability point of view, the following challenges can be highlighted:

- *Application integration and mixed-criticality*: Different applications are running on the same platform, possibly of different criticality level. The independence between the applications and the most demanding criticality shall not be endangered by applications of lower criticality.
- *Seamless dependability / trust concept up to SW and system*: efficient integration of the computing platform dedicated mechanisms into the overall dependability concept of the system
- The trend toward *highly interconnected systems* (cyber-physical systems (CPS)) leads to a concept shift from single closed systems (sensors – controller – actuators known at design time) towards open interconnected and collaborating systems of systems (intelligent control systems evolving and interacting in a dynamic environment for a bounded amount of time and sharing dependability responsibility).
- A further challenge is that safety can no longer be considered in an isolated and independent way from *security*. Since CPS are open heterogeneous interconnected systems of different manufacturers security threats are inevitable.

These challenges are aggravated by the fact that many CPS applications are inherently safety- and security-critical and adequate safety / security assurance (and certification) is thus indispensable. Safety / security co-engineering is consequently a pre-requisite for enabling full deployment of cyber-physical systems. Missing dependability evidence can be a show stopper for product release or even lead to costly recall action. On the other side, proper dependability development usually leads to reduction of V&V costs and avoid late and costly re-design [29].

Unfortunately, the established engineering methodologies are not applicable without further ado. Engineering safe and secure adaptive systems implies a huge engineering overhead due to the combinatorial complexity and the insufficient scalability of the established approaches (i.e. it would be necessary to foresee and analyze any variant a system might assume during its lifetime). For open systems (of CPS), it might even be outright impossible to build upon established approaches since the safety / security properties of the different participants (that are meant to integrate/collaborate at runtime) are not known at development time already. Moreover, existing functional safety standards even explicitly prohibit concepts like dynamic adaptation, run-time assurance or self-healing (e.g. IEC61508 [6]).

In this context, the newly started ARTEMIS EMC² project[1] aims at answering these challenges. The consortium consists of 97 partners for an overall budget of almost 100M€. The project consists of six technical work-packages and six living labs: The technical work-packages are focusing on a specific technology (e.g., SW paradigm, multi-core HW architectures, tool integration, certification), while the living labs are providing use cases from different domains (e.g., automotive, avionics, space, industrial manufacturing, internet of things).

This paper presents the solution approach that is envisioned by the EMC² WP6 "System qualification and certification" to overcome the challenges illustrated above. The approach is based on two main pillars which are the respective focus of the two technical Tasks of the WP: The co-engineering of safety and security at development time (Section 3) as well as means to shift the final certification step into runtime (Section 4).

## 2     State of the Art

The state of the art that is relevant for the solution approach envisioned by EMC² is twofold. On the one hand, there is the research question of safety and security co-engineering. And on the other hand, there is the research question of modularizing safety and security in an adequate way to enable runtime certification in the context of CPS.

Considering the first aspect, there is previous work of the project partners particularly in projects like DECOS [2] and the ARTEMIS projects SafeCer [17] and related projects like OPENCOSS [18] or SESAMO [24]. DECOS focused on the Validation and Verification (V&V) and Certification support process aiming at a component based, incremental and modular approach towards system certification. nSafeCer is aiming particularly at a compositional approach of certification and re-certification enabling re-use of pre-qualified components based on a component model using contracts as basic element and appropriate process models allowing simplified  (re-) certification, being well aware of the fact that most functional safety standards do not directly foster this approach.  Some effort is undertaken to influence relevant standards (IEC, ISO) in the long term. OPENCOSS has extended the notion of SILs (Safety Integrity levels) towards resilience and reliability (dependability), defining so-called ARRLs (Assured Reliability and Resilience Levels) of components, defining how a failure of a component influences its impact (it drops by one ARRL). By a set of composition rules similar to ISO 26262, higher level components/subsystems/systems can be built with a known ARRL. These approaches are primarily towards composability (re-use) and safety/dependability. SESAMO, on the other hand, is addressing the issue of combined safety and security management. SESAMO key elements are:

- a methodology to reduce interdependencies between safety and security mechanisms and to jointly ensure their properties

---

[1] http://www.emc2-project.eu/

- constructive elements for the implementation of safe and secure systems
- procedures for integrated analysis of safety and security
- an overall design methodology and tool-chain utilizing the constructive elements and integrated analysis procedures to ensure that safety and security are intrinsic characteristics of the system.

As for the second aspect, existing modular safety assurance approaches constitute a possible starting point for the envisioned approach. Related research typically refers to the term modular certification, which is one of the most important current trends in safety research. In the Avionics domain, Rushby [8] introduced the use of modular certification for software components in the context of IMA architectures. The main goal of this approach is to enable an incremental assurance for the certification of an IMA system. In the area of generic safety cases, another important approach in the support of modular certification was introduced by Althammer [2]. The modularization concepts introduced as part of the DECOS (Dependable Embedded Components and Systems) project have the main objective of facilitating the systematic design and deployment of integrated systems. Bate and Kelly [5] presented an approach to allow a modular construction of safety cases based on the modeling language GSN [7]. In a later publication, Kelly [13] demonstrated that many principles from the field of software architecture can be applied to managing and representing safety cases as a composition of safety case modules. Following Kelly's work, Fenn et al. [4] describe an approach extending the GSN to create modularized safety cases with the use of contracts.

Not so well known in the safety and the security community are the IEC TC 56 Dependability standards [21][22]. Although they do not directly address safety or security but rather dependability in a more general form, they provide some guidance applicable to both, safety and security, in the context of the same system and its components. [21] focuses on the Dependability Case, [22] on the issue of how to build components for trusted systems and how to build trusted systems from components. The concepts of safety cases and dependability cases are aiming at building dependable systems by design and verify them during development, predictability is the major requirement. All standards in the safety and dependability area are based on this principle by now. The security standard Common Criteria (ISO 15408)[23] classifies components according to EALs (Evaluation Assurance Levels 1-7, 7 being the highest) and specify how to identify which EAL is required for a product (relates to "component" in the CPS context) in an application. The ISO 27000 series [15][16] addresses security in an organization from a holistic system point of view, considering all factors, not only ICT.

The approaches presented so far focus on the modular safety assurance during development time (safety/security by design, predictability a major concern) and are therefore designed to support human safety engineers in their activities. Runtime assurance and certification, as it is our goal in EMC$^2$, has rarely been addressed in research up to now. Ideas for the certification at runtime were first introduced by Rushby [9][10]. He describes first ideas that it should be possible to perform formal analyses at runtime, making it possible to formally verify that a component behaves as specified during execution. However, he does not provide concrete solutions. As one possible approach, Schneider and Trapp introduced the concept of Conditional Safety Certificates (ConSerts)[1][3][11], which facilitate the modular definition of conditional safety certificates for single components and systems using a contract-like approach. This approach will be a starting point for our work in EMC² and will thus be considered in some more detail in Section 4.

# 3    Safety and Security – Trust by Design

As described in section 2, there are several approaches towards safety engineering or security engineering at design and development time for predictable critical systems. They are either based on life-cycle type processes (functional safety standards IEC 61508, IEC 61511, ISO 26262, in security e.g. the Microsoft Secure Software Development Lifecycle or the NIST Security Considerations in the System Development Life Cycle (SP 800-64)), or on system considerations (ISO 27000 series, German IT-Baseline Protection handbook). Co-engineering safety and security with generation of evidence that can be used for static evidence derived from requirements at design time and possibly as basis for runtime aspects is not state of the art. There are several approaches under development and evaluation coming either from the safety community or the security community to extend methods applicable to cover both sides of the coin, safety and security. Both are focused on the "conventional" side taking predictability as major concern.

A first (weak) approach can be taken from IEC 61508, Ed. 2.0, 2010. A working group tried to include security as an important second issue besides safety, since at this time security standards and regulations were focusing on large business systems and networks.

It was tried to align requirements for SILs (safety requirements) with related security requirements of appropriate level for products (components from CPS view point). This is based on the idea that a similar level of rigidness as defined e.g. in IEC 61508 and ISO 15408 should be applied to the SRLs on both sides (see Table 1). In case the risk and vulnerability analysis (combined safety and security analysis) provides evidence that different levels are required for both issues then the recommendations shall change.

**Table 1.** SRLs and related verification requirements (proposal)

| SRL Security Require-ments Level | Security functions and related Evaluation Assurance Levels according to ISO/IEC 15408 | Hardware, software or ASICS and related Safety Integrity Levels according to ISO/IEC 61508 |
|---|---|---|
| Low | EAL 3 + ? | SIL 1 |
| reduced | EAL 4 | SIL 2 |
| Full | EAL 5 | SIL 3 |

A combined Safety/Security Life Cycle was drawn (proposal, Fig. 1):

**Fig. 1.** A possible approach to a Unified Safety & Security Life cycle

The security management life cycle should in the end be integrated in a holistic, unified model of parallel, equivalent activities:

- Definition and Implementation of Security Policy from „Concept" to „Security Requirements Allocation" similar to the safety life cycle,
- Security during System Development (includes Security during the whole lifecycle of the system (Documentation, Evaluation and Certification)
- Maintaining Security Level during Operations (includes Maintenance, Change Management and Incident Handling), Disaster Recovery and Business Continuity Planning). This is a critical issue in context of safety certification: Security outlives rather quick its life time, so frequent updates are necessary – quite opposite to what safety people want, to avoid re-assessment and re-certification!

More details are to be found e.g. in [20][24][18]. Concerning applicable methods, some examples are FMEVA (extended Failure Mode, Effect and Vulnerability Analysis) [25], Attack Trees and State/Event Fault Trees [26][27].

Unfortunately, the approach was in the end not accepted, security should not be tackled in such detail. The conclusion was to add separate clauses into IEC 61508 everywhere where security could have an impact on safety giving advice on how to integrate the security aspect as an additional hazard (risk) for the safety-critical system, i.e. to look at the safety impact of security breaches and then derive requirements for the safety critical system, based on a joint hazard, risk and vulnerability analysis. From a complete Annex remained a few clauses only, but at least there is some pointer in IEC 61508 to the security issue in safety related systems [20].

In EMC², the Work package WP 6.2, Assurance methodologies for EMC² Systems, will focus on the assurance of safety and other qualities as well, particularly security vulnerabilities and countermeasures through system life-time and maintenance of the integrity and assurance levels. Focus will be on necessary extensions of safety & security co-analysis, co-design, combined development and V&V approaches as well as the development of appropriate runtime testing approaches and maintenance during the operational phase. This is necessary to maintain the system which was "safe and secure by design" based on the assumption of predictable behavior (static approach plus monitoring for maintenance purposes).

An additional innovative feature of EMC² is the combination of safety and security attributes as part of the assurance strategy. On one hand, dependable embedded computer systems are crucial for many applications in the fields of transportation, automation, and medicine, where a tremendous progress had been made building ultra-dependable systems out of less reliable components. A multitude of practical techniques with respect to fault masking, error detection, fault diagnosis and recovery has evolved to improve the reliability of safety-critical system. Unfortunately, almost all of these approaches focus on the safety aspect and ignore that the system can be under active and intentional malicious attack. On the other hand, securing information systems and communication are well-established topics in the security research community. Security standards for the Internet and Web services are widely-deployed in IT systems. However, the focus is on securing the information, as best described by the Confidentiality, Integrity, and Availability (CIA) triangle model. Embedded multi-core systems pose new challenges because the targets of malicious attacks are beyond the CIA aspects of information in the system: they are targeting at embedded systems control functions! For example, attackers can attempt to compromise safety through manipulation with integrity or availability attributes, or by misusing interfaces for maintenance purposes. The "foreseeable misuse" is one of the key aspects to be considered at design time.

The related innovation in the EMC² project will be to investigate, develop, and validate methodologies and technical solutions for a holistic approach to safety and security, throughout system lifetime, while taking into account the mission-critical and real-time requirements.

## 4    Safety and Security – Runtime Certification

Apart from the major challenge of co-engineering safety and security as it has been discussed in Section 3, the open and dynamic nature of the considered systems creates additional safety and security engineering challenges.

On the one hand, the capability of systems to adapt dynamically to changes in their environments (e.g. the availability of resources) generates a significant combinatorial complexity that must be dealt with in the context of the development time safety and security analyses. Any potential variant the system under investigation might assume during its lifetime must be foreseen and analyzed. Established safety engineering approaches do not provide any particular means to remediate this issue, which is not very surprising given that adaptive behavior is even prohibited by some of the most prominent current safety standards (e.g. IEC61508 [6]). It shall be noted, however, that this does not mean that adaptive (embedded) systems do not exist. In fact, many systems are adaptive as of today, but their adaptive behavior is not engineered in an adequate and explicit way. This kind of implicit adaptivity of systems makes it even more difficult to apply proper engineering methodologies to ensure their safety and security. A new way of thinking and new corresponding approaches are required in this regard, because otherwise it will hardly be possible to benefit from the full potential of CPS.

On the other hand, beyond being adaptive, the targeted systems are also open for dynamic integration in the sense of a dynamically evolving system of systems. Different systems from different manufacturers are combined at runtime in order to render higher level services that could not be rendered by one single system alone. Ensuring the safety and security of such dynamic compositions based on established engineering approaches is actually impossible per definition. We already emphasized that established approaches wholly build on development time analyses and a complete understanding of the system under development and its environment. However, for the case of open system, the system constituents of the dynamically created systems are largely unknown at development time and can thus not be analyzed in an adequate way.

A potential solution to these problems lies in shifting parts of the assurance and certification activities into runtime, when the actual system constituents and configurations are known and all relevant information can be obtained. Ultimately, this means that systems are to be enabled to (re-)certify themselves whenever dynamic adaptation or integration occurs. At this point it is clear that the amount of responsibility that is transferred to the system and into runtime is a decisive aspect. The more safety and security intelligence is shifted into runtime, the higher the flexibility that is gained. At the same time, however, the complexity of the required runtime mechanisms rises, too. And in general, it would hardly be possible to completely formalize and automate all the reasoning that is required from a safety engineer for engineering a safety concept for a given system. Therefore it must be the goal to keep the runtime aspect as light weight as possible, yet it has to be sufficient to enable dynamic adaption and integration.

A promising solution approach is to utilize modular conditional certificates as they have been proposed in [1] [3] [11]. These are post-certification artefacts, meaning that the actual certification has been conducted in the traditional way with safety engineers analyzing the system and developing an adequate safety concept. However, in contrast to closed and static system, there are certain variation points in the certificate. These are bound to formalized external dependencies that could not be resolved at development time already and shall thus be resolved at runtime. This is what makes the certificates "conditional" and provides the flexibility in the certificates that is required to be fit for a sufficiently wide range of concrete integration scenarios. Of course, the conditional certificates must also be modular, because certification needs to be conducted at the level of the units of composition of the targeted systems of systems. The concept of modular conditional certification is illustrated in Fig. 2 and elaborated in the following.

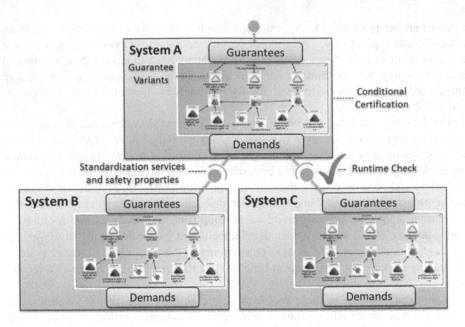

**Fig. 2.** Concept of modular conditional certificates

The conditional certificates are to be evaluated automatically and autonomously by the system at the moment of integration at runtime, based on runtime representations of the certificates of the involved units of composition. This certificate evaluation could either be realized off-board and/or on-board. Off-board checks are useful, if the integration of new systems/components or the adaptation of a given system/component does not need to happen in real-time. In this case, the emerging system can be evaluated through an off-board service (e.g., in the cloud) using more sophisticated (co-)analysis capabilities. If the integration must happen on-the-fly, or if no connection to an external service is available, the evaluation must happen on-board. In this case, the system(s) support a runtime evaluation based on efficient embedded runtime representations of the certificates and corresponding evaluation mechanisms and protocols.

Once all conditions are resolved and the evaluation is finished, an overall certificate variant can be determined for the actual composition that has been formed. In a sense, the final certification step has therewith been postponed into runtime and we could consequently speak of "runtime certification". Whenever the overall system composition changes or the system adapts itself, a re-evaluation of the conditional certificates must be conducted and the overall certificate for the composition must be updated. Such a re-evaluation might well be triggered by a minor dynamic adaptation in one of the subsystems, which, however, can easily trigger a chain reaction in relying components leading to complex reconfiguration sequences. Therefore, there is a strong interdependency between dynamic adaptations and the dynamic evaluations of the conditional certificates. An adaptation might lead to an invalidation of the current certificate and thus to a re-evaluation and to the determination of a new one. This in turn might then violate given top-level trust requirements, which might then again trigger additional adaptations to regain sufficient trust guarantees (e.g. by graceful degradation, which could imply a loss of application features).

The work on Conditional Safety Certificates (ConSerts) presented in [1][3][11]will constitute a starting point for our work. This initial approach provides promising concepts and ideas but, as of yet, lacks the maturity that would be required for industrial-strength solutions as they are envisioned by EMC². Moreover, the approach needs to be augmented in order to take additional properties beyond safety into account. This specifically concerns security, as it is one main focus of EMC² and WP6, but might also concern other less critical properties, such as properties that are related to performance.

## 5 Conclusion and Outlook

CPS have the potential to revolutionize our daily lives, but before this potential can be unlocked some important challenges need to be tackled. At the heart of these challenges, there is the need to ensure safety and security of the new generation of CPS. In this paper we outline a corresponding solution approach that is based on two main pillars, which are also the main focus of the qualification and certification work package of the EMC² project. On the one hand, we strive for sound safety security engineering and establishing integrated trust cases. And on the other hand, we deem it necessary to shift parts of the certification measures into runtime to overcome the combinatorial complexity inherent to CPS. With advances in these two fields we believe that we can get a significant step closer to the vision of safe and secure interconnected CPS and "systems of cyber-physical systems".

**Acknowledgment.** The research leading to these results has received funding from the ARTEMIS Joint Undertaking under grant agreement n° 621429 (project EMC²) and from the respective national funding authorities. Previous work was funded by the ARTEMIS JU under grant agreements n° 269265 and 295373 (projects pSafeCer and nSafeCer) and from respective national funding authorities.

## References

[1] Schneider, D., Trapp, M.: Conditional Safety Certification of Open Adaptive Systems. ACM Trans. Auton. Adapt. Syst. 8(2), Article 8, 20 pages (2013)

[2] Althammer, E., Schoitsch, E., Eriksson, H., Vinter, J.: The DECOS Concept of Generic Safety Cases - A Step towards Modular Certification. In: Proceedings of the 35th Euromicro Conference on Software Engineering and Advanced Applications, pp. 537–545 (2009)

[3] Schneider, D., Trapp, M.: Conditional Safety Certificates in Open Systems. In: Proceedings of the 1st Workshop on Critical Automotive Applications: Robustness & Safety (CARS 2010). ACM (2010)

[4] Fenn, J., Hawkins, R., Kelly, T.P., Williams, P.: Safety Case Composition Using Contracts – Refinements Based on Feedback from an Industrial Case Study. In:15th Safety Critical Systems Symposium (2007)

[5] Bate, I., Kelly, T.P.: Architectural considerations in the certification of modular systems. In: Anderson, S., Bologna, S., Felici, M. (eds.) SAFECOMP 2002. LNCS, vol. 2434, pp. 321–333. Springer, Heidelberg (2002)

[6] IEC 61508, Ed. 2.0, 2010, Part 1-7. Functional safety of electrical/electronic/programmable electronic safety related systems, International Electrotechnical Commission.

[7] Kelly, T.P, Concepts and Principles of Compositional Safety Cases. COMSA/2001/1/1, Research Report commissioned by QinetiQ (2001)

[8] Rushby, J.: Modular certification. NASA Contractor Report CR-2002-212130, NASA Langley Research Center (2002)

[9] Rushby, J.: Just-in-Time Certification. In: proceedings of the 12th IEEE International Conference on Engineering Complex Computer Systems (ICECCS 2007), pp. 15–24 (2007)

[10] Rushby, J.: Runtime certification. In: Leucker, M. (ed.) RV 2008. LNCS, vol. 5289, pp. 21–35. Springer, Heidelberg (2008)

[11] Schneider, D., Trapp, M.: A Safety Engineering Framework for Open Adaptive Systems. In: Proc. of the Fifth IEEE International Conference on Self-Adaptive and Self-Organizing Systems, SASO (2011)

[12] Moore, G.E.: Cramming more components onto integrated circuits. Electronics Magazine, 4 (1965) ISSIN 0883-4989

[13] Kelly, T.: Using software architecture techniques to support the modular certification of safety-critical systems. In: Proceedings of the Eleventh Australian Workshop on Safety Critical Systems and Software, SCS 2006, vol. 63, pp. 53–65. Australian Computer Society, Inc., Darlinghurst (2006)

[14] IEC 62443: Industrial communication networks - Network and system security. International Electrotechnical Commission

[15] ISO/IEC:27002: Information technology - security techniques - Code of practice for information security management. International Organization for Standardization (ISO), International Electrotechnical Commission (IEC)

[16] ISO/IEC 27005, Information technology — Security techniques — Information security risk management. International Organization for Standardization (ISO), International Electrotechnical Commission, IEC (2008)

[17] SafeCer (Safety Certification Safety Certification of Software-intensive Systems with Reusable Components), ARTEMIS project n° 269265/295373 (pSafeCer/nSafeCer), http://www.safecer.eu

[18] 7. OPENCOSS (Open Platform for EvolutioNary Certification Of Safety-critical Systems), European Integrated Project in FP7 , http://www.opencoss-project.eu

[19] ISO 26262 (2011/2012), Part 1- 10, "Road vehicles – functional safety"

[20] Schoitsch, E.: Safety and/vs. Security: Towards a System Engineering approach for Trust? In: Proceedings of ISSC 2013 (31st International Systems Safety Conference), IEEE Conference Proceedings, Boston, USA, August 12-16, System Safety Society, Boston (2013), Paper #134 in electronic proceedings, ISBN 978-0-9858710-1-7

[21] IEC 62741/Ed1, 2013: Reliability of systems, equipment and components. Guide to the demonstration of dependability requirements. The dependability case

[22] IEC/PAS 62814/Ed1, 2013: Dependability of Software Products Containing Reusable Components – Guidance for Functionality and Tests

[23] ISO 15408, 2009: Information technology – Security techniques – Evaluation criteria for IT security

[24] SESAMO (Security and Safety Modelling), http://www.sesamo-project.eu

[25] Schmittner, C., Gruber, T., Puschner, P., Schoitsch, E.: Security application of failure mode and effect analysis (FMEA). In: Bondavalli, A., Di Giandomenico, F. (eds.) SAFECOMP 2014. LNCS, vol. 8666, pp. 311–326. Springer, Heidelberg (2014)

[26] Steiner, M., Liggesmeyer, P.: Combination of Safety and Security Analysis - Finding Security Problems That Threaten The Safety of a System. In: SAFECOMP 2013 - Workshop DECS (ERCIM/EWICS Workshop on Dependable Embedded and Cyber-physical Systems) of the 32nd International Conference on Computer Safety, Reliability and Security (2013)

[27] Roth, M., Liggesmeyer, P.: Modeling and Analysis of Safety-Critical Cyber Physical Systems using State/Event Fault Trees. In: SAFECOMP 2013 - Workshop DECS (2013)

[28] ACROSS (Artemis project: ARTEMIS CROSS-Domain Architecture), http://www.across-project.eu

[29] Ebert, C., Jones, C.: Embedded Software: Facts, Figures and Future, pp. 42–52. IEEE Computer Society (2009)

# Introduction to the Safecomp 2014 Workshop: DEvelopment, Verification and VAlidation of cRiTical Systems (DEVVARTS '14)

Francesco Brancati[1], Nuno Laranjeiro[2], and Ábel Hegedüs[3]

[1] ResilTech s.r.l.,
Piazza Iotti, 25 - 56025 Pontedera (PI) - Italy
[2] CISUC, Department of Informatics Engineering,
University of Coimbra, Coimbra, Portugal
[3] Budapest University of Technology and Economics,
Department of Measurement and Information Systems,
Magyar tudósok krt. 2., 1117 Budapest, Hungary
francesco.brancati@resiltech.com, cnl@dei.uc.pt,
abel.hegedus@mit.bme.hu

## Introduction

The DEVVARTS '14 workshop focuses on novel methods for the development, verification and validation (V&V) and certification of Critical Systems, where the necessary effort for V&V frequently exceeds the core development time when using traditional methods. The "soft" IT industry rapidly turns to system integration based on the reuse of hardware and software components, but for safety related applications this will still evolve primarily due to the lack of composable V&V and certification. All this poses serious difficulties to companies, which are on one hand constrained to meet predefined quality goals, whereas, on the other hand, are required to deliver systems at acceptable cost and time to market. Large companies mainly follow a brute-force approach by focused large volume investment into tooling and in-house training, but even high-tech SMEs are highly vulnerable to the new challenges. Definition of methods, strategies and tools assuring an adequate and simultaneously productive V&V is one of the most challenging goals. It is hard to establish a proper tradeoff between achievable quality with a particular technique (in terms of RAMS attributes) and the costs required for achieving it. The situation is even worse in the case of integration of existing SW in a safety critical system to be certified, since, assessing products which encompass COTS software is a challenge although modern standards consider this possibility. An additional concern is the usage of recently adopted methods for SW development like MDD, since the certification of systems using software developed with these supports is at the limit of the applicability of the existing standards, and only the most recent ones are aligned with these 'modern' methods.

A. Bondavalli et al. (Eds.): SAFECOMP 2014 Workshops, LNCS 8696, pp. 192–194, 2014.

The goal of the workshop on critical systems, their development, V&V and certification is to encourage new trends and ideas about model-based design and certification, experimental assessment of safety, reliability and security, effort evaluation and prediction models for V&V activities, SW-FMEA methodologies, certifiability of critical architectures based on diversity of HW and SW COTS, component integration and V&V, tool certification, human skill aspects of V&V, design for certifiability, interactions and contradictions between safety and security from a certification point of view and techniques for dependable and secure services.

## Program

The program of DEVARTS '14 consists of 6 high-quality papers, covering the above-mentioned topics. We have separated these papers into three mini-sessions based on their focus and the topics they cover:

- Model checking approaches:
    1. "Verification of fault-tolerant system architectures using model checking" by Jussi Lahtinen ;
    2. "Verification of a real-time safety-critical protocol using a modelling language with formal data and behaviour semantics" by András Vörös, Tamás Tóth and István Majzik
- Tools:
    1. "Visualization of Model-Implemented Fault Injection Experiments" by Daniel Skarin, Jonny Vinter and Rickard Svenningsson;
    2. "Cost-Effective Testing for Critical Off-The-Shelf Services" by Fabio Duchi, Nuno Antunes, Andrea Ceccarelli, Giuseppe Vella, Francesco Rossi and Andrea Bondavalli;
- System and tool assessment:
    1. "On Security Countermeasures Ranking through Threat Analysis" by Andrea Bondavalli, Andrea Ceccarelli, Felicita Di Giandomenico, Fabio Martinelli, Ilaria Matteucci and Nicola Nostro;
    2. "Enabling Cross-domain Reuse of Tool Qualification Certification Artefacts" by Barbara Gallina, Shaghayegh Kashiyarandi, Karlheinz Zugsbratl and Arjan Geven;

## Thanks

We are grateful to the SAFECOMP organization committee and collaborators for their precious help in handling all the issues related to the workshop. We also thank all the authors of the submitted papers who manifested their interest in the workshop. With their participation the First SAFECOMP Workshop on Development, Verification and Validation of Critical Systems provides an excellent venue for cooperation and discussion for the experts in this field. Special thanks are finally due to Program Committee members and additional reviewers for the high quality and objective reviews they provided.

**Acknowledgements.** This workshop has been supported by the CECRIS (CErtification of CRItical Systems) research project (FP7-PEOPLE-IAPP-324334-CECRIS). The project aims at taking a step forward in the growing field of development, verification and validation and certification of critical systems. The project focuses on the more difficult/important points of (safety, efficiency, business, ...) of critical system development, verification and validation and certification process. The scientific objectives of the project are study both the scientific and industrial state of the art methodologies for system development and the impact of their usage on the verification and validation and certification of critical systems. Moreover the project aims at developing strategies and techniques supported by automatic or semi-automatic tools and methods for these type of activities, whose cost-quality achievements are well-predictable in order to tie costs of application of techniques to the RAMS attributes level achieved by the product being tested. The project will draw-up guidelines to support engineers during the planning of the verification & validation phases.

# Verification of Fault-Tolerant System Architectures Using Model Checking

Jussi Lahtinen

VTT Technical Research Centre of Finland,
Systems Engineering, P.O. Box 1000, FI-02044 Espoo, Finland
jussi.lahtinen@vtt.fi

**Abstract.** Model checking is a formal method that has proven useful for verifying e.g. logic designs of safety systems used in nuclear plants. However, redundant subsystems are implemented in nuclear plants in order to achieve a certain level of fault-tolerance. A formal system-level analysis that takes into account both the detailed logic design of the systems and the potential failures of the hardware equipment is a difficult challenge. In this work, we have created new methodology for modelling hardware failures, and used it to enable the verification of the fault-tolerance of the plant using model checking. We have used an example probabilistic risk assessment (PRA) model of a fictional nuclear power plant as reference and created a corresponding model checking model that covers several safety systems of the plant. Using the plant-level model we verified several safety properties of the nuclear plant. We also analysed the fault-tolerance of the plant with regard to these properties, and used abstraction techniques to manage the large plant-level model. Our work is a step towards being able to exhaustively verify properties on a single model that covers the entire plant. The developed methodology follows closely the notations of PRA analysis, and serves as a basis for further integration between the two approaches.

**Keywords:** Model checking, nuclear power plants, architecture, hardware failure, fault-tolerance.

## 1 Introduction

The verification of digital instrumentation and control (I&C) systems is challenging because of complicated control functions, and because the state spaces of the designs easily become too large for comprehensive manual inspection. Formal methods can provide more confidence on the correctness of I&C systems.

Model checking [1] is a computer-aided formal verification method that uses models quite similar to those used in simulation. However, unlike simulation, model checkers examine the behaviour of the system design exhaustively and compare it with the system specification. The specification is expressed in a suitable language, such as temporal logics, describing the permitted behaviours of a system. Given a model and a specification as inputs, a model checking algorithm determines whether the system has violated its specification. If a violating

A. Bondavalli et al. (Eds.): SAFECOMP 2014 Workshops, LNCS 8696, pp. 195–206, 2014.

behaviour is found the model checker will give a counter-example execution of the system demonstrating how the specification has been violated. In this work, we have used the model checking tool NuSMV [2], and formalised the requirements as state invariants.

We have previously applied model checking to the verification of logic designs of individual safety systems, see e.g. [3]. There is, however, also need to examine the overall system safety and fault-tolerance on the plant-level. The Finnish regulatory guides on nuclear safety (YVL guides) require that all individual safety systems are single-failure tolerant. For some systems it should also be possible to perform the safety function even if any single component fails and any other component is simultaneously out of operation due to repair or maintenance. The traditional plant-level architecture analysis methods such as fault tree analysis (FTA), failure mode and effects analysis (FMEA) and probabilistic risk assessment (PRA) are not intended for exhaustively examining the complex functionality of the digital automation systems. Model checking, on the other hand, can be used to verify the logical designs exhaustively. Thus, it is tempting to try to expand the scope of model checking to the plant-level so that the overall system behaviour could be analysed in detail. This approach could be beneficial in finding potential errors in system design that arise from a combination of a hardware failure and a software design error.

In our earlier work [4] we developed preliminary methodology for hardware fault models using a small fictitious model. In this paper we improve on this methodology. The intent is to model failures in i.e. telecommunication links, microprocessors, measurement devices, pumps and valves. The operation of the actuators and the effects of failures to how signals are interpreted in the I&C systems are modelled. The developed methodology serves as a framework for verification of high-level system properties and fault-tolerance, which has previously been quite difficult.

We have used a fictitious PRA model and created a corresponding model that can be used for model checking. The PRA model depicts a boiling water reactor (BWR) type nuclear power plant, which has four-redundant safety systems. We verified several system level safety properties, and analysed the level of fault-tolerance the plant model had with regard to these properties. We have also used simple abstractions, and simplifications to make the verification more feasible. The biggest simplification when compared to a real system is that no time delays have been implemented in the safety system logics. We have also assumed that all hardware failures are permanent. The methodology is quite compatible with PRA, and it serves as a basis for further integration between the two approaches. More details on our work can be found in a research report [5].

## 2    Related Work

Model checking has been previously used to analyse system faults and fault-tolerance. FSAP/NuSMV-SA [6] is a safety assessment platform that can be used for injecting faults into a system model and verifying the system fault-tolerance using model checking. A similar fault injection approach is described in [7], where a wheel brake system is verified using SCADE.

The Altarica language [8] was designed for formally specifying the behaviour of failing systems. Altarica is used in e.g. [9] in combination with model checking to assess safety requirements of the AIRBUS A320 hydraulic system.

Other work combining model checking and analysis of fault-tolerance is covered in e.g. [10,11,12]. In [10], a dual-redundant system for a spacecraft controller is verified using the model checker Spin. [11] and [12] are process algebra based modelling approaches for formalising fault-tolerant systems.

Our work, in contrast to the ones above, is about modelling larger systems in which many types of hardware faults are possible. The modelling methodology is built on top of the NuSMV modelling language. Our work also has a connection to PRA analysis.

## 3    Description of the Example System

The case study model used in this work is based on a PRA model of a nuclear power plant. The model depicts a fictive and simplified boiling water reactor (BWR) type nuclear power plant (NPP). In this section, the model is only briefly introduced on a general level. Detailed information on the PRA model can be found from [13] and [14].

The plant model includes eight different safety systems that are mostly four-redundant. The safety systems are divided into two separate subsystems: Reactor Protection System (RPS) and Diverse Protection System (DPS), which are implemented on different automation hardware. The RPS safety systems are: automatic depressurisation system (ADS), component cooling water system (CCW), emergency core cooling system (ECC), service water system (SWS) and residual heat removal system (RHR). The DPS safety systems are: emergency feed water system (EFW), and main feed water system (MFW). In addition, the AC power system belongs to both RPS and DPS. The model describes the operation logic of the safety systems, the hardware equipment used to implement each system, and the associated failure modes for each piece of equipment.

The safety systems read measurements, and actuate their dedicated pumps and valves when necessary to prevent damage in the reactor core. The actuation logic of the safety systems is implemented in four separate acquisition and processing unit (APU) computers. Measurements, which are also four-redundant, are separately brought to each APU. The control signals calculated by the redundant APUs are collected in several voting units (VU) that decide on sending the actuation commands to the pumps and valves.

The safety systems are designed so that the plant can survive a set of potentially hazardous events called initiating events. Five initiating events are defined: loss of coolant accident (LOCA), loss of feed water due to e.g. main feed water pump failures (LOFW), loss of online power (LOOP), disturbances in normal plant operation without the loss of primary coolant (Transient), and the loss of DC power. Depending on the initiating event there are different success criteria for the safety systems. The success criteria can be derived from event trees that exist for each initiating event.

## 4  Modelling

We used the PRA model introduced in Section 3 as reference and created a corresponding model using the NuSMV modelling language that can be used for model checking. We modelled seven out of the eight safety systems that are part of the PRA model. Only the AC power system was not included in the model due to excessive modelling effort required. The model files are available on request. We modelled the system as a discrete time model in which signal propagation is instantaneous, i.e. inputs from measurements reach the outputs of a safety system on the same clock cycle if delays are not implemented in the safety system logic. The modelling methodology was kept as modular as possible.

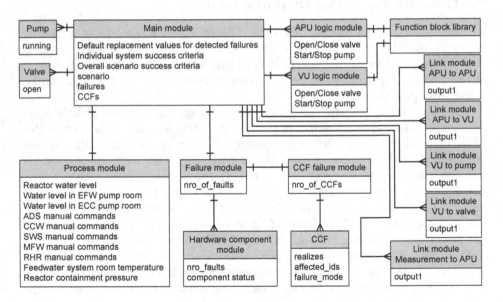

**Fig. 1.** Model composition

The main idea of the methodology is to use link modules to make connections between measurements, logic modules and equipment. The link modules are parameterised with links to the hardware that implement that link, as hardware failures may cause the received value of a variable to be interpreted differently.

The modular composition of the model is illustrated in Fig. 1. The main components of the model are the logic modules (APU and VU), the various link modules, process module, and a failure module. The connections in Fig. 1 are either one-to-one or one-to-many, and should be read as 'creates an instance of'. For example, the main module creates a single instance of the failure module.

Fig. 1 also shows some of the variables calculated and output by the modules. For example, the main module calculates the success criteria for individual safety systems and scenarios. Successful operation means for e.g. ECC that in one of the four redundancies, the pump is running and the corresponding valve is open. A large LOCA scenario is survived when both ECC and RHR systems operate successfully.

## 4.1  Logic Modules

A function block based design was manually created for each safety system. The logic design was written using a function block based approach because that has been a convention in our earlier work, see e.g. [15] for some information on how function block diagrams were modelled. The logic could be designed using the function blocks: AND, OR, NOT, and a 2-out-of-4 vote function block.

Logic was designed both for the APU computers and the voting units in separate modules. The APU computers check whether the actuation commands should be sent based on the measurement values received as input. The voting units calculate their outputs (start/open and stop/close) using 2-out-of-4 function blocks on the input signals.

## 4.2  Failure Module

As shown in Fig. 1, the failure module is used to store all instances of hardware components. Below is the hardware component type module for APU computers.

```
MODULE APU_failuremodule(id, CCFmodule)
VAR
FROZENVAR processor_status : {OK, hang_detected, hang_undetected,
    dropout_detected,dropout_undetected, delayed_detected,
    delayed_undetected, rand_detected, rand_undetected};
FROZENVAR digital_input_status : {OK, stuck_to_current_detected,
    stuck_to_current_undetected};
FROZENVAR digital_output_status : {OK, stuck_to_current_detected,
    stuck_to_current_undetected};
FROZENVAR backplane_or_powersupply_status:{OK, loss_of_function};
DEFINE
nro_faults :=  toint(processor_status != OK)
    + toint(digital_input_status != OK)
    + toint(digital_output_status != OK)
    + toint(single_failure_in_backplane) ;
single_failure_in_backplane :=
    (backplane_or_powersupply_status != OK) &
    ! CCFmodule.APU_backplane_CCF.realizes;
ASSIGN
init(backplane_or_powersupply_status):= case
    CCFmodule.APU_backplane_CCF.realizes &
```

```
            (id in CCFmodule.APU_backplane_CCF.affected_ids) :
                CCFmodule.APU_backplane_CCF.failure_mode;
            TRUE : {OK, loss_of_function};
esac;
```

The module has as parameter the hardware component id number and a reference to the module where all the CCFs are stored. Because the APU computer has many elements that can fail (processor, digital input module, digital output module, backplane and power supply), each element has its own variable indicating the status (OK or one of the failure modes) of the component. The variables are of type FROZENVAR which in the NuSMV modelling language means that the variable value cannot change after the initial time point, i.e. we assume that all faults are permanent. In addition to these variable declarations the hardware component module also calculates the number of experienced failures in the particular APU since several simultaneous failures can be possible. Since common cause failures have influence on the status of individual components the module also uses an *init* clause to force the related variable to the value dictated by the effective common cause failures. The variable *CCFmodule.APU_backplane_CCF.realizes* is a Boolean variable indicating that a common cause failure involving the APU backplane is in effect.

Failures can be either detected or undetected. Detected and undetected failures were modelled as separate failure modes following the reference material. The detection of failures is carried out by the link modules that replace the signal values with a predetermined default value in case of one of the detected failure modes is present.

The failure module is also used to decide which of the hardware components experience a failure. The decision is non-deterministic but the number of single failures and common cause failures are bound by parameters the model. All hardware failures are added up and a constraint clause (*INVAR* declaration of the NuSMV modelling language) is added to restrict the model to only those situations that are according to the failure assumptions.

The failure module creates an instance of a separate common cause failure (CCF) module that stores all the CCFs. The hardware equipment instances are given a distinct ID number when they are instantiated. The ID numbers are used for handling common cause failures. A CCF affects many hardware components, so each common cause failure is modelled by defining a set of ID numbers that are affected by the CCF, and the failure mode related to that CCF.

## 4.3   Link Modules

Link modules are used whenever some piece of information is transferred from one place to another in the plant automation. The link module executes this transfer of information but simultaneously the effects of possible faults affecting the information are taken into account. Since there are only a small number of different type of links (e.g. APU-to-APU, measurement to APU, etc.) link type modules were created that can be parameterised with equipment related to the particular link.

As an example of link module behaviour, consider a measurement of water level that is used as input on an APU computer. The read value depends on whether e.g. the measurement device or the input module of the APU has failed, and whether the failure has been detected. The link modules handle this behaviour in the model and change the perceived logical value of the measurement accordingly. The link type module for measurement-to-APU links is below.

```
MODULE LINK_MEAS_APU(in1, measurement, apu, DFLT)
VAR
prevout : boolean;
DEFINE
output1 := case
 apu.backplane_or_powersupply_status != OK : FALSE;
 apu.digital_input_status = stuck_to_current_detected : DFLT;
 apu.digital_input_status = stuck_to_current_undetected : prevout;
 measurement.status = fail_high_detected : DFLT;
 measurement.status = fail_low_detected : DFLT;
 measurement.status = drift_detected : DFLT;
 measurement.status = freeze_detected : DFLT;
 measurement.status = fail_high_undetected : TRUE;
 measurement.status = fail_low_undetected : FALSE;
 measurement.status = drift_undetected : ! in1;
 measurement.status = freeze_undetected : prevout;
 TRUE : in1;
esac;
ASSIGN
init(prevout):= FALSE;
next(prevout):= output1;
```

The parameter *in1* refers to the variable transferred by the link module, *measurement* is the measuring device from which the value is received, *apu* refers to the APU computer receiving the information, and *DFLT* is the replacement value used if a failure is detected. The transferred variable value is a Boolean variable. The TRUE value of the variable means that the threshold related to the measurement has been surpassed. The FALSE value of the variable means that the physical value is still below the related threshold. The module consists of a single case clause that defines the value of *output1*. The case clause goes through all possible failure modes of the measuring device and the APU that can influence how the variable is read and interpreted in the APU logic. In case of a detected failure (failure modes attached with "_detected") the module uses the *DFLT* value for *output1*. In case of non-detected failures the output is changed according to the failure mode. Two of the failure modes are such that the variable value freezes to the previous value. This has been modelled using a separate variable *prevout*.

## 4.4    Process Module

The process module plays the role of an environment model, and decides on the values of the physical parameters of the plant. These values are the actual physical values independent from the measured values which are suspect to faults. These physical parameters have been modelled mainly as Boolean variables instead of real valued variables. In the case study the physical parameters are mostly compared against a single limit value. From the model perspective it only matters whether the physical parameters are below or above this limit. This behaviour can be achieved using only Boolean variables.

The process module has as input the initiating event that is under examination. Four initiating events were modelled (LOCA, LOOP, LOFW, Transient) using a single enumerative variable *scenario* that determines the used initiating event. The variable *scenario* forces certain physical parameters to have a particular value. For example, in all initiating events the reactor water level becomes low. Consequently, the corresponding variables in the model shall also indicate that the reactor water level is low. The process module consists of case clauses that implement these kinds of rules for all scenarios. The variable *scenario* also has an additional possible value FREE. In this case the physical parameters of the plant experience no restrictions what so ever: the values of the parameters are selected non-deterministically.

## 4.5    Abstractions and Property Verification

In order to simplify the model we did some light abstractions. As an example, the measurement devices have a failure mode *freeze* that can be modelled using a single variable that stores the device's output at the previous time step. We made an abstraction in which we use a random variable instead. Another abstraction was to replace unneeded logic modules with interface modules. An interface module contains no function blocks, and the outputs of the module are defined as free variables. Both of these abstractions are over-approximations that preserve the truth value of universal properties (e.g. safety properties). If the over-approximated model does not have a bad state, then a bad state cannot exist in the more concrete model either.

We also concentrated on verifying simple state invariant properties only. The traditional BDD based model checking techniques were too time consuming on our case study model. Most bounded model checking techniques do not give proofs when specifications are true. We used the k-induction algorithm implemented in NuSMV that can also prove properties in some cases.

## 4.6    Modelling Choices

In our approach we modelled hardware component failures so that each component has a dedicated variable that expresses the status of that component. We then used INVAR clauses to restrict the number of simultaneous failures. This approach was much simpler and clearer than the alternative of using e.g. enumerative variables to select the failing components and failure modes. The practice of using component ID numbers, and maintaining a list of IDs affected by a common cause failure, seemed also an effective way to handle CCFs.

Another successful modelling choice was to create link type modules for different types of links that could be parameterised with the components associated with a particular link instance. A more laborious alternative would have been to bind the signals in a case-specific manner to the components that are used to transfer them, and alter the signal value according to failures in the components. This alternative approach would be laborious because a case clause would have to be written for each link instance, and the number of link instances in the model is very large. We also parameterised the link modules with the modules of the relevant equipment, instead of individual variables within the modules. This seemed to make the link modules a lot simpler.

The PRA model did not include any descriptions of time delays used in the I&C systems, and thus no timers were added to the logic modules. However, in real I&C systems timers are regularly used. Adding timers into the function block diagrams is straightforward but doing so may lead to a model that is computationally more challenging.

In our methodology we assumed that all failures were permanent. This assumption simplifies modelling, and verification times significantly. In the future, the methodology could be extended to cover non-permanent failures as well. We also did not focus on propagation of failures, where a single failure could lead to another type of failure. Propagation of a failure can also be classified as a common cause failure.

In our model the environment model is quite free. For example, the operational states of pumps and valves do not affect the physical parameters, so there are no feedbacks implemented in the model environment. It would have been technically possible to model these feedbacks but this would have overcomplicated the model. Secondly, the intention in our modelling is not to cover the process aspect of the plant in a very detailed manner.

In a more realistic I&C system some failures can be detected by the I&C unit equipment, and in case of such a detection the signal might be marked e.g. using a status bit. In a more realistic model the fault detection capabilities of a system should be modelled as part of the logical design of the system and not as a part of the link modules. In this case study, the status bits were not used or modelled since such behaviour and logic was not described in the reference material.

## 5 Results

We verified several formal specifications on the case study model, and analysed the fault tolerance of the plant with respect to these specifications. The specifications were formalised from the list of requirements in Table 1.

The first four requirements are plant-level requirements that require the inclusion of several safety systems in order to be verified.

The fault-tolerance of the plant was analysed by verifying the requirements using four different failure assumptions: 1) no single failures assumed, 2) one

**Table 1.** Requirements checked on the case study model

| Number | Requirement |
| --- | --- |
| 1 | In case of a LOCA initiating event, the plant safety systems shall fulfil the related success criteria. |
| 2 | In case of a LOFW initiating event, the plant safety systems shall fulfil the related success criteria. |
| 3 | In case of a LOOP initiating event, the plant safety systems shall fulfil the related success criteria. |
| 4 | In case of a TRANSIENT initiating event, the plant safety systems shall fulfil the related success criteria. |
| 5 | In case of a LOFW/LOOP/TRANSIENT initiating event, the EFW safety system shall start a pump and open a valve in at least one of the four redundant subsystems. |
| 6 | In case of a LOCA/LOFW/LOOP/TRANSIENT initiating event, the ECC safety system shall start a pump and open a valve in at least one of the four redundant subsystems. |
| 7 | In case of a LOOP/TRANSIENT initiating event, at least two out of the three MFW pumps shall be started. |
| 8 | In case of a LOFW/LOOP/TRANSIENT initiating event, at least four out of the eight ADS release valves shall be opened. |
| 9 | In case of a LOCA/LOFW/LOOP/TRANSIENT initiating event, at least one out of the four RHR pumps shall be started. |

single failure assumed, 3) two single failures allowed, and 4) three single failures assumed. Common cause failures were not assumed because the list of common cause failures included in the model was not extensive. The requirements were written as state invariants, and verified using the k-induction algorithm provided by the NuSMV tool. We also used the NuSMV parameters –dynamic (dynamic variable reordering) and –coi (cone of influence reduction) for better performance. The k-induction method could prove all properties on bound 1. The verification times varied from 29 s to 108 s depending on the requirement, and the failure assumptions. Memory requirements varied from 90 MB to 113 MB. The size of the state space could not be calculated for the full model. A simpler model including three (ECC, CCW, SWS) out of the seven safety systems consisted of $1.1 \times 10^{260}$ different states out of which $1.9 \times 10^{160}$ states were reachable.

Certain assumptions about the process variables had to be made as well. For example, the ECC system is stopped whenever a high water level (variables *ECCi0CL001-H1* and *ECCi0CL002-H1*) is measured in the ECC pump room. Because of this, in requirement 1 we assume that the water level does not rise. This assumption does not prevent faulty measurements of the water level. The failure assumption was made using two variables: *failures* (the number of simultaneous single hardware component failures) and *CCFs* (the number of simultaneous common cause failures). For example, the formalised property for requirement 1 assuming two single failures is:

```
INVARSPEC (failures = 2 & CCFs = 0 & scenario = LOCA & !
processmodule.ECCiOCL001-H1 & ! processmodule.ECCiOCL002-H1
-> LOCA_No_Core_Damage);
```

All requirements in Table 1 except requirement 7 are true even if two simultaneous failures are assumed. Requirement 7 becomes false in the case of two single failures. This is because the MFW system is three-redundant. In the counter-example for requirement 7 the voting modules on redundancies 1 and 2 fail. Subsequently, only the pump on train 3 is started.

## 6    Conclusions

We have presented methodology for modelling failures. The methodology serves as a framework for the verification of the fault-tolerance of the plant by taking into account the hardware configuration of the system and the various failure modes of the hardware components. We used a PRA model of a nuclear power plant as reference and created a corresponding model that can be used for model checking. We then verified the fault-tolerance of the model with respect to several properties.

Our modelling approach included several abstractions that are over-approximations. These abstractions retain the truth value of universal properties but the abstractions should be applied carefully so that the system model is always larger than the system itself.

The main challenge in verifying large plant-level models is that the resulting model can become very large. The biggest current limitation of using our methodology in practice is that adding timing behaviour to the logic modules significantly increases the complexity of the model checking problem. Using the IC3 algorithm [16] for verification is a potential approach, as well as the portfolio based approach [17].For liveness properties, a liveness to safety reduction, as described in [18], could be used.

Our work intends to bridge the gap between model checking and PRA methods. The model is entirely based on PRA reference material. This suggests that a single well-defined system-level model of the plant could be used for both PRA and model checking. We are also planning to find more synergy between the methods. For example, it may be possible to generate parts of the model checking models based on PRA analysis data sheets. We also want to find out whether the two methods can provide inputs for one another.

## References

1. Clarke, E.M., Grumberg, O., Peled, D.: Model checking. MIT Press (2001)
2. FBK-IRST, Carnegie Mellon University, University of Genova and University of Trento: NuSMV model checker v.2.5.4 (2012)
3. Lahtinen, J., Valkonen, J., Björkman, K., Frits, J., Niemelä, I., Heljanko, K.: Model checking of safety-critical software in the nuclear engineering domain. Reliability Engineering & System Safety 105, 104–113 (2012)

4. Lahtinen, J., Launiainen, T., Heljanko, K.: Model checking methodology for large systems, faults and asynchronic behaviour - SARANA 2011 work report. VTT Technology 12, VTT Technical Research Centre of Finland (2012), http://www.vtt.fi/inf/pdf/technology/2012/T12.pdf
5. Lahtinen, J.: Hardware failure modelling methodology for model checking. Research report: VTT-R-00213-14, VTT Technical Research Centre of Finland (2014), http://www.vtt.fi/inf/julkaisut/muut/2014/VTT-R-00213-14.pdf
6. Bozzano, M., Villafiorita, A.: The FSAP/NuSMV-SA safety analysis platform. International Journal on Software Tools for Technology Transfer 9(1), 5–24 (2007)
7. Joshi, A., Heimdahl, M.P.E.: Model-based safety analysis of simulink models using SCADE design verifier. In: Winther, R., Gran, B.A., Dahll, G. (eds.) SAFECOMP 2005. LNCS, vol. 3688, pp. 122–135. Springer, Heidelberg (2005)
8. Arnold, A., Point, G., Griffault, A., Rauzy, A.: The AltaRica formalism for describing concurrent systems. Fundam. Inf. 40(2,3), 109–124 (1999)
9. Bieber, P., Castel, C., Seguin, C.: Combination of fault tree analysis and model checking for safety assessment of complex system. In: Bondavalli, A., Thévenod-Fosse, P. (eds.) EDCC 2002. LNCS, vol. 2485, pp. 19–31. Springer, Heidelberg (2002)
10. Schneider, F., Easterbrook, S.M., Callahan, J.R., Holzmann, G.J.: Validating requirements for fault tolerant systems using model checking. In: ICRE, pp. 4–13. IEEE Computer Society (1998)
11. Bernardeschi, C., Fantechi, A., Gnesi, S.: Model checking fault tolerant systems. Softw. Test., Verif. Reliab. 12(4), 251–275 (2002)
12. Bruns, G., Sutherland, I.: Model checking and fault tolerance. In: Johnson, M. (ed.) AMAST 1997. LNCS, vol. 1349, pp. 45–59. Springer, Heidelberg (1997)
13. Authén, S., Holmberg, J.E.: Reliability analysis of digital systems in a probabilistic risk analysis for nuclear power plants. Nuclear Engineering and Technology 44(5), 471–482 (2012)
14. Authén, S., Gustafsson, J., Holmberg, J.E.: Guidelines for reliability analysis of digital systems in PSA context - Phase 3 status report. NKS Report NKS-277, Nordic Nuclear Safety Research, NKS (2013)
15. Pakonen, A., Mätäsniemi, T., Lahtinen, J., Karhela, T.: A toolset for model checking of PLC software. In: IEEE 18th Conference on Emerging Technologies & Factory Automation (ETFA), pp. 1–6 (September 2013)
16. Bradley, A.R.: SAT-based model checking without unrolling. In: Jhala, R., Schmidt, D. (eds.) VMCAI 2011. LNCS, vol. 6538, pp. 70–87. Springer, Heidelberg (2011)
17. Sterin, B., Een, N., Mishchenko, A., Brayton, R.: The benefit of concurrency in model checking. In: Proceedings of the International Workshop on Logic Synthesis, IWLS 2011, pp. 176–182 (2011)
18. Kuismin, T., Heljanko, K.: Increasing confidence in liveness model checking results with proofs. In: Bertacco, V., Legay, A. (eds.) HVC 2013. LNCS, vol. 8244, pp. 32–43. Springer, Heidelberg (2013)

# Verification of a Real-Time Safety-Critical Protocol Using a Modelling Language with Formal Data and Behaviour Semantics

Tamás Tóth, András Vörös, and István Majzik

Budapest University of Technology and Economics, Hungary

**Abstract.** Formal methods have an important role in ensuring the correctness of safety critical systems. However, their application in industry is always cumbersome: the lack of experts and the complexity of formal languages prevents the efficient application of formal verification techniques. In this paper we take a step in the direction of making formal modelling simpler by introducing a framework which helps designers to construct formal models efficiently. Our formal modelling framework supports the development of traditional transition systems enriched with complex data types with type checking and type inference services, time dependent behaviour and timing parameters with relations. In addition, we introduce a toolchain to provide formal verification. Finally, we demonstrate the usefulness of our approach in an industrial case study.

## 1 Introduction

Nowadays, an ever increasing number of information systems are embedded systems that have a dedicated function in a specific, often safety critical application environment (e.g., components of a railway control system). In case of safety critical systems, failures may endanger human life, or result in serious environmental or material damage, thus ensuring conformance to a correct specification is crucial for their development.

To guarantee that a system operates according to its specification, formal verification techniques can be used. These techniques are based on formal representation of both systems and their properties (requirements), which makes it possible to apply mathematical reasoning to investigate their relationship. Moreover, these methods allow verification of systems in an early phase of the development life cycle.

Since behavior of safety critical systems is often time dependent, the notion of time has to be represented in their models. The most prevalent way to model timed systems is the formalism of timed automata. However, this formalism is only suitable to describe timed behavior with respect to constant values, thus its expressive power is not sufficient to model systems with parametric behavior. Parametric timed automata, an extension of the original formalism, addresses this problem.

In this paper we introduce a formal modelling framework for supporting the efficient development of parametric timed automaton based formal models. The

A. Bondavalli et al. (Eds.): SAFECOMP 2014 Workshops, LNCS 8696, pp. 207–218, 2014.
© Springer International Publishing Switzerland 2014

modelling language is essentially based on the language of the well-know *Symbolic Analysis Laboratory* (SAL) framework[1] with extensions to simplify the work of the modellers. These extensions enable the modelling of time dependent behaviour on language level.

In the following, first we introduce the main features of language by modelling the development version of an industrial protocol. Then we present our model checking workflow and demonstrate the feasibility of it by the verification of the protocol.

**Related Work.** Our work is inspired by the *SAL* model checker [7] and its language (our extensions are introduced in Section 3). The SAL language enables compact modeling of systems in terms of (unlabeled) symbolic transition systems, however it doesn't support explicit modeling of time related behavior. The aim was to preserve compatibility so that the timed models of our extended language can still be transformed to the input of SAL. As another related tool, *UPPAAL* [1] is a model checker widely used for the verification of timed systems. It has a graphical interface and it provides efficient model checking algorithms to verify timed automata. UPPAAL models can also be transformed to our language with some restrictions: our formalism does not handle complex function declarations. Our approach has different strengths as the underlying Satisfiability Modulo Theories (SMT) technologies are efficient for even complex data structures of the modelled systems. In addition, complex synchronisation constraints can be compactly expressed in our approach. The industrial case study we use was first introduced in [8], where the SAL model checker was used for the verification. Our paper now is based on the lessons learnt from that work. Simple fault models were introduced in the case study, for a more general overview we refer the interested reader to [4,2].

## 2    The ProSigma SCAN Protocol

*ProSigma* is a microcontroller based system being developed by Prolan Ltd. Its primary role is to provide reliable communication between the modules of a railway control system. Since this functionality is highly safety critical, it has to be implemented on the highest safety integrity level, SIL4. The system consists of so-called ProSigma devices, that are interconnected in an IP based network. Each ProSigma device contains a so-called ETH unit that is responsible for data transport and so-called LG units (in object modules) that are responsible for handling field objects such as switches and signals. Communication between these units is based on the proprietary SCAN protocol. A part of the messages is forwarded within a ProSigma device, while the other messages are sent through the ETH unit to another ProSigma device addressed by the message.

A ProSigma application typically consists of a control side (e.g., a device at a supervisory control system) and an object side (e.g., a device at a field object).

---

[1] http://sal.csl.sri.com/

During connection handling, a connection is established and maintained between an LG unit of the control side and an LG unit of the object side. Connection handling includes the following two tasks:

- Establishing the connection: a link is built between the two sides.
- Object state transfer: each side sends its state to the other side.

During connection handling, the state of each connection has to be kept track of at both sides. A connection is defined by the following:

- The connected pairs - the field side has at most four, while the control side has at most one pair.
- The ETH unit providing the connection.

The connection is alive if and only if it is alive through at least one ETH unit. In the first design of the protocol, the connection handling was characterized by the following properties:

**The connection is handled** via OBJ messages (*OBJ1, OBJ2, OBJUP, OBJDOWN*). Received OBJ messages are processed on two levels. On the first level, based on the timestamps provided in the message, it has to be checked whether the message can be accepted to establish, respectively maintain the connection. On the second level, the acceptability of the object state has to be examined (the object state is more up-to-date than the one accepted last time, it is sent by the right unit, etc.).

**The connection is established** in a two-way handshake: the first message is initiating the connection, and the response to it serves as an acknowledgement. In particular, on the field side, the connection is initiated by sending *OBJ1* and is acknowledged by receiving *OBJ2*. On the control side, sending *OBJ2* initiates and receiving *OBJUP* acknowledges the connection.

LG units on the field side must establish the connection with all corresponding control sides through each ETH units independently.

**Object state is transferred** via two messages (*OBJUP, OBJDOWN*). Sending and receiving object state on an ETH channel is possible only after the LG units of the field side and the control side established connection through the ETH channel. The transfer is triggered by the ETH unit of the field side via periodic *TIMESYNC* messages to the corresponding LG units.

The following model (Figure 1) represents a connection as administered on the field and the control side, respectively, as a network of timed automata with an extended syntax that admits intuitive manipulation of data structures and handshake over multiple input and output labels.

In the model, all messages originate from either of the sides, and propagate for at least *TPropMin* and at most *TPropMax* time units. Assuming that the other parameters of the system are proportional to the propagation time, it will never be the case that a message or the object state stored in it is not acceptable due to an outdated timestamp. Thus in order to simplify the model, the timestamps of messages and acceptability checks are not included in the model (although both the altered timed automata formalism and the specification language enable their modeling).

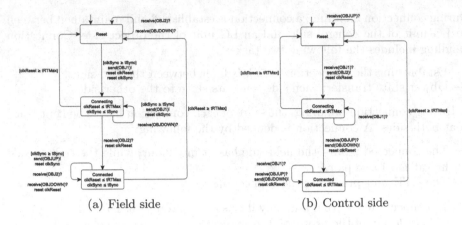

(a) Field side                    (b) Control side

**Fig. 1.** Connection handling on the field and control side

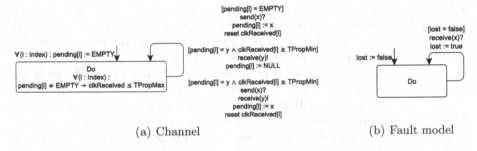

(a) Channel                       (b) Fault model

**Fig. 2.** Models of the channel and the possible fault occurrences

**Channel:** The channel serves as a communication medium between components. Its model (Figure 2(a)) has a role to store and delay messages for a certain amount of time specified by its parameters, and then dispatch them.

Initially, the channel is empty. If a message is dispatched and the channel is not full, then the message is stored. If the delay of a message is over, and some component is able to receive it, then the message is forwarded to that component. If the component instantly sends a response, then the response is stored in place of the forwarded message.

**Field side:** The model of the field side is presented on Figure 1(a).

On the field side, the connection is initially in state *Reset*. As described above, the connection establishment phase is initiated by receiving a *TIMESYNC* message from the ETH unit. For the sake of simplicity, receiving a *TIMESYNC* message is modeled with a clock *clkSync* and corresponding invariants. When the clock reaches *clkSync*, the field module sends *OBJ1* to the control side and traverses to state *Connecting*.

In state *Connecting*, the LG unit waits for *tRtMax* time units for the *OBJ2* message acknowledging the connection. If received in time, the connection is set to state *Connected*, and the object state transfer phase starts on the field side. Otherwise, as clock *clkReset* reaches *tRTMax*, the connection resets.

Object state transfer is also synchronized by *TIMESYNC* messages. When received, the field LG unit sends its state to the control side in a message *OBJUP*. If the time since the last *OBJDOWN* message received reaches *tRtMax*, the connection resets on the field side.

**Control Side:** Similarly to connection handling on the field side, initially, the connection is in state *Reset*. When receiving *OBJ1*, the LG unit sends an *OBJ2* message as response and sets the connection state to *Connecting* (Figure 1(b)) .

State *Connecting* is maintained for at most *tRtMax* time units. If no *OBJUP* is received in that interval, the connection state is set to *Reset*. For an *OBJUP* message received in time, the control LG unit sends its object state in an *OBJ-DOWN* message, and sets the connection to *Connected*. If the time since the last *OBJUP* message received reaches *tRtMax*, the connection state is set to *Reset*.

**Fault Model:** Since the system has to operate in a safety critical setting, guarantees have to be given for scenarios including unexpected events. For that purpose, the model is extended first with a simple fault model that describes loss of a single message in the channel. The fault model is depicted on Figure 2(b).

## 3   The Language

The following section demonstrates the capabilities of our extended modelling language by a step-by-step description of the model of the connection handling in the SCAN protocol.

All elements of the model are encapsulated in the context of a *specification*. A specification can have parameters that can be assigned concrete values later on. In this case, a parameter *n* is introduced to represent the capacity of the channel.

```
specification ProSigmaSpec(n : natural) {
  // Type definitions
  // Constant definitions
  // Function definitions
  // Constraint definitions
  // System definitions
  // Property definitions
}
```

To model automata locations and messages, two enumeration types are defined. Moreover, a type for timing parameters is introduced as the set of non-negative reals, and a subrange is introduced to serve as an index for messages in the channel.

```
type Location : enum { reset, connecting, connected};
type Message : enum { null, obj1, obj2, objup, objdown };
type Param : { x : real | x >= 0 };
type Index : [1 to n];
```

Other supported data types include function, array, tuple and records types, that can be combined to form more complex types.

Timing parameters can then be conveniently modeled as constants of type *Param*. To represent a concrete setting of parameters, a value is assigned to each constant.

```
const tRTMax : Param := 6.0;
const tSync : Param := 3.0;
const tPropMin : Param := 1.0;
const tPropMax : Param := 1.0;
```

However, parameters do not need to be defined explicitly, but can also be represented by constraints expressing their relationships:

```
constraint 2 * tPropMax <= tRTMax;
```

Representing the model of the channel using the language is straightforward. The channel has inputs *msgEvent* and *send* that together model the synchronization primitive *send(x)*. Received messages are stored in array *pending*, until clock *clkReceived* reaches the timeout interval. The synchronization primitive *receive(x)* is modelled by output *receive*.

```
system Channel := {
  input var msgEvent : boolean;
  input var send : Message;
  global var pending : array Index of Message;
  global var clkReceived : array Index of clock;
  output var receive : Message;
  ...
}
```

The invariant that ensures that messages are delayed for at most *tPropMax* time units can be modelled explicitly.

```
invariant forall (i : Index) : (
  pending[i] = ::null imply clkReceived[i] <= tPropMax
);
```

Analogously to invariant constraints, also urgency constraints can be specified that prohibit time to elapse in certain states.

Initial values of the variables are assigned in an *initialization* section.

```
initialization {
  let receive = ::null;
  let pending = [ i : Index | ::null ];
}
```

Similarly, transitions of the automaton can be mapped to *transition* sections. For example, the transition that dispatches a message and stores the immediate response in a single step can be modelled as follows.

```
transition async (i : Index) :
  msgEvent' and send' /= ::null and
  pending[i] /= ::null and clkReceived[i] >= tPropMin --> {
    let pending'[i] = send';
    let clkReceived'[i] = 0.0;
    let receive' = pending[i];
  }
```

The keyword *async* denotes that there is an instance of the transition for each index $i$. The formula followed by `-->` serves as the guard of the guarded command. Apostrophes mark the next state of a variable.

Transitions of the modules can then be defined in a way that complements the definition of the channel. For example, the transition of the Control module that models receiving an *OBJ1* message in location *Reset* can be specified as follows:

```
transition control_location = ::reset and
  receive' = ::obj1 --> {
    let msgEvent' = true;
    let send' = ::obj2;
    let control_location' = ::connecting;
    let control_reset'= 0.0;
  }
```

Here, *receive* is an input variable, whereas *send* and *msgEvent* are global variables. Notice that the model is modular in the sense that responsibilities of communicating modules and the channel are completely separated. Given all modules are defined, the system can be composed in the following way:

```
system ProSigma :=
  (FieldLG [] ControlLG [] FaultModel) || Channel;
```

That is, communicating modules are composed asynchronously, then the result is composed synchronously to the channel.

Temporal properties can then be defined over the composed system. For example, the model can be validated by checking the property expressing that the capacity of the array for received messages is sufficiently big:

```
property capacity : ProSigma models
  G exists (i : Index) : pending[i] = ::null;
```

The liveness property that expresses that eventually a stable connection is established is the following – note that the usual temporal operators **G** (globally) and **F** (eventually) are used:

```
property live : ProSigma models F G (
  field_location = ::connected and
  control_location = ::connected
)
```

## 4   The Verification Workflow

The semantics of the language is provided by a series of simplifying model transformations, and a mapping to an SMT problem. Figure 3 depicts the verification workflow. Dashed lines sign the possible extensions with other modelling and verification technologies.

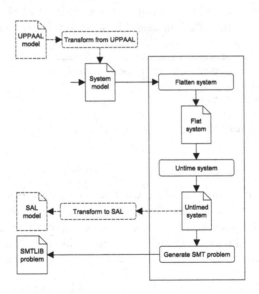

**Fig. 3.** Verification workflow

The starting point of the workflow is a model in the above language given either directly, or as a result of a transformation from other timed formalisms, e.g. *UPPAAL* [1].

As a first step, the system is automatically flattened, that is, the result of a synchronous, respectively asynchronous composition is established. This is performed by merging the variables, invariant and urgency constraints, and initialization and transition definitions of the components. For example, the following transition of the system *ProSigma* is a result of merging the two transitions presented in the previous section:

```
transition control_location = ::reset and receive^ = ::obj1 and
  msgEvent' and send' /= ::null and
  pending[1] /= ::null and clkReceived[1] >= tPropMin --> {
    let pending'[1] = send';
    let clkReceived'[1] = 0.0;
    let send' = ::obj2;
    let control_location' = ::connecting;
    let control_reset' = 0.0;
    let msgEvent' = true;
    let receive' = pending[1];
  }
```

During this step, many of the constructed transitions can be eliminated by simply checking the satisfiability of their guards with a call to the underlying SMT solver [6].

In the next step, the model is automatically "untimed" by expressing the semantics of delay transitions explicitly:

```
transition control_location = ::reset and receive^ = ::obj1 and
  msgEvent' and send' /=::null and
  pending[1] /= ::null and clkReceived[1] + d >= tPropMin --> {
    let field_location' = field_location;
    let field_reset' = field_reset + d;
    let field_sync' = field_sync + d;
    let send' = ::obj2;
    let msgEvent' = true;
    let control_location' = ::connecting;
    let control_reset' = 0.0;
    let receive' = pending[1];
    let pending' = [ i : Index |
      if i = 1 then send' else pending[i]
    ];
    let clkReceived' = [ i : Index |
      if i = 1 then 0.0 else clkReceived[i] + d
    ];
}
```

Here, a combined transition semantics [5][7] is considered, where a transition merges the effects of a delay transition, followed by a discrete transition. For that purpose, a new input variable $d$ is introduced to represent time delay. Such an untimed system model can easily be mapped to SAL or other intermediate formalisms. At the same time, transition (and initialization) definitions are completed, that is, assignments for unmodified variables (e.g., variables of asynchronous components) are made explicit. As a result, each variable (even those of some complex data type) is assigned a value in at most one assignment of a behavior definition.

The symbolic transition system represented by the model can then be easily expressed in SMT by transforming initialization and transition definitions of the system to predicates $I(\bar{x})$, respectively $T(\bar{x}, \bar{x}')$ as usual [3].

The tooling is implemented in *Eclipse*[2] using *Eclipse Modeling Framework*[3] and relating technologies.

- *Abstract syntax.* The abstract syntax of the language is implemented as a metamodel in *EMF*. It is defined as an extension of the core language suitable for defining complex data types and expressions.
- *Concrete syntax.* The textual concrete syntax is defined by an $LL^*$-parsable grammar. The textual editor is then generated using the *Xtext*[4] tooling.
- *Semantics.* Model transformations that define the semantics of the language are implemented in *Xtend*[5].
- *Well-formedness rules.* Together with other validation constraints, algorithms for type checking and type inference are implemented for the type system of the language.

The formal modeling framework supports the development and analysis of transition systems enriched with complex data types, time dependent behaviour, timing parameters with relations and also synchronous and asynchronous composition of modules. The tooling provides type checking and type inference to further improve usability.

## 5    Verification of the Protocol

To check the properties of the first design, bounded model checking in depth $k = 18$ was executed. As a result, the counterexample depicted on Figure 4. arised. On the diagram, the direction of the arrows symbolizes processing order of events occurring at the same time.

The counterexample reveals that if events occur in a particular order, the loss of even a single message can keep the connection from getting established, contrary to expectations. Due to delay and jitter in IP networks, a situation like that is possible even in practice. The situation can be prevented by modifying the control module so that it responds to *OBJ1* with *OBJ2* in state *Connecting*. The design models were updated accordingly, and the avoidance of this situation was proven by repeated verification.

---

[2] http://eclipse.org/
[3] http://eclipse.org/modeling/emf/
[4] http://eclipse.org/Xtext/
[5] http://eclipse.org/xtend/

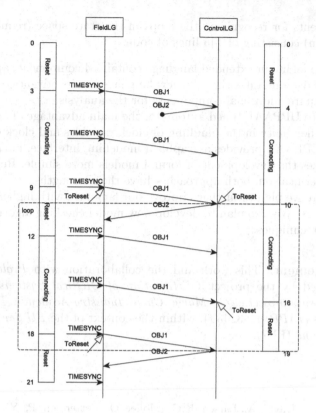

**Fig. 4.** Counterexample for the liveness property

# 6  Evaluation and Conclusion

This paper is one step towards scalable formal modelling. We proposed a modelling language to provide better support for the designers of formal models by focusing on the aspects of data semantics, time dependent behaviour, parameterization, and synchronous and asynchronous composition of components. Instead of manually coding flat transition systems, we provided automated model transformations from our extended language to more simple transition systems that can be directly mapped to the input of existing SMT solvers. This way and automated verification workflow is offered.

To evaluate the effectiveness of our language, the formal model of the introduced case study was developed in both our and the SAL languages. Comparing the results, the complexity of the developed models are the following:

The SAL model contains:

- 5 components for modelling the basic behaviour consisting of 410 lines of code,
- 2 components for supporting the proper analysis of the temporal logic specification consisting of 105 lines of code,

– 3 components for recognizing the loops in the state space (required for the verification) consisting of 145 lines of code.

The formal model in our extended language contains 4 components and 235 lines of code, which demonstrates that the new language has its advantage. Moreover, it does not require additional components for the analysis.

Compared to UPPAAL timed automata, the main advantage of our language is the greater flexibility in the handling of clock variables and clock constraints. However, as UPPAAL provides a graphical modelling interface, in case of small models it makes the development of formal models more simple. Regarding the efficiency of verification, both approaches have their strengths.

In the future we plan to further improve our language with higher level modelling constructs. We also plan to develop new model checking algorithms based on induction techniques.

**Acknowledgement.** This work and the collaboration with *Prolan Ltd.* has been supported by the project *CErtification of CRItical Systems (CECRIS, http://www.cecris-project.eu/)*, *Marie Curie Industry-Academia Partnerships and Pathways (IAPP) nr* 324334, within the context of the *EU Seventh Framework Programme* (FP7).

# References

1. Behrmann, G., David, A., Larsen, K.G., Möller, O., Pettersson, P., Yi, W.: UPPAAL - present and future. In: Proc. of 40 th IEEE Conference on Decision and Control, IEEE Computer Society Press (2001)
2. Bozzano, M., Villafiorita, A.: The fsap/nusmv-sa safety analysis platform. International Journal on Software Tools for Technology Transfer 9(1), 5–24 (2007)
3. Clarke, E., Biere, A., Raimi, R., Zhu, Y.: Bounded model checking using satisfiability solving. Formal Methods in System Design 19(1), 7–34 (2001)
4. Joshi, A., Miller, S.P., Whalen, M., Heimdahl, M.P.E.: A proposal for model-based safety analysis. In: The 24th Digital Avionics Systems Conference, DASC 2005, vol. 2, p. 13 (October 2005)
5. Kindermann, R., Junttila, T., Niemelä, I.: SMT-based induction methods for timed systems. In: Jurdziński, M., Ničković, D. (eds.) FORMATS 2012. LNCS, vol. 7595, pp. 171–187. Springer, Heidelberg (2012)
6. de Moura, L., Bjørner, N.S.: Z3: An efficient SMT solver. In: Ramakrishnan, C.R., Rehof, J. (eds.) TACAS 2008. LNCS, vol. 4963, pp. 337–340. Springer, Heidelberg (2008)
7. Pike, L.: Real-time system verification by k-induction. Tech. Rep. TM-2005-213751, NASA Langley Research Center (May 2005)
8. Tóth, T., Vörös, A., Majzik, I.: K-induction based verification of real-time safety critical systems. In: Zamojski, W., Mazurkiewicz, J., Sugier, J., Walkowiak, T., Kacprzyk, J. (eds.) New Results in Dependability & Comput. Syst. AISC, vol. 224, pp. 469–478. Springer, Heidelberg (2013)

# Visualization of Model-Implemented Fault Injection Experiments

Daniel Skarin, Jonny Vinter, and Rickard Svenningsson

Department of Electronics, SP Technical Research Institute of Sweden, Sweden
{daniel.skarin,jonny.vinter,rickard.svenningsson}@sp.se

**Abstract.** MODIFI is a fault injection tool targeting software developed as Simulink models. In this paper, we describe three techniques for visualizing fault injection results obtained using the MODIFI tool. The first technique shows the progress of a fault injection campaign, and the outcome of individual experiments, using a 3D visualization of the fault injection campaign. The second technique, referred to as sensitivity profiling, identifies parts of a model that are sensitive for a specific fault model. The third technique shows how error propagates in a Simulink model. The sensitivity profiling and error propagation techniques are based on intuitive coloring of Simulink blocks. The three visualization techniques are demonstrated using a Brake-by-Wire system.

**Keywords:** Fault injection, Simulink, Visualization.

## 1   Introduction

Model-based development of software has become more and more common over the years. Software can be designed and verified using behavioral models developed in e.g. Simulink [1], which is one of the most popular tools for this purpose. For safety-related software developed in Simulink, compliance with recommendations from functional safety standards may be required. For example, if the international standards IEC 61508 [2] or ISO 26262 [3] are used, they require that systems shall be able to handle faults, and fault injection is either recommended or mandatory according to these standards. Fault injection is an experimental method to exercise and evaluate error detection and recovery mechanisms, and it can also be used in an iterative manner to improve software robustness.

There have been some initiatives to develop fault injection support for models [4, 5, 6, 7], including the MODIFI (MODel-Implemented Fault Injection) tool [8]. The setup and execution of new fault injection experiments for Simulink models using MODIFI is done in the same manner for any Simulink model. The analyses of the fault injection experiments can be more difficult since they are application-specific and have to be tailored for each Simulink model. MODIFI analyses the output values for the experiments conducted on the Simulink model to determine failures (safety requirements violations). For a more detailed analysis, it is important to reveal error detection and propagation inside the software model. Hence, tool support that besides

A. Bondavalli et al. (Eds.): SAFECOMP 2014 Workshops, LNCS 8696, pp. 219–230, 2014.

visualizing the outcome of the experiments [8] also visualizes error propagation and sensitive blocks inside the model would be beneficial. With such support, the developer can debug the modelled software and identify robustness issues by navigating inside the target Simulink model.

This paper presents new analysis functionality in the MODIFI tool that visualizes how errors propagate through the model, and identify sensitive blocks in the model. This can be used to reveal problems and to design more robust software. We exemplify the usefulness of our approach using a Brake-by-wire model and by using both bit-flip faults and sensor fault models.

The paper is organized as follows. Section 2 presents the MODIFI tool in more detail and Section 3 explains the visualisation techniques supported by MODIFI. In Section 4, we exemplify the use of the visualization techniques on a Brake-by-Wire application developed in Simulink. Finally, conclusions are given in Section 5.

## 2     The MODIFI Fault Injection Tool

A model-based approach for software development is commonly used in the automotive industry, and Simulink [1] and TargetLink [9] are two examples of tools that can be used to develop automotive software. MODIFI is a fault injection tool for dependability assessment of software developed as Simulink models. Using this tool, non-functional properties such as error detection coverage of fault tolerance mechanisms, can be tested using Simulink models as a complement to physical fault injection tests on the target system. This method makes it possible to perform fault injection testing in early phases of the development, and the same environment is used for the development of the software, as well as functional and non-functional testing.

### 2.1     Fault Injection in Simulink Models

The objective of fault injection is to introduce artificial fault or errors in a system to test the system in presence of errors. The injection of faults using MODIFI is done by rerouting the connection between blocks in the model to also include a fault model. This is illustrated in Fig. 1 and Fig. 2, which show a Simulink model before and after MODIFI has inserted a fault injection block. The fault injection block will pass the input value to the output port unmodified unless a trigger is enabled. The trigger, which is based on the simulation time, will cause the block to apply the fault model, a bit-flip in this case, to the output. Fig. 2 also shows that MODIFI turns signals in the model into Simulink test points [10] which all have logging enabled.

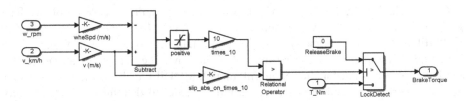

**Fig. 1.** Simulink model before fault injection

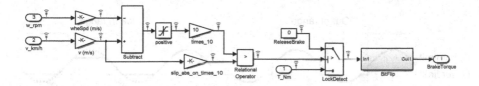

**Fig. 2.** Simulink model after insertion of a fault injection block for bit-flips

Fault injection in Simulink models can be used to identify weaknesses in a system in early phases of the development. It might also be useful for showing compliance with standards for functional safety such as ISO 26262. As stated in Part 6 of the standard [11], the test environment for software testing shall correspond to the target environment. For model-based development, testing can be performed on a model if the tests are followed by a back-to-back comparison between the model and the object code. This is done to ensure that the behaviour of the model and the code generated from it is equivalent with respect to the test objectives. The same approach is used in reference workflows described for the development of safety-related software using tools such as Simulink and TargetLink [12, 13]. Fault injection can therefore be done on Simulink models, if the tests are complemented with fault injection tests on the physical system.

## 2.2 Fault Models

MODIFI supports a wide range of fault models and can easily be extended with new fault models. In our current implementation, we provide fault models for single bit-flip faults and for sensor faults. The single bit-flip fault model is commonly used to emulate the effects of transient hardware faults, and we use this fault model to emulate the effects of hardware faults that affect registers and memory which are visible to software running on a microprocessor.

The fault models for sensors which are implemented in MODIFI are based on the ISO 26262 standard. Although the standard does not provide a generic fault model for sensors, Annex D in Part 5 [14] lists typical fault models failure modes that should be investigated when diagnostic coverage is evaluated. The standard lists the following typical failure modes for sensors: out-of-range, stuck in range, offsets, and oscillations. In addition to the previously mentioned fault modes, MODIFI also supports stuck-at and gain faults. Fig. 3 shows how MODIFI implements the different fault models for sensors. The parameters, e.g., amplitude and frequency for oscillations, are defined by the user during the configuration of a fault injection campaign.

As input when implementing support for sensor failures, we used the failure modes listed in Annex D in Part 5 of ISO 26262 but there are also other classifications of sensor failures. For example, Balaban et al. [15] discuss how sensors can supply faulty values due to, e.g., manufacturing inefficiencies, wear, and incorrect calibration or handling. They divide behaviors of faulty sensors into the following categories: bias, drift, scaling (or gain failure), noise, and hard fault. Hard faults are further divided

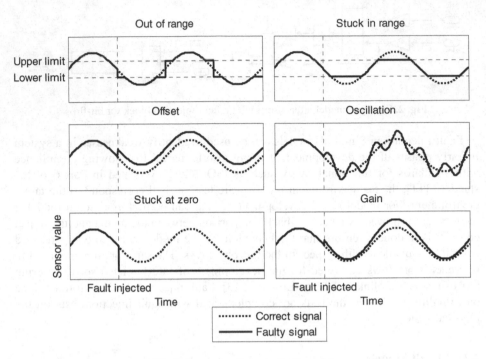

**Fig. 3.** Example of sensor fault models

into loss of signal, stuck sensor and intermittent. Ni et al. [16] present definitions and possible causes of faults, and describe faults such as outliers, spikes, stuck-at, calibration, and clipping.

# 3    Visualization of Fault Injection Experiments

The analysis of fault injection experiments is a time-consuming task that can be simplified using graphical visualization techniques. This section describes three techniques included in MODIFI that help a user in the analysis of fault injection experiments. Two of the techniques provide the user with a graphical overview of a fault injection campaign, i.e., a set of experiments. The third technique aids the user in understanding how an error propagates in a single experiment.

## 3.1    Experiment Outcomes

MODIFI shows the progress of a fault injection campaign and the outcome of individual experiments using a three-dimensional cube. Fig. 4 shows an example of a campaign with a total of 21 experiments. Each box within the cube represents one experiment, and the color of each box shows the status of the experiment.

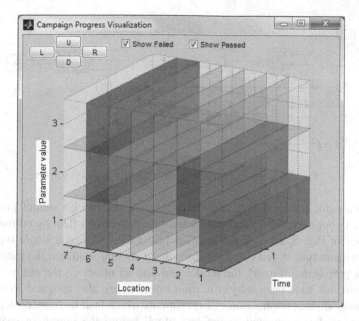

**Fig. 4.** Graphical visualization of progress and experiment outcomes using a 3D cube

For experiments which have been performed, a green color shows that the injected fault or error did not have an impact on the produced results, and a red color shows that the produced output differed from a fault-free execution of the model.

As an extensive fault injection campaign can be very time consuming to run, the cube gives the user a good overview of the progress of the experiments. It can also help to identify problems with the simulation of the model or with the setup of the campaign. For example, experiment outcomes which differ significantly from the expected behavior, e.g., Simulink throwing exceptions for several experiments, can indicate an incorrect configuration that the graphical visualization can reveal before waiting for all fault injection experiments to finish.

### 3.2    Sensitivity Profiling

One of the main purposes of performing fault injection is to identify parts of a system that is sensitive for certain kinds of faults. Such parts may require extra attention and perhaps adding or reconstructing fault handling mechanisms. MODIFI has support to aid a user in finding sensitive parts of a Simulink model by coloring it according to the outcome of a fault injection campaign. Fig. 5 shows an example of fault sensitivity profiling based on a campaign for a majority voter intended for, e.g., a Triple Modular Redundancy (TMR) system. Each block in the model which has been targeted by the fault injection campaign gets a color based on its sensitivity of the injected faults.

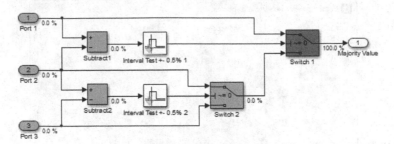

**Fig. 5.** Example of sensitivity profiling for a majority voter

A green color indicates that faults injected into the block's output ports did not propagate through the model and did therefore not have an effect on output ports. As we can see in Fig. 5, none of the injected faults that affected a single input had an impact on the output. A red color indicates that faults injected into the output ports of the block propagated through the model and had an effect on the output ports. The output ports that have been subject to fault injection are also assigned with a percentage, which indicates the fraction of experiments which lead to an incorrect output. In the figure, all faults injected in the last block before the output (a switch block) caused the output to be incorrect. This is due to the switch being a single point of failure in this implementation of the majority voter.

This visualization technique is similar to the graphical analysis described for FOCUS [17], which is a simulation environment for analyzing the fault susceptibility of VLSI designs. FOCUS includes a graphical analysis that visualizes the functional units which are affected by faults, and how faults propagate on interconnects and external pins. Techniques to visualize similar results have also been presented by Jones et al. in [18] and Munkby and Schupp in [19]. Jones et al. describe a technique to assist in the process of locating errors and faults. They use colors to map different outcomes from the execution of a program to statements in the executed program, making it possible to locate statements that are involved in executions leading to a program failure. Munkby and Schupp present a tool which visualizes the outcome of experiments using colors, similar to the technique presented by Jones et al. The tool produces a program-dependence graph with color annotations that correspond to the outcome of fault injection experiments. This graph provides an overview of instruction and fault coverage, and can also aid the user in finding patterns and anomalies.

### 3.3    Error Propagation Visualization

While sensitivity profiling describes parts of a Simulink model that are sensitive to a fault model, error propagation analysis is used to analyze how errors propagate through a model. This technique, which is applicable for a single experiment, is useful for debugging fault handling mechanisms, e.g. to ensure that fault handling mechanism are activated and that errors are properly handled by the mechanisms.

Fig. 6 shows the error propagation for an experiment with the model for a majority voter model, where a stuck at zero fault was injected during two iterations. The block where the injection was performed is marked yellow (Port 1). The fault caused the output from the upper subtract block (Subtract1) to differ from a fault-free simulation, and the faulty values propagated to the block Interval Test, but were then masked by the final switch block (Switch 1).

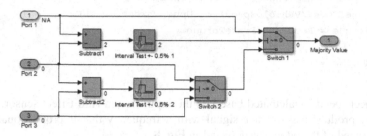

**Fig. 6.** Error propagation visualization example for a majority voter

# 4    Case Study: Brake-by-Wire Model

This section demonstrates the usage of MODIFI on a prototype brake-by-wire system which has been developed by AB Volvo for research purposes. We first give an overview of the brake-by-wire model, and then describe how MODIFI can emulate the effects of faults on the sensors that measure the wheel speed. Finally, we show how the visualization techniques can help to analyze the results from the experiments.

## 4.1    Brake-by-Wire Model

Fig. 7 shows the architecture of the brake-by-wire model. The model consists of five control units where the Global Brake Controller (GBC) is in charge of distributing the brake torque requested by the driver to four individual control units, one for each wheel of the car.

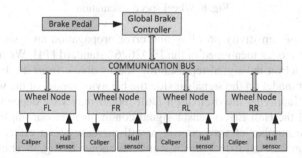

**Fig. 7.** Brake-by-wire Architecture

Each wheel node is responsible of applying the requested brake torque through the actuation of a brake caliper. The wheel node executes a simple algorithm which implements an anti-lock braking system (ABS). The algorithm can be described using the following pseudo-code:

```
IF (WheelSpeed/VehicleSpeed ) > LowerThreshold
   AND (WheelSpeed/VehicleSpeed) <  UpperThreshold THEN
   BrakeTorque = RequestedBrakeTorque
ELSE
   BrakeTorque = 0.0
ENDIF
```

The wheel speed is calculated based on the input from a Hall Effect sensor. Such a sensor may produce a sine wave signal with a frequency that is proportional to the rotational speed of the wheel, as depicted in Fig. 8.

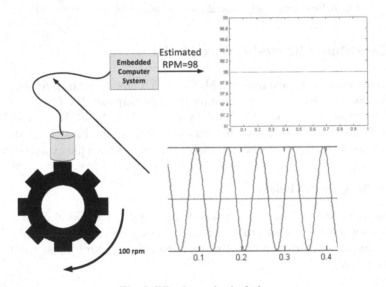

**Fig. 8.** Wheel speed calculation

To demonstrate sensitivity profiling and error propagation analysis, we apply two different failure modes mentioned in the ISO26262 standard [14]. We apply the oscillation fault model on the signal representing the feedback from the Hall Effect, and the bit-flip fault model on the signals inside the behavior model of the wheel node.

The result of applying the oscillation fault model may vary depending on the implementation of the Hall Effect sensor signal conditioner. In our implementation, we assume that the number of zero crossings will increase as an effect of oscillations superimposed on the Hall Effect sensor signal, as shown in Fig. 9. This will cause the estimated wheel speed to be higher than the actual wheel speed (154 RPM in Fig. 9 instead of 98 RPM in Fig. 8). Since we inject faults directly into the behavior model, which takes the estimated wheel speed as input, we use the offset fault model to represent an oscillation superimposed on the Hall Effect sensor signal.

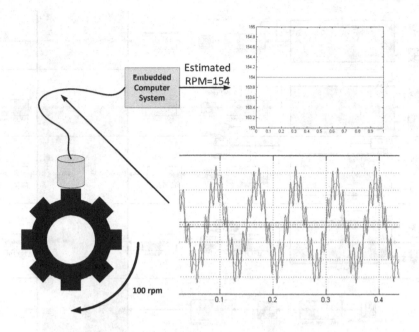

**Fig. 9.** Wheel speed calculation with Oscillation Fault Model

## 4.2    Fault Injection Results

Fig. 10 shows the sensitivity profiling for about 20 000 injections of single bit-flip faults in the brake-by-wire model. We can see that the output of the last block "LockDetect" is the most sensitive part of the model part under analysis, where 40.6% of the injected faults lead to an incorrect output. This is reasonable since there are no fault handling mechanisms after this block, and faults here will therefore affect the output. The figure also shows that no faults were injected in the output of the comparison block Relational Operator. This is because there was no fault model implemented for Booleans in the fault library used for these experiments.

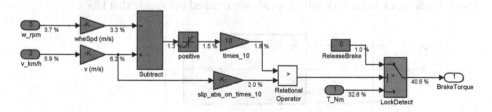

**Fig. 10.** Sensitivity profiling of a campaign with the bit-flip fault model

Fig. 11 shows an example of how error propagation is visualized for an Offset fault model that was applied on the wheel rotation input signal of the BBW model. This block is marked yellow according to the description in Section 3.3.

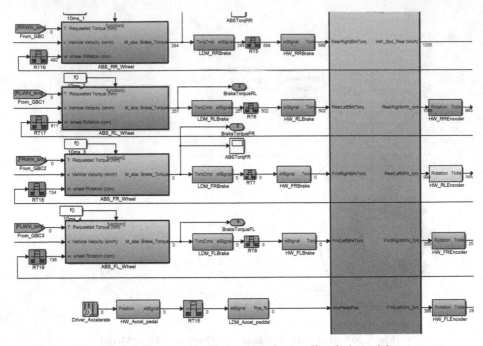

**Fig. 11.** Error propagation analysis for an offset fault model

Fig. 11 shows how the errors injected into the rotary encoder hardware propagates throughout the model. These model blocks are colored red. Some model blocks become unaffected and are colored green. Each block output signal is annotated with a number, which corresponds to the number of iterations that were affected by the injected faults. Fig. 12 shows that 809 iterations were affected on the input to the ABS_RR_Wheel block, while only 284 iterations were affected on the output port, hence errors are masked out within this block. For example, the switch Threshold_10km/h masks out errors coming from the block If v>=10km/h and errors coming from the second input port block so that only 284 errors propagate through the switch block. Further analysis can be done by more in-depth inspection of the If v>=10km/h block to find out where errors are masked out inside that block.

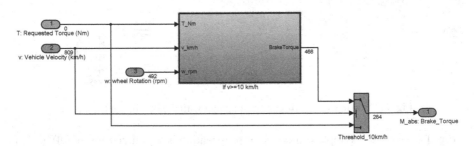

**Fig. 12.** Error propagation analysis for an offset fault model (inside block ABS_RR_Wheel)

# 5      Conclusions

Traditionally, fault injection is used as a testing method for evaluation of fault toler-ance in hardware or software. However, by using model-implemented fault injection (MIFI) as implemented in the MODIFI tool, fault injection can be used in early steps of software development. This is possible due to the increased utilization of model-based software development using tools like Simulink. Besides being used for valida-tion of fault tolerance, MIFI can be used to help developers focus on improvement of the most fault sensitive parts of a Simulink model.

We have proposed three visualization methods. The first method visualizes the outcome of experiments in a fault injection campaign using a three-dimensional cube. The second method is used for sensitivity profiling and can help developers pinpoint the most fault sensitive parts of a Simulink model. The third technique can be used for validation of fault handling mechanisms and to visualize the effect of injected faults. This error propagation analysis helps developers to ensure that fault handling mechan-isms are correctly implemented and thoroughly tested.

**Acknowledgments.** We would like to thank Mafijul Islam and Johan Haraldsson at AB Volvo for the Brake-by-Wire Simulink model used in the case study. This work was partly funded by the ARTEMIS Joint Undertaking research project VeTeSS un-der grant agreement n° 295311 and the national research project BeSafe funded by Vinnova (Swedish Governmental Agency for Innovation Systems) within the Vehicle Development Program (Diary number: 2010-02114).

# References

1. The Mathworks, Inc., http://www.mathworks.se/products/simulink/
2. IEC 61508:2010: Functional safety of electrical/electronic/programmable electronic safety-related systems
3. ISO 26262:2011: Road vehicles — Functional safety
4. Vinter, J., Bromander, L., Raistrick, P., Edler, H.: FISCADE - a fault injection tool for SCADE models. In: Proceeding of the 3rd IET Conference on Automotive Electronics, University of Warwick, UK, June 28-29 (2007) ISBN: 978-0-86341-815-0
5. Vulinovic, S., Schlingloff, B.H.: Model based dependability evaluation for automotive control functions. In: Invited Session: Model-Based Design and Test, 9th World Multi-Conference on Systemics, Cybernetics and Informatics, Florida (2005)
6. Isacson, J., Ljungberg, M.: Fault injection in Matlab/Simulink. Master's Thesis Report, Department of Computer Science and Engineering, Chalmers University of Technology, Göteborg, Sweden (2008)
7. Joshi, A., Heimdahl, M.P.E.: Model-Based Safety Analysis of Simulink Models Using SCADE Design Verifier. In: Winther, R., Gran, B.A., Dahll, G. (eds.) SAFECOMP 2005. LNCS, vol. 3688, pp. 122–135. Springer, Heidelberg (2005)
8. Svenningsson, R., Vinter, J., Eriksson, H., Törngren, M.: MODIFI: A mODel-implemented fault injection tool. In: Schoitsch, E. (ed.) SAFECOMP 2010. LNCS, vol. 6351, pp. 210–222. Springer, Heidelberg (2010)

9. dSPACE, http://www.dspace.com/en/pub/home/products/sw/pcgs/targetli.cfm
10. The MathWorks, Inc, "Simulink User's Guide"
11. ISO 26262-6:2011: Road vehicles - Functional safety - Part 6: Product development at the software level
12. Conrad, M.: Testing-based translation validation of generated code in the context of IEC 61508. Formal Methods in System Design, 35(3), 389–401 (2009)
13. Beine, M.: A Model-Based Reference Workflow for the Development of Safety-Critical Software. Embedded Real Time Software and Systems (2010)
14. ISO 26262-5:2011: Road vehicles - Functional safety - Part 5: Product development at the hardware level
15. Balaban, E., Saxena, A., Bansal, P., Goebel, K.F., Curran, S.: Modeling, Detection, and Disambiguation of Sensor Faults for Aerospace Applications. IEEE Sensors Journal 9(12), 1907–1917 (2009)
16. Ni, K., et al.: Sensor network data fault types. ACM Transactions on Sensor Networks (TOSN) 5(3), Article No. 25 (May 2009)
17. Choi, G.S., Iyer, R.K.: FOCUS: An experimental environment for fault sensitivity analysis. IEEE Transactions on Computers 41(12), 1515–1526 (1992)
18. Jones, J.A., Harrold, M.J., Stasko, J.: Visualization of test information to assist fault localization. In: Proceedings of the 24th International Conference on Software Engineering. ACM (2002)
19. Munkby, G., Schupp, S.: Improving fault injection of soft errors using program dependencies. In: Practice and Research Techniques, TAIC PART 2008. Testing: Academic & Industrial Conference. IEEE (2008)

# Cost-Effective Testing for Critical Off-the-Shelf Services

Fabio Duchi[1], Nuno Antunes[2], Andrea Ceccarelli[3], Giuseppe Vella[4],
Francesco Rossi[1], and Andrea Bondavalli[3]

[1] Resiltech S.r.l, Piazza Nilde Iotti, 25 Pontedera – PI, Italy
{fabio.duchi,francesco.rossi}@resiltech.com
[2] University of Coimbra, Polo II - Pinhal de Marrocos, 3030-329 Coimbra, Portugal
nmsa@dei.uc.pt
[3] CINI-Consorzio Interuniversitario Nazionale per l'Informatica, University of Florence
Viale Morgagni 65, I-50134, Florence, Italy
{bondavalli,andrea.ceccarelli}@unifi.it
[4] Engineering Ing. Informatica S.p.A., Viale Reg. Siciliana 7275, Palermo, Italy
giuseppe.vella@eng.it

**Abstract.** Defining cost-effective verification and validation tools is one of the
biggest research challenges of the area. Such tools speedup and reduce the cost
of the assessment of Off-The-Shelf (OTS) software components that must undergo proper certification or approval processes to be used in critical scenarios.
Previously we introduced the design of framework for testing of critical OTS
applications and services, to improve reusability, thus aiming to reduce testing
time and costs. In this paper we present an implementation of the framework
that allows applying, in a cost-effective fashion, functional testing, robustness
testing and penetration testing to web services. We present details on the implementation and we describe the procedure to use the framework to conduct
testing campaigns in web services. Finally, the framework usability and utility
is demonstrated based on a case study.

**Keywords:** testing, monitoring, critical applications, verification and validation, certification, assessment.

## 1 Introduction

Rigorous Verification and Validation (V&V) forms the fundaments of critical applications and has been largely applied in scenarios that involve life and mission critical
embedded systems. It has also been applied through years in several domains as the
railway [4] and space [14], and recently a strong effort has been made to standardize
these practices for automotive [6]. Although checking a system using V&V methods
frequently exceeds the effort needed for the core development time, it is frequently
used as a design-time quality control process for the evaluation of the compliance
between a product, service, or system [12].

As the industry rapidly turns to system integration based on the reuse of hardware
and software components, also known as Off-The-Shelf (OTS) components, it is necessary to apply rigorous V&V techniques to assess the applications. However, while

A. Bondavalli et al. (Eds.): SAFECOMP 2014 Workshops, LNCS 8696, pp. 231–242, 2014.
© Springer International Publishing Switzerland 2014

hardware OTS is nowadays widely accepted and used, software OTS still creates serious difficulties to companies, which are constrained to meet predefined quality goals while are required to deliver systems at acceptable cost and time to market. This leads to one of the biggest challenges to the V&V community: to define methods, strategies and tools able to validate a system adequately, while simultaneously keeping the cost and delivery time reasonably low. The problem grows when it is necessary to include OTS components in a critical system that has to be certified. As a matter of fact, although modern standards consider the possibility of assessing products, which encompass OTS software, this is still considered a challenge [5].

In industrial practices, *integration* and *usage* of OTS software components in critical systems is generally supported by two different assessment processes requiring both testing to understand the behavior of the component and to assess that it does not introduce hazards in the system. In the first process, whenever applicable, the activity is limited to assess the integration, verifying that the OTS component is properly wrapped in the system without affecting system's safety. In the second, a complete assessment of the OTS component is performed; this may include activities as production of documentation, reverse engineering, and static analysis, among others.

A recent work introduced the design of an advanced framework for testing and monitoring critical applications and services [1]. The idea is that by monitoring both the applications and the system where these are executing, while applying diverse forms of testing, it is possible to better detect problems, maximizing the effectiveness of the tests. The proposed framework consists of two main components: *1) Instrumented System*, a monitoring environment where the applications or services can be executed and monitored, and *2) Test and Collect,* contains a set of adaptable tools for application testing, and data storage and analysis.

This paper presents an implementation and execution of the framework in [1] for testing and monitoring of web services. The implementation includes tools that allow the user to apply to the web services different types of testing: functional, stress, robustness and penetration testing. During the different testing processes, the system variables are monitored both at middleware level (Application Server) and at operating system level. Additionally, the paper details the steps and the processes that the user must follow to use the framework to perform web services testing.

A case study was devised to evaluate the framework, focused on the services of the Liferay Portal, an enterprise web platform project that aims for immediate delivery of robust business solutions for organizations. This case study allowed us to demonstrate the flexibility, usability and utility of the framework. The results revealed the services under test performing quite well in the situations tested. Obviously, the quality of the tests performed depends on the testing tools used, but this discussion is out of the scope of this work, as the merits of each tool were evaluated and discussed in different works by their authors [2, 9].

The structure of the document is as follows. The next section presents the design of the testing framework from [1] and the implementation we developed. Section 3 presents the process to use the framework for testing web services. Section 4 presents the case study conducted while the Section 5 presents the results of the experiments. Finally, Section 7 concludes the paper.

## 2    Testing Framework

The framework aims at providing a tool-platform for automatic testing of web services, with little or even without knowledge of their internal structures. Despite the most common approach for testing OTS web services is the "black box", the tool has been designed in order to take advantages of any piece of information available.

The framework architecture is made up of two systems: i) *Instrumented System*, and ii) *Test and Collect*. The former is the system in which the web service is running; the latter is the system that is used to stimulate the web service and to collect evidences of its behavior. Although the current implementation focuses on Java Web Services running over a Tomcat 7 Application Server (AS) and a Linux CentOS 6 Operative System (OS), the proposed solution can be evolved to different platforms and Web Services Middleware (WSM).

Fig. 1 (a) shows the interactions between the two systems of the framework: the testing tool invokes methods of the web service triggering specific functionalities, and at the same time the analysis tools read information on the overall status of the operative system and service middleware.

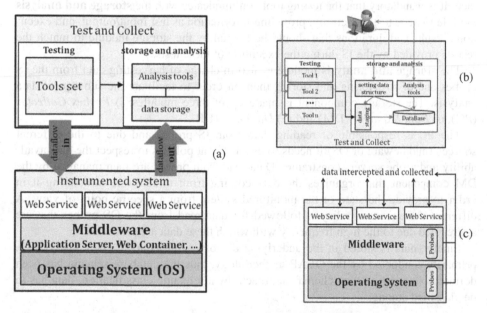

**Fig. 1.** Framework architecture: (a) overall view and interactions; (b) Detailed functioning of the Test and Collect. (c) Detailed functioning of the Instrumented System.

### 2.1    Instrumented System (IS)

Considering that weaknesses can affect the middleware layer (e.g., depleting available free memory in the heap) and the operating system layer (e.g., exchanging a huge amount of data or delaying the overall system), both of them are monitored. The middleware (AS) monitoring activity relies upon Java Management Extension (JMX) technology that is shipped with Java Runtime Environment (JRE). Although the JRE provides basic probes for monitoring the virtual machine behavior, usually the middleware enriches the set of parameters that can be monitored. This set of parameters, in turn, provides an overall picture of internal state of the middleware.

OS Monitoring activity has been supported by "System Tap"[11] with which a set of probes have been defined as two kernel modules. Due to the nature of kernel modules, the amount and the types of operations comprises in the modules affect performance and stability of system, thus, by common non-blocking IPC mechanisms, the data elaboration was moved outside the kernel modules as a user space application.

## 2.2   Test and Collect

This node is made of two components (see Fig. 1(b)): i) *testing*, and ii) *storage and analysis*. The **testing** component controls the execution of the testing tools. Although the framework is designed to be fully automated, the human interaction cannot be completely avoided at least for the test execution. The level of human interaction can vary from test to test, thus each testing tool should provide its own interaction interface. It is mandatory that the testing tool communicates with the **storage and analysis** module to trace testing activity, providing information as test input/output, and executions results and durations that should be logged by the storage module to match the results provided by the IS during the execution of these tests.

The **storage and analysis** module is also in charge of harvesting data from the IS probes and of structuring and storing them in order to facilitate the subsequent data analysis. The storage component is made up of three modules: i) *Probes Collector* (PC), ii) *Data Manager* (DM) and iii) *Database* (DB).

The PC is responsible of reading data from IS probes and due to the different sources (middleware or OS) it needs to use different policies to respect the data availability and probe servers constraints. Data read from probes are then managed by the DM component that organizes the data coming from middleware structuring it in order to provide the state of the monitored system from a specific point of view. A different management policy is followed for data read from the OS probes that are aggregated due to the high frequency with which these data are produced.

Finally, data is stored in the underlying database. Subsequent "Data Analysis" is primarily conducted by the OLAP methodology, thus the database schema has been defined following a "star schema" approach, by a semantic classification, data has to be classified among:

- *Facts* tables – represent measure on the system;
- *Dimensions* tables – represent the context in which tests has been conducted.

There are multiple facts tables, each one collecting data from a specific point of view. These tables are connected to each other by a "common" facts table. Each facts table includes correlated information such as usage of memory, usage of CPU and so forth.

# 3    Conducting Cost-Effective Testing

The framework has been developed to support different kinds of testing tools. One of the main concerns that has led to its development was the minimization of the effort needed for the adaptation of existing tool to the framework. To fit this constraint, each testing tool is seen as a different application that communicates with the framework by an interface with several optional fields. Furthermore, the interface includes the possibility to exchange files to support any kind of results produced by the testing tools.

Although tools must provide mandatory information, such as "test execution time", "test duration", and "test results" which are compulsory for having a meaningful analysis, they can provide more detailed information, such as raised exceptions or execution time of a part of the test.

Due to the loosely coupling between the testing tools and the framework, almost every existing tool can be integrated into the framework, provided that it exposes the external interface that the framework prescribes. Open source and commercial tools can be integrated as far as they provide an API or their input can be controlled and their output monitored.

The testing tools currently available allow performing functional & stress test, penetration test and robustness test. The testing framework has been developed minimizing the human interaction especially during the testing activities. With the present tools, the human interaction is indeed focused in the configuration phase, which has to be performed one time for each tool. Such tools can provide common configurations as well as they can propose a configuration that suits the testing needs.

## 3.1    Functional and Stress Testing

Functional test is a quality assurance process based on black-box approach that aims to provide a proof of implementation correctness regarding to the specifications of the software under test. The test is performed feeding the software under test with well-known values and examining the output produced.

Although common functional tests involve the test of single methods, within this context, it has been followed an approach which tackles high-level functionalities. The approach consists of a set of workflows that mimics the behavior of a software user for executing specific high-level tasks, which in turn can comprise the invocation of a huge variety of methods [3].

The workflows definition is a cornerstone of this approach and it has to be defined specifically for each service under test considering its interface and the software specification. Workflows define how and when the service interface of the software under test has to be questioned and, also, they provide the information needed for the subsequent phase of result validation. Following the black-box approach the verification is done invoking specific methods of the service for checking its internal status.

The importance of these workflows is further emphasized due to the fact that they can be used as bricks for compound and complex workflows for Stress testing. Stress testing is a form of deliberately intense testing used to determine the stability of a given system.

The tool developed for functional test, properly configured with suitable workflows, can stimulate the system under test in order to provide evidence of stability. Workflows for Stress testing have been defined from the high-level tasks identified for the functional tests by parallelizing multiple high-level tasks invoked from a variety of users and abbreviating to the minimum the delay between sequential invocations.

### 3.2     Robustness Testing

Robustness testing is a specific form of black-box testing that attempts to characterize the behavior of a system in the presence of erroneous or unexpected input conditions [7]. The tool instrumented in the testing framework implements the technique proposed in [13]. The approach consists of a set of robustness tests that is applied during execution in order to disclose both programming and design problems.

The set of robustness tests is automatically generated by applying a set of predefined rules (see detailed list in [13]) to the parameters of each operation of the web service during the workload execution. An important aspect is that rules focus difficult input validation aspects, such as: null and empty values, valid values with special characteristics, invalid values with special characteristics, maximum and minimum valid values in the domain, values exceeding the maximum and minimum valid values in the domain, and values that cause data type overflow. The robustness of the web services is characterized according to the failure modes adapted from the CRASH scale.

### 3.3     Penetration Testing

Penetration testing is nowadays one of the most used techniques by web developers to detect vulnerabilities in their applications and services. This technique assumes particular relevance in the web services environment, as many times clients and providers need to test services without having access to the source code (e.g. when testing third-party services), which prevents the use of more effective techniques that require that access. The tool instrumented in the testing framework implements a technique targeting the detection of SQL Injection vulnerabilities in web services. The tool was originally presented in [2]. Comparing to other existing web vulnerability scanners based on penetration testing, this approach presents three key improvements:

- It uses a representative workload to exercise the services and understand the expected behavior (i.e. the typical responses in the presence of valid inputs);
- It uses a more complete set of attacks. The attacks considered are a compilation of all the attacks performed by a large set of scanners plus many attack methods that can be found in the literature;
- It applies well-defined rules to analyze the web services responses in order to improve coverage and reduce false positives. These rules include comparing the

responses obtained when using malicious inputs with the normal responses (i.e. responses in the presence of a valid workload) and with the responses from classical robustness tests [8].

# 4    Case Studies: Liferay Web Services

Liferay is a free and open source Java software that was initially developed to provide an open source enterprise quality portal. Since the early stages of development, Liferay has been widely adopted for intranet as well as extranet enterprise solution. Eventually, it brought Liferay to have a big supporting community, which, together with the Liferay foundation, contributed to define a generic and extendible product.

The success passes through an extendible architecture by plugins that, in turn, encompass collaboration, social networking, and single sign on, per-component privileges policy as well as e-commerce tools. Third-party plugins are also available to provide more advanced feature such as Microsoft office integration.

A plugin can be seen as a J2EE-Servlet and is referred to as a portlet. Portlets communicate with each other using the services that each one exposes that, in turn, perform the portlets business logic. More details on Liferay can be found in [10].

Our installation of Liferay includes the version 6.0 of the portal and 83 deployed SOAP (Simple Object Access Protocol) web services. This case study aims at using the testing framework to detect flaw in a product out of the shelf. The case study encompasses Functional, Stress, Penetration and Robustness tests; all of them are further detailed in the follow.

## 4.1    Functional Tests

In order to verify the correctness of Liferay services, a study on its plugins interaction has been conducted. The necessity for the preliminary study has been felt because of the strictly correlated invocations among methods exposed by web services.

The preliminary study has been exploited to define workloads that could mimic the behavior of Liferay internal interactions. Even simple activity, like posting a message on the blog by UI interface, could involve a plethora of plugins including authentication, user information retrieving, permission checking and finally messaging service.

In order to stimulate Liferay in a way that could resemble human activities, many Workloads have been defined to cover Liferay functionalities by mimicking the behavior of human interaction. Mimicked actions encompass posting a message in the blog and in the forum, creating an event in the calendar, creating a directory-tree in the file repository and uploading a file in it.

These workloads, in order to highlight possible weakness in terms of concurrency management, have been used to define other workloads for stress tests. Those tests have been designed from the workloads defined for functional tests in order to evaluate Liferay behavior under a heavy load. For each workload, that mimics a specific action, a new one is defined as a composition of many copies of the same workload, these copies differ just for the user. The purpose of this approach is to simulate multiple users activities on Liferay, that stimulate the same services and some shared data.

The stress test, as it is designed, suits especially well when there isn't a sound knowledge of web services internal mechanism; the deeper is the knowledge of web service internals the more effective workloads can be designed.

## 4.2    Robustness Tests

Due to the preliminary study performed for the functional test, a generic knowledge of methods invocation was available to configure the tool to generate better tests. This knowledge was especially important for the tool to use values that exercise the code of the web service under test in a more complete way. After the configuration of the tool it submits the robustness tests in an automated way and reports the robustness problems found.

## 4.3    Penetration Tests

Again, the available knowledge of methods invocation was key to configure the tool to generate better workloads and attackloads. This is especially relevant for this tool as its effectiveness is depending on the completeness of its workloads. After this configuration, the test execution is a straightforward process in which the tool submits its workload and attackload to the web service and then reports the vulnerabilities found.

# 5    Tests Results

Experiment execution is made up of three phases, where just the final one is specific for the kind of test that has to be conducted. The phases are:

1. Set up Service Under Test (SUT),
2. Data Logger execution,
3. Testing tool execution.

On the first phase the service under test is started up. This phase includes also the startup of middleware and OS probes. The second phase can be launched simultaneously, as it does not read information from OS or middleware probes: it just prepares the structures needed for logging.

During test execution, the testing framework logs raw tests results and prints on the console information on the tests execution (test currently running, test duration, etc.). This information is useful for monitoring the tests execution.

Test results are collected during test execution; at the tests termination, collected data are flushed into a database.

Different tools that range from very specific tools such as R or MatLab to commonly available and general-purpose tool such as OpenOffice-Calc are installed on the Test and Collect system, connected to the database, and can be used to retrieve and analyze data.

## 5.1  Functional Test

Due to the wide usage and the extended support that Liferay received from its community since its development started, it was expected that Liferay passed all the functional tests defined.

Fig. 2 shows an extract of the workload (set of services invocations) used for creating a new event on a calendar (it includes logging in to the system, listing the available/subscribed calendars, choosing the first one and listing all the events of February, adding the new item then logging out; subsequently further invocations checks that the event was correctly recorded). The invocation correctness is verified by a visual inspection of Liferay services.

The output produced during the execution of the test is displayed on the screen of the Test and Collect system and consists of a sequence of services methods invocations. For each one of these, the HTTP response code is printed out. In a functional test is mandatory that the HTTP response code would match with the expected one.

```
- <tns:Workload name="addEventInCalendar">
  - <tns:Choreography>
    - <tns:Call portlet="Portlet_Cal_CalEventService" method="getEventsCount/1">
      - <tns:Parameters>
          <tns:Parameter name="groupId" variable="groupId"/>
          <tns:Parameter name="start">0</tns:Parameter>
          <tns:Parameter name="end">1393592163</tns:Parameter>
        </tns:Parameters>
      </tns:Call>
    - <tns:Call portlet="Portlet_Cal_CalEventService" method="getEvents/1">
      - <tns:Parameters>
          <tns:Parameter name="groupId" variable="groupId"/>
          <tns:Parameter name="start">0</tns:Parameter>
          <tns:Parameter name="end">1393592163</tns:Parameter>
        </tns:Parameters>
      </tns:Call>
    - <tns:Call portlet="Portlet_Cal_CalEventService" method="addEvent/1">
      - <tns:Parameters>
          <tns:Parameter name="title">titoloEvento</tns:Parameter>
```

**Fig. 2.** An extract of the workload to set a new Calendar event

## 5.2  Stress Test

The aim of this stress testing is to assess the ability to resist against a workload which leverage on high frequency of requests, and the results can be evaluated in term of system loads and resource usage. Table 1 shows the average CPU usage and amount of free memory; the former one is furthermore detailed distinguishing between process CPU load and system CPU load, with system CPU load that encompasses any task running on the system. Free memory is furthermore detailed as well distinguishing between free heap memory, used for java objects and free non-heap memory.

The table encompasses the experiments of 5, 10 and 100 simultaneous execution of the "New Calendar Event" workload. Data are collected 1 times per second. Table 1 shows that the CPU usage of service process remains quite stable despite the increase of the number of requests. Process CPU load, the system load as well as memory usage vary as the number of parallel requests increase. The table shows that system resources usage clearly increases due to the waits for Disk Output activities, which rise.

**Table 1.** Extract Test Results for New Calendar Event

| Parallel requests (nr) | Process CPU Load (%) | System CPU Load (%) | System Load Average | Free Heap Memory (B) | Free Non Heap Mem(B) | IO Written/ Read Data (B) |
|---|---|---|---|---|---|---|
| 5 | 0,303 | 0,382 | 1,54 | 100128920 | 24899588 | 5959 |
| 10 | 0,125 | 0,651 | 1,20 | 86411094 | 22482534 | 77344 |
| 100 | 0,134 | 0,999 | 2,34 | 84833658 | 21993838 | 184244 |

## 5.3    Robustness Tests

Fig. 3 shows an extract of the robustness test report, in which all the tests reported robustness problems. This would suggest weakness in the services, but a manual inspection revealed that while tool reports "PROBLEM", the service actually correctly identify and discard the invalid request. We explain this with the help of Fig. 4.

| fact_robustness_test_result_id | field | type | code |
|---|---|---|---|
| 1 | Field{questionId} of LONG @ [0-1001[ | ROBUSTNESS | PROBLEM |
| 2 | Field{questionId} of LONG @ [0-1001[ | ROBUSTNESS | PROBLEM |
| 3 | Field{questionId} of LONG @ [0-1001[ | ROBUSTNESS | PROBLEM |
| 4 | Field{questionId} of LONG @ [0-1001[ | ROBUSTNESS | PROBLEM |
| 5 | Field{questionId} of LONG @ [0-1001[ | ROBUSTNESS | PROBLEM |
| 6 | Field{questionId} of LONG @ [0-1001[ | ROBUSTNESS | PROBLEM |

**Fig. 3.** Extract from robustness test results

Fig. 4(a) shows an extract of a robustness test involving the Poll Service, in particular the "addQuestion" method. Liferay, relying on Axis 2 for parsing values, automatically manages the invalid value for the parameter "expirationDateMonth" rejecting the request and without passing it to the "actual" service. The rejection causes an HTTP 533 (which belongs to the "internal error" family): the tool used for robustness testing, operating at black-box, is not able to distinguish this answer from any other internal error, and consequently the "PROBLEM" code is displayed in Fig. 4(b) which shows the response that Liferay produces for the request.

```
<urn:addQuestion soapenv:encodingStyle="http://schemas.xmlsoap.org/soap/encoding/">
  <titleMapLanguageIds xsi:type="urn:ArrayOf_xsd_string" soapenc:arrayType="soapenc:string[]">
  <titleMapValues xsi:type="urn:ArrayOf_xsd_string" soapenc:arrayType="soapenc:string[]">
  <descriptionMapLanguageIds xsi:type="urn:ArrayOf_xsd_string" soapenc:arrayType="soapenc:string[]">
  <descriptionMapValues xsi:type="urn:ArrayOf_xsd_string" soapenc:arrayType="soapenc:string[]">
  <expirationDateMonth xsi:type="xsd:int">invalidNumber</expirationDateMonth>
  <expirationDateDay xsi:type="xsd:int">6</expirationDateDay>
  <expirationDateYear xsi:type="xsd:int">2000</expirationDateYear>
  <expirationDateHour xsi:type="xsd:int">5</expirationDateHour>
  <expirationDateMinute xsi:type="xsd:int">5</expirationDateMinute>
  <neverExpire xsi:type="xsd:boolean">true</neverExpire>
  <choices xsi:type="urn:ArrayOf_tns1_PollsChoiceSoap" soapenc:arrayType="mod:PollsChoiceSoap[]">
  <serviceContext xsi:type="ser:ServiceContext"> </serviceContext>
</urn:addQuestion>
```

```
<soapenv:Fault>
  <faultcode>soapenv:Server.userException</faultcode>
  - <faultstring>
      java.lang.NumberFormatException: For input string: "invalidNumber"
  </faultstring>
  - <detail>
      <ns1:hostname>testingBOX</ns1:hostname>
  </detail>
</soapenv:Fault>
```

(a)                                              (b)

**Fig. 4.** Example of robustness test: (a) request; (b) response

In general, Liferay uses Axis2 for service publishing and interface, Axis2 is responsible for parsing values passed by SOAP as well as for invoking the actual Java method which was remotely requested. The parsing phase consists also of a validation phase in which the parsed values are validated against their destination types constraints. The failure of this phase implies the subsequent rejection of the request and thus the generation of a response with HTTP code 500.

## 5.4    Penetration Tests

Fig. 5 shows an extract of the results of the penetration tests applied to Liferay Calendar Service. The extracted data, as well as the entire test results, show the robustness of Liferay against penetration attacks. All the potentially risky requests are identified and discarded by the Axis2 Layer for services interface, by the Object Relational Mapping (ORM) layer for objects persistency and by the permission checking mechanism, which constitute a cornerstone for Liferay services interoperability.

| fact_penetration_test_result_id | field | type | code | fact_id |
|---|---|---|---|---|
| 1 | Field{questionId} of LONG @ [0-1001[ | SQL | PASSED | 56151 |
| 2 | Field{questionId} of LONG @ [0-1001[ | SQL | PASSED | 56165 |
| 3 | Field{questionId} of LONG @ [0-1001[ | SQL | PASSED | 56169 |
| 4 | Field{questionId} of LONG @ [0-1001[ | SQL | PASSED | 56174 |
| 5 | Field{questionId} of LONG @ [0-1001[ | SQL | PASSED | 56204 |

**Fig. 5.** Calendar Service penetration tests result

In fact, Liferay exposes its services using Axis2, which validates the invocation parameters before passing the request to the "actual" service. Additionally, Liferay relays upon Hibernate (the ORM used), which provides an SQL parameter sanitizing service that, in turn, uses named queries that work on top of statements of the JDBC API; all those layers operate the necessary actions to avoid risks from malicious requests. Finally, the invocations involving items that the user is not authorized to use, are identified by the Liferay Permission Service.

## 6    Conclusion

This paper presents an implementation of a cost-effective testing framework for web services. The framework allows users to easily apply functional testing, stress testing, robustness testing and penetration testing to their web services. The procedure to use the framework is described and its usability is illustrated with a case study that uses the Liferay platform, composed of several web services. The framework can orchestrate the use of the tools and reduce the human effort by reutilizing the information provided at configuration time within multiple tools.

Future work includes the evaluation of the framework in different scenarios and the extension of the approach to other types of software other than web services. Additionally, the framework can be modified to use more than one Instrumented System at the same time, allowing to test more complex systems. Finally, it can be extended to take advantage of other kinds of information monitoring.

**Acknowledgements.** This work has been partially supported by the European Project FP7-2012-324334-CECRIS (CErtification of CRItical Systems), the TENACE PRIN Project (n. 20103P34XC) funded by the Italian Ministry of Education, University and Research, and the PON Ricerca e Competitività 2007 - 2013 VINCENTE (A Virtual collective INtelligenCe ENvironment to develop sustainable Technology Entrepreneurship ecosystems) project.

# References

1. Antunes, N., et al.: A monitoring and testing framework for critical off-the-shelf applications and services. In: 2013 IEEE International Symposium on Software Reliability Engineering Workshops (ISSREW), pp. 371–374 (2013)
2. Antunes, N., Vieira, M.: Detecting SQL Injection Vulnerabilities in Web Services. In: Fourth Latin-American Symposium on Dependable Computing 2009 (LADC 2009), pp. 17–24. IEEE Computer Society, Joao Pessoa (2009)
3. Ceccarelli, A., et al.: A Testbed for Evaluating Anomaly Detection Monitors Through Fault Injection. In: 5th IEEE Workshop on Self-Organizing Real-Time Systems (SORT 2014), Reno, Nevada, USA (2014)
4. IEC 61508 TC: IEC 61508, Functional Safety of Electrical/Electronic/Programmable Electronic (E/E/PE) Safety Related Systems, Part 3: Software Requirements. IEC, Geneva, Swiss (1998)
5. IEEE Computer Society. Software & Systems Engineering Standards Committee: 1012-2012 - IEEE Standard for System and Software Verification and Validation. IEEE Computer Society (2012)
6. ISO 26262: Road vehicles - Functional safety - Part 6: Product development at the software level (2011)
7. Koopman, P., DeVale, J.: Comparing the robustness of POSIX operating systems. In: Twenty-Ninth Annual International Symposium on Fault-Tolerant Computing. Digest of Papers, pp. 30–37 (1999)
8. Laranjeiro, N., et al.: Improving Web Services Robustness. In: IEEE 7th International Conference on Web Services (ICWS 2009), Los Angeles, CA, USA, pp. 397–404 (2009)
9. Laranjeiro, N., et al.: Wsrbench: An On-Line Tool for Robustness Benchmarking. In: IEEE International Conference on Services Computing, SCC 2008, pp. 187–194 (2008)
10. Liferay, Inc.: Liferay Portal, http://www.liferay.com/
11. Prasad, V., et al.: Locating system problems using dynamic instrumentation. In: 2005 Ottawa Linux Symposium, pp. 49–64 (2005)
12. Tran, E.: Verification/Validation/Certification. In: Koopman, P. (ed.) Topics in Dependable Embedded Systems. Carnegie Mellon University (1999)
13. Vieira, M., et al.: Benchmarking the Robustness of Web Services. In: 13th Pacific Rim International Symposium on Dependable Computing, PRDC 2007, pp. 322–329 (2007)
14. RTCA DO-178C/EUROCAE ED-12C - Software Considerations in Airborne Systems and Equipment Certification (2011)

# On Security Countermeasures Ranking
# through Threat Analysis

Nicola Nostro[1,2], Ilaria Matteucci[3], Andrea Ceccarelli[1], Felicita Di Giandomenico[2],
Fabio Martinelli[3], and Andrea Bondavalli[1]

[1] University of Florence, Firenze, Italy
{nicola.nostro,andrea.ceccarelli,bondavalli}@unifi.it
[2] ISTI - CNR, Pisa, Italy
f.digiandomenico@isti.cnr.it
[3] IIT-CNR, Pisa, Italy
{ilaria.matteucci,fabio.martinelli}@iit.cnr.it

**Abstract.** Security analysis and design are key activities for the protection of
critical systems and infrastructures. Traditional approaches consist first in applying a qualitative threat assessment that identifies the attack points. Results are
then used as input for the security design such that appropriate countermeasures
are selected. In this paper we propose a novel approach for the selection and
ranking of security controlling strategies which is driven by quantitative threat
analysis based on attack graphs. It consists of two main steps: i) a threat analysis,
performed to evaluate attack points and paths identifying those that are feasible, and to rank attack costs from the perspective of an attacker; ii) controlling
strategies, to derive the appropriate monitoring rules and the selection of countermeasures are evaluated, based upon the provided values and ranks. Indeed,
the exploitation of such threat analysis allows to compare different controlling
strategies and to select the one that fits better the given set of functional and security requirements. To exemplify our approach, we adopt part of an electrical
power system, the Customer Energy Management System (CEMS), as reference
scenario where the steps of threat analysis and security strategies are applied.

## 1 Introduction

The usage of Information and Communication Technology (ICT) systems in Critical
Infrastructures (CI) rapidly increases. Some of the most prominent examples of CI are
electric power systems, telecommunication networks, transportation systems. The introduction of ICT components, however, has pros and cons. The advantages are mainly
related to the management of communications among components of a CI and the control of their functionalities. On the other hand, the pervasive introduction and utilization of ICT infrastructure exposes the system to cyber security vulnerabilities. Indeed,
CI systems may occasionally fail for different reasons that go from natural disasters to
accidental failures, or malicious attacks from both insider or outsider attackers [19].

In this context, it is important to be able to analyse system architecture in order to
find possible points of failure and to provide appropriate countermeasures able to guarantee the reliability and security of the system. The goal of this paper is to describe

A. Bondavalli et al. (Eds.): SAFECOMP 2014 Workshops, LNCS 8696, pp. 243–254, 2014.

a framework for the ranking and selection of controlling strategies against security attacks. The evaluation and selection of the appropriate strategy are driven by a security model-based evaluation of the considered system. Our approach consists in synergically combining model-based quantitative security assessment and security controlling strategies definition to rank security countermeasures, and then to select the most appropriate one for guaranteeing the security of the system against a certain class of attackers. A model consists of the construction of a system's representation, based on the characteristic to be analysed and on the modelling formalism to be used. To this aim, we use the ADVISE tool [13], which allows a quantitative model-based evaluation of security properties. Such a modelling activity is helpful to identify critical attack paths, useful to realize attacks on the system under analysis, as well as the probability, time and costs to successfully achieve an attack, based on different adversary profiles and attack preferences. The measures obtained from the security analysis are then exploited to evaluate different controlling strategies, specified as process algebra operators enhanced with quantities [6,4], in order to make trade-off decisions between the cost of a strategy and the reliability of the system.

As an application use case for the proposed approach, we focus on the Costumer Energy Management Systems (CEMS) that is a service of the low voltage grids for an advanced energy management, based on tariff information and an integration of distributed energy resources (DER) for a more balanced grid stability. A basis for this control network is established by the deployment of a comprehensive Advanced Metering Infrastructure (AMI) for Automated Meter Reading (AMR), able to monitor the electricity consumption of households collected by smart meters. These connections may be subject to cyber attacks. Hence, we firstly model potential attacks to the CEMS architecture, focussing on the Man in the Middle (MIM) attack. Two profiles of attackers are considered and analysed to obtain an evaluation of the average cost of the attack. Hence, we apply each controlling strategy to MIM attack's models and we evaluate their cost to select the best one (if any) to cope with the attack.

*The paper is structured as follows:* Section 2 presents our framework for ranking security strategies according to quantitative threat analysis and Section 3 shows how our approach works on the CEMS use case scenario. Section 4 discusses the existing literature on modelling approaches, threat analysis framework, and quantitative definition and evaluation of security controlling strategies. Finally Section 5 draws conclusions and describes some ongoing and future works.

## 2   Ranking Security Strategies through Threat Analysis

The aim of this section is to describe our integration of two existing approaches, one for the model-based security assessment, and the other for quantitative security controlling strategies, in such a way to provide a novel approach for the evaluation, ranking, and selection of the best security countermeasure, if any.

A graphical representation of the workflow is depicted in Figure 1. We start from the specification of a system. The system is described by its functional and non-functional requirements. Once the system has been modelled, a threat analysis of the system is performed in order to evaluate possible risks, point of failures, and so on.

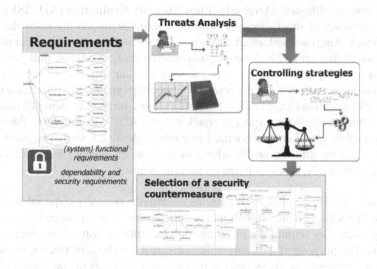

**Fig. 1.** The workflow of the proposed approach

The output of the threat analysis consists of a series of possible attacks that can be perpetrated on the system. Furthermore, the analysis provides an estimation of the cost of each attack. Given the variety of potential attackers behaviour, we define several strategies for their monitoring and controlling. Such strategies work by following the attacker's behaviour step by step. Then, we use the information on the cost of the attack, obtained through the threat analysis, in order to rank and select the controlling strategy that better fits with the system requirement. In the following we present more in detail the modelling approach and the definition of quantitative controlling strategies.

## 2.1 Modelling Approach and Threat Analysis

In this section we recall some basic notion about modelling approaches and threat analysis of a modelled system.

*Modelling Approaches.* Modelling of systems is an activity that is widely used especially in the early stages of design, in order to detect design errors, deficiencies and vulnerabilities, thus avoiding them from being detected after the deployment of the systems, which could cause serious and, in the worst case, catastrophic consequences.

Modelling consists of the construction of a system's representation based on the characteristic to be analyzed and on the modelling formalism to be used. In particular, security models shall describe how and when a security violation occurs, its impact on the system under analysis, proper countermeasures to the attack with relative costs and effects on the system. Research in security analysis has developed a variety of models, each focusing on particular levels of abstraction and/or system characteristics. Important classes of modelling approaches are represented by: Attack Trees [22], Privilege Graphs [8], Attack Graphs [23], and ADVISE [13].

In this work we adopted **ADversary VIew Security Evaluation (ADVISE)**, which extends the concept of attack graph by building executable models driven by the preferences of attack. Analyses performed through ADVISE can be tailored in order to reflect the behavior of attackers with different goals, preferences, resources, skill, knowledge and access to the system, thus specifying several attacker profiles. An attack is composed of a sequence of steps. All the potential attack steps against the system are defined as the Attack Execution Graph (AEG). Each step allows the achievement of a goal or the progress of the attack. With respect to attack graphs, ADVISE introduces the concept of time, probability, and costs associated to each single attack step. The combination of the AEG and the attacker profile allows to generate an executable model useful to produce relevant analysis output based on security metrics.

*Threat Analysis.* Threat analysis represents an activity typically required for various types of systems, in particular it finds wide application in contexts of complex systems, especially when they require the integration of multiple infrastructures, technologies, and people. The purpose of the analysis is to create a data base of threats, vulnerabilities and countermeasures, always taking into account the costs of implementation and the severity of the threats that must be handled [20]. However, identifying all the potential vulnerabilities, and the related threats of a system, especially if complex, appears to be a quite difficult process, which may take a long time, and not ensuring a full coverage. For this reason, the first step of the analysis is related to the identification of the **assets** of interest, which can be modified, damaged, and made unavailable. They can be digital (e.g., software sources, sensitive data), physical (e.g., servers), commercial (e.g., corporate brand). Once the assets have been identified they are prioritized according to their relevance, thus giving the proper weight and priority to vulnerabilities, threats, and countermeasures The output of this first step is usually represented by a simple table, where each row represents an identified asset, and columns contain an ID of the asset, a name, a description, and a priority. Afterwards, an analysis of the system's vulnerabilities and threats is carried out. At this stage, based on the reference architecture each module, component, part of the system, must be analyzed to identify the vulnerabilities and the threats. A **vulnerability** is represented by a bug, a flaw, a weakness or exposure of an application; a system, a device or a service which could lead to issues of confidentiality, integrity or availability. A **threat** represents the occurrence of a harmful event, by exploiting one or more vulnerabilities. Similarly to the assets, the output is represented by two other tables. Each row of the vulnerabilities and threats tables represents an identified vulnerability and threat, respectively. The tables produced are cross-referenced, in order to understand which threat can exploit a vulnerability to affect an asset.

## 2.2 Quantitative Controlling Strategies

Starting from the Schneider's seminal work [21], a lot of effort has been spent on formally characterizing what kind of policies can be monitored and enforced at runtime and how. In particular, the adoption of formalisms such as automata, *e.g.*, [2] or process algebras [15], allows to better define the interactions between target and enforcement mechanism as well as enforcement capabilities.

**Table 1.** Semantics definitions for quantitative control rules

$$\frac{E \xrightarrow{a,k} E' \quad F \xrightarrow{a,k'} F'}{E \triangleright F \xrightarrow{a,k*k'} E' \triangleright F'} \text{ (A)} \quad \frac{E \xrightarrow{\boxminus a,k} E' \quad F \xrightarrow{a,k'} F'}{E \triangleright F \xrightarrow{\tau,k*k'} E' \triangleright F'} \text{ (S)} \quad \frac{E \xrightarrow{\boxplus a.b,k} E' \quad F \xrightarrow{a,k'} F'}{E \triangleright F \xrightarrow{b,k} E' \triangleright F} \text{ (I)}$$

Hereafter, we adopt the process algebra formalism in order to define quantitative controlling strategies [6]. We define security *controller process algebra operator* $E \triangleright_K F$, where $E$ is the controller process, $F$ is the possible malicious system, and $K$, that ranges over $\{A, S, I\}$, i.e., *Acceptance* operator, *Suppression* operator, and *Insertion* operator, identifies the possible strategies that can be applied in order to control the behaviour of (possibly untrusted) target components by a control program.

The alphabets of $E$, $F$, and of the resulting process $E \triangleright F$ are different, as $E$ may perform *control actions* of the form $a$, $\boxplus a.b$, $\boxminus a$ for $a, b \in Act$, denoting respectively the actions of *acceptance*, *suppression*, and *insertion*, that regulate the actions of $F$, and the resulting process $E \triangleright F$ may perform internal actions, denoted by $\tau$, as a consequence of suppression. Each action of both, the controller and the target are associated to a measure. We use *semirings* for specifying quantities and for modelling two fundamental modes of composing process behaviour, either by combination of different traces, or by sequential composition.

**Definition 1.** *A semiring* $\mathbb{K} = (K, +, \times, 0, 1)$ *consists of a set* $K$ *with two binary operations* $+, \times$, *and two constants* $0, 1$, *such that* $+$ *is associative, with neutral element* $0$; $\times$ *is associative, with neutral and absorbing elements* $1, 0$; $\times$ *distributes over* $+$.

Semirings have a partial order $\sqsubseteq$, such that $k_1 \sqsubseteq k_2$ if, and only if $k_1 + k_2 = k_2$. Intuitively, $\sqsubseteq$ indicates *preference*, that is, $k_1 \sqsubseteq k_2$ can be read as $k_2$ is "better" than $k_1$.

Controlling strategies are represented by *multiple labelled transition system* ($MLTS$ for short) that are labelled transition systems where each transition is labelled by pairs $(a, k)$ where $k \in \mathbb{K}$ is a quantity associated to the effect $a$.

The *acceptance rule* (A) constrains the controller and the target to perform the same action, in order for it to be observed in the resulting behaviour. In particular, if $F$ performs the action $a$ with a measure $k'$ and the same action is performed by $E$ with a measure $k$ (so it is allowed on the system), then $E \triangleright F$ performs the action $a$ with an observed value that is the product of those of the controller and of the target, $k * k'$. This implies that any good action is allowed. Bad actions are prevented because they are not allowed by $E$.

The *suppression rule* allows to hide actions happening for an external user but leaves they happen for guaranteeing the functionality of the system. Hence, the suppression rule (S) allows the controller to hide actions of the target by performing the control action $\boxminus a$ with a measure $k$. The target *wants to* performs the action $a$ with a measure $K'$, but the action is not performed by the controlled entity and the observed result is a $\tau$ action, with the value calculated as the product $k * k'$ of the suppressing and the target action. Then $E \triangleright F$ performs the action $\tau$ that *suppresses* the action $a$, *i.e.*, $a$ becomes not visible from external observation.

The *insertion rule* (I) describes the capability of correcting some bad behaviour of the target, by inserting another action in its execution trace by performing a control action $\boxplus a$ followed by an action, e.g., $b$. The value of insertion is the value of the controller, i.e., $k$; this accounts for the fact that the target does not perform any action, but rather stays in its current state.

In the qualitative case [15], they are applied in a non-deterministic way. Hence, the approach has been extended by associating to each action a "quantity", as, for instance, the cost of an action or a benefit associated to a step [16][6]. This allows us to evaluate each strategy with respect to a certain measure and select the rule to apply according to a certain value. In particular, we consider the result of threat analysis as input values of controlling rules, in such a way to be able to combine them in the most appropriate way for maximizing the result.

Controller strategies are evaluated with respect to their *execution path*, i.e., a sequence $(a_1, k_1) \cdots (a_n, k_n)$ from the root of the process to the end of the execution. We call $\mathcal{T}(A)$ the set of paths rooted in $A$. Given a path $(a_1, k_1) \cdots (a_n, k_n)$, we define its *label* $l(t) = a_1 \cdots a_n$, and its *run weight* $|t| = k_1 \times \ldots \times k_n \in K$. We define *valuation* of process $A$ the value $\llbracket A \rrbracket = \sum_{\{t \in \mathcal{T}(A)\}} |t|$. Hence, we are able to rank different strategies and, eventually, select the "best" solution by applying the following definition.

**Definition 2 ([6]).** *Given an agent $F$, and a semiring $K$, a controller $E_2$ is better than a controller $E_1$ with respect to $F$, and we denoted it by $E_1 \sqsubseteq_{K,F} E_2$, if and only if $\llbracket E_1 \triangleright F \rrbracket \sqsubseteq_K \llbracket E_2 \triangleright F \rrbracket$.*

## 3    Use Case: Customer Energy Management System

In order to describe how the proposed approach works, in this section, we focus on the Customer Energy Management System (CEMS) as use case scenario [12]. A CEMS is an application service or device that communicates with devices in the home. It may have interfaces to the meter to read usage data or to the operations domain to get pricing or other information to make automated or manual decisions to control energy consumption more efficiently. Among the functionalities of the CEMS, the most critical operations that must be secured are: i) direct load/generation management and ii) communication of power consumption information. The CEMS can be connected to home automation devices and to the EMG by means of shared network (e.g., the home WiFi, office LAN). The use of already deployed IP network is extremely appealing however, IP-based networks, when not well secured, are subject to cyber attacks. The attack can be executed either from the Internet or from a device connected to the Home Area Network (HAN) (Figure 2) which has been previously tampered, such as a personal computer or the Local Network Access Point (LNAP), and may have special information or authorizations (e.g., Energy Management Gateway (EMG) login credentials, remote management of home automation devices).

For illustrative purpose, we concentrate on a *Man In the Middle (MIM)* attack on the CEMS model (one of the potential identified threats). In MIM attack an opponent

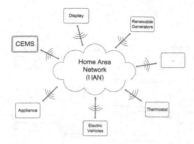

**Fig. 2.** The logical view of CEMS interconnections

captures messages exchanged between the EMG and the CEMS. It can delay the messages or alter their content to produce an undesired effect, or simply collect data without altering the content, thus causing a violation of integrity, availability or confidentiality.

Specifically, we consider two different attack goals and two different adversaries (*attackers*). The first attack aims at corrupting the messages exchanged between the CEMS and the EMG in order to compromise the integrity property. Bringing the first attack to completion with success, results in altering the electrical devices operation. The second attack goal attempts to gather (sensitive) information during the message exchange, thus leading to a violation of confidentiality property. When this attack is successfully carried out, it allows the disclosure of sensitive information about the customer or the energy supplier. Among the potential attackers, we consider two different profiles related to a *hacker* and to a *criminal* trying to achieve both the attack goals.

Due to space constraints, this section only provides a high-level description of the ADVISE model. Figure 3 shows the Attack Execution Graph of the MIM attack which aims at achieving the two identified attack goals, represented by the ovals in figure. The graph represents the attack steps the adversary has to perform in order to realize his goal. Specifically, Figure 3 shows a total number of ten attack steps (represented by rectangles). The first seven steps are common for the two different attack goals.

For both of the goals, the attacker, initially, has to gain the network access. The second attack step, called configuration step, represents the activity required to allow the attacker to intercept the messages exchange on the network, e.g., by exploiting a router with some malicious programs to intercept messages between the CEMS and the EMG. Then, the next attack steps are the generic activities an attacker has to follow to realize a (Public-Key encryption) MIM attack: *i)* Attacker intercepts a conversation request from CEMS (EMG) with its public key; *ii)* Attacker sends a conversation request to EMG (CEMS) with its own public key; *iii)* EMG (CEMS) receives request, and sends reply encrypted with attacker's key; *iv)* Attacker sends a reply encrypted with CEMS's key (EMG's key), intercepted at step i); *v)* Attacker receives from CEMS (EMG) a message encrypted with attacker's key. At this point the attacker can simply decrypt the message and get sensitive information, thus realizing one of the attack goals, or s/he can modify the message and send it to EMG (CEMS), thus achieving the other attack goal.

The attack execution graph, described above, is valid both for the hacker and criminal, whose profiles are defined through a set of specific characteristic. Specifically, the adversary profile defines a set of access domains, knowledges, and attack skills, owned

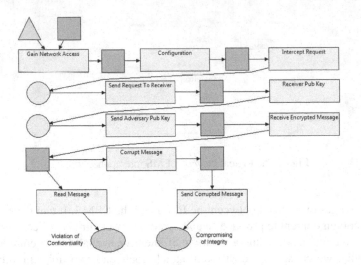

**Fig. 3.** ADVISE Attack Execution Graph for Man in the Middle attack

by the attacker before the attack begins. For each attack goal, the attacker assigns a specific payoff value, obtained by achieving that goal. Moreover, each adversary defines three attack preference weights: maximizing the payoff ($Weight_{payoff}$), e.g., achieving the attack goal; minimizing costs ($Weight_{cost}$); and minimizing the probability of being detected ($Weight_{detection}$). Each of the attack step has a specific duration of time, cost, success probability, and detection probability, which are specific for each adversary profile, based on the ability to attack. Table 2 shows the set of parameters used to define the attackers. We want to point out that the assigned values are arbitrary and they are used for illustrative purpose only. Anyway, when considering a realistic scenario such values could be derived from statistical data on the field of interest, if available. In absence of actual data, a range of plausible values could be chosen and exercised through the model in order to perform a sensitivity analysis, thus identifying the criticality of the system. For both the profiles, the adversary does not care about detection, while s/he is more attracted by the attack step cost than the potential payoff. Due to the different ability of attackers, Table 2 shows different values about success probability for each attack step, reasonably the probability to successfully get through the attack steps is higher for the hacker with respect to the criminal. ADVISE considers cost and time as unitless quantities in the model, and it is up to the modeller of taking care that all input values are in the same cost unit (Euros, Millions of Euros, etc.) and the same time unit (seconds, minutes, days, etc.). Analysis results of the average cost for the adversaries to achieve a specific attack goal are shown in Table 3. The costs reported in Table 3 are combined with the costs of controlling strategy actions in order to evaluate the cost of different quantitative controlling strategies with respect to attacks' behaviour. Indeed, such a measure can be specified through the semiring $\mathbb{C} = (\mathbb{R}^+ \cup \{\infty\}, min, +, \infty, 0)$ Due to space constraints, we just consider two simple controlling strategies, $E_1$ and $E_2$, that act differently only on the first action GainNetAccess. The first countermeasure $E_1$ modifies the behaviour by introducing an access request to identify the attacker. The

**Table 2.** Definition of Criminal and Hacker profiles

|  |  | Hacker | Criminal |
|---|---|---|---|
| Adversary Preferences | $Weight_{payoff}$ | 0.2 | 0.2 |
|  | $Weight_{cost}$ | 0.8 | 0.8 |
|  | $Weight_{detection}$ | 0.0 | 0.0 |
| Success Probability Attack Steps | Gain Network Access | 0.95 | 0.87 |
|  | Configuration | 0.95 | 0.87 |
|  | Interception Request | 0.99 | 0.9 |
|  | Send Request to Receiver | 0.99 | 0.9 |
|  | Receiver Pub Key | 0.99 | 0.9 |
|  | Send Adversary Pub Key | 0.99 | 0.9 |
|  | Receive Encrypted Message | 0.99 | 0.9 |
|  | Corrupt Message | 0.99 | 0.9 |
|  | Send Corrupt Message | 0.97 | 0.89 |
|  | Read Message | 0.99 | 0.9 |

other one, $E_2$ works by intercepting the GainNetAccess and suppressing it in order to avoid the communication between the attacker and the CEMS system.

$$E_1 = (\boxplus\text{GainNetworkAccess}, 2).(\text{SendAccessRequest}, 5).E$$
$$E_2 = (\boxminus\text{GainNetworkAccess}, 6).E$$

where $E$ is a controller process that works by suppressing all attackers' actions. In this way, even if the attacker tries to perform an attack action, it is not visible from outside so it cannot interact with the system. This means that the attacker perpetrates the attacks but it interacts only with the controller process and its execution does not alter the functionality of the target system. It is worth noticing that both the strategies we consider here do not block the execution of the attack. This is because it may halt the execution of the target system, with consequent violation of safety and resiliency requirements. In order to compare $E_1$ and $E_2$ we have to apply them on the attacker's behaviour. Since the two attackers perform the same execution path, they are the same for the two controlling strategies. To eximplify how the strategies are evaluated, we first consider the criminal attack and we assume that the cost of each action is proportional to its probability. Assuming the cost of gain network access is 10, we obtain the following:

$$E_1 \rhd C = (\boxplus\text{GainNetworkAccess}, 3).(\text{SendAccessRequest}, 5)\rhd$$
$$(\text{GainNetworkAccess}, 10).(E \rhd C')$$
$$E_2 \rhd C = (\boxminus\text{GainNetworkAccess}, 6) \rhd (\text{GainNetworkAccess}, 10).(E \rhd C')$$

Noting that the $\times$ of the semiring $\mathbb{C}$ is the $+$ of real number and the $+$ is the minimum, the evaluation of $E \rhd C'$, $[\![E \rhd C']\!] = 31$ a constant of the two evaluations, according

**Table 3.** Total average cost for an adversary to achieve a particular attack goal

|  | Corrupt Messages | Read Messages |
|---|---|---|
| Hacker | 65 | 45 |
| Criminal | 115 | 95 |

to Definition 2, the evaluation is $[\![E_1 \rhd C]\!] = min((3 + 5), 10) + 31 = 39$ while the evaluation of $E_2$ is $E_2 \rhd C = min(6, 10) + 31 = 37$. Hence the best controlling strategy is $E_2$ because it guarantees the security requirement but costs less than the $E_1$.

Let us now suppose that the hacker spends less than the criminal for gaining the access to network, e.g., it spends 6. In this case, $[\![E_1 \rhd H]\!] = min((3+5), 6) + 31 = 37$ and $E_2 \rhd H = min(6, 6) + 31 = 37$. Hence, there is no difference between the cost of the two strategies. In this case, they are both optimal.

It is worth noting that more complex strategies can be defined. However, using this method the evaluation is always an equation made of the two operations of the semiring, so it is not difficult to calculate. Furthermore, note that, even if the controlling strategies can be defined in such a way to cover all possible situations, this is not the case in real life. Thus, in order to balance between cost and likelihood we can choose, at design time, not to control all the possible attack's paths. However, the paper does not focus on this aspect, which will be tackled in future investigations.

## 4    Related Work

Security assessment relied for several years on qualitative analyses only. Leaving aside experimental evaluation and data analysis [17], [7], model-based quantitative security assessment is still far from being an established technique, despite being an active research area. Specific formalisms for security evaluation have been introduced in the literature, enabling to some extent the quantification of security. Attack trees are closely related to fault trees: they consider a security breach as a system failure, and describe sets of events that can lead to system failure in a combinatorial way [18]; they however do not consider the notion of time. Attack graphs extend attack trees by introducing the notion of state, thus allowing more complex relations between attacks to be described. Mission Oriented Risk and Design Analysis (MORDA) assesses system risk by calculating attack scores for a set of system attacks. The scores are based on adversary attack preferences and the impact of the attack on the system [11]. The recently introduced ADVISE formalism [13] extends the attack graph concept with quantitative information and supports the definition of different attackers profiles.

Recently, the interest is moving also toward the definition and quantitative evaluation of countermeasures and controlling strategies able to (partially) guarantee security of a system. In [5], the authors introduce the notion of lazy controllers, which only control the security of a system at some points in time, and based on a probabilistic modelling of the system, quantify the expected risk. In [1] the case where some actions are uncontrollable (*i.e.*, cannot be stopped) has been considered. To cope with this, the authors define which kind of policies can be enforced by using controller modelled as a Deterministic Turing Machine. In a recent approach [14], the authors deal with probabilistic cost enforcement based on input/output automata to model complex and interactive systems. Associating to each execution trace a probability and a cost measure, it is possible to evaluate the expected cost of the monitor and of the monitored systems. Also, in [9], a notion of cost is used to compare correct enforcement mechanisms (defined as state machines) with different strategies. In [10], the authors evaluate the proposed controlled strategies in order to find the optimal one by using dynamic programming. The approach is developed in the context of software monitoring, where the system is represented as a Directed Acyclic Graph, and where rewards and penalties with correcting actions are taken into account. From a different perspective, Bielova and Massacci propose in [3] a notion of distance among traces, thus expressing that if a trace is not secure, it should be edited to a secure trace close to the non-secure one.

Our approach differs from those listed above since it presents a novel approach, which combines modelling and threat analysis with quantitative controlling strategies definition. We believe that this is an advantage with respect to previous works because it allows to define focused and customized controlling strategies for each attack. Indeed, in previous work, especially in the qualitative security literature, controlling strategies are defined and applied regardless the behaviour of the attacker. On the contrary, using the analysis results, we are able to drive the selection of a controlling strategy for managing the security of the considered system. Furthermore, we describe the proposed approach through a reference scenario from the electrical power grid case study.

## 5 Conclusion and Future Works

This work represents a first step in the analysis of optimal countermeasures selection in presence of an attack. We focus on the description of a novel approach for identifying the best (the better) strategy in terms of cost of both attacker and controller among several controlling strategies. The approach is an integration of two existing framework for the model-based security assessment and the specification of quantitative controller strategies. We show how the approach works by means of the CEMS, by modelling its functionalities and analysing possible threats. We focus on Man in the Middle attack to evaluate quantitative controlling strategies. As a result, we are able to compare different strategies with respect to such attacker's behaviour and choose the one with a lower cost.

As an ongoing work, we are considering also the probability of attack as an additional aspect that leads to the identification of the optimal solution. As future work, we plan to introduce the selected controller process into the system in such a way to be able to analyse the impact of the controller on the system. This would allow us to close the loop and fully evaluate the effectiveness of the proposed solution.

**Acknowledgement.** This work has been partially supported by the TENACE PRIN Project (n. 20103P34XC) funded by the Italian Ministry of Education, University and Research, by the Regional Project POR-CREO 2007-2013 SECURE!, and by public funding from the ARTEMIS Joint Undertaking SESAMO (Grant Agreement No. 295354).

## References

1. Basin, D., Jugé, V., Klaedtke, F., Zălinescu, E.: Enforceable security policies revisited. In: Degano, P., Guttman, J.D. (eds.) POST. LNCS, vol. 7215, pp. 309–328. Springer, Heidelberg (2012)
2. Bauer, L., Ligatti, J., Walker, D.: Edit automata: Enforcement mechanisms for run-time security policies. International Journal of Information Security 4(1-2) (2005)
3. Bielova, N., Massacci, F.: Predictability of enforcement. In: Erlingsson, Ú., Wieringa, R., Zannone, N. (eds.) ESSoS 2011. LNCS, vol. 6542, pp. 73–86. Springer, Heidelberg (2011)

4. Bistarelli, S.: Semirings for Soft Constraint Solving and Programming. LNCS, vol. 2962. Springer, Heidelberg (2004)
5. Caravagna, G., Costa, G., Pardini, G.: Lazy security controllers. In: Jøsang, A., Samarati, P., Petrocchi, M. (eds.) STM 2012. LNCS, vol. 7783, pp. 33–48. Springer, Heidelberg (2013)
6. Ciancia, V., Martinelli, F., Ilaria, M., Morisset, C.: Quantitative evaluation of enforcement strategies: Position paper. In: Danger, J.-L., Debbabi, M., Marion, J.-Y., Garcia-Alfaro, J., Heywood, N.Z. (eds.) FPS 2013. LNCS, vol. 8352, pp. 178–186. Springer, Heidelberg (2013)
7. Cinque, M., Cotroneo, D., Natella, R., Pecchia, A.: Assessing and improving the effectiveness of logs for the analysis of software faults. In: 2010 IEEE/IFIP International Conference on Dependable Systems and Networks (DSN), pp. 457–466 (2010)
8. Dacier, M., Deswarte, Y.: Privilege graph: An extension to the typed access matrix model. In: Gollmann, D. (ed.) ESORICS 1994. LNCS, vol. 875, pp. 319–334. Springer, Heidelberg (1994)
9. Drábik, P., Martinelli, F., Morisset, C.: Cost-aware runtime enforcement of security policies. In: Jøsang, A., Samarati, P., Petrocchi, M. (eds.) STM 2012. LNCS, vol. 7783, pp. 1–16. Springer, Heidelberg (2013)
10. Easwaran, A., Kannan, S., Lee, I.: Optimal control of software ensuring safety and functionality. Tech. Rep. MS-CIS-05-20, University of Pennsylvania (2005)
11. Evans, S., Wallner, J.: Risk-based security engineering through the eyes of the adversary. In: Information Assurance Workshop, Proc. of the 6th Annual IEEE SMC, pp. 158–165 (2005)
12. Hägerling, C., Kurtz, F.M., Wietfeld, C., Iacono, D., Daidone, A., Di Giandomenico, F.: Security Risk Analysis and Evaluation of Integrating Customer Energy Management Systems into Smart Distribution Grids. CIRED Workshop Proc. (ed.) Accepted to be Published in the Technical Track About Telecommunications and Data Management
13. LeMay, E., Ford, M.D., Keefe, K., Sanders, W.H., Muehrcke, C.: Model-based Security Metrics Using ADversary VIew Security Evaluation (ADVISE). In: Proc. of the 8th Int. Conf. on Quantitative Evaluation of SysTems, QEST, pp. 191–200. IEEE Computer Society (2011)
14. Mallios, Y., Bauer, L., Kaynar, D., Martinelli, F., Morisset, C.: Probabilistic cost enforcement of security policies. In: Accorsi, R., Ranise, S. (eds.) STM 2013. LNCS, vol. 8203, pp. 144–159. Springer, Heidelberg (2013)
15. Martinelli, F., Matteucci, I.: Through modeling to synthesis of security automata. ENTCS 179 (2007)
16. Martinelli, F., Matteucci, I., Morisset, C.: From qualitative to quantitative enforcement of security policy. In: Kotenko, I., Skormin, V. (eds.) MMM-ACNS 2012. LNCS, vol. 7531, pp. 22–35. Springer, Heidelberg (2012)
17. Mendes, N., Neto, A., Duraes, J., Vieira, M., Madeira, H.: Assessing and comparing security of web servers. In: 14th IEEE Pacific Rim International Symposium on Dependable Computing, PRDC 2008, pp. 313–322 (2008)
18. Nicol, D., Sanders, W., Trivedi, K.: Model-based evaluation: from dependability to security. IEEE Transactions on Dependable and Secure Computing 1(1), 48–65 (2004)
19. Nostro, N., Ceccarelli, A., Bondavalli, A., Brancati, F.: A methodology and supporting techniques for the quantitative assessment of insider threats. In: Proc. of the 2nd International Workshop on Dependability Issues in Cloud Computing, pp. 1–6 (2013)
20. Practical threat analysis (pta), http://www.ptatechnologies.com/ Documents/PTA_for_Software.pdf (accessed May 2014)
21. Schneider, F.B.: Enforceable security policies. ACM Transactions on Information and System Security 3(1), 30–50 (2000)
22. Schneier, B.: Secrets & Lies: Digital Security in a Networked World, 1st edn. John Wiley & Sons, Inc., New York (2000)
23. Wang, L., Singhal, A., Jajodia, S.: Toward measuring network security using attack graphs. In: Proc. of the ACM Workshop on Quality of Protection, QoP 2007, pp. 49–54 (2007)

# Enabling Cross-Domain Reuse of Tool Qualification Certification Artefacts

Barbara Gallina[1], Shaghayegh Kashiyarandi[1],
Karlheinz Zugsbratl[2], and Arjan Geven[2]

[1] MRTC, IDT,
Mälardalen University, P.O. Box 883, SE-72123 Västerås, Sweden
{name.surname}@mdh.se
[2] TTTech, Wien, Austria
{name.surname}@tttech.com

**Abstract.** The development and verification of safety-critical systems increasingly relies on the use of tools which automate/replace/supplement complex verification and/or development tasks. The safety of such systems risks to be compromised, if the tools fail. To mitigate this risk, safety standards (e.g. DO-178C/DO330, IEC 61508) define prescriptive tool qualification processes. Compliance with these processes can be required for (re-)certification purposes. To enable reuse and thus reduce time and cost related to certification, cross-domain tool manufacturers need to understand what varies and what remains in common when transiting from one domain to another. To ease reuse, in this paper we focus on verification tools and model a cross-domain tool qualification process line. Finally, we discuss how reusable cross-domain process-based arguments can be obtained.

**Keywords:** Tool qualification processes, safety cases, process-based arguments, safety standards, DO-178C, ISO 26262, IEC 61508, Software Process Engineering Meta-model (SPEM) 2.0, Goal Structuring Notation (GSN).

## 1 Introduction

In the context of safety-critical systems engineering, software is increasingly developed and verified (semi)-automatically. Tools for code generation as well as for verification are introduced to (semi)automate/replace/supplement complex tasks. Since safety might be compromised if such tools fail, safety standards (e.g. IEC 61508 [1]) prescribe tool qualification processes (which represent process reference models for tool qualification). More recently DO-178C [2], which is going to become the de-facto standard for certifying avionic software, and more precisely its supplement DO330 has entered the scene with new requirements on the tool qualification process. This supplement provides a very detailed process which has been conceived to be used for cross-domain certification, assumed that the domain-specific documents confirm its applicability. As a consequence, since

A. Bondavalli et al. (Eds.): SAFECOMP 2014 Workshops, LNCS 8696, pp. 255–266, 2014.

compliance with the DO330 process reference model may constitute a mandatory requirement for certification purposes, companies (including TTTech) used to develop tools in compliance with either DO-178B [3] or IEC 61508 have to quickly perform a gap analysis in order to introduce adequate changes in their processes for being prepared for efficient re-certification.

In the automotive domain and within the context of intra-domain certification, we face similar circumstances such as the introduction of new standards and thus new requirements related to processes. For this case, we proposed to exploit the time for the gap analysis to reach a solution that goes beyond ad-hoc and temporary patches. More specifically, to enable flexible but compliant development processes, we proposed (and presented in [4]) to adopt a safety-oriented process line approach and model the set of prescriptive processes as a process line. The time for the gap analysis was thus used to identify and model the commonalities and variabilities among processes in order to enable reuse of process elements. The experience gathered in the automotive domain is exploited and further developed in this work. More specifically, in this paper we do not only enable reuse of process elements by modeling a cross-domain tool qualification process line, but we also enable reuse of certification artifacts by relating the process line with the corresponding family of process-based arguments related to process compliance. To do that, we show how reusable process-based arguments can be obtained from a process line. The need of harmonizing qualification guidance amongst standards is clearly stated in the perspectives discussed in [5]. The demand for reusing certification data related to the tool qualification process is explained in [6], while the motivation of providing a knowledge base concerning qualification effort is described in [7]. Our proposal for enabling reuse of process-related artifacts contributes to the satisfaction of these abovementioned needs and addresses the current problems as stated in related work and faced in practice. More specifically, the tool qualification process line contributes in engineering the harmonization of the standards. It systematizes the comparative study we performed on the set of tool qualification processes. With this, the relation between the process line and the set of corresponding process-based arguments enables reuse of certification artifacts and at the same time constitutes a knowledge base of certification strategies.

The rest of the paper is organized as follows. In Section 2, we provide essential background information. In Section 3 we present our cross-domain safety-oriented process line constituted of tool qualification processes. In Section 4, we give an intuition concerning the derivation of reusable process-based arguments from the process line. In Section 5 we discuss related work. Finally, in Section 6 we present some concluding remarks and future work.

## 2     Background

In this section, we present the background information on which we base our work. In particular, in Section 2.1 we provide essential information concerning prescriptive tool qualification processes. In Section 2.2, we briefly present

SPEM 2.0, the process modeling language used to model the tool qualification process line. In Section 2.3, we briefly present Goal Structuring Notation (GSN), the graphical notation used to argue about process compliance.

## 2.1   Tool Qualification Processes

To ensure that tools behave correctly concerning the imposed safety requirements, safety standards define tool qualification processes. These processes are typically constituted of three phases: classification, qualification, and usage [8]. During the classification phase, the tools are classified according to the level of confidence that is required to ensure their behavior is in-line with the safety requirements. Levels are named differently from one standard to another: *tool confidence levels* in the ISO 26262 [9], *tool criteria* in the DO-178C and *tool classes* in the IEC 61508. If a tool is considered to be harmless, it can be used without requiring any qualification. During the qualification phase, the tools that were considered potentially harmful, have to be qualified, i.e. manufacturers have to show absence of hazardous events (failures that might lead to accidents). Finally during the usage phase, tools can be used within the specified restrictions.

Tool qualification processes embrace two categories of tools: development tools and verification tools. In the context of this paper the focus is put on verification tools. More specifically, the work has been performed having in mind the tool qualification process related to the *TTE-Verify* tool, a verification tool of *TTEthernet* networks. As a result, those parts of the standards which deal with the active contribution to the development, e.g. code generation, are not covered in this work.

## 2.2   Safety-Oriented Process Lines and SPEM 2.0

Safety-oriented process lines [10] represent sets of safety-oriented processes that exhibit: full commonalities (equal process elements), partial commonalities (structured process elements that are partially equal), and some variabilities (e.g. optional process elements). Safety-oriented process lines can be modeled by adopting a two-phase approach consisting of a first phase aimed at modeling the domain and a second phase aimed at modeling the single processes.

SPEM (Software Process Engineering Meta-model) 2.0 [11] is the OMG's standard for systems and software process modeling. The selection of SPEM 2.0 for modeling process lines was extensively motivated in [10]. SPEM 2.0 offers support for the definition of reusable process content. Process engineers are enabled to define reusable work definition elements (e.g. tasks) as well as other process elements. An additional package called Method Plugin supports the creation of repositories for reuse of process content. SPEM 2.0 also offers support for variability modeling enabling the specification of (safety-oriented) process lines, as explored in [10] and in [4]. In Table 1, we recall some of the SPEM 2.0 graphical modeling elements that can be interrelated to model the process dynamics. In the table, we focus on the elements that we subsequently use in Section 3.

**Table 1.** Icons denoting Method Content Use elements

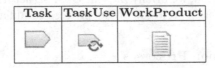

| Task | TaskUse | WorkProduct |
|------|---------|-------------|

As discussed in [12], these elements could be extended to better model safety aspects. However, currently this extension does not embrace cross-domain needs. In the context of this work, we thus take the standardized SPEM 2.0 and provide SPEM 2.0 models by using Eclipse Process Framework Composer [13], which is a SPEM 2.0-compatible open source tool for authoring development method content and publishing processes.

### 2.3   Process Compliance and GSN

Safety cases are contextualized structured arguments containing process and product-based sub-arguments. These sub-arguments are aimed at linking evidence with claims regarding system safety. In this paper, we focus on process-based arguments and more specifically on these process-based arguments that are used to show that the verification tools used to verify the software have been developed in compliance with the tool qualification process mandated by the standard. To document process-based arguments, we use the graphical notation called GSN [14]. The selection of GSN for documenting safety cases was extensively motivated in [15, 16]. GSN permits users to structure their argumentation into flat or hierarchically nested graphs (constituted of a set of nodes and a set of edges), called goal structures. To make the paper self-contained, we recall the concrete syntax of the GSN core modeling elements used in Section 4 in Figure 1. The following list provides their informal semantics:

- Goal: represents a claim about the system.
- Strategy: represents a method that is used to decompose a goal into sub goals.
- Context: represents the domain or scope in which a goal, evidence or strategy is given.
- Supported by: represents an inferential or evidential relationship. Inferential relationships declare that there is an inference between goals in the argument. Evidential relationships declare the link between a goal and the evidence used to substantiate it.
- In context of: represents a contextual relationship.

As Figure 1 shows, all the nodes are characterized by an identifier (ID) and a statement which is supposed to be written in natural language. Beyond the modeling elements presented in Figure 1, we also make use of the diamond-shaped element to characterize *to-be-developed* argumentation branches. Curly brackets within statements are used to denote variables.

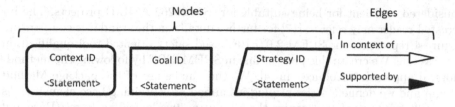

**Fig. 1.** Partial concrete syntax of GSN

# 3    A Cross-Domain Tool Qualification Process Line

As discussed in [10], whenever prescriptive processes mandated by the standards exhibit evident similarities they can be treated as a safety-oriented process line. This fosters reuse of process elements thanks to the systematic engineering of commonalities and variabilities between processes. To identify commonalities and variabilities between tool qualification processes, the guidelines provided in [10] are followed. Thus, for each standard and for each phase, the following actions are taken:

- identification of activities, tasks, steps;
- identification of the order in which activities and tasks should be performed;
- identification of the way in which tasks are grouped to form activities;
- identification of the way in which activities are grouped to form phases.

This identification requires a very detailed analysis of each of the explicit and implicit process-related pieces of information provided in the standard. Similarly to what has been done in [4], the gathered information has been documented in a spreadsheet (depicted in Figure 2) and then used to model the cross-domain process line in EPF Composer/SPEM2.0 according to the methodological framework proposed in [4].

| | Task DO178C | Task IEC61508 | Variability type |
|---|---|---|---|
| 1 | Task DO178C | Task IEC61508 | Variability type |
| 2 | Determine the tool qualification needs | Determine the tool qualification needs | partial process commonality |
| 3 | Develop Tool Operational Requirements | Create Tool Operational Requirements | partial process commonality |
| 4 | Develop Tool Operational Requirements | Create Tool Operational Requirements | partial process commonality |
| 5 | Develop the source code | Provide Tool Configuration Baseline | full process commonality |
| 6 | Create the Tool Operational Verification and Validati | Verify Tool Requirements | partial process commonality |
| 7 | Create the Tool Operational Verification and Validati | Verify Tool Requirements | partial process commonality |
| 8 | | | |

DO178C   IEC61508   ISO26262   Compatibility Matrix   +

**Fig. 2.** Cut of the spreadsheet documenting the comparative analysis

The compatibility matrix only compares DO-178C/DO330 and IEC 61508 because no classification is required anymore. The reason is that ISO 26262-8:11.4.6 states that a tool developed according to the DO330 standard can be considered sufficient for being suitable for ISO 26262 ASIL-D projects. The interested reader may refer to [17] for further details on the standards comparison. Figure 4 represents the SPEM 2.0/EPF-based safety oriented tool qualification process line. We create this process line in SPEM/EPF by following the methodological approach introduced in [4]. We thus make use of the package Method Plugin and we define a series of plug-ins aimed at containing base elements. As Figure 3 shows, we then organize them by using two logical packages (Base and Processes).

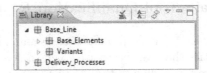

**Fig. 3.** Top-level view of the SPEM2.0/EPF-based tool qualification process line

We use Base (respectively Processes) for organizing plugins related to the Domain (Process) engineering phase. More specifically, we define one plug-in for each type of commonality (either full or partial) and variability (i.e., optional). We also define a plug-in for all the variants that are related to either partial commonalities or variabilities. In this paper, the naming convention used for tasks classified as partial commonality is that the name of DO330 is used.

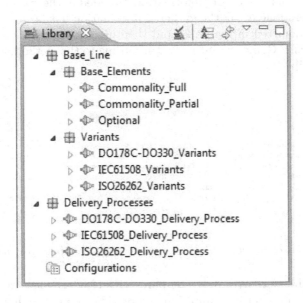

**Fig. 4.** Lower-level view of the SPEM2.0/EPF-based tool qualification process line

Figure 5 details the process elements contained in the plugin related to the full commonalities. It is in compliance with the information initially collected in the spread sheet.

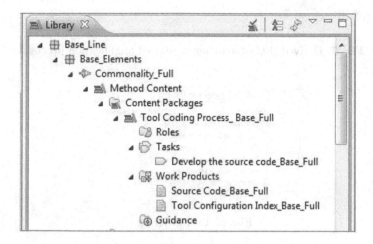

**Fig. 5.** SPEM2.0/EPF-based tool qualification process line

From Figure 5, it clearly emerges that the task named *Develop the source code* is the only full commonality.

Once a cross-domain safety-oriented process line constituted of tool qualification processes is available, (partial) commonalities as well as variabilities are clearly systematized and single processes can be easily derived. Figure 6 and Figure 7 represent the single-processes derived from the safety oriented process line by selecting and composing desired process elements.

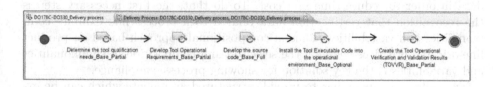

**Fig. 6.** Derived DO330-compliant tool qualification process

More specifically, to create single processes and thus populate the logical package *Delivery Processes*, full and partial commonalities must be selected. Finally to characterize single processes eventual additive as well as optional elements must also be selected. Besides selection, ordering of the process elements is necessary. This is done by setting the predecessor (as shown in Figure 8).

As it can be seen by comparing the two Figures 6 and 7, the two derived processes exhibit few variabilities in terms of tasks and thus the effort performed to

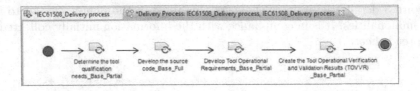

**Fig. 7.** Derived IEC 61508-compliant tool qualification process

| Presentation Name | Index | Predecessors |
|---|---|---|
| ▲ 🏛 DO178C-DO330_Delivery proc | 0 | |
| 🔲 Determine the tool qualifi | 1 | |
| 🔲 Develop Tool Operational | 2 | 1 |
| 🔲 Develop the source code_I | 3 | 2 |
| 🔲 Install the Tool Executable | 4 | 3 |
| 🔲 Create the Tool Operation | 5 | 4 |

DO178C-DO330_Delivery process

**Fig. 8.** Task ordering

be compliant with IEC 61508 can be rather easily reused to obtain the certification stamp by certification authorities responsible for checking compliance with DO330.

## 4    Enabling Reuse of Certification Artifacts

To (re)certify tools, process compliance is required. Manufacturers have to show that the qualification process mandated by the standard has been performed. When moving from one domain to another, it is crucial to reuse certification data in order to reduce time and cost. To do that, the first necessary step is the recognition that certification data related to a process line exhibits commonalities and variabilities. Thus, a compositional approach based on product line-oriented practices enabling the selection and composition of commonalities and variabilities is the key solution for showing process compliance.

Typically, a company has to provide structured arguments which can be expressed graphically or in natural language to show compliance. In this section, based on the process line presented in Section 3 and on GSN recalled in Section 2.3, we give an intuition about how such compositional and reusable process-based arguments could look like. Our goal is thereby to illustrate how reuse can be enabled and accelerated via the tool qualification process line, thus we do not show a complete process-based argument.

Figure 9, in particular, shows how the sub-goal structure (fragment of the process-compliance argumentation) can reflect the tool qualification process line.

From Figure 9 we retrieve the following argument fragment: the process is compliant with the process mandated by the standard under consideration.

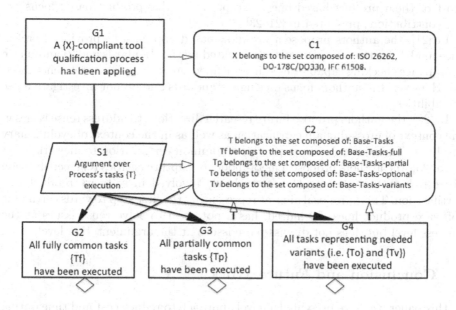

**Fig. 9.** Goal structure fragment representing a process-based argument

To support this top-level claim (G1 in Figure 9), a strategy (S1) is used to decompose it into sub-claims (G2-G4) which step by step can be more easily supported by evidence. The strategy focuses on a specific process element (i.e. task) and argues that compliance is achieved because all the common tasks and all the standard-specific tasks have been performed. From this argument fragment that only considers the initial break-down structure of the entire argumentation, it clearly emerges that:

– G2, once fully developed, can be easily fully reused.
– G3, once fully developed, can be easily partially reused.
– G4, once fully developed, cannot be reused.

Thus, the main effort during re-certification is expected to be limited to the development of G4.

## 5   Related Work

The necessity of ensuring compliance with the standards as well as the demand for reducing time and cost related to the certification process is currently providing the motivation for several research projects (e.g. [18, 19] and [20]).

To ensure compliance as well as reduce time and cost, different solutions (compliance checking, reuse, etc.) are being investigated under different perspectives, most of them product-based ones. Exceptions to this product-based focus are the contributions presented in [21–23].

In [21], the authors propose a workflow-based approach to provide: 1) reference models for the safety processes mandated by the standards and 2) automatic compliance checking capabilities of user-defined processes against reference models. However, the authors focus on single standards and do not investigate reuse possibilities.

In [22], the authors propose future research directions to address reuse issues in the context of cross-domain certification as well as in the context of evolutionary products. Their intention is to provide a common certification framework.

In [23], the authors propose a meta-model to capture entities (e.g. certification objectives with respect to the safety level) involved in software product line certification. Their proposal aims at representing the first step towards certifiable software product lines. It, indeed, has a potential to solve reuse issues at the process level but does not discuss reuse issues at the argumentation level.

# 6    Conclusion and Future Work

In this paper, we have presented a novel approach to reduce cost and time during the tool certification process. We have shown that by modeling the family of tool qualification processes via a safety-oriented process line, it is possible to identify reusable process elements and thus speed up the re-certification process when tools are expected to be used in different domains. We have also shown that these reusable process elements are reflected in the process-based arguments and thus not only qualification data (evidence) has the potential to be reused but also process-based sub-arguments. The main attention in this paper was given to the verification tools, however the approach can be extended to other tool categories as well as other kinds of safety-related processes. Due to space reasons, we also focused on process-related tasks and work products. As extensively discussed in [24], reuse also embraces all the other crucial process elements (namely, roles, work products, and guidance).

In a medium-term future, we aim at further developing our approach. First of all we will start to define a pattern for process compliance targeting cross-domain tool qualification processes. Then, we will work on providing an adequate tool-support allowing for semi-automatic generation of process-based and pattern-based arguments from process models. A master thesis on this research direction is already ongoing [25]. Finally, we also plan to introduce metrics to measure the real gain that our approach introduces.

**Acknowledgments.** This work has been partially supported by the European Project ARTEMIS SafeCer [18] and by the Swedish SSF SYNOPSIS project [19].

# References

1. IEC61508: Functional safety of electrical/electronic/programmable electronic safety-related systems (2010)
2. RTCA Inc.: Software Considerations in Airborne Systems and Equipment Certification, RTCA DO-178C (EUROCAE ED-12C), Washington DC (2013)
3. RTCA Inc.: Software Considerations in Airborne Systems and Equipment Certification, RTCA DO-178B (EUROCAE ED-12B), Washington DC (1992)
4. Gallina, B., Kashiyarandi, S., Martin, H., Bramberger, R.: Modeling a safety- and automotive-oriented process line to enable reuse and flexible process derivation. In: 8th IEEE International Workshop Quality-Oriented Reuse of Software (July 2014)
5. Camus, J.L., Dewalt, M.P., Pothon, F., Ladier, G., Boulanger, J.L., Blanquart, J.P., Quere, P., Ricque, B., Gassino, J.: Tool qualification in multiple domains: Status and perspectives. In: Embedded Real Time Software and Systems, Toulouse, France, February 5-7, vol. 7991. Springer (2014)
6. Kornecki, A.J., Zalewski, J.: Design tool assessment (December 15, 2003)
7. Kornecki, D.A.J., Zalewski, D.J.: The qualification of software development tools from the DO-178B certification perspective. CrossTalk - The Journal of Defense Software Engineering (April 2006)
8. Slotosch, O.: Model-Based Tool Qualification: The Roadmap of Eclipse towards Tool Qualification. In: Cerone, A., Persico, D., Fernandes, S., Garcia-Perez, A., Katsaros, P., Ahmed Shaikh, S., Stamelos, I. (eds.) SEFM 2012 Satellite Events. LNCS, vol. 7991, pp. 216–229. Springer, Heidelberg (2014)
9. ISO26262: Road vehicles Functional safety. International Standard (November 2011)
10. Gallina, B., Sljivo, I., Jaradat, O.: Towards a Safety-oriented Process Line for Enabling Reuse in Safety Critical Systems Development and Certification. In: Post-Proceedings of the 35th IEEE Software Engineering Workshop, SEW-35, Greece (2012)
11. Object Management Group: Software & Systems Process Engineering Meta-Model (SPEM), v2.0. Full Specification formal/08-04-01 (2008)
12. Gallina, B., Pitchai, K.R., Lundqvist, K.: S-TunExSPEM: Towards an Extension of SPEM 2.0 to Model and Exchange Tunable Safety-oriented Processes. In: Lee, R. (ed.) SERA 2013. SCI, vol. 496, pp. 215–230. Springer, Heidelberg (2013)
13. Eclipse Process Framework, http://www.eclipse.org/epf/
14. GSN: Community Standard Version 1 (November 2011), http://www.goalstructuringnotation.info/documents/GSN_Standard.pdf
15. Dardar, R., Gallina, B., Johnsen, A., Lundqvist, K., Nyberg, M.: Industrial experiences of building a safety case in compliance with iso 26262. In: IEEE 23rd International Symposium on Software Reliability Engineering Workshops (ISSREW), pp. 349–354 (2012)
16. Gallina, B., Gallucci, A., Lundqvist, K., Nyberg, M.: VROOM & cC: A Method to Build Safety Cases for ISO 26262-compliant Product Lines. In: SAFECOMP Workshop on Next Generation of System Assurance Approaches for Safety-Critical Systems (SASSUR), HAL/CNRS Report (September 2013)
17. Gallina, B., et al.: nSafeCer, D121.1: Generic process model for integrated development and certification (2014)
18. ARTEMIS-JU-269265: SafeCer-Safety Certification of Software-Intensive Systems with Reusable Components (2013), http://www.safecer.eu/

19. SYNOPSIS-SSF-RIT10-0070: Safety Analysis for Predictable Software Intensive Systems. Swedish Foundation for Strategic Research
20. FP7 OPENCOSS: Open platform for evolutionary certification of safety-critical systems
21. Chung, P.W.H., Cheung, L.Y.C., Machin, C.H.C.: Compliance flow - managing the compliance of dynamic and complex processes. Know.-Based Syst. 21(4), 332–354 (2008)
22. Espinoza, H., Ruiz, A., Sabetzadeh, M., Panaroni, P.: Challenges for an open and evolutionary approach to safety assurance and certification of safety-critical systems. In: First International Workshop on Software Certification (WoSoCER), pp. 1–6 (2011)
23. Braga, R.T.V., Trindade Jr., O., Castelo Branco, K.R., Neris, L.D.O., Lee, J.: Adapting a Software Product Line Engineering Process for Certifying Safety Critical Embedded Systems. In: Ortmeier, F., Lipaczewski, M. (eds.) SAFECOMP 2012. LNCS, vol. 7612, pp. 352–363. Springer, Heidelberg (2012)
24. Kashiyarandi, S.: Reusing Process Elements in the Context of Safety Critical Systems Development and Certification. Master's thesis, Mälardalen University, School of Innovation, Design and Engineering, Sweden (to appear)
25. Asghar Ali, E.: Deriving reusable process-based arguments from process models in the context of safety critical systems development and certification. Master's thesis, Mälardalen University, School of Innovation, Design and Engineering, Sweden (ongoing)

# 1st International Workshop on the Integration of Safety and Security Engineering (ISSE '14)

Laurent Rioux[1] and John Favaro[2]

[1] THALES Research & Technology
1, av Augustin Fresnel, F-91767 PALAISEAU Cedex
laurent.rioux@thalesgroup.com
[2] Intecs S.p.A.
via Umberto Forti 5, 56121 Pisa, Italy
john.favaro@intecs.it

## 1    Introduction

The growing complexity of critical systems is creating new challenges for safety and security engineering practices: it is now expected that delivered products implement more and more complex features, while respecting strict requirements on safety and security. For such systems, an ever-increasing portion of design effort is therefore spent on safety and security assessment and verification. Applying safety verification without considering security properties is no longer possible since safety decisions have an impact on system security properties and vice-versa.

The challenge addressed by this workshop relates to the inefficiency and ineffectiveness of combining engineering activities related to safety and security properties of the software or the system. The inefficiency relates to the costs and time required to perform both safety and security engineering. The ineffectiveness relates to the potentially redundant or contradictory solutions elaborated by the safety engineering and security engineering activities. These issues are mainly due to the clustering of these two engineering domain activities.

The purpose of the ISSE'14 workshop was to share ideas, experiences and solutions to concretely combine or integrate safety and security engineering activities. As a result, the ISSE'14 workshop aimed at providing a forum for practitioners and researchers to present contributions and share ideas on combining safety and security process, methods, tools and verification techniques and their applicability to industrial critical systems. It also aimed at promoting discussions, closer interaction, cross-fertilization of ideas, and synergies across the breadth of the safety and security research communities, as well as attracting industrial participants from different domains having a specific interest in safety and security verification.

The workshop was conceived with the intention of becoming a unique place to exchange and discuss ideas about the issues and opportunities associated with combining or integrating safety and security engineering. To that end, a questionnaire was distributed to the participants in order to capture the first elements for a community-building effort that would contribute to a sustainable series of workshops in the future.

A. Bondavalli et al. (Eds.): SAFECOMP 2014 Workshops, LNCS 8696, pp. 267–268, 2014.
© Springer International Publishing Switzerland 2014

## 2    Workshop Format

According to the stated objectives, the workshop was organized primarily as a discussion forum as opposed to a mini-conference. The morning session included summary presentations of results on safety and security integration by the organizing projects MERGE and SESAMO, followed by two invited talks and presentations of research and experience papers selected for their potential to stimulate discussion and debate, including:

- an application of Failure Mode, Vulnerabilities and Effects Analysis (FMVEA) to safety and security analysis of intelligent and cooperative vehicles;
- an adaptation of models devised for safety assessment of avionics platforms in order to analyse their security, with the aim of developing common models and tools to assess safety and security;
- a uniform approach to risk communication in distributed IT environments combining safety and security aspects.

The afternoon session was dedicated to discussions and interactions on challenges in the integration of safety and security engineering. For this, a panel including research representatives promoting different approaches animated a discussion with participation of the attendees, aiming to identify the scientific and industrial stakes in the integration of both engineering domains. The session concluded with a synthesis report agreed by the attendees. This report will be published at the next workshop.

**Acknowledgements.** The ISSE '14 workshop was supported by the following projects:

- **Multi-concerns Interactions System Engineering (MERgE).** The ITEA 2 project MERgE (www.merge-project.eu) aims to develop and demonstrate innovative concepts and design tools to address multi-concerns interactions in systems, targeting the elaboration of effective architectural solutions with a focus on safety and security.
- **Safety and Security Modelling (SESAMO).** The ARTEMIS JU SESAMO project (www.sesamo-project.eu) is addressing the root causes of problems arising with convergence of safety and security in embedded systems at architectural level, where subtle and poorly understood interactions between functional safety and security mechanisms impede system definition, development, certification, and accreditation procedures and standards. The SESAMO approach is to develop a component-oriented design methodology based upon model-driven technology, jointly addressing safety and security aspects and their interrelation for networked embedded systems in multiple domains.

# From Safety Models to Security Models: Preliminary Lessons Learnt

Pierre Bieber and Julien Brunel

ONERA-DTIM
2 Av Edouard Belin, BP 74025, F-31055 Toulouse
{Firstname.Lastname}@onera.fr

**Abstract.** We aim at developing common models and tools to assess both safety and security of avionics platforms so we studied the adaptation of models devised for Safety assessment in order to analyse security. In this paper, we describe a security modelling ana analysis approach based on the AltaRica language and associated tools, we illustrate the approach with an avionics case-study. We report lessons learnt about the convergence and divergence points between security and safety with respect to modelling and analysis techniques.

## 1 Introduction

Taking into account information security risks is a relatively new task in the development of safety-critical aircraft systems. Recent transport aircraft including Airbus A380 and Boeing B787 contain a security architecture that organizes the avionics platform in domains: aircraft control, airline information services, passenger information and entertainment Services. Security mechanisms such as firewalls and digital signature infrastructure are in place in order to control information flows and applications that belong to these domains.

In parallel to the development of these security architectures, an international effort has led to the creation of Airworthiness Security Process (AWSP) document ED-202/DO-326 [10] that standardizes the development process of aircraft systems with respect to security. This document aims at providing a joint basis for the certification of information security aspects of aircraft systems. Consequently, this document focuses on security aspects that have an effect on the safety of the aircraft, these aspects are called "Security for Safety". The document does not deal with other security aspects concerning, for instance, the protection of passenger privacy or the protection of aircraft manufacturer intellectual property. In this paper we restrict ourselves to the modelling and analysis of "Security for Safety".

The first generation of security architecture has to evolve in order to deal with new services for airlines such as remote maintenance or paper-less cockpit. An important goal for the design of new security architectures is to keep the costs of their implementation and assessment of security architecture as low as acceptable.

A. Bondavalli et al. (Eds.): SAFECOMP 2014 Workshops, LNCS 8696, pp. 269–281, 2014.
© Springer International Publishing Switzerland 2014

In the past decade an approach has been defined to help assess efficiently the safety of systems. This approach, called Model Based Safety Assessment [4], is based on the use of formal models of aircraft systems and of associated tools to automatically perform parts of the safety assessment required in the airworthiness certification process.

In this paper we describe an attempt to adapt the Model Based Safety Assessment approach in order to deal with Information Security aspects. We believe that the reuse of safety models and assessment tools should reduce the cost of security assessment. In the following of the paper, we first summarize the main aspects of the Model Based Safety Assessment methodology. Then we explain the adaptation of models to deal with security and we describe how we used two safety assessment tools to perform security analysis. Finally we list several preliminary lessons learnt.

## 2    A Summary of Model Based Safety Assessment

### 2.1    Safety Model

Model Based Safety Assessment aims at supporting the Preliminary System Safety Assessment (PSSA) [8]. Before the PSSA is performed, the Functional Hazard Analysis identifies the Failure Conditions (e.g. safety critical situations of the system) and assesses their severity on a scale going from No Safety Effect (NSE) to Catastrophic (CAT). Then, during the Preliminary System Safety Assessment, safety models (or alternatively fault-trees) are built and analysed. A safety model describes formally in which node a fault occurs and how this fault propagates inside the system architecture in order to cause a Failure Condition.

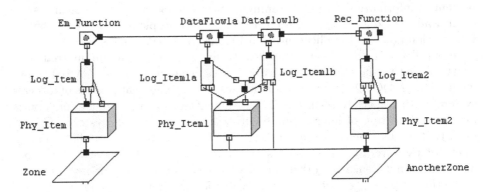

**Fig. 1.** Layered Architecture Model

As shown in the previous figure the safety model is organised into several layers :

– Functional Layer : at the top of the layers are depicted functional nodes, Em_Function is a function that emits a data flow (represented by the nodes

DataFlow1a and DataFlow1b) towards a receiver function called Rec_Function. The links relating functional nodes represent the routing of the data-flow from an emitter to the receiver. All these nodes use resources from the logical layer. The links between the logical and functional layers connect functional nodes with the logical resources that they use.

- Logical Layer: this layer groups logical nodes such as software, partitions, virtual links or network messages that implement the functional nodes. All these nodes use resources from the physical layer. The links between the logical and physical layers connect logical nodes with the physical resources that they use.
- Physical Layer: this layer groups physical nodes such as computers, mass-memory storage, network communication equipment and links. They are used to implement the logical nodes. All these nodes are located in a Zone. The links between the zone and physical layers connect physical nodes with their installation zone.
- Zone Layer: this layer describes the various installation zone of interest: cockpit, avionics bay; cabin, aircraft vicinity, airport, maintenance operation center, ...

To implement the Model Based Safety Assessment approach we have been using the AltaRica language and associated tools [2]. Each of the nodes in the previous diagram is modelled formally by an AltaRica node_ selected in a predefined library. For instance, nodes Dataflow1a and Dataflow1b are instances of the formal node DataFlow that has two inputs I and R and one output O. When it is in its correct mode and its resource is in its correct mode, this node propagates on its output the value of its input, it does not propagate any value if the node or its resource is in the lost mode and otherwise an erroneous value is propagated.

```
node DataFlow
    flow
        O: FailureType:out; I,R: FailureType:in;
    state
        Status: FailureType;
    event
        F_loss,F_error
    trans
        (Status ≠lost) |− F_loss →Status:= lost;
            (Status = ok) |− F_error →Status:= erroneous;
    assert
        O = case {
                Status=ok and R=ok: I,
                Status=lost or R=lost: lost,
                else erroneous
            };
    init
        Status:= ok;
edon
```

The **state** section declares state variables names and domains. Values of variable Status are in user defined domain FailureType that is the enumeration ok, lost, erroneous. These values denote the failure status of a node. The correct value is used when the node is working correctly, the lost value is used when the node is not producing any output, the value erroneous is used when the node is producing an output whose value deviates from what is expected. The **flow** section declares variables that are used to model data exchanged with interfaced components, the FailureType domain is used.

The **event** section declares failure events. In the **trans** section, a transition is associated with failure event. The transition associated with event F_loss may only be triggered when the node is not lost. The new value of Status is lost. The value of a state variable can only be modified by transitions.

The **assert** section, defines how the value of output O is computed using the values of inputs I and O and state variable Status.

The **init** section states that initially the component is working correctly.

A library of AltaRica nodes was developed in order to help building safety models for avionics platform architectures. This library includes AltaRica nodes that describe functional, logical and physical nodes. The library was used in order to develop safety models to assess the safety of Integrated Modular Avionics [9]. In this type of architecture, computation or communication resources are shared by several functions or data flows. Consequently, the fault of a shared physical node has an impact on all logical and functional nodes that are connected with this physical node. For instance, in the previous figure, data flows DataFlow1a and DataFlow1b are connected to the same physical node called Phy_Item1. So if Phy_Item1 is lost then both data flows would be lost.

## 2.2   Safety Analysis

The design of aeronautics safety critical systems deals with two families of faults: random faults of equipments and systematic faults in the development of the equipment, which include errors in the specification, design and coding of hardware and software. Two different approaches are used when assessing whether the risk associated with these two types of faults is acceptable. Qualitative requirements (minimal number of failures leading to a Failure Condition) and quantitative requirements (maximal probability of a Failure Condition occurrence) are associated with equipment faults whereas requirements stated in terms of Development Assurance Levels (DAL) are associated with development faults.

For both types of requirements, the first step of the safety analysis is the computation of the minimal combinations of node faults leading to the Failure Conditions. These combinations are called Minimal Cut Sets (MCS). They are used to compute the mean probability of the Failure Condition in order to assess whether the designed architecture is safe enough. The MCS are also analysed to check whether there are combinations made of a single fault event that could lead to the Failure Condition.

In order to generate the MCS we used the sequence generator from the Cecilia OCAS toolset. The tool takes as input a Failure Condition (actually it is the name of the output variable of a node representing the Failure Condition in the model) and an Order (the maximum size of the scenarios), then it computes a set of minimal sequences of events in the model that lead from the initial state to a state where the Failure Condition is satisfied. A MCS is a sequence of pairs of the form CpName.FName where, CpName is the name of a node of the AltaRica model and FName is either F_loss or F_error.

Several kind of analysis of the MCS are possible. In the domain of Integrated Modular Avionics (IMA), a first analysis can be performed on the basis of MCS that only include functional node faults. This first analysis provides an indication of the safety of the system before integrating the system on the IMA platform. Then another analysis if performed using MCS that only include physical node faults. This second analysis is used to assess the safety of the system after integration on the IMA platform. The size of both MCS can be compared in order to check whether the effect of common mode failures related wiht IMA shared resources is acceptable.

Another analysis of MCS is performed in order to check the DAL allocation. We check that the DAL allocated to each node dominates the DAL of the Failure Conditions it contributes to. A node contributes to a Failure Condition if a fault of this node appears in one of the MCS of the failure condition. Table 2 gives the basic DAL allocation rules for Failure Conditions (Sev is the severity of the Failure Condition).

| Sev | NSE | MIN | MAJ | HAZ | CAT |
|-----|-----|-----|-----|-----|-----|
| DAL | E | D | C | B | A |

Fig. 2. Basic DAL allocation

New DAL allocation rules introduced in the revised ARP4754a [8] allow to downgrade the original DAL allocated using the basic rule, in cases when nodes involved in the minimal cut sets are known to be pair-wise independent. In order to check these new rules Onera has developed the DALculator [1]. This tool uses as input a file containing MCS for a Failure Condition It also needs an indication of the reference DAL of the Failure Condition. For instance, if the DAL of the Failure Condition is B, and a MCS leading to this Failure Condition is {Cp1.F_loss, Cp2.F_loss, Cp3.F_error} then allocating DAL B to Cp1 and DAL D to Cp2 and Cp3 would be acceptable according to the new DAL allocation rules provided that Cp1 is independant from Cp2 and from Cp3. Consequently, it is possible to build highly dependable systems at DAL B with components of mixed DAL B and D.

# 3 Towards Model Based Security Assessment

## 3.1 Security Models

We aim at reusing the safety node library in order to build security models. We investigated the main Threat Conditions for the avionics platform and concluded that availability and integrity concepts in safety and security were very similar. Consequently, we propose to use the value lost also to denote the status of a component that was subject to an availability threat. We name T_block the generic threat that leads to losing the availability of an item in the architecture. We propose to use the value erroneous for the status of a component that was subject to an integrity threat. We name T_forge the related generic threat.

The main difference between Threat Conditions and Failure Conditions is that there is no direct counterpart to confidentiality in the safety domain. We first thought that, as we were interested in "security for safety", we could avoid dealing with confidentiality. But a number of security mechanisms rely on secret attributes as keys or passwords. If the confidentiality of these attributes is compromised then the security mechanism cannot work properly and this could lead to a safety problem. So we decided to deal with confidentiality. We extended the domain FailType with a new value, named public, which represents the status of a component whose confidentiality was compromised. We name T_listen the related generic threat.

The platform model was extended with an Agent layer in order to be able to relate a threat with the agent that initiates the attack. The node associated with an agent is very simple, it contains an event T_initiate that represents attack initialisation. Whenever an attack is initiated, the output of the agent node is set to the Boolean value true and this value is propagated to the items located in the zone where the agent is located.

In safety models, the propagation of a failure mode follows the links connecting nodes. We propose to use the same principle in a security model. Let's consider the example shown in the following figure. A threat in physical item Phy_item was exploited by an Agent, its status is erroneous. The picture shows the propagation of this integrity threat from Phy_Item to function Rec_Function. To ease the understanding of propagation, the colours of nodes and links depend of their current value. In the picture, erroneous components and links are coloured in red whereas components coloured in green are working properly. The propagation path starts at component Phy_item, then it goes to Log_item whose integrity is comprised due to its reliance on Phy_item, then Em_Function is also erroneous because it relies on the Log_Item. Then the integrity attack propagates through the functional layer to go from the emitter function to the receiver function.

Other types of propagations should be taken into account when dealing with security: indirect propagation through shared resources. For instance, when a logical item as a piece of software is attacked, if the computer that hosts the software is not protected this attack also contaminates the computer. And then, when the computer is attacked it is also likely that all other pieces of software hosted by the computer are contaminated. Similarly, communication links are shared by several computers. It is likely that an attack on one computer can contaminate the communication link and the connected computers. We have extended the models in order to describe this type of indirect propagation. We added event T_contaminate to nodes in the physical layer such that when one

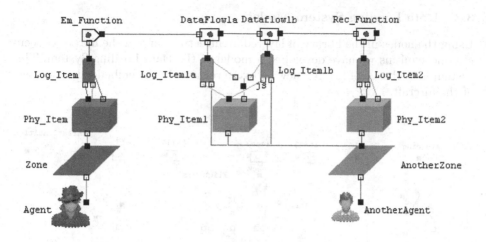

**Fig. 3.** Propagation of threats through the functional layer

of the logical node using this physical node is attacked, the attack is propagated to the physical item and to all the other logical nodes using this physical node.

### 3.2 Security Mechanism Library

Security mechanisms are nodes that cannot be reused from the safety models. We developed a library of models of security mechanisms that can be used to secure an avionics platform, this library includes models for :

- Zone Access Control: This mechanism blocks the attack initiation signal sent by an agent. This is implemented by controlling the physical access of agents into a zone of the platform. This is an organisational security mechanism.
- Physical Item Access Control: This mechanism blocks the attack initiation signal sent by an agent. This is implemented by controlling the access of agents to a physical item.
- Contamination Control: This mechanism blocks the contamination of a shared resource by an attacked logical item. This can be implemented by an Operation System partitioning service or by virtualization tools.
- Local integrity mechanism: This mechanism blocks an erroneous value and transforms it into a lost value. This could represent a message filtering device.
- End to End integrity mechanism: This mechanism is made of a pair of mechanisms: the first one prepares the proof of integrity of a value and the second one checks the integrity proof. This represents digital signature.

Each security mechanism is implemented as an AltaRica node containing assertions that formalize their influence on the propagation of threat values as (erroneous, lost or public). All the nodes in the security mechanisms library contain an event called T_bypass that voids the limiting effect of the mechanism on threat propagation.

## 3.3   Data Loading System Model

Using the nodes in the library of layered architectures and in the library of security mechanisms we have developed a model of the Data Loading System. This system is in charge of loading new software releases in the embedded computers of the aircraft.

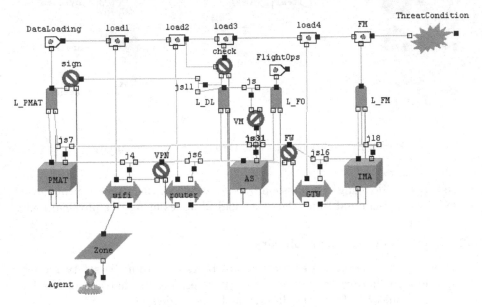

**Fig. 4.** DLCS Security Model

- Functional Layer: We have detailed the part of Data Loading functions that are related with a request for data loading initiated from a portable maintenance terminal (PMAT) that is connected via wifi to the platform. The load dataflow is emitted by the DataLoading function and is received by the Flight Management (FM) function. The load dataflow is divided into 4 nodes in order to make it easier to relate the data flow with the supporting resources. The functional layer also contains a very abstract view of the flight operation function (FlightOps). This function is described by a unique node. In this model, its role is to study the potential contamination between various functions.
- Logical Layer: The model consists of 4 logical nodes to describe the software components needed to implement the Data Loading (and part of the Flight Ops) functions. For the sake of simplicity, we have not included logical nodes for the network components (wifi, router, and GTW). In that case, data flow nodes are directly linked to physical resources.

- Physical Layer: the model includes the major physical nodes useful for the Data Loading functional chain: computers such as PMAT, AS (Avionics Server) and IMA (Integrated Modular Avionics) and communication equipment such as wifi, router and GTW (Communication Gateway).
- Zone Layer: The model contains only one zone of interest where the wifi link can be attacked. We have not modelled all the other zones of the aircraft because we have supposed that either the agents that can access the platform are trusted (pilot, cabin crew, ..) or there are sufficient organizational controls in order to stop an attack that would originate in other zones such as the cockpit, cabin or aircraft vicinity.
- Agent Layer: the model contains only one type of agent that represents the General population as we have considered, for this example, that all other types of agents are trusted.

Two kinds of security mechanisms were used in the model:

- End to End Integrity Control is used to model the signature of loads with a digital signature exchanged by the PMAT (sign component) and the AS (check component).
- Contamination Control is used three times. VM models a virtualisation service running on the AS server in order to control the contamination of logical items. VPN models a virtual private network mechanism associated with the router, FW models a firewall associated with the gateway.

## 3.4 Security Analysis

We reuse safety analysis tools that were presented earlier to assess the security of the model. We use the Cecilia OCAS Sequence Generator in order to generate threat scenarios leading to a threat condition. We want to use the DALculator in order to analyse threat scenarios in order to allocate a security level with nodes of an avionics platform.

We were interested in two Threat Conditions related with the Data Loading system:

- *"Loss of update of Flight Management software due to a Data Loading via wifi"*. We consider that this Threat Condition is moderately severe because this could potentially lead to the loss of the Flight Management system when the aircraft is on ground.
- *"Erroneous update of the Flight Management software due to a Data Loading via wifi"*. We consider that this Threat Condition is more severe because this could potentially lead to an erroneous behaviour of the Flight Management system during flight.

We generated all threat scenarios including a maximum of 6 threat events. As in the case of MCS, a threat scenario is a sequence of pairs of the form CpName.ThreatName that starts from the initial state of the system where no attack is launched and leads to a state where the system is attacked. In a threat scenario, CpName is the name of a logical node or a physical node or a security mechanism or a user name, and ThreatName is the name of the threat being activated on the component. It could be: T_forge (corruption threat), T_listen (disclosure threat), T_block (denial of service threat), init (user attack activation) , T_bypass (circumvention of a security mechanism) or T_contamination (propagation of a threat from one component to another).

Let us consider a threat scenario leading to the erroneous update of the Flight Management software.

{'Agent.T_init', 'PMAT.T_forge'}

This Threat Scenario is made of two pairs. The first pair 'Agent.T_init' means that the user called Agent is the initiator of the attack and the second pair 'PMAT.T_forge' means that a corruption attack is performed on physical node PMAT. The corruption of the physical node has a negative effect on the behaviour of the end to end integrity protection mechanisms. As this could lead to an undetected corruption of the load then it could be the case that the flight management function is updated with a corrupted load.

Let us now consider a more complex Threat Scenario leading to the loss of update of the Flight Management function. This scenario involves the propagation by the router of an attack.

{'Agent.T_init', 'router.T_contamination', 'AS.T_block', 'router.T_contamination'}

In this scenario, Agent initiates the attack. The next step is 'router.T_contamination'. This means that the router could propagate the attack initiation signal to components physically linked with the router (e.g. wifi). The following step is 'AS.T_block', which means that a denial of service attack is performed on the avionics server. The last step of the scenario is 'router.T_contamination', which means that the denial of service attack is propagated to the router and all components connected to the router. Since the router is lost (due to the propagated denial of service attack) and should be used to communicate the software load, then the software load is not received by the Flight Management function that cannot be updated.

Let us now consider another threat scenario:

{'Agent.T_init', 'router.T_contamination', 'AS.T_block', 'FW.T_bypass', 'GTW.T_contamination'}

In this scenario, Agent initiates the attack, and then the router propagates the attack initiation signal to nodes physically linked with the router. Then, a denial of service attack is performed on the avionics server. The next step of the scenario is 'FW.T_bypass', which means that the firewall is deactivated. In the last step the denial of service attack is propagated to the gateway.

Among the 13 threat scenarios that lead to the loss of the Flight Management there are 11 scenarios of size 2, and 2 of size 3. Among the 40 threat scenarios that lead to an erroneous behaviour of the Flight Management there are 9 scenarios of size 2, 21 of size 3 and 10 of size 4. All these scenarios can be reviewed in order to check whether there are enough security mechanisms in the avionics platform.

We used the DALculator tool to check the allocation of a Security Level to each of the components that appear in the threat scenarios. The Security Level of security mechanisms measures the expected efficiency of this mechanism. The Security Level for other nodes can be seen as a level of Trust in the node. The Security Level is measured using the same range of values as the DAL : from E to A.

Due to the severity of the Threat Condition *"erroneous update of the FM software due to the DLCS via wifi"* we have considered that its Security Level is B.

We have considered that the Security Level of nodes Agent and wifi is level D. This means that their trust level is very low. We considered that the Security Level of the node Flight Ops is level C because it is little bit more trusted than external entities as the Agent or the wifi network.

The solution checked by the DALculator is described in the following figure. In this solution the efficiency of the end to end integrity functions (sign and check nodes) should be rather high (level B). The trust in the resources used to check the signature is consistent as AS and L_DL should also have level B. A similar efficiency is required for VPN and VM. The level of trust in other components is rather low (level D).

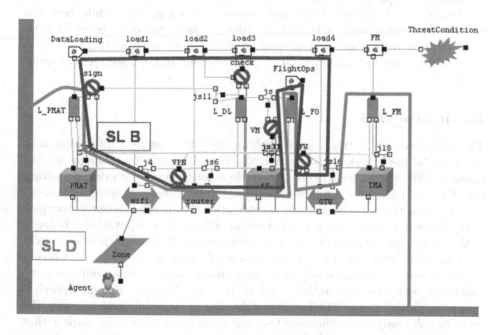

**Fig. 5.** Security Level Allocation

# 4    Conclusion

## 4.1    Preliminary Lessons Learnt

This first experiment in using AltaRica to build security models helped us to analyse convergence and divergences points between Safety and Security modelling and assessment:

- The layered model for the safety analysis of avionics platform was reused efficiently for the security model. We only had to add the Agent layer to model threat activation.
- The AltaRica code was easily extended to deal with security threats. The main addition was related with the modelling of confidentiality.
- We had to model the propagation of threats due to the use of shared resources. Although, propagation of an integrity or availability fault is a safety concern that is considered in IMA dévelopement we never included this type of propagation in the safety models we have been building so far in order to help System safety Assessment.
- The OCAS sequence generator was used successfully to generate Threat Scenarios. As the models could include both fault and threat events, it should be possible to generate scenarios that combine fault and threats in order to analyse complex requirements mixing safety and security.
- Using DAL to model the security level of nodes in the architecture was possible. Extra work is needed in order to check the consistency of DAL allocation rules with security level allocation rules such as the ISO 27005 risk reduction approach (see [3] for a comparison of DAL level and Security Level).

## 4.2    Related Work

The work described in this paper is preliminary. The most relevant related work seems to be the attack tree approach [5]. This approach proposes to use the classical fault tree notation in order to study security. As in our work, the attack tree contains basic events representing elementary threats. In some variants of the notation, the tree also include a description of the effect security barriers. In [7] the authors propose to use an extension of the fault-tree notation in order to deal with dynamic aspects of the threat propagation. Both of the previous works tend to focus on a quantitative assessment of security requirements whereas we have been working on qualitative requirements because this would be more consistent with the Airworthiness Safety process. Another relevant approach was proposed by the CORAS project [6] , this notation aims at assisting the security risk analysis. A difference between this approach and our work is that the CORAS can be applied before the security architecture is designed whereas our approach is applied once the security architecture is established.

**Acknowledgements.** The research described by this paper was partially supported by the ITEA project MERGE and DGAC project ARCS.

# References

1. Bieber, P., Delmas, R., Seguin, C.: DALculus – theory and tool for development assurance level allocation. In: Flammini, F., Bologna, S., Vittorini, V. (eds.) SAFE-COMP 2011. LNCS, vol. 6894, pp. 43–56. Springer, Heidelberg (2011)
2. Bieber, P., Seguin, C.: Safety Analysis of Embedded Systems with the AltaRica Approach. In: Industrial Use of Formal Methods: Formal Verification, ch. 3. Wiley (2013)
3. Blanquart, J.-P., Bieber, P., Descargues, G., Hazane, E., Julien, M., Leonardon, L.: Similarities and dissimilarities between safety levels and security levels. In: Proceedings of the Embedded Real-Time Systems and Software Conference (ERTS2 2012) (2012)
4. Bozzano, M., Villafiorita, A., Aakerlund, O., Bieber, P., Bougnol, C., Böde, E., Bretschneider, M., Cavallo, A., Castel, C., Cifaldi, M., Cimatti, A., Griffault, A., Kehren, C., Lawrence, B., Luedtke, A., Metge, S., Papadopoulos, C., Passarello, R., Peikenkamp, T., Persson, P., Seguin, C., Trotta, L., Valacca, L., Zacco, G.: Esacs: an integrated methodology for design and safety analysis of complex systems. In: Proceedings of ESREL 2003. Balkema Publisher (2003)
5. Kordy, B., Mauw, S., Radomirovic, S., Schweitzer, P.: Attack-defense trees. Journal of Logic and Computation 24, 55–87 (2012)
6. Lund, M.S., Solhaug, B., Stoelen, K.: Model-Driven Risk Analysis. The CORAS Approach. Springer (2010)
7. Piètre-Cambacédès, L., Bouissou, M.: The promising potential of the bdmp formalism for security modelling. In: Proceedings of the 39th Annual IEEE/IFIP International Conference on Dependable Systems and Networks (DSN 2009) (2009)
8. S. S-18 and E. W.-. committees. Arp4754a - guidelines for development of civil aircraft and systems. SAE aerospace (2010)
9. Sagaspe, L., Bel, G., Bieber, P., Boniol, F., Castel, C.: Safe allocation of shared avionics resources. In: Proceedings of the Ninth IEEE International Symposium on High-Assurance Systems Engineering (HASE 2005) (2005)
10. WG72. Ed202 - airworthiness security process specification. EUROCAE (October 2010)

# FMVEA for Safety and Security Analysis of Intelligent and Cooperative Vehicles

Christoph Schmittner, Zhendong Ma, and Paul Smith

Safety & Security Department,
Austrian Institute of Technology, Austria
{christoph.schmittner.fl,zhendong.ma,paul.smith}@ait.ac.at

**Abstract.** Safety and security are two important aspects in the analysis of cyber-physical systems (CPSs). In this short paper, we apply a new safety and security analysis method to intelligent and cooperative vehicles, in order to examine attack possibilities and failure scenarios. The method is based on the FMEA technique for safety analysis, with extensions to cover information security. We examine the feasibility and efficiency of the method, and determine the next steps for developing the combined analysis method.

**Keywords:** safety and security analysis, vulnerability and effect analysis, FMEA, FMVEA, cyber-physical system (CPS), failure mode, threat mode, intelligent vehicle.

## 1 Introduction

Cyber-physical systems (CPSs) are systems in which networked computers control physical entities. CPSs are widely used in mission-critical applications, such as in the power grid, industrial process, aerospace, and automotive domains, where safety is critical. Since CPSs increasingly rely on Information and Communication Technology (ICT), attacks in cyberspace can lead to devastating consequences in the physical world. Therefore, ensuring safety and security in the engineering process are two equally important aspects for developing systems with high availability, reliability and dependability.

In the past, safety engineering has been applied to build dependable systems out of less reliable components. A multitude of practical techniques such as fault masking, error detection, fault diagnosis, and recovery have evolved to improve the reliability of safety-critical system. Since the operations of these systems also depends on software and communicated information, malicious attacks to information security must be considered and appropriately addressed. Commonly, the focus of security can be described by the Confidentiality, Integrity, and Availability (CIA) model. A safety analysis needs to include security risks, determined by vulnerability, threat, and impact with respect to the CIA model.

This short paper presents our ongoing work for building a holistic approach to safety and security analysis for the assessment of vulnerabilities and risks of CPSs in different application domains, in which networked embedded systems are used

A. Bondavalli et al. (Eds.): SAFECOMP 2014 Workshops, LNCS 8696, pp. 282–288, 2014.

for applications with different criticality levels. Specifically, we apply the Failure Mode, Vulnerabilities and Effect Analysis (FMVEA) method [3] to the safety and security analysis of intelligent and cooperative vehicles. As a type of CPSs, vehicles in the automotive domain are very safety-critical. Intelligent vehicles are equipped with sophisticated in-vehicle embedded systems and electronic control units (ECUs) with complex software (e.g., a modern luxury car runs on 100 million lines of code [1]), and are able to communicate with other entities in a cooperative system – this introduces new security challenges that need to be addressed [8]. FMVEA has the potential to bring both safety and security into analysis. In the following, Sec. 2 introduces the FMVEA method and Sec. 3 gives an overview of the vehicle system to be analysed by FMVEA. Section 4 summarises initial results from applying FMVEA for safety and security analysis of the vehicle system, followed by the conclusion and future work in Sec. 5.

## 2   Failure Mode, *Vulnerabilities* and Effect Analysis

FMVEA [3] is a combined analysis method for safety and security. It is based on the Failure Mode and Effects Analysis, as described in IEC 60812 [6]. In the FMEA approach, each component of a system is analyzed for potential failure modes. Based on the detail level and maturity of the design, components can be HW/SW-modules or functions. A failure mode is the manner in which the component fails [6] or the manner by which a occurred fault is observed [4]. In the next step the effects of the failure mode on the system are identified. A failure mode could cause a component to cease to function and still only have a negligible effect on the functionality of the complete system. After the severity of the final effect is determined, potential causes are identified. Based on the causes, the probability of the failure mode is estimated. This process is repeated until every failure mode of the component and every component on the chosen analysis level is examined.

FMVEA extends this approach with a security analysis. Components are not only examined for failure modes, but also for threat modes. While a failure mode describes how a system quality attribute [10] fails, a threat mode describes how a security attribute of the components fails. It is the manner by which a occurred threat is observed. Causes for failing security attributes are vulnerabilities. In order to estimate the frequency of threat modes, potential attackers (threat agents) are identified. The probability of a threat mode is determined based on the threat agent and the vulnerability. The results of a FMVEA are the failure and threat modes of a system, and their causes and consequences. In addition, failure and threat modes are evaluated in terms of probability and severity. We refer the reader to [3] for a more detailed description of FMVEA.

## 3   System of Intelligent and Cooperative Vehicles

Modern intelligent vehicles include highly heterogeneous and complex systems, consisting of a combination of mechanical and electronic components – they are cyber-physical systems. Our focus is on the safety and security aspects of the hardware and software of the in-vehicle system. Although there is no one-size-fits-all general system architecture, based on [9], we derive a system architecture that includes the most important interconnected Electronic Control Units (ECUs) in modern vehicles (shown in Fig. 1). The Local Interconnect Network (LIN) for connecting sensors to ECUs and the Media Oriented Systems Transport (MOST) Bus for multimedia applications is omitted, in order to decrease complexity.

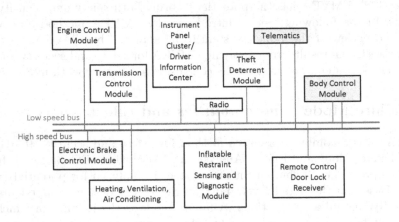

**Fig. 1.** Intelligent vehicle system architecture, including key Electronic Control Units

As can be seen in Fig. 1, the ECUs are connected to two types of vehicle buses. The Engine Control Module (ECM), Electronic Brake Control Module (EBCM) and Transmission Control Module (TCM) are safety/mission-critical components, which are connected to the high-speed bus. Meanwhile, the Remote Control Door Lock Receiver (RCDLR), Heating, Ventilation, Air Conditioning (HVAC), Inflatable Restraint Sensing and Diagnostic Module (SDM), Instrument Panel Cluster/Driver Information Center (IPC/DIC), Radio, and Theft Deterrent Module (TDM) are less safety/mission-critical components, which are connected to low-speed bus. Furthermore, the Body Control Module (BCM) and Telematics Module are connected to both the high- and low-speed bus at the same time. The choice of usage between the low-speed and high-speed bus is mostly driven by timing requirements, bandwidth and cost of the components – not security concerns. As for industrial standards, most system are connected by the Controller Areas Network (CAN) or FlexRay bus, and use AUTOSAR as the software platform.

## 4   FMVEA Analysis

As FMVEA is an extension to the SW/Functional-FMEA approach, the first step is to decompose a system into functions. We can distinguish between processing and communication functions. In [13], potential failure modes for input and output, and processing functions are listed. For the threat modes, the examples in [12] are used. Due to space restrictions, we focus on critical failure/threat modes. For the risk assessment, severity is rated from 1 (lowest) to 6 (highest). The risk number is based on the multiplication of severity and probability.

The analysis focuses on the Telematics Control Unit (TCU), because it bridges two buses with different safety-criticalities, and possesses long-range communication capability. Due to the lack of source authentication or encryption on the CAN-bus, controlling one ECU allows complete control of all other devices on the same bus. Table 1 lists some of the TCU functions given in [5]. The TCU communicates over a wireless communication infrastructure with a Telematics Network Operations System (TNOS), which provides most of the services for the telematics unit.

**Table 1.** Functions of TCUs

| Safety and Security Services | Information and Navigation | Entertainment | Diagnostics |
|---|---|---|---|
| send crash data | call technical support | receive voice commands | transmit diagnostic data |
| send vehicle position | connect wifi/bluetooth devices | connect to external media sources | receive over the air(OTA) firmware updates |
| receive door lock signal | | | |

For the purpose of analysis, we combined the functions from Table 1 with the generic failure/threat modes from [13], [12], in order to identify all potential failure/threat modes for this function. [13] is a report on the usage of the failure mode and effects analysis for the analysis of software-based systems. In a literature survey lists of failure modes are identified. We used a list which differentiates between failure modes for input/output functions (Missing data, Incorrect data, Timing of data, Extra data) and failure modes for processing functions (Halt/Abnormal termination, Omitted event, Incorrect logic, Timing/Order). For threat modes Spoofing, Tampering, Repudiation, Information disclosure, Denial of service and Elevation of privilege were considered. Afterwards we analysed each threat/failure mode for effects, causes, severity and probability.

Threat properties are based on the capabilities and motivation of the attacker. For this, we assumed an attacker with reasonable technical and operational capabilities, as described in [2], where the attacker is able to analyze the system to develop malicious input and deliver the input either by physical access or radio communication channels. System susceptibility is based on reachability and information available about the system. The attack probability is the sum of both ratings. According to ISO 26262 [7], for fault-based risks, the probability is the probability of exposure. In order to estimate risks, the values of probability and severity are multiplied. An excerpt of the detailed FMVEA analysis of TCU is given in Tab. 2.

**Table 2.** Failure Mode, Vulnerabilities and Effect Analysis of TCU

| ID | component | Vulnerability / Failure Cause | Threat Mode / Failure Mode | Threat Effect / Failure Effect | Threat Effect / System Status | System Effect | Severity | System Susceptibility | Threat Properties | Attack / Failure Probability | Risk |
|---|---|---|---|---|---|---|---|---|---|---|---|
| 1 | OTA | insufficient authentication of TNOS | Attacker masquerades itself as TNOS and sends own firmware update | Attacker deploys own firmware | same susceptibility in all system states | safety-critical, Attacker has control over the vehicle | 6 | 4 | 4 | 8 | 48 |
| 2 | OTA | wireless connection, susceptibility to jamming | Attacker interrupts OTA | Update is interrupted | Updating | none | 1 | 6 | 4 | 10 | 10 |
| 3 | OTA | disturbance while transmitting update | Update data is incorrect | incorrect firmware is applied | Updating | safety-critical, firmware could include critical faults | 6 | ... | ... | 6 | 36 |
| 4 | OTA | connection is lost | Data missing from update | Update is interrupted | Updating | none | 1 | ... | ... | 6 | 6 |
| 5 | bluetooth connection | attacker exploit buffer overflow in bluetooth implementation | The attacker could use a already connected device and extend it's privileges | Attacker is able to execute code on TCU | connected compromised device | to safety-critical, Attacker has control over the vehicle | 6 | 3 | 4 | 7 | 42 |
| 6 | external media | no congestion control at TCU | data overflow at TCU from streaming data | TCU malfunctions | streaming connection | TCU services not longer available | 3 | ... | ... | 6 | 18 |
| 7 | transmit diagnostic data | man in the middle attack on GSM base station | Attacker is manipulating diagnostic data | wrong data transmitted | system receives "limp home command" from TNOS | reduced functionality | 2 | 3 | 4 | 7 | 14 |

# 5    Conclusion and Future Work

This paper presents our ongoing work to develop a holistic approach to safety and security analysis of mission-critical CPS. While our analysis of intelligent and cooperative vehicles gives a good overview of vulnerable functions of the TCU, the risk rating was a relatively complex process. Often attacks on critical CPSs consisted of multiple steps [11]. Thus, the assignment of system susceptibility was not straightforward. FMVEA is based on the functional and software-FMEA. Both approaches are best used for an early design time assessment of systems. Similar to them the FMVEA allows to anticipate the effects of potential failures and threats during design time and thus enable to focus the development and verification effort there.

At this time, the analysis is focused on a single vehicle. In an next step we will include cooperating vehicles and analyse a system of cooperating vehicles. We will also extend the FMVEA to model and analyse multi-stage attacks. In addition, while there are many existing lists of potential failure modes for different domains, in IEC 60812 [6] or [13], potential threat modes and vulnerabilities need to be examined further. Microsoft's STRIDE (Spoofing, Tampering, Repudiation, Information disclosure, Denial of service and Elevation of privilege) was used as a generic threat mode catalogue. In future work, we will build a more specific threat catalogue for CPSs and intelligent systems in different domains. Another research direction we will follow is to apply FMVEA to other domains with different use cases, and compare it with other safety and security analysis methods such as Combined Harm Assessment of Safety and Security for Information Systems (CHASSIS).

**Acknowledgments.** Research leading to these results has received funding from the EU ARTEMIS Joint Undertaking under grant agreements no. 621429 (EMC$^2$) and from the FFG (Austrian Research Promotion Agency) on behalf of BMVIT, The Federal Ministry of Transport, Innovation and Technology.

# References

1. Charette, R.N.: This Car Runs on Code. IEEE Spectrum 46(3), 3 (2009),
   http://spectrum.ieee.org/transportation/systems/this-car-runs-on-code
2. Checkoway, S., McCoy, D., Kantor, B., Anderson, D., Shacham, H., Savage, S., Koscher, K., Czeskis, A., Roesner, F., Kohno, T.: Comprehensive Experimental Analyses of Automotive Attack Surfaces. In: Proceedings of the 20th USENIX Conference on Security (2011)
3. Schmittner, C., Gruber, T., Puschner, P., Schoitsch, E.: Security Application of Failure Mode and Effect Analysis (FMEA). In: The 33rd International Conference on Computer Safety, Reliability and Security (SafeComp) (in press, September 2014)
4. Department of Defense: MIL STD 1629A, Procedures for performing a failure mode, effect and criticality analysis (1980)
5. Hughes Systique Corporation: Automotive Telematics (2006)

6. International Electrotechnical Commission: Analysis Techniques for System Reliablity - Procedure for Failure Mode and Effects Analysis (FMEA) (2006)
7. International Organization for Standardization: ISO 26262 Road vehicles – Functional safety (2010)
8. Kargl, F., Ma, Z., Schoch, E.: Security Engineering for VANETs. In: 4th Workshop on Embedded Security in Cars (ESCAR 2006), Berlin, Germany (November 2006)
9. Koscher, K., Czeskis, A., Roesner, F., Patel, S., Kohno, T., Checkoway, S., McCoy, D., Kantor, B., Anderson, D., Shacham, H., Savage, S.: Experimental Security Analysis of a Modern Automobile. In: Proceedings of the 2010 IEEE Symposium on Security and Privacy, SP 2010, pp. 447–462. IEEE Computer Society, Washington, DC (2010)
10. Laprie, J.C.: Dependable computing: Concepts, limits, challenges. In: Proceedings of the Twenty-Fifth International Conference on Fault-Tolerant Computing, FTCS 1995, pp. 42–54. IEEE Computer Society, Washington, DC (1995)
11. Ma, Z., Smith, P.: Determining risks from advanced multi-step attacks to critical information infrastructures. In: Luiijf, E., Hartel, P. (eds.) CRITIS 2013. LNCS, vol. 8328, pp. 142–154. Springer, Heidelberg (2013)
12. Microsoft: Security Development Lifecycle - SDL Process Guidance Version 5.2. Microsoft (2012)
13. Pentti, H., Atte, H.: Failure mode and effects analysis of software-based automation systems. In: VTT Industrial Systems, STUK-YTO-TR 190 (August 2002)

# Uniform Approach of Risk Communication in Distributed IT Environments Combining Safety and Security Aspects

Jana Fruth and Edgar Nett

Otto-von-Guericke University Magdeburg,
Faculty of Computer Science, Department of Distributed Systems,
Postfach 4120, D-39106 Magdeburg, Germany
{jana.fruth,edgar.nett}@ovgu.de

**Abstract.** The trend to compose real time systems with standard IT known from conventional office domains results in heterogeneous technical environments. Examples are modern industrial process automation networks. It is a challenging task, because of potential impacts of security incidents to the system safety. For example, robot control units could be manipulated by malicious codes. The term "risk communication" is introduced, to describe alarm communication in human-machine interaction scenarios. User adapted risk communication between humans and industrial automation systems, including home robotics, can prevent hazards and/or threats to the entire system safety and security. Current safety and security risk communication standards are compared to examine the adequacy for our uniform approach. This paper focuses on alarm system standards in the industrial process automation domain and intrusion detection systems from the conventional desktop IT domain. A uniform model based approach for risk communication in distributed IT environments is introduced.

**Keywords:** uniform approach, risk communication standards, alarms, safety and security aspects, human-machine interaction.

## 1  Introduction and Motivation

Today, intelligent technical systems in industrial and consumer domains are often used to increase comfort, efficiency and safety of such systems. Applied technical components are called ubiquitous and/or embedded systems [21]. The composition of real time systems known from industrial domains with standard information technologies (IT) known from conventional office domains of organisations results in heterogeneous technical environments. Examples can be seen in systems for industrial process automation. Motivated by the need of higher efficiency, standard IT network components and/or protocols like Ethernet or TCP/IP are applied frequently [19]. One example of this is the remote maintenance of industrial field components over the Internet. Formerly, these systems are designed to be closed and separated from other external systems, providing

A. Bondavalli et al. (Eds.): SAFECOMP 2014 Workshops, LNCS 8696, pp. 289–300, 2014.

protection against cyber-attacks [10][19]. Integration of standard desktop IT in industrial domains increases the likelihood of introducing known vulnerabilities of the desktop IT network components and protocols as well as the occurrence of security[1] incidents in the industrial environment.

Historically, the environment of real time systems[2] was mainly protected against system failures by safety and reliability mechanisms. Examples include a safe system design to avoid electric shocks, safety fences in front of machines, and dead man switches to stop a running system [23] . Protection mechanisms against cyber attacks were considered as unnecessary in industrial real time systems, because of their closed and separated character [10][19]. Conventional desktop IT in organisations were protected against cyber attacks with security mechanism. Examples are confidentiality protection mechanism with encryption, authenticity protection mechanism using passwords or biometrics, and availability protection mechanism based on introducing data redundancy. The before mentioned recent fusion of real time systems with desktop IT can trigger interdependencies between security incidents and the system safety of real time systems. One example is the manipulation of robot control units for manufacturing caused by malicious codes[3] in an assembly line [14]. The malfunction of industrial robots control units could have several implications, e.g. produced workpieces could be damaged and people near the robot can be injured. Furthermore, the manufacturing of defective workpieces or the stagnation of manufacturing can result in extensive financial losses. One typical example was the famous malicious attack in the domain of industrial automation systems [24], called Stuxnet. A worm was written to manipulate Siemens control components in Iranian nuclear power plants [24]. It was not detectable for the alarm management system for various reasons, e.g. the usage of insider knowledge by Stuxnet, like the exploitation of previously unreleased security vulnerabilities of Windows and the use of stolen certificates for authentication purposes. Another reason could be the absence of any cyber attack detection system like an intrusion detection system (IDS)[4] in the plant.

In this paper the term of *risk communication* is used. Risk [11] is defined as the product of occurrence probability of a damaging event and severity of potential damage, caused by that event. In the security world the event is named threat[5], in the safety world it is called hazard[6]. Figure 1 illustrates the basis of the risk

---

[1] In this paper the term "security" is defined as computer security for information technical systems. In [11] security is specified as property of a fail-safe system, which can only enter system states, which can cause no unauthorised manipulation or retrieval of information.

[2] Real time systems are computer systems which underlay specific time conditions determined by environmental requirements [17].

[3] Malicious logic or malicious codes are software programs written by attackers to realise automated attacks on computer systems [9]. Examples are computer viruses, worms, and Trojan horses.

[4] Intrusion detection systems detect attacks based on analyses of log records of unexpected activities and known attacker activities [9].

[5] A threat is defined as potential violation of security [9].

[6] Hazards are undesirable conditions, which potential cause accidents [16].

communication approach described in this paper, based on [8] and [16]. We focus on risk communication between humans (operators, users, plant management etc.) and industrial automation systems (including home robotics). To avoid accidents, users should be aware of the critical changes in the system states, especially caused by security threats from conventional IT systems. Furthermore, their interactions have to be guided with the automation system. Application examples are previously mentioned robots in industrial domains. Another domain of robots are private households, where service robots operate autonomously and support users in various domestic tasks. At present world widely only a few autonomous domestic robots are used, but the demand is expected to increase in future [15]. Caused by limited technical abilities, current household robots can only accomplish simple tasks, like floor cleaning or law-mowing. In the future technical properties will have developed further, and the tasks of domestic robots will be more sophisticated, so those robots will be worthwhile attack targets. One potential security attack could be the malicious manipulation of the robot control (threat)(see figure 1). This attack could potentially cause undesirable robot movements (hazard), so that human users can be frightened or/and injured (accident). Two main challenges have to be considered: first, the dynamic and less predictable behaviour of security threats, and second, the difficulty in analysis and management of security risks, caused by the complexity of heterogeneous systems. One approach to solve these challenges is to warn the users of potential security threats with impacts on the safety of the system. If the system is not able to take an automatic decision, a manual selection of protection mechanisms by users against specific threats can be the alternative solution. This requires a detailed analysis of current security risks and decisions, and clarify which risks have to be communicated to the users. Furthermore, user friendly and comprehensible risk communication to safety and security novices has to be designed and realised.

Effective communication of risks to users can prevent consequences for the overall system security and safety and the personal welfare of users caused by security and safety incidents. New concepts are needed to close the gap between risk management (with people involved) and risk communication in heterogeneous technical environments to cope with potential security and safety interdependencies. A uniform model based approach is sketched in this paper.

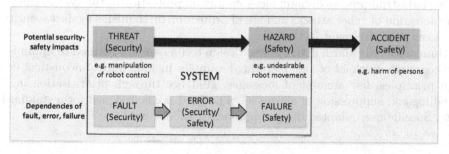

**Fig. 1.** Basis of risk communication approach (based on [8] and [16])

The paper is structured as follows: in Section 2 a short overview and a comparison of state of the art of standards for risk communication in the safety and security domain are illustrated. Furthermore, selected approaches are described regarding their contributions to our uniform approach. Section 3 describes the uniform approach for risk communication in heterogeneous domains. Section 4 concludes the paper and shows future prospects.

## 2    State of the Art: Risk Communication Standards

The following sections describe the state of the art of risk communication standards. Until now different approaches of risk communication of protection systems in both worlds, real time systems and desktop IT systems, exist. Therefore, we select two different types of standards: first, alarm management standards of the industrial process management domain (see section 2.1) and second, intrusion detection system standards and recommendations of the desktop IT domain (see section 2.2). Furthermore, we use only standards and recommendations, which are available free of charge via our library and the Internet. These are standards by the German Institute for Standardisation (DIN), including European (EU) and International (ISO) DIN norms, and recommendations by approved industrial and computer security organisations. Section 2.3 concludes the section with a comparison of current standards of risk communication using own evaluation criteria. In section 2.4 first approaches towards an uniform approach of risk communication in distributed IT environments are sketched.

### 2.1    Alarm Management Standards in the Industrial Process Management

Alarm management systems are defined as systems to detect systematic failures and principles [6]. Monitoring systems generate alarms and warning messages to provide operators with tasks in the process management. Different from warning messages, alarms need to be acknowledged by the operator. Via the acknowledgement the operator confirms that he has noticed the change of the system status. Alarms and messages have the specific task to assist the operators in alarm analysis and decision taking to realise countermeasures. Alarm management systems in the industrial process domain focus mainly on protection of the system safety. The detection of cyber attacks and use of protection mechanisms against security incidents were irrelevant in the past.

Human friendly alarm management design techniques are realised to minimise the cognitive overload of the operator. Examples include optical-acoustical design principles, few amount of messages, guidance through prioritisation, and bundling and suppression of alarms [6]. The feedback is designed for a standard user. Specific user-adapted design approaches are not used.

## 2.2    Intrusion Detection System Standards for Information Technology in Organisations

Intrusion detection is defined as active monitoring of computer systems or networks in desktop IT domains to detect attacks and misuse [1]. Intrusion detection systems are instruments, which provide IDS process (from event detection, evaluation, escalation, and documentation). An IDS detects so called cyber attacks based on analysis of log records of unexpected activities and known attacker activities [9]. The detection of malicious activities on the computer systems are the main task of IDS, so it focuses on computer security. The realisation of safety requirements is not the goal for IDS in homogeneous desktop IT systems.

IDS also applies techniques to minimise the cognitive overload of their users. Examples are optical-acoustical design principles, efforts to reduce the amount of alarm messages, prioritisation, and suppression of alarms [1]. The feedback via alarm messages is designed for a standard user, too. In IDS specific user adapted design approaches are not applied.

## 2.3    Comparison of Risk Communication Standards

This section compares risk communication standards of the industrial process management domain and desktop IT domain. The comparison is based on the following evaluation criteria:

1. The nature of content (model vs. procedure)
2. Provided phases of the human-automation interaction process (see [22]) (stage 1: information acquisition, stage 2: information analysis, stage 3: decision selection, stage 4: action implementation)
3. Advantages and properties not covered for the realisation in heterogeneous technical environments[7]

The phases of the human-automation interaction process is based on the correspondent taxonomy from Parasuraman et al. [22]. They introduced a model, which categorises four stages of functions of automation systems according to the human psychological process [18]. In the model various levels of automation from low to high are differentiated, which determine the level of guidance to the human operator by the automated system. In the first stage of *information acquisition*, input data is acquired corresponding to the sensation and perception of information by humans. While systems with high level of automation filter out most critical information, low level automation systems present all input data to the operators and guide operator's attention to most relevant data. The stage of *information analysis*, provides operators with integrating raw data, draw interferences and generating predictions. Automation function at this stage requires higher cognitive functions such as information integration and cognitive interference. Systems with high level of automation reduce the amount of information to

---

[7] The new risk communication standard is not targeted at heterogeneous technical systems as such, but at systems being safety and security critical.

one single hypothesis regarding the system state. Low level automation systems extrapolate the current information and predict future status to the operators. In the stage of *decision selection*, appropriate decisions or actions are selected from many alternatives corresponding to the cognitive stage of decision making. While high level automation systems present and/or select the optimal decision or action to the operators, low level automation systems provide the complete set of alternatives to operators. In the last stage of *action implementation* the operator is aided by the automated system by the execution of a selected action. This stage corresponds with the human cognitive status of response and execution. While low level automation systems simply assist the operators in the execution of the action, high level automation systems take over more of the control from the operator [18].

**Table 1.** Comparison of selected Risk Communication Standards / Recommendations

| Standard | Content | Advantages | Properties not covered |
|---|---|---|---|
| *Industrial process control (Safety)* | | | |
| DIN EN 62541-9 / IEC 62541 (2012) [4] | Model | 1) Formal description of alarms via a holistic information model (OPC unified architecture) 2) Exemplary models | 1) No providing of information acquisition 2) Only focus on system failures (safety) 3) No user specific model/design examples |
| NA 102 (Worksheet, 2008) [3] | Procedure | 1) Providing of all four stages 2) Holistic and interdisciplinary approach of alarm management design 3) Optical and acoustical design pattern 4) Examples of practical experiences | Only focus on system failures (safety) |
| VDI/VDE 3699, Blatt 5 (German Draft, 2013) [6] | Model | Strategies to minimise the cognitive overload of operators (e.g. minimising, automated selection, and prioritisation of alarms) | 1) No providing of information acquisition and analysis 2) Only focus on system failures (safety) 3) Only optical alarm design |
| *Desktop IT (Security)* | | | |
| ISO/IEC DIS 27039 (Draft, 2013) [5] | Procedure | 1) Providing of all four stages 2) Holistic procedure of selection, deployment and operation of IDS in an organisation | 1) Only focus on cyber attacks (security) 2) Only general description of handling of IDS alerts (information and severity of attacks) - no user specific design approaches |
| BSI - Guideline for introduction of IDS (2002) [1] | Procedure | 1) Providing of all four stages 2) Holistic procedure of selection, deployment and operation of IDS in an organisation | 1) Only focus on cyber attacks (security) 2) Only general description of alert and incident handling - no user specific design approaches |

Table 1 summarises a selected risk communication standards and recommendations. For the sake of clarity, the term "alarm" refers to both alarm and warning message in the table. The table also serves as an indicator for potential approaches which can be integrated in our new approach of a risk communication standard for heterogeneous systems. The content described in the table in column "properties not covered" is basis for our motivation for a new standard in that field. In the following, the standards and recommendations described in table 1 are specified, primarily the three standards of industrial process control and secondly the two standards in the desktop IT domain.

The DIN EN 62541-9 standard [4] is a detailed and formal description of alarms using a specific modelling language. It gains its advantage by its exemplary models, which illustrate the formal concepts. Properties not covered include the lack of the information acquisition phase, selected focus on safety incidents, as well as lack of user specific design concepts.

The NA 102 [3] is a worksheet which recommends holistic and interdisciplinary alarm design principles. It shows advantage by providing all four stages of the human-automation interaction process model, the use of optical and acoustical design pattern, and the illustration with practical examples. The standard only focuses on system failures (safety).

The VDI/VDE 3699 standard [6] describes a model for alarms and messages during process control with screens. Furthermore, user friendly design methods of alarms / messages for screens in the process control of primary control units are recommended. Properties not covered include the center on the stages of decision selection and action implementation in the human-automation interaction model, the focus on system failures (safety), and recommendations for only optical design principles.

ISO/IEC DIS 27039 [5] is a draft of a procedure, which describes an holistic approach of selection, deployment and operation of IDS in an organisation. It provides all four stages of the human-automation interaction process model, including event detection, analysis, response, and data storage. However, it fails to address cyber attacks (security) and user specific design approaches while handling IDS alerts.

BSI recommendation [1] is a guideline for the introduction of IDS in an organisation. It also provides all four stages of the human-automation interaction process model. Besides that, it also supports the holistic conception of selection, deployment and operation of IDS in an organisation (conception - integration - operation - revision). However, similar to ISO/IEC DIS 27039, it also fails to address cyber attacks (security) or user specific design approaches.

## 2.4 First Approaches towards an Uniform Approach of Risk Communication in Distributed IT Environments

This section describes three different approaches, which are parts of the previous scientific work of the first author of this publication. These approaches include parts, which could be integrated in our uniform approach of risk communication in distributed IT environments. The first model based approach [12] is introduced to realise secure data management in embedded systems. The processed data of the system are linked with specific properties of the system components to detect modifications of security properties of the system. The different views on the system could be included in our uniform approach. The second model based approach was published in [20]. It describes interdependencies between safety and security incidents for embedded systems on component level. What could also contribute to our uniform approach is the modeling of the principle of cause and effect with so called primary and secondary events. The third approach describes a user adapted multimedia-based design for the interaction between humans and industrial robots [13]. The design applies visual and acoustical information. One example is the visual and textual description of the primary security incident, which causes the warning. Furthermore, instructions to the operator are visualised, such as calling the supervisor and/or push the emergency button. It's multimedia-based design principles are used in our uniform approach to ease the user's understanding of complex contexts in heterogeneous systems. The three models alone are not sufficient for the development of a uniform approach of a risk communication for safe and secure heterogeneous systems, because they cover different aspects separately.

## 3    Uniform Approach for Risk Communication in Safety and Security Domains

As existing risk communication standards and approaches are not sufficient to solve the problems of heterogeneous systems with safety and security requirements, an uniform approach is introduced in this paper. In section 3.1 a generic system model is illustrated. Section 3.2 describes a first approach of user adapted risk communication in human-automation interaction scenarios.

### 3.1    Generic System Model

A generic model of a system seems to be promising, because of its dynamic adaptability suitable for the current risk situation. The overall system model consists of various parts, which represent specific views to the system (see also figure 2):

1. model of technical *components* of the system (including interacting persons and the environment)
2. model of the *data*, which is processed by the system
3. model of the *requirements* on the system safety and security
4. model of realised safety and security *mechanism*
5. model of *level of protection* (safety and/or security level)

The *component model* includes technical components of the system, including both hardware and software. Exemplary software components of a service robot in a household could be executable codes for movement control (see figure 2). Other parts of the component model is human, like users, who interact with

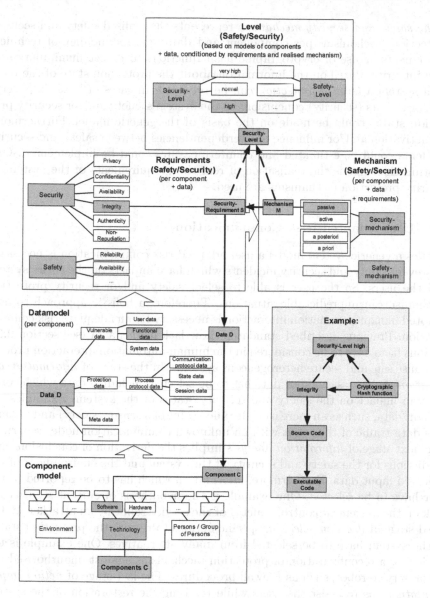

**Fig. 2.** Generic model and example of a heterogeneous system, including the safety and security properties

the technical system and the environment which influences the system from the outside, like weather conditions. The *data model* represents the data which is processed by technical components, such as functional data like source code of a robot control program. The *safety and security requirement model* describes the system's safety requirements like reliability and the requirements of the security like data integrity to detect unauthorised data manipulation. The *model of the safety and security mechanism* represents the realised safety and security protection mechanisms per component and data, e.g. redundancy of technical components or use of cryptographic hash functions to detect manipulation of data integrity. Based on the information about the protection state of the technical system a *level of protection* can be reflected. In cases of hazards (safety) and/or threats (security) conclusions to the system's safety and/or security protection status could be made on the basis of the generic model. Furthermore, the activation and/or influence of interdependencies between safety and security incidents could be estimated and countermeasures could be implemented. One existing challenge is the realisation of real time requirements of the system, if security protection mechanisms are used.

### 3.2   User Adapted Risk Communication

Besides a generic system model a user adapted risk communication is necessary to prevent safety and security incidents which have impacts on the entire system and the users. So the user is able to select safety and/or security protection mechanisms in unpredictable situations. Therefore, a holistic approach to user adapted human-automation interaction is necessary for an adequate risk communication. Previous described standards show lack in this area (see section 2.3). Various facts have to be considered in the human-automation interaction process to realise safe and secure heterogeneous systems. In the stage of *information acquisition* the necessary input data has to be selected, including data which could have an impact on the safety and security status of the system. Examples are deviant data, such as an increasing distance value of a sensor (safety) and anomalous data traffic of the robot with an unknown communication node (security). The next stage of *information analysis* implies the derivation of conclusions and predictions for the safety and security of the system and the environment of the collected input data. Furthermore, information which has to be reported to the user have to be selected. One example is the hypothesis of current security attack on the movement control (safety) of the service robot by an attacker. In the third stage of *decision selection* specific actions to restore the protection status of the system have to be selected from many alternatives. One example is the advice for a reconfiguration of protection mechanisms against unauthorised use of the service robot, such as firewall procedures. The last stage of *action implementation* has to assist the users while realising the restoration of the system status. This includes the user adapted design of the communicated data. One example is the assistance to reconfigure firewall procedures.

## 4   Conclusion and Future Work

In this paper a selection of current safety and security risk communication standards and recommendations are compared using selected evaluation criteria. We focus on alarm system standards in the industrial process automation domain and intrusion detection systems known from conventional desktop IT domain. A series of DIN standards and recommendations, which are available free of charge from approved industrial and computer security organisations, are reviewed. Current risk communication standards and recommendations offer domain-specific solutions, but are not sufficient to fulfill safety and security requirements of distributed IT environments with safety and security properties. Therefore a new model based approach is introduced.

There are still gaps concerning joint (unified) safety and security analysis, development and maintenance/operation. Therefore, further safety and security standards and approaches used in general in industrial context should be taken into account in the future. Exemplary safety standards are IEC 61508 (Functional Safety)[8] or ISO 13482 (Safety requirements for personal care robots)[7] and security standards, like ISO 15408 (Common Criteria)[2] or the ISO 2700x series (Security Management)[9]. As such, the analysis of appropriate abilities will be extended to cover security and safety requirements in heterogeneous systems.

Furthermore, in the future, our generic approach for risk communication in heterogeneous systems with safety and security requirements has to be specified and evaluated. Practical implementations on selected heterogeneous systems are planed. Exemplary systems are service robots, which manoeuvre in an environment with different obstacles and interact with persons and other technical devices. Safety and security incidents, including interdependencies, should be simulated. On the basis of our model, user specific alarm and warning messages should be generated.

**Acknowledgments.** We would like to thank Manuela Kanneberg and Kun Qian for proofreading the paper.

# References

[1] Introduction to Intrusion Detection Systems - Guideline to introduce IDS. Tech. Rep. 1.0, BSI - German Federal Office for Information Security, ConSecur GmbH (October 2002)
[2] ISO/IEC 15408: Common Criteria for Information Technology Security Evaluation (2007)
[3] NA 102: Alarm Management. Tech. rep., NAMUR (October 2008)
[4] DIN EN 62541-9 / IEC 62541: OPC unifed architecture, Part 9: Alarms and conditions (June 2013)
[5] ISO/IEC DIS 27039: Information technology - Security techniques - Selection, deployment and operations of intrusion detection systems (IDPS) (July 2013)
[6] VDI/VDE 3699 Blatt 5: Process control with screens - Alarms/messages (German Draft) (May 2013)
[7] ISO 13482: Robots and robotic devices – Safety requirements for personal care robots (2014)

---

[8] http://www.iec.ch/functionalsafety/, last access: 26. June 2014.
[9] http://www.27000.org/, last access: 26. June 2014.

[8] Avizienis, A., Laprie, J.C., Randell, B.: Fundamental concepts of dependability. Tech. rep., UCLA Computer Science Department - University of California (USA), LAAS-CNRS (France), University of Newcastle upon Tyne (UK) (2001)

[9] Bishop, M.: Computer Security: Art and Science. Addison-Wesley Professional (2003)

[10] Byres, E., Lowe, J.: The Myths and Facts behind Cyber Security Risks for Industrial Control Systems. In: VDE Congress 2004, Berlin, Germany (2004)

[11] Eckert, C.: IT-Sicherheit: Konzepte - Verfahren - Protokolle. Oldenbourg Verlag München Wien (2008)

[12] Fruth, J., Dittmann, J., Ortmeier, F., Feigenspan, J.: Metadaten-Modell für ein sicheres eingebettetes Datenmanagement. In: D-A-CH Security 2010, pp. 359–370 (2010)

[13] Fruth, J., Krätzer, C., Dittmann, J.: Design and Evaluation of Multi-Media Security Warnings for the Interaction between Humans and Industrial Robots. In: Electronic Imaging Conference 7575: Intelligent Robots and Computer Vision XXVIII: Algorithms and Techniques, IS&T/SPIE, San Francisco Airport, CA, USA, January 23-27 (2011)

[14] Fruth, J., Münder, R., Gruschinski, H., Dittmann, J., Karpuschewski, B., Findeisen, R.: Sensitising to security risks in manufacturing engineering: An exemplary VR prototype. In: Second International Workshop on Digital Engineering, pp. 39–44 (2011)

[15] IFR Statistical Department: Executive Summary: World Robotics 2013 (2013)

[16] Kopetz, H.: Real-time Systems: Design Principles for Distributed Embedded Applications. Kluwer international series in engineering and computer science. Kluwer Academic Publishers (1997)

[17] Krishna, C.M., Shin, K.G.: Real-Time Systems. McGraw-Hill (1997)

[18] Lehto, M.R., Lesch, M.F., Horrey, W.J.: Safety warnings for automation. In: Springer Handbook of Automation, pp. 671–695. Springer (2009)

[19] Lueders, S.: (No) Security in Automation!? In: VGB PowerTech, vol. 88, pp. 127–130. Essen, Germany (2008)

[20] Neubüser, C., Fruth, J., Hoppe, T., Dittmann, J.: Wechselwirkungsmodell der Safety und Security. In: D-A-CH Security 2011: Bestandsaufnahme, Konzepte, Anwendungen, Perspektiven; Tagungsband, pp. 67–78 (2011)

[21] Paar, C., Weimerskirch, A.: Embedded security in a pervasive world. Information Security Technical Report 12(3), 155–161 (2007)

[22] Parasuraman, R., Sheridan, T.B., Wickens, C.D.: A model for types and levels of human interaction with automation: IEEE Transactions on Systems Man and Cybernetics, Part A: Systems and Humans. IEEE Transactions 30, 286–297 (2000)

[23] Storey, N.: Safety-Critical Computer Systems. Addison Wesley Longman Limited (1996)

[24] Symantec: Stuxnet Introduces the First Known Rootkit for Industrial Control Systems. Symantec Offical Blog (August 2010), http://www.symantec.com/connect/blogs/ stuxnet-introduces-first-known-rootkit-scada-devices (last access June 26, 2014)

# Introduction to the Safecomp 2014 Workshop: Reliability and Security Aspects for Critical Infrastructure Protection (ReSA4CI 2014)

Silvia Bonomi[1] and Ilaria Matteucci[2]

[1] Dipartimento di Ingegneria Informatica Automatica e Gestionale
"Antonio Ruberti"
Università degli Studi di Roma "La Sapienza" Via Ariosto 25, 00185, Roma, Italy
bonomi@dis.uniroma1.it
[2] Instituto di Informatica e Telematica
Consiglio Nazionale delle Ricerche (IIT-CNR),
Via G. Moruzzi, 1 Pisa, Italy
ilaria.matteucci@iit.cnr.it

## Introduction

The ReSA4CI workshop aims at providing a forum for researchers and engineers in academia and industry to foster an exchange of research results, experiences, and products in the area of reliable, dependable, and secure computing for critical systems protection from both a theoretical and practical perspective. Its ultimate goal is to envision new trends and ideas about aspects of designing, implementing, and evaluating reliable and secure solutions for the next generation critical infrastructures. Critical Infrastructures present several challenges in the fields of distributed systems, dependability and security methods and approaches crucial for improving trustworthiness on ICT facilities. The workshop aims at presenting the advancement on the state of art in these fields and spreading their adoption in several scenarios involving main infrastructures for modern society.

Critical infrastructures (CIs) are at the hearth of any advanced civilized country. These infrastructures include among others: finance and insurance, transportation (e.g. mass transit, rails and aircrafts), public services (e.g., law enforcement, fire and emergency), energy, health care. Hence, their destruction or disruption, even partially, may, directly or indirectly, strongly affect the normal and efficient functioning of a country. The global scope and massive scale of today's attacks necessitate global situational awareness, which cannot be achieved by the isolated local protection systems residing within the IT boundaries of individual institutions. This leads to foster the investigation of innovative methodologies for gathering, processing and correlating huge amounts of data understanding anomaly behaviours and learning automatically always-evolving cyber threats with the final aim to prevent and/or mitigate their consequences.

A workshop on reliability and security aspects in the general domain of CI is motivated by the unsuitability of current approaches due to the novel challenges imposed by always smart and powerful adversaries. In fact, several works exist in

A. Bondavalli et al. (Eds.): SAFECOMP 2014 Workshops, LNCS 8696, pp. 301–303, 2014.

the literature about these research themes. However, existing solutions are usually applied to specific and closed system making them not general enough to be extended to other types of CI. The innovative and challenging aspect is to define new protection strategies in the context of complex, evolvable, and extremely heterogeneous systems and with respect to always evolving adversaries.

## Program

The program of ReSA4CI 2014 consists of and 6 high-quality papers, covering the above-mentioned topics. In particular, we can group them in two main classes according to their topic:

- **Session1: Security and Dependability of Critical Infrastructure**
  - Laura Carnevali, Marco Paolieri, Fabio Tarani, Enrico Vicario and Kumiko Tadano. "Modeling and evaluation of maintenance procedures for gas distribution networks "
  - Peter Popov, Kizito Salako and Oleksandr Netkachev. "Quantification of the Impact of Cyber Attack in Critical Infrastructures"
  - Paolo Franchin and Luigi Laura. "Probabilistic inference in the physical simulation of interdependent critical infrastructure systems"
- **Session 2. Methodologies and Analysis of Distributed Systems**
  - Cesario Di Sarno and Alessia Garofalo. "Energy-Based Detection of Multi-Layer Flooding Attacks on Wireless Sensor Network"
  - Luca Montanari, Roberto Baldoni, Claudio Ciccotelli, Federico Lombardi, Alessandro Donno and Adriano Cerocchi. "Towards a non-Intrusive Recognition of Anomalous System Behavior in Data Centers"
  - Richard M. Zahoransky, Thomas Koslowski and Rafael Accorsi. "Towards Resilience Assessment in Business Process Architectures"

Each paper was selected according to at least two reviews produced mainly by Program Committee members and a little percentage of external reviewers. Selected papers come from several countries around the world. In addition, we are glad to host two keynote speakers, Dr. Barbara Gallina and Prof. Michele Colajanni, that have contributed in the litterature about Security, Dependability, Risk Analysis, and Principles of Critical Infrastructure Protection.

## Thanks

We would like to thank the SAFECOMP organization committee and collaborators for their precious help in handling all the issues related to the workshop. Our next thanks go to all the authors of the submitted papers who manifested their interest in the workshop. With their participation the First SAFECOMP Workshop on Reliability and Security Aspects for Critical Infrastructure Protection (ReSA4CI 2014) becomes a real success and an inspiration for future workshops on this new and exciting area of research. Special thanks are finally due to Program Committee members and additional reviewers for the high quality and objective reviews they provided.

**Acknowledgement.** This workshop has been supported by

- the TENACE PRIN Project (n. 20103P34XC), that aims to study the degree of maturity of the Italian critical infrastructures in order to provide solutions to protect them.
- the SESAMO EU project , (Grant Agreement No. 295354), that addresses the root causes of problems arising with convergence of safety and security in embedded systems at architectural level.
- the PANOPTESEC FP7 EU project (Grant Agreement No. 610416), that aims at the definition of methods and tools for dynamic risk assessment and management.

# Workshop Organizers

Silvia Bonomi, University of Rome La Sapienza, Italy
Ilaria Matteucci, IIT-CNR, Italy

# Keynote Speakers

Michele Colajanni, University of Modena and Reggio Emilia, Italy
Barbara Gallina, Mälardalen University, Sweden

# Program Committee

Valentina Bonfiglio, University of Florence, Italy
Silvia Bonomi, University of Rome La Sapienza, Italy (co-chair)
Felicita Di Giandomenico, ISTI-CNR, Italy
Karama Kanoun, LAAS, France
Ilaria Matteucci, IIT-CNR, Italy (co-chair)
Alessia Milani, University of Bordeaux, France
Simin Nadjm-Tehrani, Linköping University, Sweden
Federica Paci, University of Trento, Italy
Marta Patino Martinez, Technical University of Madrid, Spain
Marinella Petrocchi, IIT-CNR, Italy
Maria Gradinariu Potop-Butucaru, UPMC Paris 6, France
Sara Tucci Piergiovanni, CEA, France

# Additional Reviewer

Francesco Santini, IIT-CNR, Italy

# Modeling and Evaluation of Maintenance Procedures for Gas Distribution Networks with Time-Dependent Parameters

Laura Carnevali[1], Marco Paolieri[1], Fabio Tarani[1],
Enrico Vicario[1], and Kumiko Tadano[2]

[1] Dipartimento di Ingegneria dell'Informazione - Università di Firenze, Italy
{laura.carnevali,marco.paolieri,fabio.tarani,enrico.vicario}@unifi.it
[2] Central Research Laboratories - NEC Corporation, Kawasaki, Japan
k-tadano@bq.jp.nec.com

**Abstract.** Gas networks comprise a special class of infrastructure, with relevant implications on safety and availability of universal services. In this context, the ongoing deregulation of network operation gives relevance to modeling and evaluation techniques supporting predictability of dependability metrics. We propose a modeling approach that represents maintenance procedures as a multi-phased system, with parameters depending on physical and geographical characteristics of the network, working hours, and evolution of loads over the day. The overall model is cast into a non-Markovian variant of stochastic Petri nets, which allows concurrent execution of multiple generally distributed transitions but maintains a complexity independent of network size and topology. Solution is achieved through an interleaved execution of fluid-dynamic analysis of the network and analytic solution of the stochastic model of the procedure. Solution provides availability measures for individual sections of the network as well as global quality of service parameters.

**Keywords:** gas distribution networks, non time-homogeneous systems, performance evaluation, Markov regenerative processes, transient stochastic state classes.

## 1 Introduction

Quantitative evaluation of availability is gaining increasing relevance for the efficient operation of gas distribution networks, led by several causes including competitive challenges raised by re-organization of utilities, issues of homeland security, demand-response control applications, and automation capabilities offered by smart monitoring and actuation devices [22]. This motivates investigation in modeling and solution methods, both in the tactic perspective supporting decision during run-time operation and in the strategic perspective related to planning of topology, localization of sensing/actuation devices and evaluation of sustainable service levels.

The problem has been widely investigated in telecommunication and power systems, yet gas networks are different in notable aspects, such as: localization

A. Bondavalli et al. (Eds.): SAFECOMP 2014 Workshops, LNCS 8696, pp. 304–315, 2014.

of failure and network reconfiguration, which may involve much less automation and may result in a large variability of timings; regulation of controllable inputs, which involves processes running on a much slower time scale; a lower level of network redundancy and a different perspective on the criticality of interruptions; flexibility in management of input pressure levels, which allows trading efficiency of operation against resilience to transient faults.

Most of the literature on the analysis and simulation of gas networks focuses on the fluid-dynamics perspective, mainly oriented to assess flow rates and pressures across network elements [14,11]. Optimization of operations has been addressed in various aspects, notably to favor efficient integration within multi-carrier systems combining provisioning of electric and gas power [19,17,16,18]. In [23] fluid-dynamic analysis of a section of a real gas network is repeated for different configurations of demand reflecting the statistics of usage in different day hours and seasons.

In a previous paper [6], we proposed a method for modeling the availability of middle/low pressure gas networks, which consists in an interleaved execution of $i$) a quasi-static fluid-dynamic analysis of the network and $ii$) a stochastic model of the failure management procedure. The latter uses non-Markovian temporal parameters, thus overcoming the limits of memoryless and unbounded support of exponential distributions. As a distinctive trait, fluid-dynamic calculations are decoupled from the non-Markovian stochastic analysis and the complexity of stochastic analysis is insensitive to topology and size of the gas network.

In this paper, the model of [6] is extended so as to capture non-homogeneous temporal parameters. As a matter of fact, failure management procedures and their impact on network operation may be affected by various time-dependent parameters, including the responsiveness of repair infrastructure and the gas consumption rate, both of which can be modeled through cycles with phases of deterministic duration. In the evaluation stage, the evolution over time of the failure management actions is analyzed through transient analysis based on stochastic state classes and generalized Markov renewal equations, as proposed in [15]. Stochastic analysis provides the probability over time of any feasible operating condition of the network after a failure. Transient probabilities are then aggregated on the basis of the results of fluid dynamics analysis, identifying service levels in each operating condition, which enables the derivation of availability measures for each node in the network.

The rest of the paper is organized in four sections. In Section 2, we present both the failure management model (Section 2.1) and the fluid-dynamics model (Section 2.2). In Section 3, we recall the salient aspects of the solution technique of [15] (Section 3.1) and we discuss how the results of stochastic transient analysis are exploited to derive transient and average availability measures (Section 3.2). In Section 4, we exemplify the proposed approach on a small-sized case study of the literature (Section 4.1) and we present the obtained transient and average availability measures (Section 4.2). Finally, conclusions are drawn in Section 5.

## 2    Model

The gas distribution network comprises a kind of hybrid system combining continuous physical variables affecting fluid dynamics (pressure and flow rate) with the temporal behaviour of actions taken to recover from a failure. This duality is coped with by the interaction of two separate models: a stochastic model is used to analyse the timings of the failure management procedure (Section 2.1), whereas a fluid-dynamics simulator is used to quantify the lack of service metrics associated with each possible set of boundary conditions (Section 2.2).

For what concerns the fluid dynamics, gas is supplied to a low-pressure distribution network from a medium-pressure transmission network through a set of regulating stations (input nodes), and it is withdrawn by end-users at a certain number of load nodes. In the perspective of analysis, input nodes have a known pressure, whereas load nodes have a known flow balance, with their pressure depending on topology and flow patterns in the network. As a first approximation, which is valid for most existing distribution networks, the flow balance at load nodes is considered to depend on the time-of-day, whereas pressure at the supply nodes is considered constant. To guarantee correct operation as well as commercial standards, pressure at each load node should exceed a given minimum threshold and should not be greater than a maximum allowed value.

Whenever a network component fails, pressure levels and flow rates may be affected, and a set of maintenance actions is undertaken in order to restore the correct operating mode. These actions usually affect network topology and flow patterns: for instance, if a leaking pipe is detected, the nearest upstream and downstream valves are closed to isolate the faulty section, while other sectioning valves may be opened to minimise the number of end-users affected. The temporal evolution of repair actions and their effects are conditioned by various time-dependent parameters: on the one hand, the duration of some phases depends on the time-of-day, i.e., on the responsiveness of the system (e.g., availability of repair personnel may be lessened or null during nighttime); on the other hand, the degradation of the quality of service perceived by end-users depends on the load level throughout the network, which in turn varies according to a cyclic daily pattern.

Without loss of generality, the failure management procedure can be conveniently abstracted as a phased-mission process [20], consisting of three phases. The first phase includes operations occurring before physical intervention on the network, e.g., organisation of work team, planning and transportation on site. This phase is considered to end when the failed component (e.g., pipe) is excluded from the network, which comprises the first variation of topology. Hence, load nodes are partitioned into three classes:

- i) *offline* nodes, disconnected from any supply node;
- ii) *online served* nodes, connected with sufficient pressure;
- iii) *online not served* nodes, connected but with pressure lower than required.

The second phase represents actions occurring while the network status is in a modified configuration with respect to regular operation. In this phase repair is performed, while pressure is concurrently controlled at some regulating station, so as to restore the correct pressure levels at online load nodes during repair.

The third phase begins when the regular topology is restored, and it includes actions that do not affect user-perceived quality of service but are necessary for the operator to close the maintenance procedure. It is worth noting that the division in three phases has a general character and can be tailored to any specific procedure, as long as there exists a single continuous phase during which the network topology is modified.

The quality of service maintained throughout the procedure is captured by various metrics of performability, including the number of nodes served with an insufficient pressure and the amount of gas requested by users and not delivered.

## 2.1   Stochastic Model

The process of failure management can be represented as a *stochastic Time Petri Net* (sTPN) [24,5] extended with features such as enabling conditions and update functions, which reproduce modeling mechanisms that are usual in such environments such as SAN networks [12] and do not change the essence of analysis. As regards sTPN syntax and semantics, the reader is referred to [24].

The model is shown in Figure 1. Two looped chains of deterministic (DET) transition are use to model the dependence of repair responsiveness (places *workHour*, *extraHour* and *nightTime*) and load levels (places *highLoad*, *medLoad* and *lowLoad*) on the time-of day. The duration of each transition corresponds

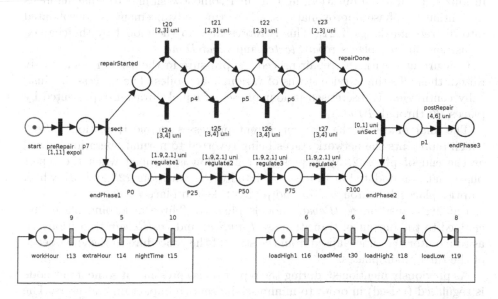

**Fig. 1.** The sTPN specification of the failure management model. IMM, DET and GEN transitions are represented by thin bars, thick gray bars, and thick black bars, respectively. The distributions associated with timed transition refer to the case study analyzed in Section 4.

to the duration of the preceding phase, while the sum of the durations of each loop amounts to 24 h, thus modeling in both cases a cyclical daily pattern.

The failure management procedure is divided in three parts. Transition *preRepair* represents actions taken during phase 1 (no network status modification). The time duration of phase 1 activities can have much different characterisation depending on organisational issues or network topology in each specific context. To illustrate the ability of the modeling and analysis technique in accommodating such difference, we use here a general (GEN) transition with an expolynomial (EXPOL) distribution over bounded support, which was derived so as to be bounded over $[1, 11]$ h and have an expected value equal to 3 h, and a variance equal to 2 $h^2$. The immediate (IMM) transition *sect* models the end of phase 1 and the beginning of phase 2.

The dependence of the repair speed on the time-of-day can be modelled by a number of parallel transitions which are alternatively enabled according to the marking of the corresponding DET loop. In doing so, an approximation is introduced following the same approach applied in [20]: when the time-of-day phase changes, two possible modelling strategies lead to different results. In the first case, the previously enabled transition is disabled and one of the mutually exclusive ones is newly enabled (thus disregarding the time elapsed since the enabling of the former, lengthening the total duration and leading to a worst-case approximation). Alternatively, at the time-of-day phase change, the previously enabled transition could be fired, thus shortening the total duration.

To restrain the impact of approximation, the repair activity is partitioned in four steps of equal duration, in a manner somehow similar to what happens in continuous phase approximations, where time advancement is consolidated into discrete markings [2,21]. This is represented in the model by the chained transitions linking places *repairStarted* and *repairDone*.

Concurrently with the repair procedure, pressure in the system is gradually raised, thus affecting service status of various load nodes. The process, intrinsically continuous, is discretised in four phases of equal duration represented by places *P0* through *P100*.

The final places of the two concurrent processes enable transition *unSect*, which represents the network status being reverted to normal operation as well as the end of phase 2. Since pressure regulation is stopped when the repair phase ends, an update function is associated with transitions *t23* and *t27*, which empties places *P0* through *P75* and puts a token in place *P100*.

Finally, transition *postRepair* models phase 3. Three absorbing places are chained to the output of transitions *sect*, *unSect* and *postRepair* transitions, so as to monitor the time elapsed from the start of the procedure to the end of each of the three main phases.

As previously mentioned, during the repair phase pressure at some input node is regulated (raised) in order to minimise the service impact on end users. The final pressure to be reached after the increase is calculated by means of the fluid-dynamic model as the minimum of two values: the minimum pressure necessary at the supply node so that all connected load nodes experience a pressure higher than the corresponding required pressure threshold, and the maximum pressure at the supply node so that no load node experiences a pressure higher than its maximum tolerated pressure. By means of the exposed modelling, a factual separation between the fluid dynamic model (whose complexity does depend on the complexity of the studied network) and the stochastic model (whose complexity does not) is achieved. In particular, the fluid dynamic model is used for two different purposes:

- to calculate the pressure increase to be imposed at the supply node in order to restore adequate pressure to all online load nodes;
- to evaluate service status at load nodes during each phase of the failure management process.

In the latter case, it is necessary to perform a certain number of analyses depending both on the load values considered (time-dependence of flow balance at load nodes) and on the number of steps representing the pressure increase process (time-dependence of pressure level at supply nodes). For each simulation, various measures representing service levels can be calculated and used as reward rates in the stochastic model.

## 2.2   Fluid-Dynamic Model

Given a set of boundary conditions, fluid-dynamic calculations are performed to assess the network state in terms of pressures at nodes and mass flow rates in pipes. In detail, two sets of equations are written to evaluate the mass balances at nodes and the pressure loss along pipelines, taking pressures at supply nodes and mass flow rates withdrawn at load nodes as inputs.

The first set of equations states that, for each node $n$, the signed sum of flow rates that enter or exit from $n$ must be equal withdrawn flow rate $Q_n^w$, i.e.,:

$$\sum_{i \in I_n^{\text{ent}}} Q_{in} - \sum_{j \in I_n^{\text{ex}}} Q_{nj} = \begin{cases} 0 & \text{if } n \text{ is a passive node} \\ Q_n^w & \text{if } n \text{ is a load node} \end{cases} \tag{1}$$

where $I_n^{\text{ent}}$ and $I_n^{\text{ex}}$ are the sets of indexes of pipelines that enter and exit from node $n$, respectively.

The second set of equations is used to calculate the pressure loss for each pipeline $m$, according to the Darcy-Weisbach formulation:

$$\delta P_m = f \cdot \frac{\delta L}{D_m} \cdot \frac{\rho V^2}{2} \tag{2}$$

where $\rho$ is the gas density, $V$ is the average gas velocity, $D_m$ is the pipeline diameter, and $f$ is the Darcy friction factor calculated by means of the Colebrook equation [10] for turbulent flows and the Poiseuille formula for laminar flows.

Combining Equations 1 and 2, a non-linear system is written and solved through an iterative procedure based on the Newton-Raphson method.

# 3  Evaluation

The model of Section 2.1 is evaluated through regenerative transient analysis based on stochastic state classes [15,24] using the Oris tool [7,4,1].

## 3.1  Quantitative Transient Analysis

The solution technique of [15] supports the transient analysis of models with multiple concurrent GEN transitions that underlie a Generalized Semi-Markov Process (GSMP) with equal-speed timers [13,9]. The state of the underlying GSMP is sampled after each transition firing and an additional timer called $\tau_{age}$ is maintained to account for the absolute elapsed time. This identifies a *transient stochastic graph* whose states are named *transient stochastic state classes* (transient classes for short), each made of a marking plus the joint support and PDF of $\tau_{age}$ and the times-to-fire of the enabled transitions. The marginal PDF of $\tau_{age}$ permits to derive the PDF of the absolute time at which a transient class can be entered, enabling the evaluation of continuous-time transient probabilities of reachable markings within a given time horizon, provided that the number of transient classes that can be reached within that time interval is either bounded or can be truncated under the assumption of some approximation threshold on the total unallocated probability.

The complexity of the solution technique can be reduced in the case that the model underlies a Markov Regenerative Process (MRP) that always reaches a regeneration point, i.e., a state where the future behavior is independent from the past behavior through which it has been reached. In this case, transient analysis is limited to the first regeneration epoch and repeated from every regenerative point, supporting the derivation of the local and global kernels that characterize the MRP behavior [8,9,3] and enabling the evaluation of the transient probabilities of reachable markings at any time through the numerical integration of generalized Markov renewal equations.

## 3.2  Evaluated Measures

Each marking in the stochastic model can be associated with a reward rate corresponding to the relevant metrics of performability. Since lack of service experienced by end-users is determined on the basis of pressure regulation status (places *P0* through *P100*) and load level (places *highLoad, medLoad, lowLoad*), reward rates are associated to the twelve reachable combinations. In particular, performability is measured through the number of non-served nodes (either offline or online with insufficient pressure) and non-served gas demand corresponding to such nodes.

Moreover, the absorbing places in the failure management model are used to evaluate the Cumulative Distribution Function (CDF) of the completion time of any of the three phases, allowing the derivation of average measures.

# 4    A Case Study

We illustrate here the gas distribution network considered in the experimental validation (Section 4.1) and we discuss the obtained results (Section 4.2).

## 4.1    Experimental Setting

Figure 2 shows a topological representation of the sample gas distribution network analyzed in the experiments. The network has a double-loop topology and is made of a supply node marked as A, six load nodes marked as B through G, and fifteen pipelines.

Operating parameters of the network components have been chosen so as to experience different degrees of network unavailability following different pipeline failures. In detail, three load levels are considered, and the correponding withdrawal rates at load nodes are reported in Table 1. Moreover, each load node is supposed to have a minimum required pressure of 20 mbar. During the regular operation of the network, the pressure in each load node is greater than the corresponding pressure threshold, so that all nodes are properly served.

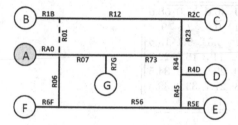

**Fig. 2.** Sample gas distribution network. The shaded nodes are supply nodes, while the others are load nodes. The dashed pipe is the one whose failure is considered.

**Table 1.** Mass flow rates of the nodes of the gas distribution network shown in Figure 2 for three different load scenarios

| Node | maxLoad (Sm$^3$/h) | medLoad (Sm$^3$/h) | minLoad (Sm$^3$/h) |
|------|---------|---------|---------|
| B | 200 | 150 | 100 |
| C | 200 | 150 | 100 |
| D | 150 | 113 | 75 |
| E | 200 | 150 | 100 |
| F | 200 | 150 | 100 |
| G | 100 | 75 | 50 |

Once a failure is detected and located, the corresponding pipe is excluded from the network and the load nodes are divided into online and offline nodes. If the failed pipe does belong to one of the main loops, no load node will be offline, whereas if the failed pipe is one of the radial connections from the main loops to a load node, one ore more of such nodes will.

For failures of pipes belonging to the ring, the pressure regulation time is characterized by assuming a pressure increase rate of 2 mbar/h and using the results of the fluid-dynamic analysis which provides the minimum pressure increase $\Delta P$ to be actuated at the supply node so that all online nodes are served.

## 4.2   Experimental Results

Without loss of generality, we illustrate the process of analysis with reference to a failure occurring at pipe *R12* as an example for discussion. Note that we deliberately focus on a failure of a pipeline that belongs to the network ring, as such failures will leave more load nodes not served than failures of radial pipelines and make pressure regulation a sensible choice.

**Fluid-Dynamic Analysis.** As a first step, a calculation is performed by excluding the failed pipe from the network and leaving every other parameter unchanged. The pressure at each node is shown in the third column of Table 2 in the *highLoad* scenario. Comparing the pressure values with those in the first column (regular operation), it can be noted that the nodes originally downstream of the failed pipe (B and C) experience a great pressure loss due to the change in flow patterns, whereas other load nodes suffer smaller decreases.

**Table 2.** Pressures at nodes during the different steps of pressure regulation and regular operation in the highLoad scenario. Shaded cells correspond to nodes not served.

| node | regular | P0 | P25 | P50 | P75 |
|------|---------|------|------|------|------|
| A | 40.0 | 40.0 | 46.0 | 52.0 | 58.0 |
| B | 38.8 | 0.0 | 0.0 | 2.8 | 9.1 |
| C | 31.1 | 3.6 | 5.5 | 9.4 | 15.6 |
| D | 21.4 | 6.8 | 11.3 | 16.5 | 22.7 |
| E | 28.1 | 18.1 | 22.9 | 28.3 | 34.5 |
| F | 31.7 | 22.8 | 27.7 | 33.2 | 39.3 |
| G | 29.7 | 8.1 | 11.0 | 15.5 | 21.7 |

From the values in Table 2, global metrics can be derived. Table 3 shows the reward rates as calculated by aggregating the results of the fluid-dynamic analysis in terms of nodes not served and demand not served.

**Table 3.** Reward rates from fluid-dynamic calculations

| scenario | P0 | P25 | P50 | P75 |
|----------|------|------|------|------|
| number of nodes not served | | | | |
| highLoad | 5 | 4 | 4 | 2 |
| medLoad | 4 | 2 | - | - |
| lowLoad | - | - | - | - |
| demand not served (Sm2/h) | | | | |
| highLoad | 850 | 650 | 650 | 400 |
| medLoad | 650 | 400 | - | - |
| lowLoad | - | - | - | - |

**Stochastic Analysis.** As a first step, the probability of having completed each phase of the procedure at time $t$ (given that procedure is started at 10 a.m.) is calculated and reported in Figure 3(a). Figure 3(b) shows the probability of being in each of the markings corresponding to a degradation of the perceived service quality at time $t$.

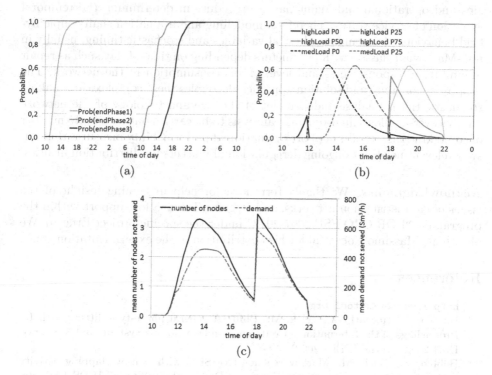

**Fig. 3.** Results of the stochastic analysis: (a) probability of completion of each phase by time $t$, (b) transient probability of being in a marking with lack of service at time $t$ and (c) expected value of nodes not served and demand not served at time $t$

Each peak refers to a different pressure level, solid lines representing high-Load scenario and dashed lines corresponding to medLoad. The four peaks lie at approximately equal distances from each other, corresponding to the duration of the regulation step (note that the "medLoad P50" line is not shown, as it brings no service disruption, but it can be inferred from the "highLoad P50" line). Figure 3(c) shows the expected values of the two lack of service measures, calculated using values in Table 3 as reward rates. Thus, considerations arise on the critical time-of-day in terms of service disruption and on the global impact of the failure, e.g., the discontinuity at 18 h corresponds to increased lack of service due to rising load in the network, which leads to lower pressure especially for nodes farther away from the supply station, while the area below the dashed curve represents the expected gas amount not sold due to the maintenance procedure.

## 5    Conclusions

Being a universal service, gas distribution networks represent a critical infrastructure with notable safety and availability issues. Their operation is cyber-physical, as the intrinsically physical infrastructure (which is geographically extended and follows deterministic laws) interacts with remote control strategies and operational and maintenance procedure in determining the temporal evolution of service status. Therefore, modelling and evaluation shall couple hybrid behaviour of continuous physical variables and stochastic timing, usually in non-Markovian classes, with parameters depending on time-of-day such as repair organisation responsiveness and level of gas consumption in the network. The proposed modelling and solution approach decouples these complexities, making stochastic timed analysis independent of the size and topology of the network and, viceversa, allows fluid-dynamic analysis to be carried out on a finite number of configurations. Results support evaluation of performability measures that answer relevant needs for ongoing deregulation of markets for distribution utilities.

**Acknowledgments.** We thank Terranova for help in gaining insight of the issues of gas distribution networks, and Regione Toscana for support within the programme "POR CRO FSE 2007-2013" under the specific project Ernesto. We also thank Massimo Nocentini for his contribution in the experimentation stage.

## References

1. http://www.oris-tool.org
2. Bobbio, A., Horváth, A., Telek, M.: Phfit: A general phase-type fitting tool. In: Proceedings of the International Conference on Dependable Systems and Networks, DSN 2002, p. 543. IEEE (2002)
3. Bobbio, A., Telek, M.: Markov regenerative SPN with non-overlapping activity cycles. In: Int. Computer Performance and Dependability Symp., IPDS 1995, pp. 124–133 (1995)
4. Bucci, G., Carnevali, L., Ridi, L., Vicario, E.: Oris: a tool for modeling, verification and evaluation of real-time systems. International Journal on Software Tools for Technology Transfer 12(5), 391–403 (2010)
5. Carnevali, L., Grassi, L., Vicario, E.: State-Density Functions over DBM Domains in the Analysis of Non-Markovian Models. IEEE Trans. on SW Eng. 35(2), 178–194 (2009)
6. Carnevali, L., Paolieri, M., Tarani, F., Vicario, E.: Quantitative evaluation of availability measures of gas distribution networks. In: VALUETOOLS (September 2013)
7. Carnevali, L., Ridi, L., Vicario, E.: A framework for simulation and symbolic state space analysis of non-markovian models. In: Flammini, F., Bologna, S., Vittorini, V. (eds.) SAFECOMP 2011. LNCS, vol. 6894, pp. 409–422. Springer, Heidelberg (2011)
8. Choi, H., Kulkarni, V.G., Trivedi, K.S.: Markov regenerative stochastic Petri nets. Perform. Eval. 20(1-3), 337–357 (1994)
9. Ciardo, G., German, R., Lindemann, C.: A characterization of the stochastic process underlying a stochastic petri net. IEEE Transactions on Software Engineering 20(7), 506–515 (1994)

10. Colebrook, C.: Turbulent flow in pipes, with particular reference to the transition region between smooth and rough pipe laws. Journal of the Institution of Civil Engineers (London) (1939)
11. Costa, A., de Medeiros, J., Pessoa, F.: Steady-state modeling and simulation of pipeline networks for compressible fluids. Brazilian Journal of Chemical Engineering 15(4), 344–357 (1998)
12. Courtney, T., Gaonkar, S., Keefe, K., Rozier, E., Sanders, W.H.: Möbius 2.3: An extensible tool for dependability, security, and performance evaluation of large and complex system models. In: IEEE/IFIP Int. Conf. on Dependable Systems and Networks (DSN), pp. 353–358 (2009)
13. Glynn, P.W.: A GSMP formalism for discrete-event systems. Proceedings of the IEEE 77, 14–23 (1989)
14. Herrán-González, A., Cruz, J.D.L., Andrés-Toro, B.D., Risco-Martín, J.: Modeling and simulation of a gas distribution pipeline network. Applied Mathematical Modelling 33(3), 1584–1600 (2009)
15. Horváth, A., Paolieri, M., Ridi, L., Vicario, E.: Transient analysis of non-Markovian models using stochastic state classes. In: Performance Evaluation (2012)
16. Koeppel, G., Andersson, G.: Reliability modeling of multi-carrier energy systems. Energy 34(3), 235–244 (2009)
17. Li, T., Eremia, M., Shahidehpour, M.: Interdependency of natural gas network and power system security. IEEE Transactions on Power Systems 23(4), 1817–1824 (2008)
18. Martínez-Mares, A., Fuerte-Esquivel, C.: Integrated energy flow analysis in natural gas and electricity coupled systems. In: North American Power Symposium (NAPS), pp. 1–7. IEEE (2011)
19. Munoz, J., Jimenez-Redondo, N., Perez-Ruiz, J., Barquin, J.: Natural gas network modeling for power systems reliability studies. In: Power Tech Conf. Proc., IEEE Bologna, vol. 4, p. 8 (2003)
20. Mura, I., Bondavalli, A.: Markov regenerative stochastic Petri nets to model and evaluate phased mission systems dependability. IEEE Transactions on Computers 50(12), 1337–1351 (2001)
21. Reinecke, P., Krauss, T., Wolter, K.: Hyperstar: Phase-type fitting made easy. In: QEST, pp. 201–202 (2012)
22. Smart Grids Task Force of the European Commission. Mission and work programme. Technical report (2012)
23. Szoplik, J.: The Gas Transportation in a Pipeline Network. In: Al-Megren, H. (ed.) Advances in Natural Gas Technology. InTech (2012) ISBN: 978-953-51-0507-7
24. Vicario, E., Sassoli, L., Carnevali, L.: Using stochastic state classes in quantitative evaluation of dense-time reactive systems. IEEE Trans. SW Eng. 35(5), 703–719 (2009)

# Quantification of the Impact of Cyber Attack in Critical Infrastructures

Oleksandr Netkachov, Peter Popov, and Kizito Salako

Centre for Software Reliability, City University London, UK
{Oleksandr.Netkachov.1,P.T.Popov,K.O.Salako}@city.ac.uk

**Abstract.** In this paper we report on a recent study of the impact of cyber-attacks on the resilience of complex industrial systems. We describe our approach to building a hybrid model consisting of both the system under study and an Adversary, and we demonstrate its use on a complex case study - a reference power transmission network (NORDIC 32), enhanced with a detailed model of the computer and communication system used for monitoring, protection and control. We studied the resilience of the modelled system under different scenarios: i) a base-line scenario in which the modelled system operates in the presence of accidental failures without cyber-attacks; ii) scenarios in which cyber-attacks can occur. We discuss the usefulness of our findings and outline directions for further work.

**Keywords:** Critical Infrastructures, Power Transmission Network, IEC 61850, stochastic modelling.

## 1    Introduction

Security of industrial control systems (ICS) used to control critical infrastructure (CI) has been extensively studied in the last few years by both industry and academia. Generally, the services offered by CI are somewhat robust with respect to single component failures of the underlying network. The reaction to multiple and cascading failures, however, is much harder to predict. Dependencies and interdependencies are an important source of risk and a significant factor in our uncertainty of risk assessment, particularly the risk due to cascading failures in which the rate and size of loss is amplified.

Although there are similarities between the ICS and the information and communication technology (ICT) systems, important differences between the two exist [1]. High availability and real-time response to events in industrial systems make some defenses against cyber-attacks widely used in ICT (e.g. patching) inadequate for ICS.

The literature rarely acknowledges other differences between the ICT and ICS, which make the detection of failures/cyber-attacks in the ICS *easier* to achieve than in the ICT. The processes that an ICS controls are generally either *directly observable* or reliable methods for indirect measurement exist. For instance, whether a power generator is connected to the power grid or not, is either directly observable or can be established reliably using sophisticated software tools such as *state estimators*.

A. Bondavalli et al. (Eds.): SAFECOMP 2014 Workshops, LNCS 8696, pp. 316–327, 2014.

The paper is organized as follows: In section 2 we state the problem of quantitative risk assessment studied in the paper. In section 3 we provide a description of the modeling framework, the approach we take to modeling cyber-attacks on ICS and a brief description of the case study used to illustrate the approach. Section 4 summarizes our findings, section 5 – the related research. Finally, section 6 concludes the paper and outlines directions for future research.

## 2    Problem Statement

In the past we developed a method for quantifying the impact of interdependencies between CI [2], which we called Preliminary Interdependency Analysis (PIA). PIA starts by a systematic search for CI interdependencies at a fairly *high level of abstraction*; interdependencies which might otherwise be overlooked. In a separate study [3] we demonstrated that although using a high level of abstraction is useful, the risk assessment results are, in general, quite sensitive to the level of abstraction. PIA acknowledges this fact via a set of refinements in model building, which invite the modeller to create hybrid models of the modelled infrastructures and choose the level of modelling abstraction that suits the specific study. The software tools developed to support the PIA method allow the modeller to quickly build complex hybrid models which combine: i) stochastic models of the elements of the modelled system, which account for functional, spatial and other *stochastic dependencies* between these elements, and ii) domain specific deterministic models, necessary in case a high fidelity analysis is sought. Such deterministic models, e.g. flow models, typically operate on a subset of modelled elements.

Cyber security of ICS has been a topic of active research recently (some important contributions are summarised in the Related Research section). Its practical importance, the need for empirical studies and the difficulties with these have been widely recognised.

A common problem with cyber security research is that it concentrates on security incidents in the ICT/ICS, while the real impact of successful attacks is rarely quantified. As a result, quantitative risk assessment is difficult. As we pointed out in the introduction, while such an approach is, to some extent, justified in ICT systems (for instance, how one assesses the impact of information theft is an open debate), with industrial systems the real impact of a cyber incident may be relatively easy to quantify. For instance, the impact of losing a generator in a power system as a result of a cyber-attack will vary between 0, in case other generators can provide additional power to compensate fully for the lost generator, to losses due to not supplying power to some consumers, in case the spare power generation capacity of the other generators in the network is insufficient to meet the current power demand. PIA models are well suited for quantitative risk assessment as they model, stochastically, both the controlled plant and the ICS. So far, however, PIA has not been used to explicitly address cyber security concerns. Bridging this gap is the *focus of this paper*. We propose to extend the PIA method by adding an Adversary model and building on the recent work by others in this direction, e.g. the ADVISE formalism [4].

# 3     Solution

Due to a lack of space we concentrate on describing the extension of the PIA method. Technical details about the newly implemented *simulation engine*, used for resilience assessment of our chosen case study, the NORDIC 32 system, in the presence of cyber-attacks will be provided in separate publications.

## 3.1     The System under Study

We use a non-trivial case study of a power transmission network to demonstrate the analysis one can undertake with the extended PIA and to evaluate how well the method scales to realistically complex industrial systems.

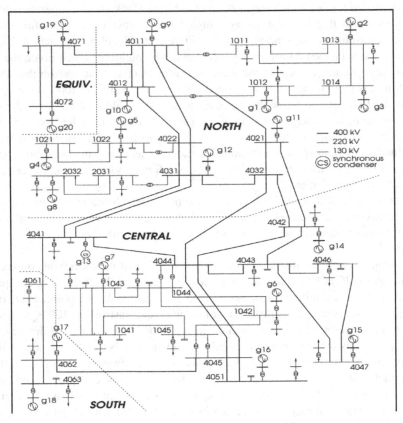

**Fig. 1.** NORDIC 32 power system topology

The system under study is shown in Fig. 1. The system model was developed by the FP7 EU project AFTER (http://www.after-project.eu/Layout/after/). It is based on a reference power transmission network, NORDIC 32, enhanced with an industrial distributed control system (IDCS) compliant with the international standard IEC

61850 "Communication networks and subsystems in sub-stations". A detailed description of the case study is beyond the scope of this paper, but a short summary is provided below.

The transmission network consists of a large number of transmission lines which connect 19 power generators and 19 loads. All connections of lines, generators and links are done in 32 sub-stations. Each sub-station is arranged in a number of bays. Each bay is responsible for connecting a single element – a line, a generator or a load – to the transmission network.

In this case study the sub-stations are assumed compliant with IEC 61850. Fig. 2 shows an example of a sub-station. The other sub-stations have similar architecture but may contain different numbers and types of bays. Some sub-stations may have generators and/or loads and all connect transmission lines.

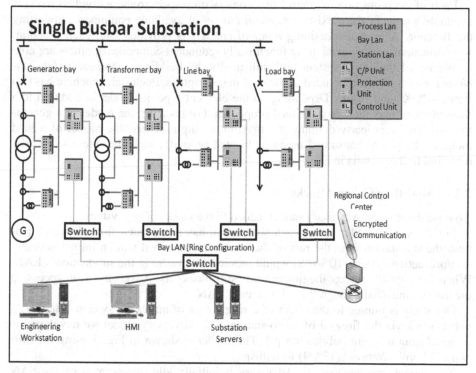

Fig. 2. An example of a sub-station compliant with IEC 61850

The sub-stations are connected via a sophisticated ICT infrastructure (not shown for lack of space), which includes a number of control centres, communication channels and data centres. At the top of the hierarchy is a National Control Centre, which communicates with 3 Regional control centres, which in turn monitor and control the operation of the sub-stations in their respective regions either via direct communication channels or via channels provided by public data centres.

Each bay is responsible for (dis)connecting one element from the transmission network. This is achieved by a set of elements – relays and electronic devices[1] of the following two types – either a protection device or a control device. The function of the protection devices is to disconnect the power elements from the transmission network, e.g. as a result of overloading of a line or of a generator. The control devices, on the other hand, are used to connect or disconnect the power elements from the network and are typically used by either the operators in the respective control centres or by "special purpose software" (SPS) designed to undertake some of the operators' functions automatically.

Each sub-station has a *Local Area Network* (LAN), which allows the local devices to communicate with each other. The LAN is protected from the rest of the world by a firewall (as shown by the "brick wall" in Fig. 2). Legitimate traffic in and out the sub-station is allowed, of course.

Each of the protection or control functions (with respect to the individual bays) is available whenever there exists a *minimal cut set* of available equipment supporting the function. A predicate defining *minimal cut sets* is provided with each function: some functions are achieved using functionally redundant components, others are not.

We model the entire system probabilistically, by building a *stochastic state machine* for each element included in the system description. Each state machine has two states – "OK" and "Fail". Depending on the element type, its model in addition to a state machine may include additional properties. For instance, the model of a generator will have a property defining the maximum output power; the model of a load includes the power consumed as an additional property, etc. The interested reader may find further details in [2].

## 3.2    Modelling Cyber-Attacks

Now we describe an Adversary model, added to the model of the system.

For the system under study, each sub-station has a dedicated firewall which isolates the sub-station from the rest of the world. We assumed that an intrusion detection/prevention system (IDS/IPS) would monitor the traffic in the sub-station's LAN. When the IDS/IPS detects illegitimate traffic it blocks the Adversary from accessing the assets controlled through the sub-station's LAN.

Our study is limited to the effect of a *single type of attack* on system behavior: a cyber-attack via the firewall of a sub-station. The Adversary model we developed is *adapted* from a recent publication [9]. The model is shown in Fig. 3 using the *Stochastic Activity Networks* (SAN) formalism.

This model assumes that the Adversary is initially idle (represented by the SAN *place labeled* "Idle"). With some regularity, defined by the *activity* Attack_interval, the Adversary launches a cyber-attack on the system by trying to penetrate the Firewall of *one* of the 32 sub-stations defined in NORDIC-32 model. The selection of the sub-station to attack is driven by either a *uniform distribution*, defined over the 32 sub-stations ("Indiscriminate attacker profile"), or by a *non-uniform distribution*, defined in a way to capture the preferences of the Adversary.

---

[1] IEC 61850 distinguishes between Intelligent Electronic Devices (IED), functions and nodes. Nodes are responsible for implementing a specific function (i.e. protection or control) and can involve several IED.

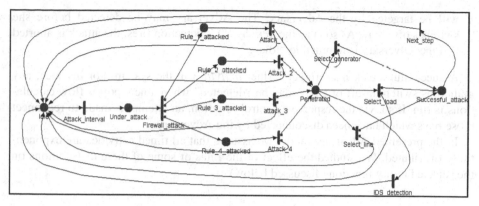

**Fig. 3.** Model of Adversary applied to NORDIC 32

We chose to model the preferences of the Adversary by setting the distribution over the set of sub-stations in such a way that the Adversary would prefer to attack either the largest generators or the largest loads ("major targets" profile). Under this profile we assumed that the Adversary is equally likely to switch off generators or loads and will never attempt to switch off a transmission line. Under the current model we also assume that the firewalls of all sub-stations are equally easy/difficult to penetrate. In fact, the SAN model in Fig. 3 is a sub-model of our Adversary model: it does not include how our Adversary chooses a sub-station. Instead, this model shows the steps that follow the Adversary's initial selection of a sub-station to attack:

— The Adversary may target each of the firewall *configuration rules*. The decision of which rule to attack is modeled by the *activity* Firewall_attack. In Fig. 3 we assume that there are 4 rules to choose between, which is just an example. The model assumes that the rules are equally likely to be chosen by an attacker – the probabilities associated with the outputs of the Firewall_attack activity are all set to 0.25.
— Once a rule is selected (modeled by the places Rule_1 – Rule_4), the Adversary spends time trying to break the selected rule, which is modeled by the *activities* Attack_1 – Attack_4, respectively. This effort may be successful or unsuccessful. In the case of a failed attempt, the Adversary returns to an idle state and may launch another attack later, likely to be on a different sub-station.
— In the case of a successful penetration through the firewall, the model enters the state "Penetrated", which in turn has three alternative options for the Adversary to proceed: to switch off a generator (in case a bay exists in the sub-station, via which a generator is connected to the grid), to switch off a load (in case a bay exists in the sub-station via which a consumer is connected to the grid) or disconnect a line from the grid (selecting at random one of those controlled by the sub-station).
— If the Adversary succeeds, she leaves the sub-station. In other words the Adversary under this model affects at most one bay per attack. This choice is modeled by the *instantaneous activity* Next_step, which returns the Adversary to the state "Idle".
— IDS/IPS is modeled by the *activity* IDS_detection, which is enabled if the model state is "Penetrated". This activity competes with the activities selecting which bay

will be targeted by the Adversary. The Adversary may be detected before she switches off a bay. As soon as the *activity* IDS_detection fires, the attack is aborted and the Adversary is returned to "Idle".

A successful attack may trigger further *activities* in the system. For instance, any malicious switching-off of a bay may be "detected" when a new power flow calculations is run. If so, via the respective control function, an attempt is made to reconnect those bays which have been disconnected by the Adversary.

In the presented Adversary model we assume that all timed activities are exponentially distributed. We studied the effect of the rates of some of these distributions on the selected utility function (discussed below).

# 4    Findings

## 4.1    Rewards

We were interested in measuring the effect of cyber-attacks on the system under study. We chose to compare the behavior of a *base-line model*, i.e. a model without cyber-attacks, with the behavior of the model in which cyber-attacks are enabled ("system under attack"). For the comparison we chose as a reward (utility function) the deviation of the supplied power, in the presence of failures and attacks, from the known maximum power supplied of 10,940 MW. This reward has been used in the analysis of power systems by others [9]. Other suitable candidates would be the size of cascades as we have done in the past [3]. We compute the reward at any state-machine event in the model and log these values during the simulations. Clearly, for every simulation run, the value of the supplied power varies over time to form a *continuous-time stochastic process*. We study the following two statistics of this process:

— The average power supplied during a simulation run. This would be lower than the *maximum* power. We selected, somewhat arbitrarily, the length of a simulation run to be the equivalent of 10 years of operation. The average over this period will vary between simulated runs, and we look at the *distribution of this average* over a number of runs.

— The *standard deviation* of the power supplied during a simulation run, as a measure of the variability of the supplied power. This statistic, too, varies between the simulation runs, and we look at the average over a number of simulation runs.

## 4.2    Studies

The studied system is non-trivial. It consists of more than 1500 modeling elements. With the chosen parameterization, based on input from domain experts, we observed a significant number (~7000 ... 32,000) of events over a single simulation run. Many of these events require power flow calculations and control optimizations, which take considerable time to complete. As a result, a single simulation run takes approximately 5 min to complete. Obtaining results with high confidence would require a large number of simulation runs: empirically we established that with ~500 simulation runs we obtain *Relative Standard Errors* (RSE) for these statistics no greater than 10%.

We completed 7 simulation campaigns which are summarized as follows:

- A base-line scenario - only accidental failures are possible and no cyber-attacks.
- A scenario with daily cyber-attacks, where substations are intelligently chosen by the attacker. Accidental network component failures occur.
- Scenarios in which we varied the cyber-attack frequency, no accidental failures:
  - Substations are *randomly* chosen by the attacker. The attacks occur with different rates: once per year, once per month, once per week or once per day.
  - Substations are *intelligently* chosen by the attacker and occur once per day.

## 4.3    Results

Our findings are summarized in the plots below.

**Attacks Only Cases**

The simulation results from this study are shown in Fig. 4.

The figure on the left shows the effect of frequency of attacks on the distribution of the supplied power when accidental component failures are ignored.  The two distributions on the left of this plot represent the case of daily attacks. The difference between the two curves is in how the Adversary chooses a target. The left most plot (labeled "Major Targets") represents the case when the Adversary chooses the 5 largest generators and loads with probabilities 0.5, 0.25, 0.1, 0.1 and 0.05, respectively: the largest generator and the largest load are chosen with 0.5 probability while the probabilities of attacking the next largest generators/loads decreases with their size. This case, thus, represents the case of an Adversary whose objective is to cause *maximum immediate* disruption. The second curve of daily attacks (second from the left in the plot) represents the system behavior with an Adversary who is indifferent between the targets, i.e. each of the sub-stations is chosen at random (with the same probability of 1/32). Clearly, the impact of such indiscriminate attacks is lower than the well targeted attacks, which is not surprising. Note that for rare attacks (which vary between once a year and once a week) the mean of the supplied power hardly differs from the maximum of 10, 940MW.  However, when the rate of attack is increased to one a day, we see a noticeable and statistically significant difference in the distributions and their means. We checked the statistical significance of the differences using *Kolmogorov-Smirnov two-sample* test at a 1% significance-level, which confirmed that in our model there is an ordering: increasing the frequency and sophistication of attacks reduces the average power supplied by the network.

The plot on the right of Fig. 4 shows the distribution of the *standard deviation* of the supplied power (calculated over the sample of 500 experiments representing each of the simulated cases). Now the ordering between the cases is reversed: the daily attacks have larger standard deviation than the cases with rarer attacks – the two plots on the right hand side of the plot represent the two cases of "daily" attacks. The case of "Major Targets" has the largest standard deviation. This indicates that the variation of the supplied power is greatest when the targets are selected so as to cause the largest immediate damage, i.e. in this cases the system's behavior is the most *erratic*.

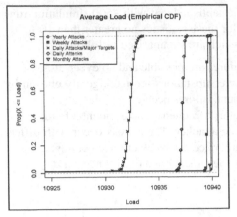
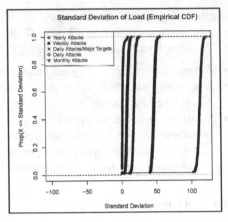

**Fig. 4.** Attacks only study: Distributions of the Mean and Standard Deviation of the supplied power

## Accidental Failures and Attacks Cases

Similar trends are observed when we enabled accidental failures (see Fig. 5). The elements of the modeled system may fail randomly and if they do – will be eventually repaired – the state machines of the modeling elements provide stochastic transitions from "Failed" states to "OK" states. We compared the case of "No Attacks", i.e. the losses were due to accidental failures only, with the case of daily "Major Targets" attacks.

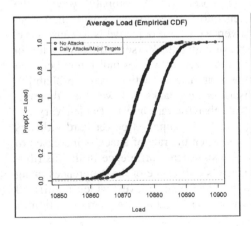
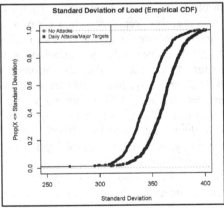

**Fig. 5.** Accidental failures and cyber-attacks: Mean and standard deviation of supplied power

The mean and standard variation of the supplied power for both cases is shown in Fig. 5. The ordering between "No Attacks" and "Major Targets" shows a trend similar to the one observed earlier: attacks decrease the mean and increase the standard deviation of the supplied power. In other words, the negative consequences of attacks have two aspects – less power is supplied and the system behaves more erratically.

# 5    Related Research

Different aspects of SCADA system security have been studied extensively.

Influential reports by both the Department of Homeland Security [8] and the National Institute of Standards and Technology (NIST) [1] provide a comprehensive discussion of current SCADA architectures and best practice approaches for their security.

Stochastic models have been used in the past to address, specifically, the cyber security of industrial control systems. For instance, Ten et. al [9] offer a model based on stochastic Petri nets, adapted for cyber security on power transmission systems. The study is similar to ours, except that Ten et. al do not provide a base line study and primarily concentrate on cyber-attacks under a fixed model parameterisation.

The ADVISE formalism [4] offers an alternative approach to stochastic modelling of a *rational* Adversary. The utility function used by ADVISE is computed based on the preferences of an adversary and on the likelihood of an attack being detected. The modelling approach allows for non-determinism – in terms of an outcome of a particular step in an attack – but any decision that the adversary would need to take during the attack is driven by her preferences, defined in the model *statically*. The formalism allows one to study *one attacker and attack-strategy at a time*; comparison of the impact of multiple, different attackers and attack-strategies requires building separate models and studies.

An interesting approach to modelling an adaptive adversary is developed by Martinelli et al [10]. The key idea there is captured by a graph describing the steps that an adversary could take, including "stepping back" in case of unsuccessful attack.

Nash equilibrium has recently become popular in cyber security research, e.g. [11]. The ideal of Nash equilibrium is attractive as it establishes, under fairly broad assumptions, the existence of the *worst consequences* from cyber-attacks without having to define, in detail, the attacks in specific contexts.

# 6    Conclusions

We described an approach to stochastic modelling of industrial control systems in which both accidental failures and cyber-attacks are treated in a unified way:

— accidental failures of the elements of the systems are modelled as stochastic state machines which allow the modeller to chose the right level of modelling abstraction (by selecting the most appropriate state machine);
— malicious behaviour of an Adversary (i.e. cyber-attacks) are modelled by stochastic state machines too, and these capture the behaviour of an adversary (their knowledge/preferences about the assets under attack);
— the dependencies between the behaviour of the modelled elements – including accidental failures and the effects of successful cyber-attacks – are modelled via a set of additional models that are either deterministic – such as power flows – or probabilistic – e.g. stochastic dependencies between the elements of the system.

We illustrated our approach on a non-trivial case study and report on the initial findings from a useful sensitivity analysis: we studied the effect, on system resilience, of varying model parameters of different threats and defenses. More specifically, we confirm that indiscriminate poorly prepared cyber-attacks will have negligible effect while attacks launched by a highly knowledgeable adversary – one capable of targeting the most critical components of power systems (large generators and consumers) – can cause significant disruption.

Our approach allows one to explore the space of possible defenses, if necessary increasing the level of detail. For instance, we could explore the possibility of deploying IDS/IPS with different coverage in the different sub-stations. One would expect that higher coverage should be associated with assets which are highly critical, but undertaking detailed modeling will allow one to be more precise in stating how much better these IDS/IPS should be in order for the negative impact of cyber-attacks to be minimized to an acceptable level.

We chose a simple attack to illustrate the approach. Extending the work to more sophisticated scenarios of attacks is straightforward. Each new attack would require a new state machine, which would define the steps of an Adversary in launching an attack, a relatively simple task. A more interesting scenario would involve distributed attacks by an intelligent adversary.

We envisage extending the work in a number of ways. Expanding the work modeling adversaries at the same level of abstraction, i.e. ignoring the specifics of the communication protocols used in the ICS. A number of attack scenarios are of immediate interest. An obvious extension of the adversary model used in this paper is one in which the adversary may attack more than one sub-station, e.g. until she eventually gets caught. Another scenario of interest would be to consider attacks which do not cause harm immediately. For instance, once access to a sub-station LAN is gained the adversary could change the thresholds of protection devices/functions. Such attacks lead to no immediate consequences for the power system, but incorrect threshold value may trip a line incorrectly in the future, e.g. as a result of even a minor accidental failure. When multiple protection thresholds are altered the problem may escalate and lead to large cascades. Finally, scenarios of simultaneous and/or coordinated attacks by multiple Adversaries (SWARM attacks) are important in practice.

Some cyber-attacks exploit deficiencies of the communication protocols. The PIA approach – building hybrid models with level of abstraction tailored to the needs of the particular study – fits the modeling task well. In a recent study [12] we recorded evidence that the PIA style of modeling scales well to such detailed models.

Last but not least, the recent work to re-engineer the tools supporting the PIA method makes it suitable to "study the future", i.e. for studies in which the system under study *evolves*. The changes may concern the system topology (e.g. the system may grow if the study period spans several decades), the model parameters (e.g. the effect of ownership change /lack of investment may impact the resilience of the system) and, not least, the cyber crime patterns may evolve over time.

**Acknowledgement.** This work has been partially supported by the EU Framework Programme 7 project AFTER ("A Framework for electrical power systems vulnerability identification, defence and Restoration", Grant agreement no: 261788), and by the EU ARTEMIS JU programme project SESAMO ("Security and Safety Modelling", Grant agreement no: 295354).

# References

1. Stouffer, K., Falco, J., Kent, K.: Guide to Supervisory Control and Data Acquisition (SCADA) and Industrial Control Systems Security, p. 164. National Institute of Standards and Technology (NIST) (2006)
2. Bloomfield, R.E., et al.: Preliminary Interdependency Analysis (PIA): Method and tool support, p. 56. Adelard LLP (2010)
3. Bloomfield, R., Buzna, L., Popov, P., Salako, K., Wright, D.: Stochastic Modelling of the Effects of Interdependencies between Critical Infrastructure. In: Rome, E., Bloomfield, R. (eds.) CRITIS 2009. LNCS, vol. 6027, pp. 201–212. Springer, Heidelberg (2010)
4. Ford, M.D., et al.: Implementing the ADVISE security modeling formalism in Möbius. In: The 43rd Annual IEEE/IFIP International Conference on Dependable Systems and Networks (DSN). IEEE, Budapest (2013)
5. Sanders, W.H.: Mobius, http://www.mobius.illinois.edu/ [cited]
6. IRRIIS. Integrated Risk Reduction of Information-based Infrastructure Systems (IRRIIS) (2006–2009), http://www.irriis.org/ [cited]
7. Hearing Before The Subcommittee On National Security, Cybersecurity: Assessing The Immediate Threat To The United States 2011, House of Representatives One Hundred Twelfth Congress First Session (2011)
8. US-CERT, Recommended Practice: Improving Industrial Control Systems Cybersecurity with Defense-In-Depth Strategies, US-CERT, p. 44 (2009)
9. Ten, C.-W., Liu, C.-C., Manimaran, G.: Vulnerability Assessment of Cybersecurity for SCADA Systems. IEEE Transactions on Power Systems 23(4), 1836–1846 (2008)
10. Krautsevich, L., Martinelli, F., Yautsiukhin, A.: Towards Modelling Adaptive Attacker's Behaviour. In: Garcia-Alfaro, J., Cuppens, F., Cuppens-Boulahia, N., Miri, A., Tawbi, N. (eds.) FPS 2012. LNCS, vol. 7743, pp. 357–364. Springer, Heidelberg (2013)
11. Johnson, B., Grossklags, J., Christin, N., Chuang, J.: Are Security Experts Useful? Bayesian Nash Equilibria for Network Security Games with Limited Information. In: Gritzalis, D., Preneel, B., Theoharidou, M. (eds.) ESORICS 2010. LNCS, vol. 6345, pp. 588–606. Springer, Heidelberg (2010)
12. Cavalieri, S., et al.: Quantitative Assessment of Distributed Networks through Hybrid Stochastic Modelling. In: Bruneo, D., Distefano, S. (eds.) Quantitative Assessments of Distributed Systems, pp. 1–39. Scrivener Publishing LLC, USA (to appear)

# Probabilistic Inference in the Physical Simulation of Interdependent Critical Infrastructure Systems

Paolo Franchin[1] and Luigi Laura[2,3]

[1] Dept of Structural and Geotechnical Engineering,
"Sapienza" University of Rome, Via A. Gramsci 53, 00197, Roma, Italy
paolo.franchin@uniroma1.it
[2] Dept. of Computer, Control, and Management Engineering "Antonio Ruberti",
"Sapienza" University of Rome, Via Ariosto 25, 00185, Roma, Italy
laura@dis.uniroma1.it
[3] Research Centre for Transport and Logistics (CTL),
"Sapienza" Università di Roma, Italy

**Abstract.** One of the main tasks that can be performed with a Bayesian Network (BN) is the probabilistic inference of unobserved values given evidence. Recently, a framework for physical simulation of critical infrastructures was introduced, accounting for interdependencies and uncertainty; this framework includes the modeling of the interconnected components of a critical infrastructure network as a BN. In this paper we address the problem of the *triangulation* of the resulting BN, that is the first step in many exact inference algorithms.

## 1 Introduction

A framework has been recently proposed for the performance simulation of Critical Infrastructures (CI) under seismic hazard, at the regional or urban scale [4]. This framework has been developed within a research project on seismic vulnerability of buildings and lifelines (SYNER-G 2012, [12]), and is thus denoted in the following as SYNER-G framework, or simply framework. It consists of a set of models, that can be jointly used to assess the impact of regional seismic hazard on CI, in terms for instance of reduced service level, or a community, e.g. in terms of social loss metrics such as displaced population [3]. The framework has also been employed to evaluate the probability distribution of a city's resilience [5], adopting the definition in Asprone et al. [1].

Inside this framework the uncertainty is described in terms of random variables and their joint probability distribution. Probabilistic dependencies are represented through a Bayesian Network whose nodes correspond to uncertain elements within the modeled physical systems and hazard, as done, e.g., in [2]. However, so far, and contrary to [2] the full power of BNs has not been exploited, and the network is used only in a forward simulation: the only probabilistic analysis methods currently employed are, indeed, the plain Monte Carlo

A. Bondavalli et al. (Eds.): SAFECOMP 2014 Workshops, LNCS 8696, pp. 328–338, 2014.

and Importance Sampling, the latter enhanced with K-means clustering [6]. The focus in the development of the framework was on the accurate description of physical interactions and of systems' performance in terms of service level (i.e. describing flows in the utility and transportation networks, rather then limiting the analysis to pure connectivity problems). The next step thus is that of adding the capability of performing Bayesian inference on unobserved components given evidence on others.

We recall that a BN [7] is a directed acyclic graph in which nodes represent the problem variables (usually random variables with a finite number of possible states); and the edges represent relationships of relevance between the joined variables. To perform efficient inference in Bayesian networks, the network graph needs to be triangulated. Note that the quality of this triangulation largely determines the efficiency of the subsequent inference, but the triangulation problem is unfortunately NP-hard [13], and there is a rich literature proposing heuristic methods, as discussed in the survey of Kjærul [8]: the range of techniques varies from *simple random elimination; maximum cardinality search* [14] to *simulated annealing* [9]. We refer the interested reader to the already mentioned survey of Kjærul [8] and to the more recent work of Larrañaga et al. [11], that employ a *genetic algorithm* approach. A more detailed coverage of BNs and inference in BNs can be found in the books [7,10].

Thus, motivated by the need of efficient inference in the SYNER-G framework, in this paper we analyze the generic BN built by this framework, i.e. associated to a Complex Infrastructure system, and provide an explicit triangulation of the corresponding *moralized graph*; our analysis, therefore, forms the basis for the explicit construction of the *junction* tree, that is the auxiliary graphical structure needed by the most typical inference engines [7].

This paper is organized as follows: in the next section we describe the few aspects of the framework that we will use as the basis of our analysis. In Section 3, we detail our main result: the triangulation of a generic BN corresponding to a CI system. Finally, we conclude in Section 4.

## 2   The Framework for Physical Simulation of Critical Infrastructures

In this section we recall the fundamental aspects of the SYNER-G framework for physical simulation of critical infrastructures. We refer the interested reader to [3,5,4,12] for more details.

For the purpose of this paper we can refer to Figure 1, which depicts an instance of the most basic CI system of systems, made up of two interconnected infrastructure systems, each with two components. In particular, system 1 is a power network with a generation node (point-like component 1) and a substation (point-like component 2). The latter provides power to a pump (point-like component 3), which is part of system 2, a water-supply network, and inputs water into a pipe (line-like component 4) that conveys it to an end-user or demand node. Figure 1 shows also a grid with six points and a simple seismic source of rectangular geometry. The seismic hazard model generates events with location within one of the active sources (in the figure just one) and of magnitude constrained by the source properties. The model then translates the corresponding energy in the local intensity at each grid point, from which it is interpolated to the sites of each component (the power source, the sub-station, the pump, the pipe centroid, etc). The state of physical damage of each component can thus be assessed based on their vulnerability and functional analysis can be carried out to determine the level of residual functionality, if any, as a consequence of the event. Uncertainty affects all of the above elements in the framework, from the seismic sources, the intensity felt at each site as a result of an earthquake, the state of components and the system performance given the physical damage. This uncertainty is modeled as anticipated with a network of random variables, described in in Figure 2. The figure actually shows a "superset" of the Bayesian Network we consider in this paper: more precisely, we do not include the third layer, i.e. the System of Systems functional model, that is regarded as a "deterministic layer". Figure 2 is the BN produced by the framework for the system of systems and seismic environment in Figure 1, and is representative of the generic BN produced by the framework. The BN has a hierarchical structure, and three portions can be identified: the top one corresponds to the distributed seismic hazard, the middle one to the components physical vulnerability, and the bottom one to the systems' (functional) models. The seismic intensity at the grid points (six in this example) has a central role not only in the BN, but, as we will see in the following, in the triangulation process. For the purpose of this paper the exact meaning of each node is not relevant, only the topology of the network is important. Nonetheless, from top to bottom, the variables are: event magnitude M, source S, event location L, inter- and intra-event errors $\eta$ and $\epsilon$, respectively (that measure deviation in the regression model that lead from magnitude and location to local intensities), local intensities at the bedrock, at grid points and components' sites, Sgr and Sr, respectively, and local intensity at the surface SS, amplification A, damage state D, rupture state B, number of leaks NL, and, finally, performance indicators PI. The gray nodes, in any part of the graph, represent represent epistemic uncertainty on the distribution parameters of other variables. More details can be found in [4]. The nodes for which we might have evidence have been colored in yellow.

The corresponding graphical representation is shown in Figure 2, that is a "superset" of the Bayesian Network we will consider in this paper: more precisely, we will not consider the third layer, i.e. the *System of Systems functional model*, that, for the moment, we consider a deterministic layer inside the framework.

## 3    Inference in the Bayesian Network Associated with the SYNER-G Framework

In this section we describe the triangulation of the generic BN produced by the framework. As a first step, we need to moralize the BN, by adding edges between common parents of a given node, and then drop the orientation from the original BN set of edges.

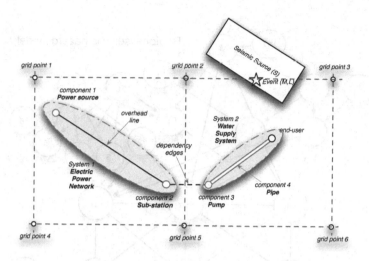

**Fig. 1.** Basic CI system of systems made up of two interconnected systems, each with two components

In Figure 2 we can see, as already mentioned, an example of a generic Bayesian Network produced by the framework. We will not consider the third layer of the figure, i.e. the *System of Systems functional model*; the nodes for which we might have evidence have been colored in yellow. From the figure is it possible to appreciate the hierarchical structure of the model, and the fact that the grid points have a central role not only in the BN, but, as we will see in the following, in the triangulation process.

## 3.1   Graph Moralization

The graph moralization is the process of turning the directed BN into an undirected graph. We refer to the BN shown in Figure 2, that is a generic Bayesian Network produced by the framework, in order to identify the common parents for each node, starting from the top part of the graph:

- Yellow nodes are the ones for which we might have evidence.
- The gray nodes, in any part of the graph, represent epistemic uncertainty on the distribution parameters of other variables, and none of these nodes have an entering edge.
- The parents of $S$ are $\theta_S$ and $M$.
- The parents of $L$ are $\theta_S$ and $S$.
- The parents of $\eta$ are $\theta_\eta$ and $S$.
- The parents of the generic $\epsilon_i$ are $\theta_\epsilon$ and $u$.
- The parents of the generic $S_{gir}$, i.e. the local seismic intensity at the generic grid point, are $\eta$, $L$, $M$ and the corresponding $\epsilon_i$.

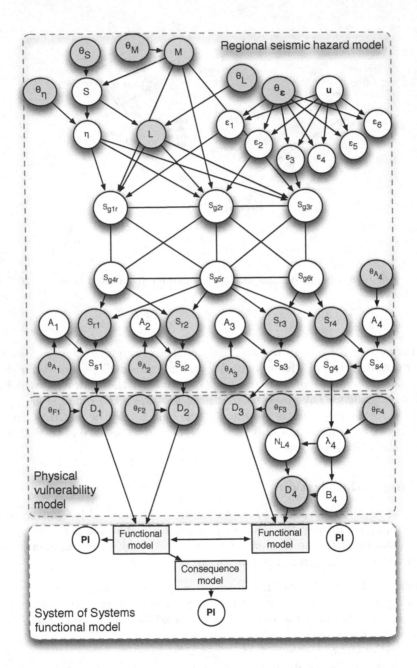

**Fig. 2.** BN representing uncertainty in the system in Figure 1: circles represent random variables, rectangles represent "analytical/numerical models", arrows represent statistical dependence among random variables or input/output to/from a model

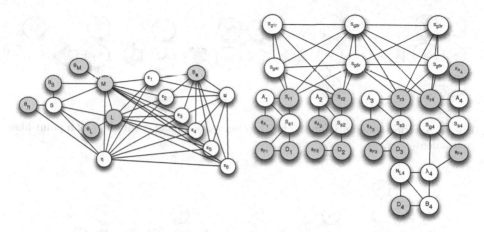

**Fig. 3.** Moral graph of the top part (left) and the bottom part (right) of the BN shown in Figure 2

- The parents of the generic $S_{ri}$ are the four grid nodes that correspond to the vertices of the grid element the corresponding component belongs to.
- The parents of the generic $A_i$ is the corresponding $\theta_{A_i}$.
- The parents of the generic $S_{si}$ are the corresponding $A_i$ and $S_{ri}$.
- In case of point-like components, such as the first three components of Figure 1, corresponding to nodes $D_1$, $D_2$, and $D_3$ in Figure 2, the parents of the generic $D_i$ node are the corresponding node $S_{si}$ and $\theta_{Fi}$.
- In case of line-like components, as the fourth component of Figure 1, corresponding to node $D_4$, there is more structure: we have in this case a variable corresponding to peak ground deformation, i.e. $S_{g4}$, that is children of node $S_{s4}$ and, together with node $\theta_{F4}$ they are the parents of node $\lambda_4$ (rate of failures per unit length). The parents of $D_4$ are the nodes $N_{L4}$ and $B_4$ that are children of node $\lambda_4$.

We show in Figure 3 left and right, respectively, the top and the bottom part of the moral graph obtained; note that we do not show the links between the two parts that are, for each generic $S_{gir}$, a connection with $\eta$, $L$, $M$ and the corresponding $\epsilon_i$. We will first simplify the two parts, and then we will reconnect them in a single figure.

## 3.2 Triangulation

As a first step in the triangulation phase consider the moral graph corresponding to the top part of the BN shown in Figure 2, i.e. the moral graph shown in Figure 3 (left). Here we see that, if we follow the elimination order $\theta_M$, $\theta_S$, $\theta_\eta$, $\theta_L$, and $S$, we are left with the graph shown in Figure 6 (left) without the need of inserting any fill-in edge.

In the case of the bottom part of the BN shown in Figure 2, we show in Figure 4 the elimination order of the subgraph that links intensity to damage

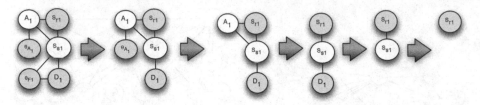

**Fig. 4.** A perfect elimination order for the "intensity-damage" subgraph of a point-like component

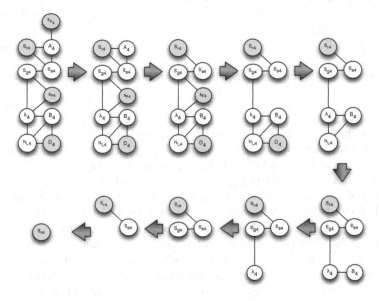

**Fig. 5.** A perfect elimination order for the subgraph "below" a line-like component

for a point-like component. It is possible to see, from both Figure 3 (right) and Figure 4, that this subgraph has a perfect elimination order. Also in the case of a line-like component there is a perfect elimination order, as shown in Figure 5.

The application of a perfect elimination order for each component transform the moral graph of the bottom part of the BN, shown in Figure 3 (right), into the one depicted in Figure 6 (right). It is important to note that, in this graph, each node corresponding to a component is a simplicial[1] node, and therefore it can be removed without adding fill-in edges. Therefore, from the original moral graph shown in Figure 3 (right), we are left only with the grid intensity nodes.

---

[1] Given an undirected graph $G = (V, E)$ and a node $X \in V$, let us denote by $nb(X)$ the set of neighbors of $X$, and by $fa(X)$ the family of $X$, i.e., the set of neighbors of $X$ plus $X$. A node $A$ is *simplicial* if $nb(A)$ is a clique or, equivalently, if $fa(A)$ is a clique.

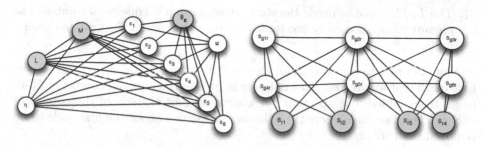

**Fig. 6.** The graphs resulting after the application of a perfect elimination order for each of the components in the moral graphs shown in Figure 3. Note that each node corresponding to a component is a simplicial node, and therefore it can be removed without adding fill-in edges.

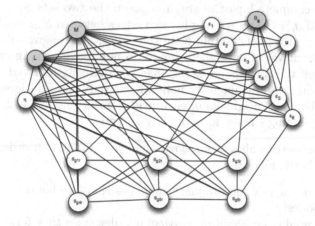

**Fig. 7.** After some elimination both in the top and the bottom part, in the picture it is shown the complete resulting graph to be triangulated

Now we can merge the top and bottom parts, in order to obtain the graph shown in Figure 7, that is the base of our analysis. Note that the above approach can be extended to any BN generated according to the framework: in particular, the resulting generic graph will have four distinct clusters:

1. The grid intensity nodes that have links, inside their cluster, according to their position in the grid: each node, indeed, is connected to the adjacent nodes in the grid. Outside the cluster, each node is connected to the corresponding $\epsilon$ node and to the $L$, $M$, $\eta$ nodes.
2. The $\epsilon$ nodes, one for each grid node. Inside this cluster there is no link, whilst outside each of them is connected to i) the $L$, $M$, $\eta$ nodes, ii) to the corresponding grid intensity node, and iii) the pair $\theta_\epsilon$ and $u$.
3. The pair of nodes $\theta_\epsilon$ and $u$, that are connected together and, both, are connected to every $\epsilon$ node.

4. The $L$, $M$, $\eta$ nodes: inside the cluster they form a clicque, whilst outside, as already mentioned, they are connected to each node of the grid and each $\epsilon$ node.

Now, in order to find a optimal elimination order for this generic graph, we first recall that we are interested not only in finding the minimal number of fill-in edges to be added, but also that our goal is to limit the size of the maximum clique. Therefore, we observe the following properties about the first node to be removed from this graph:

- If we remove either $\theta_\epsilon$ or $u$, we need to turn the subgraph made of the $\epsilon$ node into a complete graph, i.e. if we have $n$ nodes (from $\epsilon_1$ to $\epsilon_n$) we need to insert $n \cdot (n-1)/2$ edges, and form a clique of $n$ nodes.
- The same above holds for the removal of a node between $L$, $M$, and $\eta$.
- The removal of an $\epsilon$ node, let us say $\epsilon_i$ forces the insertion of the following edges: the complete bipartite graph between the two sets $S_1 = \{u, \theta_\epsilon\}$ and $S_2 = \{L, M, \eta\}$, i.e. six edges, plus two edges between $S_{gir}$ and $u$, $\theta_\epsilon$ if the node $S_{gir}$ is still in the graph. Note that, after the removal of any single $\epsilon$ node, the removal of any other $\epsilon$ node do not require the insertion of any fill-in edge if the corresponding $S_{gir}$ has been already removed.
- The removal of a grid intensity node affects only the grid intensity nodes, since all the other neighbors of each grid intensity node, i.e. $L$, $M$, $\eta$, and the corresponding $\epsilon$ node, form already a clique.

From the properties above, it follows that the elimination order for such a generic graph is the following:

1. the nodes in the grid, according to their position (see below);
2. all the $\epsilon$ nodes;
3. all the remaining nodes, in no particular order since they form a clique: all of them are simplicial nodes and, therefore, their removal do not require the insertion of any fill-in edge.

In order to complete, we need to describe a minimal elimination order of the nodes in a grid. Let us assume that the grid has $r$ rows and $c$ columns, with a total of $r \cdot c$ nodes. We observe that it is not convenient to remove any internal node, since it would leave 8 nodes with 8 edges, and therefore we would need to add 20 fill-in edges[2]. Note that the removal of corner node do not require any fill-in edge, and a subsequent removal of the node below the corner node, in the same column, requires two edges. It is easy to see that the removal of a column of $r$ nodes requires $2(r-3)$ fill-in edges (we do not need two edges for three nodes: the first and the last in the column, that are corner nodes, and the last one to be removed). And, we do not need to insert fill-in edges when we remove the last two columns. Therefore, the overall number of fill-in edges to be inserted is $2(r-3) \cdot (c-2) \approx 2cr$, i.e. twice the nodes in the grid.

---

[2] A clique with 8 nodes has $8 \cdot (8-1)/2 = 28$ edges.

Therefore, the number of fill-in edges required to triangulate the graph is the following:

1. $2(r - 3) \cdot (c - 2) \approx 2cr$ in order to remove the nodes in the grid, according to their position;
2. 6 to remove all the $\epsilon$ nodes;
3. 0 to remove all the remaining nodes, in no particular order since they form a cliques.

It follows that the overall number of fill-in edges is approximately twice the number of the grid nodes, and therefore it is linear in the number of the nodes of the whole BN.

## 4   Conclusions

In this paper we addressed the problem of the triangulation of (the moral graph of) a generic BN produced by the SYNER-G framework to describe uncertainty associated with a system of interconnected CI systems subjected to seismic hazard. The triangulation of a domain graph is the first step in order to be able to propagate inference efficiently; unfortunately, the triangulation of a graph is an NP-hard problem [13], for which several heuristics have been presented in the literature.

In this paper we analyzed the generic BN built by this framework and provided an explicit triangulation of the corresponding *moralized graph*; as already mentioned our analysis forms the basis for the construction of the *junction* tree, that is the auxiliary graphical structure needed by the most typical inference engines [7]. The algorithm is linear in the number of nodes of the BN. Future research will look into adding the system performance nodes to the BN and include them in the triangulation algorithm.

## References

1. Asprone, D., Cavallaro, M., Latora, V., Manfredi, G., Nicosia, V.: City ecosystem resilience analysis in case of disasters. In: Computer Aided Civil & Infrastructure Engineering (2013) (submitted)
2. Bensi, M.T., Der Kiureghian, A., Straub, D.: A Bayesian network methodology for infrastructure seismic risk assessment and decision support. Pacific Earthquake Engineering Research Center (2011)
3. Cavalieri, F., Franchin, P., Gehl, P., Khazai, B.: Quantitative assessment of social losses based on physical damage and interaction with infrastructural systems. Earthquake Engineering & Structural Dynamics 41(11), 1569–1589 (2012)
4. Franchin, P.: A Computational Framework for Systemic Seismic Risk Analysis of Civil Infrastructural Systems. In: Pitilakis, K., et al. (eds.) SYNER-G: Systemic Seismic Vulnerability and Risk Assessment of Complex Urban, Utility, Lifeline Systems and Critical Facilities. Geotechnical, Geological and Earthquake Engineering, vol. 31, pp. 23–56. Springer Science+Business Media Dordrecht (2014), doi:10.1007/978-94-017-8835-9_2

5. Franchin, P., Cavalieri, F.: A framework for physical simulation of critical infrastructures, accounting for interdependencies and uncertainty. In: 11th International Conference on Structural Safety & Reliability, ICOSSAR 2013, New York, NY, USA, June 16-20 (2013)
6. Jayaram, N., Baker, J.W.: Efficient sampling and data reduction techniques for probabilistic seismic lifelines assessment. Earthquake Engineering and Structural Dynamics 39(10), 1109–1131 (2010)
7. Jensen, F., Nielsen, T.D.: Bayesian networks and decision graphs. Springer, Berlin (2007)
8. Kjærul, U.: Triangulation of graphs – Algorithms giving small total state space. Technical Report R 90-09, University of Aalborg, Denmark (1990)
9. Kjærul, U.: Optimal decomposition of probabilistic networks by simulated annealing. Statistics and Computing 2, 7–17 (1992)
10. Koller, D., Friedman, N.: Probabilistic Graphical Models: Principles and Techniques. MIT Press (2009)
11. Larrañaga, P., Kuijpers, C., Poza, M., Murga, R.H.: Decomposing Bayesian networks: triangulation of the moral graph with genetic algorithms. Statistics and Computing 7, 19–34 (1997)
12. SYNER-G 2012, collaborative research project, funded by the European Union within Framework Programme 7 (2007-2013) under grant agreement no. 244061, http://www.syner-g.eu
13. Wen, W.: Optimal decomposition of belief networks. In: Proceedings of the Sixth Conference on Uncertainty in Artificial Intelligence (UAI 1990), pp. 209–224. Elsevier Science, New York (1990)
14. Tarjan, R.E., Yannakakis, M.: Simple linear-time algorithms to test chordality of graphs, test acyclicity of hypergraphs, and selectively reduce acyclic hypergraphs. SIAM Journal on Computing 13, 566–579 (1984)

# Energy-Based Detection of Multi-layer Flooding Attacks on Wireless Sensor Network

Cesario Di Sarno and Alessia Garofalo

University of Naples "Parthenope", Department of Engineering, Naples, Italy
{cesario.disarno,alessia.garofalo}@uniparthenope.it

**Abstract.** Ensuring cyber security on Wireless Sensor Network (WSN) is a challenging task since nodes are devices with very limited resources. Existing Intrusion Detection Systems (IDSs) solutions either ensure protection from attacks at one specific OSI layer, or they ensure multi-layer protection but with more relevant computational costs. In this work we propose a new solution which aims at detecting attacks at different OSI layers by minimizing the number of features required to perform intrusion detection activities on a WSN node. In this work we consider multi-layer flooding attack performed at routing and application layers; our experimental tests show that a high correlation exists between the features of these attacks available at the corresponding layers and energy consumption. This allows to use energy consumption as the only feature to detect both the attacks even if they are performed at different OSI layers.

**Keywords:** Wireless Sensor Network, Intrusion Detection System, flooding attack.

## 1 Introduction

Nowadays, different assets can be identified in our society whose compromisation could have catastrophic consequences e.g. energy production and distribution, telecommunication, water supply and others. For this reason, such assets are classified as critical [8]. Specifically, the term Critical Infrastructure (CI) is used to describe these assets that are essential for a society and must be available 365 days a year and 24 hours a day. Thus, CI monitoring is a very important task to avoid disasters. CI monitoring is often performed through IT solutions so to allow CI operators to detect anomalies which could cause failures. However, the drawback of such solutions is that they are exposed to cyber attacks.

Wireless Sensor Network (WSN) represents a possible solution to perform large scale monitoring of CIs. Specifically, the WSN is a collection of spatially deployed wireless sensors of small size that allow to monitor environment changing in a collaborative way without relying on any underlying infrastructure support. The sensors of a WSN are low-price devices with limited resources in terms of battery, memory, storage space and computational power. This implies that classic security systems as Intrusion Detection Systems (IDSs) or complex systems that perform data correlations [9] to discover security breaches cannot be

A. Bondavalli et al. (Eds.): SAFECOMP 2014 Workshops, LNCS 8696, pp. 339–349, 2014.

used as they are but they must be re-designed considering these constraints. Due to such constraints, Intrusion Detection System (IDS) solutions on WSN are typically designed to detect one single attack [12] [3].

In past works we proposed an IDS [6] for security analysis which was designed considering limited resources available as a functional requirement. In such work, only data provided at routing layer of each sensor are analyzed in order to detect specific routing attacks as sinkhole and sleep deprivation.

In this paper we focus on multi-layer flooding attacks and on solutions useful to detect them. In flooding attacks, a malicious node sends packets to a target node continuously. The goal of the attacker is to deplete the resources available on the node e.g. in order to deny the service provided by that node. By multi-layer we mean that flooding attacks can be performed at different layers of OSI model, so this security breach cannot be detected through knowledge of data belonging to a single OSI layer. In this work two types of flooding attacks are considered: path based Denial of Service (DoS) and sleep deprivation attacks, which are respectively performed at application layer and routing layer. In a path based DoS attack, e.g. random data are produced and fed to nodes through a specific path. The purpose of sleep deprivation attack is to hinder nodes from going in sleep mode and saving energy. The consequence is that the low energy resources available on WSN nodes are soon consumed and the service offered by attacked nodes is no longer available. The purpose of our analysis is to select the approach that allows detection of multi-layer flooding attacks by using a low number of features to describe these attacks. Finding the solution to this problem is a relevant task since nodes of a WSN are devices with limited resources. The analysis performed highlighted that one specific feature can be chosen among others since it contains relevant information about flooding attacks independently of the specific layer the attack is launched. Such feature is the battery consumption profile of WSN nodes; experimental results show a significant correlation between variations of battery consumption and multi-layer flooding attacks.

The paper is organized as follows: in Section 2 we discuss the state of the art of current IDSs solutions for WSNs used to perform intra-layer and multi-layer security analysis; in Section 3 we present approaches that can be used to detect path based DoS and sleep deprivation attacks; in Section 4 we show the experimental results.

## 2    Related Work

Many IDSs were proposed in literature to improve WSN cyber-security. We can divide them in two categories: 1) IDSs designed to perform security analysis on data gathered from a single OSI layer e.g. routing layer, physical layer and so on; 2) IDSs designed to perform multi-layer data correlation. IDSs belonging to the first category provide protection against a small set of cyber attacks since they are not capable of detecting multi-layer attacks and single-layer attacks; the latter occurs when the layer attacked is different from the layer monitored by the

IDS. However, single-layer IDSs are more suitable for devices with limited resources as WSN motes. Instead, IDSs belonging the second category (multi-layer IDSs) provide a better protection against cyber-attacks that involve different layers; on the other hand, such IDSs require more resources to perform cross-layer data correlations.

In [7], the authors present a hybrid model of IDS. Specifically the IDS is composed of two main components: Central Agent and Local Agent. Each Local Agent runs on a different WSN node and it is designed to perform local security analysis by using data available on that node. Also, Local Agent is primarily designed considering the limited resources of motes. The Central Agent runs on a server and it performs intensive computation using the 'alerts' received from Local Agents to validate cyber-attacks. The IDS proposed in [7] is designed to detect two cyber-attacks: sinkhole and bogus packet. These attacks are performed at routing layer, so the IDS analyzes data available at the routing protocol considered, i.e. Collection Tree Protocol (CTP) [11]. The authors do not analyze the possibility to use techniques to optimize the amount of data sent from Local Agents to the Central Agent. Instead, techniques as feature selection can be useful because a huge amount of energy cost in WSN is related to data transmission. The authors do no provide considerations about energy consumption of solution proposed.

In [6] [10] the authors improve the capabilities of the IDS whose architecture has been detailed in [7]. The purpose is to improve the detection capabilities and reduce unnecessary communications and computations related to the generation of security alerts by Local Agents, since such communications are highly energy-consuming for WSN motes. Also the Central Agent is equipped with a machine learning technique in order to improve the attack detection. Several machine learning approaches are already in use for ensuring ICT security [5]; specifically, in [6] [10] Decision Tree is used to perform data classification. Also in this case, the IDS proposed works only with data available at routing layer, specifically considering Ad Hoc On Demand Distance Vector (AODV) [16] routing protocol. Experimental tests show the effectiveness of the proposed solution to detect two attacks that affect routing protocol: sinkhole and sleep deprivation.

Authors in [4] discuss a new multi-layer IDS for WSN. Authors assume a hierarchical cluster-based network topology that divides the network into several clusters; each cluster uses a cluster head in order to communicate with the Base Station (BS), i.e. the component that typically performs computation on data collected from the WSN. IDS proposed correlates information provided by different OSI layers of the node (i.e. network, MAC and physical layers) in order to discover new security breaches. The authors focus only on the detection capabilities, so they do not propose any technique to reduce the additional energy consumption due to multi-layer correlation.

Multi-layer correlation is also used in Wireless Mesh Networks. In [17] the authors propose a multi-layer based anomaly detection model designed to be equipped on each node. The model proposed is based on machine learning algorithms to estimate profiles of nodes and perform intrusion detection through such profiles. Specifically, data provided by MAC layer and network layer are used to train different classifiers in order to discover cyber-attacks i.e. probe flooding attack, grey hole attack and black hole attack. Experimental tests show that detection capabilities of multi-layer based IDS overcome the ones in classic network IDS. However, the study does not provide details about energy consumption of their solution.

In [13] the authors propose a system that allows to analyze information provided by different layers of the OSI model in order to detect flooding attack performed at any layer i.e. application, network, MAC or physical. The authors do not show which features are selected and used at each layer to detect the flooding attack. Also, details are not provided about energy consumption. Our approach also considers flooding attack performed at both application and routing layer. However, we are interested in finding correlations between features of attacks at such layers; specifically, our purpose is to minimize the number of features necessary to perform intrusion detection of multi-layer flooding attacks.

## 3    Single-Layer and Multi-Layer Detection Approaches for WSN

In this section we focus on the study of techniques that allow to detect multi-layer flooding attacks with a low number of features. The attacks considered are: path based DoS (performed at application layer) and sleep deprivation (performed at routing layer). The solutions proposed are discussed with reference to a hybrid IDS model for WSN as shown in Figure 1 and detailed in [6]. We briefly summarize the main components of the IDS architecture shown (Local Agents and Central Agent). Local Agents are deployed on each mote and their task is: to gather data provided by a specific layer of OSI model e.g. routing layer; to process gathered data to perform security analysis. In particular, the features that describe a specific attack and their security thresholds are identified in off-line mode. Then, Local Agents use the thresholds previously identified to perform online security analysis. When a Local Agent raises a security 'alert' this is sent to the Central Agent. Central Agent performs a complete analysis using

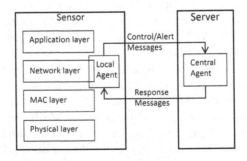

**Fig. 1.** IDS Architecture

both 'alerts' raised by node and additional information requested to/provided by neighbors of the potentially malicious node. Finally, the Central Agent generates an 'alarm' if an attack is successfully detected, otherwise the 'alert' raised is discarded. The alarm contains useful information about the security breach occurred, so the 'alarm' itself has to be stored in a secure storage [2] together with the chain of related 'alerts' that caused the 'alarm'. The purpose of a secure storage is to provide forensic evidence of the intrusion.

In order to let the IDS shown be able to detect multi-layer flooding attacks, different approaches can be chosen, each of them having different advantages and disadvantages. In the first approach, each WSN node uses two Local Agents to monitor application and routing layer. In this way each Local Agent estimates its own features and security threshold values to detect the flooding attack at the corresponding OSI layer monitored. Then, each Local Agent analyzes the data of its specific layer, and it checks in real-time that the thresholds previously established are not exceeded. If a threshold is exceeded, an 'alert' is sent to Central Agent. This approach is effective to detect multi-layer flooding attacks but there are some disadvantages that limit this solution. The nodes of a WSN are devices with limited resources in terms of memory, CPU, energy and storage space, instead Local Agents perform resource-consuming activities; e.g. memory space is necessary to store its own code and temporary results of features computation; CPU slots are required to perform jobs related to security analysis; the usage of the antenna is necessary to transmit the 'alert' to Central Agent. Moreover, e.g. the usage of two Local Agents to protect two layers involved by cyber attacks increases the usage of resources required with respect to the former solution with a single Local Agent. This has a negative impact on battery consumption. We emphasize that most of the battery consumption in a node is due to the communication module (dozens or hundreds of mA).

Another solution to detect multi-layer flooding attack is the following. Each node is equipped with a single Local Agent that analyzes data provided by both application and routing layers. In this way the Local Agent can use data gathered by both layers to detect flooding attacks. Also a feature selection algorithm can detect redundant data provided by different layers that can be discarded. This can reduce the number of features that must be monitored to detect multi-layer flooding attacks. Another advantage of this approach is that the Local Agent can transmit 'summary frames' to the Central Agent which contain information about both layers monitored. This solution allows a reduction of battery consumption with respect to a solution that computes all of the features of the layers monitored, however still a high number of features has to be computed in order to detect multi-layer flooding attacks with respect to the single-layer solution.

The last solution analyzed and chosen in this paper is to use a Local Agent which monitors features relevant to the attacks considered and independent of the specific layer the attack is performed at. For instance, in the case of multi-layer flooding attack, a relevant feature may be the energy consumption on the node. This is because a generic flooding attack can be considered layer independent, i.e. it is characterized by a malicious node that sends packets to a target node continuously. Often these packets do not have a specific purpose and they can also be malformed; however, packets received must be processed before being discarded by the node even if they contain replayed or malformed data, so energy consumption is affected by such operations in any case.

The idea proposed in this work is to use the battery consumed by each node as the only feature to be monitored to detect multi-layer flooding attacks. In particular, each Local Agent can detect the anomalous behavior of the node using a single feature, thus ensuring a lower energy and resources consumption with reference to approaches previously described. At the same time, the detection accuracy is not decreased since the Central Agent validates the anomaly detected by the Local Agent by requesting additional information. With respect to the solution with one Local Agent monitoring two different OSI levels, the approach proposed is lighter in terms of computational resources because it is based on one Local Agent per node that analyzes the values of one feature i.e. battery consumption. A lower number of computations also implies a battery-saving of the node.

## 4   Testbed and Experimental Results

An experimental testbed was simulated through Network Simulator v.3 (NS-3)[14]. In Table 1 the operating conditions implemented are described. In the first test a typical operating condition of WSNs was implemented e.g. environmental monitoring; in this scenario, each node performs environmental measurements within an area to be monitored. Measurements obtained by nodes are periodically sent to the BS which gathers those data for monitoring purposes. Typical scenarios of this kind of activities are viticulture and bridge monitoring [1] [15]. In [1] [15] authors show that a dozen of nodes are required to monitor the global area. Path based DoS and sleep deprivation attacks were also implemented in NS-3, so to reproduce two different attack scenarios which affect different OSI layers. So, two simulations were obtained and in each of them the network is affected by just one of the mentioned attacks; as stated before, our purpose was to test whether flooding attacks at two different layers can be detected by making use of the knowledge of just one parameter, specifically the battery consumption of the node.

**Table 1.** Testbed settings

| | |
|---|---|
| Network Simulator | NS-3[14] |
| Number of nodes simulated | 12 |
| Test 1 | Environmental monitoring |
| | Path based DoS attack (t≈840 [s]) |
| Test 2 | Sleep deprivation attack (t>0 [s]) |
| Nodes coverage area | 400mx300m |
| Routing Protocol | AODV |

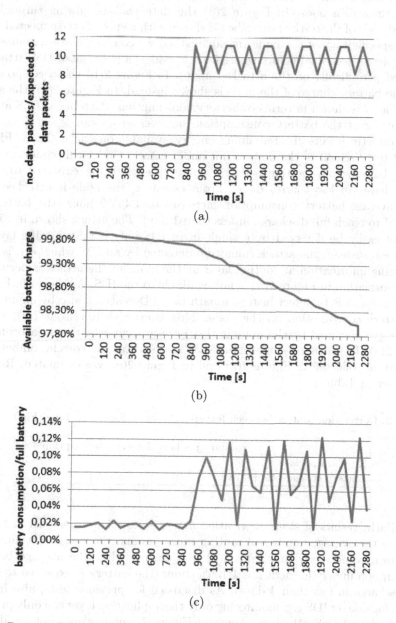

**Fig. 2.** Data packets profile, available charge and battery consumption profile on a WSN node under path based DoS attack

In Figure 2 the results of the simulation under path based DoS attack are shown, where a useful feature to detect this attack is the number of data packets flowing through a node. In Figure 2(a) the data packets flowing through an attacked node of the testbed described is shown with respect to the expected data for the specific task of the node (in our testbed we consider the environmental monitoring as described before where from t≈840 [s] a path based DoS attack is launched periodically on the attacked node). In Figure 2(b) the corresponding available battery charge of the node is shown instead. In Figure 2(c), the same battery level is shown in terms of battery consumption. Path based DoS attack does not target the battery consumption, however as we can see in figure the attack directly affects the remaining energy available on the node. In Figure 2(a), at $0 < t < 840$ [s] the node is not under attack. Under this condition, the average battery consumption is 0.857%/hour (the battery is expected to reach full discharge in less than 5 days). From t≈840 [s] the node is attacked and so the average battery consumption increases to 4.435%/hour (the battery is expected to reach full discharge in less than 1 day). The attack shown in Figure 2(a) can easily be detected by a single-layer IDS only if that specific layer is monitored. Instead, the attack cannot be detected by an IDS which e.g. is only monitoring information at routing layer at the moment the attack is occurring since information in Figure 2(a) is not available to the IDS. As shown in Figure 2(b), it is possible to detect instead a path based DoS attack also by monitoring the battery consumption on the node. This is even clearer from 2(c), where the energy consumed by the node is clearly very similar to the data profile in Figure 2(a). To prove the similarity of such information, the correlation between information collected in Figure 2(a) and in Figure 2(c) was estimated. Results are shown in Table 2.

**Table 2.** Correlation Matrix between features shown in Figure 2(a) and Figure 2(c)

|                     | No. data packets | Battery consumption |
| ------------------- | ---------------- | ------------------- |
| No. data packets    | 1                | 0.78                |
| Battery consumption | 0.78             | 1                   |

Similarly, results of sleep deprivation attack simulation are shown in Figure 3, where the average number of routing messages and the energy consumption are shown respectively in Figure 3(a) and Figure 3(b). The average battery consumption under this attack is 1.130%/hour (the battery is expected to reach full discharge in less than 4 days). As discussed for previous tests, also in this case a single-layer IDS e.g. monitoring only the application layer can only prevent the path based DoS attack as shown in Figure 2, but it would not be able to detect sleep deprivation as relevant information for this attack are available at routing layer. Sleep deprivation attack could be detected instead by a single-layer IDS placed at routing level which monitors the average number of routing messages. However, the energy consumed by the node also provides a very similar information about the ongoing attack. Thus, in both the experiments shown the

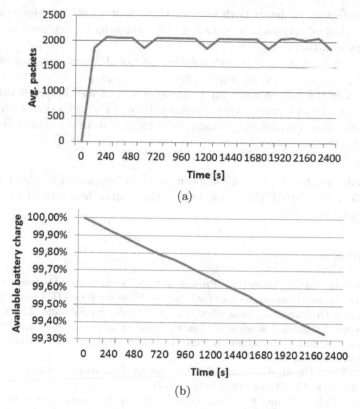

**Fig. 3.** Average routing messages and battery consumption on a WSN node under sleep deprivation attack

battery consumption is a significant feature to detect any of those attacks, as also shown by the correlation matrix in Table 2. An IDS could then monitor only the battery consumption and be able to detect multi-layer flooding attacks.

## 5    Conclusions

In this paper we focused on reducing the number of features required on WSN nodes to detect multi-layer flooding attacks. In fact, WSN nodes are devices with limited resources so intrusion detection activities should be as light as possible in order to be suitable on such devices. Experimental tests were performed through network simulator NS-3 to detect such features with respect to two flooding attacks launched at different layers, specifically path based DoS attack at application layer and sleep deprivation attack at routing layer. The two experiments performed clearly show that the same, single-layer IDS could not detect both sleep deprivation and path based DoS attacks by monitoring information available only at one specific layer. Energy consumption was found instead to be a significant feature to detect both attacks; this result allows to reduce the computational effort of intrusion detection architectures to be deployed on WSNs for this type of attacks.

In the future we plan to test such solution on Local Agents running on WSN nodes; our purpose will be to deploy one Local Agent per node where energy consumption is the only feature for local detection of multi-layer flooding attacks and one global Central Agent which validates the detection activities of Local Agents. Also, we plan to estimate the detection accuracy of such Intrusion Detection System.

**Acknowledgments.** This work has been partially supported by the TENACE PRIN Project (n. 20103P34XC) funded by the Italian Ministry of Education, University and Research.

# References

1. Sensors Mag - Smart Viticulture Project in Spain Uses Sensor Devices to Harvest Healthier, More Abundant Grapes for Coveted Albarino Wines (February 24, 2014)
2. Afzaal, M., Di Sarno, C., Coppolino, L., D'Antonio, S., Romano, L.: A resilient architecture for forensic storage of events in critical infrastructures. In: 2012 IEEE 14th International Symposium on High-Assurance Systems Engineering (HASE), pp. 48–55 (October 2012)
3. Bhattasali, T., Chaki, R., Sanyal, S.: Sleep deprivation attack detection in wireless sensor network. CoRR, abs/1203.0231 (2012)
4. Boubiche, D.E., Bilami, A.: Cross layer intrusion detection system for wireless sensor network. International Journal of Network Security & Its Applications 4 (2012)
5. Camastra, F., Ciaramella, A., Staiano, A.: Machine learning and soft computing for ict security: an overview of current trends. Journal of Ambient Intelligence and Humanized Computing 4(2), 235–247 (2013)
6. Coppolino, L., D'Antonio, S., Garofalo, A., Romano, L.: Applying data mining techniques to intrusion detection in wireless sensor networks. In: 2013 Eighth International Conference on P2P, Parallel, Grid, Cloud and Internet Computing (3PG-CIC), pp. 247–254 (October 2013)
7. Coppolino, L., D'Antonio, S., Romano, L., Spagnuolo, G.: An intrusion detection system for critical information infrastructures using wireless sensor network technologies. In: 2010 5th International Conference on Critical Infrastructure (CRIS), pp. 1–8 (September 2010)
8. Department of Homeland Security. What is critical infrastructure?
9. Ficco, M., Coppolino, L., Romano, L.: A weight-based symptom correlation approach to sql injection attacks. In: Fourth Latin-American Symposium on Dependable Computing, LADC 2009, pp. 9–16 (September 2009)
10. Garofalo, A., Di Sarno, C., Formicola, V.: Enhancing intrusion detection in wireless sensor networks through decision trees. In: Vieira, M., Cunha, J.C. (eds.) EWDC 2013. LNCS, vol. 7869, pp. 1–15. Springer, Heidelberg (2013)
11. Gnawali, O., Fonseca, R., Jamieson, K., Moss, D., Levis, P.: Collection Tree Protocol. In: Proceedings of the 7th ACM Conference on Embedded Networked Sensor Systems (SenSys 2009) (November 2009)

12. Hsu, K., Leung, M.-K., Su, B.: Security analysis on defenses against sybil attacks in wireless sensor networks
13. Khan, S., Loo, K.K., Din, Z.U.: Cross layer design for routing and security in multi-hop wireless networks. Journal of Information Assurance and Security 4, 170–173 (2009)
14. National Science Foundation and Planète group. ns-3 (2012), http://www.nsnam.org/ (last accessed November 28, 2012)
15. Hoult, N., Wu, Y., Wassell, I., Bennett, P., Soga, K., Middleton, C.: Wireless sensor networks for infrastructure monitoring: Radio propagation. Technical report, Computer Laboratory & Department of Engineering. University of Cambridge
16. Perkins, C., Royer, E., Das, S.: RFC 3561 Ad hoc On-Demand Distance Vector (AODV) Routing. Technical report (2003)
17. Wang, X., Wong, J., Stanley, F., Basu, S.: Cross-layer based anomaly detection in wireless mesh networks. In: Ninth Annual International Symposium on Applications and the Internet, SAINT 2009, pp. 9–15 (July 2009)

# Towards a Non-intrusive Recognition of Anomalous System Behavior in Data Centers

Roberto Baldoni[1], Adriano Cerocchi[2], Claudio Ciccotelli[1], Alessandro Donno[1], Federico Lombardi[1], and Luca Montanari[1]

[1] Cyber Intelligence and Information Security Research Center,
"Sapienza" University of Rome,
Via Ariosto, 25, Rome, Italy
[2] Over Technologies, Rome, Italy
{baldoni,ciccotelli,lombardi,montanari}@dis.uniroma1.it,
cerocchi@overtechnologies.it, ale.dnn@gmail.com

**Abstract.** In this paper we propose a monitoring system of a data center that is able to infer when the data center is getting into an anomalous behavior by analyzing the power consumption at each server and the data center network traffic. The monitoring system is non-intrusive in the sense that there is no need to install software on the data center servers. The monitoring architecture embeds two Elman Recurrent Networks (RNNs) to predict power consumed by each data center component starting from data center network traffic and viceversa. Results obtained along six mounts of experiments, within a data center, show that the architecture is able to classify anomalous system behaviors and normal ones by analyzing the error between the actual values of power consumption and network traffic and the ones inferred by the two RNNs.

**Keywords:** monitoring, failure prediction, dependability, critical infrastructure, data centers, power consumption, network traffic, non-intrusive, black box.

## 1 Introduction

Data centers represent the continuously-growing core infrastructure of every digital service and a basic pillar of our economy. Thus it is imperative to increase their resiliency to failures of internal components like switches, wires, servers, storage etc in order that the failure of one or a few components will not have a major degradation on the performance and on the availability of the software services hosted by the data center. Assuming that components can fail unexpectedly during service operation, to increase such resiliency there is the need of advanced monitoring system at data center scale that are able to infer if something is going wrong in order to take appropriate actions at due time. Almost all such monitoring systems are developed as intrusive software in the sense that they need to install an agent on each monitored system, sharing resources with the monitored system. Apart of the disturbance that agents can provoke to the

A. Bondavalli et al. (Eds.): SAFECOMP 2014 Workshops, LNCS 8696, pp. 350–359, 2014.

monitored system, this approach imposes a large usage of human resource to install and to keep updated the monitoring agents with the consequent explosion of operative cost. Thus a suitable approach to datacenter monitoring should minimize the deployment and management costs being also agnostic with respect to applications running in the data center. Agnosticness can be achieved by using a black-box approach to monitoring.

For black-box monitoring we mean the monitoring system can only have access to external health indicators such as: temperature, humidity, network flows, power consumption. In a previous work [5] we considered network traffic exchanges among the data center servers and their power consumption showing the there is a sharp correlation between these two metrics. In this paper we exploit this result in order to detect an anomalous behavior of data center servers.

Thus we present NiTREC, a non-intrusive monitoring architecture that takes as input data center network traffic and the aggregate of servers' power consumption. The network traffic is used to infer data center power consumption and vice versa. Thus NiTREC is able to recognize any deviation of the data center behavior by evaluating the error between inferred values and actual values. Two Elman Recurrent Networks (RNNs) are used in Nitrec to infer the aggregate power consumption and data center network traffic.

In order to assess NiTREC capabilities, we did an extensive experimental evaluation in a real data center owned by the Italian Ministry of Economy and Finance. After an accurate training of the RNNs, we show that NiTREC is able to recognize deviations from the normal system behavior with a high level of accuracy. We also compare accuracy obtained by each of the two RNNs.

## 2  Background

To better understand the architecture functioning, some details about non-intrusive monitoring and about Artificial Neural Networks are required. After these details, NiTREC architecture is presented.

*Non-intrusive Monitoring.* An intrusive approach to monitoring relies on installing software probes on each single monitored component (e.g., blade servers). The management cost of the monitoring system (installation, configuration, etc.), in terms of human and economic resources, in such complex environments can be excessive or even prohibitive for many organizations. Conversely, a non-intrusive approach does not require to install software on each server. Instead, it relies on a small number of hardware probes properly deployed leading to more affordable management costs. For this reason a non-intrusive approach is often an appealing solution, to be deployed together to legacy monitoring systems.

We considered two quantities that can be monitored without installing software on observed systems: network traffic and power consumption. Network traffic can be monitored directly at the network switches level, using network sniffers deployed in strategic positions of the data centers. Indicators like packet rate, bandwidth, message size can be in this way easily computed. Power consumption can be monitored by deploying very precise energy meters, in order to solve the problem due to the fact that blade servers-based systems aggregate the consumption. Active power, Reactive power and phase displacement can be measured.

*Artificial Neural Networks.* An *Artificial Neural Network* (ANN) is a machine learning computational model capable to approximate any non-linear function of its input, widely used for pattern recognition and forecasting. ANN are structured as a weighted interconnection system of neurons spread in levels, where the input level contains the neurons corresponding to the features, the output level contains the neurons with the estimated resulted values and in the middle, in order to improve the prediction accuracy, one or more hidden levels could be insert. The weights of each neuron interconnection are tuned by a learning algorithm, generally based on gradient-descent as the Backpropagation, the most popular one [19]. Time-series forecasting, in particular for power electric load, is a well-known problem often addressed with ANNs [11, 13, 7].

Our aim is to exploit the ANN capabilities to infer real-time power consumption starting from network traffic observation and viceversa: to infer network traffic starting from power consumption measurement. The core concept that made this possible is the correlation among the two metrics found in [5].

## 3   NiTREC Architecture

The architecture that we present here has been named NiTREC, Non-inTrusive deviation Recognizer Exploiting Correlation. It is designed to monitor in a non-intrusive way a single enclosure of a datacenter, to learn the correct system behavior and to recognize deviations from that. Considering the advantages of having a non-intrusive system to monitor and enhance resiliency of a critical infrastructure data center, we designed and implemented the NiTREC architecture so as to measure and to correlate network data and power consumption in real time, using artificial neural networks. NiTREC is able to recognize deviations from the correct system behavior after an initial phase of training. The architecture is depicted in Figure 1. The whole architecture lives inside a centralizer, an ordinary computer or a blade server, collecting measurement from the network traffic and the power consumption probes. It takes in input (i) $n$ streams of network packets[1], directly produced by $n$ probes (network sniffers that capture packets from the switches of the observed system) and (ii) a stream of power consumption data from the smart-PDUs (that measure with high precision the power consumption of the monitored enclosure) developed by Over [1]. The architecture produces in output alerts as soon as the monitoring system recognizes deviations from the correct enclosure behavior. Three modules compose the architecture, a description of them is now provided:

---

[1] In the well-known pcap format.

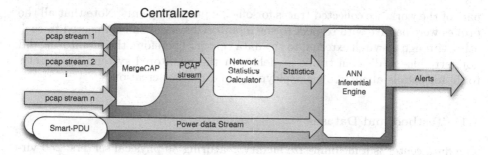

**Fig. 1.** NiTREC, a non-intrusive deviation recognizer exploiting correlation between power consumption and network traffic

*MergeCAP* a software module that takes in input $n$ streams of captured packets and gives in output a single network stream opportunely merged[2].

*Network Statistics Calculator* a software module that takes in input the network stream and, according to a set of parameters, produces in real-time indicators (e.g., message rate, bandwidth, message size, message rate per physical machine). The indicators are grouped in tuples and produced in real-time with a given frequency, for instance, one tuple per second. This led to have a snapshot of the observed system per second, for example, if we consider message rate, bandwidth, tcp messages, average message size, we would have a tuple, like the following, per second:$< sec : 3; 4387 msg/s; 14042896 bps; 2632 tcp\_msgs; 400 byte >$ meaning that during the third second of observation there have been 4387 messages, a mean bandwidth of 14042896 bit per second, 2632 tcp messages and an average message size of 400 bytes.

*ANN Inferential Engine* a software module that using indicators tuples received from the previous module and power consumption data, correlates them and according to an implementation of artificial neural network, triggers timely alerts if it recognizes deviations from correct system behavior. The ANN Inferential Engine is a crucial part of the architecture, which requires an accurate learning phase in order to build a knowledge base regarding the observed system, more details are provided in Sec. 4.

## 4    Experimental Analysis

We conducted a six months long experimental session along with Sogei s.p.a., a company of Italian Ministry of Economic and Finance (MEF) that manage the IT of the ministry. In particular we deployed the NiTREC architecture in order to monitor a single enclosure of one of the data centers of MEF. For this initial

---

[2] Merging network traces is a solved problem, several tools are available. A synchronization of the probes is required e.g., a NTP server.

part of the work, we collected traces for off-line processing only. Note that all the probes were passive with respect to the monitored system and connected to each other through a switch external to the data center. Therefore, the monitoring did not introduce additional traffic or delays in the monitored system.Please refer to [5] for details about probes deployment and dataset creation.

### 4.1   Testbed and Dataset

The data center is a medium-size facility, featuring 80 physical servers; 250 virtual servers; 20 network devices; 8 security devices; more than 50 different Web Applications; 2 Storage Area Network with more than 6 TB of disk space; more than 1000 internal users and more 80.000 external managed single users; We monitored a single enclosure that embeds 5 blade servers, 40 virtual machines, 4 network switches[3]. Each blade server has 24 cores and 64 GB of RAM. We recorded a mean packet rate around 2000 pps, with spikes from 10000 to 25000000 pps while the active power consumed is between 1550 and 1600 watts. The dataset created is composed by approximately 2.5 TB of pcap network traces and power consumption data, representing the behavior of the monitored servers from a network and power consumption point of view, during the period 31 July 2013 - 31 January 2014.

### 4.2   Neural Networks Implementation and Details

For this work we used Encog 3.2.0 [2] as machine learning framework to employ two Elman Recurrent Networks, namely: RNN1, which is designed to infer power consumption having packet rate as input and RNN2, which is designed to infer packet rate having power consumption as input. In particular, RNN1 and RNN2 are both 4-5-1 networks: 4 inputs nodes, a single hidden layer of 5 nodes and the output node. RNN1 takes as input packet rate, day, hour and power consumption at the last-seen instant. It produces as output the inferred power consumption. RNN2 takes as input power consumption and traffic rate at the last-seen instant, day and hour. It produce as output the inferred packet rate.

Both the RNNs are trained using Resilient Backpropagation algorithm[12] as long as the choice of the input node variables is due to a hybrid approach between time-series and features, as suggested in [4].

### 4.3   Preliminary Results

The idea of the experimental campaign is to evaluate the ability of the approach in recognizing deviations from normal behavior of the observed system. In particular, we evaluated two cases: estimating power consumption from packet rate and viceversa. In order to do that, we used RNN1 and RNN2 after a learning

---

[3] Network traffic has been monitored through 4 hardware probes attached to the switches.

phase. We used a small part of the dataset (10 days) as training set and a different part (3 days) as validation set. Note that the validation phase is performed off-line, using traces, but is completely equivalent to a physical deployment of the architecture, in detection mode. Not having the possibility to inject faults in the observed system[4], during the validation, we introduced a deviation in the metric used to infer the other and we observed how the deviation reflects on values inferred by the RNN. The idea behind this approach is that a deviation (e.g., an unjustified augment of power consumption), may reveal a faulty behavior of software or hardware components. We found the percent error $\delta = 100 \times |\frac{v - v_{inferred}}{v}|$ where $v_{inferred}$ is the inferred value and $v$ is the actual value to be an effective metric to detect deviations. When the percent error exceeds a given threshold $\hat{\delta}$, we trigger an alert. The threshold $\hat{\delta}$ has been chosen in order to maximize the F-measure (see below) but more complex approaches can be considered. Figure 2 and Figure 3 graph the behavior of active power, packet rate and percent error during time. The chosen threshold of percent error has been depicted and the samples over this that have been highlighted as well. In the first case, represented in Figure 2, we deployed RNN2, which infers packet rate starting from power consumption. In the first part of the graph, until 12:00, the ability of RNN2 in its inference task can be appreciated. After that, we started to progressively increase the power consumption at 12.00 causing an increase of the percent error. Even small unattended increases of power consumption quickly cause an augment of alert, due to augments of percentage error. In the second case (see Figure 3) we deployed RNN1, in order to infer power consumption starting from network traffic. Also in this case, during the first part of the graph (until time 12:00) the ability of RNN1 its inference task can be appreciated, which is better respect the RNN2 case. After that, we started to inject spare packets incrementally. The inferred power consumption started to deviate from the measured power, thus augmenting the percent error, as soon as the packet rate reached 10000 pps. In this case a more relevant deviation is required in order to have appreciable variation in the inferred value. Note that, according to the low error obtained during the period of normal functioning, an augment of the error can fairly be assumed as an uncommon situation.

In order to better evaluate the accuracy of the proposed approach in both cases, we computed the metrics reported in Tab. 1 and Tab. 2, where $N_{tp}$ (number of true positives) indicates the number of alerts correctly produced, i.e., during a deviation from the correct system behavior; $N_{tn}$ (number of true negatives) is the number of samples of percent error that correctly are under the alert threshold, i.e., during correct system behavior; $N_{fp}$ (number of false positive) is the number of alerts incorrectly produced, i.e., during correct system behavior and finally $N_{fn}$ (number of false negatives) is the number samples that incorrectly are under the alert threshold, during a deviation from the correct system behavior.

---

[4] The system is not a test environment but a real Critical Infrastructure datacenter enclosure in production.

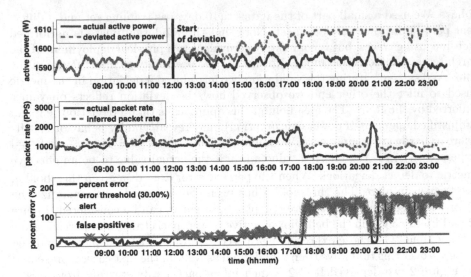

**Fig. 2.** RNN2 results. Packet rate is inferred with a good accuracy until 12:00, where the power consumption has been progressively increased causing an augment of the error. Some false positives can be seen before 9:00. The first true positive alert has been triggered at 12:00.

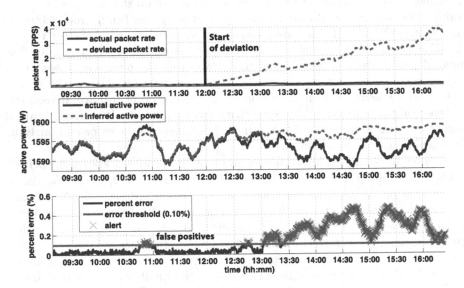

**Fig. 3.** RNN1 results. Power consumption is inferred with a better accuracy until 12:00, w.r.t. RNN2. After that, spare packets have been injected in the network trace causing an augment of the error. Some false positives can be seen before 11:00. The first true positive alert has been triggered at 12:40.

**Table 1.** RNN1 accuracy

| Precision: $p = \frac{N_{tp}}{N_{tp}+N_{fp}}$ | 85.34% |
|---|---|
| Recall (TP rate): $r = \frac{N_{tp}}{N_{tp}+N_{fn}}$ | 87.45% |
| F-measure: $F = 2 \times \frac{p \times r}{p+r}$ | 86.38% |
| FP Rate: $f.p.r. = \frac{N_{fp}}{N_{fp}+N_{tn}}$ | 3.00% |

**Table 2.** RNN2 accuracy

| Precision: $p = \frac{N_{tp}}{N_{tp}+N_{fp}}$ | 90.67% |
|---|---|
| Recall (TP rate): $r = \frac{N_{tp}}{N_{tp}+N_{fn}}$ | 71.42% |
| F-measure: $F = 2 \times \frac{p \times r}{p+r}$ | 79.90% |
| FP Rate: $f.p.r. = \frac{N_{fp}}{N_{fp}+N_{tn}}$ | 1.47% |

In both cases we can see a very low false positive rate and a F-measure of at least of 79.9%, attesting promising future developments of the approach.

## 5  Related Work

Monitoring based only on network traffic is recognized to be non-intrusive and black-box, meaning that (i) no application-level knowledge is needed to perform the monitoring [18, 3, 6], and (ii) the monitor mechanism does not install software on the monitored system [6]. In [6] CASPER is presented, a non-intrusive and black-box approach to monitor air traffic control systems. It uses network traffic only in order to represent the system health so as to recognize deviations thus triggering failure predictions. At the best of our knowledge, this is the only work that is both non-intrusive and black-box. Other monitoring systems that adopt a black-box approach are Tiresias [18] and ALERT [14], however they are intrusive as they require monitoring software installed on the monitored system. For what concern power consumption monitoring in data centers, studies have been conducted in the context of power management and energy efficiency [10, 16, 17]. None of these works, however, concerns dependability and resiliency. In [8] and [15] network traffic is monitored with the aim of consolidating traffic flows onto a small set of links and switches so as to shut down unused network elements, thereby reducing power consumption. However, there is no attempt to correlate network traffic and power consumption. In [9] a study on correlation between power consumption data and utilization statistics (CPU load and network traffic) is presented. This work shows a strong correlation between power consumption and CPU load of desktop computers. Our previous work [5] investigates the correlation between power consumption and network traffic to support the design of a non-intrusive black-box failure prediction system for improving data center resiliency. The paper reports the results of a period of experimentation conducted in one of the data centers of the Italian Ministry of Economic and Finance (MEF) during which a large dataset of network traffic and power consumption data is collected and analyzed, thus showing that correlation between these data exists in many periods. To the best of our knowledge this was the first work that explored the possibility to exploit correlation between power consumption and network traffic to support dependability of a system. In this work we used the same dataset.

# 6  Conclusions and Future Work

This work is a first step in exploiting in a non-intrusive way the correlation between network data and power consumption to recognize and predict component failures in data centers. During a preliminary 6-months long experimental campaign we created a dataset (in a completely non-intrusive way) with respect to the data center's components (network and servers). The dataset allowed us to train two neural networks in order to estimate power consumption observing network traffic and vice versa. We found that the neural networks can be used to effectively detect anomalous system behavior looking at deviations from data center network traffic and an aggregate of power consumption of each data center component. A deviation from the behavior, learnt during the training phase, can be used to trigger alerts. As future work, we need to reduce the level of granularity of the study by looking at correlation on the behavior of a single data center component. In this paper we are only considering correlation between aggregate measures, namely network traffic and power consumption. We are finally developing more complex alert techniques in order to provide a more effective detection with respect to the threshold mechanism used in this work.

**Acknowledgment.** This work was partially supported by the PRIN project TENACE. The authors would like to thank the Italian Ministry of Economy and Finance for allowing the experimentation in their data centers.

# References

[1] Over s.r.l. website, http://www.overtechnologies.com
[2] Encog Machine Learning Framework (2008), http://www.heatonresearch.com/encog/
[3] Aguilera, M.K., Mogul, J.C., Wiener, J.L., Reynolds, P., Muthitacharoen, A.: Performance debugging for distributed systems of black boxes. SIGOPS Oper. Syst. Rev. 37, 74–89 (2003)
[4] Aniello, L., Baldoni, R., Bonomi, S., Lombardi, F., Zelli, A.: An Architecture for Automatic Scaling of Replicated Services. To appear in the Proceedings of the 2nd International Conference on NETworked sYStems (NETYS), vol. 5 (2014)
[5] Baldoni, R., Caruso, M., Cerocchi, A., Ciccotelli, C., Montanari, L., Nicoletti, L.: Correlating power consumption and network traffic for improving data centers resiliency. ArXiv e-prints (May 2014)
[6] Baldoni, R., Lodi, G., Montanari, L., Mariotta, G., Rizzuto, M.: Online black-box failure prediction for mission critical distributed systems. In: Ortmeier, F., Lipaczewski, M. (eds.) SAFECOMP 2012. LNCS, vol. 7612, pp. 185–197. Springer, Heidelberg (2012)
[7] Frank, R.J., Davey, N., Hunt, S.P.: Time series prediction and neural networks. Journal of Intelligent and Robotic Systems 31(1-3), 91–103 (2001)
[8] Heller, B., Seetharaman, S., Mahadevan, P., Yiakoumis, Y., Sharma, P., Banerjee, S., McKeown, N.: Elastictree: Saving energy in data center networks. In: Proceedings of the 7th USENIX Conference on Networked Systems Design and Implementation, NSDI 2010, p. 17. USENIX Association, Berkeley (2010)

[9] Kazandjieva, M., Heller, B., Levis, P., Kozyrakis, C.: Energy dumpster diving. In: SOSP 2009: Proceedings of the ACM SIGOPS 22nd Symposium on Operating Systems Principles. ACM, New York (2009)

[10] Lefurgy, C., Wang, X., Ware, M.: Power capping: A prelude to power shifting. Cluster Computing 11(2), 183–195 (2008)

[11] Park, D.C., El-Sharkawi, M.A., Marks, R.J., Atlas, L.E., Damborg, M.J., et al.: Electric load forecasting using an artificial neural network. IEEE Transactions on Power Systems 6(2), 442–449 (1991)

[12] Riedmiller, M., Braun, H.: A direct adaptive method for faster backpropagation learning: The rprop algorithm. In: IEEE International Conference on Neural Networks, pp. 586–591. IEEE (1993)

[13] Senjyu, T., Takara, H., Uezato, K., Funabashi, T.: One-hour-ahead load forecasting using neural network. IEEE Transactions on Power Systems 17(1), 113–118 (2002)

[14] Tan, Y., Gu, X., Wang, H.: Adaptive system anomaly prediction for large-scale hosting infrastructures. In: Proc. of ACM PODC 2010, pp. 173–182. ACM, New York (2010)

[15] Wang, X., Yao, Y., Wang, X., Lu, K., Cao, Q.: Carpo: Correlation-aware power optimization in data center networks. In: 2012 Proceedings IEEE INFOCOM, pp. 1125–1133 (March 2012)

[16] Wang, X., Chen, M.: Cluster-level feedback power control for performance optimization. In: IEEE 14th International Symposium on High Performance Computer Architecture, HPCA 2008, pp. 101–110 (February 2008)

[17] Wang, X., Wang, Y.: Co-con: Coordinated control of power and application performance for virtualized server clusters. In: 17th International Workshop on Quality of Service, IWQoS, pp. 1–9 (July 2009)

[18] Williams, A.W., Pertet, S.M., Narasimhan, P.: Tiresias: Black-box failure prediction in distributed systems. In: Proceedings of IEEE International Parallel and Distributed Processing Symposium (IPDPS 2007), Los Alamitos, CA, USA (2007)

[19] Zhang, G., Patuwo, B.E., Hu, M.Y.: Forecasting With Artificial Neural Networks: the State of the Art. International Journal of Forecasting 14(1), 35–62 (1998)

# Toward Resilience Assessment in Business Process Architectures

Richard M. Zahoransky, Thomas Koslowski, and Rafael Accorsi

University of Freiburg, Germany
{zahoransky,koslowski,accorsi}@iig.uni-freiburg.de

**Abstract.** This paper investigates options to access the resilience of business process architectures, thereby connecting the two hitherto unconnected areas of Business Process Management and Information System Resilience. The overarching goal is to provide for robust and reliable business process execution even under adverse and unexpected situations. Specifically, this paper focuses on one particular resilience indicator as a basis for assessment, namely *time*. This is because timeliness and time behavior of activities in business processes directly mirror effects and impacts of a changing environment on the business process. We develop an approach based on process mining to analyze the event logs generated during the execution of processes which extract probability distributions of a process's time behavior to model the effects of occured events. A case study substantiates the applicability of the approach.

## 1 Introduction

Resilience engineering is an important aspect of dependability, safety and security in complex Information Systems (IS) in general [7,14], and Business Process Management (BPM) in particular [4,11,13]. Instead of investigating operational risks based on subjective or historical probabilities of occurrence (focus on the *cause* of events), resilience shifts attention to the *consequences* [8,13]. Resilient systems accept and manage variability rather than trying to preventively mitigate or reduce it from the outset.

Among the various resilience indicators, time behavior of a business process shows its reaction on different type of events and threats, as they delay and slow down the processing [9]. A less sensitive process architecture will show smaller delays in its execution even upon high fluctuation of resources. In this paper we focus on the timeliness and time behavior of processes for resilience assessment, addressing in particular single processes.

Notwithstanding that resilience is getting much attention in related disciplines such as Computer Science [20] or Safety Engineering [12], there is an apparent incongruity between the level of interest paid by business managers and the attention that BPM scholars have given to resilience [4,14]. BPM promises valuable development towards organizational resilience as a supportive part for applying preventive, containment and mitigation measures in the face of challenging conditions [4]. However, the majority of recent work remains on a pure conceptual level while techniques with actual implementation and validation are rare [14].

A. Bondavalli et al. (Eds.): SAFECOMP 2014 Workshops, LNCS 8696, pp. 360–370, 2014.
© Springer International Publishing Switzerland 2014

Concretely, this paper investigates the use of Process Mining (PM) for resilience detection. PM stands for automatable techniques to analyze business process models and their execution traces (logs) [1]. We developed a framework on which data from the PM is further processed on, allowing the extraction of resilience indicators. Focusing on compliance checking, we report on a case study for the manufacturing sector. The investigation follows the guidelines of [18] for conducting and reporting case studies. In particular, we used interviews to obtain: firstly, the shape of a non-trivial order-to-cash workflow; secondly, the set of concrete resilience requirements derived from the set of global business process security requirements [5]; and thirdly, the usual execution characteristics.

Our overarching goal is to bring together IS resilience and BPM, thereby casting resilience engineering into the context of enterprise systems. To this end, we present a method to model the amount of resources required as a stochastic function and to sum up the need for the whole business process, including its branches. We focus on the temporal aspects of the process and, as a resilience indicator, investigate its time behavior. In our calculations, probability distribution functions (PDF) are used instead of using classical numerical values. Using distribution functions open up the possibility of considering and measuring uncertainty and to compensate for unknown future risks and behaviors. Our method is not limited to standard distributions as in many of the previous works. Using PM, we extract the resource distribution as PDF for each activity.

In the case study used to illustrate the approach, we show that modeling the time behavior of a workflow as stochastic variable makes it possible to grasp the concept of resilience by providing a mathematical framework to deduce resilience indicators. The ultimate goal is to enable organizations to automatically identify and assess the interdependence of assets and processes, thereby lifting the approach to process architectures.

*Paper structure.* Section 2 elaborates on the research design, providing the basis of our contribution. Section 3 and 4 focus on the case study, whereas Section 5 compares our contribution with related work.

## 2    Method and Research Design

We employ the guidelines of [18] to conduct the case study. A case study is the most appropriate research methodology for this setting, as its primary objective is exploratory, with a flexible design, and collecting qualitative (instead of quantitative) data. Concretely, the case study encompasses the following steps:

1. *Case study design*: the objectives and objects of the case study are defined. This is given below.
2. *Preparation for data collection* (Sec. 3).
3. *Evidence collection*: carry out the analysis (Sec. 3.2).
4. *Analysis of collected data* (Sec. 3.3).

The "case under study" is the analysis of a real-life business process model and the log file it produces. The process comes from a medium sized company in Germany. Fig. 2 depicts the formalization of the process.

To present our approach we use a scenario based on an example workflow. This section is structured in three parts. First an introduction to the case is given. Then the requirements are stated. Third, the example is introduced. At the end the scenario is applied and analyzed.

## 2.1   Time Behavior of the Workflow - Calculus

The time distribution for the whole workflow can be calculated out of the time behavior of each activity. In our case the following rules apply:

**Sequential Activities.** Two activities with known duration pdf behave like one activity whose pdf is the convolved pdf of both activities. The convolution of two functions $f(t)$ and $g(t)$ is defined as

$$(f * g)(t) = \int f(t)g(x - \tau)\, \mathrm{d}\tau \tag{1}$$

For concrete functions, the integral becomes a sum.

The convolution can be seen as the weighted average of the two functions at moment t. The resulting function will have an area of 1, given the area under both functions is also 1. This means, if two pdfs are merged, the result will again be a pdf. As a rule of thumb, the variance increases and the mean gets shifted.

**Conditional Activities.** Convolution does not work for conditional activities. Depending on the outcome of the branch the one or the other path is taken. For computation the following procedure is done: First, each individual path is calculated. Second, each path is weighted with the probability that it is taken $(w_0 \cdots w_i)$. This number can be taken from process mining, it can be estimated or $\frac{1}{2}$ for each path, if unknown. After this, the function must be normalized. The area beneath the function must sum up to one. This is done by dividing the resulting function by its integral.

$$(f \vee g)(t) = \frac{w_0 \cdot f(t) + w_1 \cdot g(t)}{\int_0^\infty w_0 \cdot f(t) + w_1 \cdot g(t)\, \mathrm{d}t} \tag{2}$$

## 2.2   Resilience in Workflows

Different aspects must be taken into account to be able to measure the ability of a workflow to endure stress and to recover from it. According to [6], resilience may be defined as

$$R = \int_{t_0}^{t_1} 1 - Q(t)\, \mathrm{d}t$$

where $Q(t)$ is the quality of the system at time $t$. $t_0$ is the time where a shock took place and time $t_1$ after recovery of the shock. This resembles the resilience triangle [6]. In our case $Q(t)$ can be considered the on-time delivery reliability.

That is the probability that the desired outcome is reached until the deadline is due. This calculates to:

$$Q(t) = P(\text{duration} = t) = \int_0^t pdf(t)\, \mathrm{d}t = cdf(t) \tag{3}$$

where *pdf* is the resulting time distribution of the whole workflow (see Figure 1 where also deadline *d* is given). In the figure, the quality value $Q(t)$ is the shaded area below the curve. After a shock, this probability (hence, $Q(t)$) decreases and recovers again over time when new resources are built or are restored. *cdf* is the resulting cumulative probability distribution. The "R4 framework" developed by [6] points out four aspects of resilience, all of which can be used with our proposed approach:

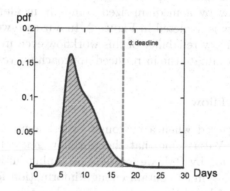

**Fig. 1.** Calculation for the quality of the given Workflow. Visualized as the shaded area below the pdf function from 0 to d.

**Robustness** is the capability to withstand a given level of stress without significant loss of function. It describes how sensitive the system is to shocks in its current state.

**Redundancy** is the extend to which elements, systems, or other units are substitutable.

**Resourcefulness** is the ability to diagnose problems and to initiate solutions by monitoring all resources and information.

**Rapidity** describes the property of the system to react fast to changes in its environment.

We plan to answer the following questions: Firstly, what guarantees can be made to the costumer regarding the duration of production? The answer will not be a simple time span but a more sophisticated calculation resulting in a pdf (workflow's completing time and related likelihood). Each activity is assigned a probability distribution used for calculations. It is later described how to obtain such distribution. Secondly, how resilient is the workflow against disruptive effects? If single activities fail, how does it affect the behavior of the whole workflow?

For this we evaluate the impact of each single activity on the whole workflow. This enables us to simulate the effect when some paths of the workflow are unavailable. To state probability values for the whole workflow, PM may be used to measure the individual time consumption of single activities. This enables us to calculate the overall workflow restrains. This is given in the next section. The PM returns historic data for instance running time. This data already includes instances where the completion of the workflow was not optimal due to different occasions, including malfunctions, external shocks or other difficulties. Instead of estimate each risk individual, they are extrapolated from the PM.

## 3    Case Study

To provide a basis for analyzing our framework within a realistic setting, an order-to-cash workflow by a medium-sized company in Germany was chosen. The example workflow is depicted in Figure 2. In our case we want to asses the resilience and the delivery reliability of this workflow even under turbulent situations. It is taken to evaluate the introduced approach for resilience assessment.

### 3.1    Example Workflow

The workflow is triggered when a customer orders a machinery, or anything that needs assembly. We assume that the workflow generates a trace inside a log. By utilizing this log by PM, we extract the timing information needed for our calculation. The log must contain enough information for the PM to work [3,13] (such as start and end time, activity ID and instance name). The timing behavior can still be extracted, even if the workflow model itself is not known.

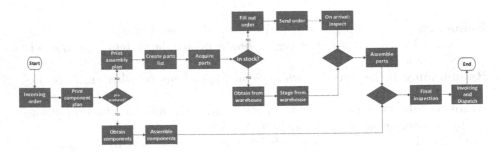

**Fig. 2.** Example workflow used in this paper. Each activity is denoted a probability density function that it will finish at the given time, see Table 1.

### 3.2    Evidence Collection

For each activity a PDF is extracted out of the process logs. Some standard activities take only short times with a low variance while customized or interrupted activities exhibit longer duration with high variability. This variability or risk is

**Table 1.** Time behavior of each single activity in the example workflow

| Activity | pdf: $(\mu, \sigma)$ or $(p, b)$ for $\gamma$-distribution |
| --- | --- |
| Incoming order | log-normal(0.2,0.4) |
| Print component plan | $\varphi$(0.5, 0.1) |
| Print assembly plan | $\varphi$(0.6, 0.15) |
| Create part list | $\gamma$(0.9, 0.7) |
| Acquire parts | $\gamma$(0.8, 0.8) |
| Fill out order | log-normal(0.1, 0.5) |
| Send order | $\gamma$(1, 0.5) |
| Arrival and inspection | log-normal(0.25, 0.5) |
| Obtain from warehouse | log-normal(0.07, 0.3) |
| Stage from warehouse | $\gamma$(0.8, 0.3) |
| Assemble parts | log-normal(1.3, 0.4) |
| Assemble Components | log-normal(0.4, 0.4) |
| Final inspection | $\varphi$(1, 0.4) |
| Invoicing and dispatch | $\varphi$(0.8, 0.3) |

modeled with a great variance in the time behavior distribution regardless the cause of delay.

In order to asses the resilience of a workflow we need information about the workflow's completing time. This might be a hard deadline or a point in time after which the service or product is no longer of value. In our example the requirement is that it must finish within a given number of days. The historic data from PM would than be used to calculate the probability that the current workflow model will end within this deadline. As this is an example workflow, no historic data is available. Hence, the time response of the single activities are described by common distribution. A short overview of the single activities are given:

## 3.3  Simulation Settings and Analysis

After applying the rules from Section 2.1, Figure 3 shows the resulting pdf and cummulative probability distributions (cdf) for the time behavior of the whole workflow. The continuous line is the result for the overall workflow. The remaning lines symbolize the individual paths within the workflow. The left figure shows the probability density scaled to one for each path. The right figure shows the overall probability that the workflow will end until the given time - the cdf. Again, for the overall workflow and for each single path of the workflow. The workflow has almost a 90 % change of finishing within 10  days under the assumption that the fastest path is taken but less than 10 % if the longest path is taken. If all OR-Splits are considered equally, the overall workfow still has a change of about 50 % to finish in that time.

It shows the probability distribution function of the duration time of the workflow. The higher its value (probability density) at time $t$, the higher is the probability that it will end at this specific point in time. Figure 3(a) shows

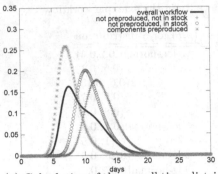

(a) Calculation of the overall time distribution for the example workflow and for each individual paths. Note: Each pdf's area is scaled to 1.

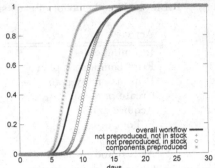

(b) Cumulative time distributions of the overall workflow and for each individual paths

**Fig. 3.** pdf calculation of the example workflow

the pdf for the overall workflow and for each of the possible paths of the workflow. For readability, the single pdfs are not weighted with their occurrence probability. Instead they are normalized so that the area accumulates to one.

Integrating the single pdf yields to the depicted cdfs in Figure 3(b). Its value shows the probability that the workflow will end until time $t$.

In this section, the results from the case study are discussed and evaluated.

## 4    Evaluation and Discussion

For our workflow, we calculated the following pdf by using the calculus from Section 3.3 as seen in Figure 1. We assume a certain deadline to depict our methodology. The calculated probability density function of the example workflow is also verified by a simulation of the workflow. In the simulation each activity is mapped to a random generator implementing the denoted probability density. The activities are started according to the structure of the workflow. Each path of an OR-decision is traversed with a probability of $\frac{1}{2}$. 100 million runs where simulated for the result depicted in figure 4.

Our evaluation shows 98.98 % probability, that the workflow is finished within 18 days even under disruptive events. As discussed previously, this value is not based on optimal or worst case scenarios as in previous works but a realistic estimate based on historic data that already includes adverse impacts. As seen in Figure 3(a), the greatest change for a delay is when parts are not preproduced and need to be ordered. The additional information can be extracted out of the time behavior: The robustness of a worklfow is expressed by the slope of the pdf. The steeper it is at the negotiated delivery time, the more susceptible the workflow is to external influences. In Figure 1, robustness can be expressed as the density of the pdf at the projected delivery time (near to zero). If an interruption happens, the workflow would take slightly longer. However, the overall

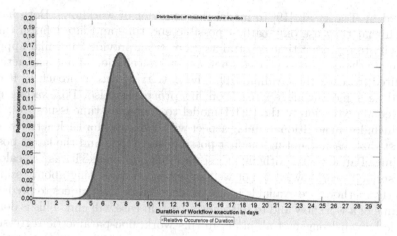

**Fig. 4.** Simulation of the needed time (100 Million runs, red bars) in the example workflow and calculated values (blue line)

probability of the intended completing time would not change significantly as the shattered area will not decrease much. The redundancy of a workflow can be calculated as the difference between actual probability of delivery compared to the negotiated delivery reliability. A higher success rate indicates a surplus on resources that increase the redundancy.

The quick and accurate information about the observed workflow further enhances the resourcefulness and rapidity of the IS: The calculations grant the possibility to react early to situations that are no longer covered by the worklfow's robustness or redundancy. Furthermore, our framework gives the possibility to compare different variations of the same workflow. This is useful for workflow engineers which start to redesign a given workflow. For each evolved design, they can compare robustness and redundancy. This also increases rapidity as the redesign process is more efficient and target-oriented.

It is now possible to rearrange the activities based on the learned numbers to further increase the operative viability (e.g. by creating the parts list in parallel to creating the components list). Despite the fact that it would slow down the best case, this modification could decrease the time required when the upper path is taken. It would therefore increase the systems capacities to absorb negative effects as the upper part is essentially involved in the delayed cases. The time behavior and thus the resilience levels of the re-designed workflow are instantaneously available as no new data is required.

## 5   Related Work and Addressed Shortcomings

Research about time behavior of workflows started in the middle of the 1970s. Ramchandani introduced timed petri nets [17] which he used to model the time response of asynchronous pipelined processors. Later, this method got adapted and used by Tsai et al. [19] to model the behavior of workflows. Both have in common that they use only earliest possible end time and latest finish time of an activity to represent time constraints. Eder et al. provided a similar approach to calculate the timeliness of a workflow or if a cancellation of optional activities is required to reach the deadline [10]. The novelty of this approach is, it could be used as a monitoring approach on life processes. Also, Pozewaunig et al. suggested an extension to the PERT model to cooperate time issues [16]. Their model includes an additional timing aspect with two cases for each activity: worst and best case, each denoting the first possible start time and the latest possible start time of an activity. Although these simplification make it easy to calculate and describe a workflow, it is not well suited when discussing about resilience. Currently, methods are available to use process mining techniques to predict the cycle time of a workflow and to tell when a certain case will end. This is done for example by van Dongen et al. in [9]. In this work, non-parametric regression of data records in event logs are used to estimate the remaining procession time of a running instance. In [2] the same question is addressed. A transition system is built to model the time behavior and to answer, if a given workflow will end in a given time-span. Also in that work, an implementation for the ProM toolbox is presented. Another way of dealing with temporal aspects of workflow is done by Pika et al. in [15]. They identified a set of Process Risk Indicators (PRI) which intend to capture the potential of delayed process executions.

Despite an undisputed value of existing works, a wide range of limitations for resilient BPM assessment exist:

Most approaches use parametric descriptions of time such as start/end time or best/worse case. Moreover, while some of todays approaches see time as a stochastic process, they often consider only Gaussian distributed values. Even the regression based method does only output single values as a possible remaining execution time and does not supply the user with a probability density function (pdf) for the remaining time. However, resilience strongly depends on the behavior between extrema (best case, worse case). The information on how the system reacts to changes in the environment lies within these two extreme boundaries (e.g. graceful degradation). The aspect of resilience can only be discussed when detailed behavior information of a workflow is given so that possible changes on a workflow model can be simulated accurately to deduce resilience key indicators. The here presented approach also gives the opportunity to test at which probability the workflow will end at which time through calculating the cumulative distribution function (cdf). Our method also makes a monitoring approach possible. When, during an active instance more information of the workflow are known, the estimation is recomputable and yields in a better forecast which can again be expressed as cdf so that a decisionmaker can efficiently judge the current instance in terms of availability, discrepancies and capable-to-promise aspects. Depending on the risk-appetite of a company the order promise can be evaluated at discretionary points and the method will return a success ratio for this point. By providing a fine grained probability value instead of providing only the information that the workflow will be delayed, our methods yields the possibility to estimate how much the workflow is delayed and at which time the delayed workflow will most likely finish. Our approach does not depend on the classification of PRI to make forecasts. Instead, by using PM on single activity basis, all risks that already occurred get encompassed and used for estimation calculations. It is also possible to use the extracted information for finished, single activities in non-finished instances.

# 6 Outlook and Conclusion

The proposed approach uses PM to create probability distributions on time behavior of worklfows. Instead of relying on an experts view who gauges the possible risk according to her experience, PM can help and automate this part. The resulting time probability provides an overall resilience estimation. Repeating this method yields in even more accurate results and finally enables a monitoring approach for resilience assessment during runtime. Our approach is not dependend on an overall workflow as each activity is considered on its own. This brings the advantage that the process log does not need to identically match the workflow, as long as the single activities correspond. A remodeled workflow can thus be simulated and compared to the original one by using the same process log. This comparison can be on different resilience dimensions to support worklfow designers to improve existing workflows. During execution of a workflow the current resilience level can be monitored and countermeasures can be initiated on run-time if the level drops.

In the future, we intend to empirically evaluate the effectiveness of the PM data with our interview partners in practice. This comparison will allow us to evaluate both, the usability and the relative benefits of our approach compared to manual exception handling. Moreover, our introduced method is not limited to evaluating timing behavior. Depending on the input functions the method can be extended to estimate economic impacts of a workflow. For instance in a more complex setup, the functions could be plotted against each other, resulting in a cost-dependent time behavior. This enables a new and throughout visibility of a workflow's resilience on run-time.

# References

1. van der Aalst, W.: Process Mining – Discovery, Conformance and Enhancement of Business Processes. Springer (2011)
2. van der Aalst, W.M., Schonenberg, M., Song, M.: Time prediction based on process mining. Information Systems 36(2), 450–475 (2011)
3. Accorsi, R., Stocker, T., Müller, G.: On the exploitation of process mining for security audits: the process discovery case. In: Proceedings of the ACM Symposium on Applied Computing, pp. 1462–1468. ACM (2013)
4. Antunes, P., Mourão, H.: Resilient business process management: Framework and services. Expert Syst. Appl. 38(2), 1241–1254 (2011), http://dx.doi.org/10.1016/j.eswa.2010.05.017

5. Atluri, V., Warner, J.: Security for workflow systems. In: Gertz, M., Jajodia, S. (eds.) Handbook of Database Security, pp. 213–230. Springer (2008)
6. Bruneau, M., Chang, S.E., Eguchi, R.T., Lee, G.C., O'Rourke, T.D., Reinhorn, A.M., Shinozuka, M., Tierney, K., Wallace, W.A., von Winterfeldt, D.: A framework to quantitatively assess and enhance the seismic resilience of communities. Earthquake Spectra 19(4), 733–752 (2003), http://earthquakespectra.org/doi/abs/10.1193/1.1623497
7. Butler, B.S., Gray, P.H.: Reliability, mindfulness, and information systems. MIS Quarterly 30(2), 211–224 (2006)
8. Caralli, R.A., Allen, J.H., Curtis, P.D., Young, L.R.: Cert resilience management model, version 1.0 (2010), http://www.worldcat.org/oclc/668434211
9. van Dongen, B.F., Crooy, R.A., van der Aalst, W.M.P.: Cycle time prediction: When will this case finally be finished? In: Meersman, R., Tari, Z. (eds.) OTM 2008, Part I. LNCS, vol. 5331, pp. 319–336. Springer, Heidelberg (2008), http://link.springer.com/chapter/10.1007/978-3-540-88871-0_22
10. Eder, J., Panagos, E., Pozewaunig, H., Rabinovich, M.: Time management in workflow systems. In: BIS 1999, pp. 265–280. Springer (1999)
11. Fenz, S., Neubauer, T., Accorsi, R., Koslowski, T.: FORISK: Formalizing information security risk and compliance management. In: 2013 43rd Annual IEEE/IFIP Conference on Dependable Systems and Networks Workshop (DSN-W), pp. 1–4. IEEE (2013)
12. Hollnagel, E., Woods, D.D., Leveson, N. (eds.): Resilience engineering: Concepts and precepts. Ashgate, Aldershot and England and and Burlington and VT (2006)
13. Koslowski, T., Zimmermann, C.: Towards a detective approach to process-centered resilience. In: Accorsi, R., Ranise, S. (eds.) STM 2013. LNCS, vol. 8203, pp. 176–190. Springer, Heidelberg (2013), http://dx.doi.org/10.1007/978-3-642-41098-7_12
14. Müller, G., Koslowski, T.G., Accorsi, R.: Resilience - A new research field in business information systems? In: Abramowicz, W. (ed.) BIS Workshops 2013. LNBIP, vol. 160, pp. 3–14. Springer, Heidelberg (2013)
15. Pika, A., van der Aalst, W.M.P., Fidge, C.J., ter Hofstede, A.H.M., Wynn, M.T.: Profiling event logs to configure risk indicators for process delays. In: Salinesi, C., Norrie, M.C., Pastor, Ó. (eds.) CAiSE 2013. LNCS, vol. 7908, pp. 465–481. Springer, Heidelberg (2013), http://link.springer.com/10.1007/978-3-642-38709-8_30
16. Pozewaunig, H., Eder, J., Liebhart, W.: ePERT: extending PERT for workflow management system. In: ADBIS, pp. 217–224 (1997), http://citeseerx.ist.psu.edu/viewdoc/download?doi=10.1.1.21.7538&rep=rep1&type=pdf
17. Ramchandani, C.: Analysis of asynchronous concurrent systems by timed petri nets. Tech. rep., Massachusetts Institute of Technology, Cambridge, MA, USA (1974)
18. Runeson, P., Höst, M.: Guidelines for conducting and reporting case study research in software engineering. Empirical Software Engineering 14(2), 131–164 (2009), http://link.springer.com/10.1007/s10664-008-9102-8
19. Tsai, J.P., Jennhwa Yang, S., Chang, Y.H.: Timing constraint petri nets and their application to schedulability analysis of real-time system specifications. IEEE Transactions on Software Engineering 21(1), 32–49 (1995)
20. Wolter, K.: Resilience assessment and evaluation of computing systems. Springer, Berlin (2012)

# Introduction to SASSUR 2014

Alejandra Ruiz[1], Tim Kelly[2], and Jose Luis de la Vara[3]

[1] ICT-European Software Institute, TECNALIA, Spain
[2] Department of Computer Science, University of York, United Kingdom
[3] Certus Centre for Software V&V, Simula Research Laboratory, Norway
alejandra.ruiz@tecnalia.com, tim.kelly@york.ac.uk
jdelavara@simula.no

The interest in and need for new safety assurance and certification approaches is undoubtedly increasing. First of all, critical systems are becoming more pervasive every day. They are used for a wide range of daily activities related to transportation, healthcare, or energy consumption, and for increasingly novel applications. Fully implantable artificial hearts and unmanned aerial vehicles are just two examples. Society increasingly depends on these systems, and on their safe operation. At the same time safety assurance and certification is becoming increasingly complex. This is a result of, for instance, evolution of regulatory practice, the increase in the size and complexity of the systems, the need for holistic assessment of cyber-physical systems, and the application of new technologies for enabling features such as autonomous, cooperative, or self-adaptive system behaviour. In addition, the application of new technologies in safety-critical systems potentially introduces new vulnerabilities that are not known yet but could affect to safety integrity.

One of the main drivers for exploring new safety assurance and certification approaches is to make it more cost-effective. Examples of accidents and near-accidents as a result of weak safety assurance and certification approaches in industry have started to gain more attention and concern general audiences. Several recalls from different car manufacturers, train accidents in Europe, and the issues with Boeing Dreamliner are some of the most recent cases. Those cases have had significant impact on the economic performance of the companies, caused reputational damage, and indicate increased risk to people and/or environment safety. System suppliers desire reductions in the cost and time associated with safety assurance. The activities currently required significantly increase the time to market, as system suppliers have to execute many safety-targeted tasks and demonstrate that they have been executed. Several studies suggest that safety assurance and certification can become prohibitively expensive in the near future unless companies adopt new practices.

Cost-effective safety assurance and certification can be tackled with many different means. These means include approaches that promote product reuse across systems and application domains, facilitate incremental and composition certification, support adequate management of system evolution, help in demonstrating compliance with safety standards, or aim to improve judgements on system safety. However, one of the

A. Bondavalli et al. (Eds.): SAFECOMP 2014 Workshops, LNCS 8696, pp. 371–374, 2014.
© Springer International Publishing Switzerland 2014

main challenges lies in ensuring that the new approaches do not introduce new safety or certification risks. The systems resulting from the application these approaches must be as safe as the systems resulting from the application of past approaches. Safety comes first. Although cost is evidently a very important aspect for any industrial project, it should not be main concern in safety-critical industries.

The Third International Workshop on Next Generation of System Assurance Approaches for Safety-Critical Systems (SASSUR 2014) aims to explore new ideas on compositional and evolutionary safety assurance and certification. In particular, SASSUR aims to provide a forum for thematic presentations and in-depth discussions about reuse and composition of safety arguments, safety evidence, and contextual information about system components, in a way that makes assurance and certification more cost-effective, precise, and scalable.

SASSUR is targeted at bringing together experts, researchers, and practitioners from diverse communities, such as safety and security engineering, certification processes, model-based technologies, software and hardware design, safety-critical systems, and applications communities (railway, aerospace, automotive, health, industrial manufacturing, etc.).

The topics of interest include:

- Industrial challenges for cost-effective safety assurance and certification
- Cross-domain product certification
- Integration of process-centric and product-centric assurance
- Compliance management of standards and regulations
- Evidence traceability
- Transparency of the safety assurance and certification processes: metrics and business cases
- Evolutionary approaches for safety and security assurance and certification
- Case-based assurance approaches
- Tools for supporting safety assurance
- Seamless development tool chain for safety critical
- Evolution of standards and trends on transport regulation
- The next challenges of safety critical development in industry
- Human factors in safety assurance and certification
- COTS or external sourcing management of evidence in safety critical system
- Mixed criticality

The papers at SASSUR 2014 address many of these topics. More concretely, the following eight papers have been accepted:

1. *Assuring Avionics - Updating the Approach for the 21st Century.* This paper explains some of the main current issues for safety assurance and certification in the avionics domain and proposes ways to mitigate them.
2. *Rethinking of Strategy for Safety Argument Development.* This paper discusses the role of strategies in safety case development and examines the application of strategies in existing argument structures.
3. *Towards a Cross-domain Software Safety Assurance Process for Embedded Systems.* This paper proposes a cross-domain software assurance process for

embedded systems, based on the reuse of safety analysis techniques and tools for product development in different domains.

4. *A Software Safety Verification Method Based on System-Theoretic Process Analysis.* This paper proposes a method for verifying software safety requirements derived at the system level in order to provide evidence of safety risk reduction.

5. *Quantifying Uncertainty in Safety Cases Using Evidential Reasoning.* This paper introduces an evidence-based approach to deal with uncertainty in human judgment on safety case development and assessment.

6. *Metamodel Comparison and Model Comparison for Safety Assurance.* This paper describes the correspondence between different meta-models or models proposed for safety assurance and certification.

7. *Does Visualization Speed up the Safety Analysis Process?* This paper reports on an experiment that shows the benefits of using visual tool support for component fault analysis.

8. *Agile Change Impact Analysis of Safety Critical Software.* This paper outlines how agile development principles can help a system supplier deal with software changes and determining their consequences for safety-critical systems.

Following the review of all the papers submitted to the workshop we are to be able to compile a high-quality programme of papers that tackle current challenges and needs in current safety assurance and certification practice. Out of the eight papers, three are authored or co-authored by practitioners. The other five papers also closely relate to practical issues, as the authors' contributions are based on insights gained into the state of the practice though industry-academia collaborations, participation in industrial projects, or analysis of existing system failure reports.

Last but not least, we hope that you enjoy SASSUR 2014.

**Acknowledgments.** We would like to thank the OPENCOSS and SafeAdapt FP7 projects, SAFECOMP 2014 organizers, SASSUR 2014 Steering Committee, Program Committee members and reviewers, and the authors of the papers submitted to the workshop for their contribution towards realising SASSUR 2014.

**Workshop Committees**

*Organization Committee*
Alejandra Ruiz - TECNALIA, Spain
Tim Kelly - University of York, UK
Jose Luis de la Vara - Simula Research Laboratory, Norway

*Steering Committee*
John Favaro - Intecs, Italy
Huascar Espinoza - TECNALIA, Spain
Fabien Belmonte- Alstom, France

# Assuring Avionics – Updating the Approach for the 21st Century

Tom Ferrell and Uma Ferrell

Ferrell and Associates Consulting, Inc., Charlottesville, Virginia, USA
{tom,uma}@faaconsulting.com

**Abstract.** This position paper outlines a number of challenges currently faced by the aerospace community in addressing system, software, and hardware safety. These challenges include increasing complexity, lagging regulatory guidance, a divergent set of design assurance guidelines, and ever advancing technology. To address these challenges, four recommendations are offered: consolidation of design assurance, increased resiliency in product design, a move to less prescriptive standards in favor of a goal-based approach, and the imposition of personnel qualification.

**Keywords:** ARP-4754, Avionics, Certification, Complexity, Design Assurance, Digital Design, DO-178, DO-254, Goal-based Assurance, Safety.

## 1 Introduction

With the publication of the original DO-178, *Software Considerations in Airborne Systems and Equipment Certification*, by the RTCA[1] in 1982, the era of design assurance as a means for assessing the safety of avionics software was born. This document introduced the basic concept that defects can be reduced in fielded software by way of documented, repeatable development processes coupled with rigorous, structured verification. This approach has served the aviation industry well and has been steadily expanded to address aeronautical data production, systems design, and airborne hardware development. This paper will argue that while effective in the past, complexity, changing regulatory oversight, and ever accelerating technical advancement mean that objective-based design assurance as currently practiced is simply unsustainable and new approaches must be found in the immediate future.

## 2 Background

DO-178 went through rapid evolution with the A version released in 1985 and a B version in 1992. DO-178B was the prevailing software guidance for twenty years until DO-178C was published in December 2011. Formally acknowledged by the US

---

[1] Refers to RTCA, Inc., a Washington DC non-profit organization that serves a Federal Advisory Committee (FAC) to the Federal Aviation Administration (FAA).

A. Bondavalli et al. (Eds.): SAFECOMP 2014 Workshops, LNCS 8696, pp. 375–383, 2014.

Federal Aviation Administration (FAA) in July 2013, DO-178C along with a standalone set of guidelines for tool qualification and three technical supplements is now the accepted means for demonstrating compliance for airborne software. The airborne distinction is important as a standalone interpretation of DO-178C known as DO-278A was also created at the same time for ground and space-based aeronautical software. While admittedly unscientific, a quick-look at page counts tells the story. The original DO-178 had sixty-seven pages. Today's engineers working on a modern Integrated Modular Avionic (IMA) platform have to be familiar with (and in many cases comply to) over a thousand pages of official RTCA publications supported by hundreds of pages of regulatory guidance. The DO-178C family of documents alone weighs in at over six hundred pages.[2]

In the early 90's when it became apparent that companies were moving their digital designs into ASICs to avoid DO-178A and then DO-178B compliance, a new push started to create a DO-178-like approach for designs implemented in silicon. This ultimately resulted in DO-254 being published in 2000. Applicable to all airborne electronic hardware, DO-254 provides objectives, activities, and data requirements for development activities from planning through transition to production. Not to be outdone, the systems community has similarly developed guidelines for design assurance. Known as Aerospace Recommended Practice (ARP) 4754A, these guidelines employ the now familiar objective-based approach which allows for relatively easy assessment by the regulatory community. While the guidelines referenced here are those employed in the US, the approaches used in Europe and other parts of the world are similar. Suffice it to say, design assurance in accordance with a documented set of objectives is THE model for gaining approval for onboard systems, software, and hardware in 2014.

At the same time design assurance has been making its way into different domains and expanding in scope, technology has continued to advance. Most people are familiar with Moore's Law which essentially states that computational power per the same unit of buying power doubles every two years. Recent advances in 3D digital design suggest that such growth will continue for some time. Most of this advancement is driven by the computational needs of consumer electronics, especially gaming. Aerospace generally represents a very small market for the large silicon houses (e.g., Intel, Xilinx, Microchip, Freescale) and hence has little influence over the market. As a result, avionics manufacturers find themselves reacting to a market where technology is constantly advancing faster than the regulatory framework can accommodate. A current challenge for avionics suppliers is the rapid shift from single-core to multi-core processors. In fact, many industry watchers are predicting that it will become increasingly difficult to find single-core processors in the marketplace. Current regulatory guidance along with DO-178C is silent on how to verify and subsequently certify multi-core designs. Work is underway on both sides of the Atlantic to tackle this problem, but initial attempts have involved only small steps. The biggest problem seems to be demonstration of determinism of multi-core designs due to the significant level of concurrency and shared resources among cores (e.g., memory, registers).

---

[2] Includes DO-178C, DO-330, DO-331, DO-332, DO-333, and DO-248C.

# 3    Compounding Problems

Determinism is but one facet of 'first principles' that serve as the foundation of modern design assurance. Other principles of concern include a never wavering emphasis on requirements-based verification or what some refer to as 'directed testing,' repeatable processes, and the objective-based demonstration of compliance. These last two items have given rise, at least in the United States, to a major regulatory focus on Stage of Involvement (SOI) reviews. Developed with the best of intent to drive consistency in the application of DO-178B, SOI reviews were intended to be checkpoints in time where the regulatory authority could assess compliance and require course corrections (via findings and observations) if adherence to the prevailing design assurance objectives was found lacking. SOI reviews have taken on a life of their own supplanting other project management milestones to become major program events. Elaborate checklists have been developed with the regulator often requiring these checklists be completed for every project, no matter the size, technique or criticality. This has given rise to what is known in industry as a 'checklist mentality' where engineering is reduced to a checklist and the process compliance focus trumps the product content.

The problem with all of this is that as complexity has grown and technology has advanced, the regulatory framework has grown bloated and the objective-based approach to design assurance is now clearly hampering innovation. Bifurcated design assurance guidelines addressing software and electronic hardware separately add to the problem. Instead of coalescing the best approaches to design assurance for digital designs regardless of implementation, the aerospace industry has created more and more objectives, activities, and data requirements for individual technologies and approaches. This specific issue has been compounded by each practitioner community introducing variations in terminology and approaches to demonstrating compliance, often explicitly to avoid confusion or comparison with another community. As examples of these differences, consider the following:

- DO-178C defines the work to be completed for a given software level while DO-254 defines the work requirement by data to be produced and submitted for review.
- DO-178C uses quality assurance while DO-254 uses the term process assurance to describe the same activities.
- ARP-4754A makes use of the same objective format as DO-178C but instead of noting items as either required or not for a given criticality level, the same concept is expressed in terms of recommendations and items to be negotiated with the regulatory authority.
- DO-254 introduces the term Top-Level Drawing to conform a piece of hardware while the FAA guidance[3] states that what is really meant is a data item similar to a Software Configuration Index such as that described in DO-178C.
- DO-178C and DO-254 identify five levels of criticality tied to possible aircraft failure categories while DO-278A introduces a sixth level even though it is still describing criticality associated with safe aircraft operations.

---

[3] FAA Order 8110.105 (change 1).

This last item is yet another example of bifurcated design assurance. Logic would demand that both ground and airborne safety-critical software used within the air traffic control system be held to the same design assurance standard. Modern air traffic control relies on collaborative decision making between pilot and ground-based controllers. Much of the situational awareness for both of these parties comes from space-based navigational aids (e.g. GPS). As Stanislaw Jerzy Lec (Polish Writer and Aphorist 1906-1966) stated very eloquently "The weakest link in the chain is also the strongest. It can break the chain."

While someone outside the aerospace industry may assume that there are solid reasons for all of these examples of variation, when pressed, even those who work with these guidelines routinely are hard-pressed to provide a solid rationale for the differences. As veterans of the standards-making process, the authors can state directly that some of the variations exist solely as a result of political or institutional influences rather than as a result of solid engineering rationale. As the assessment of guideline adherence often falls to the same regulatory personnel, the variation noted here has the effect of adding, not decreasing confusion. At the very least assessment becomes more complicated. This is before taking into account variations between regulators, another facet of this challenge as aerospace is a worldwide industry with products that must meet many sovereign state requirements.

Between the checklist-driven reviews, and the subtleties of individual domains (e.g., software, hardware, systems, airborne, ground), it is easy to see how a design assurance regiment that was originally equally focused on product correctness and process adherence has become unbalanced. Servicing the divergent guidelines and ensuring checklists are complete draws on limited resources that previously spent a large portion of their time reviewing robustness of architecture and appropriateness of designs. It is the author's assertion that far too much time is now spent on ensuring an activity is performed rather than looking in detail at the breadth and depth of the activities to ensure correctness and completeness. A side effect of this shift is a slow but steady erosion of technical skills among compliance personnel, an aspect already under serious pressure due to ever advancing technology. Before the chain of aeronautical safety breaks, a change of approach is needed.

## 4     Proposing Solutions

The rest of this paper discusses four specific changes that the authors feel will make a positive difference in addressing the problems outlined above. These four changes are as follows:

1. Consolidation of design assurance goals regardless of implementation/location.
2. Increased resiliency in design.
3. Shift from prescriptive objective-based standards to goal-based standards.
4. Imposition of personnel qualification for aerospace digital design work.

## 4.1    Consolidated Digital Design Assurance

When one picks up DO-178C, DO-254, or ARP-4754, one is struck by the commonality of many elements. Planning, requirements, design capture, testing, configuration management, and quality assurance appear in all of these documents, albeit with subtle differences in terminology, associated data requirements, or activities. As they came into being over time and were often derivative in nature, it is easy to see how we got where we are at. The time to consolidate and simplify has arrived. It is clearly possible to see how a company could produce a single set of process documents that are technology agnostic, yet the regulatory framework, and in many cases, the guidelines themselves provide impediments to such consolidation. It should also be noted that there are other incentives at work that hinder such consolidation. One such impediment is that standards bodies such as RTCA and SAE derive significant income from the sale of documents such as DO-178C.

Having different design assurance criteria for different parts of the system (DO-178 for software, DO-254 for airborne electronic hardware, and even DO-200 for aeronautical data processing) creates the opportunity for weak links in the overall design assurance chain. In many cases, the regulator tends to drive the overall compliance across domains to the same set of evaluation criteria anyway. Why not acknowledge this and abstract up a level to capture design assurance principles that can be universally applied. One should be able to characterize what constitutes a good requirement, a good test, an acceptable level of configuration management, and appropriate quality oversight, all regardless of domain or implementation technique. Dealing with the nuances of a domain could be handled through the application of technical standards solely focused on the types of error classes to be protected against with a particular technology. In other words, the processes are common and the implementation detail is contained in such a way that it can rapidly be swapped out as technology evolves. DO-178B lasted for twenty years because it was technology independent. We are rapidly losing this idea.

## 4.2    Increased Resiliency at the Digital Level

ARP-4754A requires that system designers look at the overall safety of the system and ensure that the system is both fail-safe and fault-tolerant. Theoretically, these concepts are supposed to extend into the digital domain via application of DO-178C and DO-254. Examples of how this is accomplished include safety monitors, voted processing lanes, and signal validation (e.g., data currency, range limits). Unfortunately, it is possible for companies to claim that their digital designs are safe because they've met the objectives of these documents even though there are no explicit objectives for inclusion of fail-safe and fault-tolerant aspects at the digital design level. The argument frequently given for this is that these types of constructs need to be captured in the system requirements and then flowed to the software or hardware teams for implementation. Assuming this is done, the objectives for verifying requirements should pick up such safety-related behavior.

A longstanding controversy surrounding DO-178 is its lack of specific objectives relating to 'safety-related requirements.' The identification of such requirements is required but the need for dedicated verification and treatment is less than clear. Many of the companies responsible for digital design of avionics systems do not have the systems knowledge that an airframer or system integrator has to be able to appropriately identify safety-related requirements. Without specific objectives for safety-related requirements, digital designers are not required to demonstrate that the needed engineering emphasis (including feedback to system safety) has been accomplished.

As a result of this idea that safety is really a system property, the application of DO-178C and DO-254 is restricted to assurance that requirements are properly translated into a digital implementation. While the view serves business objectives of separation of system and software/hardware requirements, such a view can introduce gaps in understanding and implementation. The topic of robustness is introduced via verification to try to address the wide range of abnormal or off-nominal conditions the digital implementation may experience. This includes addressing the age old problem that even for a modest-sized program, it is simply not possible to test all possible digital paths.

This idea of robustness has served the community well in the past but it is unclear whether this emphasis is sufficient to deal with the increasing digital complexity, especially when emergent behavior is observed. Rather than trying to eliminate every possible defect, faults should be expected and protected against. This means always instituting rigorous exception handling, always implementing redundancy, and always building in monitors at multiple levels of the implementation. Increasingly, companies are arguing that such features are unnecessary if rigorous process is applied throughout the development process. DO-330, the new tool qualification guideline even opens the door for this by introducing a new category of tools that allows for the suppression of such checks in certain scenarios. Assuming defects and increasing the inherent capabilities of the digital implementation to mitigate their effects before they can propagate to a system boundary simply makes more sense than the current path.

## 4.3    Goal-Based Standards

The proliferation of explicit objectives and data requirements that must be satisfied based on implementation approach is simply not sustainable. The major schedule slips seen on the A380 and then the Boeing 787 are due in part to late software and hardware compliance. What used to take three years now takes five and the formality driven by these standards has become so prescriptive that even a single change, no matter how trivial, late in a project can translate to weeks of rework. Research work underway on safety or assurance cases looks extremely promising for providing some relief in this area. The FAA's emphasis on an 'accountability framework' opens the door for such an approach by requiring the Applicant seeking approval of a system to clearly state their compliance (and by definition their acceptance of liability) for that system. Defining top-level safety goals and then picking the most appropriate means for satisfying those goals rather than trying to follow a one size fits all approach seems imminently better suited for the rapid technology advance, highly complex world we live in today.

There are technical and business advantages in specifying goal-based standards rather than prescriptive regulations. Setting a goal will allow alternate means of accomplishing compliance. Even though the FAA regulations are in the form of Advisory Circulars (AC) which state "This AC describes an acceptable means, but not the only means...," they simply do not provide the flexibility that could be achieved with a goal-based approach. Advisory Circulars require that the method of how the compliance is reached be equivalent to the prescribed method specified in the regulation. For example, if an equivalent method to DO-178B has to be proposed, an applicant has to prove equivalency to each and every objective of DO-178B.

Short comings of prescribed processes are that the applicant can conduct mandatory activities without paying attention to whether other activities are warranted given the engineering problem being solved or the method, tools or technology being employed. Prescriptive regulations originate in the past experience [1] and hence from known engineering problems using known solutions, methods, tools and techniques. In absence of such history, innovative solutions may be passed over given the perceived (or real) difficulties in gaining regulatory approval. Alternatively, application of existing objectives may simply not be sufficient for the new innovation and if applied, may fall short of demonstrating acceptable safety levels. A goal-based regulation allows industry to focus on the overarching goal of design assurance and safety regardless of the technical solution chosen (e.g., design, architecture, methods, tools, and underlying technology).

Increasing complexity and prescriptive standards were the topic of discussion at two technical committees of Lloyd's Register in 2011 [2]. It was agreed that goal based standards convert a culture of passive compliance to one of active ownership.

Even though goal-based requirements have huge advantages, they bring some attendant challenges [3]. These challenges include reaching an agreement on appropriateness and the gradations in the quality or quantity of evidence in demonstrating safety especially for new technology, and difficulties in specifying contracts where the safety activities and resulting evidence may not be obvious at the start of the project. These challenges mean that the transition from the current prescriptive methods to goal-based methods for compliance will be difficult.

## 4.4    Personnel Qualification

The checklists used for SOI audits along with the rote way DO-compliance is being accomplished has ushered in an era where engineering judgment is deemphasized in favor of 'just fill out the paperwork.' It is the authors' strongly held view that engineering judgment backed up by a set of defined and accredited credentials are absolutely necessary to ensuring the strong history of safety in the aerospace community is maintained. There needs to be established grounds for maintaining and demonstrating currency including the possible use of third-party accreditation. Regulators must issue interpretive material available to all users. It would help to have regulator-accepted list of training organizations for digital design topics, and recurrent technical training should be mandatory. Additionally, a mechanism for formal mentoring of aerospace safety personnel should be put in place.

Engineers, both those who develop digital systems as well as those who regulate them, play a significant role in the safety of such systems. Development engineers (shown as "the Applicant" in figure 1) balance cost, quality and correctness while the regulators ask the hard questions on safety and implication of fielding the system, proactively defending public interest and safety as affected by the system to be fielded.

Regulation for complex systems cannot be solely based on completing a process-driven checklist. The regulator is obligated to ask probing questions to ensure the system has been robustly verified and validated in light of known failures of similar systems in the past, as well as any potential failure modes identified as part of the current development activity. In a goal-based compliance environment, the author of the argument should document as to why the author believes that a system is safe and the reviewer of that argument must ask any questions so fill any gaps in those arguments. Both must have the appropriate knowledge sets to accomplish their respective roles.

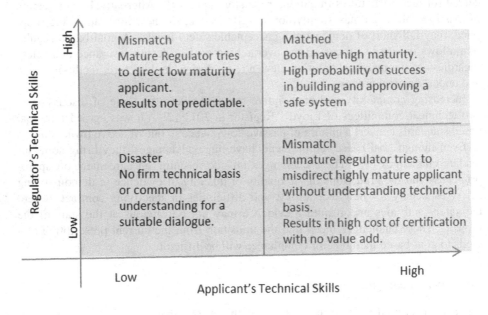

**Fig. 1.** Matching the Applicant to the Regulator

Figure 1 illustrates this point combining differently skilled regulators and applicants. The greatest chance for success is realized when both parties are highly skilled. Demanding appropriate personnel qualifications for engineers working in safety critical systems is not a new idea. Jonathan Bowen [4] argues that building of safety critical systems must be carried out in a professional and responsible manner by qualified engineers. While legislation and standards impose external pressures, education and ethical considerations help provide self-imposed guidelines.

It was the ACM Task Force on Licensing of Software Engineers working on Safety-Critical Software [5, 6] that made a distinction between licensing of engineers (using state administered board examinations) and education of engineers that is necessary and appropriate. Knight and Leveson [6] opine that it is unlikely that a reasonable test for software skills needed for safety-critical systems can be put into a multiple-choice format which is judged as passed by "minimal competence." Further, such tests cannot keep up with the technical advances. A practical solution is to impose relevant accreditation instituted via engineering programs in schools as well as changes in culture, practice and regulation.

# 5    Conclusion

This position paper has outlined a number of challenges currently faced by the aerospace community in addressing system, software, and hardware safety. These challenges include increasing complexity, lagging regulatory guidance, a divergent set of design assurance guidelines, and ever advancing technology. To address these challenges, four recommendations are offered: consolidation of design assurance, increased resiliency in product design, a move to less prescriptive standards in favor of a goal-based approach, and the imposition of personnel qualification.

# References

1. Penny, J., Eaton, A., Bishop, P., Bloomfield, R.: The Practicalities of Goal-Based Safety Regulation. In: Proc. Ninth Safety-critical Systems Symposium (SSS 2001), Bristol, UK, February 6-8, pp. 35–48. Springer, New York (2001) ISBN:1-85233-411-8
2. http://www.liwem.org/en/Documents/LIWEM_2012_presentations_ uppdaterad%20aug%202012_del3.pdf (accessed on June 30, 2013)
3. Kelly, T.P., McDermid, J.A., Weaver, R.A.: Goal-Based Safety Standards: Opportunities and Challenges. In: Proceedings of the 23rd International System Safety Conference. Proceedings Published by the System Safety Society (August 2005)
4. Bowen, J.: The Ethics of Safety Critical Systems. Communications of the ACM 43(4), 91–97 (2000)
5. http://www.cs.trinity.edu/~jhowland/cs3194/ licensing-software-engineers.pdf (accessed June 30, 2014)
6. Knight, J.C., Leveson, N.G.: Should Software Engineers Be Licensed? Communications of the ACM 45(11), 87–90 (2002)

# Rethinking of *Strategy* for Safety Argument Development

Linling Sun[1], Nuno Silva[1], and Tim Kelly[2]

[1] Critical Software, SA
Parque Industrial de Taveiro, Lote 49, 3045-504 Coimbra, Portugal
[2] Department of Computer Science, University of York
Deramore Lane, York, YO10 5GH, UK
{lsun,nsilva}@criticalsoftware.com, tim.kelly@cs.york.ac.uk

**Abstract.** A 'strategy' in Goal Structuring Notation (GSN) aims to help safety-case developers and reviewers to understand the inferences in a hierarchy of safety claims. However, the identification and elaboration of 'strategies' in argument development is not always straightforward in practice. In this paper, we revisit the role of strategies in the development of safety cases and examine the application of strategies in some existing argument structures. Four main sources of information are identified as the basis of strategy formulation. A list of generic strategy types for argument decomposition and refinement are analysed in order to facilitate the safety case development and review processes for assuring system safety.

**Keywords:** Safety Case, Assurance Case, Argument, Strategy, GSN.

## 1 Introduction

Safety cases have been increasingly accepted as an assurance technique by many industrial sectors, e.g. defence, air traffic control, railway, automobile and medical devices [1]. In the past decade, there are considerable research and application efforts placed on safety case notations, safety case life cycles, argument patterns, safety case tools and argument and evidence meta-models. However, a supportive element in the safety case development process, the 'strategy' for describing the relationships between safety claims of different levels has not been emphasized as much as other key safety case elements, e.g. claims and evidence items.

Nevertheless, in practice, inexperienced safety case developers had experienced difficulties with the application of strategies [6], e.g. 'confusing strategies with goals' or 'misunderstanding strategies as judgment branches'. Some engineers find it is helpful for argument decomposition with predefined argument decomposition patterns [6], e.g. architecture decomposition pattern. However, there are limited resources that specialized in collecting the applicable strategies for argument decomposition.

In [7], seven ways of decomposing claims in assurance cases that are identified through empirical study are listed. However, there is no guidance and examples regarding their usage in the paper. A series of reusable safety case patterns are presented in [3, 4]. However, they are aiming at guiding safety case construction with

A. Bondavalli et al. (Eds.): SAFECOMP 2014 Workshops, LNCS 8696, pp. 384–395, 2014.

existing safety criteria or safety analysis techniques, rather than summarizing and comparing ways of decomposing safety goals. In existing literature, there are multiple forms of strategies in use. The titles of the schemes in [11] are helpful descriptions of reusable strategy types that are often used in informal argumentation. In this paper, we will discuss the role of strategy in structured argumentation and present a set of generic strategy types in order to facilitate the argument development and to reduce improper usage of 'strategies'.

The paper is structured as follows. Section 2 presents the role of a strategy in argument development. Section 3 focuses on four main information sources of strategy and presents a list of typical strategies. Section 4 discusses considerations on the application of strategies. Section 5 summarises the paper and identifies the future work.

## 2  *Strategy* in Argument Development

Safety case development is an iterative process that occurs along with the other design and safety activities during the product life cycles. The two main tasks during safety case development are the development of argument structures and the collection and presentation of evidence items. Strategy, employed in the development of argument structures, is an element adopted for a better understanding of the rationale that connects lower safety claims with the higher-level claims they support. In this paper, we discuss this element in Goal Structuring Notation (GSN) terms [2], whereas it may be addressed as a different term in other structured notations, e.g. as 'Argument' element in CAE notation [10].

### 2.1  *Strategy* in GSN

GSN is one of the widely-used graphical notations for structured arguments. The notation defines a set of graphical symbols that can be used as a means of documenting and communicating arguments as to how a safety claim is true by presenting supporting sub-claims and referencing safety evidence items. The six core GSN elements are *Goals, Strategies, Solutions, Contexts, Assumptions*, and *Justifications* [2]. The core elements can be connected with two linkage elements: *SupportedBy* and *InContextOf*. The element of strategy is described in [2] as follows.

> A strategy, rendered as a parallelogram, describes the nature of the inference that exists between a goal and its supporting goal(s).

In nature, a *strategy* is a brief description of the argument approach adopted for inference from lower level safety goals to a higher-level one. It maps to 'ArgumentReasoning' [5], a meta-model element in Structured Assurance Case Metamodel (SACM) Developed by OMG System Assurance Task Force. It can be added or inserted to an existing argument structure to communicate the argument approach adopted between linked claims. It can also be adopted during the argument development process to help building up the argument structure top-down or bottom-up. However, it is worth noticing that a strategy is not a mandatory element in argument structures. A *strategy* does not support any goals by itself. It is not one of the determinate factors that affect the Boolean values of safety claims. The relations between a hierarchy of safety claims should be unchanged if a descriptive strategy is added to the existing structure.

The benefits of incorporating strategies in argument development are two-fold. Firstly, documenting *strategies* can improve the comprehension of the argument relations between a higher-level goal and its lower-level ones. Secondly, the presence of a *strategy* could help to invoke the need of presenting further information and further justification for establishing our confidence in the inference steps.

## 2.2    Argument Development Process

Guidance on safety case development is provided in [2, 9, 10]. One of them is the six-step method [2] that depicts a structured safety case development process in GSN terms. The steps of the method include [2]:

*Step 1 - Identify the goals to be supported;*
*Step 2 - Define the basis on which goals are stated;*
*Step 3 - Identify the strategy used to support the goals;*
*Step 4 - Define the basis on which the strategy is stated;*
*Step 5 - Elaborate the strategy (and back to Step 1);*
*Step 6 - Identify the basic solution.*

Three steps in the six-step method are related to *strategies*. It is obvious from the process that the elicitation of unstated rationales and context is notably enforced. A strategy may be implicit or unstated in a structured argument finally presented, but it is important during the thinking process of safety case development. According to our studies of safety case structures, it is found that this descriptive element is more informative than it was initially considered. The application of various strategies will influence the lower-level safety argument and evidence items that can be expected. Section 3 will provide a list of generic strategies as information references in order to support the proper application of strategies in future argument development.

## 3     Generic *Strategy* Types

We organise typical strategies in use in five groups, principally from the information sources from which strategies can be formulated. The four major sources include System Description, Safety Concerns, Standards and Requirements, and Logical Appeals. The generic types of strategies are observed primarily from examples of safety argument structures[1]. The types presented are intended to be informative rather than complete. The aim of presenting typical generic strategies lies in two aspects: 1) to establish prior knowledge of possible strategies to support and facilitate safety case development processes; 2) to acknowledge features of typical strategies in order to guide the development of defensible argument structures.

---

[1] We extract generic strategy types from the occurrences of various strategy types in 10 documents. Seven of them [2,3,9,12,17,21,26] include example arguments; three of them [3,4,25] include argument patterns; one of them [27] is a management document, but the requirements in it also indicate that particular strategy types should be adopted in a safety case.

## 3.1    Source 1: System Description

In any case, there is a system of our safety concern during the safety assurance process. To describe a system comprehensively, we may have varied types of information developed, refined and updated throughout its life cycle, e.g. functions, architecture, task profiles, operation modes, use scenarios, functional and non-functional properties. It has been observed as commonplace that system description of various levels of details can be used for shaping the higher level argument structure in safety cases. Some generic strategies formulated from this information source include:

*S1.1 Argument over all functions implemented by a system*
*S1.2 Argument over all subsystems/components of a system*
*S1.3 Argument over all stages of a system task*
*S1.4 Argument over all system modes*

S1.1 and S1.2 are addressed as 'functional decomposition', 'architecture breakdown' [3, 7]. They are recurrently used in reality. We expand it as an information source to cover more types of strategies in use that are related to system description.

It is straightforward to argue with the functional or architectural decomposition of a system and it is easy to implement this type of strategy due to the availability and admissibility of the associated information of a system. However, we should be aware of two pitfalls that may come along with this strategy type. Firstly, as it is always highlighted in system engineering, the interaction between various system components should not be overlooked. While we decompose the argument according to the list of functions (or components) of a system, we must append supplementary sub-goals in the argument along with other sub-goals associated with these functions - 'the interaction between functions is acceptably safe in the system context' or 'the independence between functions is adequately achieved'. Otherwise, one of the important hazard sources for system safety would be left out so that the argument validity could be seriously defected. Secondly, this type of strategy, by itself, does not drive the goals to a much more tractable level in engineering practice unless the 'acceptably safe' states of a system or subsystems are clarified. It is better to use it in combination with a strategy that is associated with the interpretation of system safety (to be discussed in Section 3.2 followed).

## 3.2    Source 2: Safety Concerns

In practice, safety should be properly specified for a specific system at the system level and be sufficiently and concretely interpreted at various system levels under study. Otherwise, the boundary of safety efforts would be unclear and unlimited. In safety argument development, both the interpretation of the meaning of an 'acceptably safe' system and the outputs from various safety analysis activities can be utilised for structuring arguments. The safety issues of a system may be addressed in a number of ways, e.g. defining undesired events associated with a system, presenting a list of hazards for a system or its components, and identifying the contributing factors to a specific failure condition.

Some generic strategies observed in use include:

*S2.1 Argument over undesired events*
*S2.2 Argument over factors contributing to undesired events or conditions*
*S2.3 Argument over hazardous contributions of a component to a system*
*S2.4 Argument over measures adopted*
*S2.5 Argument over a quantitative goal*

The first generic type, S2.1, is actually based on a more concrete depiction of our safety concerns. This type of claim decomposition has been addressed as 'concretion' in [7] and 'Interpretation and particularization' in [13], which intends to restate a safety claim in less vague forms.

S2.2 and S2.3 have a common basis – the relationships between hazardous conditions and undesired events. But they are viewing the relationship in different directions. S2.2 is more commonly presented in arguments, for example, '*Argument over all hazards identified*', '*Argument over all failure conditions identified*'. Chen et al are concerned that the difficulty of justifying the completeness of hazard analysis may lead to unsound assurance case if the argument structure is driven by hazard analysis results [14]. However, a consideration of negative conditions such as hazards lies in the heart of safety business. As the completeness issue is embedded in inductive reasoning, it is unnecessary to avoid structuring safety argument around hazards of components/functions at various levels of system structure, which is the most direct way to address safety considerations in argument claims. As a kind of partial remedy, we would recommend to place more rigors in hazard identification and to invoke context justification and updates in time if that strategy is adopted in usage [16].

Compared to S2.2, S2.3 is less frequently adopted in practice. However, it is good practice to take into account the top system-level context in a separate safety case of a subsystem. For example, the top level goal in 'High Level Software Safety Argument Pattern Structure' [4] is decomposed with this type of strategy. In that pattern, the goal '*{software Y} is acceptably safe to operate within {system Z}*' is supported by a sub-goal '*The contribution made by {software Y} to {system Z} hazards is acceptable*'. During the development and assurance of complex components of a system, it is helpful to consider the contribution by the components to higher-level system hazards at the beginning of argument decomposition, rather than to define the undesired events or attributes of the components directly.

S2.4 is commonly adopted to support a safety goal associated with a particular hazard or undesired event. There are different kinds of safety measures in a system life cycle, e.g. including design decisions, protective devices, monitor or alarm systems, barriers, operational procedures. When a safety measure is adopted, we need to carefully analyze whether it is effective, if there are conditions under which it is effective and if there are new hazards introduced. These factors should be considered in argument development, or the argument could be weak for attack. For example, an auto brake is employed when a moving device is over a prescribed speed limit. A condition of its effectiveness could be that the measurement of the real-time speed of the device is working and is accurate. Furthermore, we also need to consider what may happen if the auto brake is in functioning accidently within the speed limit.

Besides the control measures over a hazardous condition, there is another common means of demonstrating that an undesired event or condition is acceptable (as presented by S2.5) - to set a quantitative safety goal, such as '*The likelihood of a hazardous condition is lower than $1 \times 10^{-6}$*'. We need to consider if the quantitative parameter required is measurable or checkable at implementation and to consult authorities for their agreement of the parameter threshold suggested.

## 3.3    Source 3: Standards and Requirements

From the view of regulators and developers, it is a straightforward way to construct arguments for certification and audits by stating applicable standards and requirements and demonstrating that they have been met. Safety requirements for a system may be directly taken from safety legislation, regulations, and standards in a specific domain, imposed by statements in a contract, formulated on the basis of safety or hazard analysis, or derived from other safety requirements [15]. Claims in safety cases are similar to requirements in some sense. But a claim is an instance of statements that can be true or false [5] that is to be or has been justified; whereas requirements are statements depicting the desired features of a system which are to be realised in system development. Typical strategies observed in use include:

*S3.1 Argument of compliance with all applicable standards and regulations*
*S3.2 Argument of satisfaction of all (safety) requirements specified in system development.*

S3.1 is commonly considered by industries with prescriptive regulations. S3.2 is a direct way from the developers' viewpoint. However, it would be difficult to learn whether the requirements have addressed hazards sufficiently, if the links between requirements of a system and hazards in the system are lost. The 'focus on requirements can obscure underlying hazards' [17]. The argument constructed based on the hierarchy of requirements is a compliance argument that can contribute to safety assurance argument. The compliance argument may have not presented the rationale of how safety risk is controlled. Or if the requirements stated are primarily process-related, e.g. compliance with DO-178B, the system could be in a state that it is ready for certification but with unclear relation to its safety achieved [18,19].

One way in practice is to strengthen the decomposed argument on the basis of satisfying requirements with 'requirement validity arguments'. The requirement validity argument should include the following aspects [20]: 1) various level requirements are defined with a description of their relations to undesired events or conditions at a system level or hazards at component levels; 2) the decomposition of requirements has maintained the requirement validity throughout the hierarchy of requirements.

There is research work [19, 21] that intends to build explicit relationships between requirements from regulatory standards and the hazards addressed by the requirements. The work is valuable, which will benefit the communication and confidence establishment indeed. Due to the diversity of regulations, standards, requirements and development practice in various industrial sectors, further work needs to be undertaken to diminish ineffective usage of this type of strategy.

### 3.4    Source 4: Logical Appeals

This source of information takes argument approaches from the argumentation domain, from which the concept of safety cases is originated. Arguments have been used as means of inquiry and communication for persuasion in many scenarios where there is some disagreement. Previously, while formulating strategies in argument development, the argumentation domain was not discussed with prominence, although the users may have been using those logic skills inadvertently.

Through studying the argument approaches in logic literature [22-24], some generic types of strategies used in safety arguments are extracted as follows.

*S4.1 Argument by Causation*
*S4.2 Argument by Comparison*
*S4.3 Argument from Two Sides*
*S4.4 Argument from Authority or Expert*
*S4.5 Argument by Eliminative Induction*

The 'causation'[22] in S4.1covers three different kinds of relationships. The causal factor could be a necessary condition of the conclusion, or a sufficient condition of the conclusion, or be both necessary and sufficient for the conclusion. S4.1 is the logical basis of S2.2 and S2.3 (presented in Section3.2). It is necessary to differentiate causation and correlation. A correlation is incapable of authorising the inference unless the suspected causal relationship out of a correlation can be verified.

In argumentation, S4.2 *Argument by Comparison* is more often to be addressed as analogical reasoning, or argument by analogy [22,23]. The conclusion of one thing is withdrawn on the basis of comparison of it with another thing or itself in another context. The subject being compared should bear similar features; accordingly, we suppose some unknown features of the subject will be just like the features of its comparable counterpart. Nevertheless, the differences between the subject and its counterpart should be analysed in order to avoid loose and misleading analogies that bring logical fallacies. In safety domain, comparison has been adopted for justification of a safety claim regularly. For example, a safety goal of an engine can be supported by sub-goals on the acceptable engine usage in a similar context in another project [9].

S4.3 *Arguing from two sides* means to present both information in favour of the conclusion and how information against the conclusion is dismissed. This type of strategy aims to mitigate the effect of confirmation bias, i.e. the possible intention of neglecting information that refutes our goals and emphasizing supportive facts only in human reasoning [22]. It has been used for considering counterevidence in some safety argument structures [9, 25]. For example, '*Sufficient confidence exists in evidencing Goal X*' is supported by '*Sufficient confidence exists in supportive evidence provided for Goal X*' and '*Sufficient confidence exists in acceptable risk associated with counter evidence for Goal X*'(adapted from [25]). If there exists any potential counter evidence generated in system development, e.g. a failed test, the user should present the information in safety argument and justify that the problem identified in the test has been properly handled and the problem in the failed test is no longer relevant to the top goal.

However, this type of strategy will significantly expand the size of argument structures. In addition to the difficulty regarding to the management of the size of the structure, the counter evidence and claims may be difficult to obtain in reality, which may suppress the argument development in the opposing side. Therefore, users need to be careful with putting efforts on one side or another unreasonably.

In inductive reasoning, 'Argument from authority' is the name of one of the typical fallacies [22]. However, the analysis and reviews carried out by experts are occasionally used as evidence in safety cases. It is very dangerous to appeal to an expert blindly without scrutiny, analysis and justification of how a conclusion is derived from their knowledge or experience. But we should not deny the usefulness of expert opinions in safety analysis and reviews. What we need to do is to ask for explicit presentation of the reasoning logic performed by experts and to examine if the fallacious conditions have been adequately mitigated. The fallacious conditions that may fail the argument based on expert opinions [22] include the area of knowledge of the experts, the interests of experts and the consistency between expert opinions. If a group of independent experts are available for an issue, it would be helpful to ensure the consistency and agreement between the opinions from different experts.

We should also note that expert opinions may be against the safety claim to be justified. In this situation, it is very important to examine the reasons provided by an authority or expert. When properly removed or handled, the questions or problems raised by experts should be addressed in the updated safety case.

'Eliminative Induction' is proposed in [26] as the principle for confidence arguments. Defeaters, doubts or reasons for the truth of claims, are identified and used for decomposing a confidence argument structure. However, it may be inappropriate if we try to use it in a primary safety argument. As we explained before, counter evidence and claims for safety goals should be considered in safety case development. But we should not argue only from one-side in a primary safety argument without positive safety evidence, because it will make the argument incomplete and may bring 'arguing from ignorance' fallacy. We recommend arguing from two sides in primary safety arguments.

To consider logic appeals in safety arguments brings us another viewpoint of refining argument structures. Further study on other argument approaches that exist in generic argumentative situations may introduce us new generic strategies for safety argument development. We need to carefully examine potential logical fallacies while adopting strategies from logic appeals.

## 3.5    Source 5: Others

In reality, the usage of strategies is more miscellaneous. Three supplementary ones are presented as examples of other sources as they are less significant as the strategy types listed in the four major sources.

*S5.1 Argument on the basis of a timeline*
*S5.2 Argument by appeal to one or more evidence types*
*S5.3 Argument over the product and the process perspectives*

A timeline aims to review a series of ordered events that occur in the life cycle of an entity under study. The entity is a subject that carries a certain function the user needs and has its own life cycle, e.g. a system, a subsystem, a component, a software module, or a variable. The timeline for a system could be the whole product life-cycle or part of it, e.g. its development process, or its installation, operation and decommissioning process. The decomposition of a safety claim is realized by considering the claim at different stages in a timeline. The argument over a system task profile is also an example of the argument over a timeline.

A timeline is usually related to a process. It provides a simplified view of an entity, rather than other details such as activities implemented, resources needed or outcomes generated throughout a process. It could be a subtype of the Source 1. But it is worthwhile to put it separately to underline its existence and features.

In theory, S5.2 is specialized particularly in connecting a safety claim with evidence result assertions [2], a proposition that can be made from the source data of safety evidence and can be used to support domain claims in safety arguments. In reality, many safety cases are not presented with evidence result assertions, unless the author wants to highlight the evidence types to be relied upon. For example, *'Argument by proof using automated theorem provers'*[12].

We should prepare answers for the following questions if we think about using this strategy during argument development. Is there an item of evidence directly support the claim? Is the type of evidence relevant to the claim? Is there any other type of evidence that may support the claim? Is it necessary to have several types of evidence? Can the branch of argument be closed with evidence presented? If one or more evidence types are chosen, what kind of confidence argument should be considered?

S5.3 is actually a strategy that is used to combine the branch of primary safety argument with the branch of confidence argument under one top-level safety goal. With the progress of research in safety cases in recent years, it is recommended to separate the two parts in order to have the skeleton of safety clearer [16]. The elements in a process argument, such as the competence of an analyst or reviewer, may contribute to the overall quality of safety activities. But they would not exclude the possibility of errors or defects in system analysis and design and would not demonstrate the effectiveness of the control of risks directly. Therefore, we need to balance our efforts involved in the two parts, avoiding losing sight and focus of product arguments in safety cases.

# 4    Discussions

## 4.1    Comparison of Strategy Types

There is some degree of overlap of the five groups of strategies. However, it provides a view of strategies from different viewpoints. Each group has its own advantages. The strategies came from Source 1 are based upon the 'part-whole' relationship and set more focus on the decomposition, easily mapping with the system description at different stages. The strategies from Source 2 put more emphasis on the problems to be solved. It helps us to gain the view of how safety is considered and handled in the project. The strategies from Source 3 are practical and closely linked with the development process and the certification needs of a system. The strategies from Source 4 concentrate more on seeking mechanisms for providing supportive reasons, rather than intuitive decomposition and refinement of a higher-level goal.

The argument structures in reality are complicated and the strategies linking claims, if they are explicitly presented, are depicted in varied viewpoints. We wish the strategy types presented in the paper will bring about a clearer understanding of potential argument approaches and facilitate proper usage of strategies in safety argument development.

## 4.2    Application of Strategies

The strategy types presented in Section 3 may be considered in the Step 3 of the six-step method, which provide more choices for potential lower-level argument structures. In addition, the following aspects should be considered while describing argument approaches.

1. The identification and adoption of strategies does not exclude the identification of direct evidence for a goal, instead, the two activities can go in parallel. This is important, especially for searching for support for intermediate safety goals. For example, a higher level safety requirement for a software package may be supported by a number of lower level safety goals set for individual software units that associated with that package. At the same time, it may be supported by evidence such as a system level testing result.
2. It is acceptable practice to adopt and use two strategies of different types in combination to support the decomposition and refinement of one claim. If more than one strategy is chosen to advance the argument, we need to examine and ensure that no identical lower level goals are repetitively represented. Moreover, proper evidence assertions should be adopted if a single item of evidence is referenced by more than one claim. One interesting point is that if there is a case that different strategies lead to sub-goals that contradict each other, it may indicate that the definition or understanding of the higher level safety goal is insufficient, ambiguous, or inconsistent.
3. A generic strategy type can be used repeatedly in argument decomposition at different stages. However, the contexts and justifications associated with the instance of that strategy type is varied according to the goal with which it is linked.
4. Strategies are unnecessarily always explicitly presented in the graphical representation of an argument. If the comprehension is adequately achieved, obvious 'strategies' can be left implicit while an argument structure of smaller size is preferred. However, the context and the justification associated with the implicit strategies should not be neglected and should be addressed in confidence arguments.
5. The types of strategies presented may also be considered for helping to integrate lower-level safety goals to a higher-level safety goal. As described by [2], sometimes, an argument can be constructed bottom-up. While constructing arguments with a bottom-up approach, the user rarely has the freedom to select a strategy.

But with some common 'strategies' used in top-down argument construction in mind, the user can have a better view of potential higher-level goals that may be inferred and the user may put together relevant lower-level goals/evidence assertions more efficiently in order to jointly support a single higher-level goal.

## 5    Conclusion

In this paper, we have presented the major sources of information that the strategy for safety argument development may come from. In addition to the traditional approach argument decomposition based on the rule of 'divide and conquer', we have suggested to adopt strategies from the argumentation domain – logical appeals. The benefits of our work, we anticipate to evaluate in our ongoing work, include: provision of prior knowledge of reusable generic strategy types, reduction of inappropriate usage of argument strategies, a clear sense of justification needed for various strategy types, and improvement in understanding of inferences that are unclearly described in safety reviews. Furthermore, the generic types of strategies may also be used as an information source in the development of future safety case patterns.

In the future, we hope to carry on our work in the following directions. Firstly, we will perform a more extensive study of argument structures from available literature and industrial reports in order to examine the coverage and appropriateness of the classification. Secondly, we will examine the existence and coverage of the strategy types presented in the paper by performing survey to safety case practitioners. Thirdly, we will implement a real industrial case study of safety case development with mapping and application of the identified strategy types in order to check the applicability and effectiveness of the strategy types as instructive references. In addition, we would consider providing domain-specific application guidance on the usage of argument strategies in system assurance, taking account of the features of systems, the attributes to be assured and specific industrial needs. As a long term goal, we hope to put forward the practical application of argument approaches in assurance of more attributes of critical systems.

**Acknowledgments.** This work has been partially supported by the project "CECRIS – CErtification of CRItical Systems", FP7 - Marie Curie (IAPP) number 324334.

## References

1. Evidence: Using safety cases in industry and healthcare. The Health Foundation, London (2012)
2. GSN Working Group, GSN Community Standard Version 1, Origin Consulting (York) Limited (2011)
3. Kelly, T.P.: Arguing Safety: A Systematic Approach to Managing Safety Cases. PhD Thesis, Department of Computer Science, University of York, UK (1998)
4. Hawkins, R., Kelly, T.: A Software Safety Argument Pattern Catalogue. The University of York, York (2013)

5. OMG, Structured Assurance Case Metamodel (SACM), Version 1.0. (2013)
6. Yamamoto, S., Matsuno, Y.: An evaluation of argument patterns to reduce pitfalls of applying assurance case. In: 2013 1st International Workshop on Assurance Cases for Software-Intensive Systems, ASSURE. (2013)
7. Bloomfield, R., Bishop, P.: Safety and Assurance Cases: Past, Present and Possible Future – an Adelard Perspective. In: Dale, C., Anderson, T. (eds.) Making Systems Safer, pp. 51–67. Springer, London (2010)
8. Toulmin, S.E.: The Uses of Argument. University Press, Cambridge (1958)
9. Spriggs, J.: GSN - The Goal Structuring Notation (A Structured Approach to Presenting Arguments). Springer (2012)
10. Bloomfield, R., et al.: ASCAD–Adelard safety case development manual. Adelard (1998)
11. Yuan, T., Kelly, T.: Argument Schemes in Computer System Safety Engineering. Informal Logic 31(2), 89–109 (2011)
12. Denney, E., Pai, G., Pohl, J.: Automating the Generation of Heterogeneous Aviation Safety Cases. Technical Report NASA/CR-2011-215983, NASA Ames Research Center (2011)
13. Kelly, T.: A Six-Step Method for the Development of Goal Structures. York Software Engineering, Flixborough (1997)
14. Chen, Y., Lawford, M., Wang, H., Wassyng, A.: Insulin Pump Software Certification. In: Gibbons, J., MacCaull, W. (eds.) FHIES 2013. LNCS, vol. 8315, pp. 87–106. Springer, Heidelberg (2014)
15. MOD, Defence Standard 00-56 Safety Management Requirements for Defence Systems, Part 1: Requirements, Issue 4 (2007)
16. Hawkins, R., et al.: A New Approach to creating Clear Safety Arguments. In: Dale, C., Anderson, T. (eds.) Advances in Systems Safety, pp. 3–23. Springer, London (2011)
17. Weinstock, C.B., Goodenough, J.B.: CMU/SEI-2009-TN-018 Towards an Assurance Case Practice for Medical Devices, Carnegie Mellon University (2009)
18. Dodd, I., Habli, I.: Safety certification of airborne software: An empirical study. Reliability Engineering & System Safety 98(1), 7–23 (2012)
19. Holloway, C.M.: Towards understanding the DO-178C / ED-12C assurance case. In: System Safety, incorporating the Cyber Security Conference 2012 (2012)
20. Hawkins, R., Habli, I., Kelly, T.: The Principles of Software Safety Assurance. In: The 31st International System Safety Conference, Boston, Massachusetts, USA (2013)
21. Birch, J., et al.: Safety Cases and Their Role in ISO 26262 Functional Safety Assessment. In: Bitsch, F., Guiochet, J., Kaâniche, M. (eds.) SAFECOMP. LNCS, vol. 8153, pp. 154–165. Springer, Heidelberg (2013)
22. Govier, T.: A practical study of argument. Cengage Learning, Wadsworth (2010)
23. Dowden, B.H.: Logical Reasoning (2012),
    http://www.csus.edu/indiv/d/dowdenb/4/
    Logical%20Reasoning.pdf (accessed March 1, 2014)
24. Walton, D.N., Reed, C., Macagno, F.: Argumentation schemes. Cambridge University Press (2008)
25. Sun, L.: Establishing Confidence in Safety Assessment Evidence. PhD Thesis, Department of Computer Science, University of York, UK (2012)
26. Goodenough, J.B., Weinstock, C.B., Klein, A.Z.: Eliminative induction: A basis for arguing system confidence. In: 2013 35th International Conference on Software Engineering, ICSE (2013)
27. Post-Closure Safety Case for Geological Repositories - Nature and Purpose. Nuclear Energy Agency, OECD (2004)

# Towards a Cross-Domain Software Safety Assurance Process for Embedded Systems

Marc Zeller, Kai Höfig, and Martin Rothfelder

Siemens AG, Corporate Technology
Otto-Hahn-Ring 6, 81379 Munich, Germany
{marc.zeller,kai.hoefig,martin.rothfelder}@siemens.com

**Abstract.** In this work, we outline a cross-domain assurance process for safety-relevant software in embedded systems. This process aims to be applied in various different application domains and in conjunction with any development methodology. With this approach we plan to reduce the growing effort for safety assessment in embedded systems by reusing safety analysis techniques and tools for the product development in different domains.

## 1 Introduction

The importance of safety-relevant software systems in many application domains of embedded systems, such as aerospace, railway, health care, automotive and industrial automation, is continuously growing. Thus, along with the growing system complexity, also the need for safety assessment as well as its effort is increasing drastically in order to guarantee the high quality demands in these application domains. However, this trend is contrary to industry's aim to reduce development costs and time-to-market of new products.

The goal of safety assessment is to identify all failures that cause hazardous situations and to demonstrate that their probabilities are sufficiently low. In the application domains of safety-relevant software the safety assurance process is defined by the means of safety standards. The requirements of these standards must be met in order to enable argumentation that the system is safe. To reduce development costs and the time-to-market, one possible approach is to develop a safety assurance process which is applicable to multiple applications domains of embedded systems (e.g. like the IEC 61508 standard [3]). In this paper, we present an approach towards a safety assurance process for software which is applicable across different application domains of embedded systems. This process aims to be applicable with various development methodologies used in different domains and tries to use common safety analysis techniques as far as possible. Hence, it builds the foundation for the future development of methods and tools for safety assurance which can be applied across domains of safety-relevant software systems. Thus, safety analysis techniques and tools as well as artifacts produced during the safety assurance process may be reused for the safety assessment of different kinds of products. Especially, in areas where embedded systems are highly related to software product-lines or heterogeneous

A. Bondavalli et al. (Eds.): SAFECOMP 2014 Workshops, LNCS 8696, pp. 396–400, 2014.
© Springer International Publishing Switzerland 2014

systems-of-systems, a cross-domain safety analysis process will reduce the effort needed to fulfill the requirements of the respective safety standard significantly.

This paper is organized as follows: In Sec. 2 we present relevant related work. Then, we outline our approach for a cross-domain safety assurance process. The benefits of this process are discussed in Sec. 4. This paper is concluded and an outlook to future work is given in the last section.

## 2    Related Work

Today, numerous standards related to functional safety of software are existing (cf. [1]). These standards provide the rules and guidelines as basis for the safety assurance process of safety-relevant systems in specific domains. Since each domain-specific safety standard defines a specific vocabulary and covers the complete safety life-cycle, each domain has evolved its individual safety assurance process. Since we focus on the safety assurance process of software, we will further consider only safety standards related to software. These standards are: the DO-178C in aeronautics, the ISO 26262 in automotive, IEC 60880 & 62138 in the area of nuclear power plants, the EN 50128 in railway, the IEC 62304 in health care, and the ECSS-Q-ST-80C in space. Moreover, IEC 61508 will be considered which covers the industrial automation domain. However, only parts of the safety process defined in the IEC 61508 standard are related to software, since the scope of this standard is much broader.

In order to enable cross-domain harmonization of the safety assurance process and the sharing of common techniques and tools, first attempts to identify similarities and dissimilarities have already been performed in [1,2,5,6,7]. As a result of these previous analyses the following similarities between the examined standards have be identified:

- Common notion of safety and certification
- Linear progressing safety process with dedicated phases
- Combined hazard assessment and risk analysis to derive safety requirements
- Criticality levels as means to allocation safety (integrity) requirements to system elements
- Verification activities are driven by the safety requirements
- Safety case provides evidence that safety requirements are fulfilled which is needed for certification

Moreover, the following divergences have be identified:

- Varying definition of criticality levels
- Different approaches for the allocation of safety requirements
- Specific verification & validation processes

Based on a number of identified similarities of the safety standards in the transportation sector, [7] already outlines a generic safety assessment process integrated into a concrete system development process. However, only safety standards from the transportation domain are analyzed and recent developments in safety regulations (e.g. the ISO 26262) are not considered. In our work, we aim at finding a cross-domain safety assurance process applicable to any domain-specific software development process.

## 3   Cross-Domain Safety Assurance Process

According to the similarities and divergences of the analyzed safety standards related to software, we outline a cross-domain safety assurance process (see Fig. 1). This process consists of generic and domain-specific steps which must be executed in each of the considered domains as well as steps which are only necessary in specific domains.

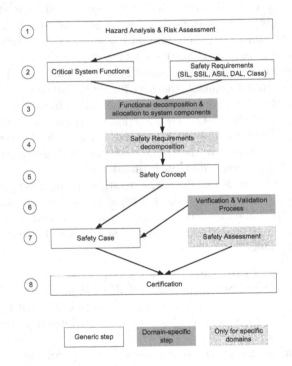

**Fig. 1.** Cross-domain software safety assurance process

The software safety assurance process starts with the *Hazards Analysis & Risk Assessment (HARA)*. This step aims to determine safety-relevant systems functions, the safety requirements of these functions (maximum tolerable failure probabilities) as well as the potential demands for additional safety functions. The different safety standards generally agree on common HARA techniques [6].

As a result of the HARA, safety requirements are derived. According to [1], all safety standards introduce criticality categories, so-called *Criticality Levels* (e.g. the Safety Integrity Levels (SILs) in IEC 61508) to quantify the safety requirements. In all domains, the criticality levels characterize the consequences of failures (severity) combined with a notion of their occurrence probability. However, in each domain the acceptability frontiers of risk differs due to divergences in the definition of severity and risk occurrence [2].

The next phase in the assurance process is the allocation of criticality levels to system elements as well as the functional decomposition. This step is domain-specific due to the differences between safety standards. In aeronautics, nuclear, railway and space the fist categorized element is a (top level) function. Then the criticality levels are derived according to functional decomposition and allocated to the system elements implementing the top-level functions. In the automotive domain, however the criticality levels are allocated first to safety goals and derived to safety requirements and system elements.

Furthermore, a decomposition of the criticality levels is possible in railway and space domain (according to generic rules) as well as in the aeronautics and automotive domain (according to specific rules) [2]. But this phase of the safety assurance process is only possible in these domains.

As a next step, the *Safety Concept* is derived. It is defined as the specification of the safety requirements, their allocation to system elements and their interaction necessary to achieve safety goals [4]. The construction of the safety concept is a generic step which is compliant to all considered safety standards. However, the necessary content of the safety concept may differ from domain to domain.

Within the next phase, the developed software is verified and validated. The verification and validation techniques (such as source code verification, unit testing, integration testing, etc.) and the process itself are defined or recommended by the domain-specific safety standards.

Finally, the *Safety Case* is compiled to argue that the system is safe. The safety case is derived from the safety concept and extended by results of the verification & validation process to prove that the safety requirements have been fulfilled. A safety case is a concept applicable across all domains. However, in aerospace and railway a so-called *Safety Assessment* is required additionally to show the conformity to the standard [5]. The evidence for system safety provided by the safety case forms the basis for safety certification.

# 4   Discussion

The cross-domain safety assurance process outlined in Sec. 3 is applicable to any development process or methodology, since none of the process steps directly include a reference to the system development. Hence, our approach may be used along with state-of-the-art approaches in system/software engineering such as component-based and model-based development as well as software-product-lines.

Our approach solely consists of 8 different process steps which are all not new in the area of safety engineering. Thus, established safety analysis techniques (such as *Hazard and Operability Studies (HAZOP)*, *Failure Mode and Effects Analysis (FMEA)*, *Fault Tree Analysis (FTA)*, etc.) can be applied and no new safety analysis methodologies need to be developed.

More than the half of the phases in our process are generic. Therefore, the techniques and tools used in these steps can be applied in various application domains. The domain-specific steps only differ in methods for the allocation of criticality levels to the system elements and the requirements for software verification & validation. However, also common techniques and tools can be applied in these phases but have to be adapted to the domain-specific requirements respectively. There are only two process phases which are solely relevant to particular safety standards. For these steps domain-specific techniques and tools must be provided separately.

## 5   Conclusions and Outlook

The cross-domain assurance process for safety-relevant software in embedded systems, outlined in this paper, aims to be applied in various different application domains. Thus, supporting the cost-efficient system development as well as the reuse of techniques and tools for the safety analysis. However, not all of the process steps can be realized in a generic and domain-independent way. But our approach is independent from concrete development methodologies and can be applied along with component-based and model-based design. Moreover, common safety analysis techniques can by applied in most process steps.

Future work will include a more refined description of each phases of the cross-domain safety assurance process including applicable techniques and tools. Moreover, we will evaluate our approach in different application domains.

## References

1. Baufreton, P., Blanquart, J., Boulanger, J., Delseny, H., et al.: Multi-domain comparison of safety standards. In: Proceedings of the 5th Int. Conf. on Embedded Real Time Software and Systems, ERTS2 (2010)
2. Blanquart, J.P., Astruc, J.M., Baufreton, P., Boulanger, J.L., et al.: Criticality categories across safety standards in different domains. In: Proceedings of the 6th Int. Conf. on Embedded Real Time Software and Systems, ERTS2 (2012)
3. Int. Electrotechnical Commission (IEC): IEC 61508: Functional safety of electrical/electronic/programmable electronic safety related systems (1998)
4. Int. Organization for Standardization (ISO): ISO 26262: Road vehicles - Functional safety (2011)
5. Ledinot, E., Astruc, J.M., Blanquart, J.P., Baufreton, P., et al.: A cross-domain comparison of software development assurance standards. In: Proceedings of the 6th Int. Conf. on Embedded Real Time Software and Systems, ERTS2 (2012)
6. Machrouh, J., Blanquart, J.P., Baufreton, P., Boulanger, J.L., et al.: Cross domain comparison of system assurance. In: Proceedings of the 6th Int. Conf. on Embedded Real Time Software and Systems, ERTS2 (2012)
7. Papadopoulos, Y., McDermid, J.A.: The potential for a generic approach to certification of safety critical systems in the transportation sector. Reliability engineering & system safety 63(1), 47–66 (1999)

# A Software Safety Verification Method Based on System-Theoretic Process Analysis

Asim Abdulkhaleq and Stefan Wagner

Institute of Software Technology, University of Stuttgart,
Universitätsstraße 38,70569 Stuttgart, Germany
{Asim.Abdulkhaleq,Stefan.Wagner}@informatik.uni-stuttgart.de
http://www.iste.uni-stuttgart.de/se.html

**Abstract.** Modern safety-critical systems are increasingly reliant on software. Software safety is an important aspect in developing safety-critical systems, and it must be considered in the context of the system level into which the software will be embedded. STPA (System-Theoretic Process Analysis) is a modern safety analysis approach which aims to identify the potential hazardous causes in complex safety-critical systems at the system level. To assure that these hazardous causes of an unsafe software's behaviour cannot happen, safety verification involves demonstrating whether the software fulfills those safety requirements and will not result in a hazardous state. We propose a method for verifying of software safety requirements which are derived at the system level to provide evidence that the hazardous causes cannot occur (or reduce the associated risk to a low acceptable level). We applied the method to a cruise control prototype to show the feasibility of the proposed method.

**Keywords:** STPA approach, software safety analysis, temporal logic, safety verification, formal verification methods.

## 1   Introduction

A safety-critical system is a system that can cause undesired loss or harm to human life, property, or the environment, whereas safety-critical software is software that can contribute to such loss or harm [1]. A software cannot directly cause loss or harm, but it may control some equipment that may cause accidents [2]. Therefore, many examples of safety systems which have failed due to software related faults: the loss of Ariane 5 [4], Therac-25 [3], and more recently Boeing 777-200 [8] and the Toyota Prius. Many software related accidents and major losses are the result of incompleteness or other flaws in the software requirements, not coding errors [1]. Safety is a system problem; therefore, to understand the safety aspects of software, it is necessary first to understand the general field of system safety.

STPA (System-Theoretic Process Analysis) [5] is an approach developed by Leveson to identify safety requirements and constraints at the system level. In STPA, the system is seen as a set of control loops (comprising interacting components involving software) which interact with each other. STPA uses the existing

A. Bondavalli et al. (Eds.): SAFECOMP 2014 Workshops, LNCS 8696, pp. 401–412, 2014.

knowledge about a system to guide the safety analysis process; therefore, it is not necessary to have knowledge about the details of implementation.

## 1.1   Problem Statement

Typically, software verification focuses on proving the functional correctness of software and demonstrating that the software fully satisfies all functional requirements [16]. However, they cannot make it safe and the correctness of software cannot ensure the software is safe, or reduce the risk. Therefore, the software must be analyzed regarding the safety aspect and verified against its safety requirements at the system level [7]. As STPA is a new technique, which has proven to be effective on establishing the safety requirements and constraints at the system level (e.g. Space Shuttle Operations [18], Japanese Exploration Agency (JAXA) [19]); it has not been used for identifying software safety requirements in the system context and verifying the software against them.

## 1.2   Research Objectives

The overall objective of this research is to fill this gap and investigate the possibility of verifying safety-critical software against safety requirements and constraints which are derived at the system level by using STPA. To control the associated risk of the safety-critical software, we first need to identify the potential hazards and then demonstrate that a potential hazardous cause cannot occur, i.e., the software cannot contribute to an unsafe state. The main purpose of applying STPA to software in the context of a system in our method is to understand the software hazardous causes early to develop corresponding software safety requirements which should be taken into consideration. The second purpose is to reduce the amount time and effort of safety analysis and verification at the code level.

## 1.3   Contribution

For that, we propose a method which provides a link between the safety analysis at the system level and safety verification at the code level. This method enables the safety analyst to extract the software safety requirements at the system level and verify them at the code level.

## 2   Background

We give background information on the three main topics which we use in the proposed method: STPA, safety verification, and formal specification and verification:

## 2.1  STPA

STPA [5] is a top-down system engineering approach to system safety; therefore, it can be applied early in the system development process or before a design has been created to generate high-level safety requirements and constraints. In contrast to traditional safety analysis techniques, which are based on reliability theory, STPA is more powerful in terms of identifying more causal factors and hazardous scenarios, particularly those related to software, system design and human behaviour [6]. STPA identifies systematic failures such as software design errors, hardware design errors, requirements specification errors and other operational procedures.

STPA is implemented in four steps [6]: (1) establish the fundamentals of analysis; (2) identify potentially hazardous control actions; (3) use the identified potentially hazardous control actions to create safety requirements and constraints; and (4) determine how each potentially hazardous control action could occur. In step 1, the safety analyst must identify the accidents or losses which will be considered, hazards associated with these accidents, and specify safety requirements (constraints). After establishing the fundamentals, the safety analyst must draw a preliminary (high-level) functional control structure of the system. In step 2, the analyst has to use the control structure as a guide for investigating the analysis to identify the potentially unsafe control actions. Then he or she translates them to corresponding safety constraints. In step 3, the analyst has to identify the process model variables for each controller (automated controller or human) in the control loop and analyze each path to determine how each potentially hazardous control actions could occur. At the end of the process, a recommendation for the system design should be developed for additional mitigations.

## 2.2  Software Safety Verification

The first step of safety verification is to verify that the software requirements are consistent with or satisfy safety constraints. Safety verification exists to provide evidence that associated risk has been reduced or eliminated [1]. Safety verification is not the same as functional verification. Functional verification assures that the software fully satisfies its specifications, while safety verification uses the results of the safety analysis process to assure that the software meets the safety requirements [20]. The safety verification can be done in two ways [1]: (1) static analysis which looks over the code and design documents of the system (e.g. fault tree, formal verification); and (2) dynamic analysis requires the execution of the software to check all of the systems safety features. Static analysis is the same as a structured code review. Systems can be proven to match requirements, but it will not catch any safety states that the requirements miss [1]. The dynamic analysis has the ability to catch unanticipated safety problems, but it cannot prove that a system is safe (e.g. software testing).

SFTA (Software Fault Tree Analysis) [1] is a static analysis technique which is primarily used to discover all potential faults such as faulty inputs or software bugs that could occur in software. SFTA has also been used for verifying software code. Leveson stated in [1] that SFTA is applicable only to small-sized software. Because the complete generating of a tree is not possible for large software.

### 2.3    Formal Specification and Verification Techniques

Formal verification is a very active area of research, and many promising techniques and methodologies have been invented for verifying computing systems. Theorem proving and model checking are common methods used today. Formal verification entails a mathematical proof showing that a system satisfies its desired property or specification. To do this, the property of interest must be modeled in a mathematical structure (e.g. temporal logic). Temporal Logic has been proposed by Pnueli [9] as an appropriate formalism in the specification and verification of concurrent programs. Many different versions of temporal logic have been used in the verification process such as Linear-Time Temporal Logic (LTL), and Computation Tree Logic (CTL) [23] which have been broadly used to express safety properties in a formal notation. An LTL formula consists of atomic propositions, Boolean operators ($\neg, \vee, \wedge, \leftrightarrow, \rightarrow, true, false$) and temporal operators ($\bigcirc$ next, $\square$ always, $\lozenge$ eventually, $\mathcal{U}$ until, $\mathcal{R}$ release). CTL is an extension of classical logic that allows reasoning about an infinite tree of state transitions. Model checking is a very popular formal verification technique and has been used widely in the verification of software. It first involves building a finite state machine as a formal model of a system, and then verifying whether the property, written in some temporal logic, holds or not through an exhaustive search of the system state space. Model checkers can be used also for testing purposes to generate test cases [10].

## 3    Software Safety Verification Method Based on STPA

The safety analysis of safety-critical software provides the safety requirements which need to be tested. Safety verification shall be performed to verify a correct incorporation of software safety requirements [24]. Verification must show that hazards have been eliminated or controlled to an acceptable level of risk. Figure 1 shows the proposed method of software safety verification based on STPA at the system level. The method includes three main steps: (1) safety analysis of software at the system level; (2) formalization of safety requirements and constraints; and (3) verification and testing at the code level.

### 3.1    Safety Analysis of Software at the System Level (Step 1)

This step aims at analyzing the software in the context of the system to identify the potential hazardous causes of software that could lead or contribute to an accident. At this step, the safety analyst will apply STPA to the requirements specification of the whole system. Then he/she will extract the requirements relevant to the software in the context of the system. The safety control structure of a system will include the software in the control loop as the main component

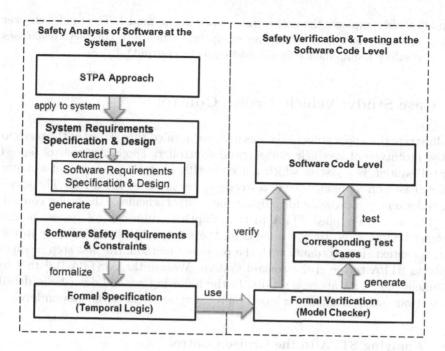

**Fig. 1.** Overview of software safety verification method

(controller) to depict the interactions between software and other parts of the system (SW/HW components). Each unsafe control action in this context will be documented with four types of hazardous control actions [5]: *Not Providing Causes Hazard, Providing Causes Hazard, Wrong Timing/Order,* and *Stopped Too Soon/Applied Too Long.* At the end of this step, the safety analyst will translate each hazardous control action of software identified by STPA into the corresponding safety constraints and requirements in the system context.

## 3.2 Formalization of Safety Requirements and Constraints (Step 2)

Up to this step, the safety requirements of the software are identified. These safety requirements must be formalized using temporal logic (e.g. LTL, CTL) to be able to verify them in the next step.

## 3.3 Verification and Testing at the Code Level (Step 3)

This step aims to verify the software at the code level against the safety requirements which are expressed in the formal specification in step 2. After formalizing the safety requirements, this step can be done in two different ways: 1) using a model checker for formal verification [22], or 2) using a model checker to generate corresponding test cases [17]. A model checker takes as input a model of the software and the property of interest, which is written in temporal logic and then effectively explores the entire state space of the model. The model checker generates counterexamples which can easily be turned into complete test cases with the safety requirements (input and expected output).

# 4   Case Study: Vehicle Cruise Control

To illustrate the application of the method, we applied three steps of the method to the prototype of a vehicle cruise speed controller. The cruise control (speed control) system is a system which automatically controls the speed of a motor vehicle based on a preset value of a steady speed given by the driver. The speed controller unit is a program for judging the control scheme of the cruise control. In [11], we have applied STPA to the adaptive cruise control system at the abstract system level. Here, we focus on the safety analysis of software in the system context. In accordance with the proposed method, the first step involves applying STPA to the cruise control system. We use the A-STPA [12] tool to document the STPA analysis results. In the following, we will describe in detail the software safety verification based on a safety analysis at the system level.

## 4.1   Applying STPA to the Cruise Control

The results of applying STPA to the cruise controller at the system level are as follows:

1. **Analysis of Fundamentals:** The safety analyst must first establish the following fundamentals:
   - **Software Description:** The software of the cruise control (controller) maintains the vehicle speed automatically without pressing the accelerator pedal. It does it by sending the adjust throttle position to move as necessary to maintain the specified speed under varying conditions. The throttle is moved by a throttle actuator. The cruise control software maintains the speed of the vehicle on the occurrence of one of these events: (1) driver engages the brake, (2) the engine stops running, (3) the driver turns the ignition off, and (4) the driver turns the cruise control off. The controller receives signals from several sensors such as rotation sensor, brake pedal sensor, gear box sensor, and engine status sensor.
   - **Software Level Goals:** G.1: Control the speed of the vehicle.
   - **Accident:** AC1: The accident to be considered is a sudden acceleration of the vehicle which leads to a crash with another vehicle and the occupants are injured while the cruise control is in operation.
   - **The Related Software Level Hazards:**
     H.1: Unintended acceleration or deceleration of the vehicle when the cruise control is in active mode.
     H.2: The current speed value on the user interface is different from the actual speed of vehicle.

- **Design Requirements:**
  DR.1: The target speed must be between 40 $km/h <= vt <= 100\ km/h$.
  DR.2: The software shall notify the driver when trouble is detected.
  DR.3: It shall keep the acceleration rate within 0.25 and 0.4 m/sec.
- **Safety Constraints:**
  SC1: The controller shall keep the current speed of the vehicle below or equal to the desired speed.
  SC2: The cruise control shall not engage at the speed < 25 mph (40kph).
- **Safety Control Structure Diagram:** Figure 2 shows the control structure diagram which depicts the interaction between the software and other components in the system.

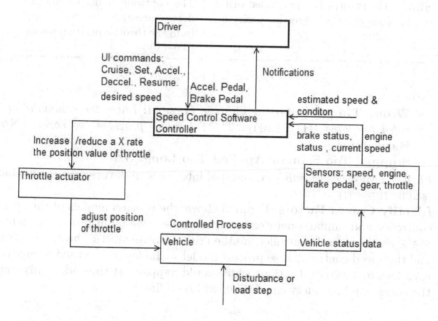

**Fig. 2.** Safety control structure of cruise control software at the system level

2. **Identify Unsafe Control Actions:** Based on the control structure diagram (Fig. 2), we can identify the potentially unsafe control actions of the software at the system level which can lead to critical error. For example, the control Action: *Provide throttle position command (out)* can be documented as follows:

  - **Not Providing Causes Hazard:** *Throttle position command provided but not received by the throttle actuator when the cruise control is engaged (on)* [**H1**]
  - **Providing Causes Hazard:** *The throttle position is commanded while the cruise control is inactive (off)* [**H1**]. *The throttle position commanded with incorrect value of the throttle position* [**H1**].

Table 1. Examples of safety requirements which are derived by STPA

| #code | Hazardous control actions | Safety Requirements and Constraints |
|-------|---------------------------|-------------------------------------|
| SR1 | Throttle position command provided but not received by the throttle actuator when the cruise control is engaged (on). | The throttle actuator must receive the adjustment throttle position command when it is commanded by controller. |
| SR2 | The throttle position command is commanded while the cruise control is disengaged (off). | The controller must prevent rogue commands to the throttle when cruise control is off. |
| SR3 | The throttle is commanded with incorrect X throttle position value. | The controller must be able to detect incorrect voltages issuing from the throttle position sensor (0.9-4.0v). |

- **Wrong Timing or Order Causes Hazard: Late**: *the command provided too late*   [**H1**]. **Early**: *The command provided too early*   [**Not Hazardous**]
- **Stopped Too Soon or Applied Too Long**: *N/A*

Each hazardous cause will be translated into software-level safety constraints (see in Table 1.)

3. **Identify Causal Factors:** Figure 3 shows the process models of the speed controller and human operator as an example. The main process variables of the cruise control controller are the cruise control states, throttle control, and the speed control. These process model variables can be used to analyze each hazardous control actions which could happen. At the end of this step, the corresponding safety constraints will be refined.

## 4.2   Formalising the Safety Requirements

After identifying the safety commitments, we can translate them into formal specifications to be able to verify them with formal verification methods in the next step. Based on the classification of safety requirements for formal verification which are described in [13] by Friedemann, we mapped the four types of the hazardous control action classifications to the formal specification.

**Mapping Safety Requirements to a Formal Specification:** The mapping process starts with taking the set of the process model variables of the software (software states variables) which are identified in the last step of STPA to understand the main states of the software. To translate the safety requirements into a formal specification, first, we write them as informal textual requirements, i.e. if we consider the safety constraint **SC2**:*The cruise control shall not engage*

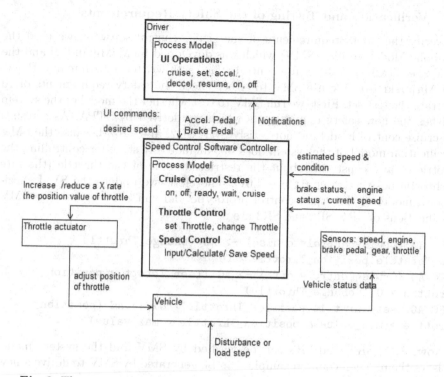

**Fig. 3.** The process model of the cruise control software at the system level

*at the speed* < 25 *mph* (40 *kph*). Second, we translate the textual descriptions to formal textual description by using the control flow statements (*IF- Then, Wait- Until, Wait- For, Do- Until*), for example:

**IF** *CruiseControl (inactive)* **and** *Read_speed(actual_speed)* <25 *mph* **Then** *CruiseControl (inactive)*

Finally, we translate them into an LTL specification, for example:

□ ( CruiseControl (off) ∧ *Read_Speed(speed_data)* < 25 *mph*) → □ CruiseControl (off)

Examples of formal specifications of software safety requirements which are derived from the STPA safety analysis at the system level are:

- **SR1:** □ *CruiseControl(cruise)* → □ *(change_Throttle ∧* set_Throttle (position_Throttle) )
- **SR2:** □ CruiseControl (off)  → □ ¬*(set_Throttle(position_Throttle)* ∨ *change_Throttle)*
- **SR3:** □ *set_Throttle(position_Throttle)* → □ *(position_Throttle > min_value ∧ position_Throttle < max_value)*

## 4.3    Verification and Testing of the Safety Requirements

To verify the safety requirements of the cruise control software, we used the Symbolic Model Verifier (SMV) which was developed by McMillan [14] and the SMV specification of the cruise control which was written by Ammann, Black, and Majurski [10]. We use SMV to either check the safety requirements or to generate the test set. First, we run SMV to test whether the model of the system satisfies the new safety requirements which we derived by STPA. As a result, the cruise control model did not satisfy SR1, SR2, and SR3, because the SMV specification model of the system does not include any state for controlling the throttle or any constraint about the restricted value of the throttle (the rate of throttle position value 0.09v - 4.0v). Therefore, we update the SVM specification model of the cruise control prototype and run SMV again. The SMV specifications of SR1, SR2 and SR3 are :

```
SPEC AG (CruiseControl= cruise) -> AG (change_Throttle &
set_Throttle.position_Throttle > 0)
SPEC AG (CruiseControl= off ) -> AG !(set_Throttle.position_
Throttle > 0 | change_Throttle)
SPEC AG (set_Throttle.position_Throttle > 0) -> AG (position_
Throttle > min_value & position_Throttle < max_value)
```

Now, SR1, SR2, and SR3 can be verified by SMV and the system model satisfies them. Then counterexamples can be generated by SMV to derive a new test suite.

## 5    Related Work

There is a large body of existing work on using formal verification for safety properties, safety verification by using SFTA, and generating test cases by using a model checker. Here, we discuss some of the most closely related work.

Leveson et al. [7] explain software fault tree analysis as a method for safety verification at the code level to be used on a more complex language involving such features as concurrency and exception handling. They consider the application of the safety analysis procedures to requirements modeling and specification languages. Kristen et al. [15] investigates how the results of one safety analysis technique, fault trees, are interpreted as software safety requirements by using interval logic to be used in the program design process. They interpreted fault trees as temporal formulas and how such formulas can be used for deriving safety requirements for software. Friedemann[13] propose the classification of safety requirements for the formal verification of software models of industrial automation systems. He expresses the safety requirements by using computation tree logic. The main reason of developing this classification is to handle difficulties in formal specification of safety requirements by software engineer. Recently, Black[17] shows how to generate test cases by using model checking.

The previous work focused on using the formal verification methods to verify that the software fulfills its specification (functional correctness). However, not all software errors can lead to the critical error that may lead to an accident. Safety properties (e.g. deadlocks, unexpected behavior, etc.) also are a special interest in formal verification. There have been a lot of work to verify safety properties at the code level. Verifying safety requirements, which are derived by using the traditional hazard analysis techniques such as FTA and SFTA, is an active area in verifying safety-critical systems. However, FTA and SFTA are difficult to apply to different parts of the safety related system (e.g. interaction between components). They evaluate only the possibility of occurrence, not the likelihood and appear to be scalable for software, but they have limitation. For example, the root node can only describe a known failure and they are labor-intensive and thus costly for large-size software [21].

Since safety of software cannot be analyzed without taking into account the system context, we take the advantages of STPA at the system level to construct a method for verifying safety requirements derived at the system level by using STPA. The method starts with safety analysis of software in the context of the system level by using STPA to derive the high-level safety requirements and constraints. The potential hazards identified during STPA will be translated into a set of verifiable safety requirements. The safety verification uses these verifiable safety requirements to prove that the software satisfies these requirements.

## 6  Conclusions and Future Work

In this paper, a method of software safety verification at the system level based on STPA is proposed. We investigated the application of the STPA structure to software, and we found that STPA can be directly used for software. We mapped the results of the STPA safety analysis to a formal specification to be able to verify safety requirements at the software code level. The limitation of the method is that the formal specification is done manually which may lead to much effort to construct and check the potential combinations of relevant states. Therefore, we are exploring the automation of this step and integrate it with our A-STPA tool as future work. Furthermore, we plan in-depth case studies to improve the method by applying it to real safety-critical software in industry. We plan also to investigate the effectiveness of using the proposed method during an ISO 26262 life cycle in the automotive industry.

## References

1. Leveson, N.G.: Safeware: System Safety and Computers. ACM, New York (1995)
2. McDermid, J.A.: Issues in developing software for safety critical systems. Reliability Engineering & System Safety 32, 1–24 (1991)
3. Leveson, N.G., Turner, C.S.: An investigation of the Therac-25 accidents. Computer 26(7), 18–41 (1993)
4. Llons, J.L.: ARIANE 5: Flight 501 Failure. Technical Report, Inquiry Board (1996)
5. Leveson, N.G.: Engineering a Safer World: Systems Thinking Applied to Safety. Engineering systems. MIT Press (2011)

6. Leveson, N.G.: An STPA Primer. Engineering systems. MIT Press (2013)
7. Leveson, N.G., Cha, S.S., Shimeall, T.J.: Safety verification of Ada Programs Using Software Fault Trees. IEEE Software 8(4), 48–59 (1991)
8. ATSB Transport safety Investigation Report, In-Flight Upset Event 240 km North-West of Perth, WA Boeing Company 777-200, 9M-MRG (2005)
9. Pnueli, A.: The temporal logic of programs. In: 18th Annual Symposium on Foundations of Computer Science, pp. 46–57 (1977)
10. Ammann, P.E., Black, P.E., Majurski, W.: Using Model Checking to Generate Tests from Specifications. In: Proceedings of the Second IEEE International Conference on Formal Engineering Methods, ICFEM 1998 (1998)
11. Abdulkhaleq, A., Wagner, S.: Experiences with Applying STPA to Software-Intensive Systems in the Automotive Domain. In: Proc. 2013 STAMP Conference, MIT, USA (2013)
12. Abdulkhaleq, A., Wagner, S.: An Open Tool Support for System-Theoretic Process Analysis. In: Proc. 2014 STAMP Conference, MIT, USA (2014)
13. Friedemann, B.: Classification of Safety Requirements for Formal Verification of Software Models of Industrial Automation Systems. In: Proceedings of the 13th Conference on Software and Systems Engineering and their Applications, ICSSEA 2000 (2000)
14. McMillan, K.L.: Symbolic Model Checking. Kluwer Academic Publishers, Norwell (1992)
15. Hansen, K.M., Ravn, A.P., Stavridou, V.: From safety analysis to software requirements. IEEE Transactions on Software Engineering 24(7), 573–584 (1998)
16. Tracey, N., Clark, J., McDermid, J., Mander, K.: Integrating Safety Analysis with Automatic Test-Data Generation for Software Safety Verification. In: Proceedings of the 17th International Conference on System Safety (1999)
17. Black, P.E.: Test Generation Using Model Checking and Specification Mutation. IT Professional 16(2), 17–21 (2014)
18. Stringfellow, M.V., Leveson, N.G., Owens, B.D.: Safety-Driven Design for Software-Intensive Aerospace and Automotive Systems. Proceedings of the IEEE 98(4), 515–525 (2010)
19. Ishimatsu, T., Leveson, N.G., Thomas, J.P., Fleming, C.H., Katahira, M., Miyamoto, Y., Ujiie, R., Nakao, H., Hoshino, N.: Hazard Analysis of Complex Spacecraft Using Systems-Theoretic Process Analysis. Journal of Spacecraft and Rockets 51(2) (2014)
20. Hardy, T.L.: Essential Questions in System Safety: A Guide for Safety Decision Makers. AuthorHouse (2010)
21. Lutz, R., Nikora, A.: Failure Assessment in System Health Management with Aerospace Applications, 1st edn. John Wiley & Sons (2011), Johnson, S.B., et al (eds.)
22. Brock, B.C., Hunt, W.A.: Formally Specifying and Mechanically Verifying Programs for the Motorola Complex Arithmetic Processor DSP. In: Proceedings of the 1997 IEEE International Conference on Computer Design: VLSI in Computers and Processors, ICCD 1997, October 12-15, pp. 31–36 (1997)
23. Kapur, R.: CTL for Test Information of Digital ICS. Springer (2002)
24. NASA.: Software Safety, NASA Technical Standard, NASA-STD 8719.13A (1997)

# Quantifying Uncertainty in Safety Cases
# Using Evidential Reasoning

Sunil Nair[1], Neil Walkinshaw[2], and Tim Kelly[3]

[1] Simula Research Laboratory, Norway
[2] Department of Computer Science, University of Leicester, United Kingdom
[3] Department of Computer Science, University of York, United Kingdom
sunil@simula.no, n.walkinshaw@mcs.le.ac.uk,
tim.kelly@york.ac.uk

**Abstract.** Dealing with uncertainty is an important and difficult aspect of analyses and assessment of complex systems. A real-time large-scale complex critical system involves many uncertainties, and assessing probabilities to represent these uncertainties is itself a complex task. Currently, the certainty with which safety requirements are satisfied and the consideration of the other confidence factors often remains implicit in the assessment process. Many publications in the past have detailed the structure and content of safety cases and Goal Structured Notation (GSN). This paper does not intend to repeat them. Instead, this paper outlines a novel solution to accommodate uncertainty in the safety cases development and assessment using the *Evidential-Reasoning approach* - a mathematical technique for reasoning about uncertainty and evidence. The proposed solution is a bottom-up approach that first performs low-level evidence assessments that makes any uncertainty explicit, and then automatically propagates this confidence up to the higher-level claims. The solution would enable safety assessors and managers to accurately summarise their judgement and make doubt or ignorance explicit.

**Keywords:** safety, safety assessment, safety case, confidence argument, evidence, evidential reasoning, human factors, expert judgement, uncertainty, confidence.

## 1 Introduction

Goal-based system safety standards such as DS 00-56 (MoD 2004a) often require the construction and provision of a safety case - *a structured argument, supported by a body of evidence, that provides a compelling, comprehensible and valid case that a system is safe for a given application in a given environment* [1]. The assessor needs to establish confidence that the safety case adequately addresses the identification and mitigation of hazards. Unfortunately, both evidence and argument will typically be imperfect and uncertainties in the assessment of safety cases are unavoidable.

A major challenge in developing a good safety case is to determine what type of evidence and how much of this evidence is *sufficient* to satisfy the safety case claims.

A. Bondavalli et al. (Eds.): SAFECOMP 2014 Workshops, LNCS 8696, pp. 413–418, 2014.
© Springer International Publishing Switzerland 2014

Expert judgement plays a vital role in this process. However, the developer or the assessor can never be 100% certain that all hazards were mitigated. Furthermore, uncertainties might exist from secondary issues, such as who created the safety case, who was responsible for generating the evidence, what types of tools and techniques were used, etc. These confidence factors often tend to be implicit considerations in the development and assessment of safety cases.

This paper proposes a novel approach to explore these factors and provide a mathematically sound framework for assessing safety cases using Evidential Reasoning (ER) [2]. The uncertainty of the expert´s judgement is captured in this approach through a series of questions (specific for different evidence types), gauging their confidence in the supporting evidence. ER provides a mechanism by which this low-level confidence information can be propagated up the hierarchy of a structured safety case represented in GSN. The ER algorithm [2] allows us to calculate an aggregate *belief function* for the top-level claim, which explicitly captures any uncertainty in the expert´s judgement from the lower-level confidence ratings. Eliciting the expert´s confidence factors for different evidence types and providing a scale of uncertainty, will allow both developers and regulators to more accurately summarise their opinion and make any doubt or ignorance explicit. This assessment framework will help safety case assessment to be more systematic and consistent, thereby providing increased assurance on the safety of the system.

The rest the paper is organized as follows. Section 2 outlines the background of the paper. Section 3 presents the research agenda and proposed solution. Section 4 presents our conclusions.

## 2 Background

This section introduces the background on expert judgement in safety and ER. We also review related work.

### 2.1 Confidence and Uncertainty in Safety Assessment

Recent studies have shown that determining the confidence in the safety of a system as a whole and, as a part of that process, confidence in individual pieces of evidence is challenging for both industry [3] and academia [4]. The strong reliance of judgment-based processes has led to the current situation where expert judgment may be considered as a *de facto* method for assessing safety of a system in practice [3]. Despite the pervasive and predominant use of expert judgment in safety assessment, few systematic investigations on handling uncertainty have been performed to date.

Improving safety case development and argumentation has been a major research interest in the past. The notion of confidence arguments and assurance deficits were introduced to support the safety case development [5]. Studies have also dealt with confidence factors and criteria used in safety assessments [6, 7]. Past studies [8-10] have detailed the notion of uncertainty in safety cases and provided ways to handle them e.g., using Bayesian Belief Networks (BBN) [11]. Although plausible, BBN rely heavily on their probability tables, which in turn rely on the availability of prior probability information. This reliance upon the prior probability information, which is often complicated to obtain, makes it difficult to provide a thorough assessment on confidence where the assessor is ignorant or doubtful.

## 2.2    Evidential Reasoning (ER)

The general challenge of reasoning about multifaceted decision problems, where the underlying data is subject to varying degrees of (un-)certainty is well-established. In the late 60's, Dempster and Schäfer proposed that the subjective beliefs of individuals could be expressed as `belief functions' in their `Theory of Evidence' (DS-theory) [12, 13]. In a belief function, the possible range of beliefs is represented as a Likert-scale (e.g., 0 is very bad and 5 is excellent), and the subjective belief is represented as a distribution over this scale (where total ignorance is represented as an empty function). They then showed how such belief functions could be combined to yield aggregate beliefs for multi-faceted decision problems.

In reality (e.g., the assessment of safety cases), decision problems tend be structured; certain factors may feed-in to each other, and can form more complex, hierarchical belief structures. ER [2] is an extension of DS-theory that enables the aggregation of belief functions, where the factors are arranged in a hierarchical structure. The root-node represents the final decision one wishes to make. Branch nodes represent contributory factors. Branches can be given different weights, indicating the extent to which they contribute to the overall decision. Leaf-nodes represent points at which one can present ones own belief functions. ER then provides the mathematically sound basis by which to combine the belief-functions provided in the leaf-nodes, and to propagate them up to the root.

# 3    Research Agenda

Our overall goal is to develop a tool-supported framework to improve and support expert judgment in safety assessments. Following on from preliminary work using ER to assess software quality [14], we intend to apply ER to provide an automated, mathematically sound basis for the assessment of the expert's confidence in safety-claims, as set out with confidence arguments.

The proposed high-level procedure is shown in Figure 1. A typical GSN confidence argument will allow structuring of claims and the supporting arguments that increase confidence. The satisfaction of the low-level claims relies on the solution (evidence) supporting them. Through a series of generic and specific questions about the solution, the expert will set out their assessment (ranging from a scale of 0 – 5) and their confidence (a quantified value of confidence level e.g., in percentage) in the satisfaction of the claim. ER will then propagate these beliefs through the GSN structure to yield an overall assessment of the system. Crucially, any ignorance or uncertainty about a claim will be made explicit in the overall assessment as well. Some sample generic questions are shown in the Figure 1.

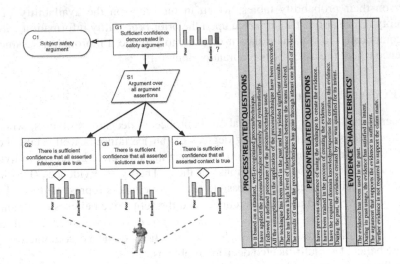

**Fig. 1.** High-level application of ER on GSN confidence argument and sample questions

To achieve the above-mentioned goal we formulate will require us to address the following key research questions (RQs):

*RQ1. What information makes experts gain or lose confidence in the claim, its arguments, and the supporting evidence?*

This RQ aims to understand the expert´s decision-making process. It attempts to identify the various factors and criteria for individual evidence types that influence the confidence of the expert. The key challenge here would be to identify through systematic examination the specific questions to establish the underlying belief functions in ER. Different evidence types are likely to have specific factors that influence the expert´s confidence and these needs to be identified. An initial attempt to answer this RQ was through interviews with experts [10].

*RQ2. How can the confidence in goal structured safety cases be quantified along with uncertainties with the help of ER?*

This RQ aims at adaptation of ER approach to a goal structured safety case. We need to identify ways in which the confidence can be quantified in the argument patterns proposed [5]. We also need to identify ways in which the assurance deficit is captured and communicated to the assessor. As a potential challenge, we need to account for the fact that the confidence arguments are not necessarily tree-structured. We need to identify an approach that enables feeding the answers to the questions (see RQ1) into the ER framework and efficiently propagate these lower-level belief values to the top-level claims. Implementation of the approach with a scalable tool support is also a major step in this RQ.

# 4     Conclusion

This paper has introduced our position in relation to a potential assessment framework that enables quantification of uncertainties and confidence in safety case with the help of the Evidential Reasoning. The framework enables assessors and developers to explicitly quantify any ignorance or doubt they have in the assessment of the lower level solutions. The ER algorithm will propagate these confidence values as *belief functions* to the top-level claims while maintaining the GSN structure. Our preliminary investigations on safety case assessment have shown the importance of identifying and building confidence arguments to support the core safety argument and effectively quantify the confidence and the assurance deficit. This will greatly improve the clarity and consequently the comprehension of the arguments and help reduce the overall size of the core argumentation.

We plan to take some initial steps towards answering the research questions in the near future by systematically identifying factors that influence expert's confidence and how to elicit them. Initial steps have already been taken towards this objective [10]. We also plan to implement the framework as a scalable tool that enables safety case development using GSN and assessment through the adaption of ER on confidence arguments. The tool support would be validated with experts to identify its usefulness in practice. This task would require collaboration among system suppliers and safety assessors in order to investigate the potential of the proposed approach.

**Acknowledgments.** The research leading to these results has received funding from the FP7 programme under grant agreement n° 289011 (OPENCOSS) and from the Research Council of Norway under the project Certus SFI.

# References

1. Interim Defence Standard 00-56 Part 1 - Issue 5, in, UK MOD (2014)
2. Yang, J.-B., Xu, D.-L.: On the evidential reasoning algorithm for multiple attribute decision analysis under uncertainty. IEEE Transactions on Systems, Man, and Cybernetics, Part A 32(3) (2002)
3. Nair, S, et al.: The State of the Practice on Evidence Management for Compliance with Safety Standards, Simula Research Laboratory, Techincal Report (2013)
4. Nair, S., et al.: An Extended Systematic Literature Review on Provision of Evidence for Safety Certification. Information and Software Technology 56(7), 689–717 (2014)
5. Hawkins, R., et al.: A new approach to creating clear safety arguments. In: Advances in Systems Safety, pp. 3–23 (2011)
6. Hamilton, V.: Criteria for Software Evidence, Goal-based standards require evidence-based approaches. Safety Systems 16, 1 (2006)
7. Nair, S, et al.: Understanding the practice of Safety Evidence Assessment: A Qualitative Semi-Structured Interview Study. Technical report, Simula Research Laboratory (2014)
8. Denney, E., Pai, G.: A lightweight methodology for safety case assembly. In: Ortmeier, F., Lipaczewski, M. (eds.) SAFECOMP 2012. LNCS, vol. 7612, pp. 1–12. Springer, Heidelberg (2012)

9. Weaver, R., et al.: Gaining confidence in goal-based safety cases. In: Developments in Risk-based Approaches to Safety, pp. 277–290 (2006)
10. Ayoub, A., Kim, B., Lee, I., Sokolsky, O.: A systematic approach to justifying sufficient confidence in software safety arguments. In: Ortmeier, F., Lipaczewski, M. (eds.) SAFECOMP 2012. LNCS, vol. 7612, pp. 305–316. Springer, Heidelberg (2012)
11. Denney, E., et al.: Towards measurement of confidence in safety cases. In: ESEM (2011)
12. Dempster, A.P.: A generalization of Bayesian inference. Journal of the Royal Statistical Society, Series B 30, 205–247 (1968)
13. Shafer. G.: A Mathematical Theory of Evidence. Princeton University Press (1976)
14. Walkinshaw. N.: Using evidential reasoning to make qualified predictions of software quality. In: PROMISE (2013)

# Metamodel Comparison and Model Comparison for Safety Assurance

Yaping Luo, Luc Engelen, and Mark van den Brand

Eindhoven University of Technology,
P.O. Box 513, 5600 MB, Eindhoven, The Netherlands
{y.luo2,l.j.p.engelen,m.g.j.v.d.brand}@tue.nl

**Abstract.** In safety-critical domains, conceptual models are created in the form of metamodels using different concepts from possibly overlapping domains. Comparison between those conceptual models can facilitate the reuse of models from one domain to another. This paper describes the mappings detected when comparing metamodels and models used for safety assurance. We use a small use case to discuss the mappings between metamodels and models, and the relations between model elements expressed in mappings. Finally, an illustrative case study is used to demonstrate our approach.

**Keywords:** Metamodel Comparison, Model Comparison, Conceptual Model, Mapping, Safety Assurance.

## 1 Introduction

In safety-critical domains, safety assurance is usually costly and time-consuming due to the amount of manual work involved. Model-driven engineering techniques could be used to reduce the high costs for safety assurance [5] [6] [8]. Different models are created for different applications in those domains. Moreover, metamodels that are used to express those models could be different. Consequently, reusing those models from one context to another is a big challenge.

The background of our work is OPENCOSS, a European project aimed at cross-domain reuse of safety-assurance data. As one of the key challenges of the OPENCOSS project is to define a common conceptual framework for specifying certification assets [1], a generic metamodel (GMM) for safety standards (IEC 61508, ISO 26262, EN 50128, DO 178B, etc.) has been developed as a part of this framework [10]. It includes most of the common concepts and relations between different standards and domains for safety certification. The benefits of the GMM are sharing of patterns of certification assessments, and support for cost-effective re-certification between different standards [1] [10]. However, when introducing this GMM to the companies in safety-critical domains, their current way of working must be changed to conform to the GMM, and extra effort will be required. In practice, those companies want to get the benefits of the generic metamodel while minimizing the required changes to do so. Additionally, because

A. Bondavalli et al. (Eds.): SAFECOMP 2014 Workshops, LNCS 8696, pp. 419–430, 2014.
© Springer International Publishing Switzerland 2014

the concepts in the GMM are limited and generic, some ambiguities will arise when interpreting and using those concepts.

To address those issues, in [4], we present a metamodel transformation approach to facilitate the process of creating metamodels for a specific safety standard, domain or company. As a result, a family of metamodels is generated throughout a metamodel transformation sequence. The traceability information of those metamodels needs to be stored, maintained and analyzed for metamodel consistency. Besides, one of the key tasks to reduce the safety assurance cost is to find the reusable data from models conforming to similar metamodels. Thus, metamodel comparison and model comparison are vital. The comparison results can be described as mappings between metamodels or between models and used for supporting safety-assurance data reuse.

Our main focus is the results of metamodel comparison and model comparison. We call this kind of mapping comparative mappings. In comparative mappings, the similarities and differences between the source model and the target model not only depend on metamodel comparison, but also model comparison. In other words, even if the results of comparison between metamodels are known, the comparison between models still need to be done manually. However, the former comparison can facilitate the latter one by specializing which type of models can be compared.

In this paper, we discuss our previous metamodel transformation approach to take into account comparative mapping support. We define two levels of comparative mapping: conceptual mapping and concrete mapping. Conceptual mapping shows the relations between different conceptual models or metamodels. Concrete mapping shows the relations between models. Then we introduce four comparative mapping types to express the relations between model elements. Finally, an illustrative case study from the OPENCOSS project is used to demonstrate our approach.

## 2   Metamodel Transformation

The current generic metamodel proposal oversimplifies the modeling needs of safety engineers and assessors. This can lead to overgeneralization, additional manual work, and less support for automatic consistency checks. In our previous work, we introduced domain-specific metamodels to address this [4]. By refining the GMM, we create domain-specific metamodels. In this way, the ambiguities in the GMM are mitigated. It can also prevent safety engineers from making interpretation mistakes while creating models. Additionally, domain-specific metamodels only need to be defined once by the best expert(s) available in a certain domain. Figure 1 recapitulates our approach for metamodel refinement. A metamodel transformation is executed, which takes the GMM along with those domain concepts described in the metamodel refinement language (MMRL) as inputs, and produces a specific metamodel (SMM) as output. Finally, a graphical editor, based on the SMM, can be automatically generated, which facilitates safety engineers in building their models using concepts from their own domain. More information of our approach and MMRL can be found in [4].

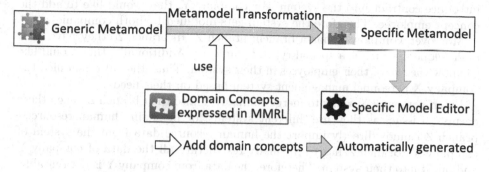

Fig. 1. Overview of our approach

By repeatedly applying refinement specifications to conceptual models, a family of conceptual models can be created (Figure 2). Those conceptual models include standard conceptual models, company conceptual models, project conceptual models, etc. By a family of conceptual models, we means a closely related set of metamodels, where each metamodel in the set (except the root metamodel) can be defined in terms of an existing metamodel from the same set with a number of changes. For example, an IEC 61508 metamodel can be refined into an ISO 26262 metamodel in the automotive domain or an EN 50128 metamodel in the railway domain with different refinement specifications. Therefore, the elements in each of the metamodels can be traced back to a refinement specification (or the corresponding intermediate metamodel) or the metamodel that formed the starting point of the family.

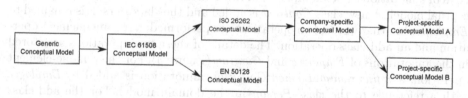

**Fig. 2.** By successively refining metamodels, a family of closely related metamodels is created. For clarity, the metamodel transformations and the domain concepts introduced by refinement specifications of Figure 1 are not shown in this figure.

## 2.1   A Small Use Case

To simplify the issue and demonstrate our approach in a clear and easy way, we use a small use case from the personnel management domain. The scenario is as follows: there are two companies, company X and company Y. They bought the same personnel management system from a software supplier. Then they find they need to improve that system in order to make it fit to their situations. For company X, they would like to use the concept employee instead of person, and introduce contract into the system. For company Y, they would like to add the concept employee. Therefore the system gets modified by both companies.

Moreover, company X has a branch: branch Z. In branch Z, they have a lot of developers, which is a special type of employee. Additionally, they would like to know the age of their employees in their system. Thus, they also modified the company X personnel management system based on their needs.

Later, company X wants to merge company Y into their branch Z. Then there occurs an issue, as they use different systems for managing human resources, branch Z cannot directly import the human resource data from the system of company Y. Branch Z has to manually restructure all the data of company Y and put it into their system. Therefore, the data from company Y is not reusable. However, there are some similarities between the personnel systems of branch Z and company Y. They start to think how to find the similarities and relations to support the data reuse, and then reduce the merge cost. For instance, for the same person, his/her resume can be reused from company Y system to Branch Z system.

**Our Implementation for the Use Case.** Figure 3 illustrates the sequence of transformations for the aforementioned use case. There is a domain model of the original personnel management system, which represents the relations between *Person* and *Resume*. Through the metamodel refinement process, it can be refined into the corresponding parts in the company X conceptual model, the branch Z conceptual model, and the company Y conceptual model. Therefore, in this family of conceptual models, there are four metamodels. The traceability information of the refinement process is stored in metamodels themselves in the form of annotations. For example, from the domain model to the company X conceptual model. A new class *Contract* is added and the class *Person* is renamed to *Employee*. In other words, two operations are performed: a rename-element operation and an add-class operation. The details of these two operations are stored in the annotations of *Employee* and *Contract*(Figure 3). For the rename-element operation, a *refine.renameElementOperation* annotation is added to *Employee* with a reference to the class *Person* in the domain model. For the add-class operation, a *refine.addClassOperation* annotation is added to the class *Contract*. Because the class *Contract* is new, there is no class in the domain model that can be referred to. Thus, the reference of the *refine.addClassOperation* annotation is the class *Contract* itself.

Similarly, from the company X conceptual model to the branch Z conceptual model, an attribute *age* is added to the existing class *Employee* and *Developer* is introduced as a new type of *Employee*. The information of the corresponding operations is logged in the new annotations of attribute *age* and class *Developer*. The annotation of attribute *age* refers to the class *Employee* in the company X conceptual model, while the annotation of the class *Developer* refers to itself. Note that, the old annotations are kept from the company X conceptual model.

For each element (concept and relation) in the family of conceptual models, its annotation keeps all its traceability information in the transformation sequence.

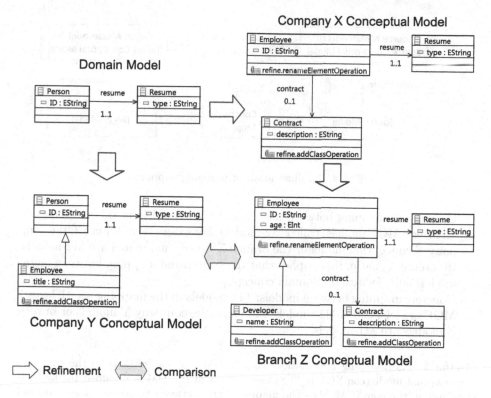

**Fig. 3.** A small example for the sequence of transformations

Therefore, the concepts and relations in the metamodels can be related across metamodels by tracing their relationships through their annotations. Furthermore, the traceability information can be obtained and analyzed for comparative mappings between metamodels, which will be discussed in the next section.

## 3   Mapping Support

In this section, we discuss the comparative mapping between metamodels and between their instances. And the relation types between concepts and between instances are described in terms of mappings.

### 3.1   Mappings: Between Conceptual Models and between Models

From a usability perspective, there are two levels of comparative mapping: mappings between concepts and mappings between instances of concepts (on a concrete level). These mappings are illustrated in Figure 4 and can be described as follows:

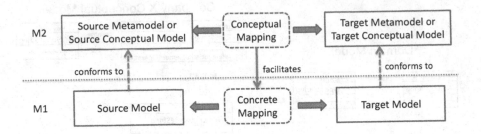

**Fig. 4.** An illustration of mapping support

- Conceptual mapping between metamodels: The models in this mapping are all layer 2 MOF models, called M2-models. For example, in Figure 3, the company Y conceptual model or the branch Z conceptual model are M2-models. In a reuse scenario, this implies that the conceptual mapping between metamodels only focuses on domain concepts.
- Concrete mapping between models: The models in the mapping are all layer 1 MOF models, called M1-models. For example, company Y models or branch Z models are M1-models.

**Listing 1.** The mapping information from the domain model(DM) to the company X conceptual model(comXCM): The class *Person* in the DM is renamed to the class *Employee* in the comXCM, thus the mapping type between these two classes are full mapping (line 3-7). The class *Contract* in the comXCM is a newly added class, then there is no mapping for this class (line 8-12). The class *Resume* in the comXCM is copied from the DM, so this class is fully mapped to the class *Resume* in the DM (line 13-17).

```
1   <?xml version="1.0" encoding="UTF-8" standalone="no"?>
2   <mappings>
3     <mapping mappingType="0" sourceClass="domainModel.Person"
4                       targetClass="comXConceptualModel.Employee">
5       <operator>Rename</operator>
6       <reason>Rename an existing class</reason>
7     </mapping>
8     <mapping mappingType="3" sourceClass="null"
9                       targetClass="comXConceptualModel.Contract">
10      <operator>AddClass</operator>
11      <reason>null</reason>
12    </mapping>
13    <mapping mappingType="0" sourceClass="domainModel.Resume"
14                      targetClass="comXConceptualModel.Resume">
15      <operator>NotModified</operator>
16      <reason>The class is copied from original MM.</reason>
17    </mapping>
18  </mappings>
```

The conceptual mappings can be implemented through metamodel transformations. In Section 2, a refinement of the Domain Model(DM) is described. The refinement specifications involve the changes made from the DM to a targeted metamodel. The corresponding conceptual mapping from the DM to a targeted metamodel is documented in the metamodel transformation. For example, Listing 1 shows the mapping information from the domain model to the company X conceptual model in the form of XML. The comparisons between different metamodels (except the DM) can be achieved by analyzing the mapping documents of each metamodel. Listing 2 shows the comparison results between the company Y conceptual model and the branch Z conceptual model. The relations in the comparison are expressed in terms of mappings. The conceptual mappings can facilitate the concrete mappings between models. For example, in Listing 2, class *Person* in the company Y conceptual model can be mapped to class *Employee* or class *Developer* in the branch Z conceptual model. On the model level, we need to find which specific person can be mapped to employee, and which should be mapped to developer.

**Listing 2.** The result of comparison between the company Y conceptual model (comYCM) and the branchZ conceptual model(ZCM): One full mapping is found between the class *Resume* in the comYCM and the class *Resume* in the ZCM. One partial mappings are found: the mapping from the class *Person* in the comYCM to the class *Employee* in the ZCM. There possible mappings are discovered: the mapping from the class *Employee* in the comYCM to the class *Developer* in the ZCM, and to the class *Employee* in the ZCM, and the mapping from the class *Person* in the comYCM to the class *Developer* in the ZCM.

```
1   <?xml version="1.0" encoding="UTF-8" standalone="no"?>
2   <mappings>
3     <mapping mappingType="2" sourceClass="comYConceptualModel.Employee"
4                      targetClass="branchZConceptualModel.Developer">
5       <reason>Intermediate concept is:domainModel.Person</reason>
6     </mapping>
7     <mapping mappingType="2" sourceClass="comYConceptualModel.Employee"
8                      targetClass="branchZConceptualModel.Employee">
9       <reason>Intermediate concept is:domainModel.Person</reason>
10    </mapping>
11    <mapping mappingType="2" sourceClass="comYConceptualModel.Person"
12                      targetClass="branchZConceptualModel.Developer">
13      <reason>Intermediate concept is:domainModel.Person</reason>
14    </mapping>
15    <mapping mappingType="1" sourceClass="comYConceptualModel.Person"
16                      targetClass="branchZConceptualModel.Employee">
17      <reason>Intermediate concept is:domainModel.Person</reason>
18    </mapping>
19    <mapping mappingType="0" sourceClass="comYConceptualModel.Resume"
20                      targetClass="branchZConceptualModel.Resume">
21      <reason>Intermediate concept is:domainModel.Resume</reason>
22    </mapping>
23  </mappings>
```

## 3.2   Mapping Types: Between Concepts and between Instances

Relations between concepts indicate whether concepts in their definition or nature are the same. Relations between instances also include the instantiation or content of the concepts. In this paper, for consistency, we use comparative mappings to represent relations. For example, hazard concepts from Mil Std 822 and the ISO 26262 standard can relate with each other from a conceptual point of view. However, if the underlying severity categories are different, the relation should indicate only a partial mapping. Essentially, four types of mapping are identified in this paper:

- Full mapping: the elements in the mapping are identical. In a reuse scenario, this implies that the characteristics of the element (such as its form, its attributes, and its references) are not changed.
- Partial mapping: there are some similarities between the elements. The similarities and differences can be analyzed and documented in the mapping document.
- Possible mapping: there is a possibility that a mapping can be found between the elements. Further analysis of the elements needs to be done to make sure that there are some similarities between them.
- No mapping: there is insufficient similarity between the elements to permit a mapping to take place.

In our implementation, we use "0", "1", "2", "3" to represent full mapping, partial mapping, possible mapping, and no mapping respectively. For example, in of Listing 1 (line 3), the mapping type "0" means that the mapping between the class *Person* in the domain model and the class *Employee* in the company X conceptual model is full mapping. The reason for that is the class *Employee* is renamed from the class *Person* without changes. Moreover, the mapping types also indicate priority where Level 3 is the highest. If the priority level of an existing mapping between two concepts is lower than a newly discovered mapping, the priority level between those two concepts will be changed to the new one.

## 4   Results

As mentioned before, the current generic metamodel proposal oversimplifies the modeling needs of safety engineers and assessors. This can lead to overgeneralization, additional manual work, and less support for automatic consistency checks. To address this, extended metamodels are refined from the GMM; For our demonstration, we use a family of metamodels from safety-critical domains. All of these metamodels are derived from the GMM. The details of the GMM are defined in [10]. Figure 5 shows an extract of an ISO 26262 metamodel from the automotive domain (ISOMM). Figure 6 shows an extract of a DO 178C metamodel from the avionic domain (DOMM).

Both of those two metamodels are from the same aforementioned family. From these two figures, we can see that the traceability information of this family is

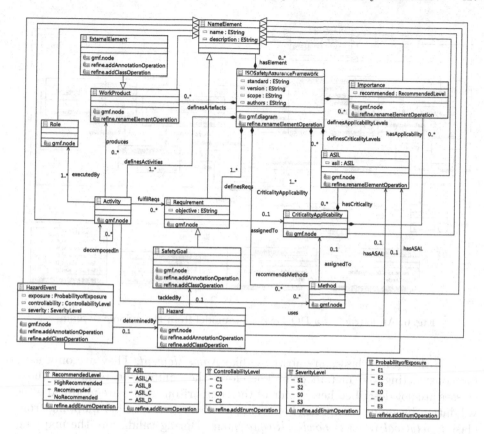

**Fig. 5.** An extract of an ISO 26262 metamodel from the automotive domain

kept in the annotations of the metamodels. After analysing this traceability information and comparing these two metamodels, some results can be obtained automatically:

- There are five possible mappings from the ISOMM to the DOMM: from class *Importance* to class *ApplicabilityLevel*; from class *ASIL* to class *SoftwareLevel*; from class *SafetyGoal* to class *HighlevelRequirement*; from class *SafetyGoal* to class *LowlevelRequirement*; and from class *CriticalityApplicability* to class *CriticalityApplicability*.
- There are four partial mappings from the ISOMM to the DOMM: from class *ExternalElement* to class *Artefact*; from class *SafetyGoal* to class *Requirement*; from class *Requirement* to class *HighlevelRequirement*; and from class *Requirement* to class *LowlevelRequirement*.
- There are five full mappings from the ISOMM to the DOMM: from class *WorkProduct* to class *Artefact*; from class *Requirement* to class *Requirement*; from class *Artefact* to class *Artefact*; from class *Method* to class *Method*; from class *Role* to class *Role*.

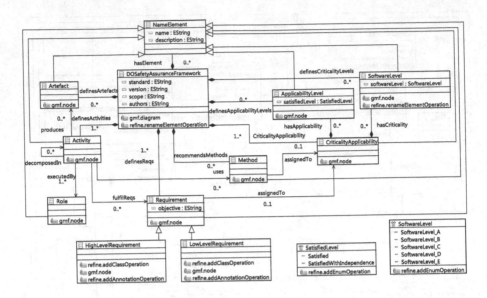

**Fig. 6.** An extract of a DO 178B metamodel from the avionic domain

Note that some classes are abstract, like *NameElement*. They are only used for constructing the metamodels. Therefore, the comparison results of those classes are not described here. Some of the comparison results are modified after validation by domain experts. For example, there is a possible mapping from class *SafetyGoal* to class *LowlevelRequirement*. During validation, the mapping type between these two class is changed to no mapping.

The conceptual mappings can be used in two scenarios. Firstly, they could be used for supporting concrete mappings. A concrete mapping can be found in the model level only if there exists a conceptual mapping at the metamodel level. For instance, if there is no mapping between class *SafetyGoal* and class *LowlevelRequirement*, then at the model level, all instances of *SafetyGoal* can not be mapped to the instances of *LowlevelRequirement*. Secondly, because those metamodels are used as domain-specific conceptual models in safety cases [5], the conceptual mappings between them can be used for supporting safety case reuse.

## 5  Related Work

Related research is found in metamodel refinement, traceability management, and metamodel matching.

**Metamodel Refinement.** Metamodel refinement is strongly related with metamodel evolution and metamodel adaptation. In [11], the use of transformation patterns in the form of QVT relations for metamodel refinement is introduced. By introducing new concepts, the target metamodel can be extended though model transformation. A model change language with a number of migration rules is presented in [7] for defining metamodel changes. It is a high-level visual language and designed for describing metamodel evolution. Our approach presented in this paper is discussed in the context of safety-critical domains and focuses on metamodel refinement with metamodel transformation rather than metamodel evolution. Metamodel evolution is caused by external factors, whereas metamodel refinement is a design process.

**Traceability Management.** In [9], a model-driven framework for traceability management, called iTrace, is developed, which enables the analysis of traceability information of the different models involved in the software development cycle. Also, in [2], traceability visualization in model transformations has been done to facilitate traceability analysis. In this paper, we focus on traceability management of metamodels rather than models, and we propose to use metamodel refinement specifications to support traceability management and the analysis of traceability information.

**Metamodel Matching.** Metamodel matching techniques support the detection of mappings between two metamodels. Those mappings are used to generate a model transformation between two metamodels. In [3], metamodel matching for automatic transformation generation is discussed. The metamodels used for metamodel matching are created independently for the same kind of applications. However, in this paper, the metamodels are all derived from the same original metamodel. The information of those mappings is defined in refinement specifications and stored with the metamodels in the sequence of transformations. Besides, those comparative mappings can not only be used for generating a model transformation, but also for supporting safety case reuse.

# 6   Conclusions and Future Work

In this paper, we have presented our approach to take into account comparative mapping support in the context of conceptual modeling. The study of comparative mapping support between conceptual models or metamodels in safety-critical domains is a promising approach to improve the understanding between different domains or companies at the conceptual level and, consequently, the reuse of safety assurance data at the model level. Based on our previous research, conceptual models are also used for constructing safety cases. In this case, the mappings found between conceptual models can support safety case reuse.

The main contribution of this work is insight into traceability management and mapping support in the sequence of transformations. The traceability information is stored in metamodels themselves, which is easy to be maintained and analyzed. Meanwhile for each refinement of metamodels, a mapping specification is generated along with the target metamodels. A comparison between different conceptual models or metamodels can be obtained by analyzing the related mapping specifications.

As future work, we will study and implement the applications of comparative mappings. For example, how to support safety case or evidence reuse based on conceptual mappings. In addition, we envisage to study detecting comparative mappings in the model level automatically or semi-automatically.

**Acknowledgements.** The research leading to these results has received funding from the FP7 programme under grant agreement n° 289011 (OPENCOSS).

# References

1. OPENCOSS: Deliverable D4.1 - Baseline for the common certification language (2013), http://www.opencoss-project.eu/node/7
2. van Amstel, M.F., van den Brand, M., Serebrenik, A.: Traceability Visualization in Model Transformations with TraceVis. In: Hu, Z., de Lara, J. (eds.) ICMT 2012. LNCS, vol. 7307, pp. 152–159. Springer, Heidelberg (2012)
3. Falleri, J.-R., Huchard, M., Lafourcade, M., Nebut, C.: Metamodel Matching for Automatic Model Transformation Generation. In: Czarnecki, K., Ober, I., Bruel, J.-M., Uhl, A., Völter, M. (eds.) MoDELS 2008. LNCS, vol. 5301, pp. 326–340. Springer, Heidelberg (2008)
4. Luo, Y., van den Brand, M., Engelen, L., Klabbers, M.: From Conceptual Model to Safety Assurance. In: Conceptual Modeling (accepted for publication, 2014)
5. Luo, Y., van den Brand, M., Engelen, L., Klabbers, M.: A Modeling Approach to Support Safety Certification in the Automotive Domain. In: ICSEng 2014 (accepted for publication, 2014)
6. Luo, Y., van den Brand, M., Engelen, L., Favaro, J., Klabbers, M., Sartori, G.: Extracting Models from ISO 26262 for Reusable Safety Assurance. In: Favaro, J., Morisio, M. (eds.) ICSR 2013. LNCS, vol. 7925, pp. 192–207. Springer, Heidelberg (2013)
7. Narayanan, A., Levendovszky, T., Balasubramanian, D., Karsai, G.: Automatic Domain Model Migration to Manage Metamodel Evolution. In: Schürr, A., Selic, B. (eds.) MODELS 2009. LNCS, vol. 5795, pp. 706–711. Springer, Heidelberg (2009)
8. Panesar-Walawege, R.K., Sabetzadeh, M., Briand, L.: Using UML Profiles for Sector-Specific Tailoring of Safety Evidence Information. In: Jeusfeld, M., Delcambre, L., Ling, T.-W. (eds.) ER 2011. LNCS, vol. 6998, pp. 362–378. Springer, Heidelberg (2011)
9. Santiago, I., Vara, J.M., de Castro, M.V., Marcos, E.: Towards the Effective Use of Traceability in Model-Driven Engineering Projects. In: Ng, W., Storey, V.C., Trujillo, J.C. (eds.) ER 2013. LNCS, vol. 8217, pp. 429–437. Springer, Heidelberg (2013)
10. de la Vara, J.L., Panesar-Walawege, R.K.: SafetyMet: A Metamodel for Safety Standards. In: Moreira, A., Schätz, B., Gray, J., Vallecillo, A., Clarke, P. (eds.) MODELS 2013. LNCS, vol. 8107, pp. 69–86. Springer, Heidelberg (2013)
11. Wachsmuth, G.: Metamodel Adaptation and Model Co-adaptation. In: Ernst, E. (ed.) ECOOP 2007. LNCS, vol. 4609, pp. 600–624. Springer, Heidelberg (2007)

# Does Visualization Speed Up the Safety Analysis Process?

Ragaad AlTarawneh[1], Max Steiner[2], Davide Taibi[3],
Shah Rukh Humayoun[1], and Peter Liggesmeyer[2]

[1] Computer Graphics and HCI
[2] Software Engineering: Dependability
[3] Software Engineering: Processes and Measurement
University of Kaiserslautern
Gottlieb-Daimler-Str. 67663 – Kaiserslautern, Germany
{tarawneh,steiner,taibi,humayoun,liggesmeyer}@cs.uni-kl.de

**Abstract.** The goal of this paper is to present our experience in utilizing the power of the information visualization (InfoVis) field to accelerate the safety analysis process of Component Fault Trees (CFT) in embedded systems. For this, we designed and implemented an interactive visual tool called ESSAVis, which takes the CFT model as input and then calculates the required safety information (e.g., the information on minimal cut sets and their probabilities) that is needed to measure the safety criticality of the underlying system. ESSAVis uses this information to visualize the CFT model and allows users to interact with the produced visualization in order to extract the relevant information in a visual form. We compared ESSAVis with ESSaRel, a tool that models the CFT and represents the analysis results in textual form. We conducted a controlled user evaluation study where we invited 25 participants from different backgrounds, including 6 safety experts, to perform a set of tasks to analyze the safety aspects of a given system in both tools. We compared the results in terms of accuracy, efficiency, and level of user acceptance. The results of our study show a high acceptance ratio and higher accuracy with better performance for ESSAVis compared to the text-based tool ESSaRel. Based on the study results, we conclude that visual-based tools really help in analyzing the CFT model more accurately and efficiently. Moreover, the study opens the door to thoughts about how the power of visualization can be utilized in such domains to accelerate the safety assurance process in embedded systems.

**Keywords:** Embedded Systems, Safety Analysis, Information Visualization.

## 1 Introduction

Embedded systems are widely used in our daily life. Embedded systems are classified as electronic devices that incorporate a computer system into their implementations [1]. Some examples of these systems are control systems in cars,

A. Bondavalli et al. (Eds.): SAFECOMP 2014 Workshops, LNCS 8696, pp. 431–443, 2014.

airplanes, railroad crossings, and washing machines. Generally, they are not centralized in one component but are distributed among a set of components, which represent the system parts. In fact, these systems are mostly composed of two types of components: software components and hardware components. These two types of components collaborate with each other through a set of interfaces. This results in complex structures inside these systems [1]. Due to the frequent usage of these systems, safety and reliability aspects are essential and critical from the end users' perspective. Both aspects guarantee a working system without any unexpected errors and risks. Consequently, maintaining these systems in terms of ensuring safe situations requires intensive study of those critical situations that might bring the underlying system to some undesired state [2].

The process of analyzing failures is necessary to trace the reasons that may lead to a specific hazard in the system's lifetime. Therefore, many techniques have been proposed to trace the failure propagation paths within the set of cooperating components in technical systems. The Fault Tree Analysis (FTA) technique is one of the common modeling techniques that help to understand the failure mechanisms in technical systems [3, 4]. The Component Fault Tree (CFT) technique extends the FTA concept by introducing additional information about the underlying system structure. Therefore, CFTs are used to depict the failure scenarios in complex embedded systems in which a safety scenario for the underlying system is depicted as a directed acyclic graph and the root of this model is the top event of interest [2,4]; see Fig. 1 to check the difference between the FT and the CFT.

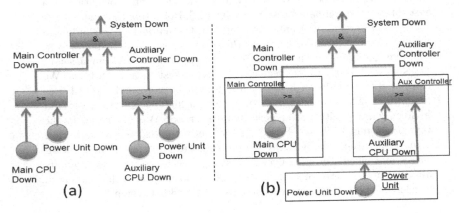

**Fig. 1.** The Fault Tree (FT) concept (a) vs. the Component Fault Tree (CFT) concept (b)

The process of detecting possible failures in embedded systems is normally performed by *safety experts*, who identify the failure mechanisms using CFT analysis in order to trace all possible reasons for each specific top-level event during the system's lifetime. Their objective is to find all possible safety-critical components that might trigger the underlying hazard. They design this model based on all possible failure relations between the system components related to the specified top event. After building the CFT model, they start analyzing the safety scenario to determine all safety-critical components in order to maintain these components to keep the system in a safe mode. The result of this analysis helps the *system engineers*, who are responsible for maintaining all system components and for fixing the overall system in order to make it safer from the end users' perspective. This iterative interaction process between safety experts and system engineers supports the maintenance process of these complex embedded systems.

Visualizing the safety aspects of embedded systems is comparatively a new field. As the complexity of an embedded system is increased, the corresponding component fault tree size is also increased, which makes it difficult to handle the failure detection process. The information visualization (InfoVis) field can play an important role in speeding up the system developing process because it eases the steps of finding the important information from both the system and the user perspective. Also, it helps to reduce the errors that may be made by humans while searching for the relevant information. For example, Markus Weber in [5] mentions that 30% of people's time is wasted in looking for the important information. Moreover, visualization supports interaction with the data and automates the steps of the information-extracting process.

In this work, we ran an empirical study to compare two tools: **ESSAVis** (**E**mbedded **S**ystems **S**afety **A**spects **Vis**ualizer) [6,7], an interactive visual tool for analyzing and visualizing component fault trees, and **ESSaRel** (**E**mbedded **S**ystems **S**afety and **R**eliability Analyser), a text-based tool for modeling, editing, and partly analyzing component fault trees [8]. This study aims to answer the question of whether a visualization-based system like ESSAVis can accelerate the process of analyzing failure scenarios in complex systems more than traditional tools like ESSaRel. ESSaRel was selected in this work because it was the only tool at the moment of evaluation study that edits and models CFT models. As expected, our results show that that visual-based tools offer better support for analyzing the CFT model by providing more accurate and efficient results than non-visual tools.

The remainder of the paper is structured as follows: In Section 2, we provide some related work. In Section 3, we give an overview of both tools. In Section 4, we highlight the user evaluation study we performed to investigate the differences between using the two tools. Finally, we conclude the work and list the possible future directions in Section 5.

## 2   Related Work

To generate a CFT model manually, highly skilled and experienced engineers analyze the system. To achieve this, they need insights about the system and an overview of the failure modes and their consequences at a particular time. Performing this process manually requires plenty of concentration, but it is still error-prone due to the difficulties in understanding the whole system. To tackle the above-mentioned concern, many tools have been proposed in the literature to help the safety experts model and understand the safety mechanisms of complex systems. Many existing tools propose visualizing this by showing a tree structure of the failure. Most of these tools visualize the fault tree in 2D representations such as ESSaRel [8, 9], UWG3 [2], and Cecilia OCAS [10].

In the above-mentioned tools, the node-link diagram is used to show the relations between the infected system parts, while simple primitive shapes are used to show components of the Fault Tree (FT): e.g., small circles for representing basic events and a small rectangle for showing the gate (the logical connector) between two basic events. These tools also use color and/or text to depict other types of information, such as the gate type. These kinds of tools are useful for modeling the failure relations between the system parts, but they do not provide options for analyzing the failure path or the set of critical parts in the underlying system.

In spite of the facility provided for editing and modifying the FT structure in these tools, they generally lack the ability to analyze the FT itself and to present an overall view of the current failure mechanism. However, ESSaRel provides a textual description of some safety aspects of the CFT model. For example, the set of minimal cut sets in the current scenario is included together with information about the related set of components and the failure connections among them, all this data can be grouped into one xml file. This xml file is the input of our ESSAVis tool [6], where we extract the safety data related to each component and then arrange the set of components to be ready for the visualization process. However, ESSaRel [8] is the only tool in the above-mentioned tools that can model a CFT. Therefore, we used ESSaRel as the opponent tool to the ESSAVis tool in our study.

## 3   Introduction to ESSAVis and ESSaRel

ESSAVis [6, 7] is a visual-based tool that takes an xml file representing the CFT model as input. The file describes the top-event situation by presenting the list of components together with the list of basic events in each component that are required to trigger this top event. Each basic event has a real value between 0 and 1 indicating its probability of failing. Moreover, the file contains the failure relations between these components using the information about the gate connections.

ESSAVis parses this information and converts the model to a graph model in a way that the set of vertices $V$ contains the list of components and the set of inclusion edges $E$ contains the structural relations between these components, while the set of adjacency edges $F$ contains the failure relations between the system elements. Furthermore, a component may contain other components or leaves, with leaves in this context being basic events in the system. ESSAVis visualizes this graph model using a multi-level orthogonal layout algorithm [11] (see Fig. 2b). Moreover, ESSAVis provides different interaction techniques for navigating through the graph. For example, it allows the user to expand and close nodes on demand [12], as shown in Fig. 2a. It also distinguishes between different

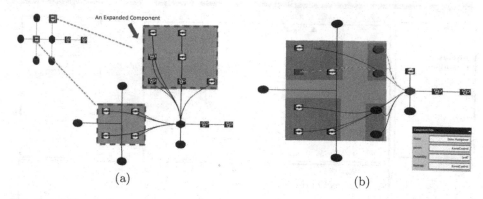

(a)                                                        (b)

**Fig. 2.** (a) Expanding the required component to extract its internal structure, and (b) the failure path between several components, with the corresponding parts highlighted in red

component types using different textures and shapes. For example, the root of the graph corresponding to the top event is represented as a hexagon shape, basic events are represented as blue cycles, and the components are represented by blue boxes.

ESSAVis arranges the important safety information in a menu called the Safety Information Menu. Users can trigger this menu by clicking the right mouse button. This menu contains three main tabs. The first one shows the list of components in the current CFT model together with their number of basic events. The second tab contains a list of all the basic events and their probabilities in the CFT model, while the third tab contains a list of all the minimal cut sets in the CFT model with the option to sort them based on their probabilities or their sizes. In each tab, ESSAVis provides two buttons to allow users to highlight the selected elements in the list and then expand them to show their place in the visualized CFT model. Moreover, ESSAVis provides animation to show the failure relations between two selected elements in the visualization (see Fig 2b).

Fig. 3 shows the main interface view of ESSaRel [8], which has previously been used in industry (CESAR Project Report 2010, p. 43) [9]. The main centered window (i.e., the CFT window) is for editing the safety model. This is achieved by dragging the small graphical shapes and dropping them into this window's drawing area. This area is useful for depicting the participating components and the connections among them. The right window in the figure is used to show the system structure through the hierarchy of the components in the current safety scenario. This helps to detect the structural relations between the parent components and their children. ESSaRel is considered a powerful tool for editing the safety model [8]. However, it lacks the ability to show an overall view of the safety scenario. This makes the process of tracing a failure rather difficult.

ESSaRel helps safety experts in "modeling" the CFT model. It is an editor that offers basic functionalities required to model safety-critical scenarios in technical systems. It offers a multi-view feature to present the multi-level concept in the

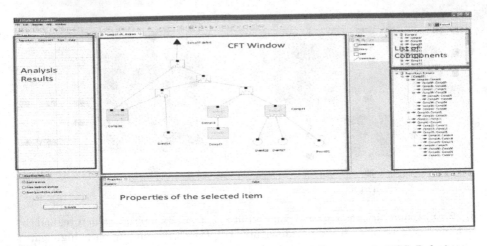

**Fig. 3.** The ESSaRel interface. Red rectangles show different main ESSaRel views.

CFT model. Therefore, the internal structure of a specified component is hidden on the upper level. Users can select a specific component by using the mouse, which results in opening a new window showing the internal structure of the component. Although this facility helps safety experts to modify the internal structure of the required component, it makes it difficult to understand the overall system structure because the new view does not preserve the relations between the current level and the upper level. ESSaRel shows the structural relations among the system's components in a side-view explorer (see right side of Fig. 3), where all the incorporated components in the current scenario are listed hierarchically according to their relations in the system. Again, the system structure shows the list of all collaborating components; however, it does not present the component-subcomponent relations visually. The user needs to open a new view to see the subcomponents' structure. Therefore, in order to explore the internal structure of each component, the user needs to select the required component to allow displaying the next level of details. As mentioned above, the view opens in a new window without any indication of the previous level, which makes it difficult to investigate the internal structure of each component and identify the main reasons that cause a problem in the upper-level component. Furthermore, tracing the failures between the multiple levels in the CFT model is also quite a difficult task in this approach. This leads to difficulties in tracing the failure propagation path between the required components.

## 4    The Empirical Study

The goal of our study was to analyze ESSAVis and ESSaRel for the purpose of comparing their *accuracy*, *speed*, and *user acceptance* in analyzing component fault tree models from the end users' perspective (i.e., the safety experts' perspective). In order to compare the results for the two platforms, we identified a set of metrics by means of a GQM model [13]:

- *Metrics for accuracy:* percentage of correct answers for each task.
- *Metrics for speed:* time needed for each task.
- *Metrics for efficiency:* accuracy/speed.
- *Metrics for acceptance:* perceived usefulness, perceived ease of use, attitude toward using the tool, behavioral intention to use the tool, actual use of the system.

We combined these metrics as suggested by the Technology Acceptance Model [14]. Further it was important for us to collect the participants' feedbacks on how to improve the tool. For this purpose, we chose an open-ended questionnaire form so as to add their comments. We formulate the study hypotheses as:

- **H1:** ESSAVis is more accurate than ESSaRel.
- **H2:** ESSAVis is faster than ESSaRel.
- **H3:** ESSAVis is more efficient than ESSaRel.
- **H4:** ESSAVis has a higher level of user acceptance compared to ESSaRel.

## 4.1  Study Design and Procedure

Based on the identified goal and hypotheses, we designed this study as a controlled experiment under laboratory conditions with a maximum time-frame of two hours per participant. The participants executed a set of tasks on both platforms. To reduce learning effects, we randomized the participants of each sub-group in such a way that half of the participants ran the experiment first on ESSAVis and then on ESSaRel, while the other half did it the other way around.

To assure a basic level of knowledge on both tools, a 30-minute tutorial was provided for each tool. Since the participants from the safety expert sub-group already had thorough knowledge of using ESSaRel, they were excluded from the ESSaRel training session. We allowed all the participants to ask further questions during the training session and during the test in case of any technical issue. We ran the study with 25 researchers from the department of Computer Science in our university. 21 participants were males, while the remaining 4 participants were females. The participants were divided into groups based on their backgrounds (4 were robotics experts, 6 were safety experts, 4 were software engineers, and the remaining 11 were visualization researchers). The study was performed in the required time frame, never exceeding 1 hour time frame for each test. The study was based on 4 tasks to be performed on a common safety scenario with components renamed in order to avoid any learning effects. At the end of each task, we reported the participants answeres and their time to achieve that task, to evaluate accuracy (H1) and speed (H2). Then, in order to assess user acceptance (H4), we asked participants to fill in two questionnaire forms. The first questionnaire form was based on eight questions, where each question offered six different options based on a Likert scale (scaled from 0 to 5 to show the degree of agreement with each question from the participant's perspective; the sixth option was "Don't know") [15]. The second one was opened questionnaire, to get their general feedback.

The experiment was performed using a desktop environment, with the participants seated in front of the computer. They interacted with the platform with a normal mouse and a keyboard. We allowed the participants to try the target platform before starting the tasks and encouraged them to ask for more details about any interaction technique during the test.

### 4.2 Task Description

The defined safety scenario we used in our study describes one of the possible situations where the RAVON [16] robot can hit other solid objects. The assumption of this scenario is that RAVON moves forward in a moderate drive mode. Moreover, there is no water on the road nor are there any unexpected slopes or gradients. The components of this possible hazard comprise 48 compound components in the RAVON structure, with 70 basic events that can appear in different locations of the CFT model simultaneously. However, due to the test constraints, we decided to include only part of the scenario. The scenario we used in our test consisted of 25 components with more than 33 basic events. We designed the tasks based on a common process to analyze fault trees [17]. The test consisted of four main tasks for both tools:

- **Task 1:** Find the Minimal Cut Set (MCS) lists. This included two sub-tasks:
    - **Task 1.1:** Sort them according to their size.
    - **Task 1.2:** Sort them according to their probability values.
  To accomplish this task in ESSAVis, the participants were trained to trigger the safety menu and then select the minimal cut set tab. This shows the list of all minimal cut sets in the current CFT model (critical minimal cut sets are the ones with fewer than three basic events). Further, ESSAVis provides the option of sorting this list based on sizes or on probabilities. In ESSaRel, the list of minimal cut sets is shown together with their size information. However, there is no option to sort this list, which could be easily fixed if the ESSaRel developers consider adding this option in the future. The MCS is also considered to be critical if it has a high probability of failing. In our test, we specified the probability threshold to be $> 1 \cdot 10^{-12}$.
- **Task 2:** Find the components that are affected by the most critical MCSs. This task required the participants to investigate both the CFT visualization and the list of minimal cut sets. This task depended on the results of the previous task, as participants found the most critical cut sets from the previous task. In ESSAVis, it is possible to accomplish this task by selecting the critical minimal cut sets from the safety menu, then clicking the Expand-to-Show button and finally clicking the Mark-as-Failing button at the bottom of the menu. In this case, ESSAVis opens the compound components until the required components appear and then it highlights them in red. The names of these components can be obtained by hovering the mouse pointer over the highlighted parts. The situation in ESSaRel is different, as

it does not provide this kind of interactions. The participants were expected to search manually for these components in the CFT representation based on the information from the previous task.

- **Task 3:** What are the interactions/connections of components **CX** and **CY** with respect to system failures?

  In this task, the participants were given two components and were asked to give the logical connections between them. These two components were on different levels without any structural connection between them. The only relation between them was the failure relation. This task can be accomplished in ESSAVis by clicking on the two specified components and then noting the color of the top event node. If the top-event node becomes red, this means that both components are in one minimal cut set and have an AND relationship; otherwise (if the color is blue) they are not. In ESSaRel, the participants were expected to navigate through the CFT model manually and keep in mind the logical connections between these two components. However, some of the safety experts used the minimal cut set information and determined whether these two components were in one minimal cut set or not; if they were, they knew that these components have an AND relationship, otherwise they do not affect the top event.

- **Task 4:** Find the events that have the highest impact on the safety level of the system. (**Hint**) Find the events that are in the most critical MCSs.

  This task can be achieved in two ways, either the basic event with the highest probability to fail or the one that occurred in the most critical minimal cut set has to be found. Therefore, for this task we collected four different answers (two possibilities for both tools). In ESSAVis, the information about the probability of each basic event is listed in the basic events tab of the Safety-Menu, while in ESSaRel it is shown in a properties panel. The minimal cut set information was available through a menu in both tools. However, in ESSaRel participants should navigate manually through the CFT to extract the basic-event probability.

## 4.3   Results and Discussion

In this section, we discuss the results for each hypothesis. Detailed results can be found in Table 1, Table 2 and Figure 4.

Results were analyzed by performing the following steps: (1) We performed a descriptive analysis of the collected data. (2) We tested the data for normality using a Shapiro-Wilk test [18]. (3) Since the data were not normally distributed, we performed a Median test for independent samples or a Wilcoxon Signed-Rank test for dependent samples with a significance level of 0.05 to test our hypotheses.

Table 1 provides descriptive statistics on the analysis together with the results of the T-Test. As shown by this table, the results are statistically relevant for accuracy and acceptance, but not significant for time and efficiency. We assume this is due to the different populations that took part in the study.

The analysis of the results for the first hypothesis (**H1**) shows that ESSAVis was always more accurate, or at least provided the same accuracy as ESSaRel.

**Table 1.** Statistical information showing the differences between the two tools

|  | Accuracy | | Time | | Acceptance | | Efficiency | |
|--------|---------|---------|---------|---------|---------|---------|---------|---------|
| Method | ESSAVis | ESSaRel | ESSAVis | ESSaRel | ESSAVis | ESSaRel | ESSAVis | ESSaRel |
| Mean | 0.86 | 0.66 | 98.99 | 256.39 | 4.19 | 2.67 | 1.32E-02 | 4.77E-03 |
| Median | 0.84 | 0.68 | 101.21 | 151.42 | 4.08 | 2.52 | 7.50E-03 | 4.13E-03 |
| Std | 0.12 | 0.18 | 65.78 | 272.52 | 0.27 | 0.46 | 9.69E-03 | 3.05E-03 |
| T-Test | 1.00E-01 | | 3.14E-01 | | 6.11E-07 | | 1.50E-01 | |

In both sub-tasks 1.1 and 1.2, ESSAVis outperformed ESSaRel (15% more in Task 1.1 and 274% more in Task 1.2). The difference is not due to the visualization power of ESSAVis, but to the lack of some features in ESSaRel. The same results are also reflected in Task 2 (ESSAVis was 24% more accurate than ESSaRel) and in Task 3 (ESSAVis was 9% more accurate than ESSaRel). Anyway, due to the low complexity of Task 3, we can claim that there were no significant differences between the two tools in this task regarding accuracy. Finally, in Task 4 ESSAVis also outperformed ESSaRel by 10% in terms of accuracy. We think this is because the participants in ESSaRel needed to perform the analysis manually in order to get the answers.

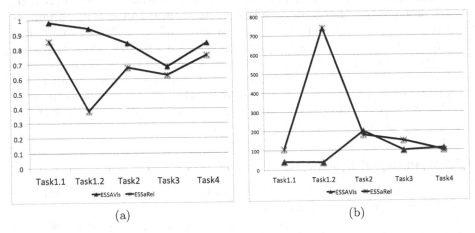

(a)                                                        (b)

**Fig. 4.** (a) Average accuracy per task. (b) Average time (in seconds) to achieve the task.

Taking into account the time needed to run the tasks (**H2**), our hypothesis was always confirmed since ESSAVis always provided faster results than ESSaRel. The time required for both sub-tasks 1.1 and 1.2 was lower in ESSAVis than in ESSaRel (2.54 times lower in Task 1.1 and 18.94 times in Task 1.2). This time difference is considered to be significant for such simple tasks. We believe that this variation is due to the automation provided by ESSAVis, as it automates the calculation process for the minimal cut set probabilities. In Task 2, ESSAVis equalled ESSaRel in terms of the time needed to perform the tasks (200 seconds in ESSAVis and 187 seconds in ESSaRel). Since some participants were new to ESSAVis but familiar with ESSaRel, we expect an improvement on this task after someone becomes familiar with ESSAVis. Task 3 required 33% less time with ESSAVis (100 seconds vs. 150 seconds) while Task 4 required nearly the same time. ESSAVis provides this information using different methods, like the basic events tab or the minimal cut set tab in the Safety Menu. Specifically, in this task we observed that the safety experts outperformed all other participants because they knew how to get this answer. The average time for them was 93 seconds compared to 124 seconds for the other participants. So we think this is due to the experience level of the participants. In ESSaRel, all participants regardless of their background performed this task at a relatively similar speed, which was 101 seconds on average. We think this can be improved if the participants get trained and used to the ESSAVis tool.

**Table 2.** Average accuracy and average time in seconds of all tasks for all users

| Tool | Metric | Task 1.1 | Task 1.2 | Task 2 | Task 3 | Task 4 |
|------|--------|----------|----------|--------|--------|--------|
| ESSAVis | Accuracy | 0.98 | 0.94 | 0.84 | 0.68 | 0.84 |
|  | Time | 41.96 | 39.13 | 200.44 | 101.21 | 112.23 |
|  | Efficiency | 2.34E-02 | 2.40E-02 | 4.19E-03 | 6.72E-03 | 7.50E-03 |
| EssaRel | Accuracy | 0.85 | 0.38 | 0.68 | 0.63 | 0.76 |
|  | Time | 107.36 | 740.33 | 181.5 | 151.42 | 101.35 |
|  | Efficiency | 7.96E-03 | 5.15E-04 | 3.73E-03 | 4.13E-03 | 7.50E-03 |

The results for efficiency (**H3**) all confirm our hypothesis. ESSAVis was nearly 200% more efficient in Tasks 1.1 and 1.2, 13% better in Task 2, 59% better in Task 3, and identical in Task 4. The results for user acceptance (**H4**), based on the Technology Acceptance Model, show that most of the participants accepted ESSAVis more than ESSaRel (22 participants out of 25). The main reasons for the higher acceptance of ESSAVis were the interaction facilities (22 out of 25) and the visual support provided by ESSAVis (18 out of 25).

## 5    Conclusion and Future Work

In this paper, we reported on a controlled experiment aimed at comparing the accuracy, the time needed, and the acceptance of ESSAVis (an interactive visual platform) and ESSaRel (an editor for CFT models) in analyzing a CFT model. After introducing related works, we provided an overview of both tools, highlighting the pros and cons of visualization techniques in safety analysis. Then we designed and ran an empirical study under laboratory conditions to answer our research questions.

The study was designed using an experimental design and was conducted with 25 participants (researchers in computer science), who ran both systems on a common set of tasks. The tasks consisted of those basic tasks that are necessary to measure the criticality of the top-event situation. The goal was to measure how visualization can help to speed up the process of safety analysis in complex embedded systems. The results show that the participants provided more accurate results when using ESSAVis instead of ESSaRel (between 9% and 24% more accurate, depending on the task). Moreover, the participants performed all tasks relatively faster with ESSAVis and with higher efficiency than when using ESSaRel.

The results are not only due to the visualization capabilities of ESSAVis but also to the automation process of the algorithm that is required to calculate the probability of each minimal cut set. We also observed that the majority of participants preferred ESSAVis rather than ESSaRel due to its intuitiveness and the different interaction techniques provided. At the same time, the results show the need to train users in interpreting the results of their queries using ESSAVis. One of the valuable findings was that in some tasks, there was no significant difference between the two platforms. This indicated us to the need for possible improvements in ESSAVis, as it lacks some options that are necessary for the safety analysis process. For example, ESSAVis does not visualize the gate information explicitly, as it conveys the logical connections between nodes implicitly. However, this needs to be fixed in the next version of ESSAVis. In the future, we aim to add this feature in order to improve the tool's use in the safety analysis process of complex embedded systems. Moreover, we intend to perform further evaluation studies with the new features in different environments in order to guarantee the feasibility and effectiveness of the tool.

# References

1. Lee, E.A., Seshia, S.A.: Introduction to Embedded Systems - A Cyber-Physical Systems Approach, 1 edn. Lee and Seshia (2010)
2. Kaiser, B., Liggesmeyer, P., Mäckel, O.: A new component concept for fault trees. Reproduction 33, 37–46 (2003)
3. Bozzano, M., Villafiorita, A.: Design and Safety Assessment of Critical Systems. CRC Press (Taylor and Francis), an Auerbach Book (2010)
4. Kaiser, B., Gramlich, C., Förster, M.: State/event fault trees - a safety analysis model for software-controlled systems. Reliability Engineering System Safety 92, 1521–1537 (2007)
5. Weber, M.: A survey of semantic annotations for knowledge management. DFKI GmbH, p. 1 (2008)
6. AlTarawneh, R., Bauer, J., Keller, P., Ebert, A.: Essavis: A 2Dplus3D visual platform for speeding up the maintenance process of embedded systems. In: BCS HCI 2013 (2013)
7. AlTarawneh, R., Bauer, J., Humayoun, S.R., Ebert, A., Liggesmeyer, P.: Enhancing understanding of safety aspects in embedded systems through an interactive visual tool. In: IUI Companion 2014, pp. 9–12. ACM (2013)
8. Software Engineering Research Group: Dependability Kaiserslautern University, Essarel Tool: Embedded systems safety and reliability analyser (2014), http://essarel.de
9. CESAR Project: cesar project report (2010), http://www.cesarproject.eu

10. Bieber, P., Bougnol, C., Castel, C., Heckmann, J.-L., Kehren, C., Seguin, C.: Safety assessment with altarica - lessons learnt based on two aircraft system studies. In: 18th IFIP World Computer Congress, Topical Day on New Methods for Avionics Certification, p. 26 (2004)

11. Gelfand, N., Tamassia, R.: Algorithmic patterns for orthogonal graph drawing. In: Whitesides, S.H. (ed.) GD 1998. LNCS, vol. 1547, pp. 138–152. Springer, Heidelberg (1999)

12. AlTarawneh, R., Johannes, S., Humayoun, S.R.: Clue: An algorithm for expanding clustered graphs. In: 7th IEEE Pacific Visualization Symposium (PacificVis 2014), Yokohama, Japan (2014)

13. Basili, V.R., Caldiera, G., Rombach, H.D.: The goal question metric approach. In: Encyclopedia of Software Engineering. Wiley (1994)

14. Venkatesh, V., Morris, M.G., Davis, G.B., Davis, F.D.: User acceptance of information technology: Toward a unified view. MIS Q. 27, 425–478 (2003)

15. Dix, A., Finlay, J.E., Abowd, G.D., Beale, R.: Human-Computer Interaction, 3rd edn. Prentice-Hall, Inc., Upper Saddle River (2003)

16. Proetzsch, M.: Development Process for Complex Behavior-Based Robot Control Systems. RRLab Dissertations. Verlag Dr. Hut (2010) ISBN: 978-3-86853-626-3

17. Vesely, W.: Fault Tree Handbook with Aerospace Applications. NASA (2002)

18. Shapiro, S.S., Wilk, M.B.: An analysis of variance test for normality (complete samples). Biometrika 52, 591–611 (1965)

# Agile Change Impact Analysis of Safety Critical Software

Tor Stålhane[1], Geir Kjetil Hanssen[2], Thor Myklebust[2], and Børge Haugset[2]

[1] Norwegian University of Science & Technology, Trondheim, Norway
tor.stalhane@idi.ntnu.no
[2] SINTEF ICT, Trondheim, Norway
{ghanssen,thor.myklebust,borge.haugset}@sintef.no

**Abstract.** Change Impact Analysis (CIA) is an important task for all who develops and maintains safety critical software. Many of the safety standards that are used in the development and use of systems with a certified safety integrity level (SIL) requires changes of such systems to be initiated by a CIA. The resulting CIA report will identify planned changes that may threaten the existing safety level. The challenge with CIA is that there are no practical guidelines on how to conduct and report such an analysis. This has led to a practice where most changes lead to extensive up-front analysis that may be costly and delay the change process itself. In this paper we propose a new strategy for CIA based on the principles of agile software development and the SafeScrum approach to establish a more efficient in-process impact analysis. We discuss several benefits of this approach, like resource savings, shorter time to initiate the change process, better prioritization and management of the change process, and others.

**Keywords:** Safety critical systems, agile software development, SafeScrum, change impact analysis, IEC61508.

## 1 Introduction

Change impact analysis (CIA) is an important task for anybody who develops and maintains safety critical systems such as gas and fire detection systems, railway signaling systems and process control systems. Several standards and directives require that a CIA has to be done when a system with an approved safety integrity level is to be changed – e.g., IEC 61508 [1] and the EN 5012X series [2]. A CIA produces a CIA report (CIAR), which is an important input both to the development team implementing the changes and to the assessor who will approve the changes according to the relevant standards. Although several standards require a CIA to be performed there are no practical guidelines available. This is a major concern as change of complex software systems is a highly demanding task [3, 4] and even more so for safety critical systems. However, we need to strike a balance between what should be done – the standard's domain – and how it should be done, which to a large degree should be left to the development organization. We have provided guidance for CIA in a previous paper [5]. The key principle of our approach is to split the CIA into two phases. Phase 1 is performed for a group of changes when needed and before starting the

A. Bondavalli et al. (Eds.): SAFECOMP 2014 Workshops, LNCS 8696, pp. 444–454, 2014.

change process. This is more efficient than the present ad-hoc practice where all changes from the systems requirements specification (SRS) are evaluated together. See our previous paper for details on this [ibid]. For phase 2 we suggest to perform the rest of the CIA as part of the development process itself. This process is described in this paper. We are motivated by the potential effect that lies in the principles of agile software development [6-9] of safety critical systems and believe that our previously described SafeScrum [10] method can be extended to facilitate an efficient in-process CIA – see section 2. The work on SafeScrum and the more recent development on agile CIA have been done as part of a four year Norwegian research project SUSS (Agile Development of Safety-critical Software).

The approach with a two phase agile CIA that is described in this paper is conceptual and not yet applied in industry. However, the author team has complimentary expertise in the domain with one expert on assessment of safety critical systems according to important standards like IEC 61508 and EN50128, one expert in development and evaluation of safety critical systems and two experts on agile software development and process improvement. We relate this work to our previous suggestion for an agile approach of developing safety critical systems [10] where development is done incrementally and iteratively, and where the management of requirements, assessment and impact analysis is done concurrently.

Our approach is based on extensive discussions in the collegium of experts, investigation of relevant literature and standards, and also through verification of ideas with leading industry partners developing SIL 2 and SIL 3 systems. There is, however, little difference between SIL 3 and SIL 4 when it comes to software. There is thus no reason why the approach should not work also for SIL 4 as well.

The key ideas promoted in this paper are that we provide practical expert guidelines on how to achieve a two-phase agile CIA process as well as on details on the SafeScrum process, and discuss expected savings from effectuating such a process. Our motivation is that there are no guidelines on how to perform and document a CIA at all, and that an agile approach will improve the current industrial practice.

The rest of the paper is organized as follows: Section 2 explains the background for CIA and gives a short summary of some of the relevant literature while Section 3 drafts an agile approach of developing safety critical systems. Section 4 provides the details on how to perform an *agile* CIA. Section 5 discusses some of the benefits we expect from this approach. Finally, section 6 concludes our work and provides directions for further work on these topics.

## 2    Background

### Change Impact Analysis of Safety Critical Systems

Development and evolution of safety critical software such as fire detection systems or ship controlling systems must comply with extensive safety standards and regulations in order to be approved for use. This also means that changes and extensions of such systems must undergo an assessment to update the certificate. For a system with an established SIL, planned changes to code and architecture are evaluated to see if the system will still meet the requirements specified in the standard after the changes. This is required by several standards, but there are no concrete guidelines on how to perform the analysis and how to document it in a CIAR.

The established practice is to perform the CIA upfront of the new development, have it accepted and then initiate the change and development process without any further CIA. This may represent a problem as the change process potentially can disclose problems with the planned change that the CIA didn't foresee. Also, doing the complete CIA upfront means that the change process cannot start until the analysis is fully completed. In a previous paper [5] we argue that it can be a good idea to perform the CIA in two phases; Phase 1 is performed upfront of development, similar to the common practice today but shorter in time and with less details. Phase 2 CIA is done as an integrated part of the development process itself.

## Related Work

A search for related work has shown several papers on the traceability problem related to CIA. Another topic of research that is published extensively is the effect of incremental changes e.g. in object-oriented development. We have also seen some publications on research on the effect of process change. However, we have seen no papers on the problems of change impact analysis in agile development of safety critical software apart from one of our own recent papers [11]. The closest is a quote from a paper by Jose Luis de la Vara and Rajwinder Kaur Panesar-Walawege on their meta-model SafetyMet [12] where they identify this topic as an area of future research.

B. Li et al. [13] has published the result of a survey, where they have identified 23 change impact analysis methods. Another survey, performed by S. Lehnert [14] has reviewed 150 approaches and related literature. We will not go through all these methods in detail. Instead, we will look at two of the methods reviewed by B. Li et al. and two papers that are not mentioned in either survey.

The first paper we will study in some more details is written by M. Acharya and B. Robinson from ABB [15]. The authors have developed a new framework for change impact analysis based on slicing and developed a tool for this, called Imp. This tool is designed to seamlessly integrate with the nightly build process. The approach is tested in an experiment with 30 changes in two versions of the same system and seems to work well. However, it still has the same weakness as most other change impact analysis methods – it must start with the original and the changed code.

The second paper that we will discuss is written by M.S. Kilpinen et al. [16]. This paper discusses change impact analysis for the whole system – hardware and software. In addition, they do not assume that changes have been done before the change impact analysis is performed. The experiences reported stems from a Rolls Royce project for developing a jet engine controller. Design changes were managed through an *informal* change impact process early in the detailed design and a more formal process when the design baseline had been defined. Their most important observation is that "the system engineers tend only to use their experience and knowledge of the system rather than any systematic method to brainstorm on the impact on the system requirements given to embedded software". In relation to this, we should keep in mind Lindvall and Sandahl's observation [17] that "software engineers tend to perform impact analysis intuitively. Despite this common practice, many software engineers do not predict the complete change impact."

Based on this short survey there seems to be little tool support for change impact analysis decision support, which is what we need. Knowing post festum that the change was a bad idea is important but it is much cheaper to know this before we start to change anything.

## 3   SafeScrum

Agile software development is a way of organizing the development process, emphasizing direct and frequent communication, frequent deliveries of working software increments, short iterations, active customer engagement throughout the whole development life cycle and change responsiveness rather than change avoidance. This can be seen as a contrast to waterfall-like models, which emphasize thorough and detailed planning, and design upfront and consecutive plan conformance. We do not believe that an agile approach is appropriate for all steps needed when developing a safety-critical system. Thus, SafeScrum has come up with the idea of separation of concerns, as shown in figure 1, based on the process described in IEC 61508. Note that several requirements specified in IEC 61508-3, annex A (normative) and annex B (informative) will influence the Scrum process. We have also added an activity where trace information is collected.

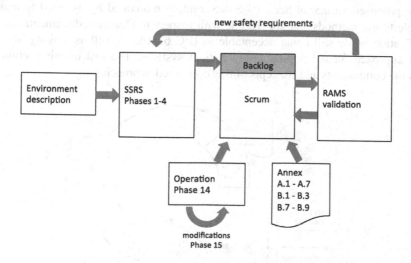

**Fig. 1.** Separation of concerns

Several agile methods exist, whereof *extreme programming* [16] and *Scrum* [7] are the most commonly used. Figure 2 explains the basic concepts of SafeScrum.

The process starts with initial planning, which is short and results in a prioritized list of requirements for the system called *the product backlog*. Developers also *estimate* the implementation cost per backlog item. The following development is organized as a series for *sprints* (iterations) that each lasts a few weeks. Each sprint starts with sprint planning, followed by test and development, a sprint review and a retrospective. Typically, developers will apply the principles of *test-driven development* [13] where automated tests are developed *before* the code.

In the *sprint planning meeting*, the top items from the product backlog is transferred to the *sprint backlog* – adding up to the amount of resources available for the period. These requirements will be implemented in the following sprint. Each working day starts with a *scrum*, which is a short meeting where each member of the development team (1) explains what she/he did the previous work day, (2) any impediments or problems that need to be solved and (3) planned work for the work day. Problems related to relevant safety standards should be discussed with the assessor as soon as possible after the meeting.

Each sprint *releases* an *increment* which is a running or demonstrable part of the final system. The increment is *demonstrated* for the customer(s), which will decide which backlog items that have been resolved and which that need further work. Based on the results from the demonstration the next sprint is planned. The product backlog is revised by the customer and is potentially changed / reprioritized. This initiates the sprint-planning meeting for the next sprint. When all product backlog items are resolved and / or all available resources are spent, the final product is released. Final tests can be run to ensure completeness.

The proposed variant of Scrum – SafeScrum, is motivated by the need to make it possible to use methods that are flexible with respect to planning, documentation and specification while still being acceptable to IEC 61508, as well as making Scrum a useful approach for developing safety critical systems. The rest of this section explains the components and concepts of this combined approach.

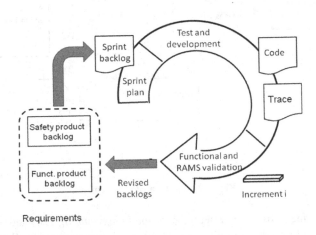

**Fig. 2.** SafeScrum process model

Our model has three main parts. The first part consists of the IEC 61508 steps needed for developing the environment description and then the phases 1- 4 (concept, overall scope definitions, hazard and risk analysis and overall safety requirements). These initial steps result in the initial requirements of the system that is to be developed. This is the key input to the second part of the model, which is the Scrum process. The requirements are documented as *product backlog items*. A product backlog is a list of all functional and safety related system requirements, prioritized by the customer. We have observed that the safety requirements are quite stable (e.g. the response time has to be less than the Process safety time for a fire alarm system), while the functional requirements may change considerably over time. Development with a high probability of changes to requirements will favour an agile approach.

Due to the focus on safety requirements, we propose to use two product backlogs: one *functional product backlog*, which is typical for Scrum projects, and one *safety product backlog*, which is used to handle safety requirements. The safety requirements will come from three sources (1) applicable standards, (2) safety analysis – e.g. HazOp – and (3) from the system's customer. It is not necessary to have two physically separated backlogs – adding a tag to the safety product backlog items will suffice. Adding a second backlog is an extension of the original Scrum process and is needed to separate the frequently changed functional requirements from the more stable safety requirements. With two backlogs we can keep track of how each item in the functional product backlog relates to the items in the safety product backlog, i.e. which safety requirements that are affected by which functional requirements. This can be done by using simple cross-references in the two backlogs. It can also be supported with an explanation of how the requirements are related if this is needed to fully understand a requirement. One of the participating companies includes the backlog and the necessary linking in a Jira tool. Using a tool like Jira enables us to adapt the process depending on whether a requirement is safety critical or not.

In order to be performed in an efficient manner, traceability requires the use of a supporting tool. There exist several process-support tools that can manage this type of traceability in addition to many other process support functions. One out of many examples is Jira plus RMsis.

To make Scrum conform to IEC 61508, the final validation in each iteration should be done both as a validation of the functional requirements and as a RAMS (Reliability, Availability, Maintainability, and Safety) validation, to address specific safety issues. If appropriate, the independent safety validator should take part in this validation for each sprint. If we discover deviations from the relevant standards, the assessor should be involved as quickly as possible as he is normally not involved in the validation for each sprint. Using an iterative and incremental approach means that the development project can be continuously *re-planned* based on the most recent experience with the growing product. This principle is related to the well-known principle of the Deming/Shewhart cycle [18]. Between the iterations, it is the duty of the customer or product owner to use the most recent experience to re-prioritize the product backlogs.

In addition to the re-planning mentioned above, applying the RAMS validation process to each increment will also give risk and hazard analyses a gradually evolving scope. This will improve the quality of these analyses. Even if the increments cannot be installed at the customer's site, they can still be tested and run as part of a system simulation. In addition, safety analysis performed on small increments can be more focused and thus give better results [19].

As the final step, when all the sprints are completed, a final RAMS validation will be done. Given that most of the developed system has been incrementally validated during the sprints, we expect the final RAMS validation to be less extensive than when using other development paradigms. This will also help us to reduce the time and cost needed for certification, enabling a shorter time to market. We also expect that it will be quicker and less expensive to perform updates to an existing system this way.

## 4    Agile Change Impact Analysis

The proposed agile CIA-approach is organized as two phases. Phase 1 analysis is done before the change implementation process and resembles the present practice, but requires less effort and time because some analysis is postponed to phase 2. This also means that the change and development process will start earlier. See Myklebust et al. [5] for details on phase 1. In the following of this paper we look into the details of what we call phase 2 CIA.

The key principle of phase 2 is that the impact analysis is performed continuously and in synchronization with the SafeScrum development process. This is based on the same principle of simultaneity that justifies the idea of doing formal assessment as an integrated part of the SafeScrum development process itself [10]. In practical terms, this phase 2 in-process CIA is implemented as an extension to the SafeScrum process (see section 3) and more specifically, the sprint review meeting and the sprint-planning meeting. (See in-line references to figure 3 - ✿):

**Sprint-Planning Meeting ✿:** Each sprint starts with a planning meeting where the team estimates, selects and details items from the product backlog and moves them to the sprint backlog to fill up the available resources (working days) for the upcoming sprint ✿. With respect to the CIA we suggest that the team considers any effects the detailing of requirements and design decisions [20] might have for system's safety. The important question is: *will the requirement and design affect the safety?* A potential aid to use for decision support is Failure Mode and Effects Analysis (FMEA) [21]. Potential issues and un-clarities should be resolved immediately – either by reconsidering the requirement or the design. In case the requirement needs to be reconsidered, the product owner must be consulted. Alternatively, the design of the solution must be reconsidered. The product owner is not normally a part of the Scrum planning meeting so we suggest that the product owner is available, or that he can be contacted in cases where he needs to make decisions. One of our industrial partners uses the business manager and the manager of development here. All CIA issues that are raised and resolved during the planning meeting should also be documented in the CIAR ❸.

**Sprint-Review Meeting ❹:** After the completion of a sprint, the product owner joins the Scrum team to evaluate the outcome and results of the sprint. This involves approving or disapproving the recent sprint result ❺, often based on a demonstration by the team. The product owner will revise the product backlog and decide whether there are items that should be removed, changed or re-prioritized ❻. This is done using the most recent knowledge of the problem that is being solved and the solution that is being developed to solve the problem. For each change, the team will evaluate the impact of the change and consider whether it has an impact on the safety integrity level of the system. In cases where the team is not able to make this judgment they need to clarify this with relevant roles such as safety managers, product management, sales, and others – in general roles that are in positions to make a qualified judgment.

The dual backlog, which is an important concept in SafeScrum, will be an important aid to raise attention to changes that may affect the safety integrity level because of the potential relationships between functional requirements and safety requirements. If a functional requirement has a strong influence on one or more safety requirements we might consider moving it to the safety requirements backlog. Also, backlog items should be stated in the form of user stories explaining **who** the user role is, **what** the goal is (what the product owner wants to achieve), and **why** the user story is required (the rationale). This information is useful in order to evaluate the effect on the safety integrity level.

Identified issues need to be discussed either right away or in the following sprint review meeting, possibly also involving the product owner. This may result in further additions to the product backlog. Furthermore, all issues that are identified, and

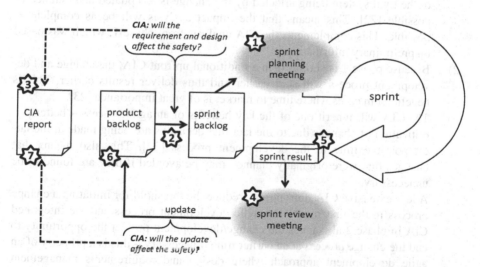

**Fig. 3.** SafeScrum in-process (phase 2) change impact analysis

resolved, should be documented. This becomes important input to the CIAR ⚙, which grows incrementally in parallel with the system. We suggest that this should be the responsibility of the Scrum master. The updated CIAR becomes important information for the external assessor, which also is given a closer role in the development process [10].

## 5    Discussion

To quote an anonymous developer: "After the first sprint, everything is maintenance of an existing system". For the CIA we need to consider two types of changes: (1) changes to existing safety requirements and (2) changes that will influence code that directly or indirectly belongs to a safety requirement.   All such changes can be categorized into one of two classes: simple and not simple. For simple changes we consider it to be enough if the developer categorizes the change as simple, perform a CIA and documement why he has made this decision. For the other cases, and especially those that concern safety requirements, we need to have a more elaborate CIA.

- Use trace information to see which parts of the code that will be affected
- Check the code for potential impact on safety in a code review
- Make a decision – change or not – and write a report. Note that the CIA reports will later be an important input for the assessor.

Changes to the safety requirements in the product backlog should always go through a CIA.   We see several benefits of our two-phase CIA:

1) An in-process CIA is done when it is practical to do it, when the knowledge of the total system being affected by the change is as updated and detailed as possible [22]. This means that the impact analysis will be as complete as possible. This complements the CIA analysis from phase 1, which was based on preliminary information.

2) Because phase 1 is shorter than a traditional upfront CIA, the change and development process will start earlier and thus deliver results earlier. This is beneficial in cases where time to market is of great importance [23].

3) The CIA will inherit one of the key benefits of an agile process – better prioritization of changes due to the fact that decisions are being made at the latest possible time in the development process [22]. This also means that changes that were originally planned may be avoided if they are found to be unnecessary.

4) A less extensive CIA upfront may reduce the threshold for initiating a change process in the first place. The agile development process and the integrated CIA in phase 2 also gives the change/development project the opportunity to end the change process at an earlier time if necessary – this is a property of an agile development approach where design and requirements management

may be adjusted during the course of the project. This can e.g. be a decision that is made by the product owner that sees that the (prioritized) changes that have been implemented so far are sufficient and that the product should enter the market. Thus, the change process becomes more flexible and controllable.

5)   A classical CIAR is useful both to developers and to assessors, but we argue that the incremental CIAR will be even more valuable. It produces more updated information since it is made progressively during the system development, but also because the developers are continuously involved in the process and that they don't have to rely on a document that might be outdated.

6)   A phase 2 approach like the one we have drafted will contribute to a more streamlined and synchronized process where impact analysis, development and assessment are done concurrently, instead of – as today – sequentially.

# 6    Conclusions and Future Work

The motivation for this paper is the need for a better way of analyzing and managing changes in a certified safety critical software system. Based on our knowledge of the industry we see a tendency to stick with traditional approaches of heavy upfront analysis. We also see that the obligatory standards that the industry needs to adhere to are weak on providing practical guidelines on *how* to perform the CIA. Thus, we have described how a modern software engineering process like Scrum can be adapted to improve the CIA and address some of the main limitations. We have also discussed what we expect will be the benefits and earnings from applying this approach.

One limitation of our work though is that the proposed agile CIA is currently being evaluated in an industrial context. However, the author team behind this paper has an extensive and complimentary expertise that is unique and we have chosen to develop and present our ideas here as an invitation to the academic community as well as the industry to consider ways of improving the CIA process. We would strongly encourage our peers to comment on our ideas and to try them out in practice.

To develop these ideas further we have started two pilot projects using the agile CIA approach in Norwegian industry[1]. The results of these empirical studies will be reported in following publications. Another important thread of activity is our engagement in the IEC 61508 standardization committee where one of the authors holds a position. Our goal is to encourage changes in the next revision of this important standard and to incorporate practical industrially proven guidelines like we have suggested in this paper.

**Acknowledgements.** This work was partially funded by the Norwegian research council under grant #228431 (the SUSS project). Research has been done in collaboration with Autronica Fire & Security AS.

---

[1] http://www.sintef.no/safescrum

# References

[1] IEC, 61508:2010 Functional Safety of Electrical/Electronic/Programmable Electronic Safety-related Systems (E/E/PE, or E/E/PES)

[2] EN 5012X series. Railway applications

[3] Lehman, M.M., Ramil, J.F.: Software evolution - Background, theory, practice. Information Processing Letters 88, 11 (2003)

[4] Lehman, M.M., Ramil, J.F.: An Approach to a Theory of Software Evolution. Presented at the IWPSE, Vienna, Austria (2001)

[5] Myklebust, T., Stålhane, T., Hanssen, G.K., Haugset, B.: Change Impact Analysis as required by safety standards, what to do? Presented at the Probabilistic Safety Assessment & Management Conference (PSAM12), Honolulu, USA (2014)

[6] Agile Manifesto (2009), http://www.agilemanifesto.org/

[7] Schwaber, K., Beedle, M.: Agile Software Development with Scrum. Prentice Hall, New Jersey (2001)

[8] Takeuchi, H., Nonaka, I.: The New New Product Development Game. Harward Buisiness Review (1986)

[9] Dingsoyr, T., Nerur, S., Balijepally, V., Moe, N.B.: A decade of agile methodologies: Towards explaining agile software development. Journal on Systems and Software 85, 1213–1221 (2012)

[10] Stålhane, T., Myklebust, T., Hanssen, G.K.: The application of Scrum IEC 61508 certifiable software. Presented at the ESREL, Helsinki, Finland (2012)

[11] Myklebust, T., Stålhane, T., Hanssen, G.K., Haugset, B.: Change Impact Analysis as required by safety standards, what to do? Presented at the Probabilistic Safety Assessment & Management Conference, Hawaii, USA (2014)

[12] de la Vara, J.L., Panesar-Walawege, R.K.: SafetyMet: A Metamodel for Safety Standards. In: Moreira, A., Schätz, B., Gray, J., Vallecillo, A., Clarke, P. (eds.) MODELS 2013. LNCS, vol. 8107, pp. 69–86. Springer, Heidelberg (2013)

[13] Li, B., Sun, X., Leung, H., Zhang, S.: A survey of code-based change impact analysis techniques. Software Testing, Verification and Reliability 23, 613–646 (2012)

[14] Lehnert, S.: A Review of Software Change Impact Analysis. Ilmenau University of Technology, Department of Software Systems / Process Informatics, Germany (2011)

[15] Acharya, M., Robinson, B.: Practical change impact analysis based on static program slicing for industrial software systems. Presented at the 33rd International Conference on Software Engineering (ICSE 2011), Honolulu, USA (2011)

[16] Kilpinen, M.S., Clarkson, P.J., Eckert, C.M.: Change Impact Analysis at the Interface of System and Embedded Software Design. Presented at the International Design Conference, Dubrovnik (2006)

[17] Lindvall, M., Sandahl, K.: How Well do Experienced Software Developers Predict Software Change? Journal on Systems and Software 43, 19–27 (1998)

[18] Deming, W.E.: Out of the Crisis. The MIT Press, Cambridge (2000)

[19] Vuori, M.: Agile Development of Safety-Critical Software.pdf. Tampere University (2011)

[20] Armitage, J.: Are agile methods good for design? Interactions 11, 14–23 (2004)

[21] IEC, 60812: Analysis techniques for system reliability - Procedure for failure mode and effects analysis (FMEA), 2nd edn. (2006)

[22] Poppendieck, M., Poppendieck, T.: Lean Software Development: An Agile Toolkit for Software Development Managers. Addison Wesley, New Jersey (2003)

[23] Baskerville, R., Ramesh, B., Levine, L., Pries-Heje, J., Slaughter, S.: Is "Internet-speed" software development different? IEEE Software 20, 70–77 (2003)

# Author Index